D0994736

Essential
Revision Notes
for MRCP

PASTEST
Dedicated to your success

Essential
Revision Notes
for MRCP

edited by

Philip A Kalra MA MB BChir FRCP MD

Consultant Nephrologist and Honorary Lecturer
Hope Hospital, Salford Royal Hospitals Trust and
The University of Manchester

PASTEST
Dedicated to your success

©PASTEST
Egerton Court
Parkgate Estate
Knutsford
Cheshire WA16 8DX

Telephone: 01565 752000

All rights reserved. No part of this publication may be reproduced, stored in a retrieval system, or transmitted, in any form or by any means, electronic, mechanical, photocopying, recording or otherwise without the prior permissions of the copyright owner.

First published 1999
Reprinted 1999

ISBN: 1 901198 06 5

A catalogue record for this book is available from the British Library.

The information contained within this book was obtained by the authors from reliable sources. However, whilst every effort has been made to ensure its accuracy, no responsibility for loss, damage or injury occasioned to any person acting or refraining from action as a result of information contained herein can be accepted by the publishers or authors.

PasTest Revision Books and Intensive Courses

PasTest has been established in the field of postgraduate medical education since 1972, providing revision books and intensive study courses for doctors preparing for their professional examinations.

Books and courses are available for the following specialties: **MRCP Part 1 and Part 2 (General Medicine and Paediatrics), MRCOG, DRCOG, MRCGP, DCH, FRCA, MRCS, PLAB.**

For further details contact:

PasTest, Freepost, Knutsford, Cheshire WA16 7BR
Tel: 01565 752000 Fax: 01565 650264
E-mail: enquiries@pastest.co.uk

Design and typesetting by **EDITEXT**, Charlesworth, Derbyshire (01457 857622).
Printed and bound by Hobbs the Printers, Totton, Hampshire.

Contents

List of Contributors   *vii*

Preface   *ix*

CHAPTER

1. **Cardiology**   *1*
   A Bakhai and N Peters

2. **Clinical Pharmacology, Toxicology and Poisoning**   *59*
   M Caulfield

3. **Dermatology**   *83*
   G Gupta

4. **Endocrinology**   *101*
   CM Dayan

5. **Gastroenterology**   *141*
   J MacDowall

6. **Genetics**   *187*
   L C Wilson

7. **Genito-urinary Medicine and AIDS**   *203*
   B Goorney

8. **Haematology**   *221*
   K Patterson

9. **Immunology**   *259*
   M J McMahon

10. **Infectious Diseases**   *285*
    W Weir

Contents

11. **Metabolic Diseases**   *309*
D J O'Donoghue

12. **Molecular Medicine**   *349*
K Talbot

13. **Nephrology**   *387*
P A Kalra

14. **Neurology**   *439*
G Rees

15. **Ophthalmology**   *487*
K Smyth

16. **Psychiatry**   *507*
C Bench

17. **Respiratory Medicine**   *539*
D A Wales

18. **Rheumatology**   *587*
M J McMahon and S Allard

19. **Statistics**   *619*
A M Wade

Bibliography   *635*

Index   *639*

Contributors

Simon Allard BSc MBBS MD FRCP
Consultant Physician and Rheumatologist, Department of Rheumatology, West Middlesex University Hospital, Isleworth, Middlesex *Rheumatology*

Ameet Bakhai MBBS MRCP
Specialist Registrar in Cardiology, Academic Cardiology Unit, Division of the National Heart and Lung Institute, Imperial College School of Medicine, St Mary's Hospital, London *Cardiology*

Christopher Bench MBBS MRCPsych
Senior Lecturer, Division of Neuroscience and Psychological Medicine, Imperial College School of Medicine, London *Psychiatry*

Mark Caulfield MBBS MD MRCP (UK)
Reader in Clinical Pharmacology/Consultant Physician, Department of Clinical Pharmacology, St Bartholomew's and the Royal London School of Medicine and Dentistry, London *Clinical Pharmacology*

Colin M Dayan MA MBBS FRCP PhD
Consultant Senior Lecturer in Medicine, University Division of Medicine, Bristol Royal Infirmary, Bristol *Endocrinology and Diabetes*

Ben Goorney MBChB FRCP
Consultant Genito-Urinary Physician, Department of Genito-Urinary Medicine, Hope Hospital, Salford *Genito-urinary Medicine and AIDS*

Girish Gupta MBChB MRCP
Specialist Registrar, Department of Dermatology, Glasgow Royal Infirmary, Glasgow *Dermatology*

Philip A Kalra MA MB BChir FRCP MD
Consultant Nephrologist, Department of Renal Medicine, Hope Hospital, Salford *Nephrology*

Jennifer MacDowall MBChB MRCP (UK)
Specialist Registrar in Gastroenterology, Department of Gastroenterology, Blackburn Royal Infirmary, Blackburn *Gastroenterology*

Mike McMahon BSc MBChB MRCP (UK)
Consultant Physician and Rheumatologist, Department of Rheumatology, Dumfries and Galloway Royal Infirmary, Dumfries *Immunology & Rheumatology*

Donal J O'Donoghue BSc MBChB FRCP
Consultant Renal Physician, Department of Renal Medicine, Hope Hospital, Salford *Metabolic Diseases*

Keith Patterson FRCP FRCPath
Consultant Haematologist, Department of Haematology, University College London Hospitals, London *Haematology*

Geraint Rees BA BMBCh MRCP (UK)
Lecturer, Institute of Neurology, University College London *Neurology*

Katherine Smyth MBChB MRCP FRCOpth
Specialist Registrar in Ophthalmology, Manchester Royal Eye Hospital, Manchester *Ophthalmology*

Kevin Talbot BSc MBBS MRCP
Specialist Registrar, Department of Neurology, Radcliffe Infirmary, Oxford *Molecular Medicine*

Angie Wade BSc MSc PhD
Lecturer in Medical Statistics, Department of Epidemiology and Public Health, Institute of Child Health, London *Statistics*

Deborah A Wales MBChB MRCP FRCA
Specialist Registrar in Respiratory Medicine, North West Lung Centre, Wythenshawe Hospital, Manchester *Respiratory Medicine*

William R C Weir FRCP FRCP (Edin)
Consultant Physician, Department of Infectious and Tropical Diseases, Coppett's Wood Hospital, London *Infectious Diseases*

Louise C Wilson BSc MBChB MRCP
Consultant in Clinical Genetics, Mothercare Institute for Clinical Genetics and Fetal Medicine, Institute of Child Health, London *Genetics*

Preface

Despite the availability of innumerable comprehensive textbooks of medicine, and short paperbacks that concentrate on MRCP questions and answers, a major hiatus remains for the prospective MRCP candidate. Where is the textbook that provides detailed summary notes in the topics highly relevant for both Part 1 and Part 2 of the MRCP, and yet presents the material in a user-friendly format, rather than in turgid text or only stand-alone lists?

We certainly believe that **Essential Revision Notes for MRCP** will fill this gap. Our philosophy has been to produce a book that, although not attempting to cover comprehensively the wide syllabus of medicine, covers all the areas that are important for the MRCP candidate to understand and remember. Each chapter has been written by a specialist in the subject. Authors have been asked to concentrate on topics which are most important, poorly understood, or most relevant to the MRCP; the chapters are flavoured by the authors' unique insights into their subjects. Those subjects which are less frequently involved in the MRCP exams, namely Ophthalmology, Dermatology, Genetics and Statistics, receive wide and detailed coverage with the intention that the candidate be reassured that there is no need to look elsewhere for revision of these important, yet 'fringe' subjects. A unique chapter on Molecular Medicine is included, and this contains key basic science that is applied to medicine and which underpins an understanding of topics within other chapters.

The overall result is a book which is up-to-date, sufficiently detailed to bridge the gap between the short text and the comprehensive textbook, but most importantly, that is easy to read. The format, which includes short sections of concise text, bullet-points and tables, is ideal for facilitating revision. Although aimed primarily at MRCP candidates, the book will also be of value to ambitious medical students, and for those doctors studying other post-graduate curricula (e.g. FRACP) in medicine.

I would finally like to acknowledge the impressive contributions of all the chapter authors who managed to adhere to a tight brief, particularly with regard to the style of the book. Also, many thanks are due to Freydis Campbell for her initiative and enthusiasm, and to other members of the PasTest team, including Jane Bowler, Cathy Dickens and especially Sue Harrison, who have all ensured that the project has culminated in a book of which we are all proud.

Philip Kalra

Dedicated to my wife, Marian, for her patience and understanding, mum and dad and to Michael (12 months old) for his unique help in sorting the manuscripts.

Chapter 1
Cardiology

CONTENTS

1. **Cardiac investigations**   3
    1.1   Common aspects of the ECG
    1.2   Echocardiography
    1.3   Nuclear cardiology: myocardial perfusion imaging (MPI)
    1.4   Complications of diagnostic coronary arteriography
    1.5   Exercise stress testing
    1.6   24-hour ambulatory blood pressure monitoring

2. **JVP, arterial pulse and heart sounds**   9
    2.1   Jugular venous pulse
    2.2   Arterial pulse associations
    2.3   Cardiac apex
    2.4   Heart sounds

3. **Valvular disease and endocarditis**   13
    3.1   Murmurs
    3.2   Mitral stenosis
    3.3   Mitral regurgitation
    3.4   Aortic regurgitation
    3.5   Aortic stenosis (AS)
    3.6   Tricuspid regurgitation
    3.7   Prosthetic valves
    3.8   Infective endocarditis

4. **Congenital heart disease**   22
    4.1   Atrial septal defect (ASD)
    4.2   Ventricular septal defect (VSD)
    4.3   Patent ductus arteriosus (PDA)
    4.4   Coarctation of the aorta
    4.5   Eisenmenger's syndrome
    4.6   Tetralogy of Fallot

5. **Arrhythmias and pacing**   26
    5.1   Complete heart block (CHB)
    5.2   Re-entrant tachycardias
    5.3   Atrial arrhythmias
    5.4   Ventricular arrhythmias and long QT syndromes
    5.5   Temporary pacing and ablation procedures

6. **Ischaemic heart disease**   33
    6.1   Angina
    6.2   Myocardial infarction
    6.3   Thrombolysis
    6.4   Coronary artery interventional procedures

7. **Other myocardial diseases**   41
    7.1   Cardiac failure
    7.2   Hypertrophic cardiomyopathy (HCM)
    7.3   Dilated cardiomyopathy (DCM)
    7.4   Restrictive cardiomyopathy
    7.5   Myocarditis
    7.6   Cardiac tumours
    7.7   Alcohol and the heart
    7.8   Cardiac transplantation

8. **Pericardial disease**   47
    8.1   Constrictive pericarditis
    8.2   Pericardial effusion
    8.3   Cardiac tamponade

9. **Disorders of major vessels**   49
    9.1   Pulmonary hypertension
    9.2   Venous thrombosis and pulmonary embolism
    9.3   Systemic hypertension
    9.4   Aortic dissection

Appendix I: Normal cardiac physiological values   55

Appendix II: Summary of important large trials in ischaemic heart disease 56

Cardiology

1. CARDIAC INVESTIGATIONS

1.1 Common aspects of the ECG

Both the axis and sizes of QRS vectors give important information. Axes are defined:

- $-30°$ to $+90°$: normal
- $-30°$ to $-90°$: left axis deviation
- $+90°$ to $+180°$: right axis deviation
- $-90°$ to $-180°$: indeterminate axis.

The causes of common abnormalities are given below.

Causes of common abnormalities in ECG

- **Causes of left axis deviation**
  Left bundle branch block (LBBB)
  Left anterior hemi block (LAHB)
  Left ventricular hypertrophy (LVH)
  Primum atrial septal defect (ASD)
  Cardiomyopathies
  Tricuspid atresia

- **Low voltage ECG**
  Pulmonary emphysema
  Pericardial effusion
  Myxoedema
  Severe obesity
  Incorrect calibration
  Cardiomyopathies
  Global ischaemia
  Amyloid

- **Causes of right axis deviation**
  Infancy
  Right bundle branch block (RBBB)
  Right ventricular hypertrophy
    (e.g. lung disease, pulmonary
    embolism, large secundum ASD,
    severe pulmonary stenosis, Fallot's)

- **Abnormalities of ECGs in athletes**
  Sinus arrhythmia
  Sinus bradycardia
  1° heart block
  Wenckebach phenomenon
  Junctional rhythm at rest
  Right axis deviation
  Criteria for LVH

Short PR interval

This is rarely less than 0.12 s; the most common causes are those of pre-excitation involving accessory pathways or of tracts bypassing the slow region of the AV node; other causes do exist.

- **Pre-excitation**
  Wolff–Parkinson–White (WPW) syndrome
  Concealed accessory pathway
  Low–Ganong–Levine syndrome (short PR syndrome)

- **Other**
  Ventricular extrasystole falling after P wave
  AV junctional rhythm (but P wave will usually be negative)
  Low atrial rhythm
  Coronary sinus escape rhythm

Causes of tall R waves in V1

It is easy to spot tall R waves in V1. This lead largely faces the posterior wall of the left ventricle and the mass of the right ventricle. As the overall vector is predominantly towards the bulkier LV in normal situations, the QRS is usually negative in V1. This balance is reversed in the following situations:

- Right ventricular hypertrophy
- RBBB
- Posterial infarction
- Dextrocardia
- Wolff–Parkinson–White (WPW) **type A** (ventricular conduction starts via a left posterior accessory pathway, i.e. towards V1)
- Hypertrophic cardiomyopathy (septal mass greater than posterior wall).

Bundle branch block and ST segment abnormalities

Complete bundle branch block is a failure or delay of impulse conduction to one ventricle from the AV node, requiring conduction via the other bundle, and the transmission within the ventricular myocardium; this results in abormalities of the normally iso-electric ST segment.

- **Causes of left bundle branch block (LBBB)**
  Ischaemic heart disease (recent or old MI)
  Left ventricular hypertrophy (LVH)
  Aortic valve disease
  Cardiomyopathy
  Myocarditis
  Post-valve replacement
  Right ventricular pacemaker

- **Causes of right bundle branch block (RBBB)**
  Normal in young
  Right ventricular strain
    (e.g. pulmonary embolus)
  Atrial septal defect
  Ischaemic heart disease
  Myocarditis
  Idiopathic

- **Causes of ST elevation**
  Early repolarization
  Acute myocardial infarction
  Pericarditis (saddle-shaped)
  Ventricular aneurysm
  Coronary artery spasm
    during angioplasty

- **Other ST-T wave changes (not elevation)**
  Ischaemia
  Digoxin therapy
  Hypertrophy
  Post-tachycardia
  Hyperventilation
  Oesophageal irritation
  Cardiac contusion
  Mitral valve prolapse
  Acute cerebral event (e.g. subarachnoid haemorrhage)
  Electrolyte abnormalities

Q waves may be permanent (reflecting myocardial necrosis) or transient (suggesting failure of myocardial function, but not necrosis).

- **Pathological Q waves**
  Transmural infarction
  LBBB
  Wolff–Parkinson–White syndrome
  Hypertrophic cardiomyopathy
  Idiopathic cardiomyopathy
  Amyloid heart disease
  Sarcoidosis
  Neoplastic infiltration
  Progressive muscular dystrophy
  Friedreich's ataxia
  Myocarditis (may resolve)
  Dextrocardia

- **Transient Q waves**
  Coronary spasm
  Hypoxia
  Hyperkalaemia
  Cardiac contusion
  Hypothermia

Potassium and ECG changes

There is a reasonable correlation between plasma potassium and ECG changes.

- **Hyperkalaemia**
  Tall T waves
  Prolonged PR
  Flattened/absent P waves

- **Very severe hyperkalaemia**
  Wide QRS
  Sine wave pattern
  Ventricular tachycardia/ventricular fibrillation/asystole

- **Hypokalaemia**
  Flat T waves, occasionally inverted
  Prolonged PR
  ST depression
  Tall U waves

1.2 Echocardiography

Diagnostic uses of echocardiography

Conventional echocardiography is used in the diagnosis of:

- Pericardial effusion and tamponade
- Valvular disease (including large vegetations)
- Hypertrophic cardiomyopathy, dilated cardiomyopathy, LV mass and function
- Cardiac tumours and intracardiac thrombus
- Patent ductus arteriosis; coarctation of the aorta

- **Stress echo**: infarction and ischaemia, hibernation
- **Contrast echo**: atrial septal defects/ventricular septal defects, coronary perfusion.

Potential uses of transoesophageal echo

Transoesophageal echo (TOE) provides much clearer pictures, particularly of posterior structures, and is therefore useful in the following:

- Diagnosis of aortic dissection or atheroma
- Suspected atrial thrombus
- Assessment of vegetations or abscesses in endocarditis
- Prosthetic valve dysfunction or leakage
- Intra-operative assessment of ventricular function or valve repair or septal resection
- Technically sub-optimal transthoracic echocardiogram.

1.3 Nuclear cardiology: myocardial perfusion imaging (MPI)

Perfusion tracers such as thallium or technetium can be used to gauge myocardial blood flow, both at rest and during tachycardia, that is induced by drugs or exercise. Tracer uptake is detected using tomograms and displayed in a colour scale in standard views.

Lack of uptake may be:

- **Physiological**: due to lung or breast tissue absorption
- **Pathological**: reflecting ischaemia, infarction or other conditions in which perfusion abnormalities also occur (e.g. HCM or amyloidosis).

MPI may be used to:

- Detect infarction or ischaemia
- Investigate atypical chest pains
- Assess ventricular function
- Determine prognosis and detect myocardium that may be re-awakened from hibernation with an improved blood supply (e.g. after coronary bypass grafting).

1.4 Complications of diagnostic coronary arteriography

There are usually few complications (totalling ~ 5%); these include contrast allergy, local haemorrhage from puncture sites with subsequent occurrence of thrombosis, false aneurysm or AV malformation. Vasovagal reactions are common. Other complications are:

- Coronary dissection (particularly the right coronary artery (RCA) in women) and aortic dissection or ventricular perforation.
- Air or atheroma embolism: in either the coronary or other arterial circulations with consequent ischaemia or strokes.
- Ventricular dysrhythmias: may even cause death in the setting of left main stem disease.
- Mistaken cannulation and contrast injection into the conus branch of the RCA will cause ventricular fibrillation.
- Overall mortality rates are quoted at < 1/1000 cases.

1.5 Exercise stress testing

This is used in the investigation of coronary artery disease, exertionally induced arrhythmias, and in the assessment of cardiac workload and sinus node function. Exercise tests also give diagnostic and prognostic information post-infarction, and generate patient confidence in rehabilitation after MI.

The main contraindications to exercise testing include those conditions where fatal ischaemia or arrhythmias may be provoked, or those patients in whom cardiac function may be severely and acutely impaired by exertion. These include the following.

- Severe aortic stenosis or HCM with marked outflow obstruction
- Acute myocarditis or pericarditis
- Pyrexial or 'flu'-like illness
- Severe left main stem disease
- Untreated congestive cardiac failure
- Unstable angina
- Dissecting aneurysm
- Adults with complete heart block
- Untreated severe hypertension

Indicators of positive exercise test result

The presence of each factor is additive in the overall positive prediction of coronary artery disease.

- Development of anginal symptoms
- A fall in BP of >15 mmHg or failure to increase BP with exercise
- Arrhythmia development (particularly ventricular)
- Poor workload capacity (may indicate poor left ventricular function)
- Failure to achieve target heart rate (allowing for beta-blockers)
- >1 mm down-sloping or planar ST segment depression, 80 ms after the J point
- ST segment elevation
- Failure to achieve 9 min of the Bruce protocol due to any of the points listed

Exercise tests have **low specificity** in the following situations.

- Ischaemia in young women with atypical chest pains
- Atrial fibrillation
- LBBB
- Wolff–Parkinson–White syndrome
- Left ventricular hypertrophy
- Digoxin or beta-blocker therapy
- Anaemia
- Hyperventilation
- Biochemical abnormalities such as hypokalaemia

1.6 24-hour ambulatory blood pressure monitoring

The limited availability and relative expense of ambulatory blood pressure monitoring prevents its use in all hypertensive patients. Specific areas of usefulness are in the following situations.

- Assessing for 'white coat' hypertension
- Borderline hypertensive cases that may not need treatment
- Evaluation of hypotensive symptoms
- Identifying episodic hypertension (e.g. in phaeochromocytoma)

- Assessing drug compliance and effects (particularly in resistant cases)
- Nocturnal blood pressure dipper status (non-dippers are at higher risk)

2. JVP, ARTERIAL PULSE AND HEART SOUNDS

2.1 Jugular venous pulse (JVP)

This reflects the right atrial pressure (normal to 3 cm above the clavicle). This should fall with inspiration, which increases venous return by a suction effect of the lungs and with expansion of the pulmonary beds. However, if the neck veins are distended by inspiration this implies that the right heart chambers cannot increase in size due to restriction by fluid or pericardium: **Kussmaul's Sign**.

Normal waves in the JVP

a wave:	Due to atrial contraction — active push up SVC and into right ventricle (may cause an audible S4)
c wave:	An invisible flicker in the x descent due to closure of the tricuspid valve, before the start of ventricular systole
x descent:	Downward movement of the heart causes atrial stretch and drop in pressure
v wave:	Due to passive filling of blood into atrium against a closed tricuspid valve
y descent:	Opening of tricuspid valve with passive movement of blood from right atrium to right ventricle (causing an S3 when audible)

Continues ...

... Continued

Pathological waves in the JVP

a waves:	Lost in atrial fibrillation, giant in tricuspid stenosis or in pulmonary hypertension with sinus rhythm. (Atrial septal defect will exaggerate the natural a and v waves in sinus rhythm.)
Giant V(S) waves:	Merging of the a and v into a large wave (with a rapid y descent) as pressure continues to increase due to ventricular systole in patients with tricuspid regurgitation
Steep x descent:	Occurs in states where there is atrial filling only due to ventricular systole, i.e. compressed atrial states with tamponade or constrictive pericarditis
Rapid y descent:	Occurs in states where high flow occurs with tricuspid valve opening (e.g. tricuspid regurgitation (high atrial load) or constrictive pericarditis) — vacuum effect. A slow y descent indicates tricuspid stenosis.
Cannon waves:	Atrial contractions against a closed tricuspid valve due to either a nodal rhythm, a ventricular tachycardia, ventricular-paced rhythm (regular), complete heart block or ventricular extrasystoles (irregular). They occur regularly but not consistently in type 1 second degree heart block.

Non-pulsatile JVP elevation occurs with SVC obstruction.

2.2 Arterial pulse associations

- **Collapsing**: aortic regurgitation, arterio-venous fistula, patent ductus arteriosus or other large extra-cardiac shunt.
- **Slow rising**: aortic stenosis (delayed percussion wave).
- **Bisferiens**: a double shudder due to mixed aortic valve disease with significant regurgitation (tidal wave second impulse).
- **Jerky**: hypertrophic obstructive cardiomyopathy.
- **Alternans**: severe left ventricular failure.
- **Paradoxical**: an excessive reduction in the pulse with inspiration (drop in systolic BP >10 mmHg) occurs with left ventricular compression, tamponade, constrictive pericarditis or severe asthma as venous return is compromised.

Causes of an absent radial pulse

- Dissection of aorta with subclavian involvement
- Iatrogenic: post-catheterization
- Peripheral arterial embolus
- Takayasu's arteritis
- Trauma

2.3 Cardiac apex

An absent apical impulse

The apex may be impalpable in the following situations:

- Obesity/emphysema
- Right pneumonectomy with displacement
- Pericardial effusion or constriction
- Dextrocardia (palpable on right side of chest)
- Asystole.

Apex associations

Palpation of the apex beat (reflecting counterclockwise ventricular movement striking the chest wall during isovolumic contractions) can detect the following pathological states:

- **Heaving**: left ventricular hypertrophy (and all its causes).
- **Thrusting/hyperdynamic**: high left ventricular volume (e.g. in mitral regurgitation, AR, PDA).
- **Tapping**: palpable first heart sound in mitral stenosis.
- **Displaced and diffuse/dyskinetic**: left ventricular impairment and dilatation; dilated cardiomyopathy, myocardial infarction.
- **Double impulse**: with dyskinesia is due to left ventricular aneurysm; without dyskinesia in HCM.
- **Pericardial knock**: constrictive pericarditis.
- **Parasternal heave**: due to right ventricular hypertrophy (e.g. ASD, pulmonary hypertension, chronic obstructive airways disease, pulmonary stenosis).

2.4 Heart sounds

Abnormalities of first heart sound (S1): closure of mitral and tricuspid valves

Loud	Soft	Split	Variable
Mobile mitral stenosis	Immobile mitral stenosis	RBBB	Atrial fibrillation
Hyperdynamic states	Hypodynamic states	LBBB	Complete heart block
Tachycardic states	Mitral regurgitation	VT	
Left to Right shunts	Poor ventricular function	Inspiration	
Short PR interval	Long PR interval		

Abnormalities of second heart sound (S2): closure of aortic then pulmonary valves (<0.05 s apart)

Intensity	Splitting	
Loud	*Fixed*	*Single S2*
Systemic hypertension (loud A2)	ASD	Severe PS/AS
		Hypertension
Pulmonary hypertension (loud P$_2$)	*Widely split*	Large VSD
	RBBB	Fallot's tetralogy
Tachycardic states	Pulmonary stenosis	Eisenmenger syndrome
ASD (loud P$_2$)	Deep inspiration	Pulmonary atresia
	Mitral regurgitation	Elderly
Soft		*Reversed split S2*
Severe aortic stenosis		LBBB
		Right ventricular pacing
		PDA
		Aortic stenosis

Third heart sound (S3)

Due to the passive filling of the ventricles on opening of the AV valves audible in normal children and young adults. Pathological in cases of rapid left ventricular filling (e.g. mitral regurgitation, VSD, CCF and constrictive pericarditis).

Fourth heart sound (S4)

Due to the atrial contraction that fills a stiff left ventricle, such as in left ventricular hypertrophy, amyloid, HCM and left ventricular ischaemia. It is absent in atrial fibrillation.

Causes of valvular clicks

- **Aortic ejection**: aortic stenosis $\pm$ bicuspid aortic valve.
- **Pulmonary ejection**: pulmonary stenosis
- **Mid-systolic**: mitral valve prolapse.

3. VALVULAR DISEASE AND ENDOCARDITIS

3.1 Murmurs

Benign flow murmurs are soft, short systolic murmurs heard along the left sternal edge to the pulmonary area, without any other cardiac auscultatory, ECG or chest X-ray abnormalities. Thirty per cent of children may give an innocent flow murmur.

Cervical venous hum: continuous when upright and is reduced by lying; occurs with a hyperdynamic circulation or with jugular vein compression.

Large A-V fistula of the arm: may cause a harsh flow murmur across the upper mediastinum.

Effect of posture on murmurs: standing significantly increases the murmurs of mitral valve prolapse and HCM only. Squatting increases cardiac afterload and therefore decreases the murmur of HCM whilst increasing most other murmurs such as ventricular septal defect, aortic, mitral and pulmonary regurgitation, and aortic stenosis.

Effect of respiration on murmurs: inspiration accentuates right-sided murmurs by increasing venous return, whereas held expiration accentuates left-sided murmurs. The strain phase of a Valsava manoeuvre reduces venous return, stroke volume and arterial pressure, decreasing all valvular murmurs but increasing the murmur of HCM.

Classification of particular murmurs

- **Mid/late systolic murmur**
  Innocent murmur
  Aortic stenosis or sclerosis
  Coarctation of the aorta
  Pulmonary stenosis
  HCM
  Papillary muscle dysfunction
  Atrial septal defect (due to high
    pulmonary flow)

- **Mid-diastolic murmurs**
  Mitral stenosis or 'Austin Flint' due to aortic regurgitant jet
  Carey Coombs (rheumatic fever)
  High AV flow states (ASD, VSD, PDA,
    anaemia, mitral regurgitation, tricuspid regurgitation)
  Atrial tumours (particularly if
    causing AV flow disturbance)

- **Continous murmurs**
  PDA
  Ruptured sinus of valsalva aneurysm
  Large arterio-venous fistula
  ASD
  Anomalous left coronary artery
  Intercostal AV fistula

3.2 Mitral stenosis

Two-thirds of patients presenting with this are women. The most common cause remains chronic rheumatic heart disease; rarer causes include congenital disease, carcinoid, SLE and mucopolysaccharidoses (glycoprotein deposits on cusps). Stenosis may occur at the cusp, commisure or chordal level.

- Anticoagulation for atrial fibrillation protects from 17x increased risk of thrombo-embolism.

Mitral balloon valvuloplasty

Valvuloplasty using an Inove balloon requires either a trans-septal or a retrograde approach and is used only in suitable cases where echo shows:

- The mitral leaflet tips and valvular chordae are not heavily thickened, distorted or calcified
- The mitral cusps are mobile at the base
- There is minimal or no mitral regurgitation
- No left atrial thrombus is seen on TOE.

Features of severe mitral stenosis

- **Symptoms**
  Dyspnoea with minimal activity,
    haemoptysis
  Dysphagia (due to
    LA enlargement)

- **Chest X-ray**
  Left atrial or right ventricular
    enlargement
  Splaying of subcarinal angle (>90°)
  Pulmonary congestion or
    hypertension
  Pulmonary haemosiderosis

- **Echo**
  Doming of leaflets
  Heavily calcified cusps
  Direct orifice area <1.0 cm²

- **Signs**
  Long diastolic murmur
  Close proximity of opening snap
    to S2 (lost if valves not mobile)
  Right ventricular heave or loud P2
  Pulmonary regurgitation
    (Graham-Steell murmur)
  Tricuspid regurgitation

- **Cardiac catheterization**
  PCW end diastole: LVEDP gradient
    >15 mmHg
  LA pressures >25 mmHg
  Elevated right ventricular and
    pulmonary artery pressures
  High pulmonary vascular resistance
  Cardiac output <2.5 l/min/m²
    with exercise

3.3 Mitral regurgitation

The full structure of the mitral valve includes the annulus, cusps, chordae and papillary musculature and abnormalities of any of these may cause regurgitation. The presence of symptoms, and increasing left ventricular dilatation are indicators for surgery in the chronic setting. Operative mortalities are 2–7% for valvular replacements in patients with NYHA grade 2–3 symptoms. Valve repairs (when possible) have better mortality rates.

When left ventricular impairment leads to annular dilatation, mitral regurgitation may be functional and this is commonly encountered. However, the other main causes are as follows:

- Chronic rheumatic disease
- Disorders of collagen such as
    Marfan's syndrome
- Ischaemic (e.g. papillary muscle
    dysfunction)

- Endocarditis
- Connective tissue diseases
- Idiopathic
- Associated with an atrial septal defect
    or with HCM

Indicators of the severity of mitral regurgitation

- Left ventricular enlargement due to overload
- Presence of S3
- Mid-diastolic flow murmur
- Praecordial thrill, signs of pulmonary hypertension or congestion.

Signs of predominant mitral regurgitation in mixed mitral valve disease

- Soft S1; S3 present
- Left ventricular enlargement with thrusting apex
- ECG showing left ventricular hypertrophy and left axis deviation.

Mitral valve prolapse (MVP)

This condition occurs in 5% of the population and is commonly over-diagnosed (depending on the echocardiography criteria applied). The patients are usually females and may present with chest pains, palpitations or fatigue. Squatting increases the click and standing increases the murmur, but the condition may be diagnosed in the absence of the murmur by echo. Often there is myxomatous degeneration and redundant valve tissue due to deposition of acid mucopolysaccharide material. Antibiotic prophylaxis before dental or surgical interventions should be recommended for those with a murmur. Several conditions are associated with MVP, and patients with the condition are prone to certain sequelae.

Sequelae of mitral valve prolapse:

- Embolic phenomena
- Rupture of mitral valve
- Dysrhythmias with QT prolongation
- Sudden death
- Cardiac neurosis.

Conditions associated with mitral valve prolapse

- Coronary artery disease
- Cardiomyopathy — DCM/HCM
- PDA
- Pseudoxanthoma elasticum
- Myocarditis
- Muscular dystrophy
- Polycystic kidney disease
- Secundum ASD
- WPW syndrome
- Marfan's syndrome
- Osteogenesis imperfecta
- SLE; polyarteritis nodosa
- Left atrial myxoma

3.4 Aortic regurgitation

Patients with severe chronic aortic regurgitation (AR) have the largest end-diastolic volumes of those with any forms of heart disease and also have a greater number of non-cardiac signs. AR may occur acutely (as in dissection or endocarditis) or chronically when the left ventricle has time to accommodate.

● **Causes of aortic regurgitation**
  Valve inflammation
    Chronic rheumatic
    Infective endocarditis
    Rheumatoid arthritis; SLE
    Hurler's syndrome
  Aortitis
    Syphilis
    Ankylosing spondylitis
  Aortic dissection/trauma
  Hypertension
  Bicuspid aortic valve
  Ruptured sinus of valsava aneurysm
  VSD with prolapse of (R) coronary cusp
  Disorders of collagen
    Marfan's syndrome (aortic aneurysm)
    Hurler's syndrome
    Pseudoxanthoma elasticum

● **Eponymous signs associated with AR**
  Quincke's sign — nail bed fluctuation of capillary flow
  Corrigan's pulse — (waterhammer); collapsing radial pulse
  Corrigan's sign — visible carotid pulsation
  De Musset's sign — head nodding with each systole
  Duroziez's sign — audible femoral bruits with diastolic flow (indicating moderate severity)
  Traube's sign — 'pistol shots' (systolic auscultatory finding of the femoral arteries)
  Austin Flint murmur — functional mitral diastolic flow murmur
  Argyll–Robertson pupils — aetiological connection with syphilitic aortitis

Indications for surgery

Acute severe AR will not be tolerated for long by a normal ventricle and therefore requires prompt surgery, except in the case of infection where delay for antibiotic therapy is preferable (if haemodynamic stability allows). At 10 years, 50% of patients with moderate chronic AR are alive, but once symptoms occur deterioration is rapid.

Features of AR indicative of the need for surgery

- **Symptoms of dyspnoea/LVF**
  Reducing exercise tolerance

- **Rupture of sinus of valsalva aneurysm**

- **Infective endocarditis not responsive to medical treatment**

- **Enlarging aortic root diameter in Marfan's syndrome with AR**

- **Enlarging heart**
  End systolic diameter >55 mm at echo
  Pulse pressure >100 mmHg
  Diastolic pressure <40 mmHg
  Lengthening diastolic murmur
  ECG: lateral lead T wave inversion

3.5 Aortic stenosis (AS)

Patients often present with the classic triad of symptoms: angina, dyspnoea and syncope. Echo and cardiac catheterization gradients of >60 mmHg are considered severe and are associated with a valve area <0.5 cm². The gradient may be reduced in the presence of deteriorating left ventricular function or mitral stenosis, or significant aortic regurgitation.

- **Causes of AS**: may be congenital bicuspid valve (usually male children, who present in sixth decade), degenerative calcification (common in the elderly) and post-rheumatic disease.
- **Subvalvular** causes of aortic gradients include HCM and subaortic membranous stenosis, while **supravalvular** stenosis is due to aortic coarctation, or William's syndrome (with elfin facies, mental retardation, hypercalcaemia).
- **Sudden death**: may occur in AS or in subvalvular stenosis due to ventricular tachycardia. The vulnerability to ventricular tachycardia is due to LVH.
- **Complete heart block**: may be due to calcification involving the upper ventricular septal tissue housing the conducting tissue. This may also occur post-operatively (after valve replacement) due to trauma.
- **Calcified emboli**: may arise in severe calcific AS.
- All symptomatic patients should be considered for surgery: operative mortality for AS is predominantly related to the absence (2–8%) or presence (10–25%) of left ventricular failure.

Indicators of severe AS

- Symptoms of syncope or LV failure
- Signs of left ventricular failure
- Soft single S2 or paradoxically split A2
- Presence of praecordial thrill
- Slow rising pulse with narrow pulse pressure
- Late peaking of long murmur

3.6 Tricuspid regurgitation (TR)

Aetiologies for severe TR include the following:

- Functional, due to right ventricular dilatation
- Infection due to intravenous drug abuse
- Carcinoid (nodular hepatomegaly and telangiectasia)
- Post-rheumatic
- Ebstein's anomaly: tricuspid valve dysplasia with a more apical position to the valve. Patients have cyanosis and there is an association with pulmonary atresia or ASD, and less commonly, Fallot's tetralogy.

3.7 Prosthetic valves

Valve prostheses may be metal or tissue (bioprosthetic). Mechanical valves are more durable but tissue valves do not require full lifelong anticoagulation. All prostheses must be covered with antibiotic therapy for dental and surgical procedures; they have a residual transvalvular gradient across them.

Mechanical valves
- **Starr–Edwards**: ball and cage — ESM in aortic area and an opening sound in mitral position are normal.
- **Bjork–Shiley**: single tilt disc — audible clicks without stethoscope.
- **St Judes/Carbomedics**: double tilt discs with clicks.

Tissue valves
- **Carpentier–Edwards**: porcine three-cusp valve — 3 months' anticoagulation needed until tissue endothelialization. No need for long-term anticoagulation if patient in sinus rhythm.
- **Homografts**: usually cadaveric and, again, need no long term anticoagulation.

Infection of prosthetic valves
- Mortality is still as high as 60% depending on the organism
- Within 6 months of implantation is usually due to colonization by *Staphylococcus epidermidis*
- Septal abscesses may cause PR interval lengthening
- Valvular sounds may be muffled by vegetations; new murmurs may occur
- Mild haemolysis may occur, and is detected by the presence of urobilinogen in the urine
- Dehiscence is an ominous feature requiring urgent intervention.

Anticoagulation in pregnancy

Warfarin may cause fetal haemorrhage and has a teratogenicity risk of 5–30%. This risk is dose-dependent and abnormalities include chondrodysplasia, mental impairment, optic atrophy, and nasal hypoplasia. The risk of spontaneous abortion may be increased. At 36 weeks it is advised to switch to intravenous heparin for delivery. Breast-feeding is not a problem with warfarin. In all cases, consideration of the health of the mother should be paramount.

3.8 Infective endocarditis

Groups affected by endocarditis	% of all cases of endocarditis
Chronic rheumatic disease	30
No previous valve disease	40
Intravenous drug abuse	10
Congenital defects	10
Prosthetic	10

- *Streptococcus viridans* (α haemolytic group) are still the most common organisms, occurring in 50% of cases.
- Marantic (metastatic-related) and SLE-related (Libman–Sacks) endocarditis are causes of non-infective endocarditis.

See also previous section on 'Prosthetic valves'.

- **Poor prognostic factors in endocarditis**
  Prosthetic valve
  Staphylococcus aureus infection
  Culture-negative endocarditis
  Depletion of complement levels

- **Indications for surgery**
  Cardiac failure
  Extensive valve incompetence
  Large vegetations
  Septic emboli
  Septal abscess
  Fungal infection
  Antibiotic-resistant endocarditis

Antibiotic prophylaxis

This is indicated in the following.

- Past history of infective endocarditis
- Prostheses
- HCM
- Use with pacemaker and defibrillator implantations
- Certain types of valve disease
- Most congenital heart disease (except unclosed secundum ASD)
- Balloon valvotomies
- Shunt closure devices

Prophylaxis should be used to cover:

- All dental procedures
- All surgical, obstetric and gynaecological procedures, including an uncomplicated vaginal delivery when placenta handling may cause bacteraemia
- Cover of gastroscopies and trans-oesophageal echocardiography (though very low risk) and rigid bronchoscopies
- Cover of those patients with mitral valve prolapse if murmur present or mitral regurgitation detectable on echocardiogram.

4. CONGENITAL HEART DISEASE

Causes of congenital acyanotic heart disease*

- **With shunts**
  Aortic coarctation (with VSD
   or PDA)
  Ventricular septal defect
  Atrial septal defect
  Patent ductus arteriosus
  Partial anomalous venous drainage
   (with ASD)

- **Without shunts**
  Congenital aortic stenosis
  Aortic coarctation

Causes of cyanotic heart disease

- **With shunts**
  Fallot's tetralogy (VSD)
  Severe Ebstein's anomaly (ASD)
  Complete transposition of great
   vessels (ASD ± VSD/PDA)

- **Without shunts**
  Tricuspid atresia
  Severe pulmonary stenosis
  Pulmonary atresia
  Hypoplastic left heart

*Associated shunts

4.1 Atrial septal defect (ASD)

Atrial septal defects (ASDs) are the most common congenital defects found in adulthood. Rarely, they may present as stroke in young people, due to paradoxical embolus that originated in the venous system and reached the cerebral circulation via right to left shunting. Fixed splitting of the second heart sound is the hallmark of an uncorrected ASD. There are three main sub-types:

- **Secundum (70%)**: central fossa ovalis defects often associated with mitral valve prolapse (10–20% of cases). ECG shows incomplete or complete RBBB with *right* axis deviation. Note that the **patent foramen ovale** (slit-like deficiency in the fossa ovalis) occurs in 25% of the population, but this does not allow equalization of atrial pressures, unlike ASD.
- **Primum (15%)**: sited above the atrio-ventricular valves, often associated with varying degrees of mitral regurgitation and thus usually picked up earlier in childhood. ECG shows RBBB, left axis deviation, 1° heart block. Associated with Down's, Klinefelter's and Noonan's syndromes.
- **Sinus venosus (15%)**: defect in the upper septum, often associated with anomalous pulmonary venous drainage directly into the right atrium.

Operative closure is recommended with pulmonary to systolic flow ratios above 1.5:1. Closure of secundum defects may be performed via cardiac catheterization.

Holt–Oram syndrome: (triphalangeal thumb with ASD) is a rare syndrome (autosomal dominant with incomplete penetration). It is associated with absence (or reduction anomalies) of the upper arm.

Lutembacher's syndrome: a rare combination of an ASD with mitral stenosis (the latter is probably rheumatic in origin).

Investigations for ASDs

Right atrial and right ventricular dilatation may be seen on any imaging technique as may pulmonary artery conus enlargement. Other characteristic features are:

- **Chest X-ray**: pulmonary plethora
- **Echo**: paradoxical septal motion, septal defect and right to left atrial contrast flow during venous injection with Valsalva manoeuvre
- **Catheterization**: pulmonary hypertension: raised right ventricular pressures and step up in oxygen saturation between various parts of the right circulation (e.g. SVC to high RA). Left ventricular cavity shape may be characteristic.

4.2 Ventricular septal defect (VSD)

Ventricular septal defects are the most common isolated congenital defect (2/1000 births; around 30% of all congenital defects), spontaneous closure occurs in 30–50% of cases (usually muscular or membranous types).

- Irreversible pulmonary changes may occur from 1 year of age, with vascular hypertrophy and pulmonary arteriolar thrombosis, leading to Eisenmenger's syndrome.
- Parasternal thrill and pansystolic murmur are present. The murmur may be ejection systolic in very small or very large defects. With large defects the aortic component of the second sound is obscured, or even a single/palpable S2 is heard; a mitral diastolic murmur may occur.

There is a high risk of SBE with defects of any size and thus antibiotic prophylaxis is necessary.

Once Eisenmenger's complex develops, the thrill and LSE murmur abate and signs are of pulmonary hypertension ± regurgitation and right ventricular failure. Surgery should occur earlier to avoid this situation.

- **Other cardiac associations of VSD**
  PDA (10%)
  Aortic regurgitation (5%)
  Pulmonary stenosis
  ASD
  Fallot's tetralogy
  Coarctation of aorta

- **Types of VSD**
  Muscular
  Membranous
  Atrio-ventricular defect
  Infundibular
  Into right atrium (Gerbode defect)

4.3 Patent ductus arteriosus (PDA)

Patent ductus arteriosus (PDA) is common in premature babies, particularly female infants born at high altitude; also if maternal rubella occurs in the first trimester. The connection occurs between the pulmonary trunk and the descending aorta, usually just distal to the origin of the left subclavian artery. PDA often occurs with other abnormalities.

Key features of PDA

- A characteristic left subclavicular thrill
- Enlarged left heart and apical heave
- Continuous 'machinery' murmur
- Wide pulse pressure and bounding pulse

Signs of pulmonary hypertension and Eisenmenger's syndrome develop in about 5% of cases. Indomethacin closes the duct in about 90% of babies while intravenous prostaglandin E_1 may reverse the natural closure (useful when PDA associated with coarctation, hypoplastic left heart syndrome and in complete transposition of the great vessels). The PDA may also be closed thoracoscopically or percutaneously by use of a 'clam shell' or other device.

4.4 Coarctation of the aorta

Coarctation may present in infancy with heart failure, or in adulthood (third decade) with hypertension, exertional breathlessness or leg weakness. This 'shelf-like' obstruction of the aortic arch, usually distal to the left subclavian artery, is 2–5 times more common in males and is responsible for about 7% of congenital heart defects.

Treatment is by surgical resection, preferably with end-to-end aortic anastomosis, or by balloon angioplasty for recurrence after surgery (which occurs in 5–10% of cases). Complications may occur despite resection/repair and these include hypertension, heart failure, berry aneurysm rupture, premature coronary artery disease and aortic dissection (in the third or fourth decade of life).

- **Associations of coarctation**

  Cardiac:
  Bicuspid aortic valve (and thus
    AS ± AR) in 10–20%
  PDA
  VSD
  Mitral valve disease
  Non-cardiac:
  Berry aneurysms (Circle of Willis)
  Turner's syndrome
  Renal abnormalities

- **Signs of coarctation**

  Hypertension
  Radio-femoral delay of arterial pulse
  Absent femoral pulses
  Mid-systolic or continuous murmur
    (infraclavicular)
  Subscapular bruits
  Rib notching on chest X-ray
  Post-stenotic aortic dilatation
    on chest X-ray

4.5 Eisenmenger's syndrome

Reversal of left to right shunt, due to massive irreversible pulmonary hypertension (usually due to congenital cardiovascular malformations) leads to Eisenmenger's syndrome. Signs of development include:

- Decreasing intensity of tricuspid/pulmonary flow murmurs
- Single S2 with louder intensity, palpable P2; right ventricular heave
- Appearance of Graham–Steell murmur due to pulmonary regurgitation
- 'V' waves due to TR (which may be audible)
- Clubbing and central cyanosis.

Eisenmenger's syndrome

- **Causes**
  VSD (termed Eisenmenger's complex)
  ASD
  PDA

- **Complications of Eisenmenger's syndrome**
  Right ventricular failure
  Massive haemoptysis
  Cerebral embolism/abscess
  Infective endocarditis (rare)

4.6 Tetralogy of Fallot

The most common cause of cyanotic congenital heart disease (10%) usually presenting after age 6 months (as the condition may worsen after birth).

Key features

- Pulmonary stenosis (causes the systolic murmur)
- Right ventricular hypertrophy
- VSD
- Overriding of aorta
- Right-sided aortic knuckle (25%)

Clinical features	Possible complications of Fallot's tetralogy
Cyanotic attacks (pulmonary infundibular spasm)	Endocarditis
Clubbing	Polycythaemia
Parasternal heave	Coagulopathy
Systolic thrill	Paradoxical embolism
Palpable RV heave	Cerebral abscess
Soft ESM (inversely related to pulmonary gradient)	Ventricular arrhythmias
Single S2 (inaudible pulmonary closure)	
ECG features of right ventricular hypertrophy	

- Cyanotic attacks worsen with catecholamines, hypoxia and acidosis. The murmur lessens or disappears as the right ventricular outflow gradient increases.
- Squatting reduces the right to left shunt by increasing systemic vascular resistance; it also reduces venous return of acidotic blood from lower extremities, and hence reduces infundibular spasm.
- The presence of a systolic thrill and an intense pulmonary murmur differentiates the condition from Eisenmenger's syndrome.
- A Blalock shunt operation results in weaker pulses in the arm from which the subclavian artery is diverted to the pulmonary artery.

5. ARRHYTHMIAS AND PACING

Atrial fibrillation remains the most common cardiac arrhythmia, with incidence increasing with age (Framingham data indicate a prevalence of 76/1000 males and 63/1000 females aged 85–94 years).

Use of the term 'supraventricular tachycardia' (SVT) is best avoided as it is imprecise, particularly as radiofrequency ablation is changing the face of treatment in this condition. Ventricular tachycardia and fibrillation are life-threatening conditions, but implantable defibrillators and catheter or surgical ablation are now additional treatments to conventional pharmacological therapy.

5.1 Complete heart block (CHB)

Untreated acquired CHB is associated with mortality that may exceed 50% at one year, particularly in patients aged over 80 years and in those with non-rheumatic structural heart disease.

- CHB is the most common reason for permanent pacing.
- It occurs mostly with right coronary artery occlusion, when related to an infarction, as the AV nodal branch is usually one of the distal branches of the right coronary artery.
- CHB rarely (3–7% of patients) requires permanent pacing when it occurs after acute infarction.
- In patients with an anterior infarct CHB is a poor prognostic feature, indicating extensive ischaemia.
- Congenital cases may be related to connective tissue diseases. However, in patients having normal exercise capacities, recent studies show that prognosis is not as benign as was previously thought and pacing is therefore recommended.

5.2 Re-entrant tachycardias

- Characteristically produces a delta wave on the ECG due to early pathway-mediated ventricular activation (NB. Lown–Ganong–Levine syndrome: accessory pathway without delta wave) and thus has a short PR interval. The delta wave is lost with tachycardia if conduction via the pathway is retrograde (ventricle to atrium).
- Usually presents in adolescents with a narrow complex tachycardia (AV re-entry tachy-cardia) with the P wave occurring visibly and shortly after the QRS, rather than buried in the QRS as in AV nodal re-entry tachycardias (where the atria and ventricles depolarize simultaneously). In 90% of cases there is retrograde conduction via an accessory pathway — hence narrow tachycardia.
- Vagal manoeuvres may help, as may beta-blockers, flecainide and amiodarone.
- Digoxin and verapamil may accelerate conduction down the accessory pathway by blocking the AV node and **therefore should be avoided**.
- Radio frequency ablation is the treatment of choice; it incurs a 1% risk of CHB.

Wolff–Parkinson–White syndrome (WPW)

Occurring in 0.15% of healthy individuals, WPW is associated with an accessory pathway that connects the atrium and ventricle; this mediates the tachycardia, but more seriously, it can predispose to unopposed conduction of atrial fibrillation to the ventricle.

- **Associations with WPW**: Ebstein's anomaly (may have multiple pathways), HCM, mitral valve prolapse, thyrotoxicosis.

5.3 Atrial arrhythmias

Atrial flutter

The atrial rate is usually between 250–350 beats/min with a ventricular response of 150 beats/min. This may vary between a 1:1 ratio (with chemically slowed flutter) to 1:4 (with AV nodal disease). Isolated atrial flutter (without atrial fibrillation) is rare and has a lower association with thromboembolism; however, at the present time anticoagulation is often recommended with prolonged flutter.

- Ventricular response may be slowed by increasing the vagal block of the AV node (e.g. carotid sinus massage) or by adenosine which 'uncovers' the flutter waves on ECG
- Most likely arrhythmia to respond to DC cardioversion with low energies (e.g. 25 volts)
- Amiodarone and solatol may chemically cardiovert, slow the ventricular response or act as prophylactic agents
- Radiofrequency ablation is curative in up to 90% of cases.

Atrial fibrillation (AF)

This arrhythmia is due to multiple wavelet propagation in different directions. It may be paroxysmal, persistent (but 'cardiovertable') or permanent, and in all three states is a risk factor for strokes. Treatment is aimed at ventricular rate control, cardioversion, recurrence prevention and anticoagulation. Atrial defibrillators are now available.

Associations with atrial fibrillation

- Dilated left atrium
  (>4.5 cm)
- Thyroid disease
- IHD
- WPW
- Pericarditis
- Pulmonary embolus
- Atrial myxomas

- Mitral valve disease
- Left ventricular hypertrophy
- Acute alcohol excess/chronic
  alcoholic cardiomyopathy
- Post-coronary artery bypass graft (CABG)
- ASD
- Pneumonia
- Bronchial malignancy

The overall risk of systemic emboli is 5–7% annually (higher with rheumatic valve disease); this falls to 1.6% with anticoagulation. **Trans-oesophageal echocardiography** may exclude atrial appendage thrombus but cannot predict development of a thrombus in the early stages post-cardioversion; anticoagulation is therefore always recommended for prolonged atrial fibrillation.

- **Risk factors for stroke with non-valvular AF**

  Previous history of CVA or
   TIA (risk ↑ x 22.5)
  Diabetes (x1.7)
  Hypertension (x1.6)
  Left ventricular impairment
  Left atrial enlargement

- **Risk factors for recurrence of AF after cardioversion**

  Long duration (>1–3 years)
  Rheumatic mitral valve disease
  Left atrium size >5.5 cm
  Older age (>75 years)
  Left ventricular impairment

5.4 Ventricular arrhythmias and long QT syndromes

Ventricular tachycardia (monomorphic)

Ventricular tachycardia (VT) has a poor prognosis when left ventricular function is impaired. After the exclusion of reversible causes such patients may need implantable defibrillators and anti-arrhythmic therapy.

- Ventricular rate is usually 120–200/min
- Patients should be DC cardioverted when there is haemodynamic compromise; overdrive pacing may also terminate VT
- Amiodarone, sotalol, flecainide and lignocaine may be therapeutic adjuncts or prophylactic agents; magnesium may also be useful.

Associations of ventricular tachycardia

- Myocardial ischaemia
- Hypokalaemia or severe hyperkalaemia
- Long QT syndrome (see below)

- Cardiomyopathies
- Congenital abnormalities of the right ventricular outflow tract (VT with LBBB and right axis deviation pattern)

Features favouring ventricular tachycardia (VT) in broad complex tachycardia

It is often difficult to distinguish VT from SVT with aberration (disordered ventricular propagation of a supraventricular impulse); VT remains the most common cause of a broad complex tachycardia, especially with a previous history of myocardial infarction (MI). The following ECG observations favour VT:

- Capture beats: intermittent SA node complexes transmitted to ventricle
- Fusion beats: combination QRS from SA node and VT focus meeting and fusing (causes cannon waves)
- Right bundle branch block (RBBB) with LAD
- Very wide QRS >140 ms
- Altered QRS compared to sinus rhythm
- V leads concordance with all QRS vectors, positive or negative
- Dissociated P waves: marching through the VT
- History of ischaemic heart disease: very good predictor
- Variable SI
- HR <170 beats/min with no effect of carotid sinus massage.

Ventricular tachycardia (polymorphic) — torsades des pointes

Anti-arrhythmic agents may predispose to torsades as the arrhythmia is often initiated during bradycardia. The VT is polymorphic, with QT prolongation when patient is in sinus rhythm.

- Intravenous magnesium and K^+ channel openers may control the arrhythmia, whereas isoprenaline and temporary pacing may prevent bradycardia and hence the predisposition to VT
- May be due to QT prolongation of any cause (see below).

Long QT syndromes (including Romano Ward; Jervell–Lange–Neilsen)

Abnormally prolonged QT intervals may be familial or acquired, and are associated with syncope and sudden death, due to ventricular tachycardia (especially torsades des pointes). Mortality in the untreated symptomatic patient with congenital abnormality is high but some patients may reach the age of 50–60 years despite repeated attacks. Causes and associations are shown opposite.

Causes and associations of prolonged QT intervals

- **Familial**
  Jervell–Lange–Neilsen syndrome
  Romano Ward syndrome

- **Ischaemic heart disease**

- **Metabolic**
  Hypocalcaemia
  Hypothyroidism
  Hypothermia
  Hypokalaemia

- **Rheumatic carditis**

- **Mitral valve prolapse**

- **Drugs**
  Quinidine
  Erythromycin
  Amiodarone
  Tricyclic antidepressants
  Phenothiazines
  Probucol
  Non-sedating antihistamines
  (e.g. terfenadine)

- The QT is >540 ms (normal = 380–460 ms)
- Ninety per cent are familial, with chromosome 3, 7 or 11 defects (Romano Ward is autosomal dominant inheritance, Jervell–Lange–Neilsen is autosomal recessive and associated with congenital sensorineural deafness)
- Arrhythmias may be reduced by a combination of beta-blockers and pacing.

Cardiac causes of electro-mechanical dissociation (EMD)

When faced with a cardiac arrest situation it is important to appreciate the list of causes of electro-mechanical dissociation (EMD).

- Severe hypovolaemia or massive haemorrhage
- Massive pulmonary embolism
- Aortic dissection
- Electrolyte disturbance
  (e.g. severe hyperkalaemia)
- Severe acidosis
- Prosthetic valve dysfunction

- Severe hypoxia
- Cardiac tamponade
- Tension pneumothorax
  (unilateral or bilateral)
- Drugs/toxin overdose
- Acute hypothermia
- Massive myocardial infarction

5.5 Temporary pacing and ablation procedures

Temporary pacing

The ECG will show LBBB morphology (unless there is septal perforation when it is RBBB). Pacing may be ventricular (right ventricle apex) or atrio-ventricular (atrial appendage and right ventricle apex) for optimized cardiac output.

Complications include:

- Crossing the tricuspid valve during insertion causes ventricular ectopics, as does irritating the outflow tract.
- Atrial or right ventricular perforation and pericardial effusion.
- **Pneumothorax**: internal jugular route is preferable to subclavian as it minimizes this risk and also allows control after inadvertent arterial punctures.

Permanent pacing

More complex permanent pacing systems include rate-responsive models which use piezocrystal movement sensors or physiological triggers (respiratory rate or QT interval) to increase heart rates. Although more expensive they avoid causing pacemaker syndrome and they act more physiologically for optimal left ventricular function.

● **Indications for temporary pacing**	● **Indications for permanent pacing**
Asystole	Chronotrophic incompetence (inability
Haemodynamically compromised	to appropriately increase heart rate
bradycardia	with activity)
Prophylaxis of myocardial	Post-AV nodal ablation for arrhythmias
infarction complicated by second	Neurocardiogenic syncope
degree or complete heart block	Hypertrophic cardiomyopathy
Pre-operatively for	Dilated cardiomyopathy (may pace
trifascicular block	more than two chambers)
Prior to cardiac interventions or	Long QT syndrome
pacemaker replacement	Prevention of atrial fibrillation
Prevention of some tachyarrhythmias	Post-cardiac transplantation
Overdrive termination of various	Chronic atrio-ventricular block
arrhythmias (e.g. atrial flutter, VT)	

Radio frequency ablation

Radio frequency ablation is heat-mediated (65°C) protein membrane disruption causing cell lysis without the risk of coagulum forming on the electrode tip. Using cardiac catheterization (with electrodes in right- or left-sided chambers) it interrupts electrical pathways in cardiac structures. Excellent results are obtained with accessory pathways, His–Purkinje system tachycardias or for AV nodal ablation. Technically more difficult in atrial flutter (where a line of block across the atrium is required) and in VT (ventricular myocardium much thicker than atrial). Complete heart block and pericardial effusions are rare complications.

6. ISCHAEMIC HEART DISEASE

Cardiovascular disease remains the largest cause of death in the UK, accounting for almost 250,000 deaths (77,000 from myocardial infarction) in 1994 (compared to 140,000 deaths from malignant disease).

Risk factors for coronary artery disease (CAD)

- **Primary**
  Hypercholesterolaemia (LDL)
  Hypertension
  Smoking

- **Unclear**
  Low fibre intake
  Hard water
  High plasma fibrinogen levels
  Raised Lp (a) levels
  Raised Factor VII levels

- **Protective factors**
  Exercise
  Moderate amounts of alcohol
  Low cholesterol diet
  Increased HDL:LDL

- **Secondary**
  Reduced HDL cholesterol
  Obesity
  IDDM
  NIDDM
  Family history of CAD
  Physical inactivity
  Stress and personality type
  Gout and hyperuricaemia
  Race (Asians)
  Low weight at 1 year of age
  Male sex
  Chronic renal failure
  Increasing age
  Low social class
  Increased homocystine levels
    and homocystinuria

Smoking and its relationship to cardiovascular disease

Smokers have an increased incidence of the following cardiovascular complications:

- Coronary artery disease
- Malignant hypertension
- Ischaemic stroke
- Morbidity from peripheral vascular disease

- Sudden death
- Subarachnoid haemorrhage
- Mortality due to aortic aneurysm
- Thromboembolism in patients taking oral contraceptives

Both active and passive smoking increases the risk of coronary atherosclerosis by a number of mechanisms. These include:

- Increased platelet adhesion/aggregation and whole blood viscosity
- Increased heart rate; increased catecholamine sensitivity/release
- Increased carboxyhaemoglobin level and, as a result, increased haematocrit
- Decreased HDL-cholesterol and vascular compliance
- Decreased threshold for ventricular fibrillation.

6.1 Angina

Other than the usual forms of stable and unstable angina, those worthy of specific mention include:

- **Decubitus:** usually on lying down — due to an increase in LVEDP or associated with dreaming, cold sheets, or coronary spasm during REM sleep.
- **Variant (Prinzmetal):** unpredictable, at rest, with transient ST elevation on ECG. Due to coronary spasm, with or without underlying arteriosclerotic lesions.
- **Syndrome X:** associated with ST depression on exercise test, but angiographically normal coronary arteries. May reflect very small vessel disease and/or abnormal ventricular function. Ischaemia can be proven by assessment of lactate in the coronary sinus after atrial pacing. Usually affects middle-aged menopausal women after hysterectomy.
- **Vincent's angina:** nothing to do with cardiology; infection of pharyngeal and tonsillar space!

Causes of non-anginal chest pains

- **Pericardial pain**

- **Aortic dissection**

- **Mediastinitis**
  Associated with trauma,
  pneumothorax or diving

- **Pleural**
  Usually with breathlessness in
  pleurisy, pneumonia,
  pneumothorax or a large
  peripheral pulmonary embolus

- **Musculoskeletal**

- **Gastrointestinal**
  Including osesophageal, gastric,
  gallbladder, pancreatic

- **Hyperventilation/anxiety**
  Reproduction of sharp infra-mammary
  pains on forced hyperventilation is
  a reliable test

- **Mitral valve prolapse**
  May be spontaneous, sharp,
  superficial, short-lived pain

Symptomatic assessment of angina

The Canadian cardiovascular assessment of chest pain is useful for grading the severity of angina:

- **Grade I**: angina only on strenuous or prolonged exertion
- **Grade II**: angina climbing two flights of stairs
- **Grade III**: angina walking one block on the level (indication for intervention)
- **Grade IV**: angina at rest (indication for urgent intervention).

6.2 Myocardial infarction

Myocardial infarction (MI) occurs with an annual incidence of 5/1000 in the UK. The mortality associated with MI remains high, with a 40% out-of-hospital and 3–20% in-hospital mortality rate, and overall mortality of 13–27% at 28 days post-MI.

- **Posterior infarction** (a tall R wave in V1 with ST depression in leads V1–V3): no clear benefit of thrombolysis has been shown as few patients have been enrolled into major trials, especially as ECG interpretation is often difficult when the presentation is not with inferior infarct. Sixty per cent are due to right coronary artery disease.
- **Sub-endocardial (non-Q wave) infarctions**: have not been shown to benefit from thrombolysis. They have a low inpatient but high (65%) 1-year mortality (compared to 34% for Q-wave infarcts) and they should be investigated early and aggressively.

- If an **inferior infarct** is complicated by CHB with a broad complex escape rhythm, atropine, isoprenaline and temporary pacing should be considered before thrombolysis. Narrow complex escape rhythms are more stable. A two-week post-MI period is appropriate to allow the return of sinus rhythm before considering permanent pacing.
- The right coronary artery (RCA) is the dominant vessel (over left circumflex) in 85% of patients. As this gives off branches to SA and AV nodes, heart block and a larger infarct would be observed if a dominant RCA is occluded.

Although **warfarin** provides no general benefit, it may reduce the overall CVA rate (1.5–3.6%) in those patients with mural left ventricular thrombus on echo after a large anterior MI, and is thus recommended for up to 6 months after the infarction.

Cardiac enzymes

A number of markers of cardiac damage are now available. The following table is a guide to the timing of the initial rise, peak and return to normality.

Marker	Initial rise	Peak	Return to normal	Notes
Creatine phosphokinase*	4–8 h	18 h	2–3 days	CPK-MB is main cardiac isoenzyme
Myoglobin	1–4 h	6–7 h	24 h	Low specificity from skeletal muscle damage
Troponin I	3–12 h	24 h	3–10 days	Undergoing evaluation; appears to be sensitive and specific marker
Heart fatty acid binding protein	1.5 h	5–10 h	24 h	(As for troponin)
Lactate dehydrogenase (LDH)	10 h	24–48 h	14 days	Cardiac muscle mainly contains LDH

*Creatine phosphokinase has three isoenzymes of which the CPK-MB isoenzyme is more cardiac-specific, although numerous other organs possess the enzyme in small quantities. A ratio of CPK-MB: CPK of > 2.5:1 has been suggested as very specific for MI in the context of chest pain. This is inaccurate in situations of significant acute or chronic skeletal injury where CPK levels will be high.

Complications of MI

Since the advent of thrombolysis, complication rates have been reduced (e.g. halved for percarditis, conduction defects, ventricular thrombus, fever, Dressler's syndrome). All complications may be seen with any type of infarction, but the following are the most common associations.

- **Anterior infarctions**

  Late VT/VF
  Left ventricular aneurysm
  Left ventricular thrombus and
    systemic embolism (usually
    1–3 weeks post-MI)
  CHB (rare)
  Ischaemic mitral regurgitation
  Congestive cardiac failure
  Cardiac rupture — usually at
    days 4–10 with EMD
  VSD with septal rupture
  Pericarditis and pericardial effusion
    (**Dressler's** syndrome with high
    ESR, fever, anaemia, pleural
    effusions and anti-cardiac muscle
    antibodies is seen occasionally)

- **Inferior infarctions**

  Higher re-infarction rate
  Inferior aneurysm — with mitral
    regurgitation (rare)
  Pulmonary embolism (rare)
  CHB and other degrees of heart block
  Papillary muscle dysfunction and
    mitral regurgitation
  Right ventricular infarcts need high
    filling pressures (particularly if
    posterior extension)

Post-MI rehabilitation

After myocardial infarction, a patient should take 2 months off work and 1 month's abstinence from sexual intercourse and driving (see below). Cardiac rehabilitation is particularly important for patient confidence. Depression occurs in 30% of patients.

Fitness to drive
The DVLA provides extensive guidelines for coronary disease and interventions, but the essential points are:

- Ordinary drivers do not need to inform the DVLA of cardiac events unless a continuing disability results. Driving should be avoided for 1 month after MI, CABG, unstable angina or pacemaker insertion, and for 1 week after percutaneous coronary angioplasty (PTCA).
- Vocational drivers (HGV etc.) must inform the DVLA. They should not recommence driving until 3 months post-MI or CABG, and they must be symptom free and able to

complete the first three stages of a Bruce protocol safely, (off treatment for 24 hours), without symptoms, signs or ECG changes.
- Implantation of cardiac defibrillators usually results in permanent revocation of a driving licence.

6.3 Thrombolysis

Thrombolysis is beneficial up to 6 hours after pain onset but may be given for up to 12 hours in the context of continuing pain or deteriorating condition. Recanalization after thrombolysis occurs in 70% (15% without) of patients and results in a higher, earlier CPK rise (but a lower total CPK release). Reperfusion arrhythmias are common within the first 2 hours after thrombolysis. Theoretically (but generally impractical at this stage) primary angioplasty is better than thrombolysis for acute MI if performed within the first few hours.

Tissue plasminogen activator (TPA) and similar recombinant agents are 5–7 times more expensive than streptokinase (SK) and should be used only in patients to whom SK has previously been administered, those with proven streptococcal throat infections, or in hypotensive patients. The absolute added mortality benefit for large anterior MI in younger patients presenting within 4 hours is only 1% above SK.

Contraindications to thrombolysis

Although there are numerous relative contraindications where the risk/benefit considerations are individual to the patient (e.g. a large anterior infarct in a patient where access to primary PTCA is unavailable), there are several absolute contraindications to thrombolysis.

Contraindications to thrombolysis

- **Absolute**
  Active internal bleeding or
    uncontrollable external bleeding
  Suspected aortic dissection
  Recent head trauma (<2 weeks)
  Intracranial neoplasms
  History of proven haemorrhagic
    stroke or cerebral infarction
    <2 months earlier
  Uncontrolled blood pressure
    (>200/120 mmHg)
  Active untreated diabetic
    haemorrhagic retinopathy

- **Relative**
  Pregnancy
  Traumatic prolonged cardio-pulmonary
    resuscitation
  Bleeding disorders
  Recent surgery
  Probable intracardiac thrombus
    (e.g. AF with mitral stenosis)
  Anticoagulation or INR >1.8

Groups particularly benefiting from thrombolysis (determined by the GUSTO, ISIS 2 and ISIS 3 trials) include:

- Large anterior infarction
- Pronounced ST elevation
- Elderly (>75 years)
- Poor left ventricular function or LBBB, or systolic BP <100 mmHg
- Early administration: within 1 hour of pain onset.

Summary of clinical trials in patients with acute MI†

Agents used for acute MI	Mortality in treated group (%)	Mortality in control subjects (%)	Number treated to save 1 life	Trials involved
Aspirin	9.4 (at 5 weeks)	11.8	42	ISIS 2
Thrombolytics	10.7* (at 21 days)	13.0*	43*	GISSI 1*, ISIS 2, TIMI II, GUSTO
Beta-blockers	3.9 (at 7 days)	4.6	143	ISIS 1
ACE inhibitors	35.2* (after 39-month mean follow-up)	39.7*	22*	SAVE, SOLVD*, AIRE
Lipid lowering therapy (patients with average cholesterol)	10.2 (after 5 years)	13.2	33	CARE (note endpoints included second non-fatal MI and cardiac deaths)
Heparin with aspirin and any form of thrombolysis	8.6	9.1	200	Meta-analysis of 68,000 patients

†See also Appendix 2: 'Important trials in ischaemic heart disease'.
*Data from that particular trial.

Continues...

... Continued

Agents used for acute MI	Mortality in treated group (%)	Mortality in control subjects (%)	Number treated to save 1 life	Trials involved
Magnesium: contradictory data but no mortality reduction				LIMIT 1, 2, ISIS 4
Nitrates: no clear benefit				ISIS 4, GISSI 3
Warfarin: no proven benefit above aspirin after thrombolysis				

6.4 Coronary artery interventional procedures

After **percutaneous coronary angioplasty** (PTCA) the recurrence or re-stenosis rate is 30% within 3 months (without stent insertion) and 40–60% for total occlusions that are successfully dilated. Eighty per cent of lesions are suitable for PTCA (particularly discrete, proximal, uncalcified, unoccluded lesions which are away from side branches or the division of a vessel, and without thrombus). There is an acute occlusion rate of 3% with angioplasty that requires urgent bypass grafting.

Stenting is useful for dissection flaps impeding flow after angioplasty and after angioplasty in saphenous vein grafts. Diabetic subjects in particular benefit from stenting. Chronic total occlusions have better long term outcomes when stented after successful angioplasty. Other important considerations in coronary intervention are:

- Vessels < 2.5 mm in diameter have sub-optimal results after stenting whilst vessels > 4.5 mm in diameter rarely require it if the flow is good.
- **Ticlopidine** for 1 month is now used instead of warfarin to reduce 'in-stent' re-stenosis (see Chapter 2, *Clinical Pharmacology, Toxicology and Poisoning*).
- Balloon pumping is useful for proximal left anterior descending (LAD) disease or mainstream stenting in patients with poor left ventricular function.
- In patients with three-vessel disease, PCTA and CABG are comparable in price, but the former requires more repeat procedures.
- **Reopro** is an excellent adjunct during angioplasty in the presence of thrombus; it acts by inhibiting GP IIb/IIIa glycoprotein on platelets (see Chapter 2, *Clinical Pharmacology, Toxicology and Poisoning*).

Coronary artery bypass grafting (CABG)

Coronary artery bypass grafting has clear benefits in specific groups of patients with chronic coronary artery disease (when compared to medical therapy alone). Analysis has previously been limited because randomized trials included small numbers and were performed several decades ago; patients studied were usually males aged <65 years. The population now receiving CABG has changed, but so has medical therapy.

- Prognostic benefits shown for symptomatic, significant left main stem disease (Veteran's Study), symptomatic proximal three-vessel disease and in two-vessel disease which includes proximal LAD artery (CASS data).
- Patients with moderately impaired left ventricular function have greater benefit, but those with poor left ventricular function have greater operative mortality. Overall mortality is <2%, rising to between 5% and 10% for a second procedure. Eighty per cent of patients gain symptom relief.
- Peri-operative graft occlusion is around 10% for vein grafts, which otherwise last 8–10 years. Arterial grafts (internal mammary, gastro-epiploic) have a higher patency rate but long term data is awaited.
- A 'Dressler-like' syndrome may occur up to 6 months post-surgery.
- Minimally invasive CABG involves the redirection of internal mammary arteries to coronary vessels without the need for cardiac bypass and full stenotomy incisions. Recovery times following this procedure are extremely short.

7. OTHER MYOCARDIAL DISEASES

7.1 Cardiac failure

Cardiac failure can be defined as the pumping action of the heart being insufficient to meet the circulatory demands of the body (in the absence of mechanical obstructions). A broad echocardiographic definition is of an ejection fraction (EF) <40% (as in the SAVE trial, which enrolled patients for ACE inhibitors post-MI). Overall five-year survival is 65% with EF <40%, compared to 95% in those with EF >50%.

The ejection fraction is, however, only a guide and is dependent on other pre-load and after-load factors.

- **Pre-load**: will affect left ventricular end-diastolic pressure
- **After-load**: will affect left ventricular systolic wall tension.

Other echocardiographic features of LV dysfunction include reduced fractional shortening, LV enlargement and paradoxical septal motion.

The New York Heart Association (NYHA) classification is a helpful indication of severity:

NYHA class	Symptoms	One-year mortality
I	Asymptomatic with ordinary activity	5–10%
II	Slight limitation of physical activities	15%
III	Marked limitation of physical activities	30%
IV	Dyspnoeic symptoms at rest	50–60%

7.2 Hypertrophic cardiomyopathy (HCM)

Characteristic features of HCM

- Jerky pulse with large tidal wave as outflow obstruction is overcome
- Large 'a' waves in JVP
- Double apical impulse (palpable atrial systole in sinus rhythm)
- LSE systolic thrill (turbulence) with harsh ESM radiating to axilla
- Often accompanied by mitral regurgitation.

Important points to remember

- Associations with Friedreich's ataxia, WPW, phaeochromocytoma, familial lentiginosis.

- ESM *increases* with: GTN, digoxin and standing, due to volume reduction in diastole; ESM *decreases* with: squatting, beta-blockers, valsalva release, handgrip.

- Avoid digoxin (if in sinus rhythm), nitrates, atropine, inotropes, diuretics (unless in LVF).

- Cardiac catheterization abnormalities include a 'banana' or 'spade-shaped' left ventricular cavity in systole, mitral regurgitation and 'sword fish' narrowing of the left anterior descending artery.

- Autosomal-dominant in half the patients, associated with chromosomes 1, 11, 14 or 15. May also result from a gene mutation which leads to myocardial disarray and varying expression of hypertrophy. Prevalence <0.2% of the general population. Life expectancy is variable with symptoms and investigations determining risk of sudden death.

- **Sudden death** may be due to catecholamine-driven extreme outflow obstruction, ventricular fibrillation related to accessory pathway — transmitted AF, or massive MI. Sudden death may occur without hypertrophy. Annual mortality of 2.5% in adults and 6% in children.

- Poor prognostic features include young age of diagnosis, family history or sudden death and syncopal symptoms, but there is no correlation with the left ventricular outflow tract gradient.

- Pregnancy is possible, but haemorrhage, prolonged vaginal delivery effort and epidural analgesia are best avoided; antibiotic prophylaxis and counselling are advised.

- Therapeutic options include beta-blockers, calcium antagonists, amiodarone, dual chamber pacing, internal defibrillators, surgical myomectomy or therapeutic septal infarction.

Echocardiographic features of HCM (none are diagnostic)

- Asymmetrical septal hypertrophy: septum > 30% thicker than left ventricular posterior wall
- Left ventricular outflow tract gradient ± turbulence
- Premature closure of aortic cusps
- Almost complete obliteration of left ventricular cavity

- Systolic anterior motion of anterior mitral valve cusp probably due to venturi effect (see on M mode)
- Tip thickening of anterior mitral cusp where it strikes the septum
- Hypertrophy which may only be apical

7.3 Dilated cardiomyopathy (DCM)

Dilated cardiomyopathy (DCM) is a syndrome of global ventricular dysfunction and dilatation, usually with macroscopically normal coronary arteries (if causes of ischaemic cardiomyopathy are excluded). Aetiology is often undetermined and the condition is more common in males and Afro-Carribeans. There is often LBBB or poor R wave progression on ECG and anticoagulation is commonly warranted as the incidence of AF and ventricular thrombus is high.

Causes of DCM

- Alcohol
- Undiagnosed hypertension
- Autoimmune disease
- Nutritional deficiency (e.g. thiamine and selenium)
- Muscular dystrophies

- Viral infections (e.g. Coxsackie and HIV)
- Peripartum
- Drugs (e.g. doxorubicin)
- Infiltration (e.g. haemochromatosis, sarcoidosis)

7.4 Restrictive cardiomyopathy

This produces identical symptoms to constrictive pericarditis (see section 8.1) but surgery is of little use in restrictive cardiomyopathy. The ventricles are excessively rigid and impede diastolic filling. AF may supervene and stagnation of blood leads to thrombus formation.

- **Myocardial causes**

  Idiopathic
  Scleroderma
  Amyloid (see below)
  Sarcoid
  Haemochromatosis
  Glycogen storage disorders
  Gaucher's disease

- **Endomyocardial causes**

  Endomyocardial fibrosis
  Hyper-eosinophilic syndromes
    (including Loeffler's)
  Carcinoid
  Malignancy or radiotherapy
  Toxin-related

Cardiac amyloidosis

Cardiac amyloidosis behaves like restrictive cardiomyopathy but it may also be accompanied by pericardial thickening (due to nodular deposition), pericardial effusion and, rarely, tamponade. It is important to avoid digoxin in amyloid cardiac disease because of the risk of heart block and asystole.

7.5 Myocarditis

Myocarditis may be due to many different aetiological factors (e.g. viral, bacterial, fungal, protozoal, autoimmune, allergic and drugs). It may be difficult to differentiate it from DCM, but the following features may help:

- Usually young patient
- Acute history
- Prodrome of fever, arthralgia, respiratory tract infection, myalgia
- Neutrophilia
- Slight cardiomegaly on chest X-ray
- Episodes of VT, transient AV block and ST/T wave changes
- Elevated viral titres
- Cardiac enzymes raised (with normal coronary arteries).

Rheumatic fever

This follows a group A streptococcal infection; pancarditis usually occurs and valvular defects are long term sequelae. The cardiac histological marker is the Aschoff nodule. Patients are treated with penicillin and salicylates or steroids.

Critiera for diagnosis include the need for evidence of preceeding β-haemolytic streptococcal infection (raised ASOT, positive throat swab or history of scarlet fever), together with two major (or one major and two minor) Duckett–Jones criteria (see below).

Rheumatic fever (Duckett–Jones diagnostic criteria)

- **Major criteria**
  Carditis
  Polyarthritis
  Chorea
  Erythema marginatum
  Subcutaneous nodules

- **Minor criteria**
  Fever
  Arthralgia
  Previous rheumatic heart disease
  High ESR and CRP
  Prolonged PR interval on ECG

7.6 Cardiac tumours

Myxomas are the most common cardiac tumours, comprising 50% of most pathological series.

- **Autopsy incidence** of <0.3%; more common in females (2:1) and in the left atrium; usually benign (75%). May cause sudden death due to outflow obstruction across the mitral or tricuspid valves, or embolization symptoms in 40% of cases. May recur in 5–10% of cases despite resection, hence the need for annual TOE up to 5 years.
- **Signs**: fever and weight loss occur in 25%. There may be transient mitral stenosis, early diastolic 'plop', clubbing, Raynaud's phenomenon (rare), pulmonary hypertension. Usually the rhythm is sinus.
- **Investigations**: WCC high, platelets low, haemolytic anaemia or polycythaemia, raised immunoglobulins, raised ESR in 60% (thought to be due to secretion of interleukin 6).
- Avoid left ventricular catheterization; use TOE to diagnose and resect surgically.
- Other tumours include: papillomas, fibromas, lipomas, angiosarcomas, rhabdomyosarcomas and mesotheliomas.

7.7 Alcohol and the heart

Acute alcoholic intoxication is the most common cause of paroxysmal atrial fibrillation amongst younger individuals. Chronic excessive intake over 10 years is responsible for a third of the cases of DCM in Western populations; alcohol is also aetiologically related to hypertension,

CVA, arrhythmias and sudden death. Atrial fibrillation may be the first presenting feature (usually between the ages of 30–35 years).

Pathological mechanisms

- Direct myocardial toxic effect of alcohol and its metabolites
- Toxic effect of additives (e.g. cobalt)
- Secondary effect of associated nutritional deficiences (e.g. thiamine)
- Effect of hypertension

Treatment includes nutritional correction and — most importantly — complete abstinence from alcohol, without which 50% will die within 5 years. Abstinence may lead to a marked recovery of resting cardiac function.

Beneficial mechanisms of modest amounts of alcohol

- Favourable effects on lipids (50% of this benefit is due to raised HDL levels)
- Anti-thrombotic effects (perhaps by raising natural levels of t-PA)
- Anti-platelet effects (changes in prostacyclin:thromboxane ratios)
- Increase in insulin sensitivity
- Antioxidant effects of red wine (flavonoids and polyphenols)

7.8 Cardiac transplantation

With over 2500 heart-only transplants being performed in the USA each year, most often for intractable coronary disease and cardiomyopathy (44%), survival rates have been estimated at 80% at 1 year, 75% at 3 years and 40–50% at 10 years. Myocarditis is yet another indication; transplantation during the acute phase does not worsen prognosis, but myocarditis may recur in the donor heart.

The major complications encountered after transplantation include accelerated coronary atheroma, lymphoma, skin cancer (and other tumours) and CRF (due to cyclosporin A toxicity).

8. PERICARDIAL DISEASE

8.1 Constrictive pericarditis

Rare in clinical practice, it presents in a similar way to restrictive cardiomyopathy, i.e. with signs of right-sided heart failure (hepatomegaly, raised JVP, ascites and oedema) due to restriction of diastolic filling of both ventricles. It is treated by pericardial resection.

Other specific features include:

- Diastolic pericardial knock at the time of the y descent of the JVP which reflects the sudden reduction of ventricular filling — 'the ventricle slaps against the rigid pericardium'.
- Soft heart sounds.
- Severe pulsus paradox rarely occurs and indicates the presence of a co-existent tense effusion.
- Thickened, bright pericardium on echocardiography.

Causes of constrictive pericarditis

- Tuberculosis (usually post-pericardial effusion)
- Mediastinal radiotherapy
- Pericardial malignancy
- Drugs (e.g. hydralazine, associated with a lupus-like syndrome)

- Post-viral (especially haemorrhagic) or bacterial pericarditis
- Following severe uraemic pericarditis
- Trauma/post-cardiac surgery
- Connective tissue disease
- Recurrent pericarditis

Signs common to constrictive pericarditis and restrictive cardiomyopathy

- Raised JVP with prominent x + y descents
- Atrial fibrillation

- Non-pulsatile hepatomegaly
- Normal systolic function

Some key features distinguish constrictive pericarditis from restrictive cardiomyopathy:

- Absence of LVH in constrictive pericarditis
- Absent calcification on chest X-ray, prominent apical impulse and conduction abnormalities on ECG, which are features of restrictive cardiomyopathy.

However, a combination of investigations, including cardiac CT, MRI and cardiac biopsy, may be necessary to differentiate the two conditions.

8.2 Pericardial effusion

A slowly developing effusion of 2 litres can be accommodated by pericardial stretching and without raising the intrapericardial pressure. The classical symptoms of chest discomfort, dysphagia, hoarseness or dyspnoea (due to compression) may be absent. A large effusion can lead to muffled heart sounds, loss of apical impulse, occasional pericardial rub, small ECG complexes and eventually electro-mechanical dissociation.

Other key features are:

- **Pulsus alternans**: variable left ventricular output and right ventricular filling.
- **Pulsus paradoxus**: exaggerated inspiratory fall in systolic BP (mechanism described in section 2.2)
- **Electrical alternans on ECG**: 'swinging QRS axis'.
- **Globular cardiac enlargement on chest X-ray**.

Causes of pericardial effusion

- All causes as listed for constrictive pericarditis
- Aortic dissection
- Iatrogenic due to pacing or cardiac catheterization
- Ischaemic heart disease with ventricular rupture
- Anticoagulation associated with acute pericarditis

8.3 Cardiac tamponade

In contrast, if a small amount of intrapericardial fluid (e.g. <200 ml) accumulates rapidly, it can significantly limit ventricular filling, reduce cardiac output and elevate intracardiac pressures (particularly right-sided initially). Thus the 'y' descent due to right ventricular filling with tricuspid valve opening is lost as right ventricular pressures are high, and the 'x' descent of right atrium filling due to right ventricular contraction is prominent. The right atrium collapses in diastole as a result of impaired filling and high intrapericardial pressures. In early diastole even the right ventricle may collapse.

Common signs of cardiac tamponade

- Elevated systemic venous pressure
- Tachypnoea
- Systolic hypotension
- Paradoxical pulse
- Tachycardia
- Diminished heart sounds

Treatment is by urgent drainage — usually under echocardiographic control. Surgical 'pericardial' windows may be necessary for chronic (e.g. malignant) effusions.

9. DISORDERS OF MAJOR VESSELS

9.1 Pulmonary hypertension

It is important to determine whether pulmonary hypertension is secondary to an under-lying condition as this may be treatable. The most common cause of secondary pulmonary hypertension is COPD.

Causes of pulmonary hypertension

- **Primary pulmonary hypertension**

Secondary causes

- Chronic parenchymal lung disease (e.g. COPD)
- Chronic pulmonary thromboembolism
- Chronic hypoxia (high altitude, polio, myasthenia)
- Intravenous drug abusers with recurrent embolic vegetations
- HCM
- Cor triatrium
- Constrictive pericarditis and restrictive cardiomyopathy
- Appetite suppressants (e.g. fenfluramine)
- Left atrial myxoma

Primary pulmonary hypertension (PPH)

Primary pulmonary hypertension constitutes less than 1% of all cases of pulmonary hypertension. PPH has an incidence of 2 per million and is a disease of children and young adults, with the ratio of females:males (2:1). One in ten cases are familial. PPH is associated with connective tissue diseases and the vasculitides. The pulmonary arteries become dilated and abnormally thickened; there is dilatation of the proximal pulmonary vessels with thick-walled, obstructed 'pruned' peripheral vessels. As a consequence of the high pulmonary pressure the right ventricle undergoes marked hypertrophy.

Three types of PPH are recognized:

- Primary plexogenic pulmonary arteriopathy
- Thrombotic pulmonary arteriopathy
- Pulmonary veno-occlusive arteriopathy.

Patients present with gradual worsening exertional dyspnoea and, in the later stages, angina of effort and syncope occur. Fatigue is common and haemoptysis may occur.

- Signs include: cyanosis, right ventricular heave, loud P_2, tricuspid regurgitation, peripheral oedema and acites.
- Untreated the median survival is approximately 3 years.

Treatment of primary pulmonary hypertension

- Advise avoidance of strenuous exercise and recommend contraception, as pregnancy is harmful.

- Anticoagulation to avoid thrombus formation *in situ* in the pulmonary arteries and also pulmonary embolism.

- Calcium channel antagonists have been used to lower pulmonary (and systemic) pressure.

- Diuretics are helpful in the management of right heart failure.

- Prostacyclin (PGI_2), a potent pulmonary and systemic vasodilator, is used, particularly to bridge patients to transplantation. The drug has an extremely short half-life and has to be given by continuous intravenous infusion, usually through a tunnelled central venous catheter. It is also very expensive.

- Continuous ambulatory inhaled nitric oxide is being developed, and this would provide good pulmonary vasodilatation, but without systemic effect.

The chief therapeutic option is transplantation, as other treatments are of limited benefit, or are difficult to administer.

Summary of available treatments for pulmonary hypertension

- **General**
  Address secondary causes
   where possible
  Digoxin even in patients with
   sinus rhythm
  Diuretics for symptoms
  Ambulatory supplemental oxygen
   for some
  Anticoagulation

- **Vasodilator therapy
  (only helps some subjects)**
  Adenosine infusions or boluses
  Nitric oxide inhalation, nitrates
   (chronic infusion)
  Calcium channel blockers
  PGI_2 or PGE (chronic infusion)

- **Surgical options
  (in selected cases)**
  Heart–lung or single/double lung
   transplant
  Atrial septostomy (only if no
   resting hypoxia)

9.2 Venous thrombosis and pulmonary embolism (PE)

The true incidence of pulmonary embolism is unknown but PE probably accounts for 1% of all admissions. Predisposing factors are discussed in Chapter 8, *Haematology*.

One or more predisposing risk factors are found in 80–90% of cases. The oral contraceptive increases the risk of DVT/PE 2–4 times. However, thromboembolism is rare in women taking oestrogens without other risk factors.

Clinical features

Nearly all patients have one or more of the following symptoms: dyspnoea, tachypnoea or pleuritic chest pain. With a large pulmonary embolus patients may present with collapse. Hypoxaemia may be present with moderate or large pulmonary emboli.

Investigations

- **Chest X-ray**
  May be normal; pleural-based wedge-shaped defects described classically are rare and areas of oligaemia may be difficult to detect

- **D-dimer**
  Will be raised in PE but the test is non-specific

- **Helical CT scanning**
  Will demonstrate pulmonary emboli in the large pulmonary arteries but may not show small peripheral emboli

- **ECG**
  May show sinus tachycardia and, in massive PE, features of acute right heart strain; non-specific S-T segment and T-wave changes occur

- **Arterial blood gases**
  Show a low or normal pCO_2 and may show a degree of hypoxaemia

- **Ventilation/perfusion (V/Q) scanning**
  Shows one or more areas of ventilation perfusion mismatching

- **Pulmonary angiography**
  Remains the 'gold standard', but this is under-used

In each case a clinical assessment of the probability of PE should be made. As demonstrated in the PIOPED study:

- Cases of high clinical probability combined with a high probability V/Q scan are virtually diagnostic of PE.
- Similarly, cases of low clinical suspicion combined with low probability or normal V/Q scans make the diagnosis of PE very unlikely.
- All other combinations of clinical probability and V/Q scan result should be investigated further.
- Patients who present with collapse need urgent echocardiography, helical CT scan or pulmonary angiogram to demonstrate pulmonary embolus.

Management

In all cases of moderate or high clinical probability of PE, anticoagulation with heparin should be started immediately after baseline coagulation studies have been taken. If unfractionated heparin is used, an initial loading dose of 5000–10,000 units should be given intravenously followed by a continuous infusion of 1300 IU/hour (adjusted according to the results of the APTT which should be 1.5–2.5 × the control). Low molecular weight heparin, given as a once daily subcutaneous injection, has recently been licensed for the treatment of PE; no monitoring is required. Patients should be treated with heparin for at least five days; during that time warfarin is introduced and the heparin is discontinued once the INR is 2–3 times the control.

- Warfarin is continued for 3–6 months in most cases; for PE occurring post-operatively, 6 weeks' anticoagulation is adequate. In recurrent PE, anticoagulation should be for longer periods (e.g. 1 year) and consideration should be given to life-long treatment.
- In cases of collapse due to massive PE, thrombolysis with streptokinase or rtPA given by peripheral vein should be considered. This should be avoided when the embolic material is an infected vegetation (e.g. i.v. drug abusers).
- Occasionally, pulmonary embolectomy is used for those with massive PE where thrombolysis is unsuccessful or contraindicated.
- Inferior vena caval filters should be considered in patients where anticoagulation is contraindicated or in those who continue to embolize despite anticoagulation.

9.3 Systemic hypertension

Guidelines for treatment continually adapt to new clinical evidence, but the threshold for treatment should now be BP >160/90 mmHg, or even lower if there is evidence of target organ damage or the presence of other risk factors (e.g. diabetes mellitus). Stepped antihypertensive therapy is probably outmoded as 50% of patients will be uncontrolled by monotherapy, and therapeutic gains with 2–3 agent low-dose therapy far outweigh the incidence of side-effects.

- Investigation of **phaeochromocytomas:** recommend three 24-hour urinary VMAs on a vanilla-free diet (and off all drugs). Urinary metadrenalines may also be measured.

- Hypertension **increases the risk** (Framingham data) of: stroke (x7); cardiac failure (x4); coronary artery disease (x3); peripheral vascular disease (x2).

- Potassium salt should be substituted for sodium salt where possible.

- **Drugs to avoid in pregnancy**: diuretics, ACE inhibitors, angiotensin II receptor blockers. **Drugs with well-identified risks preferred in pregnancy**: beta-blockers (especially Labetalol), methyldopa and hydralazine.

- Young Black men have a poor response to ACE inhibitors, thiazides and beta-blockers as they are salt conservers by background, and so are resistant to renin manipulation and particularly likely to develop the side-effects of impotence.

9.4 Aortic dissection

Two-thirds of tears occur in the ascending aorta with about one-fifth occurring in the descending aorta. Mortality is highest in the first few hours if the dissection is untreated. The differential diagnosis for ascending dissection includes MI if the vulnerable right coronary ostium is involved (giving rise to an inferior infarct pattern). This is particularly important when considering thrombolysis; aortic regurgitation provides supportive evidence of the diagnosis.

Associations with aortic dissection

- Systemic hypertension
  (present in 80%)
- Marfan's syndrome
- Cystic medial degeneration
  (rare in the absence of Marfan's
  syndrome)
- Noonan's, Turner's syndromes
- Trauma

- Aortic coarctation
- Congenital bicuspid aortic valve
  (present in 10–15% and dissection is
  therefore associated with aortic stenosis)
- Giant cell arteritis
- Pregnancy (particularly in patients with
  Marfan's syndrome)
- Cocaine abuse

- **Involvement of ascending aorta
  may cause**

  Aortic regurgitation
  Inferior myocardial infarction
  Pericardial effusion (including
    cardiac tamponade)
  Carotid dissection
  Absent or decreased subclavian pulse

- **Medical therapy to be
  considered for**

  Old, stable dissections (> 2 weeks)
  Uncomplicated dissection of
    descending aorta
  Isolated arch dissections

Investigations for aortic dissection

- TOE, aortic MRI or contrast-enhanced spiral CT scans all have a high diagnostic
  sensitivity, but CT rarely identifies the site of tear or the presence of aortic regurgitation
  or coronary involvement.
- MRI is of the highest quality but is contraindicated in patients with pacemakers, certain
  vascular clips and metal valve prostheses.
- TOE is probably the most widely used investigation as it is available in the acute situation
  and has high sensitivity and specificity.
- Aortography is no longer the gold standard and coronary angiography is applicable only
  when deciding on the need for concomitant CABG.

APPENDIX I

Normal cardiac physiological values

ECG

- PR interval 0.12–0.20 s
- QRS duration <0.10 s

- QTc (males) 380 ms
  (females) 420 ms
- QRS axis −30° to +90°

Indices of cardiac function

- Cardiac index = Cardiac output/body surface area = 2.5–4.0 l/min/m^2

- Stroke volume index = Stroke volume/BSA = 40–70 ml/m^2

- Systemic vascular resistance (SVR) = $\dfrac{80 \times (A_o - RA)^*}{\text{Cardiac output}}$ = 770–1500 dyn/s/cm^{-5}

- Ejection fraction = proportion of blood ejected from left ventricle = 50–70%

Cardiac catheterization pressures (mmHg)		Criteria for significant oxygen saturation step-up	
Mean right atrial	0–8	SVC/IVC to RA	>7% (e.g. ASD)
Right ventricular systolic	15–30	RA to RV	>5% (e.g. VSD)
End diastolic	0–8	RV to PA	>5% (e.g. PDA)
		Any level:	
		SVC to PA	>7%
Pulmonary artery systolic	15–30		
End diastolic	3–12		
Mean	9–16		
Pulmonary artery wedge			
a	3–15	Usual saturations (SaO$_2$)	
v	3–12	Venous	65–75%
		Arterial	96–98%
Left atrial mean	1–10		
Left ventricular systolic	100–140		
End diastolic	3–12		
Aortic systolic	100–140		
End diastolic	60–90		
Mean	70–105		

*A_o = mean aortic pressure; RA = mean right atrial pressure

APPENDIX II

Summary of important large trials in ischaemic heart disease

ISIS 1: *International Study of Infarct Survival 1 (N = 16,027)*
Atenolol i.v. during MI and orally for 7 days. Fifteen per cent reduction in 7-day mortality which was mostly on days 0–2 (reduced cardiac rupture or cardiac arrest). Note, this was in the pre-thombolysis era. However, trial of metoprolol after thrombolysis (TIMI 2B) showed a lower early death and non-fatal re-infarction rate also (though not statistically significant — probably due to low numbers).

ISIS 2: *International Study of Infarct Survival 2 (N = 17,187)*
Assessing the role of aspirin and i.v. streptokinase either alone or in combination; showed a reduction in 5-week vascular mortality with either treatment (23% and 25% respectively) individually and 42% reduction when they were combined.

ISIS 3: *International Study of Infarct Survival 3 (N = 41,299)*
Compared streptokinase, t-PA and APSAC (anisoylated plasminogen streptokinase activator complex) and also randomized patients between aspirin against aspirin and subcutaneous heparin. Found no significant 35-day mortality differences between the three thrombolysis regimes, although haemorrhagic stroke rates were higher in the t-PA arm. The addition of subcutaneous heparin tended to improve 1-week mortality at the expense of increased bleeding rates, but there was no difference at 1 month.

ISIS 4: *International Study of Infarct Survival 4 (N = 58,050)*
Comparison of 5-week mortality on separate or combined use of oral nitrates, oral captopril or i.v. magnesium in addition to traditional therapies. No effects were found with magnesium or nitrates (which were well-tolerated). However, a small (7%) but significant benefit was seen with captopril which was sustained to 1 year.

GUSTO 1: *Global Utilisation of Streptokinase and t-PA for Occluded Coronary Arteries Trial 1 (N = 41,021)*
A complex trial comparing a mixture of accelerated and standard t-PA and streptokinase regimes together with a mixture of subcutaneous and i.v. heparin regimes. Although a small benefit of t-PA and i.v. heparin over streptokinase was shown (14%), there was a small increase in the risk of haemorrhagic stroke with the former arm. Some authors suggested this data implies a benefit of t-PA over streptokinase for high-risk groups.

AIRE: *Acute Infarction Ramipril Efficacy study (N = 2006)*
Post-infarction patients with early clinical or radiological evidence of heart failure were enrolled to receive ramipril or placebo, excluding patients with severe or resistant heart failure. At 15 months the mortality difference was 27% which has since been shown to be sustained (31% at 5 years).

SAVE: *Survival And Ventricular Enlargement study (N = 2231)*
Captopril given to patients with post-MI ejection fraction <40% had a 19% mortality reduction in the 3–5-year follow-up, with fewer re-infarctions and heart failure re-admissions.

CAST: *Cardiac Arrhythmia Suppression Trial (N = 1727)*
Assessing the effects upon mortality of flecainide, encainamide and moricizine (by suppression of arrhythmias post-MI). Although effective at Holter suppression of ventricular ectopics, mortality with encainamide and flecainide was higher than with placebo (4.5% versus 1.2%).

CONSENSUS: *Co-operative North Scandinavian Enalapril Survival Study (N = 253)*
Effects of addition of enalapril in severe heart failure (NYHA V). This study was terminated early due to the consistent benefits in the enalapril group, with a 40% at 6-month and 31% at 1-year mortality reduction (due to improvement in left ventricular function).

CONSENSUS II: *Co-operative North Scandinavian Enalapril Survival Study II (N = 6090)*
Effect of early enalapril administration (i.v. then oral) after acute MI did not show any specific mortality difference and, in fact, rates were slightly higher in the treatment group; postulated due to hypotension causing coronary perfusion compromise.

4S: *Scandinavian Simvastatin Survival Study (N = 4444)*
Anginal or post-infarction patients with cholesterol between 5.5–8.0 mmol/l showed a 33% event reduction at a median of 5.4 years when placed on simvastatin, for a total mean cholesterol reduction of 25%.

CARE: *Cholesterol And Recurrent Events trial (N = 4159)*
At 5 years, 24% endpoint (fatal coronary or non-fatal myocardial events) reduction in patients with not only high but also average cholesterol values post-infarction.

WOSCOPS: *The West of Scotland Coronary Prevention Study (N = 4159)*
Men between 45–65 years, without overt coronary disease, with cholesterol >4 mmol/l were randomized to receive pravastatin or placebo for 5 years, and had a 22% all-cause mortality reduction with a 20% total cholesterol reduction. This was an extremely important primary prevention study.

Chapter 2
Clinical Pharmacology, Toxicology and Poisoning

CONTENTS

1. **Drug metabolism and interactions**   61
   1.1   Genetic polymorphisms of drug metabolism
   1.2   Liver enzyme induction
   1.3   Liver enzyme inhibition
   1.4   Failure of the combined oral contraceptive pill

2. **Prescribing in particular clinical states**   63
   2.1   Drugs and breast feeding
   2.2   Pregnancy and drug therapies
   2.3   Prescribing in liver disease and liver failure
   2.4   Prescribing in renal failure

3. **Individual drugs and those used in specific clinical conditions**   65
   3.1   Cardiology
   3.2   Endocrinology
   3.3   Gastroenterology
   3.4   Neurology
   3.5   Psychiatry
   3.6   Rheumatology
   3.7   Miscellaneous

4. **Specific adverse effects**   76
   4.1   Secondary amenorrhoea due to drugs
   4.2   Bronchospasm
   4.3   Dyskinesia and dystonia
   4.4   Gynaecomastia
   4.5   Hypothyroidism
   4.6   Drug-induced liver disease
   4.7   Drugs provoking myasthenia
   4.8   Photosensitivity
   4.9   Drug-induced vasculitis

5. Poisoning   **79**
    5.1   Aspirin overdose
    5.2   Carbon monoxide
    5.3   Ethylene glycol
    5.4   Paracetamol overdose
    5.5   Quinidine and quinine
    5.6   Theophylline overdose
    5.7   Tricyclic antidepressant overdose
    5.8   Haemodialysis for overdose or poisoning

Clinical Pharmacology, Toxicology and Poisoning

1. DRUG METABOLISM AND INTERACTIONS

1.1 Genetic polymorphisms of drug metabolism

Genetic determination of enzyme activity may alter the susceptibility of an individual to adverse drug reactions. For example, the slow acetylator phenotype is possessed by 50% of UK citizens and may be associated with specific adverse effects:

- Isoniazid-induced peripheral neuropathy
- Drug-induced lupus.

Drug-induced lupus is associated with slow acetylation and possession of HLA DR4. Unlike autoimmune SLE, male and female incidence are equal. Laboratory findings include antibodies to histones and single-stranded DNA. Clinical features include:

- Butterfly rash
- Arthralgia
- Pleurisy.

Renal involvement (except with **hydralazine**) or neuropsychiatric manifestations are unusual.

Drugs causing a lupus erythematosus-like syndrome

- Phenytoin
- Isoniazid
- Procainamide
- Penicillin
- Chlorpromazine
- Tetracyclines

- Hydralazine
- Beta-blockers
- Lithium
- Sulphonamides
- Clonidine
- Methyldopa

Poor metabolizers of debrisoquine have reduced activity of another liver enzyme which potentiates the effects of metoprolol and nortriptyline.

1.2 Liver enzyme induction

Many drugs either induce or inhibit liver enzyme systems. Important alterations in the metabolism of concomitantly prescribed drugs may result. Induction of microsomal enzymes of the cytochrome P450 system occurs over days because it requires transcription and translation of the genetic code to produce more enzyme. This may lead to treatment failure with the following agents:

- Warfarin
- Phenytoin
- Theophyllines
- Oral contraceptive pill.

The drugs which cause this effect can be remembered by the mnemonic:

PC BRAS

(**P**henytoin, **C**arbamazepine, **B**arbiturates, **R**ifampicin, **A**lcohol (chronic excess), **S**ulphonylureas.)

1.3 Liver enzyme inhibition

Inhibition of liver enzymes is an instant phenomenon and this may potentiate the effects of drugs such as:

- Warfarin
- Phenytoin
- Carbamazepine
- Theophyllines
- Cyclosporin.

Drugs which are liver enzyme inhibitors may be recalled by the mnemonic:

ODEVICES

(**O**meprazole, **D**isulfiram, **E**rthyromycin, **V**alproate, **I**soniazid, **C**imetidine (and ciprofloxacin), acute **E**thanol intoxication, **S**ulphonamides.)

1.4 Failure of the combined oral contraceptive pill

Any condition that leads to impaired absorption of the components of the contraceptive pill (e.g. traveller's diarrhoea) may result in its failure as a contraceptive agent.

In addition:

- The oestrogenic component of the oral contraceptive may be metabolized more rapidly in the presence of liver enzyme inducers (see previous page), leading to pill failure, but enzyme inhibitors have no effect.
- Pill failure may also result from concomitant antibiotic usage. For example, ampicillin, amoxycillin and tetracyclines may damage gut flora that deconjugate bile salts thereby interrupting enterohepatic cycling of the oestrogenic component.

2. PRESCRIBING IN PARTICULAR CLINICAL STATES

2.1 Drugs and breast feeding

Infants under one month of age are at greatest risk from drugs excreted in breast milk because they have immature metabolism and excretion. Drugs which are definitely excreted in breast milk and are contraindicated during breast feeding include:

- **Amiodarone**: thyroid anomalies
- **Cytotoxics and chloramphenicol**: blood dyscrasia.

Other drugs that should not be taken by breast-feeding mothers are:

- **Gold**: haematological reactions and renal impairment
- **Iodides**: thyroid disturbance
- **Oestrogens**: feminization of male infants
- **Lithium**: involuntary movements
- **Indomethacin**: has been reported to cause seizures.

2.2 Pregnancy and drug therapies

During the first 16 weeks of pregnancy, drugs may exert **teratogenic** effects on the fetus leading to malformations. Particular associations are:

- **Sodium valproate** and **retinoids**: neural tube defects
- **Phenytoin**: facial fusion abnormalities such as cleft lip and palate
- **Warfarin**: abnormalities of long bones and cartilage
- **Lithium**: cardiac abnormalities.

Later in pregnancy some drugs may cross the placenta and harm the fetus:

- **Carbimazole**: neonatal goitre (which may even be large enough to obstruct labour)
- **Gentamicin**: VIIIth nerve deafness in the newborn.

63

2.3 Prescribing in liver disease and liver failure

In liver failure the toxic substances normally cleared by the organ may impair central nervous system function, and the latter may lead to abnormal responses to some drugs. Opioids in particular may cause coma due to altered brain sensitivity. Similarly, benzodiazepines may accumulate and depress the central nervous system. There have been reports of hepatic encephalopathy occurring after starting these drugs. Thiazides and loop diuretics may cause hypokalaemia, thereby provoking encephalopathy. Other important aspects of drug metabolism in liver disease are listed below:

- Drugs excreted via the bile, such as rifampicin, may accumulate in patients with obstructive jaundice.
- Hypoalbuminaemia, resulting from cirrhosis, may reduce available binding sites for protein bound drugs (e.g. phenytoin) to very low levels.
- Reduced clotting factor synthesis means an increased risk of bleeding for patients taking warfarin.
- Patients with advanced liver disease retain salt and water due to secondary hyperaldosteronism; the resulting ascites and oedema can be worsened by non-steroidal anti-inflammatory drugs and steroids.

2.4 Prescribing in renal failure

Consideration of drug metabolism is important in patients with renal failure, as nephrotoxic agents may exacerbate renal damage (especially in patients with acute renal failure) and other drugs, especially those which are water soluble and therefore eliminated largely by the kidneys, may accumulate in patients with a low glomerular filtration rate (GFR), leading to toxic effects.

Drugs which accumulate and cause toxicity in patients with severe renal failure (GFR < 10 ml/min) include:

- **Penicillins** and **cephalosporins** (high dose): lead to encephalopathy
- **Digoxin**: cardiac arrythmias, heart block
- **Erythromycin**: encephalopathy.

Nephrotoxic drugs may lead to an acute deterioration of renal function in patients with chronic renal failure, and they can severely exacerbate renal damage in acute renal dysfunction. If treatment is considered essential (e.g. gentamicin or parenteral vancomycin for staphylococcal infections) then levels should be carefully monitored, otherwise such agents should be avoided in these patient groups. Examples of nephrotoxic drugs include:

- Aminoglycosides
- Amphotericin
- Non-steroidal anti-inflammatory drugs.

Other drugs may have more specific nephrotoxic effects, such as gold-induced proteinuria or nephrotic syndrome, which is usually due to membranous glomerulonephritis. (See also Chapter 13, *Nephrology*.)

3. INDIVIDUAL DRUGS AND THOSE USED IN SPECIFIC CLINICAL CONDITIONS

3.1 Cardiology

Abciximab (Reopro)

This chimeric monoclonal antibody irreversibly binds GpIIb/IIIa glycoprotein receptors in platelets, preventing the final common pathway of platelet activation and aggregation. It has a potent long term antiplatelet effect after intravenous bolus/infusion. Licensed now for high risk angioplasty (EPIC trial), it prevents acute thrombosis and chronic restenosis within coronary arteries and has recently been shown to be beneficial for unstable angina (EPILOG–Stent trial). Risks of thrombocytopenic haemorrhage are low and reversed by platelet administration. Abciximab should be used only once in a particular patient.

Adenosine

Adenosine is a purine nucleoside with a half-life of 8–10 seconds. It acts via specific adenosine receptors, activating K^+ channels, in sinoatrial and atrioventricular nodes to cause sinus node arrest, so terminating supraventricular tachycardia (SVT). Its chief therapeutic use is to distinguish between SVT and ventricular tachycardia. The action of adenosine may be inhibited by aminophylline and potentiated by dipyridamole, which interferes with its metabolism.

Side-effects of adenosine

- Facial flushing
- Chest tightening
- Bronchospasm (avoid in asthmatic patients)
- Anxiety

Amiodarone

Amiodarone has anti-arrhythmic action which spans all categories of the Vaughan-Williams classification. Its main action is to prolong the refractory period, and thus the QT interval, on the ECG. Amiodarone may be used to control supraventricular and ventricular arrhythmias. It may prolong the lifespan of patients with recurrent VT or hypertrophic cardiomyopathy.

- It is iodine-containing and has a very long half-life (26–127 days).
- Protein binding can displace digoxin or warfarin, so increasing their actions.
- Given intravenously, the anti-arrhythmic action occurs within a few hours; given orally this may take 1–3 weeks.
- Amiodarone is the least negatively inotropic anti-arrhythmic with the exception of digoxin.
- Hyperthyroidism may result from enhanced peripheral de-iodination of thyroxine to T_3.
- Hypothyroidism arises from increased production of reverse T_3 in the liver.

Side-effects of amiodarone

- Reversible corneal microdeposits
- Metallic taste
- Alveolitis
- Slate grey discoloration of skin
- Arrhythmias (torsades)
- Hypothyroidism
- Ataxia
- Peripheral neuropathy
- Hepatitis
- Photosensitivity
- Hyperthyroidism

Angiotensin receptor blockers

Angiotensin II receptor (type AT1) antagonists do not inhibit bradykinin breakdown (unlike ACE inhibitors) and so do not provoke cough. They provide more specific AT1 receptor antagonism at tissue level, and are indicated for treatment of hypertension. It is expected that licensing will extend their use post-myocardial infarction, and for treatment of heart failure. They have very few side-effects.

Angiotensin converting enzyme (ACE) inhibitors

ACE inhibitors reduce mortality in all grades of heart failure and may reduce death after myocardial infarction, probably by reducing deleterious remodelling. They are contraindicated in bilateral renal artery stenosis and should be used with caution in severe renal impairment.

- Dry cough may accompany their use; this may be due to persistence of bradykinin and is more common in women, who have more sensitive cough reflexes.
- Hypersensitivity to ACE inhibitors is manifest as angio-neurotic oedema.
- Potassium may rise during therapy due to inhibition of aldosterone production by ACE inhibitors.

Digoxin

Digoxin increases block at the atrioventricular node and so is used to slow ventricular conduction in atrial fibrillation and flutter. It has some minimal use as a positive inotropic agent in heart failure; indeed, recent trial evidence suggests digoxin reduces morbidity but not mortality in heart failure.

- Eighty-five per cent of a digoxin dose is eliminated unchanged in the urine; it can therefore accumulate in renal impairment.
- The steroid-like structure of digoxin has occasionally caused gynaecomastia in chronic use.
- Digoxin has a narrow therapeutic window, above which toxic effects are often seen.

Digoxin toxicity

Any arrhythmia may occur with digoxin toxicity; the most common is heart block but even atrial fibrillation has been observed. Pulsus bigeminus is indicative of a ventricular ectopic coupled to a normal QRS complex on the ECG and this may herald digoxin toxicity.

- However, note that 'reversed tick' ST segment depression is commonly seen in the inferior and lateral leads on the ECG, and represents a sign of *digoxin therapy* and not specifically toxicity. First-degree heart block is also seen in patients with sinus rhythm who take digoxin.
- Electrolyte imbalances which may predispose to digoxin toxicity include hypokalaemia, hypomagnesaemia and hypercalcaemia.
- Amiodarone may displace digoxin from tissue binding sites leading to toxicity, whereas quinidine/quinine and calcium antagonists may interfere with tubular clearance of digoxin leading to accumulation and risk of toxic effects.

Toxic effects of digoxin

- Yellow vision (xanthopsia)
- Anorexia
- Arrhythmias (e.g. atrial fibrillation, heartblock)

- Nausea/vomiting
- Diarrhoea

Flecainide

A class 1c agent used for treatment of ventricular arrhythmias, pre-excitation syndromes and for chemical cardioversion of acute atrial arrhythmias. The CAST trial suggested that flecainide is pro-arrhythmic post-myocardial infarction; it should be avoided in left ventricular impairment. Its half-life is about 16 hours; other main side-effects are vertigo and visual disturbance.

HMG CoA reductase inhibitors

HMG CoA reductase inhibitors up-regulate low density lipoprotein (LDL) receptors thereby reducing LDL by 30% and increasing the clearance of cholesterol, and increasing high density lipoprotein (HDL). Most statins have minimal effects on triglycerides. However, although atorvastatin may reduce triglycerides, mortality data are still awaited.

- Statins reduce mortality after myocardial infarction in men who have high cholesterol ('4 S' study).
- They have recently been shown to be effective in reducing primary mortality from ischaemic heart disease (WOSCOP trial).
- Statins rarely cause rhabdomyolysis (frequency 1/100,000), but this is more likely in patients with renal impairment or when given with a fibrate; drug-induced hepatitis may also occur.

Nicorandil

A K$^+$ channel opener that induces arterial vasodilatation, it also possesses a nitrate component that promotes venous relaxation. Used as an antianginal agent. Side-effects are transient headache, flushing and dizziness. In large doses it may cause hypotension with a reflex tachycardia.

Thiazide diuretics

Thiazides are associated with a series of **dose-dependent** metabolic effects:

- Hyponatraemia, hypokalaemia and hypomagnesaemia; a hypochloraemic alkalosis may result.
- Raised plasma urate may occur due to reduction of tubular clearance of urate; rarely, gout may be precipitated.
- Diabetic glycaemic control may worsen on thiazides due to impaired insulin release; tissue-based insulin resistance, and cholesterol may rise, at least temporarily.
- Thiazide diuretics may also cause postural hypotension, photosensitivity and impotence (mechanism unclear).

Rare dose-independent side-effects of thiazide diuretics

- Pancreatitis
- Agranulocytosis
- Thrombocytopenia

Ticlopidine

This is a novel antiplatelet agent which probably acts via GpIIb/IIIa glycoprotein. Its uses include secondary stroke prevention, treatment of unstable angina and post-coronary stent insertion. It is at least as effective as aspirin. Severe (but reversible) neutropenia occurs in 1% of users and diarrhoea in 20%. Intrahepatic cholestasis and marrow aplasia have also been reported.

3.2 Endocrinology

Carbimazole

Carbimazole acts by inhibiting a peroxidase which catalyses all phases of thyroid hormone production from the amino acid tyrosine. It takes at least 6 weeks to reduce blood levels of thyroid hormones. Therefore, somatic symptoms of hyperthyroidism, such as tachycardia and anxiety, are best suppressed by beta blockers (e.g. propranolol).

- Agranulocytosis may occur within the first 16 weeks of therapy and in the event of a sore throat patients should be advised to seek medical help.
- The drug crosses the placenta; however, if it is given in low dose in pregnancy, fetal hypothyroidism may be prevented.

Hormone replacement therapy

On average, over a third of a woman's life is in the post-menopausal phase, yet only 12% receive hormone replacement therapy (HRT); 60–75% of menopausal women will experience vasomotor symptoms and these will be reduced by HRT.

- Without HRT, women aged 70 years have a 50% reduction in bone mass and one in two will have an osteoporosis-related fracture.
- HRT therefore leads to 50% reduction in fractures and may reduce ischaemic heart disease by 20% and stroke by 15%; this may be at the expense of an increased risk of breast cancer.
- See also Chapter 4, *Endocrinology*, section 4.4.

3.3 Gastroenterology

Mesalazine and olsalazine

Mesalazine and olsalazine differ from sulphasalazine in being purely 5-amino salicylic acid (5-ASA) molecules which are split for local action in the colon. They suppress local inflammation in ulcerative colitis.

- They have some systemic side-effects including nausea, abdominal pain, headache and sometimes worsening of colitis.
- Rare side-effects of mesalazine and olsalazine include reversible pancreatitis, blood dyscrasias and interstitial nephritis (with mesalazine).

Sulphasalazine

Sulphasalazine consists of a sulphonamide molecule plus 5-ASA. It is used in the treatment of ulcerative colitis, and also as a disease-modifying anti-rheumatic in rheumatoid arthritis.

The sulphonamide moiety frequently leads to gastrointestinal upset. Other key features are as follows:

- Oligospermia, leading to male infertility, may occur but this is usually reversible on stopping sulphasalazine.
- Patients may note orange discoloration of body fluids.
- Slow acetylators may experience more toxicity with sulphasalazine due to exposure to higher levels of the sulphonamide constituent.
- Rare side-effects of sulphasalazine include Stevens–Johnson syndrome, blood dyscrasias (especially agranulocytosis and aplasia) and nephrotic syndrome.

3.4 Neurology

Treatment of Parkinson's disease

Enhanced dopaminergic transmission is central to the medical management of Parkinson's disease:

- **Selegiline** is a type B monoamine oxidase inhibitor (MAO-B); inhibition of monoamine oxidase potentiates dopamine and reduces end-dose akinesia. It was thought that selegiline might also retard progression of Parkinson's disease by preserving dopaminergic neurones. This is now known to be untrue.
- **Amantadine** potentiates dopamine by preventing its re-uptake into pre-synaptic terminals.
- **Levodopa** (L-dopa) is absorbed in the proximal small bowel by active transport, but the presence of amino acids (and thus meals) may reduce absorption. It is a pro-drug which must be converted to dopamine within the nigro-striatal pathway. The drug is largely metabolized by catechol-o-methyl transferase.
- After 8 years of therapy with L-dopa, 50% of patients will have choreo-athetoid dyskinesia and end-dose akinesia. By this time many patients will have deteriorated to pre-treatment levels of disability due to progression of Parkinson's disease.

Side effects of L-dopa

- Involuntary movements (dyskinesia) occur commonly
- Psychosis (depression or mania)
- Postural hypotension
- Nausea and vomiting
- Cardiac arrhythmias

Treatment of epilepsy

Recent developments in the therapeutics of epilepsy have concentrated on agents which interact with neurotransmitters.

- Glutamic acid is an excitatory central nervous system neurotransmitter; **lamotrigine** inhibits it, so suppressing seizures. The side-effects of lamotrigine include mood changes, maculopapular rashes, influenza-like symptoms and Stevens–Johnson syndrome.
- Gamma amino butyric acid (GABA) is an inhibitory central nervous system neurotransmitter. Gabapentin and vigabatrin potentiate GABA and thus may be used to treat seizures.
- **Vigabatrin** is used for refractory epilepsy, potentiating GABA by irreversible inhibition of GABA transaminase. Side-effects of vigabatrin include mood disturbance and psychosis in 5%.
- **Diazepam** also terminates seizures by indirectly interacting with GABA transmission. It stimulates the benzodiazepine receptor in the brain which in turn enhances the affinity of the neighbouring GABA receptor for its neurotransmitter.
- **Carbamazepine** is a derivative of the tricylic antidepressants and is useful for epilepsy and also neural pain (e.g. trigeminal or post-herpetic neuralgia). Patients commonly experience headaches and diplopia on starting carbamazepine and 5–15% of patients can develop a generalized morbilliform rash.
- **Sodium valproate** is used in absence attacks and temporal lobe epilepsy. It inhibits liver enzymes and may potentiate other anti-epileptics such as phenytoin. It may cause alopecia, with curly regrowth after stopping the drug.

Adverse effects of valproate

- Thrombocytopenia
- Ataxia
- Amenorrhoea
- Alopecia

- Hepatitis (sometimes fatal)
- Weight gain
- Gynaecomastia
- Liver enzyme inhibition

Sumatriptan

Sumatriptan is a 5-HT agonist used during the acute phase of migraine. It maintains vasoconstriction and prevents headache associated with the vasodilator phase of migraine. It must not be given in hemiplegic migraine, or within 24 hours of ergotamine, as intense vasospasm may lead to permanent neurological damage.

Side-effects of sumatriptan

- Chest pain
- Flushing
- Drowsiness
- Vasospasm
- Fatigue

3.5 Psychiatry

Chlorpromazine

Chlorpromazine blocks many different receptors; for example, it acts as a dopamine blocker, an alpha blocker, anticholinergic and antihistamine. Due to prolongation of the QT interval on the ECG, ventricular tachycardia may result (particularly when used in high dose).

Adverse effects of chlorpromazine

- Dystonias
  (including oculogyric crisis)
- Photosensitivity
- Agranulocytosis
- Ventricular tachycardia
  (prolonged QT)
- Neuroleptic malignant syndrome
- Tardive dyskinesia (chronic use)
- Contact dermatitis and purple
  pigmentation of the skin

Lithium

Lithium carbonate is used for prophylaxis in bipolar affective disorder, for treatment of acute mania/hypomania and to augment antidepressants in recurrent or resistant depression. It is also used to treat aggressive behaviour in patients with learning disabilities. It has a narrow therapeutic range (0.5–1 mmol/l). Toxic effects occur at levels > 2.0 mmol/l.

- **Toxicity** is more likely in renal impairment or when there are imbalances of electrolytes; it may also arise when lithium excretion is impaired by thiazide and loop diuretics, ACE inhibitors and non-steroidal anti-inflammatory drugs.
- Lithium may cause **histological changes** in the kidney and it has been recommended that long term treatment is reviewed every 2–3 years.
- **Polyuria** arises due to nephrogenic diabetes insipidus; lithium prevents anti-diuretic hormone (ADH) from interacting with the collecting duct receptor, so leading to water loss. There is a compensatory increase in ADH release.

Toxic and side-effects of lithium

- **(At 1–2 mmol/l)**
  Coarse tremor
  Blurred vision
  Muscle weakness
  Anorexia and vomiting
  Diarrhoea
  Ataxia and dysarthria
  Drowsiness

- **(Severe toxicity >2 mmol/l)**
  Hyper-reflexia
  Circulatory failure
  Oliguria
  Convulsions
  Coma
  Toxic psychoses
  Death

Side-effects of lithium*

- **Common**
  Fine tremor (in about 15% of patients
  Oedema
  Polyuria
  Weight gain
  Nausea
  Loose motions
  Polydypsia
  Leucocytosis

- **Rare**
  Hypothyroidism
  Worsening of psoriasis and acne
  Interstitial nephritis
  Goitre

*May arise despite therapeutic range dosing

- Antacids, theophylline and acetazolamide lead to decreased plasma lithium carbonate.
- CNS toxicity has been described with SSRIs, carbamazepine and phenytoin, methyldopa, antipsychotics (especially haloperidol), calcium channel blockers and sumatriptan.

3.6 Rheumatology

Penicillamine

Penicillamine is used as a disease-modifying agent in rheumatoid arthritis and also to chelate cysteine in cystinuria and copper in Wilson's disease, respectively. In the first 6 weeks of therapy reversible loss of taste may occur. This may resolve without stopping the drug.

- After 4–18 months of therapy, proteinuria due to membranous glomerulonephritis may ensue.

- Thrombocytopenia and neutropenia may result from penicillamine therapy; patients should be warned to seek medical advice if a sore throat or ready bruising develop.
- Myasthenia, drug-induced lupus and Stevens–Johnson syndrome have also been reported.

Treatment of gout

Allopurinol inhibits xanthine oxidase, the enzyme which converts purines into uric acid, and so prevents gout. However, commencement of therapy will occasionally provoke an acute attack of gout. Established gouty tophi may regress with chronic use of allopurinol.

- Azathioprine, a pro-drug, is converted to 6-mercaptopurine in the body and may accumulate causing bone marrow toxicity in patients receiving allopurinol.
- The renal clearance of cyclophosphamide may also be impeded in patients receiving allopurinol and this again leads to marrow toxicity.

Colchicine inhibits macrophage migration into a gouty joint but its use is limited by the frequent occurrence of diarrhoea. It has therefore been said that with colchicine 'you run before you can walk'!

3.7 Miscellaneous

A detailed description of the mechanism of action, important pharmacokinetics and characteristic or serious side-effects of commonly used antibacterial, antiviral and antihelminthic agents is provided in Chapter 10, *Infectious Diseases and Tropical Medicine*.

Ciprofloxacin

This 4-quinolone inhibits DNA bacterial gyrase, an enzyme which prevents supercoiling of bacterial DNA; it has activity against both Gram-positive and Gram-negative organisms. It is a liver enzyme inhibitor and particularly potentiates theophylline. Ciprofloxacin is not recommended for children under 12 years of age (except in cystic fibrosis) because of the potential for bony anomalies (which have been shown in pre-pubertal animal models).

Side-effects of ciprofloxacin

- Diarrhoea
- Arthralgia
- Anaphylaxis
- Sedation (which may affect driving)
- Photosensitivity
- Seizures
- Impaired motor function

- The **seizures** occur because ciprofloxacin can compete with the inhibitory neurotransmitter, GABA, within the brain.

Cyclosporin A

Cyclosporin A is used to reduce transplant rejection and it has significantly improved graft survival. It causes dose-dependent nephrotoxicity and has a narrow therapeutic range. The risk of toxicity is therefore assessed by therapeutic drug monitoring. (See also Chapter 13, *Nephrology*.)

Gum hyperplasia is common; it is increased in individuals with poor oral hygiene, and also those concomitantly taking dihydropyridine calcium-channel blockers. As with most immunosuppressives, there is an increased risk of skin and lymphoproliferative malignancy with long term therapy.

Adverse effects of cyclosporin A

- Hirsutism
- Hypertension
- Oligodystrophy
- Nephrotoxicity
- Liver dysfunction
- Fluid and potassium retention
- Burning hands and feet
  (especially during 1st week of therapy)
- Gum hyperplasia

Cytotoxics

The majority of cytotoxic agents have the potential to cause marrow suppression.

Specific side-effects of cytotoxic agents

- **Methotrexate**
  May cause severe mucositis and myelosuppression which is prevented by the use of folinic acid rescue. During chronic administration pneumonitis and liver fibrosis may occur

- **Vincristine** and **vinblastine**
  Cause a reversible peripheral neuropathy

- **Cisplatinum**
  May cause ototoxicity, nephrotoxicity (interstitial nephritis), hypomagnesaemia and peripheral neuropathy

- **Doxorubicin**
  May cause skin irritation and cardiomyopathy

- **Bleomycin**
  Causes dose-dependent lung fibrosis; it is one of the least myelotoxic chemotherapeutic agents

Retinoids

Oral retinoids are indicated for treatment of severe psoriasis and acne that is resistant to other therapies. They are teratogenic, leading to neural tube defects. Like other vitamin A derivatives they may cause benign intracranial hypertension. Dryness of mucous membranes leading to intolerance of contact lenses has been noted during treatment with retinoids.

High-dose retinoids can rarely cause diffuse interstitial skeletal hyperostosis.

Adverse effects of retinoids

- Alopecia
- Hypertriglyceridaemia
- Thrombocytopenia
- Reduced night vision
- Dry mucous membranes
- Skeletal abnormalities
  (with high doses)

- Photosensitivity
- Mood changes
- Hepatitis
- Teratogenicity
- Benign intracranial hypertension

---

4. SPECIFIC ADVERSE EFFECTS

4.1 Secondary amenorrhoea due to drugs

Dopamine inhibits prolactin release and so dopamine blocking drugs, such as chlorpromazine and cimetidine (but not ranitidine) may provoke hyperprolactinaemia, and hence, amenorrhoea. Sodium valproate may also cause amenorrhoea.

4.2 Bronchospasm

Bronchospasm may be induced by **aspirin** and **non-steroidal anti-inflammatory drugs**, particularly in patients with late onset asthma. Sensitivity to these agents is thought to relate to pharmacological effects on prostaglandin metabolism; the effect is not immunological, and thus it is termed 'pseudoallergic'.

- **Adenosine** should be avoided in asthma, as it may cause bronchoconstriction via stimulation of adenosine receptors found in bronchial smooth muscle.
- Even **cardioselective beta-blockers**, such as atenolol, may provoke bronchospasm.
- **Sodium chromoglycate** is a mast cell stabilizer; it is an inhaled, preventative agent in asthma. However, bronchospasm has occasionally been reported, because chromoglycate is administered as a dry powder.

- **N-acetyl cysteine** may cause bronchospasm and anaphylaxis when given as an antidote to paracetamol overdose.

4.3 Dyskinesia and dystonia

Both dopamine agonists and antagonists can lead to movement disorders.

- Drugs with **dopamine-like effects** that are used to treat Parkinson's disease may cause dyskinesia (L-dopa, bromocriptine, lysuride and pergolide).
- **Dopamine blocking agents** such as phenothiazines (chlorpromazine) or butyrophenones (haloperidol) may also cause dyskinesias.
- Fluoxetine and paroxetine, **serotonin re-uptake inhibitors** used in the treatment of depression, have both been associated with dystonias.

4.4 Gynaecomastia

Gynaecomastia can complicate treatment with drugs that are oestrogen-like in action or anti-androgens.

Osetrogen-like action	Anti-androgen action
<ul><li>Stilboestrol</li><li>Digoxin</li><li>Spironolactone</li></ul>	<ul><li>Cimetidine</li><li>Cyproterone acetate — *dianette*</li><li>Luteinizing hormone releasing hormone (LHRH) analogues (e.g. goserelin)</li></ul>

4.5 Hypothyroidism

Impaired thyroid hormone production may result from:

- Lithium
- Amiodarone
- Carbimazole
- Propylthiouracil
- Radio-iodine.

4.6 Drug-induced liver disease

Drug-induced liver disease may represent either dose-dependent or dose-independent effects.

- Dose-dependent liver disease includes paracetamol poisoning, fatty change due to tetracyclines and alcoholic hepatitis.
- Dose-independent liver disease usually involves either **hepatitis** or **cholestasis**; it generally has an allergic basis and may on occasion be associated with liver failure.

Drug-induced hepatitis occurs with

- Isoniazid
- Phenytoin
- Methyldopa
- HMG CoA reductase inhibitors

- Pyrazinamide
- Valproate
- Amiodarone

Causes of drug-induced cholestasis

- Chlorpromazine
- Carbamazepine

- Erythromycin
- Sulphonylureas

- Liver tumours may be associated with use of androgens and oestrogens (which can also cause Budd–Chiari malformations); liver fibrosis may accompany methotrexate treatment.

4.7 Drugs provoking myasthenia

- **Aminoglycosides**, certain **beta-blockers** (propranolol, oxprenolol), **phenytoin**, **lignocaine**, **quinidine** and **procainamide** may all impair acetylcholine release, leading to worsening or unmasking of myasthenia.
- **Penicillamine** may cause formation of antibodies against the acetylcholine receptor, and a syndrome indistinguishable from myasthenia results. This resolves in two-thirds of cases after penicillamine withdrawal.
- **Lithium** may also cause myasthenia-like weakness by impairing synaptic transmission.

4.8 Photosensitivity

Drugs causing photosensitivity

- Loop and thiazide diuretics
- Amiodarone
- Retinoids
- Sulphonylureas
- Oral contraceptives

- Tetracyclines
- Ciprofloxacin
- Psoralens
- Griseofulvin
- Piroxicam

4.9 Drug-induced vasculitis

Drug-induced vasculitis can affect the skin or internal organs.

Drugs causing vasculitis

- Sulphonamides
- Captopril
- Hydralazine
- Thiazides

- Penicillin
- Cimetidine
- Allopurinol
- Quinidine

5. POISONING

5.1 Aspirin overdose

The adverse effects of salicylate poisoning are due to direct stimulation of the respiratory centre in the CNS (respiratory alkalosis) and to metabolic stimulation, which leads to the accumulation of organic acids.

Early features of poisoning

- Hypokalaemia
- Respiratory centre stimulation in the CNS, and hence alkalosis
- Tinnitus
- Sweating

Later features of poisoning

- Metabolic acidosis
- Hypoprothrombinaemia
- Hypoglycaemia
- Pulmonary oedema
- Acute renal failure

Key aspects of management of salicylate poisoning involve:

- Emesis or lavage
- Activated charcoal
- Correction of electrolyte and metabolic abnormalities
- **Forced alkaline diuresis**: infusion of 0.9% saline (0.5 litres), followed by similar volumes of 5% dextrose and then 1.26% bicarbonate, in rotation, at a maximum infusion rate of 1.5–2 l/hour, to a total of 6 litres. The urinary pH should be maintained at 7.5–8.5.
- **Haemodialysis**: for very severe salicylism (blood salicylate >750 mg/l), refractory to forced diuresis.

5.2 Carbon monoxide

Carbon monoxide binds to haemoglobin with high affinity (>200 times that of oxygen); poisoning leads to decreased haemoglobin oxygen-carrying ability, and consequent tissue anoxia. Normal carboxyhaemoglobin levels are <3% in non-smokers and 5–6% in smokers; at 10–30% exposed patients usually only complain of headaches and mild exertional dyspnoea.

Signs of marked toxicity (carboxyhaemoglobin 30–60%)

- Agitation and confusion
- Bullous lesions
- Muscle necrosis
- Hypertonia and hyperreflexia
- Acute renal failure
- Pink mucosae
- Hyperpyrexia
- Vomiting
- ECG changes and arrhythmias

- Severe toxicity is associated with coma, convulsions and cardio-respiratory arrest.
- Treatment is with 100% oxygen by mask; hyperbaric oxygen (2.5 atmospheres pressure) will decrease the elimination half-life of carbon monoxide (from 4 hours to 22 minutes) but this is not often available on site.
- Neuropsychiatric changes may develop over several weeks after recovery from poisoning and these include intellectual deterioration, personality change, cerebral and cerebellar damage, and midbrain damage (Parkinson's disease).

5.3 Ethylene glycol

Poisoning with ethylene glycol has the clinical appearance of alcohol intoxication with cerebellar symptoms and signs in the first 12 hours, but without any smell of alcohol. Subsequent breakdown of ethylene glycol to oxalate causes metabolic acidosis; there is a raised anion gap due to the presence of exogenous organic acid, as well as a raised osmolar gap.

Within 2–3 days acute tubular necrosis results due to cellular damage by calcium oxalate crystals. Cardiac failure with pulmonary oedema may ensue.

Treatment for ethylene glycol poisoning

- **Sodium bicarbonate**
  To reduce acidosis

- **Intravenous ethanol**
  Can inhibit ethylene glycol
  metabolism

- **Calcium**
  To correct hypocalcaemia

- **Haemodialysis**
  Active elimination of ethylene glycol
  is by haemodialysis

5.4 Paracetamol overdose

Overdose with paracetamol is one of the most common causes of self-poisoning. Early features are minor (nausea and vomiting) but hepatic or renal failure occur later; liver damage peaks at 3–4 days after ingestion. Paracetamol is normally metabolized by glucuronidation in the liver. Toxicity arises because excess oxidation products are formed in overdose; these overwhelm the capacity for endogenous detoxification (glutathione) and the active metabolite binds to liver cell macromolecules, causing necrosis.

- The international normalized ratio (INR), or prothrombin ratio, is the most sensitive indicator of liver damage. Hypoglycaemia is a feature of advanced liver damage.
- Poor prognosis is indicated by an INR above 3.0, raised serum creatinine or plasma pH <7.3 more than 24 hours after overdose.
- Patients taking enzyme inducers such as phenytoin have an increased risk of hepatic necrosis after paracetamol poisoning.
- Renal failure may sometimes develop before liver necrosis due to mixed function oxidases generating the same dangerous metabolites within the renal parenchyma.
- N-acetyl cysteine binds the hepatotoxic metabolites; it improves prognosis in paracetamol poisoning even after hepatic encephalopathy has developed. It is now administered continuously until the INR has returned to normal.

5.5 Quinidine and quinine

Quinidine and quinine poisoning may result in blurred vision and abdominal pain due to anticholinergic effects. Other features are:

- **Arrhythmias**: because these drugs prolong the QT interval on the ECG
- **Hypotension**: may occur due to alpha adrenoceptor blockade
- **Tinnitus** and **irreversible blindness**.

5.6 Theophylline overdose

Theophylline causes tachycardia and may trigger arrhythmias in overdose due to phospho-diesterase inhibition. These are more likely in the presence of severe acidosis or hypokalaemia, the latter due to intractable vomiting. Seizures and confusion can occur.

- Treatment is with activated charcoal (which significantly reduces theophylline absorption) and correction of fluid and electrolyte depletion. Upper gastrointestinal endoscopy may be useful to remove tablet residuum that can remain within the stomach for many hours.
- Haemodialysis, or preferably, charcoal haemoperfusion, is indicated for patients with severe toxicity (plasma theophylline >60 mg/l).

5.7 Tricyclic antidepressant overdose

Tricyclic antidepressants have anti-cholinergic (pupillary dilatation, confusion and tachycardia) and alpha-blocking (hypotension) side-effects. Sympathomimetic overactivity results.

- Prolonged QT interval on the ECG may predispose to ventricular arrhythmias; the QRS complex is widened in severe toxicity, which may be a prelude to cardiogenic shock. These cardiac abnormalities are best treated with magnesium and pacing.
- The seizure threshold is also reduced and status epilepticus may ensue; abnormalities of thermoregulation can also occur.
- Treatment is supportive, with emesis, gastric lavage and use of activated charcoal. Fluid and electrolyte balance should be maintained; diazepam is used for convulsions.

5.8 Haemodialysis for overdose or poisoning

Drugs or poisons which are poorly removed by haemodialysis are those with a large volume of distribution (e.g. amiodarone and paraquat) or those which are highly protein-bound (e.g. digoxin and phenytoin).

Removal of drugs or toxins by haemodialysis/haemoperfusion

- **Haemodialysis effective**
  Lithium
  Barbiturates
  Alcohol
  Methanol
  Ethylene glycol
  Salicylate

- **Charcoal haemoperfusion**
  Paracetamol metabolites
  Theophylline

Chapter 3
Dermatology

CONTENTS

1. **Structure and function of skin**   85
   1.1   Structure
   1.2   Function

2. **Hair and nails**   86
   2.1   Disorders of hair
   2.2   Disorders of nails

3. **Specific dermatoses**   88
   3.1   Psoriasis
   3.2   Eczema (dermatitis)
   3.3   Lichen planus
   3.4   Erythema multiforme
   3.5   Erythema nodosum

4. **Bullous eruptions**   92

5. **The skin in connective tissue disorders**   93
   5.1   Systemic sclerosis
   5.2   Rheumatoid arthritis
   5.3   Dermatomyositis

6. **The skin in systemic diseases**   94
   6.1   Sarcoidosis
   6.2   The porphyrias
   6.3   Pyoderma gangrenosum
   6.4   Diabetes
   6.5   HIV/AIDS

7. **Generalized pruritus**   95

8. **Cutaneous markers of internal malignancy**   **96**
    8.1   Genetically determined syndromes with skin manifestations
    8.2   Skin disease as paraneoplastic features

9. **Disorders of pigmentation**   **98**

10. **Drug eruptions**   **99**

Dermatology

1. STRUCTURE AND FUNCTION OF SKIN

1.1 Structure

The skin consists of three distinctive layers: epidermis, dermis and subcutaneous fat. The dermo-epidermal junction separates the epidermis from the dermis.

- **Epidermis**: this forms the outermost layer and is the largest organ in the body. The principal cell is the keratinocyte.
- **Dermis**: contributes 15–20% of total body weight and provides nutrition to the epidermis. The dermis contains two main proteins: collagen, which provides strength, and elastin, which gives the skin its elasticity.
- **Dermo-epidermal junction**: an important structure separating the epidermis from the dermis. Anomalies of this can give rise to some of the blistering disorders.

1.2 Function

The skin has numerous functions, all of which are designed to protect the rest of the body.

- **Barrier properties**: the skin acts as a two-way barrier, preventing the inward or outward passage of fluid and electrolytes.
- **Mechanical properties**: the skin is highly elastic and so can be stretched or compressed.
- **Immunological function**: the skin provides defence against foreign agents. In the epidermis, antigen presentation is carried out by Langerhans' cells.
- **Sensory function**: the skin perceives the sensations of touch, pressure, cold, warmth and pain.
- **Endocrine properties**: as a result of exposure to ultraviolet B radiation, vitamin D3 is synthesized from previtamin D3.
- **Temperature regulation**: the rich blood supply of the dermis plays an important role in thermoregulation.
- **Respiration**: the skin plays a minor role in gaseous exchange with the environment.

2. HAIR AND NAILS

2.1 Disorders of hair

The first signs of hair follicles appear in the region of the eyebrows, upper lip and chin at about nine weeks' gestation. By 22 weeks the full complement of follicles is established. Hair abnormalities comprise either excessive hair growth or hair loss.

Excessive hair growth can be androgen-independent 'hypertrichosis' or androgen-dependent 'hirsutism'.

Causes of hypertrichosis

- **Congenital/hereditary**
  Congenital hypertrichosis
    lanuginosa
  Porphyrias
  Epidermolysis bullosa
  Hurler's syndrome

- **Drugs**
  Diazoxide
  Minoxidil
  Cyclosporin
  Streptomycin

- **Acquired**
  Acquired hypertrichosis
    lanuginosa

- **Other**
  Malnutrition
  Anorexia nervosa

- **Endocrine**
  Hypothyroidism
  Hyperthyroidism

Causes of hirsutism

- **Ovarian**
  Polycystic ovary syndrome
  Ovarian tumours

- **Adrenal**
  Congenital adrenal hyperplasia
  Cushing's disease
  Prolactinoma

- **Androgen therapy**

Loss of hair is called alopecia and can be scarring or non-scarring. Scarring alopecia is loss of hair with destruction of the hair follicles. Non-scarring alopecia is when the hair follicles are preserved. A good example of this is the 'exclamation mark' hair seen in alopecia areata.

Causes of scarring alopecia

- **Hereditary**
  Ichthyosis

- **Physical injury**
  Burns
  Radiotherapy

- **Bacterial**
  Tuberculosis
  Syphilis

- **Fungal**
  Kerion

- **Others**
  Lichen planus
  Lupus erythematosus
  Morphea
  Sarcoidosis
  Cicatricial pemphigoid

Causes of non-scarring alopecia

- **Alopecia areata**

- **Endocrine**
  Hypopituitary state
  Hypothyroidism
  Hyperthyroidism
  Hypoparathyroidism
  Pseudohypoparathyroidism
  Diabetes mellitus
  Pregnancy

- **Drugs**
  Carbimazole
  Thiouracil
  Heparin
  Warfarin
  Lithium
  Oral contraceptive pill

Alopecia areata is associated with nail dystrophy, cataracts, vitiligo, autoimmune thyroid disease, pernicious anaemia and Addison's disease.

2.2 Disorders of nails

Nails are derived from keratin. This is a protein complex, which gives the nail its hard property. The nail can be affected in a variety of skin and systemic disorders.

Causes of nail changes associated with skin disorders

- **Psoriasis**: nail changes include onycholysis, nail pitting, hyperkeratosis, pustule and occasional loss of nail.

- **Fungal**: signs include discolouration, onycholysis and thickening of the nail.
- **Bacterial**: usually due to staphylococcal infections. Pseudomonas infections give a green discolouration to the nail.
- **Lichen planus**: nail changes occur in 10% of cases, with thinning of the nail plate and longitudinal.linear depressions. Occasionally there is destruction of the nail (pterygium).
- **Alopecia areata**: pitting, thickening and ridging of the nail (sandpaper nail) is seen.
- **Dermatitis**: coarse pits, cross-ridging and onycholysis may be seen.

Causes of nail changes associated with systemic disease

- **Koilonychia**: the nails are thin, brittle and concave. There is an association with iron deficiency anaemia.
- **Yellow nail syndrome**: the nails are yellow and excessively curved. Associations include recurrent pleural effusions, chronic bronchitis, bronchiectasis, nephrotic syndrome and hypothyroidism.
- **Nail–patella syndrome**: loss of ulnar half of the nails, usually the thumbnail, is seen. Associations include small patellae, bony spines over posterior iliac crests, renal abnormalities, over-extension of joints and laxity of the skin.
- **Beau's lines**: these are transverse depressions in the nail due to temporary arrest in growth. They usually occur after a period of illness or infection.
- **Half and half nails**: the proximal nail bed is white and distal, pink or brown. They are associated with chronic renal failure and rheumatoid arthritis.

Causes of onycholysis

- **Idiopathic**: excessive manicuring or wetting
- **Dermatological disease**: psoriasis, fungal infection, dermatitis
- **Systemic disease**: impaired peripheral circulation, hypothyroidism, hyperthyroidism
- **Trauma**.

3. SPECIFIC DERMATOSES

3.1 Psoriasis

This is a genetically determined, inflammatory and proliferative disorder of the skin, occurring in 1–2% of the UK population. Its aetiology is unknown but there is an association with HLA Cw6 in skin disease and HLA B27 in psoriatic arthropathy. The disease is more common in the second and sixth decades, with females generally developing psoriasis at an earlier age than males.

Psoriasis tends to affect the extensor surfaces and demonstrates the Köbner phenomenon. Other affected areas include the scalp, nails, genitalia and flexures.

Variants of psoriasis

- Pustular — generalized pustular, palmo-plantar pustulosis
- Guttate
- Chronic plaque
- Erythrodermic.

Associations with psoriasis

- **Arthropathy**: distal inter-phalangeal joint disease, large single joint oligoarthritis, arthritis mutilans, sacro-iliitis and psoriatic spondylitis have all been described.
- **Gout**: this is due to deposits of urate crystals.
- **Malabsorption**: Crohn's and ulcerative colitis are associated with psoriasis.

Factors which can exacerbate psoriasis

- **Trauma**.
- **Infection**: guttate psoriasis can be provoked by streptococcal throat infection.
- **Endocrine**: psoriasis generally tends to improve during pregnancy and deteriorate in the post-partum period.
- **Drugs**: beta-blockers, lithium, antimalarials and the withdrawal of oral steroids can exacerbate psoriasis.
- **Alcohol**.
- **HIV**.

Causes of the Köbner phenomenon

- Psoriasis
- Lichen planus
- Vitiligo
- Viral warts
- Molluscum contagiosum
- Bullous pemphigoid

Causes of erythroderma

- Psoriasis
- Eczema
- Mycosis fungoides
- Adverse drug reactions
- Underlying malignancy
- Pemphigus foliaceous

3.2 Eczema (dermatitis)

Eczema is an inflammatory skin disorder with characteristic histology and clinical features, that include itching, redness, scaling and a papulovesicular rash. Eczema can be divided into two broad groups, exogenous or endogenous.

- Exogenous eczema — irritant dermatitis, allergic contact dermatitis
- Endogenous eczema — atopic dermatitis, seborrhoeic dermatitis, pompholyx.

Seborrhoeic dermatitis is a red, scaly rash caused by *Pityrosporum ovale*. The eruption occurs on the scalp, face and upper trunk and is more common in young adults and HIV patients.

Pompholyx is characterized by itchy vesicles occurring on the palms and soles.

Atopic dermatitis is a characteristic dermatitic eruption associated with a personal or family history of atopy. The age of onset is usually between two and six months, with males being more affected than females. The disease is chronic but tends to improve during childhood. The flexural sites are commonly affected and features include itching, exudative papules or vesicles, dryness and lichenification. There is an increased risk of bacterial (staphylococcal or streptococcal) and viral (*Herpes simplex*) infection.

3.3 Lichen planus

This presents as an itchy, shiny, violaceous, flat-topped, polygonal, papular rash with white lines on the surface known as Wickham's striae. Other affected sites include mucous membranes, genitalia, palms, soles, scalp and nails.

Causes of white lesions in the oral mucosa

- Lichen planus
- Leucoplakia
- Chronic candidiasis
- Chemical burns.

3.4 Erythema multiforme

This is usually a maculo-papular, targetoid rash, which can occur anywhere, including the palms, soles and oral mucosa. The aetiology is unknown but thought to be associated with infections, mainly viral. Stevens–Johnson syndrome, on the other hand, is more likely to affect mucosal surfaces and is thought to be associated with drug reactions.

Causes of erythema multiforme

- **Infections**
  Herpes simplex virus
  Mycoplasma
  Psittacosis
  Rickettsiae
  HIV
  Hepatitis B virus
  Orf
  Infectious mononucleosis
  Mumps

- **Drug reactions**
  Barbiturates
  Penicillin
  Sulphonamides

- **Others**
  Lupus erythematosus
  Polyarteritis nodosa
  Wegener's granulomatosis
  Underlying malignancy
  Sarcoidosis

3.5 Erythema nodosum

This is a hot, tender, nodular, erythematous eruption lasting three to six weeks, which is more common in the third decade and in females.

Causes of erythema nodosum

- **Bacterial infection**
  Streptococcal throat infection

- **Mycoses**

- **Sarcoidosis**

- **Tuberculosis**

- **Malignancy**

- **Viral/chlamydial infection**

- **Other infections**
  Salmonella gastroenteritis,
  Campylobacter colitis

- **Inflammatory bowel disease**

- **Drugs**
  Penicillin
  Tetracyclines
  Oral contraceptive pill
  Sulphonamides
  Sulphonylureas

4. BULLOUS ERUPTIONS

This is a rare group of disorders characterized by the formation of bullae. The development of blisters can be due to congenital, immunological or other causes. The level of split within the epidermis or within the dermo-epidermal junction determines the type of bullous disorder.

Causes of bullous eruptions

- **Congenital**
  Epidermolysis bullosa

- **Others**
  Staphylococcal scalded skin syndrome
  Toxic epidermal necrolysis
  Diabetic bullae
  Chronic renal failure
  Haemodialysis

- **Immunological**
  Pemphigus
  Bullous pemphigoid
  Cicatricial pemphigoid
  Herpes gestationis
  Dermatitis herpetiformis

- **Drug overdose**
  Barbiturates

Epidermolysis bullosa is the term used for a group of genetically determined disorders characterized by blistering of the skin, palms, soles and mucosae, especially the mouth and oesophagus.

Pemphigus is a group of disorders characterized by blistering of the skin and mucous membranes.

Bullous pemphigoid is a disorder characterized by large tense blisters found mainly on lower limbs in the elderly. Oral mucosal involvement is rare.

Cicatricial pemphigoid is a rare, chronic blistering disease of the mucous membranes and skin, which results in permanent scarring, particularly of the conjunctivae.

Dermatitis herpetiformis is an itchy, vesiculo-bullous eruption mainly occurring on the extensor areas. The majority of patients have asymptomatic gluten-sensitive enteropathy.

5. THE SKIN IN CONNECTIVE TISSUE DISORDERS

5.1 Systemic sclerosis

This is a rare, multisystem, connective tissue disease of unknown aetiology, characterized by fibrosis of the skin and visceral organs and accompanied by the presence of relatively specific antinuclear antibodies. The incidence peaks in the fifth and sixth decades and females are more affected than males.

Skin changes in systemic sclerosis

- Facial telangiectasia
- Restricted mouth opening
- Peri-oral puckering
- Smooth shiny pigmented indurated skin
- Raynaud's phenomenon with gangrene
- Sclerodactyly
- Pulp atrophy
- Dilated nail fold capillaries
- Ragged cuticles
- Calcinosis cutis
- Livedo reticularis
- Leg ulcers

5.2 Rheumatoid arthritis

Specific skin changes in rheumatoid arthritis

- Rheumatoid nodules
- Nail fold infarcts
- Vasculitis with gangrene
- Pyoderma gangrenosum.

5.3 Dermatomyositis

Specific skin changes in dermatomyositis

- Heliotrope rash around eyes
- Red plaques on extensor surfaces of finger joints
- Dilated nail fold capillaries.

6. THE SKIN IN SYSTEMIC DISEASES

6.1 Sarcoidosis

Skin lesions are found in approximately 25% of patients with systemic sarcoid and can occur in the absence of systemic disease.

- Erythema nodosum
- Scar sarcoid
- Lupus pernio
- Scarring alopecia.

6.2 The porphyrias

Skin signs are not seen in acute intermittent porphyria. In congenital erythropoietic porphyria patients have brown teeth which fluoresce red under Wood's light giving the 'werewolf' appearance.

- Photosensitivity
- Blister formation
- Scarring with milia
- Hypertrichosis.

6.3 Pyoderma gangrenosum

This is a painful ulcerating disease that typically occurs on the legs.

Causes of pyoderma gangrenosum

- **Gastrointestinal**
  Ulcerative colitis
  Crohn's colitis

- **Rheumatological**
  Rheumatoid arthritis
  Ankylosing spondylitis

- **Liver**
  Chronic active hepatitis
  Primary biliary cirrhosis
  Sclerosing cholangitis

- **Haematological**
  Leukaemia
  Lymphoma
  Myeloproliferative disorders

- **Others**
  Diabetes mellitus
  Thryoid disease
  Sarcoidosis
  Wegener's disease

- **Other malignancies**

6.4 Diabetes

Skin signs in diabetes mellitus

- Necrobiosis lipoidica
- Disseminated granuloma annulare
- Diabetic rubeosis
- Candidiasis and infection
- Vitiligo
- Neuropathic foot ulcers.

Diabetic rubeosis is an odd redness of the face, hands and feet thought to be due to diabetic microangiopathy.

6.5 HIV/AIDS

Skin disease is common, affecting 75% of patients who can be at any stage of HIV disease. (See Chapter 7, *Genito-urinary Medicine and AIDS*.)

7. GENERALIZED PRURITUS

Pruritus is an important skin symptom and occurs in dermatological diseases such as atopic eczema. In the absence of localized skin disease or skin signs, patients should be fully investigated to exclude an underlying cause.

Causes of generalized pruritus

- **Obstructive liver disease**

- **Haematological**
  Iron deficiency anaemia
  Polycythaemia

- **Endocrine**
  Hyperthyroidism
  Hypothyroidism
  Diabetes mellitus

- **Chronic renal failure**

- **Malignancy**
  Internal malignancies
  Lymphoma

- **Drugs**
  Morphine

- **Other**
  Pregnancy
  Senility

8. CUTANEOUS MARKERS OF INTERNAL MALIGNANCY

There are numerous skin changes associated with internal malignancy. These can be either genetically determined syndromes with cutaneous manifestations, where there is a recognized predisposition to internal malignancy, or paraneoplastic syndromes, where the cutaneous signs are significantly associated with malignancy of various organs.

8.1 Genetically determined syndromes with skin manifestations

Most of these diseases have an autosomal dominant inheritance.

- **Gardner's syndrome**: epidermal cysts, lipomas and fibromas are associated with colonic carcinoma.

- **Peutz–Jeghers syndrome**: mucocutaneous pigmentation is associated with mainly gastrointestinal malignancy.

- **Howel–Evans syndrome**: tylosis (palmo–plantar keratoderma) has been reported with oesophageal carcinoma.

- **Torre–Muir syndrome**: sebaceous tumours are associated with gastrointestinal malignancy.

- **Cowden's disease**: tricholemmomas (facial nodules) and warty hyperplasia of the mucosal surface is associated with breast and thyroid carcinoma.

- **Neurofibromatosis**: the presence of six or more café-au-lait macules, axillary freckling and neurofibromas is associated with malignant schwannomas and astrocytomas.

- **Tuberous sclerosis**: angiofibromas, together with periungual fibromas, shagreen patches and ash-leaf macules are associated with sarcomas and rhabdomyomas.

- **Gorlin's syndrome**: mucosal neuromas are associated with medullary thyroid carcinoma and phaeochromocytoma (multiple endocrine neoplasia type 2b).

- **von-Hippel Lindau syndrome:** café-au-lait macules and haemangiomas are associated with vascular tumours of the central nervous system, phaeochromocytoma, renal and pancreatic carcinoma.

- **Sturge–Weber syndrome**: port wine stain associated with ipsilateral vascular meningeal malformation and epilepsy.

- **Wiskott–Aldrich syndrome**: a sex-linked recessive disease characterized by eczema, immunodeficiency and an increased risk of lymphoma and leukaemia.

- **Chediak–Higashi syndrome:** a fatal autosomal recessive disease with recurrent bacterial infections and widespread infiltration with lymphocytes suggesting a lymphoma.

- **Ataxia telangiectasia:** an autosomal recessive disease characterized by mucocutaneous telangiectasia and an increased risk of lymphoma and leukaemia.

8.2 Skin disease as paraneoplastic features

Dermatological features can be seen in all types of malignant disease but some are more common in certain types of neoplasia.

Specific dermatological features and the common types of maligancy with which they are associated

- **Acanthosis nigricans:** gastrointestinal adenocarcinoma
- **Acanthosis palmaris (tripe palms):** bronchial carcinoma
- **Acanthosis palmaris with nigricans:** gastrointestinal adenocarcinoma
- **Generalized pruritus:** lymphoma
- **Dermatomyositis (in adults):** bronchial, breast and ovarian tumours
- **Erythema gyratum repens:** bronchial carcinoma
- **Acquired hypertrichosis lanuginosa:** gastrointestinal and bronchial tumours
- **Necrolytic migratory erythema:** glucoganoma
- **Migratory thrombophlebitis:** pancreatic carcinoma
- **Acquired ichthyosis:** lymphoma
- **Pyoderma gangrenosum:** myeloproliferative tumours
- **Erythroderma:** lymphoma and leukaemia
- **Clubbing:** bronchial carcinoma
- *Herpes zoster*: myeloproliferative tumours.

Other causes of acanthosis nigricans

- Internal malignancy
- Insulin-resistant diabetes mellitus
- Familial
- Acromegaly
- Cushing's disease

- Obesity
- Oral contraceptive pill
- Nicotinic acid
- Hypothyroidism

9. DISORDERS OF PIGMENTATION

The major colour determinant of the skin is melanin. This is produced by melanocytes, which are found in the basal layer of the epidermis. Pigmentary disorders usually present with either hypopigmentation or hyperpigmentation.

Causes of hypopigmentation

- **Genetic**
  Albinism
  Phenylketonuria
  Tuberous sclerosis

- **Chemical**
  Chloroquine

- **Infections**
  Pityriasis versicolor

- **Endocrine**
  Hypopituitarism

- **Autoimmune**
  Vitiligo

- **Post-inflammatory**
  Eczema
  Psoriasis
  Lupus erythematosus

Causes of hyperpigmentation

- **Genetic**
  Peutz–Jeghers syndrome
  Xeroderma pigmentosum
  Albright's syndrome

- **Metabolic**
  Cirrhosis
  Haemochromatosis
  Porphyria
  Renal failure

- **Drugs**
  Oral contraceptive pill
  Minocycline
  Amiodarone

- **Endocrine**
  Addison's disease
  Cushing's syndrome
  Nelson's syndrome
  Pregnancy

- **Nutritional**
  Malabsorption
  Carcinomatosis
  Kwashiokor
  Pellagra

- **Post-inflammatory**
  Lichen planus
  Eczema
  Secondary syphilis
  Cutaneous amyloid

10. DRUG ERUPTIONS

The incidence of drug eruptions is approximately 2%. One-third are thought to be fixed drug eruptions, one-third exanthematous and one-fifth urticarial.

Urticaria is a transient, itchy, erythematous rash characterized by the presence of weals. It is thought to occur due to histamine release from mast cells, but other agents such as prostaglandins and leukotrienes have also been implicated. Angio-oedema is similar to urticaria, but histologically, there is greater swelling of the subcutaneous tissue and clinically, mucosal sites are affected.

Drugs causing urticaria

- Penicillin
- Salicylates
- Quinidine
- Cephalosporin
- Angiotensin converting enzyme inhibitors
- Hydralazine

A **fixed drug eruption** is one that tends to recur in the same site each time the drug is administered. Clinically, the eruption is discrete, raised, round or oval and can occasionally blister.

Drugs causing a fixed drug eruption

- Tetracyclines
- Barbiturates
- Dapsone
- Chlordiazepoxide
- Phenolphthalein
- Sulphonamides
- Benzodiazepines
- Non-steroidal anti-inflammatory drugs
- Quinine
- Paracetamol

Lupus erythematosus-like syndrome is a relatively rare disorder, in which a number of drugs have been implicated. (See Chapter 2, *Clinical Pharmacology, Toxicology and Poisoning.*) Drug-induced photosensitivity and drug-induced vasculitis are also covered in that chapter.

Other diseases aggravated by sunlight

- Lupus erythematosus
- Dermatomyositis
- Xeroderma pigmentosum
- Herpes simplex infection
- Porphyrias (except acute intermittent)
- Pellagra
- Carcinoid syndrome

Chapter 4
Endocrinology

CONTENTS

1. **Hormone action**   103
    1.1   Types of hormone
    1.2   Hormones that act at the cell surface
    1.3   Hormones that act intracellularly
    1.4   Hormone resistance syndromes

2. **Specific hormone physiology**   106
    2.1   Hormones in illness
    2.2   Hormone changes in obesity
    2.3   Hormones in pregnancy
    2.4   Investigations in endocrinology
    2.5   Growth hormone
    2.6   Prolactin
    2.7   Adrenal steroids
    2.8   Thyroid hormone metabolism
    2.9   Renin–angiotensin–aldosterone
    2.10   Calcium, PTH and vitamin D
    2.11   Atrial natriuretic peptide (ANP)

3. **The pituitary gland**   112
    3.1   Anatomy
    3.2   Pituitary tumours
    3.3   Diabetes insipidus
    3.4   Acromegaly
    3.5   Growth hormone deficiency in adults

4. **The thyroid gland**   116
    4.1   Hyperthyroidism and hypothyroidism
    4.2   Causes of thyrotoxicosis
    4.3   Thyroid cancer and nodules
    4.4   Drugs and the thyroid
    4.5   Autoimmunity and eye signs in thyroid disease
    4.6   Thyroid function tests

5. **Adrenal disease and hirsutism**   **120**
    5.1   Cushing's syndrome
    5.2   Congenital adrenal hyperplasia (CAH)
    5.3   Hypoadrenalism
    5.4   Polycystic ovarian syndrome (PCOS) and hirsutism

6. **Phaeochromocytoma and multiple-endocrine neoplasia (MEN)**   **126**
    syndromes

7. **Puberty/growth/intersex**   **128**
    7.1   Normal puberty
    7.2   Precocious puberty
    7.3   Delayed puberty/short stature
    7.4   Intersex

8. **Diabetes mellitus**   **131**
    8.1   Risk factors and clinical features of Type 1 and Type 2 diabetes
    8.2   Diagnostic criteria for diabetes
    8.3   Secondary diabetes
    8.4   Drugs used in Type 2 diabetes
    8.5   Glycated haemoglobin (HbA1, HbA1c)
    8.6   Microvascular and macrovascular complications of diabetes
    8.7   Autonomic neuropathy

9. **Hypoglycaemia**   **137**
    9.1   Hypoglycaemia in diabetes
    9.2   Hypoglycaemia unrelated to diabetes

10. **Hyponatraemia and SIADH**   **138**

Endocrinology

1. HORMONE ACTION

There are three main types of hormone:

- Amine
- Steroid
- Peptide.

Knowing which category a particular hormone fits into makes it possible to guess much of its physiology. Vitamin D and thyroxine are exceptions to this, as shown below.

1.1 Types of hormone

- **Amine**: catecholamines, serotonin, **thyroxine**
- **Steroid**: cortisol, aldosterone, androgens, oestrogens and progestogens and **vitamin D**
- **Peptide**: everything else! (made up of a series of amino-acids).

Thyroxine is chemically an amine hormone but, like vitamin D, it acts like a steroid.

Amines/peptides	Steroids
Short half-life (mins)	Longer biological half-life (hours)
Secretion may be pulsatile	
Act on a cell surface receptor	Act on an intracellular receptor
Often act via a second messenger	Act on DNA to alter gene expression

This information can be used to predict hormone action. For example, aldosterone is a steroid hormone so it must have a biological half-life of several hours, bind to an intracellular receptor and affect gene transcription. Glucagon is not a steroid or an amine so it must be a polypeptide hormone which has a short circulation half-life, acts via a cell-surface receptor and probably utilizes a second messenger (cAMP in fact).

1.2 Hormones that act at the cell surface

Peptide and amine hormones act at the cell surface via specific membrane receptors. The signal is transmitted intracellularly by one of three mechanisms:

- Via cyclic AMP
- Via a rise in intracellular Ca^{++} levels
- Via receptor tyrosine kinases.

If in doubt, assume the action of a peptide or amine hormone (excluding thyroxine) is via cAMP unless it is insulin or has the word 'growth' in its name, in which case it is likely to act via a receptor tyrosine kinase.

Via cyclic AMP	Via Ca^{++}	Via receptor tyrosine kinases
Adrenaline (β receptors)	GnRH	Insulin
All pituitary hormones		
except GH, PRL	TRH	Growth hormone, prolactin
Glucagon	Adrenaline (α receptors)	'Growth factors': IGF-1, EGF
Somatostatin		

AMP = Adenosine monophosphate; GnRH = Gonadotrophin releasing hormone; GH = Growth hormone; PRL = Prolactin; TRH = Thyrotrophin releasing hormone; IGF-1 = Insulin-like growth factor 1; EGF = Epidermal growth factor.

Cyclic AMP and G proteins

Hormone receptors linked to cyclic AMP (e.g. TSH receptor) typically have seven transmembrane domains. The receptor does not directly generate cAMP but acts via a separate 'G-protein' on the cell surface which, in turn, interacts with the cAMP generating enzyme, adenylate cyclase, on the cell surface. (See diagram in Chapter 12, *Molecular Medicine*.)

Hormones that raise the level of cAMP intracellularly (all hormones in this category except somatostatin), act via a stimulatory G-protein, 'G$_s$'. Hormones that lower the level of cAMP somatostatin act via an inhibitory G-protein, 'G$_i$'.

G proteins are important in endocrinology because mutations in G$_s$ have been found to be associated with certain diseases:

- **Acromegaly**: 40% of patients with acromegaly have an activating somatic mutation of G_s in their pituitary tumour. As a result, the cells are always 'switched on' and continuously make GH (resulting in acromegaly).
- **McCune–Albright syndrome**: an activating mutation of G_s early in embryonic development causes hyperfunction of one or more endocrine glands, e.g. gonads (precocious puberty), GH (acromegaly), adrenal gland (Cushing's), thyrotoxicosis or hyperparathyroidism. The syndrome is associated with café au lait spots and polyostotic fibrous dysplasia. Because the mutation occurs after the zygote stage, affected individuals are a mosaic and different patterns of tissue involvement may be seen between individuals.
- **Pseudohypoparathyroidism** (Albright's hereditary osteodystrophy): 50% of cases are due to an inactivating germ-line mutation in G_s resulting in dysmorphic features (including short 4th or 5th metacarpal) and resistance to a variety of hormones that act via cAMP including parathyroid hormone, T_3 and gonadotrophins.

Intracellular Ca⁺⁺

The G proteins activated by some hormone receptors use intracellular Ca^{++} as a second mesenger. The G protein activates the cytoplasmic enzyme phospholipase C (PLC) which releases the small molecule inositol triphosphate (IP3) from membrane phospholipids. IP3 in the cytoplasm then releases Ca^{++} from stores in the endoplasmic reticulum. The Ca^{++} subsequently affects cell metabolism by binding to the protein calmodulin.

Receptor tyrosine kinases

The insulin, growth hormone (GH), prolactin and growth factor receptors do not use second messengers. The receptors themselves can act as enzymes which phosphorylate ('kinase activity') other proteins when hormone is bound at the cell surface. This is followed by a cascade of proteins phosphorylating other proteins until gene transcription in the nucleus is modulated.

1.3 Hormones that act intracellularly

Steroids, vitamin D and thyroxine are sufficiently lipid soluble that they do not need cell surface receptors but can diffuse directly through the cell membrane. They then bind to receptors in the cytoplasm which results in shedding of heat shock proteins that protect the empty receptor. The hormone–receptor complex migrates into the nucleus where the complex alters the transcription of a large number of genes (see diagram in Chapter 12, *Molecular Medicine*).

1.4 Hormone resistance syndromes

The following are conditions of hormone resistance with the site of the defect shown.

Receptor defect	Second messenger	Unknown
Laron dwarfism	Pseudohypoparathyroidism	Type 2 diabetes
Leprechaunism		
Nephrogenic DI		
Testicular feminization		
Vitamin D-dependent		
rickets type II		

Testicular feminization is now known as androgen resistance syndrome.

2. SPECIFIC HORMONE PHYSIOLOGY

2.1 Hormones in illness

During illness/stress, the body closes all unnecessary systems down 'from the top', e.g. the thyroid axis closes down by a fall in TRH, TSH and T_4/T_3. It is orchestrated by the hypothalamus, not by the end organs. Hormones involved in the stress response may rise.

Hormones which fall	May rise (stress hormones)
TSH, T_4/T_3*	GH (though IGF-1 falls)
LH FSH	ACTH, glucocorticoids
Testosterone, oestrogen	Adrenaline
Insulin (starvation)	Glucagon (starvation)
	Prolactin

*In this case conversion of T_4 to T_3 is inhibited so T_3 falls more than T_4.

TSH = Thyroid-stimulating hormone; GH = Growth hormone; IGF-1 = Insulin-like growth factor 1; LH = Luteinising hormone; FSH = Follicle-stimulating hormone; ACTH = Adrenocorticotrophic hormone.

In starvation alone, without illness, all hormones fall except glucagon. In anorexia nervosa there is also stress: all hormones fall except glucagon, GH and glucocorticoids.

2.2 Hormone changes in obesity

In the absence of other diseases developing (e.g. Type 2 diabetes) the following changes are seen.

- Hyperinsulinaemia
- Increased cortisol turnover but not hypercortisolism
- Increased androgen levels in women

- Reduced GH
- Conversion of androgens to oestrogens
- All bad lipid changes (low HDL, high LDL and triglyceride)

2.3 Hormones in pregnancy

As a general rule, most hormone levels rise in pregnancy. Insulin resistance develops, causing a rise in circulating insulin levels. Insulin requirements are highest in the last trimester but fall slightly in the last four weeks of pregnancy.

Other key features of hormone metabolism in pregnancy are as follows:

- **Prolactin** levels rise steadily throughout pregnancy and in combination with oestrogen prepare the breast for lactation. Post-partum surges of prolactin and oxytocin are generated by the nipple stimulation of breast-feeding. However, after several weeks prolactin levels fall almost to normal even if breast-feeding continues.
- **LH/FSH** from the pituitary are no longer necessary after conception for continued pregnancy (although the pituitary does double in size) — the placenta takes over.
- **Thyroid axis.** Thyroid binding globulin (TBG) levels rise in the first trimester causing a rise in total T_4 and total T_3. However, HCG from the placenta shares its alpha-subunit with TSH and very high levels in the first trimester can cause true mild thyrotoxicosis (not just a binding protein rise), especially associated with hyperemesis gravidarum. Note that T_4 and T_3 do not cross the placenta very efficiently but sufficient T_4 does cross to prevent a fetus with congenital hypothyroidism becoming hypothyroid until after birth.

2.4 Investigations in endocrinology

The plasma level of almost all hormones varies through the day (because of pulsatile secretion, environmental stress or circadian rhythms) and is influenced by the prevailing values of the substrates they control. This makes it hard to define a 'normal range'. For example, insulin values depend on the glucose level, GH levels depend on whether a pulse of GH has just been released or the blood sample is taken in the trough between pulses.

Dynamic testing is therefore frequently used, i.e. suppression or stimulation tests. The principle is, 'If you think a hormone level may be high, suppress it; if you think it may be low, stimulate it'.

- **Suppression tests** are used to test for hormone EXCESS — e.g. dexamethasone suppression for Cushing's syndrome, glucose tolerance for GH in acromegaly.
- **Stimulation tests** are used to test for hormone DEFICIENCY — e.g. synacthen tests for hypoadrenalism, insulin-induced hypoglycaemia for GH deficiency and/or hypoadrenalism.

2.5 Growth hormone

This is secreted in pulses lasting 30–45 minutes separated by periods when secretion is undetectable. The majority of GH pulses occur at night ('children grow at night'). In response to GH pulses, the liver makes insulin-like growth factor -1 (IGF-1, previously called somatomedin C), the plasma level of which is constant and which mediates almost all the actions of GH, i.e. GH does not act directly. The effective levels of IGF-1 are influenced by changes in the level of its six binding proteins (IGF-BP I-6).

2.6 Prolactin

Prolactin causes galactorrhoea but not gynaecomastia (oestrogen does this). Raised prolactin levels are essentially the only cause of galactorrhoea, although occasionally prolactin levels in the normal range can cause milk production in a sensitized breast. Raised prolactin levels also 'shut down' the gonadal axis 'from the top' (hypothalamic level) resulting in low GnRH, LH and oestrogen/testosterone levels. Surprisingly, prolactin is a stress hormone and levels rise after an epileptic fit.

Prolactin release from the pituitary is under **negative** control by dopamine from the hypothalamus. Oestrogens (the pill, preganancy) and nipple stimulation raise prolactin.

Prolactin is raised by

- Phenothiazines (*not* tricyclics)*
- Damage to hypothalamus
  (e.g. radiation)
- Pregnancy
- Nipple stimulation

- Anti-emetics (e.g. metoclopramide)
- Damage to pituitary stalk
  (e.g. pressure from a pituitary tumour)
- Oestrogens
- Polycystic ovary syndrome

Prolactin is suppressed by

- Bromocriptine (dopamine agonist)
  and related drugs

*Female psychiatric patients may complain of galactorrhoea — doctors often do not believe them but they are right and it is due to the doctor's treatment!

Gynaecomastia

This is due to a decreased androgen:oestrogen ratio in men. Gynaecomastia is unrelated to galactorrhoea (which is always due to prolactin). Breast enlargement is not necessary to make milk.

Causes of gynaecomastia:

- Pubertal (normal)
- Obesity — not true gynaecomastia
- Hypogonadism (e.g. Klinefelter's, testicular failure)
- Cirrhosis, alcohol
- Hyperthyroidism
- Drugs: including spironolactone, digoxin, oestrogens, cimetidine, anabolic steroids, marijuana
- Tumours, including adrenal or testicular making oestrogen; lung, pancreatic, gastric making HCG; hepatomas converting androgens to oestrogens.

2.7 Adrenal steroids

These act intracellularly to alter the transcription of DNA to mRNA (see Section 1, Hormone Action). Surprisingly, the mineralocorticoid (aldosterone) and glucocorticoid receptors have an equal affinity for cortisol. However, the cellular enzyme **11-beta hydroxysteroid dehydrogenase** 'protects' the mineralocorticoid receptor by chemically modifying any cortisol that comes near the receptor to an inactive form while having no effect on aldosterone itself. Inactivating mutations of this enzyme or inhibition of it by liquorice causes 'apparent mineralocorticoid excess' since cortisol (which circulates at much higher concentrations than aldosterone) is able to stimulate the mineralocorticoid receptor.

	Relative glucocorticoid effect	Relative mineralocorticoid effect	Duration of action
Cortisol = hydrocortisone	1	+	Short
Prednisolone	4	+/–	Medium
Dexamethasone	30	–	Long
Fludrocortisone	10	+ + +	

2.8   Thyroid hormone metabolism

More than 95% of thyroid hormones are bound to plasma proteins in the circulation, predominantly thyroid binding globulin (TBG) and thyroid binding prealbumin (TBPA). T_4 (L-thyroxine, four iodine atoms per molecule) has a half-life of seven days (so if a patient is in a confused state it is possible to administer his/her total weekly dose of thyroxine once a week). It is converted partly in the thyroid and partly in the circulation to T_3 (L-thyronine, three iodine atoms per molecule), which is the active form and has a half-life of one day.

The same (monodeiodinase) enzyme that converts T_4 to T_3 also converts reverse T_3 (rT_3, inactive) to T_2 (see diagram). The enzyme is inhibited by illness, propranolol, propylthiouracil, amiodarone and ipodate (gall bladder X-ray contrast). This reduces the level of active hormone, T_3 with little change or a rise in T_4. rT_3 levels rise (T_4 spontaneously converts to rT_3 if the monodeiodinase is not available) but rT_3 is *not* detected in laboratory tests of T_3 levels.

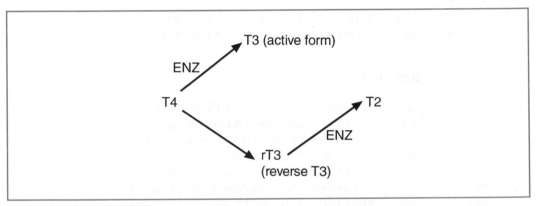

Metabolism of thyroid hormones. ENZ = Deiodinase enzyme — the same enzyme converts T_4 to T_3 and rT_3 to T_2

It is said that you should, 'Never measure thyroid function tests on ITU as you will not be able to interpret them'. In illness TSH and free T_3 levels fall ('sick euthyroidism'). The only interpretable finding in sick patients is a raised free T_3 — this would almost definitely indicate thyrotoxicosis.

2.9 Renin–angiotensin–aldosterone

Aldosterone secretion is controlled almost completely by the renin–angiotensin system, not by ACTH. The initial letters of the zones of the adrenal cortex from outside inwards spell 'GFR', like glomerular filtration rate: glomerularis, fasciculata, reticularis. Aldosterone is the 'outsider hormone' and is made on the 'outside' (zona glomerulosa).

Renin is released from the JGA (juxtaglomerular apparatus) of the kidney in response to low Na^+ delivery or reduced renal perfusion. Renin is an enzyme which converts angiotensinogen to angiotensin I (10 amino-acids). ACE (angiotensin converting enzyme) in the lung converts angiotensin I to angiotensin II which is the active form. ACE also breaks down bradykinin: ACE inhibitors (e.g. captopril) are believed to cause cough by causing a build up of bradykinin in the lung.

The renin–angiotensin system is designed to restore circulating volume. It is therefore activated by hypovolaemia (see above) and its end product, angiotensin II has three actions which restore volume:

- Releasing aldosterone from the adrenal (retains Na^+, excretes K^+ in the distal tubule)
- Vasoconstriction (powerful)
- Induction of thirst (powerful).

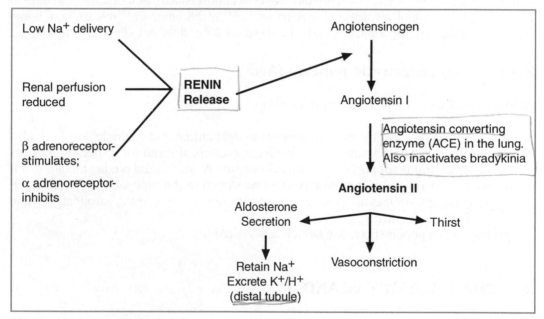

The renin-angiotensin system

2.10 Calcium, PTH and vitamin D

(See also Chapter 11, *Metabolic Diseases*.)

Plasma calcium is tightly regulated by parathyroid hormone (PTH) and vitamin D acting on the kidney (PTH), bone (PTH) and the gut (vitamin D).

PTH controls Ca^{2+} levels minute to minute by mobilizing Ca^{2+} from bone and inhibiting Ca^{2+} excretion from the kidney. Vitamin D has a more long term role, predominantly by promoting Ca^{2+} absorption from the gut. Its actions on the kidney and bone are of lesser importance.

Precursor vitamin D, obtained from the diet or synthesized by the action of sunlight on the skin, requires activation by two steps:

- 25-hydroxylation in the liver
- 1-hydroxylation in the kidney.

PTH can promote 1-hydroxylation of vitamin D in the kidney, i.e. it can activate vitamin D thereby indirectly stimulating Ca^{2+} absorption from the gut.

Calcitonin (from the C-cells of the thyroid) behaves almost exactly as a counter-hormone to PTH (secreted by high Ca^{2+}, acts to lower serum Ca^{2+} by inhibiting Ca^{2+} release from bone) but its physiological importance is in doubt (thyroidectomy does not affect Ca^{2+} levels).

2.11 Atrial natriuretic peptide (ANP)

ANP physiology can be predicted from its name.

- **Atrial**: it is synthesized by the myocytes of the right atrium and ventricle
- **Natriuretic**: it causes a natriuresis (urinary excretion of sodium). It thereby *reduces* circulating volume (opposite of renin–angiotensin). As you would predict therefore, it is secreted in conditions of *hypervolaemia* — via stretch of the right atrial and ventricular walls. It also antagonizes the other actions of angiotensin II by causing vasodilatation and reduced thirst/salt craving
- **Peptide**: it is a peptide hormone (which acts via cAMP).

3.   THE PITUITARY GLAND

3.1 Anatomy

The anatomical relations of the pituitary are important as enlarging pituitary tumours may press on surrounding structures.

- **Above**: optic chiasm (causing bitemporal hemianopia if compressed), pituitary stalk, hypothalamus, temporal lobes
- **Below**: sphenoid sinus (in front and below to allow transphenoidal surgery), nasopharynx
- **Lateral**: cavernous sinus, internal carotid arteries, III, IV, V_1, V_2 and VI cranial nerves.

Expanding pituitary tumours may also compromise remaining anterior pituitary function but very rarely affect posterior pituitary hormones.

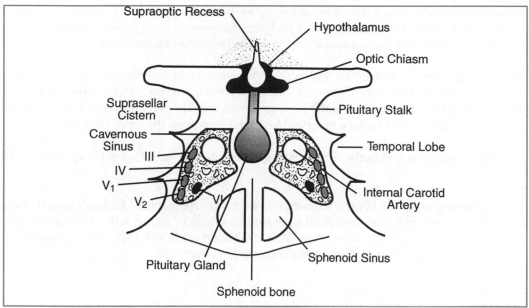

Schematic sagittal section through the pituitary to show its relation to surrounding structures

3.2 Pituitary tumours

A microadenoma is a pituitary tumour less than 1 cm in size. The size and frequency of pituitary tumours are related.

Large — non-secreting (typically chromophobe)	50% of all tumours
Large — prolactinomas in men	25% of all tumours
Medium — acromegaly (typically 'acidophil', 70% are >1 cm)	12% of all tumours
Small — Cushing's disease (often undetectable on CT/MRI, typically basophil)	5–10% of all tumours
Small — TSH-secreting	1% — very rare

Many 'non-secreting' tumours stain immunochemically for FSH or LH and some secrete excess gonadotrophin, but hypergonadism is never seen so these tumours are effectively silent (non-functioning).

Prolactinomas in women are usually picked up at the microadenoma size due to menstrual disturbance.

Nelson's syndrome arises after adrenalectomy for pituitary-dependent Cushing's syndrome (Cushing's disease). The small tumour is no longer suppressed by high steroid levels and can become very invasive. Local tumour effects and hyperpigmentation result.

Pituitary apoplexy is sudden enlargement of the pituitary by haemorrhage into a tumour, typically causing the combination of headache, neck stiffness and sudden blindness associated with cardiovascular collapse due to hypopituitarism. Treatment is with steroid replacement and urgent surgery for visual loss (to decompress the optic chiasm).

Forty per cent of **acromegaly** (GH tumours) arise because of a G-protein mutation (see section 1.2).

Craniopharyngiomas are benign tumours that arise from remnants of Rathke's pouch. Two-thirds arise in the hypothalamus itself (suprasellar), one-third in the sella. They are usually cystic, frequently calcify, often recur after aspiration and, although they represent an embryonic remnant, they not infrequently present in adulthood.

3.3 Diabetes insipidus

To cause **cranial diabetes insipidus** (DI), the hypothalamic nuclei (supraoptic and paraventricular) need to be damaged — it is not sufficient simply to compress the posterior pituitary as vasopressin can be secreted directly from the hypothalamus itself. Pituitary tumours therefore rarely cause DI.

Major causes of cranial diabetes insipidus

- Idiopathic
- Craniopharyngiomas
- Infiltrative processes of the hypothalamus (e.g. sarcoid, histiocytosis X)
- Trauma
- Pituitary surgery
- Lymphocytic hypophysitis
- Dysgerminomas

Causes of nephrogenic diabetes insipidus

Reduced action of ADH on the kidney may be due to several causes

- **Primary**
  Childhood onset
    X-linked/dominant
    abnormality in tubular ADH receptor

- **Secondary (common)**
  Hypercalcaemia
  Hypokalaemia
  Renal disease (particularly if it
    involves the medullary interstitium)
  Lithium
  Democlocycline

3.4 Acromegaly

The common features of acromegaly are well known (hand and foot enlargement, coarse facial features, overbite of the lower jaw, splaying of teeth) but the following also occur:

Diabetes
Sleep apnoea
Multinodular goitre
Hypertension
2 x increase in death from
  cardiovascular disease
Enlarged testes
Raised phosphate
Raised triglycerides

Arthropathy — often pseudogout
Carpal tunnel syndrome
Increase in malignancies,
  especially colonic polyps
Cardiomyopathy
Left ventricular hypertrophy
Renal stones (hypercalciuria)
Raised prolactin, galactorrhoea,
  menstrual change

Acromegaly is almost always due to a growth hormone (GH) secreting pituitary tumour. Rarely the condition is due to ectopic GH releasing hormone (GHRH) secretion from a tumour (typically carcinoid) which stimulates the normal pituitary. Acromegaly is diagnosed by failure of GH to suppress to less than 2 mU/L at any time in a standard glucose tolerance test (GTT). This may produce a double diagnosis as the GTT may diagnose acromegaly induced diabetes at the same time.

First-line treatment is transphenoidal surgery to the pituitary tumour (or transcranial surgery if there is a large suprasellar extension of tumour). The cure rate depends on the initial tumour size. Alternative therapies are octreotide (long-acting analogue of somatostatin), pituitary radiotherapy or bromocriptine (effective in less than 20% of cases). After treatment of acromegaly most signs do not regress. Features of active disease are increased sweating and oedema of hands and feet which can regress after therapy.

3.5 Growth hormone deficiency in adults

GH is required for growth in children. It was thought to have little function in adults but recently the following have been ascribed to **adult GH deficiency**:

- Reduced muscle, increased fat
- Low mood
- Raised lipids
- Reduced left ventricular function
- Osteoporosis.

4. THE THYROID GLAND

4.1 Hyperthyroidism and hypothyroidism

The common features of hyperthyroidism (e.g. weight loss, tremor, palpitations) and hypothyroidism (e.g. weight gain, dry skin, slowing up) are well-known but questions are often asked on the more unusual features. The following are 'recognized' features of the two major thyroid syndromes.

	Hyperthyroidism	**Hypothyroidism**
General	Weight gain (rarely) Gynaecomastia	Weight gain Serous effusions (pleural, pericardial, ascites, joint)
	Occult in elderly Hair loss	Hair loss
Gynae	Amenorrhoea Raised sex hormone binding globulin (SHBG)	Menorrhagia Infertility
GI	Diarrhoea	Constipation
Muscle	Proximal myopathy Periodic paralysis (especially Chinese)	Raised creatine kinase Chest pain (muscular) Muscle cramps

Continues ...

... Continued

	Hyperthyroidism	**Hypothyroidism**
CVS	Dyspnoea Atrial fibrillation with high stroke rate High output cardiac failure	Hypercholesterolaemia Ischaemic heart disease
Bone	Osteoporosis Hypercalcaemia	
Neuro	'Apathetic thyrotoxicosis'	Deafness Ataxia, confusion, coma
Eyes	Eye signs (see Section 4.5)	Periorbital oedema
Blood	Leucopenia Microcytic anaemia	Macrocytic anaemia Microcytic if menorrhagia
Skin	Urticaria	Dry, orange (caroteinaemia)

Amenorrhoea is predictable in hyperthyroidism because of associated weight loss. In hypothyroidism, everything slows down except the periods! The menorrhagia can cause a microcytic anaemia in contrast to the more usual macrocytosis. In both conditions there may be subfertility. In the GI tract, the symptoms of hyperthyroidism are almost indistinguishable from those of anxiety. The diarrhoea is actually more like the increased bowel frequency before an examination.

- A patient with hypothyroidism could present in A&E with chest pain and have raised CKs like a myocardial infarct. The chest pain may be muscular, but it may also be myocardial ischaemia — the raised cholesterol of hypothyroidism accelerates atheroma.
- Both hyperthyroidism (if Graves' disease) and hypothyroidism can cause periorbital oedema. See note in Section 4.5 on eye signs in thyrotoxicosis.
- The leucopenia of thyrotoxicosis often causes confusion: thionamide drugs (e.g. carbimazole) used as treatment also commonly cause a lymphopenia. Both of these are separate from the agranulocytosis that rarely occurs with thionamide drugs.
- In hyperthyroidism the urticaria due to the disease itself can cause confusion with the maculopapular rash which develops in 10% of patients treated with thionamide drugs.

Side effects of anti-thyroid drugs (carbimazole, prophylthiouracil)

- **Common**
  Rash
  Leucopenia

- **Rare**
  Agranulocytosis
  Aplastic anaemia
  Hepatitis
  Fever
  Arthralgia

(See also Chapter 2, *Clinical Pharmacology, Toxicology and Poisoning*)

4.2 Causes of thyrotoxicosis

The three common causes of thyrotoxicosis are:

- Graves' disease
- Toxic multinodular goitre
- Toxic (hot) nodule.

In all these conditions all or part of the gland is overactive and the gland takes up a normal or increased amount of radioiodine.

In the following rare conditions, there is thyrotoxicosis without increased production of new hormone by the thyroid gland itself, i.e. radioiodine uptake is suppressed.

- Excess thyroxine ingestion
- Thyroiditis: post-viral (De Quervain's), postpartum or silent thyroiditis
- Ectopic thyroid tissue, e.g. lingual thyroid or ovary (struma ovarii)
- Iodine administration: gland is still active but cold iodine competes for radioiodine in scanning.

4.3 Thyroid cancer and nodules

Only 5–10% of thyroid nodules are malignant (the rest are adenomas). Thyroid cancer virtually never causes hyperthyroidism so 'hot nodules' can usually be presumed to be benign. In order of increasing malignancy and decreasing frequency the thyroid epithelial cancers are:

- Papillary
- Follicular
- Anaplastic.

Lymphomas occur in Hashimoto's disease. Medullary thyroid cancer is from the C-cells (calcitonin), not from the thyroid epithelium. Serum calcitonin is a tumour marker for this cancer which often occurs in families, sometimes as part of the multiple endocrine neoplasia type 2 syndrome (see section 6).

4.4 Drugs and the thyroid

- **Lithium**
  Inhibits T_4 release from the gland causing hypothyroidism

- **Oestrogens**
  Raised thyroid binding globulin (TBG) and hence 'total' T_4/T_3

- **Frusemide**
  Displaces T_4/T_3 from TBG (reducing total T_4/T_3)

- **Interferon**
  Induces antithyroid autoantibodies and hypothyroidism

- **Amiodarone**
  Inhibits T_4 to T_3 conversion, increasing reverse T_3
  High iodine content can cause hyper- or hypothyroidism

- **Aspirin**
  Displaces T_4/T_3 from TBG (reducing total T_4/T_3)

- **Phenytoin**
  Displaces T_4/T_3 from TBG and increases T_4 metabolism

4.5 Autoimmunity and eye signs in thyroid disease

In areas such as the UK where there is no iodine deficiency, more than 90% of spontaneous hypothyroidism is due to autoimmunity. Antithyroglobulin autoantibodies are present in 60% of cases and antimicrosomal antibodies (now identified as antithyroid peroxidase antibodies) are present in up to 90%. Antibodies that block the TSH receptor may also be present. Similar antibodies are present in Graves' disease but the anti-TSH receptor antibodies are stimulatory, causing the thyrotoxicosis. The term LATS (long acting thyroid stimulator) referring to this stimulatory antibody is no longer used.

The eye signs in thyroid disease are shown in the table below (see also Chapter 15, *Ophthalmology*). Retro-orbital inflammation and swelling of the extra-ocular muscles is only seen in Graves' disease. The target of the antibody or T-cell reaction causing this inflammation is not known for certain and eye disease activity can occur in the absence of thyrotoxicosis.

Thyrotoxicosis from any cause	Graves' disease only
Lid retraction	Soft tissue signs: periorbital
Lid lag	oedema, conjunctival injection, chemosis
	Proptosis/exophthalmos
	Diplopia/ophthalmoplegia
	Optic nerve compression causing visual failure

4.6 Thyroid function tests

TSH is the most sensitive measure of thyroid status in patients with an intact pituitary. T_4 and T_3 are over 95% protein bound, predominantly to TBG. The following alter TBG levels and hence total but not free hormone levels.

Conditions which alter thyroid binding globulin (TBG)

- **Raised TBG**
  Pregnancy
  Oestrogen
  Hepatitis
  Congenital TBG abnormality

- **Low TBG**
  Nephrotic syndrome
  Congenital TBG abnormality

5. ADRENAL DISEASE AND HIRSUTISM

5.1 Cushing's syndrome

Cushing's syndrome refers to the sustained over-production of cortisol (hypercortisolism) which causes:

- Centripetal obesity with moon face
- 'Buffalo hump'
- Hirsutism
- Recurrent infections
- Osteoporosis
- Oligomenorrhoea
- Hypokalaemia
- Striae
- Acne
- Proximal muscle weakness
- Hyperglycaemia
- Psychiatric disturbances
- Hypertension

If untreated, death is usually due to infection. Other than due to steroid treatment, Cushing's syndrome is rare. In the first instance, it needs to be distinguished from simple obesity. Once Cushing's syndrome is confirmed, the cause needs to be identified.

The diagnosis is made in two phases.

Tests to confirm hypercortisolism (Cushing's syndrome)

- Loss of diurnal variation (midnight cortisol not lower than morning cortisol)
- Overnight dexamethasone suppression test (1 mg at midnight then 9 am cortisol)
- Low-dose dexamethasone suppression test (0.5 mg qds for 48 hours)
- Urinary free cortisol (24-hour collection).

If one or more of these are positive then one can proceed to localization. NB: Depression or alcoholism can both cause cortisol over-production ('pseudo-Cushing's'). If these conditions are present, further investigation is very difficult.

Tests to localize the cause of Cushing's syndrome

Possible causes of Cushing's syndrome are:

- Adrenal tumour
- Pituitary tumour (Cushing's disease)
- Ectopic production of ACTH — either from cancer (e.g. small cell cancer of lung) or from a bronchial adenoma (often very small)
- Ectopic production of corticotrophin releasing hormone (CRH) (very rare).

MRI scanning of the adrenal or pituitary alone cannot be relied on to localize the cause. Firstly, the tumours of the pituitary causing Cushing's disease are often too small to see, and secondly, incidental tumours of both the pituitary and adrenal are common and may not be functional. Tests used to identify the causes of Cushing's syndrome are shown overleaf.

Tests used to identify causes of Cushing's syndrome

	Adrenal	Pituitary	Ectopic
ACTH	Suppressed	Mid-range	High
High dose dexamethasone suppression	No change in cortisol	Suppression of cortisol	No change
CRH stimulation test	No change	Rise in ACTH and cortisol	No change
Metyrapone	Rise in 11-deoxy-cortisol <220 fold	Rise in 11-deoxy-cortisol >220 fold	Rise in 11-deoxy-cortisol <220 fold
Petrosal sinus ACTH	Equals peripheral level	Higher than peripheral level	Equals peripheral level

- 'Under pressure' (i.e. at high doses), pituitary adenomas behave like a normal pituitary in dynamic endocrine testing, whereas adrenal or ectopic sources do not. A positive response to high dose suppression (2 mg qds for 48 hours) is >10% suppression of plasma cortisol or 24-hour urine-free cortisol.
- With modern assays, an undetectable ACTH level with confirmed hypercortisolism is sufficient for a diagnosis of an adrenal source.

Bilateral adrenalectomy will cure the hypercortisolism of pituitary dependent Cushing's syndrome but loss of the suppression by the high cortisol levels may allow a pre-existing pituitary adenoma to grow very rapidly, causing local damage and general pigmentation (Nelson's syndrome).

Endocrine causes of obesity

- Steroid excess (Cushing's syndrome)
- Hypothyroidism
- Hypothalamic tumours (hyperphagia)
- Prader–Willi syndrome
- GH deficiency.

5.2 Congenital adrenal hyperplasia (CAH)

Two enzyme defects account for 95% of all CAH:

- 21-hydroxylase (90%)
- 11-hydroxylase (5%).

17-hydroxylase, 3-beta-hydroxysteroid dehydrogenase and cholesterol side-chain cleavage enzyme defects are very rare.

The following are true of all enzyme defects causing CAH.

- Autosomal recessive
- Plasma ACTH is high
  (renin is high if salt-losing)
- Can cause ambiguous genitalia in females (not 17-hydroxylase or side chain enzyme)
- Can have a minor, late-onset form resembling polycystic ovarian syndrome
- Antenatal steroid therapy to the mother has been used
- Both gene deletions and point mutations can occur
- Can cause male precocious puberty (not 17-hydroxylase or side chain enzyme)
- Treat with glucocorticoids ± mineralocorticoids at night
- Surgery may be required to correct ambiguous genitalia/cliteromegaly

---

Differentiating features in congenital adrenal hyperplasia

	21-Hydroxylase	11-Hydroxylase	17-Hydroxylase/ side chain enzyme
Frequency	90% cases	5% cases	Very rare
Presentation in female	Virilizing, intersex 70% salt-losing*	Virilizing hypertension low K+	Non-virilizing (intersex in boys)
Biochemistry	Raised 17-hydroxy- lase progesterone	Raised 11- dehydroxy- cortisol	

*Salt-losing individuals can have Addisonian crises soon after birth.

5.3 Hypoadrenalism

In the UK, spontaneous hypoadrenalism is most commonly due to autoimmune destruction of the adrenal glands (Addison's disease — adrenal autoantibodies present in 70% of cases). Vitiligo is present in 10–20% of cases. Other causes include TB, HIV or haemorrhage into the adrenal glands and anterior pituitary disease (secondary hypoadrenalism). Hypoadrenalism after withdrawal of longstanding steroid therapy is similar to secondary hypoadrenalism.

The following are 'recognized' features of hypoadrenalism:

- **Biochemical**: raised urea, hypoglycaemia, hyponatraemia, hyperkalaemia, raised TSH, hypercalcaemia.
- **Haematological**: eosinophilia, lymphocytosis, normocytic anaemia.
- **Clinical features**: weight loss, abdominal pain, psychosis, loss of pubic hair in women, hypotension, auricular cartilage calcification, increased pigmentation.

Hyperkalaemia and increased pigmentation are absent in secondary hypoadrenalism since there are low levels of circulating ACTH and mineralocorticoid continues to be secreted via the renin–angiotensin–aldosterone system.

5.4 Polycystic ovarian syndrome (PCOS) and hirsutism

Hirsutism is the increased growth of terminal (dark) hairs in androgen-dependent areas. Virilization is temporal hair recession (male pattern), breast atrophy, voice change, male physique and (most important) cliteromegaly. Hirsutism and acne are invariably also present.

Causes of hirsutism

Ovarian	Adrenal	Drugs
PCOS (>90% of cases)	CAH (may be late-onset)	Minoxidil
Virilizing tumour	Cushing's/	Phenytoin
	adrenal carcinoma	Diazoxide
		Cyclosporin
		Androgens

A serum testosterone >4.5 nmol/l (normal <1.8), recent onset of hirsutism and signs of virilization in women should prompt a search for other causes (e.g. a tumour). Dehydroepiandrostenedione (DHEA) is a weak androgen produced in the adrenal only.

- Measure the 17-hydroxyprogesterone after stimulation with ACTH to check for late-onset 21-hydroxylase deficiency (partial enzyme deficiency).
- Other than androgens, the drugs listed strictly cause hypertrichosis, an increase in vellus hair, rather than an increase in androgen-sensitive terminal hairs (see Chapter 4, *Dermatology*).

Polycystic ovarian syndrome

There is no widely recognized definition and up to 20% of women have a degree of hirsutism. The following are recognized associations of PCOS.

- **Clinical features**: obesity, acanthosis nigricans, oligomenorrhoea, polycystic ovaries, subfertility, hypertension, premature balding in male relatives, hirsutism.
- **Biochemical**: insulin resistance and hyperinsulinaemia, raised testosterone, raised LH/ FSH ratio, raised prolactin low HDL.

6. PHAEOCHROMOCYTOMA AND MULTIPLE-ENDOCRINE NEOPLASIA (MEN) SYNDROMES

Phaeochromocytomas are rare tumours of the adrenal medulla or ganglia of the sympathetic nervous system. They are the 'tumour of 10%':

- 10% are outside the adrenal glands — paragangliomas (including organ of Zuckerkandl)
- 10% are multiple (e.g. bilateral)
- 10% are malignant
- 10% are familial.

The malignancy of a phaeochromocytoma is defined by the presence of metastases; like most endocrine tumours, histology is not a reliable guide to malignant potential. Diagnosis is by measurement of urinary catecholamines.

Familial phaeochromocytomas

- Multiple endocrine neoplasia Type II (see below)
- Von Hippel–Lindau syndrome (retinal and cerebral haemangioblastomas and renal cystic carcinomas)
- Spontaneously in some families (not associated with a syndrome)
- von Recklinghausen's disease (neurofibromatosis — 1–2%)
- Carney's Triad:
  Gastric leiomyosarcoma,
  pulmonary chondroma,
  Leydig testicular tumour

Important features of phaeochromocytomas

- 70% have persistent rather than episodic hypertension
- Extra-adrenal tumours do not make adrenaline (they secrete noradrenaline/dopamine)
- They give characteristically a 'bright' (white) signal on T_2-weighted MRI scan
- Phaeochromocytomas may produce chromogranin A
- The triad of headache, sweating and palpitations is said to be >90% predictive
- Hypotension or postural hypotension may occur particularly if adrenaline is produced
- MIBG (m-I-131-L-benzylguanidine) scanning may help localization
- Pre-operative preparation is with alpha adrenergic blockade (e.g. phenoxybenzamine) *before* beta blockade

Causes of episodic sweating and/or flushing

- Oestrogen/testosterone deficiency (e.g. menopause, castration)
- Carcinoid syndrome (flushing, diarrhoea, wheeze)
- Phaeochromocytoma (sweat but do not flush)
- Hypoglycaemia (in diabetes)
- Thyrotoxicosis (not usually episodic)
- Systemic mastocytosis (histamine release)
- Allergy.

Multiple endocrine neoplasia (MEN) syndromes are syndromes with multiple benign or malignant endocrine neoplasms. They should not be confused with polyglandular autoimmune syndromes which relate to autoimmune endocrine diseases.

MEN-I	MEN-IIA	MEN-IIB
Genetics		
menin gene	*ret* gene	
Chromosome 11	Chromosome 10	
Tumours		
Parathyroid	Parathyroid	Parathyroid
Pituitary	Phaeochromocytoma	Phaeochromocytoma
Pancreas	Medullary thyroid	Medullary thyroid
(Carcinoid)	cancer	cancer
(Adrenal adenomas)		Marfanoid
		Mucosal neuromas

- MEN-I was formerly known as Werner's syndrome. MEN-IIA was known as Sipple's syndrome. All MEN syndromes are autosomal dominant. Genetic (DNA-based) screening is being introduced for MEN-II and may follow for MEN-I. The MEN-II mutation in *ret* activates the protein. Inactivating mutations of *ret* are seen in Hirschsprung's disease.
- All MEN syndromes can be associated with hypercalcaemia. This is usually due to hyperplasia of all four parathyroids, not a single parathyroid adenoma as with sporadic hyperparathyroidism. Hypercalcaemia is often the first manifestation in MEN-I.
- Gastrinomas and insulinomas are the most common pancreatic tumours in MEN-I. Of the pituitary tumours, prolactinomas are the most common, followed by acromegaly and Cushing's disease.

Medullary thyroid cancer (MTC) is always malignant, secretes calcitonin and is preceded by C-cell hyperplasia. Prophylactic thyroidectomy may be performed to prevent this most serious manifestation. The MTC in MEN-II is less aggressive than sporadic MTC.

Secondary hypertension

Ninety-five per cent of hypertension is idiopathic, 5% is due to renal disease and around 0.05% has an endocrine cause. (See also Chapter 13, *Nephrology*.)

- **Renal**: intrinsic renal disease (e.g. glomerulonephritis, polycystic kidney disease), renal artery stenosis
- Coarctation of the aorta (hypertension in upper limbs only)
- **Endocrine**: Conn's syndrome, Cushing's syndrome, phaeochromocytoma, acromegaly, apparent mineralocorticoid excess*
- **Other**: alcohol, obesity.

7. PUBERTY/GROWTH/INTERSEX

7.1 Normal puberty

In 95% of children, puberty begins between ages 8–13 in females and 9–14 in males. The mean age of menarche is 12.8 years. The events of puberty occur in a particular order, although the later stages then overlap with the earlier ones.

Order of events in normal puberty

(Earliest events listed first)

- **Male**
  Scrotal thickening (age 9–14)
  Testicular enlargement (>2 ml)
  Pubic hair
  Phallus growth
  Growth spurt (age 10–16)
  + increasing bone age

- **Female**
  Breast development (age 8–13)
  Growth spurt
  Pubic hair
  Menstruation (age 10–16)
  + increasing bone age

---

*Three rare genetic syndromes that clinically resemble Conn's syndrome:

- 11-beta hydroxysteroid dehydrogenase deficiency
- Liddle's syndrome (activation of renal sodium channel)
- Glucocorticoid suppressible hyperaldosteronism.

7.2 Precocious puberty

True precocious puberty is rare. It is diagnosed if multiple signs of puberty develop before age 8 in females and age 9 in males accompanied by increased growth rate, accelerated bone age and raised sex steroid levels. Isolated premature breast development (thelarche) or the appearance of pubic hair alone (from adrenal androgens — adrenarche) are both benign conditions if no other stages of puberty are entered.

True 'central' gonadotrophin-dependent precocious puberty	Other causes (gonadotrophin-independent)
• Idiopathic	• Adrenal, overian tumour
	• CAH (males)
• Other CNS disease (e.g. hydrocephalus, encephalitis, trauma)	• Testotoxicosis (males)
	• Exogenous oestrogen (females)
	• McCune–Albright syndrome
	• Follicular cysts (females)
• CNS hamartoma (e.g. pineal)	• Profound hypothyroidism

McCune–Albright syndrome is more common in girls — see Section 1.2 on activated G-proteins.

7.3 Delayed puberty/short stature

Short stature in children is often due to delayed puberty and hence the two problems are usually grouped together. Three per cent of children are 'statistically delayed', i.e. for girls no breast development by age 13 or menses by age 15 and for boys no testicular enlargement by age 14. The majority will have 'constitutional delay' and will later enter puberty spontaneously. However, there is no endocrine test that can reliably distinguish constitutional delay from other organic causes of delayed puberty.

In investigation, systemic diseases or syndromes that can cause delayed puberty should be excluded before considering pituitary testing. A karyotype (for Turner's syndrome) should always be requested in girls (see overleaf).

Causes of delayed puberty/short stature

General causes	Occult systemic disease	Syndromes causing delayed puberty/short stature
Overt systemic disease	Renal failure/ renal tubular acidosis	Turner's (XO)
Social deprivation	Crohn's /coeliac disease	Noonan's ('Male Turner')
Anorexia, excess exercise	Hypothyroidism	
Chemotherapy/gonadal irradiation	Asthma	Androgen insensitivity (testicular feminization — XY female)
Cranial irradiation		Polycystic ovarian syndrome (delayed menarche only)
		Kallman's (XY) anosmia
		Klinefelter's (XXY) — males
	Anterior pituitary disease	Prader–Willi
	Hyperprolactinaemia	
	Isolated GH deficiency	

In Turner's syndrome, Noonan's syndrome, androgen insensitivity and Klinefelter's syndrome raised LH and FSH are present. **Kallman's syndrome** is due to failure of GnRH secreting neurons to migrate to the hypothalamus. Gene cloned. There is no test currently available to distinguish this from constitutional delay.

Turner's syndrome (XO) (see Chapter 6, *Genetics*) occurs in 1 in 2500 live births. The typical features (web neck, widely spaced nipples, wide carrying angle) may be absent. A karyotype should always be requested in girls with short stature/delayed puberty since the final height can be increased by early treatment with high doses of growth hormone.

Klinefelter's syndrome (XXY) (see Chapter 6, *Genetics*) occurs in 1 in 1000 live births but is usually undiagnosed until adulthood. Testosterone production is around 50% of normal, but is sufficient to allow secondary sexual characteristics and normal height to develop. Patients usually come to attention because of small testes, gynaecomastia or infertility.

7.4 Intersex

(See also Chapter 6, *Genetics*.) Ambiguous genitalia at birth require urgent diagnosis with steroid profile and karyotype to assign the appropriate sex of rearing and identify the risk of a salt-losing crisis (CAH). Causes can be grouped as follows.

Virilized female (XX)	Non-masculinized male (XY)

CAH (21-OH or 11-OH)
Maternal androgen ingestion
	Unusual CAH (17-hydroxylase/side-ch/3-beta-OH)
	Androgen resistance:
	  receptor defect ('testicular feminization')
	  5-alpha-reductase deficiency

8. DIABETES MELLITUS

Diabetes may be defined as chronic hyperglycaemia at levels sufficient to cause microvascular complications:

- 85% of cases are due to insulin resistance of unknown origin (Type 2, maturity-onset, non-insulin dependent)
- 10% of cases are due to autoimmune destruction of the pancreatic islets causing insulin deficiency (Type 1, juvenile-onset, insulin dependent)
- Around 5% of cases are due to miscellaneous secondary causes (see Section 8.3).

8.1 Risk factors and clinical features of Type 1 and Type 2 diabetes

The table overleaf summarizes the differences between Type 1 and Type 2 diabetes. Note that Type 2 diabetes is more common in non-Caucasian races and that despite being 'late-onset', is more strongly inherited than the juvenile-onset form.

Comparison between Type 1 and Type 2 diabetes

	Type 1	Type 2

Genetics	Both parents affected:
	  10–20% risk for child
	Identical twins:
	  50% concordance
	HLA DR3/4 (95%)
	HLA-DR2, DQasp57
	  protective
	Caucasians
		Both parents affected:
		  70–100% risk for child
		Identical twins:
		  up to 90% concordance
		No HLA association
		
		Asian, Black, Pima Indians

Autoantibodies	60–90% Islet Cell Ab (ICA)
	  positive at diagnosis
	35% risk of diabetes in
	  5 years if ICA-positive
	3% of sibs ICA-positive
		No association with antibodies

Other risk factors		Impaired glucose tolerance Gestational diabetes (50% diabetic in 10 years)
Incidence	Approx 1/10,000/year	Approx 1/1000/year
Prevalence	Approx 1/1000	Approx 2/100

Clinical (at diagnosis)	Age < 30
	Weight loss
	Ketosis prone
	Insulin-deficient
	Autoimmune aetiology
		Age > 40 (except MODY — see
		  below)
		Overweight
		Ketone negative
		Insulin-resistant
		Associated with 'syndrome X'
		  (hypertension, IHD,
		  hyperinsulinaemia,
		  glucose intolerance,
		  hypertension, etc.)
		Amyloid deposition in islet

In addition to insulin-resistance, there is relative failure of the beta cells in Type 2 diabetes: they are unable to maintain the very high insulin levels required.

Rule of 10s (approximate)

- Incidence of Type 1 — 0.01%
- Prevalence of Type 1 = incidence of Type 2 — 0.1%
- Prevalence of Type 2 (10x Type 1) —1% (actually closer to 2%).

Maturity-onset diabetes of the young (MODY) is the term used to describe Type 2 diabetes occuring in patients under the age of 25 with a strong family history. Single gene defects in glucokinase or the transcription factors HNF1α or HNF4α have been identified in more than 80% of cases.

8.2 Diagnostic criteria for diabetes

WHO (1985) criteria (see table below) use a 75 g oral glucose tolerance test. The two-hour value always 'trumps' the fasting value. Values use **venous plasma** — values are lower with capillary sample or whole blood. The American Diabetes Association (ADA) has recently adopted a diagnosis based on a fasting blood sample alone with a value > 7.0 mmol/l or random glucose > 11.0 mmol/l on two occasions with symptoms. The WHO (1998) has also proposed reducing the fasting to 7.0 mmol/l but retaining the oral glucose tolerance test.

	Normal	IGT	Diabetes	Gestational diabetes*
Fasting	< 7.8	< 7.8	> 7.8	> 5.8
2-hour	< 7.8	7.8–11.1	> 11.1	> 9.2

*Figures for gestational diabetes are controversial.

In impaired glucose tolerance (IGT) glucose levels are insufficient to cause microvascular complications but there is still an increased macrovascular risk (see overleaf). Twenty per cent or more of individuals with IGT will progress to Type 2 diabetes within 10 years. The ADA defines IGT as a fasting glucose > 6.0 mmol/l and < 7.8 mmol/l and refers to it as impaired fasting glucose.

Most people with normal glucose tolerance will have fasting glucose < 6.5 mmol/l.

8.3 Secondary diabetes

A variety of conditions can lead secondarily to chronic hyperglycaemia fulfilling the criteria of diabetes either by reducing insulin secretion (Type 1-like) or by increasing insulin resistance (Type 2-like). A pigmented rash in the axillae, neck and groin (acanthosis nigricans), is seen in many conditions associated with insulin resistance.

Causes of secondary diabetes

- **Insulin deficiency**
  Pancreatitis
  Haemochromatosis
  Pancreatic cancer/surgery
  Cystic fibrosis
  Somatostatin

- **Insulin resistance**
  Polycystic ovarian syndrome
  Cushing's, steroid use
  Acromegaly
  Glucagonoma
  Phaeochromocytoma
  Insulin-*receptor* defect or signalling
  Leprechaunism
  Anti-insulin *receptor* antibodies
  Partial lipodystrophy

8.4 Drugs used in Type 2 diabetes

Three different categories of drug are used to lower glucose levels in Type 2 diabetes. A gradual decline in insulin reserve leads to an increasing requirement for medication over time and 10–30% of Type 2 diabetes patients ultimately require insulin therapy to achieve satisfactory glycaemic targets.

Drug	Action/comments
Sulphonylureas	Increase insulin secretion
Biguanides (e.g. metformin)	Reduce insulin resistance (less hepatic glucose production) Do not cause hypoglycaemia but risk of lactic acidosis
Alpha-glucosidase inhibitor (acarbose)	Slows carbohydrate absorption, not complicated by hypoglycaemia

A fourth class of drug, PPAR-gamma blockers (e.g. troglitazone) lower insulin resistance but have recently been withdrawn in the UK because of cases of liver failure.

8.5 Glycated haemoglobin (HbA1, HbA1c)

Red cell haemoglobin is non-enzymically glycated at a low rate according to the prevailing level of glucose. The percentage of glycated haemoglobin provides an accurate estimate of mean glucose levels over the preceding six weeks and correlates well with the risk of microvascular complications. HbA1c is a more specific fraction of glycosylated haemoglobin than HbA1 and values are 1–2% lower. There is no standard assay for either test and reference must be made to local ranges. Modern assays for glycated haemoglobin are rarely misleading but the following conditions should be considered if the results do not correlate with home glucose monitoring results.

Abnormally low HbA1c	Abnormally high HbA1c
Haemolysis	Persistent HbF (fetal haemoglobin)
Increased red cell turnover	Thalassaemia
Blood loss	Uraemia (carbamylated Hb)
HbS or HbC	

8.6 Microvascular and macrovascular complications of diabetes

Long term diabetic complications are due to vascular damage. Damage to the microvasculature and its consequences (see table) correlates well with levels of glycaemic control and can be delayed or prevented by maintaining near normal glucose levels. Microvascular complications take a minimum of five years to develop even with poor glycaemic control. However, they may be apparently present 'at diagnosis' in Type 2 diabetes as hyperglycaemia has often been present for many years prior to diagnosis.

In contrast, macrovascular disease appears not to be related to the level of glycaemic control. Macrovascular disease is responsible for most of the increased mortality in diabetes.

Micro- and macrovascular complications of diabetes

Microvascular	Macrovascular
Eye (90%)*	Ischaemic heart disease
Neuropathy (70–90%)*	Peripheral vascular disease
Nephropathy (30–40%)*	CVA, hypertension
Microalbuminuria (25–250 mg/day)	
Macroalbuminuria (>250 mg/day)	
Chronic renal failure	
HbA1c dependent	HbA1c independent
	(Also present in IGT)

*Approximate percentages of diabetics who will have this complication to some degree during their lifetime.

The risk of MI is doubled in diabetes and the risk of amputation is increased by 15–25 times. Ischaemic heart disease rates in diabetes are equal in men and women, i.e. the relative protection women normally have is lost. The increased risk is not explained by cholesterol levels which are little different from the general population. Proteinuria is a strong risk factor for ischaemic heart disease in diabetes.

Neuropathy (70–90%) and retinopathy (90%) occur in virtually all patients if control is not perfect and diabetes is present for long enough, but only around one-third of patients develop nephropathy (30–40%), mostly within 20 years.

The incidence of microvascular complications was reduced by around 50% in the 'Diabetes Control and Complications Trial' (DCCT) by tight control.

8.7 Autonomic neuropathy

Autonomic complications of diabetes occur in very long-standing disease and include the following:

- Postural hypotension
- Gustatory sweating
- Cardiac arrhythmia ('dead-in-bed'): hence the rationale for use of β-blockade to reduce cardiovascular mortality
- Gastroparesis
- Generalized sweating
- Diarrhoea
- Reduced appreciation of cardiac pain

9. HYPOGLYCAEMIA

9.1 Hypoglycaemia in diabetes

Hypoglycaemia can occur in diabetic patients taking either insulin or sulphonylurea drugs. In patients on insulin, failure of the normal counter-regulatory responses (sympathetic nervous system activation, adrenaline and glucagon release) may develop in long standing insulin-treated diabetes, particularly in the presence of frequent hypoglycaemic episodes. This results in **hypoglycaemia unawareness**. The patient has no warning of impending neurological impairment and cannot take appropriate action (glucose ingestion). More frequent hypoglycaemic episodes result, exacerbating the problem — 'hypos beget hypos'. Hypoglycaemia awareness can be restored by relaxing control to allow a prolonged (3-month) hypoglycaemia free period. As yet there is no proof that hypoglycaemia unawareness is more common with human as compared with animal insulin.

9.2 Hypoglycaemia unrelated to diabetes

True hypoglycaemic episodes unrelated to diabetes therapy are rare. A blood sugar of 2.5 mmol/l or less should be documented, associated with appropriate symptoms which resolve after treatment (e.g. food). A supervised 72-hour fast can be used to precipitate and document an episode, particularly to diagnose an insulinoma.

Causes can be classified as follows:

- **Fasting**
  Insulinoma
  Tumour (IGF-2)
  Hypoadrenalism
  Alcohol
  Severe liver failure
  Factitious (insulin or sulphonylurea)
  Drugs (pentamidine, quinidine)
  Anti-insulin antibodies (delayed
     post-prandial release of insulins)

- **Post-prandial**
  Post-gastrectomy
  Idiopathic (rare)

10. HYPONATRAEMIA AND SIADH

Antidiuretic hormone (ADH or vasopressin) is synthesised in magnocellular neurons in the supraoptic and paraventicular nuclei of the hypothalamus and stored in the posterior pituitary. ADH is released in response to rising plasma osmolality and acts on the distal tubule and renal collecting ducts to increase water permeability. Water is reabsorbed and the urine becomes more concentrated. When the ADH system is working normally, 'the urine should reflect the blood', that is, concentrated urine should occur when the plasma osmolality is high and vice versa.

However, hypovolaemia is also a strong signal for ADH relsease and in the presence of hypovolaemia ADH will be secreted even if the osmolality is low. This explains the hyponatraemia seen in renal, cardiac and liver failure as well as following excessive sodium loss (e.g. diarrhoea). Other stimuli can also commonly override control of ADH secretion by osmolarity (see SIADH below).

Syndrome of inappropriate ADH secretion (SIADH)

Many common stimuli override the control of osmolality and cause inappropriate amounts of ADH to be secreted, causing hyponatraemia. Sodium concentration should be high in the urine (excluding hypovolaemia), renal, adrenal and thyroid function should be normal and diuretic therapy needs to be excluded before SIADH is diagnosed. Treatment is by fluid restriction or, if necessary, oral demeclocycline.

Causes of inappropriate secretion of ADH include:

- Nausea
- Fits
- Other CNS/lung insults
- Chlorpropamide
- Head injury
- Tumours making ectopic ADH (e.g. bronchus)
- Pain
- Pneumonia
- Smoking
- Carbamazepine
- CVAs

If a tumour is the cause, it is usually obvious: a search for malignancy beyond a chest X-ray is not required in SIADH.

Smoking makes you pass less urine (releases ADH), drinking (alcohol) makes you pass more (inhibits ADH secretion).

Causes of hyponatraemia

Hyponatraemia can be divided into three categories.

- 'Real'
- Pseudohyponatraemia: high triglycerides, high protein (e.g. myeloma), normal serum osmolality
- Dilutional: high glucose, ethanol, mannitol.

To define the cause, a careful history for diarrhoea, drug use (especially diuretics) and oedema, combined with measurement of plasma osmolality and urine sodium are the most useful factors. Hypoadrenalism is the most important diagnosis not to miss, since untreated it can result in death.

Causes of hyponatraemia

Urine sodium (mmol/l)	Hypovolaemia present	Eu/Hypervolaemia +/- oedema
> 20	Diuretics, Hypoadrenalism Salt-losing nephropathy	SIADH Hypothyroidism Renal failure
< 10	Vomiting, diarrhoea Loss of other fluid	CCF, cirrhosis, nephrotic syndrome

~

Chapter 5
Gastroenterology

CONTENTS

1. **Anatomy and physiology of the GI tract**   143
    1.1   Oesophagus
    1.2   Stomach
    1.3   Pancreas
    1.4   Liver
    1.5   Small intestine
    1.6   Colon
    1.7   Gut hormones
    1.8   Metabolism of haematinics

2. **Disorders of the oesophagus**   148
    2.1   Achalasia
    2.2   Reflux oesophagitis
    2.3   Other causes of oesophagitis
    2.4   Barrett's oesophagus
    2.5   Oesophageal carcinoma

3. **Disorders of the stomach**   151
    3.1   Peptic ulcer disease
    3.2   Zollinger–Ellison syndrome
    3.3   Gastric carcinoma

4. **Disorders of the pancreas**   154
    4.1   Acute pancreatitis
    4.2   Chronic pancreatitis
    4.3   Pancreatic carcinoma

5. **Small bowel disorders**   157
    5.1   Coeliac disease
    5.2   Carcinoid tumours
    5.3   Whipple's disease
    5.4   Angiodysplasia

6. **Nutrition**   **160**
    6.1   Diarrhoea
    6.2   Malabsorption

7. **Large bowel disorders**   **163**
    7.1   Crohn's disease and ulcerative colitis
    7.2   Pseudomembranous colitis
    7.3   Familial polyposis coli
    7.4   Peutz–Jeghers syndrome
    7.5   Irritable bowel syndrome
    7.6   Colorectal cancer
    7.7   Carcinoma complicating inflammatory bowel disease

8. **Gastrointestinal infections**   **168**
    8.1   Gastroenteritis
    8.2   Gastrointestinal tuberculosis

9. **Hepatology**   **170**
    9.1   Jaundice
    9.2   Gallstone disease
    9.3   Ascites
    9.4   Cirrhosis
    9.5   Portal hypertension and varices
    9.6   Hepatic encephalopathy
    9.7   Viral hepatitis
    9.8   Chronic hepatitis
    9.9   Primary biliary cirrhosis
    9.10   Haemochromatosis
    9.11   Wilson's disease
    9.12   Hepato-biliary tumours

Gastroenterology

1. ANATOMY AND PHYSIOLOGY OF THE GI TRACT

1.1 Oesophagus

The oesophagus is 25 cm long, and is composed of outer longitudinal and inner circular muscle layers. In the upper part these are both striated muscle and in the lower part both are smooth muscle, with the myenteric plexus lying between the two layers. The mucosa is lined with squamous epithelium.

Lower oesophageal sphincter pressure is maintained at 15–35 mmHg, and the usual pH is 5–7.

1.2 Stomach

At the gastro-oesophageal junction the squamous epithelium of the oesophagus changes to columnar epithelium. Secretions total approximately 3 litres per day. In gastric pits there are chief cells producing pepsin, and parietal cells (fuelled by $H^+K^+ATPase$) producing hydrochloric acid and intrinsic factor. Mucus and bicarbonate are produced from surface cells.

Innervation is both parasympathetic via the vagus (motor and secretory supply) and sympathetic via Meissner's and Auerbach's plexus. Blood supply is derived from the coeliac trunk.

The control of gastric acid secretion is summarized in the diagram overleaf.

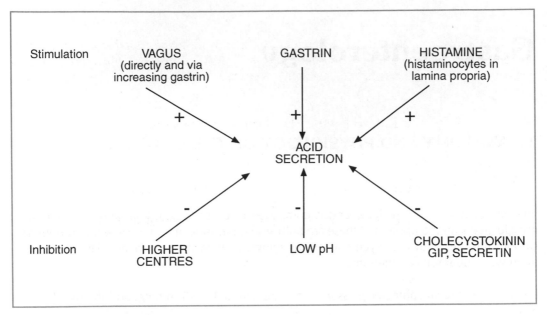

Control of gastric secretion

1.3 Pancreas

1200–1500 ml of alkaline fluid, containing proteins and electrolytes, is secreted daily. Ninety-eight per cent of the pancreatic mass consists of exocrine acini of epithelial cells; the islets of Langerhans from which endocrine secretion occurs make up the remaining 2%. Innervation is via the coeliac plexus.

Pancreatic secretions

- **Exocrine**
   (from acini of epithelial cells)
   Trypsinogen
   Chymotrypsinogen
   Pancreatic amylase
   Lipase

- **Endocrine**
   (from islets of Langerhans)
   Glucagon from α cells
   Insulin from β cells
   Somatostatin from δ cells
   Pancreatic polypeptide

1.4 Liver

Blood supply is from the hepatic artery and portal vein (bringing blood from the gut and spleen); drainage is via the hepatic vein into the inferior vena cava. Between 250 and 1000 ml of bile is produced daily; stimulation of release from gallbladder is by cholecystokinin.

Enterohepatic circulation of bile salts

Bile salts secreted into small intestine
↓
Deconjugation then reabsorption in terminal ileum
↓
Bound to albumin and returned to liver via portal vein

1.5 Small intestine

This is 2–3 metres in length with the villi and enterocytes providing a huge surface area which allows the absorption of up to 6 litres daily. The main function of the small intestine is absorption, with most taking place in the duodenum and jejunum. However, it also has an important immune role with lymphoid aggregates throughout, especially in the form of Peyer's patches in the ileum.

There is secretion of approximately 2 litres of alkaline fluid with mucus and digestive enzymes daily, from the enterocytes of the villi, Paneth's cells at the bases of the crypts of Lieberkühn and Brunner's glands.

Blood supply from the mid-duodenum onwards is derived from the superior mesenteric artery.

1.6 Colon

This is 90–125 cm in length and its main function is the absorption of water, sodium and chloride. Typically 1–1.5 litres are absorbed daily but the system can cope with up to 5 litres per day. Secretion of mucus, potassium and bicarbonate also takes place.

The blood supply is derived from the superior mesenteric artery up to the distal transverse colon; the inferior mesenteric artery supplies the remainder.

1.7 Gut hormones

The response to a meal is regulated by complex hormonal and neural mechanisms. Secretion of most hormones is determined by the composition of intestinal contents.

Major gut hormones

Hormone	Source	Stimulus	Action
Gastrin	G cells in antrum	Gastric distension Amino acids in antrum	Secretion of pepsin, gastric acid and intrinsic factor
Cholecystokinin-pancreozymin (CCK-PZ)	Duodenum and jejunum	Fat, amino acids and peptides in small bowel	Pancreatic secretion Gallbladder contraction Delays gastric emptying
Secretin	Duodenum and jejunum	Acid in small bowel	Pancreatic bicarbonate secretion Delays gastric emptying
Motilin	Duodenum and jejunum	Acid in small bowel	Increases motility
Vasoactive intestinal peptide (VIP)	Small intestine	Neural stimulation	Inhibits gastric acid and pepsin secretion Stimulates secretion by intestine and pancreas
Gastric inhibitory peptide	Duodenum and jejunum	Glucose, fats and amino acids	Inhibits gastric acid secretion Stimulates insulin secretion Reduces motility
Somatostatin	D cells in pancreas	Vagal and β-adrenergic stimulation	Inhibits gastric and pancreatic secretion
Pancreatic polypeptide	PP cells in pancreas	Protein-rich meal	Inhibition of pancreatic and biliary secretion

1.8 Metabolism of haematinics

Iron

Total body iron is between 4 and 5 g, with iron content being maintained by control of absorption in the upper small intestine. Most iron intake is in the Fe^{3+} form and approximately 5–10% of that consumed is absorbed. Iron is better absorbed from foods of animal than of plant origin.

- **Increased absorption**
  Increased erythropoiesis
  (e.g. pregnancy)
  Decreased body iron
  (e.g. GI blood loss)
  Vitamin C*
  Gastric acid*

- **Decreased absorption**
  Partial/total gastrectomy
  Achlorhydria
  Disease of small intestine
  (e.g. Crohn's disease, coeliac disease)
  Drugs
  (e.g. desferrioxamine)

*Gastric acid and vitamin C promote reduction of Fe^{3+} to Fe^{2+} which is more easily absorbed.

For a more detailed account of iron metabolism see Chapter 8, *Haematology*.

Folate

The usual requirement for this nutrient is approximately 50–200 µg/day. It is present in green vegetables. Absorption takes place in the duodenum and jejunum, thus deficiency may occur with coeliac disease, Crohn's disease or any other small bowel pathology. Dietary folate is converted into 5-methyltetrahydrofolate which enters the portal blood. Deficiency may also develop if the demands of the body increase, for example in haemolysis, pregnancy and in patients being treated with antimetabolites such as methotrexate. Clinical deficiency results in a macrocytic anaemia.

Vitamin B12

Adults require 1–2 µg of dietary vitamin B12 daily. This is predominantly obtained from foods of animal origin. It is tightly protein bound and is released by peptic digestion. Oral B12 binds to intrinsic factor in the stomach and is then absorbed in the terminal ileum. Thus deficiency can occur for several reasons:

- Dietary deficiency in vegetarians or vegans
- Post-gastrectomy (lack of intrinsic factor)
- Terminal ileal disease
- Blind loops.

The **Schilling test** determines whether deficiency is due to malabsorption in the terminal ileum or to lack of intrinsic factor (e.g. post-gastrectomy, pernicious anaemia).

1. Administer orally labelled B12.
2. Administer i.m. unlabelled B12 to saturate body binding sites.
3. Assay amount of labelled B12 excreted in urine (>10% in normal subjects).
4. Repeat above with concurrent administration of intrinsic factor: the amount excreted will rise if B12 deficiency was due to lack of intrinsic factor and is now corrected.

In pernicious anaemia, autoantibodies to gastric parietal cells result in B12 deficiency, atrophic gastritis and achlorhydria. Approximately 1% of the population aged over 50 years is affected, with a female preponderance and a familial tendency.

Autoantibodies to gastric parietal cell present in 90%, and autoantibodies to intrinsic factor present in 50%. Pancytopenia may occur and other autoimmune disease may be present. The risk of gastric cancer is increased threefold.

2. DISORDERS OF THE OESOPHAGUS

2.1 Achalasia

Achalasia is a condition of unknown aetiology resulting in failure of normal peristalsis and lack of relaxation of the lower oesophageal sphincter. The incidence is approximately 1/100,000 per year, occurring at any age but rare in children.

It is demonstrable on manometry or barium studies, resulting in oesophageal dilation with a smooth distal 'rat-tail' stricture. Chest X-ray may show an air/fluid level behind the heart. Presentation is usually with dysphagia which, unlike other types of stricture, may affect solids and liquids from the outset.

Regurgitation, pain and weight loss may occur. There is a risk of recurrent aspiration. Squamous carcinoma is a late and rare complication.

Treatment is with endoscopic dilatation or surgical myotomy.

2.2 Reflux oesophagitis

Acid reflux is extremely common. The development of reflux oesophagitis depends on a number of factors.

- **GI factors**
  Acid content of refluxate
  Mucosal defences in oesophagus
  Gastric/oesophageal motility
- **Extra-GI factors**
  Obesity
  Smoking
  Alcohol and coffee intake
  Intake of large meals

The correlation between symptoms and endoscopic appearances is poor; severe symptoms are compatible with a normal gastroscopy. The gold standard for diagnosis is oesophageal pH monitoring.

Clinical sequelae include chest pain, dysphagia, stricturing and iron deficiency anaemia.

Treatment is with H_2 antagonist or proton pump inhibitor; severe symptoms may merit surgery to avoid long term acid suppression.

2.3 Other causes of oesophagitis

Candidal oesophagitis may occur in patients who are immunosuppressed, on antibiotics or steroids, or suffering from diabetes mellitus. It can be diagnosed if barium swallow shows an irregular, 'moth-eaten' oesophagus or by white patches seen on endoscopy — biopsy will confirm diagnosis.

Chemical oesophagitis may be caused by drugs such as NSAIDs, tetracycline and potassium chloride tablets.

2.4 Barrett's oesophagus

This is found in 10–20% of patients with endoscopic oesophagitis. It consists of extension of the columnar gastric epithelium up into the oesophagus to replace the normal squamous epithelium. It is usually caused by chronic acid exposure. It is accepted to be premalignant, although estimates of the rate of transformation to adenocarcinoma vary widely from 30 to 100 times greater than the normal population. Treatment is of the underlying reflux disease; the benefits of regular endoscopic screening and biopsy to detect dysplastic change are still controversial.

Hiatus hernia is extremely common, especially with increasing age and obesity. The majority are asymptomatic incidental findings. There are two types.

* Sliding 80% — may cause aspiration and acid reflux
* Rolling 20% — may obstruct or strangulate.

Hiatus hernia can be diagnosed either on endoscopy or with barium studies. Treatment is with acid suppression. Surgical correction may sometimes be warranted.

2.5 Oesophageal carcinoma

Most oesophageal carcinomas are squamous carcinoma; adenocarcinoma is rare unless arising from ectopic gastric mucosa or Barrett's oesophagus. The incidence is rising and also increases with advancing age. The majority of tumours arise in the mid-thoracic portion of the oesophagus.

* **Risk factors**
  Smoker
  High alcohol intake
  Achalasia
  Barrett's oesophagus
  Chinese or Russian ethnicity
  Tylosis (autosomal dominant palmar
    and plantar keratosis —
    very high risk)

* **Clinical features**
  Pain and dyspepsia
  Progressive dysphasia for
    liquids then solids
  Weight loss

Oesophageal carcinoma is often asymptomatic until a late stage, resulting in poor survival figures. Diagnosis is by endoscopy or barium swallow (this shows a stricture with irregular shouldering, unlike the smooth outline of a benign peptic stricture). CT scanning is used for staging, although the accuracy is very poor especially for lymph node spread; laparoscopy may be useful. Endoscopic ultrasound is far more accurate but is not widely available.

Treatment

* Surgery
  Radical, high operative mortality
  Improves five-year survival to
    approximately 10%.
* Endoscopic dilatation and stenting

* Radiotherapy } used alone or
* Chemotherapy } in combination
    (e.g. cisplatin,   with surgery
    5-fluorouracil)

Over 50% of patients have local or distant spread such that palliation is the only option. The average five-year survival is approximately 5%.

3. DISORDERS OF THE STOMACH

3.1 Peptic ulcer disease

This is a common problem, with an estimated incidence for duodenal ulcer of 150 and 30 per 100,000 in men and women, respectively. Incidence peaks at approximately 60 years of age. Acid-suppressing drugs and an understanding of the role of *Helicobacter pylori* have revolutionized treatment and mortality, removing the need for surgery in all but a very few cases.

Patients over the age of 45 or with sinister symptoms, such as weight loss, should be investigated by endoscopy and biopsy to exclude carcinoma. Gastric ulcers should be re-scoped after treatment to ensure resolution. For younger patients presenting with dyspeptic symptoms many practitioners advocate only assessment of *H. pylori* status (e.g. by serology or breath testing) and eradication therapy if this is positive, without the need for endoscopy. This will result in ulcer healing in over 95%.

Peptic ulcer disease

- **Increased incidence**
  High alcohol intake
  NSAID use
  High-dose steroids
  Male sex
  Smoking
    ($\uparrow$ acid, $\downarrow$ protective prostaglandins)
  H. pylori colonization

- **Clinical symptoms**
  Epigastric pain
  Pain radiating to back
  Vomiting
  May be relapsing/remitting
  Weight loss
  Iron deficiency anaemia
  Acute haemorrhage*

*Duodenal ulcers are the most common cause of upper GI haemorrhage.

- **Treatment**
  Remove precipitating factors
  Acid-suppressing drugs
  Eradication of *H. pylori*
  Surgery if perforation/pyloric stenosis

Causes of upper gastrointestinal haemorrhage

- **Common**
  Duodenal ulcer — 35%
  Gastric ulcer — 20%
  Gastric erosions — 18%
  Mallory–Weiss tear — 10%

- **5% or less**
  Duodenitis
  Oesophageal varices
  Oesophagitis
  Upper GI neoplasia

- **Rare (1% or less)**
  Angiodysplasia
  Hereditary haemorrhagic telangiectasia
  Portal hypertensive gastropathy
  Aorto-duodenal fistula

Helicobacter pylori

This is a Gram-negative spiral bacillus, increasingly recognized for its role in peptic ulcer disease. Incidence increases with age — more than half of those over 50 years of age are colonized by *H. pylori* in gastric antral mucosa. *H. pylori* has been detected in 70% of patients with gastric ulcer and in 90% of patients with duodenal ulcer compared with 50% of control subjects.

Detection of *Helicobacter pylori*

- Antral biopsy at endoscopy with haematoxylin/eosin or Giemsa stain.
- Urease testing — the bacillus secretes a urease enzyme which splits urea to release ammonia. A biopsy sample is put into a jelly containing urea and a pH indicator; this will thus change colour if *H. pylori* is present.
- ^{14}C breath testing — the patient ingests urea labelled with ^{14}C; CO_2 produced by urease is detected in the exhaled breath.
- Serology (stays positive after treatment).

H. pylori causes chronic gastritis and predisposes to eventual gastric carcinoma, thus all patients with peptic ulceration found to be positive should undergo eradication therapy. Effective eradication should be assessed by either repeat biopsies or breath testing.

Relapse of peptic ulcer disease after *H. pylori* eradication is less than 5% per year, compared with more than 60% without. Evidence to support eradication of *H. pylori* in patients with non-ulcer dyspeptic symptoms is currently dubious. Eradication regimes vary but usually involve triple therapy of a proton pump inhibitor and two antibiotics (e.g. metronidazole and clarithromycin).

3.2 Zollinger–Ellison syndrome

This is a rare condition with an incidence of 1/1,000,000 population. Gastrin-secreting adenomas cause severe gastric and/or duodenal ulceration — the tumour is usually pancreatic in origin, although it may arise in the stomach, duodenum or adjacent tissues. Fifty to sixty per cent are malignant, 10% are multiple neoplasms. It may occur as part of the syndrome of Multiple Endocrine Neoplasia type I in which case malignancy is more likely.

Clinical signs

- **Pain and dyspepsia**
  From multiple ulcers
- **Steatorrhoea**
  From acid-related inactivation of
    digestive enzymes and mucosal
    damage in the upper small bowel

- **Diarrhoea**
  Due to copious acid secretion

Diagnosis is suggested by very high serum fasting gastrin levels, with little further increase with pentagastrin, and elevated basal gastric acid output. There is a rise in gastrin with secretin (unlike high gastrin secondary to achlorhydria). CT scanning may be useful to locate the adenoma and assess for hepatic metastases, although 40% of adenomata are smaller than 1 cm and thus difficult to detect on CT.

Treatment

- **High-dose acid suppression**
  (e.g. omeprazole 80–120 mg o.d.)
- **Surgical resection of adenoma**
  (May be possible)

- **Somatostatin analogues**
  To reduce gastric secretion and
    diarrhoea
- **Chemotherapy**
  (Although poor response) and
    embolization may be used
    for hepatic metastases

The five-year survival rate is 80% for a single resectable lesion but falls to 20% if hepatic metastases present.

3.3 Gastric carcinoma

The incidence of gastric carcinoma is decreasing in the Western world but it still remains one of the commonest causes of cancer deaths. It usually takes the form of an adenocarcinoma, most commonly in the pyloric region; however, the incidence of carcinoma occurring in the cardia is rising. There is very little early detection in the UK, unlike Japan where the extremely high incidence of the disease merits an intensive screening programme. Most patients have local spread at the time of diagnosis, making curative resection unusual.

Gastric carcinoma

- **Risk factors**
  Japanese
  Pernicious anaemia
  Chronic atrophic gastritis
  Blood group A
  Male sex
  High dietary salt intake
  Gastric resection (increased bile reflux)

- **Clinical presentation**
  Dyspepsia (often only symptom)
  Epigastric pain
  Weight loss
  Early satiety
  Iron deficiency anaemia
  Haematemesis/melaena

Prognosis is similar to that of colorectal cancer if detected at an early stage when potentially curative resection is possible; otherwise five-year survival is poor. Adjuvant chemotherapy before and after surgery may improve prognosis, although patients are often too unwell post-operatively to receive the second course.

4.   DISORDERS OF THE PANCREAS

4.1 Acute pancreatitis

Acute pancreatitis is a common and potentially fatal disease. Mortality in hospital remains at 7–10%, usually due to multi-organ failure or peripancreatic sepsis. Scoring systems, such as the APACHE II or that developed by Imrie in Glasgow, aim to identify those patients at high risk by assessing factors such as age, urea, hypoxia and white cell count. Obstruction of the pancreatic duct by gallstones accounts for over 50% of cases, most of the rest being alcohol-related. Four per cent are thought to have a viral aetiology; all other causes are rare. Oxygen free radicals are thought to participate in the tissue injury.

Acute pancreatitis

- **Causes**
  Gallstones
  Alcohol
  Viral (e.g. mumps, Coxsackie B)
  Trauma
  Drugs
    (e.g. azathioprine, oral contraceptive
    pill, frusemide, steroids)
  Hypercalcaemia
  Hyperlipidaemia
  Post-surgery to bile duct/endoscopic
    retrograde cholangiopancreatography
    (ERCP)

- **Poor prognostic indicators**
  Age > 55 years
  WCC > 15×10^9/l
  Urea > 16 mmol/l
  pO_2 < 60 mmHg (< 8 kPa)
  Calcium < 2 mmol/l
  Albumin < 32 g/l
  Glucose > 10 mmol/l
  LDH > 600iu/l
  (Severe attack if more than
    three factors are present)

- **Early complications**
  Adult respiratory distress syndrome
  Acute renal failure
  Disseminated intravascular coagulation

- **Late complications**
  Abscess
  Pseudocyst
  Splenic vein thrombosis

Clinical presentation is usually with abdominal pain and vomiting. A degree of hypotension is present in approximately 60%. Amylase (in blood, urine or peritoneal fluid) is raised, usually to at least four times normal values. An X-ray may show a sentinel loop of adynamic small bowel adjacent to the pancreas.

Treatment is supportive with fluids and analgesia; the presence of three or more poor prognostic indicators suggests that referral to ITU should be considered. Prophylactic antibiotics have now been shown to be of benefit. In severe pancreatitis of gallstone aetiology where jaundice and cholangitis are present, early ERCP to achieve duct decompression is of established value. Any patient with a biliary aetiology should have cholecystectomy during the same admission once the acute symptoms have settled.

4.2 Chronic pancreatitis

Chronic pancreatitis is an inflammatory condition characterized by irreversible damage to the exocrine, and later to the endocrine tissue of the pancreas. Most cases are secondary to alcohol but it is occasionally due to cystic fibrosis or haemochromatosis. There is a male predominance, often with a long history of alcohol abuse.

Chronic pancreatitis

- **Clinical signs**
  Malabsorption and steatorrhoea
  Abdominal pain radiating to the back, often relapsing
  Diabetes mellitus

- **Diagnosis**
  X-ray may show speckled calcification, present in 50–60% of advanced cases
  CT is the most sensitive for detection of pancreatic calcification
  ERCP shows irregular dilation and stricturing of the pancreatic ducts; MRCP is
    increasingly being used as a non-invasive method of imaging
  Pancrealauryl and PABA (P-aminobenzoic acid) testing are of use to assess
  exocrine function — both these involve ingestion of an oral substrate which is
  cleaved by pancreatic enzymes and can then be assayed in the urine

Treatment is with pancreatic enzyme supplementation and abstention from alcohol. Sixty per cent survive for 20 years — death is usually from complications of diabetes or alcohol.

4.3 Pancreatic carcinoma

Carcinoma of the exocrine pancreas is responsible for more than 6000 deaths per year in the UK, with an incidence of 110–120 per million, rising to 800–1000 per million over the age of 75. Seventy to 80% arise in the head of the pancreas; those in the tail are often silent in the early stages and present at an advanced stage.

The risk is increased 2–3-fold in smokers, and also possibly in those with diabetes, although it has been suggested this is an early symptom of carcinoma rather than a risk factor. Alcohol does not increase the risk.

Clinical signs include abdominal pain radiating through to back, weight loss and obstructive jaundice in 80–90%. The exocrine and endocrine functions are usually maintained.

Ultrasound and CT are both useful diagnostic tools, although ERCP is probably of most use, enabling stenting to relieve jaundice and pruritus.

Between 10 and 20% of patients are suitable for surgery and perioperative mortality is high. Radiotherapy and chemotherapy are under evaluation but so far have been shown to confer little survival benefit. Median survival remains 2–3 months from diagnosis, with one- and five-year survival rates of 10% and 3%, respectively.

5. SMALL BOWEL DISORDERS

The small bowel is the main site of absorption of nutrients for the body. Thus small bowel diseases such as coeliac or Crohn's disease often result in malabsorption and malnutrition.

Small bowel pathology can be difficult to diagnose because of the inaccessibility of this part of the GI tract. Special investigations, such as enteroscopy or white cell scanning, may be of use in addition to more routine tests such as gastroduodenoscopy or barium studies.

5.1 Coeliac disease

Also known as gluten-sensitive enteropathy, this common and underdiagnosed condition is caused by a permanent gluten intolerance to the gliadin fraction of wheat. Affecting 0.1–0.2% of the population, onset may be at any age. The incidence is greatly increased in western Ireland and it has been postulated that this is due to increased reliance on potatoes rather than wheat products as a source of carbohydrate. Thus those affected with gluten intolerance continued to thrive and reproduce.

HLA B8 DRW3 is present in 90%. Pathologically, gliadin provokes an inflammatory response which results in partial or total villous atrophy in the proximal small bowel; this reverses on a gluten-free diet but recurs on re-challenge.

Coeliac disease

- **Clinical picture**
  Diarrhoea
  Oral aphthous ulcers
  Weight loss
  Growth retardation
  General malaise
  Unexplained anaemia

- **Diagnosis**
  Upper GI endoscopy with
    jejunal biopsy
  Antiendomysial antibody
  Antigliadin antibody — may become
    negative after treatment

- **Complications**
  Anaemia — folate, B12 or iron
  Increased malignancy*
  Hyposplenism
  Dermatitis herpetiformis — very pruritic, improves with dapsone
  Osteomalacia

  *There is an increased risk of all GI malignancies but especially small bowel lymphoma, occurring in approximately 6% of cases. This risk returns to almost normal with treatment of the disease.

Treatment is by strict diet with complete avoidance of wheat, rye, oats and barley. Patients may also need folate, iron and calcium supplements. Failure to respond to treatment is usually due to non-compliance (often unwittingly) with diet. However, supervening pathology, such as lymphoma, should always be excluded.

Ten per cent of first-degree relatives will develop coeliac disease at some time. However, it is not felt of value routinely to screen the relatives of those affected unless they have symptoms to suggest the diagnosis.

Other causes of villous atrophy:

- Whipple's disease
- Hypogammaglobulinaemia
- Lymphoma
- Tropical sprue.

5.2 Carcinoid tumours

These are surprisingly common; it is estimated that carcinoid tumours are an incidental finding in up to 1% of post-mortems. Carcinoid **syndrome**, however, is extremely rare. Carcinoid tumours arise from the enterochromaffin cells of intestinal mucosa, which are neuroendocrine cells found in the lamina propria throughout the gut. The most common GI sites are the appendix (from which site metastasis is rare) and the ileum.

The tumours secrete serotonin and therefore can be detected by assay of the metabolite 5-hydroxyindoleacetic acid (5-HIAA) in the urine. Serotonin causes bronchoconstriction and increased gut motility, resulting in the symptoms documented below. Histamine and adrenocorticotrophin may also be synthesized.

Carcinoid syndrome occurs only when secondaries in the liver release serotonin into the systemic circulation; any hormone from non-metastatic gut carcinoids will be metabolized in the liver.

Clinically the following may occur:

- Diarrhoea
- Bronchospasm
- Local effect of the primary (e.g. obstruction, intussusception)

- Flushing
- Right heart valvular stenosis (left heart may be affected in bronchial carcinoid or if an ASD is present)

Treatment depends on the site of the primary and presence of metastases. Many carcinoids are very slow growing, with patient survival of more than 20 years. With widespread metastases five-year survival varies from zero to 25%, the better figures reflecting the less aggressive nature of appendiceal primaries. Treatment options include:

- **Surgical resection**
  Good prognosis if no metastases

- **Methysergide and cyproheptadine**
  For diarrhoea

- **Resection or embolization**
  Of hepatic metastases

- **Phenoxybenzamine**
  For flushing

Carcinoid may occasionally cause pellagra due to tumour uptake of tryptophan (the precursor of nicotinic acid).

5.3 Whipple's disease

This is an uncommon condition usually affecting middle-aged men, although there are case reports in women and children. The aetiology is unknown; an infective agent has been postulated but not identified.

Jejunal biopsy shows deposition of macrophages containing PAS positive granules within villi. There is a clinical syndrome of diarrhoea, malabsorption, arthropathy, and lymphadenopathy. Patients may benefit from long term tetracycline.

5.4 Angiodysplasia

Although most commonly occurring in the caecum and ascending colon, angiodysplasia is included here because of the diagnostic challenge it may present when occurring in the small intestine. Angiodysplasia may be found throughout the GI tract and its frequency in the population is unknown. It is a significant cause of acute haemorrhage, or more usually, obscure chronic GI blood loss.

Diagnosis

- **Gastroscopy/colonoscopy**
  May detect gastric and large
    bowel lesions

- **Mesenteric angiography**
  Only of use if currently bleeding;
    if so, will localize source in
    approximately 40%

- **Small bowel enteroscopy**
  The investigation of choice if
    the above fail to determine the site
    of bleeding

- **Technetium red cell scans**
  Of little use as fail to localize the
    source in 85%

Treatment is by heat or laser coagulation at endoscopy or by embolization of the bleeding point during angiography. Surgery may be indicated if the lesions are very numerous or if there is severe bleeding. Drug therapy with danazol is thought to reduce the risk of bleeding but is poorly tolerated by many patients.

6. NUTRITION

The maintenance of adequate nutrition requires three main criteria to be fulfilled.

1. **Intact GI tract**
   This may be compromised by resections resulting in a short bowel syndrome, or by fistulas such that segments of bowel are bypassed. As different nutrients are absorbed from different parts of the gut a variety of clinical sequelae may occur depending upon the segment of bowel affected (e.g. B12 deficiency after terminal ileal resection, iron deficiency after partial gastrectomy).

2. **Ability to absorb nutrients**
   Impairment of absorptive function may be caused by mucosal damage such as occurs in Crohn's or coeliac disease, or after radiation damage. Motility problems resulting in accelerated transit times may reduce absorption.

3. **Adequate intake**
   This is dependent both on the motivation to maintain an adequate oral intake, often lacking in sick or elderly patients, and on the composition of the diet.

Inability to maintain nutrition is an indication to provide supplementation by one of the three routes listed below. The underlying disease will determine which is appropriate.

- **Oral**: obviously the most simple form but relies on a conscious patient with an intact swallowing mechanism. High protein or carbohydrate drinks may be used to provide good nutritional intake in a small volume.
- **Enteral**: useful when swallowing impaired (e.g. in neurological disease) or when high volume intake is needed. May take the form of a simple nasogastric tube, or a percutaneous gastrostomy (PEG) or jejunostomy which can be inserted endoscopically or surgically. Can be for short or long term supplementation.
- **Parenteral**: this is intravenous feeding, either to supplement enteral nutrition or to provide total support in the case of complete intestinal failure.

Problems with parenteral nutrition

- Central venous access needed

- Patient/carer must be sufficiently movitated and competent to master aseptic techniques and care for venous line

- Electrolyte abnormalities may occur — need for careful monitoring; also need to monitor trace elements such as zinc and selenium

- Risk of sepsis — line infections, right heart endocarditis

Examples of specific nutritional deficiencies are covered in Chapter 11, *Metabolic Diseases*.

6.1 Diarrhoea

Diarrhoea is difficult to define. It is accepted as >200 ml of stool per day but also as increased frequency and decreased consistency. There is a wide variety of causes (as illustrated below), which may result in diarrhoea by differing mechanisms.

Classification is useful:

- Acute or chronic
- Large bowel (often smaller amounts, may contain blood or mucus)
- Small bowel (often voluminous, pale and fatty).

Causes of diarrhoea

- **Osmotic**
  (osmotic agent draws water into gut)
  Osmotic laxatives
  Magnesium sulphate
  Lactase deficiency*
  Stops with fasting

- **Secretory**
  (failure of active ion absorption ± active ion secretion)
  Infection (e.g. *E. coli*, cholera)
  Malabsorption
  Bile salts (↑ deposition into bowel after cholecystectomy)
  Continues with fasting

- **Altered motility**
  (altered peristalsis or damage to autonomic nervous system)
  Irritable bowel syndrome
  Thyrotoxicosis
  Post-vagotomy
  Diabetic autonomic neuropathy
  Stops with fasting

* Lactase deficiency may be congenital (possibly severe) or acquired, and often occurs in the setting of viral gastroenteritis or coeliac disease. Complete exclusion of lactose from diet usually not necessary — there is often a threshold below which symptoms are absent.

Investigations for diarrhoea

- **History and examination vital, including rectal examination**
  History may be suggestive of large or small bowel cause; examination *per rectum* to exclude overflow or rectal tumour

- **Sigmoidoscopy/colonoscopy**
  If large bowel cause suspected

- **Folate and iron assay**
  If small bowel cause suspected

- **Gastroscopy**
  With duodenal biopsy if small bowel cause suspected

- **Biochemistry**
  Electrolyte disturbance; include thryoid function tests

- **Stool microscopy and culture**
  Including examination for ova, cysts and parasites

- **Three-day faecal fat assay**
  If small bowel cause suspected

- **Small bowel radiology**
  If small bowel cause suspected

Treatment depends on the underlying disease process, which should obviously be treated if possible. Loperamide or codeine reduce gut transit time and thus may control symptoms.

6.2 Malabsorption

Malabsorption may be defined as a failure to absorb sufficient exogenous nutrients or reabsorb endogenous substances such as bile salts. It may be caused by a multiplicity of factors since normal absorption depends on gut structure, motility and secretion of hormones and enzymes. Malabsorption frequently, but not necessarily, results in diarrhoea. Clinical presentation depends on the type and site of defect, and includes weight loss and general ill health, osteomalacia, or specific nutritional deficiencies such as of B12 and folate, or hypoalbuminaemia. Investigation is as for diarrhoea. Specific tests for malabsorption include:

- **Schilling test**
  See earlier

- **^{14}C breath testing**
  To detect overgrowth (although the most accurate test remains quantitative bacteriological assay of jejunal aspirates)

- **Xylose absorption test**
  Give 25 g oral xylose, assay amount excreted in urine, expect >20% in urine if small bowel absorption normal

Causes of malabsorption

- **Structural abnormalities**
  Coeliac disease*
  Crohn's disease*
  Post-surgical resections*
  Bacterial overgrowth due to
    blind loops

- **Motility abnormalities**
  Thyrotoxicosis
  Drugs (e.g. neomycin)
  Diabetes

- **Secretion abnormalities**
  GI tract infection
    (e.g. *Giardia*, amoebiasis)
  Chronic pancreatitis*
  Cystic fibrosis

*Common causes in the UK.

7.   LARGE BOWEL DISORDERS

7.1 Crohn's disease and ulcerative colitis

Crohn's disease and ulcerative colitis are both chronic relapsing inflammatory disorders of the gastrointestinal tract. Their aetiology is still unknown, and it is likely that a variety of factors may be involved in a genetically predisposed individual. Possible aetiological agents include *Mycobacterium paratuberculosis*, although detection of this by polymerase chain reaction has produced inconclusive evidence. It is possible that, even if present, this may be opportunistic infection of damaged mucosa rather than a causal factor. Perinatal infection with measles virus has also been postulated but again remains inconclusive — it may be that viral infection affects immune modulation which predisposes to the later development of inflammatory bowel disease. The use of NSAIDs and the oral contraceptive pill have also been implicated but mechanisms remain unclear.

The major similarities and differences between the two disorders are detailed overleaf.

Crohn's disease

Affects any part of the GI tract from mouth to anus. Commonly terminal ileum, colon, anorectum. May be 'skip lesions' of normal mucosa between affected areas.

Ulcerative colitis

Always involves rectum and extends confluently into the colon. Terminal ileum may be affected by 'backwash ileitis' but remainder of gut unaffected.

- **Pathology**

Crohn's disease	Ulcerative colitis
Transmural inflammation	Mucosa and submucosa only involved
Non-caseating granulomata (in 30% only)	Mucosal ulcers
Fissuring ulcers	Inflammatory cell infiltrate
Lymphoid aggregates	Crypt abscesses
Neutrophil infiltrates	

- **Clinical**

Crohn's disease	Ulcerative colitis
Abdominal pain prominent and frequent fever	Diarrhoea, often with blood and mucus
Diarrhoea ± blood p.r.	Fever
Anal/perianal/oral lesions	Abdominal pain less prominent
Stricturing common, resulting in obstructive symptoms	

- **Associations**

Crohn's disease	Ulcerative colitis
Increased incidence in smokers (50–60% smokers)	Decreased incidence in smokers (70–80% non-smokers)
Skin disorders:	Increased incidence of:
erythema nodosum (5–10%)	primary biliary cirrhosis
pyoderma gangrenosum (0.5%)	chronic active hepatitis
iritis/uveitis (3–10%)	sclerosing cholangitis
Joint pain/arthritis (6–12%)	Other systemic manifestations occur
Cholelithiasis (common)	but less common than in Crohn's
Clubbing	disease
Depression	

- **Diagnosis**

Crohn's disease	Ulcerative colitis
Barium studies:	Barium studies
cobblestoning of mucosa	pseudopolyps between ulcers
rosethorn ulcers	loss of haustral pattern
strictures	featureless shortened colon
skip lesions	Sigmoidoscopy with biopsy may be
Endoscopy with biopsy	sufficient
Isotope leucocyte scans useful to diagnose active small bowel disease	

Continues ...

... Continued

Crohn's disease	**Ulcerative colitis**

- **Complications**

Crohn's disease	Ulcerative colitis

Fistulae: entero-enteral
  entero-vesical
  entero-vaginal
  perianal
Carcinoma — mildly increased risk
  of colonic malignancy (see later)*
B12 deficiency common (decreased
  absorption in terminal ileal disease)
Iron deficiency anaemia
Abscess formation
	Fistulae do not develop
	Toxic megacolon (uncommon —
	  usually an indication for urgent
	  colectomy)
	Increased risk of carcinoma*
	  20 x 20 years of disease
	  preventative colectomy of value
	Iron deficiency anaemia

*The value of screening endoscopy for carcinoma in ulcerative colitis and Crohn's disease is very much in debate. Some units advise endoscopies every 2–3 years for patients who have had the disease for more than 10 years.

Treatment is similar for both Crohn's disease and ulcerative colitis, although the latter may be more amenable to topical drug therapy:

- **5 ASA compounds**: (e.g. sulphasalazine, mesalazine). These are used to maintain remission and reduce relapse and may be topical or oral. Side-effects include rash, infertility, agranulocytosis, headache, diarrhoea and renal failure.
- **Steroids**: topical, oral or parenteral. Newer preparations such as budesonide aim to target the small bowel with fewer systemic side-effects.
- **Azathioprine**: used as a steroid-sparing agent. There are dose-dependent side-effects of pancreatitis, aplastic anaemia and hepatic/renal toxicity.
- **Nutritional support**: enteral or parenteral. An elemental diet is effective in inducing remission.
- **Surgery**: recurrence occurs in 30–60% of patients after surgery in Crohn's disease; multiple resections may result in malabsorption due to insufficient remaining bowel. Surgery in ulcerative colitis may be curative (e.g. panproctocolectomy).

7.2 Pseudomembranous colitis

This is acute colitis due to the enterotoxin of *Clostridium difficile*, usually precipitated by broad spectrum antibiotics. It is common in the elderly or chronically ill, and mortality may be as high as 20%. Patient-to-patient spread in hospital is common. Diagnosis is by demonstration of the toxin in stools or by endoscopy (which shows inflamed mucosa with yellow pseudomembranes). Treatment is with oral vancomycin or metronidazole

7.3 Familial polyposis coli

This is an autosomal dominant condition, the gene is located on the long arm of chromosome 5. Estimates of the incidence vary from one in 7000 to one in 30,000 of the population in the UK.

Multiple adenomata occur throughout the colon; if untreated, malignancy is inevitable, often when patients are aged only 30 or 40 years. Patients need regular endoscopy and eventual prophylactic colectomy in view of the high risk of malignant change. Screening of family members is essential.

7.4 Peutz–Jeghers syndrome

This is an autosomal dominant condition in which multiple hamartomatous polyps occur throughout the GI tract (particularly in the small bowel). Patients may have mucocutaneous pigmentation and perioral freckles. Lesions may lead to GI haemorrhage and may undergo malignant change (carcinoma is increased twelve-fold in patients with this condition).

7.5 Irritable bowel syndrome

This is a functional bowel disorder, and therefore a diagnosis of exclusion if the FBC, ESR and sigmoidoscopy at least are normal. Irritable bowel syndrome is the commonest cause of attendance at GI clinic, with a female preponderance.

Clinical signs associated with irritable bowel syndrome

- Constipation or diarrhoea
- Abdominal pain

- Bloating, often relieved by defaecation
- Extra-GI symptoms such as back pain, urinary frequency, anxiety and depression are common

---

Antispasmodics, increased dietary fibre, antidepressants, hypnotherapy and psychotherapy are all of proven benefit.

7.6 Colorectal cancer

This is the second most common cause of cancer death in the UK, with an incidence of approximately 30/100,000 in the UK. Because of its frequency, screening of the asymptomatic population by faecal occult blood testing has been evaluated but not found to be worthwhile, partly due to poor patient compliance. Colorectal cancer usually occurs from the sixth decade on and the incidence increases with advancing age.

Pathologically, it is an adenocarcinoma usually arising from tubular and villous adenomatous polyps (although in inflammatory bowel disease, malignant change arises directly from the mucosa). The commonest sites are the rectum and sigmoid.

Colorectal cancer

- **Increased incidence**
  Male sex
  Inflammatory bowel disease, especially ulcerative colitis
  Familial polyposis coli
  Diet low in fibre, fruit and vegetables
  Diet high in fat and red meat
  Cholecystectomy (bile salts 'dumped' in colon)

- **Clinical signs**
  These depend on the site of the lesion; all can cause weight loss and obstructive symptoms.

- **Right-sided**
  Iron deficiency anaemia
  Abdominal pain
  Abdominal mass

- **Left-sided**
  Blood p.r.
  Altered bowel habit
  Abdominal mass

- **Rectum**
  Blood p.r.
  Tenesmus

- **Complications**
  Local spread to organs and lymph nodes
  Metastasis to liver, lung, brain and bone
  Obstruction ± perforation

Treatment of colorectal cancer consists of surgery (for cure) or symptomatic relief depending on **Duke's staging**.

- **Stage**
  A — confined to mucosa and submucosa
  B — extends through muscularis propria
  C — regional lymph nodes involved
  D — distant spread

- **Five-year survival**
  80% +
  60–70%
  30–40%
  0%

Radiotherapy may be used as an adjuvant, particularly to reduce tumour bulk before surgery.

Adjuvant chemotherapy (e.g. 5-fluorouracil post-operatively) has been shown to improve prognosis for patients at Duke's stages B and C, toxicity is low so quality of life tends to be good. Serial monitoring of carcinoembryonic antigen (CEA), a glycoprotein from gastrointestinal epithelia, may be of use in detecting recurrence.

7.7 Carcinoma complicating inflammatory bowel disease

The risk of carcinoma associated with inflammatory bowel disease is increased if:

- Onset occurs at less than 15 years of age
- Disease duration has been longer than 10 years
- There is widespread disease (e.g. total colitis)
- The disease takes an unremitting course
- Compliance with treatment and follow-up is poor.

Screening for colonic cancer by colonoscopy every 3 years is indicated if one or more adenomatous colonic polyps present, if there is longstanding ulcerative colitis or if the patient has a strong family history of colonic carcinoma.

8. GASTROINTESTINAL INFECTIONS

AIDS and the gut is covered in Chapter 7, *Genito-urinary Medicine and AIDS*.

8.1 Gastroenteritis

Most gastrointestinal infections in the UK are viral or self-limiting bacterial infections such as *Staphylococcus aureus* or *Campylobacter*. Treatment is symptomatic with antidiarrhoeals (such as loperamide) and oral rehydration therapy (ORT) in patients who are at risk of dehydration. ORT utilizes the capacity of the small bowel to absorb chloride, sodium and water via a glucose-dependent active transport channel that is not disrupted by infections. More intensive therapy is confined to those systemically unwell or immunosuppressed.

The following are some of the more important gastrointestinal infections. (See also Chapter 10, *Infectious Diseases and Tropical Medicine*.)

Amoebiasis

- Infection is due to *Entamoeba histolytica* with faecal–oral spread.
- The clinical spectrum ranges from mild diarrhoea to dysentery with profuse bloody stool; a chronic illness with irritable bowel-type symptoms may also occur. Colonic or hepatic abscesses occur, the latter commonly in the setting of a severe amoebic colitis.
- Treatment is with metronidazole.

Campylobacter

- Gram-negative rods.
- Clinically, patients are often systemically unwell with headache and malaise prior to the onset of diarrhoeal illness. Abdominal pain may be severe, mimicking an acute abdomen.
- Erythromycin may be indicated if symptoms are prolonged.

Cholera

- Infection is due to *Vibrio cholerae* (Gram-negative rods) which colonize the small bowel; spread is faecal–oral. A high infecting dose is needed as the bacteria are susceptible to gastric acid.
- A severe toxin-mediated diarrhoea occurs with rice–water stool which may exceed 20 litres per day. Dehydration is the main cause of death especially in young or elderly; mortality is high without rehydration treatment.
- Tetracycline may reduce transmission.

Giardiasis

- Infection is due to *Giardia lamblia* (a flagellate protozoan) which colonizes the duodenum and jejunum; spread is faecal–oral.
- Bloating and diarrhoea (not bloody) occur; malabsorption may occur with small intestine colonization. Asymptomatic carriage is common and duodenal biopsy may be necessary to make the diagnosis.
- Treatment is with metronidazole.

Salmonella

- A Gram-negative bacillus with multiple serotypes divided into two main groups: those causing typhoid and paratyphoid (enteric fever), and those causing gastroenteritis. Spread is faecal–oral.
- Diarrhoea (may be bloody) occurs, with or without vomiting and abdominal pain.
- Treatment is with ciprofloxacin or trimethoprim. Chronic asymptomatic carriage is rare (less than 1% compared with 3–4% in typhoid/paratyphoid).

Shigella

- Gram-negative rods. Spread is faecal–oral with a very low infecting dose of organisms needed owing to its high virulence.
- The clinical spectrum ranges from diarrhoeal illness to severe dysentery depending on the infecting type: *S. sonnei, S. flexneri, S. boydi, S. dysenteriae.*
- Diarrhoea (may be bloody), vomiting, abdominal pain.
- Treat if severe with ampicillin or tetracycline although there is widespread resistance.

8.2 Gastrointestinal tuberculosis

This is common in developing countries, and causes ileo–caecal TB or TB peritonitis. There has been a recent resurgence in patients with AIDS. The infection may occur secondary to pulmonary TB as a result of swallowing infected sputum or by haematogenous spread; it may also result from drinking unpasteurized milk.

Clinical features are often non-specific such as malaise, fever and weight loss, as well as diarrhoea and abdominal pain. Ultrasound, barium studies or CT may suggest the diagnosis but biopsy, either by laparoscopy or endoscopy is confirmative.

9. HEPATOLOGY

9.1 Jaundice

Jaundice is one of the most common symptoms of liver disease, caused by the accumulation of bilirubin in the tissues. Bilirubin is formed as the end product of catabolism of haem-containing compounds and is clinically detectable at a level of > 30 μmol/l. The formation and excretion of bilirubin is shown opposite.

The most common causes of jaundice in the UK are alcoholic liver disease, gallstones and tumours of the liver and pancreas.

Hyperbilirubinaemia may occur because of excess production or decreased elimination of bilirubin. Jaundice can thus be broadly divided into three categories depending on the site of the pathology.

Prehepatic

(Excess production of bilirubin or failure of uptake into the liver.)

- Haemolysis causing excess haem production
- Congenital hyperbilirubinaemia (e.g. Gilbert's syndrome, Crigler–Najjar syndrome (see below)).

Bilirubin is unconjugated and insoluble, thus it does not appear in the urine — acholuric jaundice.

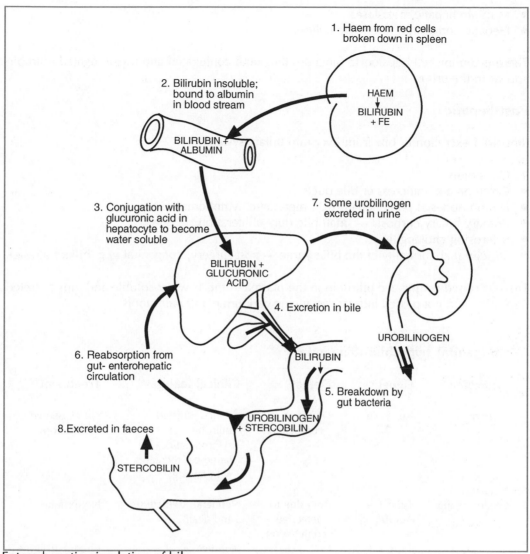

1. Haem from red cells broken down in spleen

HAEM
↓
BILIRUBIN
+ FE

2. Bilirubin insoluble; bound to albumin in blood stream

BILIRUBIN + ALBUMIN

3. Conjugation with glucuronic acid in hepatocyte to become water soluble

7. Some urobilinogen excreted in urine

BILIRUBIN + GLUCURONIC ACID

4. Excretion in bile

UROBILINOGEN

6. Reabsorption from gut- enterohepatic circulation

BILIRUBIN

5. Breakdown by gut bacteria

8. Excreted in faeces

UROBILINOGEN + STERCOBILIN

STERCOBILIN

Entero-hepatic circulation of bile

Hepatic

(Defect at level of hepatocyte.)

- Viral infection (e.g. hepatitis A, B, EBV)
- Drugs (e.g. phenothiazines)
- Wilson's disease
- Rotor and Dubin–Johnson syndromes (see overleaf)
- Cirrhosis

- Multiple hepatic metastases
- Hepatic congestion in cardiac failure.

There is diminished hepatocyte function, thus both conjugated and unconjugated bilirubin appear in the urine.

Post-hepatic

(Impaired excretion of bile from liver into biliary system.)

- Gallstones
- Carcinoma of pancreas or bile ducts
- Lymph nodes at porta hepatis (e.g. metastatic, lymphomatous)
- Primary biliary cirrhosis — small bile duct obliteration
- Sclerosing cholangitis
- Structural abnormality of the biliary tree — post-surgery, congenital (e.g. biliary atresia).

There is raised conjugated bilirubin in the plasma — this is water-soluble and thus excreted into urine and not passed into faeces, giving dark urine and pale stools.

Congenital hyperbilirubinaemia

Syndrome	Genetics	Defect	Clinical features	Treatment
Gilbert	Aut Dom	Defect in conjugation	↑ Unconjugated bilirubin Asymptomatic ± jaundice, increases with fasting	Nil as benign condition
Crigler–Najjar	Type 1 — Aut Rec	Both due to defective conjugation	Neonatal kernicterus and death	None; fatal
	Type 2 — Aut Dom		Jaundice as neonate/child; survive to adulthood	Phenobarbitone to ↓ jaundice
Dubin–Johnson	Aut Rec	Defect in hepatic excretion	Jaundice with right upper quadrant pain and malaise	Nil as benign condition
Rotor	Aut Dom	Defect in uptake and storage of bilirubin	↑ Conjugated bilirubin	Nil as benign condition

Aut Dom = autosomal dominant; Aut Rec = autosomal recessive.

Investigation of jaundice

The mainstay of investigation is ultrasound to identify whether duct dilation is present, suggesting an obstructive cause. If so, ERCP is likely to be the investigation of choice and may allow intervention to relieve obstruction at the same time. Liver biopsy may be helpful if dilation is absent, but is contraindicated in the presence of uncorrected coagulation disorders and is technically difficult if ascites is present. Full biochemical, viral and autoimmune screening including for antimitochondrial and smooth muscle antibodies is obviously useful in all cases as well as a detailed history and examination.

Biochemical screen
Viral screen
Autoimmune screen

⇩

Ultrasound scan

⇩   ⇩

duct dilation   no duct dilation

⇩   ⇩

ERCP +/- CT   Liver Biopsy

Investigation of jaundice

Liver function tests in jaundice

The pattern of derangement of liver biochemistry can provide an indication as to the site of pathology. The presence of conjugated or unconjugated hyperbilirubinaemia is of particular value. Alkaline phosphatase, as a ductal enzyme, tends to rise markedly in obstructive lesions.

Liver function tests in jaundice

	Unconjugated bilirubin	Conjugated bilirubin	ALT/AST	Alk phos	Gamma GT
Pre-hepatic	↑↑	Normal	Normal	Normal/↑	Normal/↑
Hepatic	Normal	↑↑	↑↑	Mod ↑	Mod ↑
Post-hepatic	Normal	↑	Mod ↑	↑↑↑	↑↑

9.2 Gallstone disease

Gallstones are one of the commonest causes of jaundice, usually presenting a cholestatic picture. Approximately 1 litre of bile is secreted by the hepatocytes each day. Half of this drains directly into the duodenum whilst the remainder is stored and concentrated in the gallbladder by removal of sodium, chloride, bicarbonate and water. CCK then stimulates its release.

Stones are found in 10–20% of the population (with a female preponderance) but are asymptomatic in the majority. There are two stone types: 80% are cholesterol stones, composed of at least 70% pure cholesterol with or without bile pigment and calcium. The remaining 20% are bile pigment stones.

Gallstones

- **Risk factors for stone formation**
  Female sex
  Increasing age
  Drugs
    (e.g. oral contraceptive pill, clofibrate)
  Crohn's disease
  Haemolysis (pigment stones)

- **Clinical presentation**
  Acute/chronic cholecystitis
  Biliary colic
  Cholestatic jaundice if duct obstruction
  Pancreatitis
  Cholangitis
  Gallstone ileus

NB. Stones may form in the common bile duct even after cholecystectomy

Diagnosis in most cases may be established by ultrasound ± ERCP. MRCP is useful as a non-invasive investigation but, unlike ERCP, does not allow therapeutic intervention. Definitive treatment is by cholecystectomy. ERCP with sphincterotomy and balloon clearance of the common bile duct may be indicated for duct stones. Medical treatment with ursodeoxycholic acid can be used to dissolve cholesterol stones; however, this is extremely slow and should be reserved only for patients who are unfit for other treatment.

9.3 Ascites

Ascites is defined as the accumulation of free fluid within the peritoneal cavity. It can be subdivided into transudate or exudate depending on whether the protein content is less or greater than 30 g/l, respectively. The most common causes in the UK are cirrhosis and malignant disease.

- **Transudate**
  Portal hypertension
  Nephrotic syndrome
  Malnutrition
  Cardiac failure
  Budd–Chiari syndrome
  Myxoedema

- **Exudate**
  Hepatic or peritoneal malignancy
  Intra-abdominal TB
  Pancreatitis

The **treatment** of ascites depends on the aetiology. Transudates respond to fluid restriction, low sodium intake and diuretic therapy, to promote sodium and water excretion via the kidneys. Paracentesis may be used for tense ascites or ascites which is not responding to diuretics. However, paracentesis may result in a further shift of fluid from the intravascular space into the peritoneal cavity with the risk of circulatory collapse. This can be avoided by bolstering the circulation via the concurrent administration of intravenous albumin. Exudates can be safely paracentesed without protein replacement.

9.4 Cirrhosis

Cirrhosis is characterized by the irreversible destruction and fibrosis of normal liver architecture with some regeneration into nodules.

There are four stages of pathological change.

1. Liver cell necrosis
2. Inflammatory infiltrate
3. Fibrosis
4. Nodular regeneration.

Regeneration may be macronodular (e.g. alcohol- or drug-induced), micronodular (e.g. viral hepatitis) or mixed, but a more useful categorization is according to the aetiological agent.

Cirrhosis

- **Causes**
  Alcohol (most common in the UK, approximately 30% of all cases)
  Hepatitis B or C
  (most common worldwide)
  Cryptogenic
  Primary biliary cirrhosis
  Haemochromatosis
  Wilson's disease
  Alpha-1-antitrypsin deficiency

- **Clinical signs**
  Jaundice
  Palmar erythema
  Spider naevi
  Splenomegaly
  Acites

Evidence of chronic liver disease may or may not be present.

Diagnosis of cirrhosis is definitively made by biopsy, although this can be difficult as the liver may be small and shrunken in end-stage disease. Transjugular biopsy is possible.

Treatment is aimed at the removal of causal factors such as alcohol. Specific treatments include interferon for viral hepatitis and ursodeoxycholic acid for primary biliary cirrhosis. Transplantation is the best hope but many patients are not suitable. **Contraindications for liver transplantation include:**

- Poor cardiac reserve
- Co-morbidity such as HIV infection or severe respiratory disease
- Failure to abstain from alcohol.

There is no definitive cut-off regarding age but patients over 70 years are less likely to be suitable.

Conditions which may be amenable to hepatic transplantation

- **Fulminant hepatic failure**
  (e.g. due to hepatitis C or
  paracetamol toxicity)

- **Primary biliary cirrhosis**

- **Hepatitis B**
  Although frequent recurrence after
  transplant — reduce using pre-
  transplant treatment with interferon

- **Cholangiocarcinoma**
  Most too extensive at presentation

- **Alcohol**
  If abstained for more than 6 months
  and likely to continue to do so

- **Wilson's disease**

- **Haemochromatosis**

- **Hepatocellular carcinoma**
  If not multifocal, < 5 cm and no
  evidence of vascular invasion

9.5 Portal hypertension and varices

Portal hypertension occurs as a result of increased resistance to portal venous flow. Pressure in the portal vein rises and is said to be pathological when > 12 mmHg, although pressures of up to 50 mmHg may occur. The spleen enlarges and anastamoses may open between the portal and systemic circulation. Some of the collaterals, which most commonly occur at the oesophago-gastric junction, umbilicus and rectum, may become very large with a risk of bleeding.

A variety of conditions may cause portal hypertension; in the UK the single most common is cirrhosis secondary to alcohol.

Causes of portal hypertension

- Cirrhosis due to any cause
- Portal vein thrombosis
- Budd–Chiari syndrome
  (thrombosis or obstruction of portal
  vein due to tumour, haematological
  disease or the oral contraceptive pill)

- Tumours such as cholangiocarcinoma
  or hepatocellular carcinoma
- Constrictive pericarditis
- Right heart failure

Variceal haemorrhage

Thirty per cent of patients with varices will bleed at some point with a mortality of 50% for that episode. The majority of survivors will rebleed with a mortality of 30%. Bleeding is often catastrophic as many patients also have coagulopathy as a result of their underlying liver disease.

Primary prevention of haemorrhage

All patients with cirrhosis of the liver should have upper GI endoscopy to determine the presence or absence of varices. If there are none, or only very small varices, no treatment is required except regular endoscopic review every 2–3 years. Larger varices in patients with no history of variceal haemorrhage should be treated with prophylactic beta-blockade (or nitrates if beta-blockers are contraindicated). This reduces portal pressure and significantly reduces the risk of haemorrhage.

Treatment of variceal haemorrhage

After resuscitation and correction of any coagulopathy the treatment of choice is early gastroscopy with band ligation of the varices (now shown to be superior to injection sclerotherapy). Temporary balloon tamponade may be useful if endoscopy is not imme-diately available. Vasoactive drugs, such as octreotide, are widely used but should not be viewed as a substitute for endoscopy and banding. Bleeding which does not respond to these measures may be an indication for emergency transjugular intrahepatic porto-systemic shunting (TIPSS).

Secondary prevention of haemorrhage

Patients should undergo repeated band ligation until varices are eradicated. Beta-blockade should be given as this reduces the risk of rebleeding by up to 40%. Recurrent haemorrhage may be an indication for TIPSS.

Transjugular Intrahepatic Porto-Systemic Shunting (TIPSS)

This involves placement of a shunt under radiological screening which decompresses the portal venous system. As it is less invasive than surgery it may be a useful rescue procedure for patients with recurrent or resistant haemorrhage who are not fit for surgery. The major problems are that shunting may precipitate hepatic encephalopathy (this occurs in up to 24%, but seems more responsive to treatment than encephalopathy from other causes), and shunt blockage. In the latter case a second shunt may be 'piggy-backed' across the first. TIPSS may be particularly helpful as a palliative procedure in patients with recurrent haem-orrhage due to malignancy.

9.6 Hepatic encephalopathy

Hepatic encephalopathy is a neuropsychiatric syndrome which may complicate acute or chronic liver disease from any cause. Symptoms include confusion, falling level of consciousness, vomiting, fits and hyperventilation. Renal failure may often supervene — the chance of recovery from hepato-renal failure is extremely poor. The underlying mechanisms are complex but the absorption of toxins such as ammonia from bacterial break-down of proteins in the gut is thought to play a major part. Portosystemic shunting of blood occurs — toxins thus bypass the liver and cross the blood–brain barrier.

The most common causes of **acute hepatic encephalopathy** are fulminant viral hepatitis and paracetamol toxicity which are potentially fully reversible. Indicators of poor prognosis are:

- Worsening acidosis
- Rising prothrombin time
- Falling Glasgow Coma Scale.

These patients should be referred to a specialist centre as they may need transplantation.

Chronic hepatic encephalopathy may supervene in chronic liver disease of any type. It is often precipitated by:

- Alcohol
- Drugs
- GI haemorrhage
- Infections
- Constipation.

It is characterized by a flapping tremor, decreased consciousness level and constructional apraxia.

Treatment of hepatic encephalopathy

- Screen for and treat sepsis aggressively — if ascites is present consider bacterial peritonitis and perform a diagnostic ascitic tap
- Strict fluid and electrolyte balance
- Low protein diet
- Laxatives to clear the gut and thus reduce toxin absorption; neomycin is now rarely used
- Remove or treat precipitants

Mortality is high, especially if renal failure supervenes when the mortality approaches 50%.

9.7 Viral hepatitis

The six major hepatitis viruses are described below, but further types are already postulated. Hepatitis B and C in particular are major causes of morbidity and mortality worldwide, although recent advances in treatment with interferon and other antivirals have improved the outcome in certain groups.

- **Hepatis A**
  Spread: faecal–oral
  Virus: RNA
  Clinical: anorexia, jaundice, nausea, joint pains, fever
  Treatment: supportive
  Chronicity: no chronic state
  Vaccine: yes.

- **Hepatitis B**
  Spread: blood-borne (e.g. sexual, vertical, congenital transmission)
  Virus: DNA
  Clinical: acute fever, arteritis, glomerulo-nephritis, arthropathy
  Treatment: supportive; chronic HBV may respond to interferon (the effectiveness of anti-viral agents lamivudine and famciclovir are under evaluation)
  Chronicity: 5% → chronic carriage (risk of cirrhosis and hepatocellular carcinoma)
  Vaccine: yes.

- **Hepatitis C**
  Spread: blood-borne, sexual
  Virus: RNA
  Clinical: acute hepatitis — less severe than A or B, fulminant failure rate
  Treatment: interferon for chronic HCV; combination with ribavarin more promising with chronic hepatitis
  Chronicity: 60–80% → chronic carriage (risk of cirrhosis and hepatocellular carcinoma) (20% at risk of cirrhosis and hepatocellular carcinoma)
  Vaccine: no.

- **Hepatitis D (delta agent)**
  Spread: blood-borne (dependent on concurrent hepatitis B infection for replication)
  Virus: incomplete
  Clinical: exacerbates established hepatitis B infection and increases risk of hepatic failure and cirrhosis
  Treatment: interferon of limited benefit
  Chronicity: increases incidence of cirrhosis in chronic HBV
  Vaccine: no.

- **Hepatitis E**
  Spread: faecal–oral
  Virus: RNA
  Clinical: acute self-limiting illness but mortality (fetal and maternal) in 25% of pregnancies
  Treatment: supportive
  Chronicity: no chronic state
  Vaccine: no.

- **Hepatitis G**
  Spread: blood-borne
  Virus: RNA
  Clinical: doubtful relevance; 20% of drug users with chronic HCV infected with G
  Treatment: viraemia may decline with interferon
  Chronicity: unknown — may cause cirrhosis and hepatocellular carcinoma
  Vaccine: no.

Interferon in viral hepatitis

Interferon is predominantly of benefit in patients suffering from chronic hepatitis B and C. In hepatitis B, there is a response in 40% of chronic carriers. The response is poorer in Asian patients. The response is likely to be very poor if the patient is also infected with HIV and thus treatment is not usually indicated in this group. In hepatitis C, there is a response in 50% of chronic carriers but 50% of these will relapse despite treatment.

Hepatitis B serology

Detectable antigens/antibodies and significance:

- **HBsAg**: present in acute infection; if present longer than 6 months = chronic hepatitis
- **HBeAg**: present in acute or chronic infection; signifies high infectivity
- **HBcAg**: present in acute or chronic infection; found only in liver tissue; present for life
- **AntiHBs**: signifies immunity after vaccination or acute infection
- **AntiHBe**: signifies declining infectivity and resolving infection
- **AntiHBc IgM**: signifies recent acute infection; lasts less than 6 months
- **AntiHBc IgG**: is a lifelong marker of past acute or chronic infection; does not signify immunity or previous vaccination

Other causes of acute hepatitis include:

- Drugs (e.g. halothane, amiodarone, carbon tetrachloride)
- Alcohol
- Other viruses (e.g. Epstein–Barr, yellow fever, CMV, rubella, Herpes simplex)
- Other infections (e.g. malaria).

9.8 Chronic hepatitis

Chronic hepatitis is defined as any hepatitis persisting for longer than 6 months. The main differentiation is between chronic persistent hepatitis, which is a benign condition with a good prognosis, and the more serious chronic active hepatitis.

Chronic persistent hepatitis

This is defined as a benign inflammatory reaction lasting longer than 6 months. It will remit spontaneously after several months or years. Biopsy (necessary to exclude chronic active hepatitis) shows portal fibrosis but no piecemeal necrosis. Patients are often asymptomatic; there may be hepatomegaly but signs of chronic liver disease are absent. Liver biochemistry is often normal except for elevated aspartate aminotransferase.

Causes include:

- Viral hepatitis
- Drugs
  (e.g. methyldopa, isoniazid, cytotoxics)
- Alcohol.

Because of its benign nature, treatment is not indicated.

Chronic active hepatitis (CAH)

This is an aggressive persistent hepatitis characterized by piecemeal necrosis on biopsy. Progression to cirrhosis with the associated risk of hepatocellular carcinoma is common.

Causes include:

- Hepatitis B ± hepatitis D
  (20% of all CAH; not responsive to steroids but may respond to interferon — see earlier)

- Alpha-1 antitrypsin deficiency

- Hepatitis C
  (see earlier)

- Autoimmune
  (see below)

- Wilson's disease

Autoimmune 'lupoid' hepatitis

This condition occurs predominantly in female patients. Other autoimmune disease is often present and patients are usually ANF positive. It responds to steroids and azathioprine but the majority progress to cirrhosis, although 90% are alive at 5 years and may be candidates for transplantation.

9.9 Primary biliary cirrhosis

Primary biliary cirrhosis accounts for approximately 5% of deaths due to cirrhosis. The cause is unknown although factors point to an autoimmune aetiology, especially the strong association with other autoimmune disease such as rheumatoid arthritis, Sjögren's syndrome and CREST syndrome. Histologically, progressive inflammation and destruction of small intrahepatic ducts leads to eventual cirrhosis. Ninety per cent of patients are female, often in middle age. There are four stages of primary biliary cirrhosis:

1. Destruction of interlobular ducts.
2. Small duct proliferation.
3. Fibrosis.
4. Cirrhosis.

Primary biliary cirrhosis

- **Clinical features**
  Cholestatic jaundice
  Xanthelasmata due to
    hypercholesterolaemia
  Skin pigmentation
  Clubbing
  Hepatosplenomegaly
  Portal hypertension ± varices
  Osteoporosis and osteomalacia

- **Diagnosis**
  Antimitochondrial antibody present
    in 95%
  Predominantly raised alkaline phosphatase
    — often raised in advance of symptoms/
    signs
  Raised IgM
  Liver biopsy showing the features listed
    above

Treatment is symptomatic; cholestyramine relieves pruritus. Penicillamine is of doubtful benefit. Liver transplant remains the only hope of cure. Rising bilirubin levels are an indication of disease approaching end stage and transplant should be considered in suitable patients.

9.10 Haemochromatosis

This is an autosomal recessive disorder of iron metabolism leading to deposition in the liver, pancreas, pituitary and myocardium. See Chapter 11, *Metabolic Diseases*.

9.11 Wilson's disease

This is an autosomal recessive disorder of copper metabolism causing deposition in the liver, basal ganglia and cornea (Kayser–Fleischer ring). See Chapter 11, *Metabolic Diseases*.

9.12 Hepato-biliary tumours

There are a number of types of primary hepatic malignancy, all of which are rare. Secondary tumours, however, are common, typically metastasizing from the stomach, colon, breast and lung.

Treatment of metastatic tumours is usually not indicated as the disease process is far advanced, although chemotherapy may slow progression in selected patients.

Hepatocellular carcinoma

This is rare in the UK (1–2/100,000 population) but the incidence is increased 20–30 times in Africa, Asia and Japan.

Incidence is increased by:

● Hepatitis B (commonest cause worldwide) and hepatitis C virus
● Cirrhosis from any cause
● Aflatoxin — a carcinogen from the mould *Aspergillus flavus* which may contaminate food
● Long term oral contraceptive use.

Raised serum alpha-fetoprotein (AFP) may suggest the diagnosis, and in association with ultrasound, has been suggested as an appropriate annual screening for patients with cirrhosis.

Treatment	Prognosis
No treatment	Five-year survival <25%
Resection	Only 5–15% are suitable, with 20% operative mortality; five-year survival <30%
Transplant	Very few patients are suitable — they should have single tumours smaller than 5 cm with no vascular or metastatic spread; five-year survival 90%
Chemotherapy/ ethanol injection into tumour	Palliative with little survival benefit

Cholangiocarcinoma

This is an uncommon adenocarcinoma arising from the biliary epithelium.

Predisposing factors:

- Sclerosing cholangitis
- Choledochal cyst or other biliary tract abnormality
- Liver fluke infection
- Carolli's disease (dilation of the intrahepatic bile ducts predisposing to infection and stone formation).

Treatment	Prognosis
No treatment	Average survival 2 months
Resection	Less than 20% of patients are suitable; average survival approximately 3 years
Transplant	Very few patients are suitable but this gives the best prognosis

Carcinoma of the gall bladder

This adenocarcinoma occurs in the elderly but is uncommon. It has usually spread by the time of diagnosis.

Benign hepatic adenoma

The incidence of this is increased in patients who have been taking oral contraceptives for longer than 5 years and also with the use of anabolic steroids. It is usually asymptomatic but may rarely cause intraperitoneal bleeding.

Hepatic haemangioma

This is common, and is often an incidental finding on ultrasound. It is benign but may occasionally rupture.

Chapter 6
Genetics

CONTENTS

1. **Chromosomes**   189
    1.1   Common sex chromosome aneuploidies
    1.2   Common autosomal chromosome aneuploidies
    1.3   Microdeletion syndromes

2. **Mendelian inheritance**   193
    2.1   Autosomal dominant (AD) conditions
    2.2   Autosomal recessive (AR) conditions
    2.3   X-linked recessive (XLR) conditions
    2.4   X-linked dominant (XLD) conditions

3. **Molecular genetics**   196
    3.1   DNA (deoxyribonucleic acid)
    3.2   RNA (ribonucleic acid)
    3.3   Polymerase chain reaction (PCR)

4. **Trinucleotide repeat disorders**   196
    4.1   Fragile X syndrome

5. **Mitochondrial disorders**   197

6. **Genomic imprinting**   197

7. **Important genetic topics**   198
    7.1   Ambiguous genitalia
    7.2   Cystic fibrosis
    7.3   Neurofibromatosis (NF)
    7.4   Tuberose sclerosis (TS)
    7.5   Marfan's syndrome

Genetics

1. CHROMOSOMES

Within the nucleus of somatic cells there are 22 pairs of autosomes and one pair of sex chromosomes. Normal male and female karyotypes are 46,XY and 46,XX respectively. The presence of too many or too few chromosomes is called **aneuploidy**.

Chromosomes are divided by the centromere into a short 'p' arm ('petit') and long 'q' arm. **Acrocentric** chromosomes (13, 14, 15, 21, 22) have the centromere at one end.

Lyonization is the process whereby in a cell containing more than one X chromosome, only one is active. Selection of the active X is usually random and each inactivated X chromosome can be seen as a Barr body on microscopy.

Mitosis occurs in somatic cells and results in two diploid daughter cells with nuclear chromosomes that are genetically identical both to each other and the original parent cell.

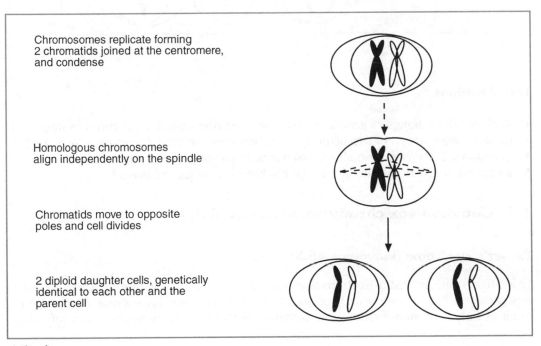

Chromosomes replicate forming 2 chromatids joined at the centromere, and condense

Homologous chromosomes align independently on the spindle

Chromatids move to opposite poles and cell divides

2 diploid daughter cells, genetically identical to each other and the parent cell

Mitosis

Meiosis occurs in the germ cells of the gonads and is also known as 'reduction division' because it results in four **haploid** daughter cells, each containing just one member (homologue) of each chromosome pair and all genetically different. Meiosis involves two divisions (**meiosis I and II**). The reduction in chromosome number occurs during meiosis I and is preceded by exchange of chromosome segments between homologous chromosomes called **crossing over**. In males the onset of meiosis and spermatogenesis is at puberty. In females, replication of the chromosomes and crossing over begins in fetal life but the oocytes remain suspended prior to the first cell division until just before ovulation.

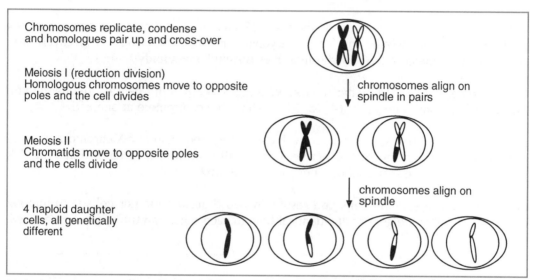

Chromosomes replicate, condense and homologues pair up and cross-over

Meiosis I (reduction division) Homologous chromosomes move to opposite poles and the cell divides

chromosomes align on spindle in pairs

Meiosis II Chromatids move to opposite poles and the cells divide

chromosomes align on spindle

4 haploid daughter cells, all genetically different

Meiosis

Translocations

- **Reciprocal:** exchange of genetic material between non-homologous chromosomes
- **Robertsonian:** fusion of two acrocentric chromosomes at their centromeres (e.g. 14;21)
- **Unbalanced:** if chromosomal material has been lost or gained overall
- **Balanced:** if no chromosomal material has been lost or gained overall.

1.1 Common sex chromosome aneuploidies

Turner's syndrome (karyotype 45,X)

This affects one in 2500 liveborn females but it is a frequent finding amongst early miscarriages. Patients are usually of normal intelligence. They have streak ovaries which result in failure of menstruation, low oestrogen with high gonadotrophins and infertility.

Normal secondary sexual characteristics may develop spontaneously or be induced with oestrogens. Short stature throughout childhood with failure of the pubertal growth spurt is typical. Final height can be increased by early treatment with growth hormone. Other features may include the following.

Features of Turner's syndrome

- Webbed or short neck
- Shield chest with widely spaced nipples
- Renal abnormalities (e.g. horseshoe kidney, duplicated ureters, renal aplasia) in approximately 1/3
- Low hairline
- Cubitus valgus (wide carrying angle)
- Cardiovascular abnormalities, particularly aortic coarctation in 10–15%
- Non-pitting lymphoedema in approximately 1/3

Triple X syndrome (karyotype 47,XXX)

These patients show little phenotypic abnormality but tend to be of tall stature. Intelligence is typically reduced compared with siblings but usually falls within normal or low–normal limits. Mild developmental and behavioural difficulties are more common. Fertility is normal but the incidence of early menopause is increased.

Klinefelter's syndrome (karyotype 47,XXY)

This affects 1 in 600 newborn males. Phenotypic abnormalities are rare prepubertally other than a tendency to tall stature. At puberty, spontaneous expression of secondary sexual characteristics is variable but poor growth of facial and body hair is common. The testes are small in association with azoospermia, testosterone production around 50% of normal and raised gonadotrophins. Gynaecomastia occurs in 30% and there is an increased risk of male breast cancer. Female distribution of fat and hair and a high-pitched voice may occur but are not typical. Intelligence is generally reduced compared with siblings but usually falls within normal or low–normal limits. Mild developmental delay (especially speech) and behavioural problems are more common.

47,XYY males

These males are phenotypically normal but tend to be tall. Intelligence is usually within normal limits but there is an increased incidence of behavioural abnormalities.

1.2 Common autosomal chromosome aneuploidies

Down's syndrome (trisomy 21)

Down's syndrome affects one in 700 live births overall and is usually secondary to meiotic non-disjunction during oogenesis, which is more common with increasing maternal age. Around 5% of patients have an underlying Robertsonian translocation, most commonly between chromosomes 14 and 21. Around 3% have detectable **mosaicism** (a mixture of trisomy 21 and karyotypically normal cells) usually resulting in a milder phenotype. Phenotypic features include the following.

Phenotypic features of Down's syndrome

- Brachycephaly
- Protruding tongue
- Single palmar crease, 5th finger clinodactyly, wide sandal gaps between 1st and 2nd toes

- Upslanting palpebral fissures, epicanthic folds, Brushfield spots on the iris
- Hypotonia and moderate mental retardation

The following are more common in patients with Down's syndrome.

Common features of Down's syndrome

- Cardiovascular malformations in 40%, particularly atrioventricular septal defects (AVSD)
- Haematological abnormalities, particularly acute lymphoblastic leukaemia (ALL), acute myeloblastic leukaemia (AML) and transient leukaemias

- Gastrointestinal abnormalities in 6%, particularly duodenal atresia and Hirschprung's disease
- Hypothyroidism
- Cataracts in 3%
- Alzheimer's disease in the majority by 40 years of age

Edwards' syndrome (trisomy 18 [eighteen])

This typically causes intrauterine growth retardation, a characteristic facies, prominent occiput, overlapping fingers (2nd and 5th overlap 3rd and 4th), rockerbottom feet (vertical talus) and short dorsiflexed great toes. Malformations, particularly congenital heart disease, diaphragmatic hernias, renal abnormalities and dislocated hips, are more common. Survival beyond early infancy is rare but associated with profound mental handicap.

Patau syndrome (trisomy 13)

Affected infants usually have multiple malformations, including holoprosencephaly and other CNS abnormalities, scalp defects, microphthalmia, cleft lip and palate, post-axial polydactyly, rockerbottom feet, renal abnormalities and congenital heart disease. Survival beyond early infancy is rare and associated with profound mental handicap.

1.3 Microdeletion syndromes

These are caused by chromosomal deletions that are too small to be seen microscopically but involve two or more adjacent genes. They can be detected using specific fluorescent probes (fluorescent *in situ* hybridization (**FISH**)).

Examples of microdeletion syndromes.

- **Di George syndrome** (parathyroid gland hypoplasia with hypocalcaemia, thymus hypoplasia with T-lymphocyte deficiency, congenital cardiac malformations particularly interrupted aortic arch and truncus arteriosus, cleft palate, learning disability) due to microdeletions at 22q11
- **William's syndrome** (supravalvular aortic stenosis, hypercalcaemia, stellate irides, mental retardation, cocktail party manner) due to microdeletions involving the elastin gene on chromosome 7.

2. MENDELIAN INHERITANCE

2.1 Autosomal dominant (AD) conditions

These result from mutation of one copy (allele) of a gene carried on an autosome. All offspring of an affected person have a 50% chance of inheriting the mutation. Within a family the severity may vary (**variable expression**) and known mutation carriers may appear clinically normal (**reduced penetrance**). Some conditions, such as achondroplasia and neurofibromatosis (type 1), frequently begin *de novo* through new mutations arising in the egg or (more commonly) in the sperm.

Examples of autosomal dominant (AD) conditions*

Achondroplasia
Ehlers–Danlos syndrome (most)
Facioscapulohumeral dystrophy
Familial adenomatous polyposis coli
Familial hypercholesterolaemia
Gilbert's syndrome
Huntington's chorea

Marfan's syndrome
Neurofibromatosis types 1 and 2
Porphyrias (except congenital
  erythropoietic which is autosomal
  recessive)
Tuberose sclerosis
von Willebrand's disease

*Conditions prefixed 'hereditary' or 'familial' are usually autosomal dominant.

2.2 Autosomal recessive (AR) conditions

These result from mutations in both copies (alleles) of an autosomal gene. Where both parents are carriers each of their offspring has a one in four (25%) risk of being affected, and a 50% chance of being a carrier.

Examples of autosomal recessive (AR) conditions

Alkaptonuria
Ataxia telangiectasia
β-thalassaemia
Congenital adrenal hyperplasia
Crigler–Najjar (severe form)
Cystic fibrosis
Dubin–Johnson
Fanconi anaemia
Galactosaemia
Glucose-6-phosphatase deficiency
  (von Gierkes)*
Glycogen storage diseases

Homocystinuria
Haemochromatosis
Mucopolysaccharidoses
  (all except Hunter's syndrome)
Oculocutaneous albinism
Phenylketonuria
Rotor (usually)
Sickle-cell anaemia
Spinal muscular atrophy
Wilson's disease
Xeroderma pigmentosa

*Do not confuse with glucose-6-phosphate dehydrogenase deficiency (favism) which is X-linked recessive.

Most metabolic disorders are autosomal recessive — remember the exceptions.

2.3 X-linked recessive (XLR) conditions

These result from a mutation in a gene carried on the X chromosome and affect males because they have just one gene copy. Females are usually unaffected but may have mild manifestations as a result of lyonization. This form of inheritance is characterized by the following.

- No male-to-male transmission (an affected father passes his Y chromosome to all his sons)
- All daughters of an affected male are carriers (an affected father passes his X chromosome to all his daughters)
- Sons of a female carrier have a 50% chance of being affected and daughters have a 50% chance of being carriers.

Examples of X-linked recessive (XLR) conditions

Alport's syndrome (usually)	Hunter's syndrome (MPS II)
Becker muscular dystrophy	Lesch–Nyhan syndrome
Duchenne muscular dystrophy	Ocular albinism
Fabry's disease	Red–green colour blindness
Fragile X syndrome	Testicular feminization syndrome
Glucose-6-phosphate dehydrogenase deficiency (favism)	Wiskott–Aldrich syndrome
Haemophilias A and B (Christmas disease)	

2.4 X-linked dominant (XLD) conditions

These are caused by a mutation in one copy of a gene on the X chromosome but both male and female mutation carriers are affected. Because of lyonization, females are usually more mildly affected and these disorders are frequently lethal in males, for the reasons outlined above.

- There is no male-to-male transmission
- All daughters of an affected male are affected
- All offspring of an affected female have a 50% chance of being affected.

Examples of X-linked dominant (XLD) conditions include vitamin D-resistant rickets and incontinentia pigmenti.

3. MOLECULAR GENETICS

3.1 DNA (deoxyribonucleic acid)

DNA is a **double-stranded** molecule composed of purine (adenine + guanine) and pyrimidine (cytosine and thymine) bases linked by a backbone of covalently bonded **deoxyribose sugar** phosphate residues. The two anti-parallel strands are held together by hydrogen bonds which can be disrupted by heating and reform on cooling.

- **Adenine (A)** pairs with **thymine (T)** by two hydrogen bonds
- **Guanine (G)** pairs with **cytosine (C)** by three hydrogen bonds.

3.2 RNA (ribonucleic acid)

DNA is **transcribed** in the nucleus into messenger RNA (mRNA) which is **translated** by ribosomes in the cytoplasm into a polypeptide chain. RNA differs from DNA in that:

- It is **single-stranded**
- Thymine is replaced by **uracil**
- The sugar backbone is **ribose.**

3.3 Polymerase chain reaction (PCR)

This is a widely used method for generating large amounts of DNA from very small samples. PCR can be adapted for use with RNA providing the RNA is first converted to DNA. For a more detailed account see Chapter 12, *Molecular Medicine.*

4. TRINUCLEOTIDE REPEAT DISORDERS

(See also Chapter 12, *Molecular Medicine.*) These conditions are associated with genes containing stretches of repeating units of three nucleotides and include the following.

Trinucleotide repeat disorders

- Fragile X syndrome XLR
- Huntington's chorea AD
- Spinocerebellar ataxia AD

- Myotonic dystrophy AD
- Freidreich's ataxia AR

In normal individuals the number of repeats varies slightly but remains below a defined threshold. Affected patients have an increased number of repeats, called an **expansion**, above the disease-causing threshold. The expansions may be unstable and enlarge further in successive generations causing increased disease severity ('**anticipation**') and earlier onset, e.g. **myotonic dystrophy**, particularly congenital myotonic dystrophy following transmission by an affected mother.

4.1 Fragile X syndrome

This causes mental retardation, macro-orchidism and seizures and is often associated with a cytogenetically visible constriction on the X chromosome. The inheritance is X-linked but complex. Among controls there are between six and 55 stably inherited trinucleotide repeats in the FMR1 gene. People with between 55 and 230 repeats are said to be premutation carriers but are unaffected. During oogenesis in female premutation carriers the triplet repeat is unstable and may expand into the disease causing a range (230 to >1000 repeats) known as a **full mutation**. All males and around 50% of females with the full mutation are affected.

5. MITOCHONDRIAL DISORDERS

(See also Chapter 12, *Molecular Medicine*.) Mitochondria are **exclusively maternally inherited**, deriving from those present in the cytoplasm of the ovum. They contain copies of their own **circular 16.5 kilobase chromosome** carrying genes for several respiratory chain enzyme subunits and transfer RNAs. Mitochondrial genes differ from nuclear genes in having no introns and using some different amino-acid codons. Within a tissue or even a cell there may be a mixed population of normal and abnormal mitochondria known as **heteroplasmy**. Different proportions of abnormal mitochondria may be required to cause disease in different tissues, known as a **threshold effect**. Disorders caused by mitochondrial gene mutations include the following:

- **MELAS** (**m**itochondrial **e**ncephalopathy, **l**actic **a**cidosis, **s**troke-like episodes)
- **MERRF** (**m**yoclonic **e**pilepsy, **r**agged **r**ed **f**ibres)
- Mitochondrially inherited diabetes mellitus and deafness
- Leber's hereditary optic neuropathy (NB other factors also contribute).

6. GENOMIC IMPRINTING

For most genes both copies are expressed but for some genes, either the maternally or paternally derived copy is preferentially used, a phenomenon known as genomic imprinting. The best examples are the Prader–Willi and Angelman syndromes, both caused by either cytogenetic deletions of the same region of chromosome 15q or by **uniparental disomy** of chromosome 15 (where both copies of chromosome 15 are derived from one parent with no copy of chromosome 15 from the other parent).

Prader–Willi	**Angelman**
• **Clinical**	
Neonatal hypotonia and poor feeding	'Happy puppet', unprovoked laughter/clapping
Moderate mental handicap	Microcephaly, severe mental handicap
Hyperphagia + obesity in later childhood	Ataxia, broad-based gait
Small genitalia	Seizures, characteristic EEG
• **Genetics**	
70% deletion on **p**aternal chromosome 15	80% deletion on maternal chromosome 15
30% maternal uniparental disomy 15 (i.e. no paternal contribution)	2–3% paternal uniparental disomy 15 (i.e. no maternal contribution) remainder due to subtle mutations

7. IMPORTANT GENETIC TOPICS

This section includes short notes on conditions that form popular exam topics. See also homocystinuria (Chapter 11, *Metabolic Diseases*) and muscular dystrophy (chapters 12, *Molecular Medicine*, and 14, *Neurology*).

7.1 Ambiguous genitalia

(See also 'intersex' in Chapter 4, *Endocrinology*.)

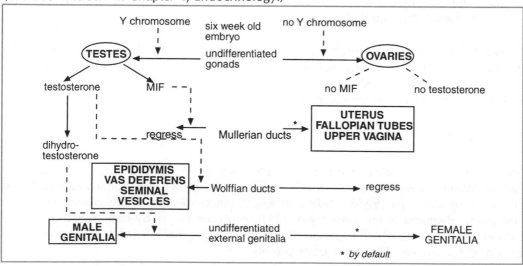

Outline of normal development of the reproductive tract and external genitalia.

198

The six-week embryo has undifferentiated gonads, Mullerian ducts (capable of developing into the uterus, Fallopian tubes and upper vagina), Wolffian ducts (capable of forming the epididymis, vas deferens and seminal vesicles) and undifferentiated external genitalia.

In the presence of a Y chromosome the gonads become testes which produce testosterone and Mullerian inhibiting factor (MIF). Testosterone causes the Wolffian ducts to persist and differentiate and, after conversion to dihydrotestosterone (by 5 α-reductase), masculinization of the external genitalia. MIF causes the Mullerian ducts to regress.

In the absence of a Y chromosome the gonads become ovaries which secrete neither testosterone nor MIF. In the absence of testosterone the Wolffian ducts regress and the external genitalia feminize. In the absence of MIF, the Mullerian ducts persist and differentiate.

The causes of **ambiguous genitalia** divide broadly into those resulting in undermasculinization of a male fetus, those causing masculinization of a female fetus, and those resulting from mosaicism for a cell line containing a Y chromosome and another which does not. They are summarized in the diagram below.

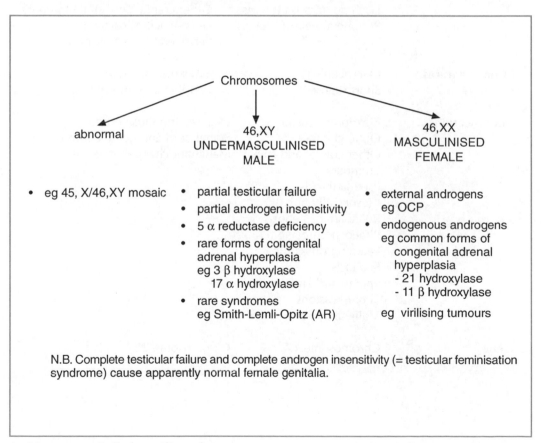

Chromosomes

abnormal

46,XY
UNDERMASCULINISED
MALE

46,XX
MASCULINISED
FEMALE

- eg 45, X/46,XY mosaic

- partial testicular failure
- partial androgen insensitivity
- 5 α reductase deficiency
- rare forms of congenital adrenal hyperplasia eg 3 β hydroxylase 17 α hydroxylase
- rare syndromes eg Smith-Lemli-Opitz (AR)

- external androgens eg OCP
- endogenous androgens eg common forms of congenital adrenal hyperplasia - 21 hydroxylase - 11 β hydroxylase

eg virilising tumours

N.B. Complete testicular failure and complete androgen insensitivity (= testicular feminisation syndrome) cause apparently normal female genitalia.

Ambiguous genitalia — outline of causes

7.2 Cystic fibrosis

This results from mutations in the **CFTR** (cystic fibrosis transmembrane regulator) gene and the **ΔF508** mutation (deletion of three nucleotides coding for a phenylalanine residue) accounts for 75% of mutations in Caucasians. Around 15% of cystic fibrosis mutations cannot be detected so that molecular testing cannot exclude a diagnosis of cystic fibrosis.

7.3 Neurofibromatosis (NF)

There are two forms of NF which are clinically and genetically distinct.

	NF1	NF2
Major features	≥ 6 café-au-lait patches (CALs) Axillary/inguinal freckling Lisch nodules on the iris Peripheral neurofibromas	Bilateral Acoustic neuromas (vestibular schwannomas) Other cranial and spinal tumours Lens opacities/cataracts Peripheral schwannomas
Minor features	Macrocephaly Short stature	CALs (usually < 6) Peripheral neurofibromas
Complications	Plexiform neuromas Optic glioma (2%) Other cranial and spinal tumours Pseudarthrosis (especially tibial) Renal artery stenosis Phaeochromocytoma Learning difficulties Scoliosis Spinal cord and nerve compressions Malignant change/sarcomas	Deafness/tinnitus/vertigo Spinal cord and nerve compressions Malignant change/sarcomas
Gene	Chromosome 17	Chromosome 22

7.4 Tuberose sclerosis (TS)

There are at least two separate genes that cause TS, on chromosomes 9 and 16.

Clinical features of tuberose sclerosis

- **Skin/nails**
  Ash-leaf macules
  Shagreen patches
    (especially over the lumbosacral
    area)
  Adenoma sebaceum (facial area)
  Subungual/periungual fibromas

- **Kidneys**
  Renal cysts

- **Neuro-imaging**
  Intracranial calcification (periventricular)
  Subependymal nodules

- **Eyes**
  Retinal hamartomas

- **Heart**
  Cardiac rhabdomyomas, detectable
    antenatally, usually regressing
    during childhood

- **Neurological**
  Seizures
  Mental handicap

7.5 Marfan's syndrome

This results from mutations in the fibrillin gene on chromosome 15. Intelligence is usually normal.

Clinical features of Marfan's syndrome

- **Musculoskeletal**
  Tall stature with disproportionately
    long limbs (dolichostenomelia)
  Arachnodactyly
  Pectus carinatum or excavatum
  Scoliosis
  High, narrow arched palate
  Joint laxity
  Pes planus

- **Heart**
  Aortic root dilatation and dissection

- **Eyes**
  Lens dislocation (typically up)
  Myopia

- **Skin**
  Striae

Chapter 7
Genito-urinary Medicine and AIDS

CONTENTS

1. **Sexually transmitted disease**   205
    1.1   Gonorrhoea
    1.2   Syphilis
    1.3   *Chlamydia* infections

2. **Basic epidemiology and virology of HIV/AIDS**   206
    2.1   Epidemiology
    2.2   The virus
    2.3   Seroconversion and the HIV antibody test
    2.4   Centre for Disease Control (CDC) classification of HIV/AIDS

3. **Respiratory diseases associated with HIV/AIDS**   209
    3.1   *Pneumocystis carinii* pneumonia (PCP)
    3.2   Pulmonary tuberculosis
    3.3   Other respiratory diseases

4. **Gastrointestinal diseases in patients with HIV/AIDS**   211
    4.1   Oral/oesophageal conditions
    4.2   Diarrhoea/abdominal pain
    4.3   Biliary and pancreatic disease
    4.4   Ano-rectal conditions

5. **HIV/AIDS-related neurological disorders**   213
    5.1   Direct neurotropic effects of HIV
    5.2   Neurological infections
    5.3   Ophthalmic disorders

6. **Malignant disease in patients with HIV/AIDS**   216
    6.1   Kaposi's sarcoma

7. **HIV/AIDS-related skin disease**   216

8. **Drug therapies in HIV/AIDS patients**   **218**
    8.1   Specific therapy of common opportunistic infections
    8.2   Anti-retroviral therapy

Genito-urinary Medicine and AIDS

1. SEXUALLY TRANSMITTED DISEASE

The incidence of sexually transmitted disease (STD) has increased dramatically over the past 40 years both globally and in the UK. As well as the more 'traditional' diseases such as syphilis and gonorrhoea, a wider spectrum of diseases transmitted by sexual contact has increasingly been recognized (e.g. oro–anal transmission of enteric infections such as giardiasis and hepatitis A). HIV infection arrived on the scene in the late 1970s.

1.1 Gonorrhoea

Transmission is primarily sexual; there is a large asymptomatic reservoir. *Neisseria gonorrhoea* is a capsulated organism, and it therefore resists phagocytosis. Benzyl penicillin is the most appropriate treatment unless resistance is present at which stage either tetracycline or ceftriaxone can be used.

Disseminated (bacteraemic) infection is ten times more common in women. Responsible strains are nearly always highly susceptible to penicillin. Pharyngeal infection is often asymptomatic. Ophthalmia neonatorum is treated with 1% silver nitrate, or tetracycline or erythromycin eye drops.

1.2 Syphilis

Transmission is primarily sexual, congenital or, rarely, by blood transfusion. Penicillin is the drug of choice, or alternatively tetracycline. **Concurrent HIV infection increases the risk of neurosyphilis**, even if the primary syphilitic infection is correctly treated. All *in vitro* attempts to culture *Treponema pallidum* have been unsuccessful to date. Diagnosis is by serology or by dark ground microscopy of **fresh** material from chancres or secondary syphilitic rash.

In the secondary and tertiary stages a positive VDRL indicates active disease; fluorescent treponemal antigen (FTA) and *Treponema pallidum* immobilization (TPI) are more specific tests, but these remain positive after successful treatment.

1.3 Chlamydia infections

Non-gonococcal urethritis (NGU) due to *Chlamydia trachomatis* is the most common cause of STD in the Western world. Serovars D to K are responsible. It is also a major cause of pelvic inflammatory disease in women, prostatitis/epididymitis in men. Neonatal conjunctivitis and diffuse interstitial pneumonia are both complications of serovars D to K; infection is acquired by passage through an infected birth canal.

- **Trachoma** (corneal scarring) is caused by serovars A, B and C.
- **Lymphogranuloma venereum (LGV)** is due to serovars L1, L2 and L3.

Both pneumonia and conjunctivitis need systemic treatment with erythromycin. Tetracycline is the drug of choice for adults.

2. BASIC EPIDEMIOLOGY AND VIROLOGY OF HIV/AIDS

2.1 Epidemiology

HIV/AIDS is a global disease. Of the estimated 30 million people infected with HIV, 19 million are from sub-Saharan Africa.

In the UK the cumulative incidence of HIV (1998) is approximately 30,000, and of AIDS 15,000.

The following are the estimated routes of transmission in the current UK AIDS population:

- Sexual intercourse between men (55%)
- Sexual intercourse between men and women (30%)
- Injecting drug abuse (7%)
- Blood and blood products (5%).

Risk factors facilitating sexual transmission include:

- Seroconversion and advancing stage of disease
- Concurrent ulcerative disease of the genitalia.

Materno–fetal transmission occurs in 12–19% of pregnancies in patients with HIV/AIDS.

The risk of transmission from mother to baby can be reduced by:

- Delivery by Caesarean section
- Avoidance of breast feeding
- Anti-retroviral therapy.

2.2 The virus

Human retrovirus is a member of the lentivirus family. It contains RNA which is transcribed to DNA via a reverse transcriptase enzyme. The main target sites of action of anti-retroviral drugs are reverse transcriptases and proteases. There are two types of human immunodeficiency virus:

- **HIV-1**: (previously known as HTLV III) is prevalent world-wide
- **HIV-2**: is common in West Africa.

Pathogenesis

The HIV virus has tropism for the following CD4 cells:

- T-helper lymphocytes
- B-lymphocytes
- Macrophages
- CNS cells.

It causes progressive immune dysfunction, characterized by CD4 cell depletion. Impairment of immunity is primarily cell-mediated, but as the disease progresses there is general immune dysregulation.

The following laboratory markers are associated with disease progression:

- Decreased CD4 lymphocyte count (normal $> 500/mm^3$ or $0.5 \times 10^9/l$). In the USA, a CD4 count of $< 200/mm^3$ is regarded as AIDS, irrespective of the presence of clinical disease
- Polyclonal gammopathy
- Increased $\beta2$ microglobulin
- Increased neopterin (an inflammatory marker, indicative of cytokine production).

2.3 Seroconversion and the HIV antibody test

After inoculation the window or seroconversion period can be up to 3 months; HIV antibody may not be detectable during this time. The HIV P4 antigen may be detectable during seroconversion. Current antibody tests detect HIV-1 and HIV-2. Approximately one-third of patients develop clinical seroconversion illnesses.

Seroconversion illnesses

- Fever
- Malaise
- Diarrhoea
- Meningo-encephalitis

- Rash
- Sore throat
- Lymphadenopathy
- Arthralgia

2.4 Centre for Disease Control (CDC) classification of HIV/AIDS

The CDC classification is adopted in the USA and most developed countries. HIV infection is not synonymous with AIDS; the latter is a stage of severe immunodeficiency characterized by opportunistic infections and/or tumour.

CDC classification of HIV/AIDS

- **Stage 1**
  Primary seroconversion illness

- **Stage 2**
  Asymptomatic

- **Stage 3**
  Persistent generalized
  lymphadenopathy

- **Stage 4a**
  AIDS-related complex
  (i.e. advanced HIV disease,
  but having none of the features
  of stages 4b–d)

- **Stages 4b–d**
  AIDS: patient may have
  opportunistic infection or tumours,
  which are termed 'AIDS indicator'
  illnesses

3. RESPIRATORY DISEASES ASSOCIATED WITH HIV/AIDS

3.1 *Pneumocystis carinii* pneumonia (PCP)

Pneumonia is the most common opportunistic infection and clinical presentation of AIDS. *Pneumocystis carinii* pneumonia (PCP) constitutes 40% of all AIDS-defining illness.

The symptoms of PCP include dry cough, dyspnoea, fever and malaise. There are remarkably few abnormal signs on chest examination.

Investigations for PCP

- **Chest X-ray**: abnormal in 90% of subjects. Typical appearance — bilateral mid- and lower-zone shadowing and interstitial shadowing. Atypical chest X-ray findings are found in 10% of PCP cases and include: cavitation, upper zone opacities, pneumothorax or unilateral consolidation. Effusions are rare.
- **Pulse oximetry**: hypoxia in 90% of PCP patients; pO_2 falls with exercise.
- **Identification of pneumocystis cysts**.

- Samples obtained by inducing sputum or from broncho-alveolar lavage (BAL) can be stained with silver or immunofluorescent antibody. Sensitivity for detection of cysts is 90%. If BAL is negative, lung biopsy should be performed.

Poor prognostic features in PCP include respiratory failure, and disease of an advanced stage.

- Treatment is with high-dose co-trimoxazole or intravenous pentamidine or atovaquone; there is a high incidence of intolerance to co-trimoxazole with nausea, vomiting, rash, leucopenia and thrombocytopenia.
- Steroids have been shown to improve prognosis in those with pO_2 <8 kPa (60 mmHg).

There is a 50% risk of recurrence within 12 months. PCP prophylaxis is always given to patients with a CD4 count <200/mm³ and to those who have already had an episode of PCP.

3.2 Pulmonary tuberculosis

Between 2.5 and 5% of AIDS patients are co-infected with Mycobacterium tuberculosis. Extra-pulmonary disease is more common in these patients, and there is a major problem with drug resistance, which is eight times more common than in the general population. Drug resistance can be identified rapidly by rifampicin probe PCR.

Other atypical features include:

- Lymphatic involvement
- Atypical appearance on chest X-ray
- Occurs at any stage of HIV disease, and at any level of CD4 count
- Multi-drug resistance
- Atypical mycobacterial infections — usually *Mycobacterium avium intracellulare*.

If suspected, the diagnosis should be obtained with multiple sputum examination for acid-fast bacilli.

3.3 Other respiratory diseases in HIV/AIDS

Other causes of respiratory disease in HIV/AIDS

- **Viral**
  Cytomegalovirus (CMV)
  Herpes simplex
  Epstein–Barr virus
  Adenovirus
  Influenza

- **Fungal**
  Candida
  Histoplasmosis
  Cryptococcus
  Nocardia

- **Bacterial**
  Streptococcus pneumoniae
  Staphylococcus aureus
  Mycobacterium tuberculosis
  Mycobacterium avium intracellulare

- **Protozoal**
  Toxoplasma

- **Tumour**
  Kaposi's sarcoma (see section 6.1)
  Non-Hodgkin's lymphoma

Radiological appearance of other infections

- **Cavitation**: *M. tuberculosis, Nocardia, S. aureus*
- **Consolidation**: *Streptococcus pneumoniae*, Toxoplasma
- **Effusion**: S. aureus (Kaposi's sarcoma may also cause effusion).

4. GASTROINTESTINAL DISEASES IN PATIENTS WITH HIV/AIDS

There are four main presentations:

- Oral/oesophageal disease
- Abdominal pain/diarrhoea
- Biliary/pancreatic disease
- Ano-rectal symptoms.

4.1 Oral/oesophageal conditions

Ninety per cent of patients will develop an oral/oesophageal condition.

- Oral and oesophageal candidiasis
- Periodontal disease (including gingivitis)
- Herpes simplex
- Lymphoma

- Oral hairy leukoplakia
- Aphthous ulcers
- Kaposi's sarcoma
- Cytomegalovirus

These conditions may be asymptomatic, or patients may have dysphagia or odynophagia.

4.2 Diarrhoea/abdominal pain

Weight loss and malnutrition is very common (90%) in patients with any stage of HIV infection. In Europe, 50% of HIV patients suffer diarrhoea. Specific enteropathogens can be isolated in 60% of cases.

Enteropathogens found in HIV

- **Bacteria**
  Salmonella
  Campylobacter
  Shigella

- **Protozoal**
  Giardia lamblia

- **Viral**
  Cytomegalovirus

- **Opportunistic organisms**
  Bacterial
  Atypical mycobacteria (*M. avium intracellulare* with CD4 < 100/mm^3)

  Protozoal
  Isospora belli
  Cryptosporidia
  (intracellular protozoan)
  Microsporidia

Clinical presentation can be with watery diffuse diarrhoea as exemplified by *Cryptospoiridium*, or abdominal pain and bloody diarrhoea (e.g. cytomegalovirus procto-colitis).

- **Cryptosporidiosis**: the cause of 15% of HIV-associated diarrhoeas. It is a coccidian parasite which invades the gastrointestinal tract.
- **Salmonella**: much more frequent in HIV-infected patients than in the general population. More likely to cause bacteraemia and recurrence is common.

The investigation of infective diarrhoea includes the following:

- Identification of organisms in stool samples: microscopy and culture for pathogens, ovae and parasites.
- If stool specimen negative, stain with Ziehl–Neelsen for *Cryptosporidium*.
- Sigmoidoscopy/colonoscopy with biopsy: with culture of the specimen for viruses, mycobacteria, bacteriology and mycology. Histological appearances are often important.

Gastrointestinal tumours

These may also cause abdominal pain and diarrhoea.

- Kaposi's sarcoma
- Intra-abdominal lymphoma (often aggressive non-Hodgkin's B cell lymphoma).

4.3 Biliary and pancreatic disease

The two most common presentations are **cholangiopathy** and **pancreatitis**.

- **Cholangiopathy**: due to *Cryptosporidium*, cytomegalovirus, or *Microsporidium*
- **Pancreatitis**: this can be induced by drugs used in HIV treatment (e.g. DDI (didanosine), or DDC (zalcitabine) which are both reverse transcriptase inhibitors), or by the biliary organisms listed above.

4.4 Ano-rectal conditions

These usually present with proctitis and the following.

• **Symptoms**	• **Causative organisms**
Anal discharge	Herpes simplex
Tenesmus	Gonorrhoea
Pruritus ani	Non-specific/*Chlamydia*
Rectal bleeding	Wart virus
Diarrhoea	Syphilis

5. HIV/AIDS-RELATED NEUROLOGICAL DISORDERS

Neurological disease is the first presentation of AIDS in 10% of HIV patients. An acute self-limiting lymphocytic meningitis may occur at the time of seroconversion. Later, chronic neurological syndromes or opportunistic infections will occur in 75% of patients with established AIDS (or advanced HIV disease), i.e. neurological disease is usually a late feature, occurring after other AIDS-defining illnesses such as PCP. The most common cause is the neurotropic effect of the virus itself.

Clinical presentation may be:

- **Focal**: hemiparesis, fits
- **Generalized**: drowsiness, confusion, behavioural change
- **Asymptomatic**: in early HIV disease.

Patients may also develop proximal myopathy, or drug-induced (e.g. DDI) neuropathy and myopathy.

5.1 Direct neurotropic effects of HIV

These include:

- AIDS dementia complex (see below)
- Vacuolar myelopathy
- Neuropathy (see below).

Neurotropic disorders are diagnosed with the help of:

- **CSF analysis**: raised protein, mild pleocytosis
- **CT brain scan**: cerebral atrophy
- **Nerve conduction studies**: distal symmetric sensory neuropathy.

AIDS dementia is the most frequent neurological condition of HIV infection, and is directly caused by the virus. Impairment of concentration and memory leads to progressive decline in widespread cognitive function. Occasionally psychiatric symptoms may be prominent. The EEG shows generalized slowing with no specific features, and imaging demonstrates cortical atrophy.

Sensorimotor neuropathy associated with HIV/AIDS usually has mild sensory symptoms and signs. Less commonly, a mononeuritis multiplex or a chronic painful myelopathy may develop.

5.2 Neurological infections

Opportunistic infections of the CNS are common.

Causes of focal neurological disease

- *Toxoplasma gondii*
  Cerebral abscess

- *Mycobacterium tuberculosis*
  Meningitis
  Tuberculosis abscess

Causes of generalized neurological disease

- *Cryptococcus neoformans*
  Meningitis

- **Cytomegalovirus**
  Encephalitis/retinitis
  Peripheral neuropathy

- **Papovavirus**
  Progressive multifocal leukoencephalopathy PML
  `caused by JC virus`

Specific CNS infections

Cerebral toxoplasmosis is the most common CNS infection (90% of focal lesions) and occurs in 10% of AIDS patients. The organism is the crescentic trophozoite form of *Toxoplasma gondii*.

- **Investigations**: CT brain scan: solitary or multiple ring — enhancing lesions. *Toxoplasma* IgG serology is of little value, because of the high background prevalence.
- First-line anti-toxoplasma therapy is pyrimethamine given with sulphadiazine.
- **Prognosis**: 10% mortality with first episode; 25% of patients have residual neurological deficit.
- It is important to differentiate from primary CNS lymphoma causing a space-occupying lesion.

Cryptococcal meningitis is due to a 'budding' yeast, it occurs in 5–10% of AIDS patients. It presents with an encephalopathic illness, in which meningism may be absent.

- Cryptococcal antigen is present in blood and CSF in 90% of cases
- **India ink stain**: positive in 70% of CSF samples.

`Rx – amphotericin`
`flucytosine`

Neurosyphilis; the co-existence of HIV and syphilis can result in aggressive and atypical neurosyphilis. Previous syphilis infection may re-activate. The following features are recognized:

- Myelopathy
- Retinitis
- Meningitis
- Meningovascular.

Diagnosis: from syphilis serology (rising VDRL) and CSF, although serology may be modified by immune dysfunction.

Treatment: first-line therapy is i.m. procaine penicillin and probenecid for 15–21 days.

5.3   Ophthalmic disorders

AIDS may affect the lids or any layer of the eye.

Ophthalmic features of AIDS

- Molluscum contagiosum of lids

- Episcleritis and keratitis

- Uveitis

- Choroidal granulomas

- Cytomegalovirus retinitis

- Neuro-ophthalmic manifestations
  (e.g. cranial nerve palsies, optic
  neuritis, sequelae to CNS infection
  or space occupying lesion)

- Kaposi's sarcoma of the eyelids
  or conjunctiva

- Retinal changes
  Haemorrhages, cotton wool spots
  oedema and vascular sheathing

- Toxoplasmosis
  May develop acquired disease
  or reactivation of pre-existing
  disease

- Candida endophthalmitis

Retinitis is common and may be caused by HIV itself (non-specific microangiopathy which is present in 75% of HIV patients) or by CMV.

CMV retinitis usually occurs when the CD4 count is <50/mm³. This is the most common AIDS-related opportunistic infection in the eye (occurring in 25% of patients).

- **Symptoms**: blurred or loss of vision; floaters
- **Signs**: soft exudates, and retinal haemorrhages
- **Prognosis**: initially unilateral eye involvement; ultimately both eyes are affected.

6. MALIGNANT DISEASE IN PATIENTS WITH HIV/AIDS

Malignant disease is the most common in HIV infected patients. The relative frequency of the most common tumours is:

- Kaposi's sarcoma (83%)
- Non-Hodgkin's lymphoma (13%)
- Primary CNS lymphoma (4%).

6.1 Kaposi's sarcoma

This occurs in 10–15% of HIV patients as the first AIDS-defining presentation. The tumour is derived from vascular or lymphatic endothelial cells.

- **Clinical presentation**: cutaneous or systemic involvement. Purplish plaque/nodular lesions. The most common systems involved are the gastrointestinal tract (30% of patients with Kaposi's sarcoma of the skin also have gastrointestinal involvement); lymph nodes and the respiratory system. Patients with pulmonary Kaposi's have cough, dyspnoea and infiltrates, lymphadenopathy or effusion on chest X-ray.
- **Diagnosis**: clinical appearance (or biopsy in difficult cases).

7. HIV/AIDS-RELATED SKIN DISEASE

Dermatological diseases are extremely common in HIV patients (affecting 75%), especially in those who have AIDS. During the acute HIV illness, patients may develop an asymptomatic maculo-papular eruption affecting the face and trunk. During seroconversion, they may also develop marked seborrhoeic dermatitis. As the disease progresses to AIDS, the development of tumours and atypical infections is seen.

Dermatological associations of HIV disease

- **General dematoses**
  Psoriasis
  Eczema
  Seborrhoeic dermatitis
  Folliculitis

- **Fungal/yeast infections**
  *Pityrosporum ovale**
  Candidiasis*
  Cryptococcus neoformans
  Histoplasma capsulatum

- **Malignancy**
  Kaposi's sarcoma
  Lymphomas
  Cervical intra-epithelial neoplasia*
  Intra-oral squamous carcinoma

- **Viral infections**
  Herpes zoster/Herpes simplex
  Epstein–Barr virus
  Human papilloma virus*
  Cytomegalovirus
  Molluscum contagiosum*

- **Bacterial infections**
  Tuberculosis
  Syphilis
  Bacillary angiomatosis
  Staphylococcus aureus

Kaposi's sarcoma occurs in approximately 30% of patients diagnosed with AIDS. Features marked * are common in HIV patients.

Skin disease may also result from drug-induced reactions:

- **Co-trimoxazole**: generalized maculo-papular rash
- **Zidovudine**: nail pigmentation
- **Ciprofloxacin**: increases risk of severe skin reaction.

8. DRUG THERAPIES IN HIV/AIDS PATIENTS

8.1 Specific therapy of common opportunistic infections

Infection	First-line drugs	Side-effects
Pneumocystis pneumonia	Co-trimoxazole (oral or i.v.)	Rash, bone marrow toxicity, nausea and fever
	Pentamidine (i.v.)	Hyper/hypoglycaemia, pancreatitis, hypotension
Cerebral toxoplasmosis	Pyrimethamine Sulphadiazine	Bone marrow suppression, fever, gastrointestinal reactions
Cryptococcal meningitis	Amphotericin Flucytosine	Chills, fever, gastrointestinal reactions
CMV retinitis	Ganciclovir Foscarnet *Cidofovir*	Bone marrow suppression Renal impairment *Nephrotoxicity*

8.2 Anti-retroviral therapy

Anti-retroviral therapy is usually given as combination therapy with the following aims:

- Complete suppression of viral replication
- Obtaining a synergistic effect from combination therapy
- Reducing the risk of viral resistance emerging.

The commonly used anti-retroviral drugs are specific reverse transcriptase inhibitors and protease inhibitors.

- **Reverse transcriptase inhibitors**

  Zidovudine (AZT): may cause
  bone marrow suppression

  Lamivudine (ZTC)

  Didanosine (DDI): side-effects
  include peripheral neuropathy,
  pancreatitis

- **Protease inhibitors**

  Indinavir: side-effects are
  crystalluria, hepatic impairment

  Ritonavir

  Saquinavir

Routine monitoring of patients on anti-retroviral therapy includes:

- **Clinical assessment**: examination of mouth (for ulcers and candidiasis), skin, lymph nodes, chest, fundoscopy and weight
- CD4 lymphocyte count
- HIV viral RNA load.

Chapter 8
Haematology

CONTENTS

1. **Anaemias** 223
   1.1 Causes of macrocytosis
   1.2 Causes of microcytosis
   1.3 Red cell morphology
   1.4 Sickle cell disease
   1.5 Aplastic anaemia

2. **Iron metabolism** 228
   2.1 Assessment of iron status
   2.2 Sideroblastic anaemia

3. **Haemolysis** 230
   3.1 General features and causes of haemolysis
   3.2 The antiglobulin (Coombs') test
   3.3 Microangiopathic haemolytic anaemia (MAHA)

4. **Disorders of leucocytes** 232
   4.1 Leucocytosis
   4.2 Leucoerythroblastic change
   4.3 Neutropenia

5. **Haematological malignancies** 236
   5.1 Acute leukaemias
   5.2 Specific chromosome abnormalities in leukaemia/lymphoma
   5.3 The French–American–British (FAB) classification of acute leukaemia
   5.4 Chronic myeloid leukaemia (CML)
   5.5 Chronic lymphocytic leukaemia
   5.6 Non-Hodgkin's lymphomas (NHL)
   5.7 Myeloma
   5.8 Thrombocytosis (platelets $> 500 \times 10^9/l$)
   5.9 Uses of α-interferon in haematological malignancy
   5.10 Myelodysplasias (myelodyplastic syndromes — MDS)
   5.11 Bone marrow transplantation

6. **Coagulation**   246
    6.1   The coagulation mechanism and detection of factor deficiencies
    6.2   Haemophilia
    6.3   von Willebrand's disease
    6.4   Disseminated intravascular coagulation (DIC)
    6.5   Vitamin K dependent coagulation factors (II, VIII, IX, X)

7. **Thrombosis**   250
    7.1   Thrombosis and the pill
    7.2   Thrombophilia
    7.3   Therapeutic fibrinolysis
    7.4   Low molecular weight heparins (LMWH)

8. **The spleen**   254
    8.1   Causes of splenomegaly
    8.2   Splenectomy
    8.3   Causes of hyposplenism

9. **Blood transfusion**   256
    9.1   Transfusion-transmitted infection
    9.2   Blood filters
    9.3   Platelet support in marrow failure
    9.4   Indications for the transfusion of fresh frozen plasma

Haematology

1. ANAEMIAS

Anaemia is defined as a reduction in the concentration of circulating haemoglobin. The normal haemoglobin level varies with age and sex; neonates having a relative polycythaemia, infants having a lower haemoglobin level than adults, and women lower levels than men.

Common features of anaemias

- Pallor
- Decreased oxygen-carrying capacity (shortness of breath on exertion, tiredness)

- Increased cardiac output (palpitations, haemic ejection murmurs, cardiac failure in the elderly)

Examination of a bone marrow aspirate allows microscopic examination of the maturing erythroid cells. Normal maturation is termed **normoblastic erythropoiesis**. In conditions where there is interference with DNA synthesis, for example due to lack of vitamin B12 or folate, morphological abnormalities are seen. These include chromatin deficiency, premature haemoglobinization, giant metamyelocytes and other morphological features which, put together, are termed **megaloblastic erythropoiesis**.

Anaemia may be classified by its cause, for example iron deficiency anaemia, but often the cause is not known at the start of investigations so the usual method of classification uses the red cell size (MCV) to classify the anaemias:

- **Macrocytic**: anaemia with large red cells
- **Microcytic**: anaemia with small red cells
- **Normocytic**: anaemia with normal red cell size.

1.1 Causes of macrocytosis

Macrocytosis with a megaloblastic bone marrow

- **B12 deficiency**: pernicious anaemia most common

- **Folate deficiency**
- **Drugs**: methotrexate, hydroxyurea, cytosine, azathioprine.

Many other chronically administered cytotoxics also affect nucleic acid synthesis.

Macrocytosis with a normoblastic bone marrow

- **Reticulocytosis**: young cells are big cells
- **Liver disease**
- **Alcohol**
- **Myxoedema** (but check not the associated autoimmune disease pernicious anaemia!)
- **Pregnancy**: usually mild.

Liver disease is associated with anaemia because of interference with manufacture of the lipid envelope of red cells, associated with abnormal liver function tests and target cells on blood film. Alcohol has a direct toxic effect on the marrow and may cause liver disease or folate deficiency.

Macrocytosis associated with haematological diseases with their own special features

- **Myelodysplasia**: associated with cytopenias, monocytosis and dysplastic morphology (with blasts when transforming to AML)
- **Myeloma**: look for paraprotein, high ESR, leucoerythroblastic blood picture
- **Myeloproliferative disorders**: polycythaemia rubra vera, essential thrombocythaemia, myelofibrosis, CML
- **Aplastic anaemia**: look for pancytopenia with hypoplastic bone marrow.

1.2 Causes of microcytosis

- **Iron deficiency anaemia**: look for pencil cells, check Fe/TIBC or ferritin
- **Thalassaemia trait**: look for Mediterranean/Asian origin, check Hb A2 level (elevated)
- **Anaemia of chronic disease**: often normocytic, usually obvious disease
- **Sideroblastic anaemia**: the MCV in this disorder may be low, normal or high (see below)
- **Aluminium toxicity**: affecting some haemodialysis patients (now uncommon).

1.3 Red cell morphology

Sometimes morphological abnormalities of the red cells are sufficiently characteristic to suggest a diagnosis. These may be commented on in blood film reports. Abnormalities of red cell shape are termed **poikilocytosis**.

Type of poikilocytosis	Found in
Tear drops	Myelofibrosis
Helmet cells and fragmented cells	Microangiopathic haemolysis
Pencil cells	Iron deficiency (with hypochromic microcytes)
Elliptocytes	Hereditary elliptocytosis
Sickle cells	Sickle cell diseases (with target cells)

Other red cell morphological changes

- **Spherocytes**: found in any cause of haemolysis but particularly hereditary spherocytosis and autoimmune haemolytic anaemia.
- **Target cells**: found in liver disease, post-splenectomy, iron deficiency, thalassaemia and haemoglobinopathies.
- **Polychromasia**: young red cells, implies a high reticulocyte count if this is measured.
- **Dimorphic blood picture**: two populations of red cells. Easily spotted using modern blood counters which can provide a graph of cell size and/or haemoglobin content. It is caused by treatment of a haematinic deficiency (the new normal red cells contrast with the persisting cells characteristic of the anaemia); it may also be seen after transfusion of normal red cells to a patient with macro- or microcytosis and occasionally in combined deficiency when separated in time (e.g. patient with folate deficiency then becomes iron deficient). In primary sideroblastic anaemia the clone of abnormal erythroblasts produce abnormal red cells which contrast with those being produced by residual normal erythropoiesis.

1.4 Sickle cell disease

The sickle cell diseases consist of homozygous sickle cell anaemia (Hb SS), haemoglobin SC disease (Hb SC) and haemoglobin S beta thalassaemia trait (Hb S Thal). The clinical manifestations of sickle cell disease are mainly due to occlusion of small blood vessels by log-jams of sickled red cells. Precipitating causes may be hypoxaemia, infection and dehydration, but often no cause is identified for a vaso-occlusive crisis.

Clinical syndromes recognized in sickle cell disease

- **Simple pain crisis**: due to infarction of red bone marrow, a common problem in sickle cell disease. Deep-seated bone pain often requires opiate analgesia. Vigorous hydration may shorten the duration of the crisis. Hypoxaemia should be corrected and infection treated with antibiotics.

- **Sickle dactylitis**: infarction of the small bones of the hands or feet may be the earliest manifestation of sickle cell disease. Local pain and swelling result, with possible long term deformity.
- **Splenic sequestration crisis**: in adults the spleen has usually atrophied by repeated infarction but children may have enlarged spleens and sometimes the spleen may rapidly enlarge (over hours) and be painful. This is associated with massive retention of sickled red cells in the spleen resulting in severe anaemia with requirement for urgent transfusion.
- **Localized areas of splenic infarction:** results in pleuritic pain in the left hypochondrium radiating to the left shoulder, sometimes associated with rubs.
- **Thrombotic stroke**: fortunately this is relatively rare but it may be catastrophic and is an indication for urgent exchange transfusion.
- **Pulmonary infarction–chest syndrome**: may be associated with infection. It is another serious complication of sickle cell disease, often requiring exchange transfusion.
- **Priapism**: painful sustained penile erection due to sickling of red cells in the corpora cavernosa. It may require surgical intervention and lead to impotence.
- **Other areas of sickle infarction**: the retina may be affected, particularly in haemoglobin S-C disease leading to retinal detachment and blindness. Infarction of the placenta may lead to fetal loss and small-for-weight babies. Intractable leg ulcers are common in countries where the ankles are not protected by shoes and socks. Avascular necrosis of the head of femur may be seen in adults.

Aplastic crisis

This is a syndrome of severe anaemia with a lower reticulocyte count and bilirubin level than usual for the patient. It is usually due to parvovirus B19 infection. In normal people this infection results in a mild febrile illness with infection of red cell precursors in the bone marrow causing shutdown of marrow red cell production for a few days. In patients with increased red cell turnover, such as sickle cell disease, a precipitous drop in haemoglobin level may result from a short shutdown in red cell production. Aplastic crisis may be found in other patients with sickle cell disease and those with other congenital haemolytic anaemias associated with a high red cell turnover.

Transfusion in sickle cell disease

Because the oxygen dissociation curve of sickle haemoglobin is shifted to the right, oxygen is more easily released from haemoglobin to the tissues. Anaemia is therefore well tolerated and blood transfusion for the correction of anaemia is rarely required except in aplastic or sequestration crisis. For severe sickle problems exchange transfusion with non-sickling HbA containing red cells is required. To be effective the percentage of haemoglobin A needs to be raised to 80–90% and care needs to be taken not to increase the haematocrit which may lead to stagnation and increased sickling.

1.5 Aplastic anaemia

This is a pancytopenia secondary to marrow hypoplasia.

Aplastic anaemia

Causes:

- **Idiopathic**: most cases are in fact autoimmune
- **Drugs**: an idiosyncratic reaction to drugs such as gold, phenylbutazone and chloramphenicol
- **Post-hepatitis**: viruses that are toxic to hepatocytes may also kill bone marrow stem cells
- As a predictable reaction to chemotherapy or radiation.

Treatment:

- **Supportive**: red cell transfusion for correction of anaemia, antibiotics for infections, platelet transfusion for thrombocytopenic bleeding
- **Immunosuppression**: high-dose steroids, anti-lymphocyte globulin, cyclosporin
- **Stimulation of residual marrow activity**: anabolic steroids
- **Bone marrow transplantation**: only in severe cases, particularly in children with an HLA-matched sibling.

2.   IRON METABOLISM

A representation of the body's iron economy is shown in the figure below.

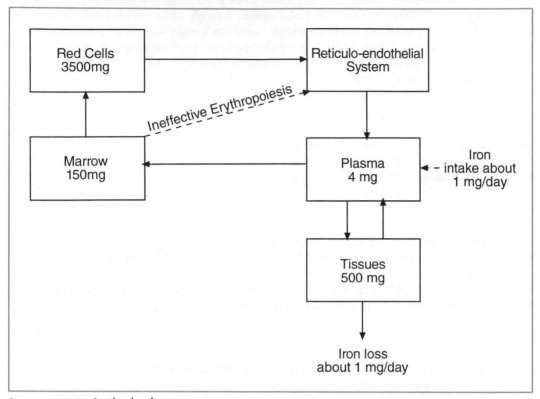

Iron economy in the body

Iron absorption may be greatly increased in iron deficiency, but iron excretion cannot be increased in case of iron overload. Most iron in the body lies within red cells, so chronic bleeding is a potent cause of iron deficiency.

The marrow normally contains stainable iron but it is possible to have no stainable iron in the bone marrow but a normal haemoglobin level. The converse is not true, however, in iron deficiency anaemia the marrow will not contain stainable iron. In megaloblastic anaemias, haemoglobinopathies and myelodysplasia, red cells may die and enter the reticuloendothelial system without leaving the bone marrow — this is termed **ineffective erythropoiesis**.

2.1 Assessment of iron status

- **Serum iron**: on its own, not very useful. Serum iron is reduced in patients with inflammatory disease. False elevations may be found if the patient is taking iron at the time of the test (stop the day before). Serum iron should always be measured with total iron binding capacity (TIBC).
- **Total Iron Binding Capacity (TIBC), transferrin**: always measure with serum iron. In iron deficiency the TIBC is increased, reflecting the body's desire to mop up and conserve all free iron molecules. False elevation of the TIBC may be found in pregnancy and oestrogen administration.
- **Transferrin saturation**: may be calculated by dividing the TIBC by the serum iron. Low in iron deficiency, high in iron overload. More useful than serum iron or TIBC assessed on their own.
- **Serum ferritin**: a major transport and storage form of iron which is high in iron overload states and low in iron depletion. It is one of the acute phase proteins, so like CRP, fibrinogen and immunoglobulins it is increased in inflammatory illness. If the ESR is increased then the serum ferritin may not be an accurate reflection of iron stores. It is also released from damaged liver cells, so if the patient has a transaminitis then it will be falsely elevated.
- **Iron stain**: on particles from bone marrow aspirate. This is the gold standard, but it is invasive!
- **Serum soluble transferrin receptor**: the latest index for measuring iron status, being high in iron deficiency and low in iron overload. It is still a research tool but shows promise.

2.2 Sideroblastic anaemia

In this disorder there is a failure to incorporate iron into the haemoglobin molecule, due to a biochemical block, and it accumulates in the mitochondria. These become poisoned and are visible as iron granules lying in a ring around the erythroblast nucleus. Hence the diagnostic feature is **ring sideroblasts** in the bone marrow.

Causes of sideroblastic anaemia:

- **Congenital**: rare, pyridoxine responsive
- **Acquired — primary**: one of the myelodysplastic disorders
- **Acquired — secondary**: alcohol, malignancy in the body, drugs (e.g. anti-tuberculous), connective tissue disorders, heavy metal poisoning.

3.   HAEMOLYSIS

Destruction of red cells may occur in the:

- circulation (*intravascular*)
- reticuloendothelial system (*extravascular*).

If haemolysis is intravascular then the haemoglobin liberated from red cells will be conserved in the body by binding to plasma proteins. Initially this will be haptoglobin so haptoglobin levels will be reduced. Then albumin will bind free haemoglobin, forming methaemalbumin, which may be detected by a positive Schumm's test. Without a protein to bind to, the haemoglobin will pass through the glomerulus to appear in the urine — **haemoglobinuria**.

3.1 General features and causes of haemolysis

The anaemia is commonly macrocytic and associated with:

- **Elevated reticulocyte count**: >2%
- **Jaundice**: pre-hepatic, unconjugated, water-insoluble bilirubin. Therefore NOT found in urine, but **urobilinogen** may be found in urine — due to increased breakdown products of porphyrins secreted into the bile and reabsorbed from the bowel. Detected by simple stick test
- **Abnormal red cell morphology**: particularly spherocytes (see above).

Causes of haemolysis

- **Mainly intravascular**
  Immediate haemolytic transfusion
    reaction
  Paroxysmal cold haemoglobinuria
  Micro-angiopathic haemolytic anaemia
  Glucose-6-phosphate dehydrogenase
    deficiency
  Infections — malaria
  Phosphokinase deficiency
  Paroxysmal nocturnal haemoglobinuria

- **Mainly extravascular**
  Warm autoimmune haemolytic
    anaemia
  Cold haemagglutination disease
  Haemolytic disease of the newborn
  Hereditary spherocytosis
  Haemoglobinopathies
    (e.g. sickle cell disease)

3.2 The antiglobulin (Coombs') test

The direct antiglobulin test detects antibody on the patient's red cells. The antibody coating on the red cells may be:

- **Opsonizing:** making the red cells attractive to the phagocytes of the reticuloendothelial system.
- **Complement fixing:** causing a local enzymatic explosion blowing a hole in the red cell envelope.
- **Agglutinating:** in which case the red cell clumping may be visible in the test tube without resorting to a Coombs' test to discover the antibody.

The indirect antiglobulin test detects antibody in the patient's serum. This involves incubation of serum with test red cells bearing various surface antigens. This test is most frequently used as part of the 'cross-match' or compatibility test. The donor's red cells are mixed with the recipients serum and if there is incompatibility a positive indirect antiglobulin test will result.

3.3 Microangiopathic haemolytic anaemia (MAHA)

Fibrin strands are laid down in small blood vessels and these chop up red cells (like a wire cheese cutter). The red cells reseal themselves if not too badly damaged and circulate as helmet cells or if multiply chopped, as fragmented cells. All the features of haemolysis will be present, as well as reticulocytosis due to increased marrow activity.

Haematological features of microangiopathic haemolytic anaemia:

- Anaemia
- Helmet cell
- Fragmented cells
- Polychromasia
- Reticulocytosis.

Sometimes thrombocytopenia and consumption coagulopathy may be associated, depending on diagnosis.

Causes:

- Disseminated intravascular coagulation (DIC)
- Haemolytic uraemic syndrome (HUS)
- Thrombotic thrombocytopenic purpura (TTP)
- Malignant hypertension
- Severe pre-eclampsia.

TTP
HUS

4. DISORDERS OF LEUCOCYTES

4.1 Leucocytosis

An elevated white cell count may be due to an increase in any of the individual types of white cell in the blood and should prompt examination to determine if there is a neutrophilia, lymphocytosis or, more rarely, an increase in other types of white cell to give a leucocytosis.

Neutrophilia (>7.5 x 10⁹/l)

This is by far the commonest cause of a leucocytosis. If acute it may be associated with young neutrophils (band cells) in the blood or 'left shift'.

Causes of neutrophilia

- **Bacterial infections**
  Localized or generalized

- **Metabolic disorders**
  (e.g. uraemia, acidosis, gout,
  eclampsia, poisoning)

- **Malignant neoplasms**
  Particularly when associated
  with tissue necrosis

- **Inflammation or necrosis**
  (e.g. myocardial infarction, trauma,
  vasculitis)

- **Corticosteroid therapy**

- **Myeloproliferative disorders**
  (e.g. chronic granulocytic leukaemia,
  myelofibrosis, essential
  thrombocythaemia,
  polycythaemia rubra vera)

Lymphocytosis (>3.5 x 10⁹/l)

The morphology of the lymphocytes may give valuable clues. For example, in acute viral infections the lymphocytes may show morphological abnormalities termed 'reactive changes' and in chronic lymphocytic leukaemia the mature-looking small lymphocytes characteristic of the disease are fragile and become crushed during the spreading of the blood film — 'smear cells'.

Causes of lymphocytosis

- **Acute viral infections**
  (e.g. influenza, glandular fever,
    rubella, mumps, acute HIV)

- **Chronic lymphocytic leukaemia**

- **Thyrotoxicosis**

- **Chronic infections**
  (e.g. TB, brucella, hepatitis,
    syphilis)

- **Other chronic leukaemias and
  lymphomas**

A lymphocytosis is normal in infancy

Eosinophilia (>0.5 x 10^9/l)

In the developed world allergic disorders are the main cause of eosinophilia.

Causes of eosinophilia

- **Allergies**
  (e.g. asthma, hay fever, drugs)

- **Skin diseases**
  (e.g. eczema, psoriasis,
    dermatitis herpetiformis)

- **Tropical eosinophilia**

- **Hypereosinophilic syndrome**
  (See below)

- **Eosinophilic leukaemia**
  (Very rare)

- **Parasites**
  (e.g. ankylostomiasis, ascariasis,
    filariasis, trichinosis, toxocariasis)

- **Neoplasms**
  (e.g. Hodgkin's disease)

- **Miscellaneous conditions**
  (e.g. sarcoidosis, polyarteritis
    nodosa, eosinophilic granuloma)

Hypereosinophilic syndrome

This condition is associated with a high eosinophil count, up to 100 x 10^9/l. The aetiology is obscure. Some cases are myeloproliferative disorders equivalent to eosinophilic variants of chronic myeloid leukaemia, some are T-cell lymphomas which produce large amounts of cytokines such as IL5, which stimulate eosinophil proliferation. Treatment is with steroids and hydroxyurea. See also Chapter 17, *Respiratory Medicine*.

Hypereosinophilic syndrome

- **Clinical features**
  Weight loss
  Rashes
  Fever
  Peripheral neuropathy
  Oedema
  Cardiac disturbances

- **Pathological features**
  Acute arteritis
  Pericarditis
  Cardiac mural thrombus
  Chronic endocardial fibrosis
  Pulmonary abnormalities
  Splenomegaly

Monocytosis (>0.8 x 10^9/l)

Monocytes are tissue phagocytes ('dustbin lorries') *en route* to the tissues to phagocytose and digest dead cells and other debris.

Causes of monocytosis

- **Recovery**
  (From chemotherapy or radiotherapy)

- **Chronic inflammatory disease**
  (e.g. sarcoidosis, Crohn's, ulcerative colitis, rheumatoid arthritis, SLE)

- **Myelodysplastic syndromes**
  (and chronic myelomonocytic leukaemia)

- **Infections**
  (e.g. TB, brucella, kala-azar, typhus, bacterial endocarditis, malaria, trypanasomiasis)

- **Hodgkin's disease**
  (and other neoplasms)

- **Acute myelomonocytic leukaemias**
  (when associated with increased blast cells)

4.2 Leucoerythroblastic change

This is defined as the presence of nucleated red cells and primitive white cells of any type in the peripheral blood. There are two major causes; either the normal cells inhabiting the bone marrow are being evicted by a marrow infiltration, or the patient has acute severe illness.

Causes of a leucoerythroblastic blood picture

- **Invasion of marrow space**
  Tumour (metastatic carcinoma), leukaemia, myeloma, lymphoma, myelofibrosis, osteopetrosis, storage disease (e.g. Gaucher's disease)

- **Severe illness**
  (e.g. severe haemolysis, massive trauma, septicaemia)

4.3 Neutropenia

This is defined as a neutrophil count less than $2 \times 10^9/l$. Below $1 \times 10^9/l$, some risk of infection exists; below $0.5 \times 10^9/l$ this may be severe and such patients, if in hospital, will usually be isolated and subject to a regimen of care including prophylactic antiseptic mouthwashes and anti-fungal agents and avoidance of foods with a high bacterial load. In the event of significant fever a broad-spectrum antibiotic regimen reserved for 'febrile neutropenia' is instituted.

Causes of neutropenia

- **Associated with intercurrent viral infections**

- **Idiosyncratic drug reactions**
  (e.g. carbimazole)

- **Collagen diseases**
  (e.g. SLE, rheumatoid)

- **Meylodysplasia**

- **After chemotherapy or radiotherapy**

- **Racial** (e.g. in Blacks or Arabs)

- **Hypersplenism**
  Often low platelet count and haemoglobin as well

- **Marrow infiltration**
  May be associated with leucoerythroblastic change

235

5. HAEMATOLOGICAL MALIGNANCIES

These may be broadly divided into:

- Leukaemias
- Lymphomas
- Myelodysplasias
- Myeloproliferative disorders.

Acute leukaemias are characterized by primitive blast cells in the bone marrow and blood, chronic leukaemias with an excess of mature cells in the marrow and blood. In leukaemias the malignant cells lie mainly in marrow and blood, whereas in the lymphomas they lie mostly in lymph nodes. There is an overlap, however, so many cases of lymphoblastic lymphoma have marrow involvement by cells of the disease in addition to enlargement of thymus and lymph nodes.

5.1 Acute leukaemias

Acute	Chronic
Myeloid (AML)	Myeloid (CML (CGL))
Lymphoid (ALL)	Lymphoid (CLL)

Acute lymphoblastic leukaemia:

- Predominantly affects children
- Remission may be induced with non-myelosuppressive chemotherapy
- CNS involvement common
- >60% cure rate with chemotherapy
- Further classified by immunological surface markers.

Acute myeloid leukaemia:

- Predominantly affects adults
- Marrow hypoplasia required to induce remission
- CNS involvement unusual
- >30% cure rate with chemotherapy
- Further classified by morphological appearance (see below).

How to identify the leukaemic blast cell

- **Morphology**: often this is not helpful as myeloblasts look similar to lymphoblasts. One give-away is the presence of Auer rods which are diagnostic of AML
- **Cytochemistry**: the leukaemic cells are tested for their biochemical activities. Important cytochemistry tests in acute leukaemia: Sudan black (stains lipid material in AML); Periodic Acid Schiff (PAS) (stains carbohydrate material in ALL); Esterase (stains monocytic variants of AML)
- **Immunological surface markers**: these are particularly useful in ALL when they allow classification into T-cell, B-cell and other immunological types.

Treatment strategies in acute leukaemia

Bone marrow transplantation is a powerful treatment for acute leukaemia, as it also harnesses the power of graft-versus-leukaemia effect. It is a risky treatment, however, and this risk increases with age. The total body irradiation also results in sterility. Chemotherapy treatment also carries risks, so patients with acute leukaemia are therefore stratified by prognostic indicators so that appropriate treatment can be selected.

Prognostic indicators in acute leukaemia

Acute lymphoblastic leukaemia:

- Height of presenting white cell (blast) count*
- Age (less than 1 year or over 10 years worsen prognosis)*
- Sex (males do worse)*
- Cytogenetics (see below)
- Immunophenotype (B-cell ALL is poor prognosis and T-cell ALL usually has a high presenting white count — see below).

Acute myeloid leukaemia:

- Cytogenetics (see above)
- Age (over 60s do worse)
- Response to first course of chemotherapy.

---

* Highest presenting white cell count, age and sex may be combined in the Medical Research Council's risk algorithm.

5.2 Specific chromosome abnormalities in leukaemia/lymphoma

Cytogenetic techniques

Morphological examination of the chromosomes of malignant haematological cells is possible by culturing them in tissue culture medium and then 'freezing' the cell in division with the chromosomes spread out (metaphase arrest) by adding colchicine or vincristine which poison the spindle apparatus. The cells are then swollen in hypotonic salt solution and the cell suspension is dripped onto glass microscope slides so that the cells split open releasing a cloud of contained chromosomes. This is examined under the microscope and usually analysed with the aid of a computerized image analysis system. The chromosomes are arranged in order of their length to form a karyotype (see Chapter 6, *Genetics*). Cytogenetic abnormalities are found in two-thirds of cases of AML and three-quarters of cases of ALL.

Chromosome abnormalities in leukaemia and lymphoma are important for the following reasons.

● They act as a marker of the disease, indicating remission or relapse.

● Some have a prognostic significance. If the prognosis is especially bad (e.g. Philadelphia chromosome in childhood ALL) then a high-risk treatment such as bone marrow transplantation may be employed early in treatment. If the prognosis is especially good (e.g. t(8;21) in adult AML) then conventional chemotherapy may be employed without a transplant unless the patient relapses.

● Some of the abnormal DNA sequences that result from chromosomal translocation can be amplified by the polymerase chain reaction to allow the detection of incredibly small amounts of residual leukaemia. The prognostic significance of this minimal residual disease is now being investigated in international trials.

Many of the chromosomal abnormalities in leukaemia and lymphoma are translocations, involving the exchange of material between chromosomes. For example, t(9;22) involves a reciprocal translocation between chromosomes 9 and 22. Chromosome 22 comes off worst in this exchange, gaining only a small amount of extra material. The abnormally shortened long arms of this chromosome are visible morphologically as the Philadelphia chromosome (see opposite).

Cytogenetic abnormality	Found in
t(9;22)	Philadelphia chromosome in CML
t(15;17)	Acute promyelocytic leukaemia (M3) — see 5.3 below
t(8;21)	AML with differentiation (M2) — better prognosis
inv(16)	(Inversion of the long arm of chromosome 16) Acute myelomonocytic leukaemia (AML M4) with marrow eosinophilia (M4Eo)
Hyperdiploidy	(More than 47 chromosomes) Childhood ALL — better prognosis
t(1;19)	Childhood pre-B ALL
t(8;14)	ALL L3 Burkitt type
5q-	Myelodysplastic syndrome (refractory anaemia) with abnormal megakaryocytes particularly in women (loss of part of the long arm of chromosome 5)
t(14;18)	Follicular NHL — found in 3/4 of cases

5.3 The French–American–British (FAB) classification of acute leukaemia

This morphological classification is widely used for AML but in ALL has been largely supplanted by the immunophenotype. It depends on the degree of differentiation of the leukaemic cells and whether a recognizable tendency to differentiate along one of the myeloid pathways (e.g. monocytic) is present. As with any morphological classification it is rather subjective and there will be some cases which would be best classified between grades, e.g. M2½!

FAB Type	Description
M0	Acute myeloid leukaemia undifferentiated — no morphological feature to distinguish it from ALL
M1	Acute myeloid leukaemia with recognizable myeloid features such as Auer rods
M2	Acute myeloid leukaemia with a few cells differentiating to the promyelocyte stage
M3	Acute promyelocytic leukaemia — see below
M4	Myelomonocytic leukaemia
M5	Pure monocytic leukaemia
M6	Acute erythroleukaemia
M7	Acute megakaryoblastic leukaemia

Acute promyelocytic leukaemia (AML M3)

- Majority of leukaemic cells are abnormal hypergranular promyelocytes
- Auer rods and collections of Auer rods (Faggots) common
- Strongly Sudan black/peroxidase positive
- Characteristic chromosome abnormality t(15;17), involving retinoic acid receptor gene alpha (RARA)
- Variant M3 (M3v) is **hypo**granular but otherwise the same.

The disease and its treatment are associated with acute fibrinolysis/DIC — tranexamic acid is used to block fibrinolysis and heavy platelet and fresh frozen plasma support are needed. Remission can be induced with all-*trans* retinoic acid (ATRA) — a differentiating agent which also helps with the coagulopathy. Prognosis is good providing death from DIC does not occur during induction.

5.4 Chronic myeloid leukaemia (CML)

CML is a disease of middle age, the majority of patients presenting with tiredness, weight loss and sweating. Splenomegaly is found in 90% of cases. If the white cell count is very high (over 500 x 10^9/l) then problems associated with hyperleucocytosis may be found: visual disturbance, priapism, deafness. Eventually almost all patients transform to blast crisis in 1–10 years. This may be myeloid, lymphoid or mixed transformation. At this stage it is very difficult to treat.

Blood and marrow features of CML

- High white cell counts 100–500 x 10^9/l
- Absolute basophilia and eosinophilia
- Platelet count high, normal or low
- Low neutrophil alkaline phosphatase (NAP) score
- Increased blood colony forming cells (stem cells)
- High serum B12 due to production of a B12 binding protein by white cells
- Massive neutrophilia with left shift
- Anaemia in relation to height of WBC
- Philadelphia chromosome (see below)
- Marrow hyperplasia sometimes with increased reticulin (fibrosis)

Philadelphia chromosome (Ph)

This is a balanced translocation between chromosomes 9 and 22, termed t(9;22). Ninety per cent of cases of CML have Ph chromosome; the breakpoints are at the *bcr* gene on 22 and *abl* gene on 9. The majority of Ph-negative CML cases have a translocation at the *molecular* level.

Ph is also found in:

- 5% childhood ALL
- 25% adult ALL
- 1% adult AML.

It carries a bad prognosis if found in these diseases. The protein product of the hybrid gene has protein tyrosine kinase activity.

5.5 Chronic lymphocytic leukaemia

This is the most indolent of the chronic leukaemias. Many cases are discovered as an incidental finding when blood counts are done for some other reason, such as health screening.

- Commonest cause of a lymphocytosis in the elderly
- 95% of cases are of B-cell lineage
- Mature-looking lymphocytes and smear cells on the blood film
- Progression through lymphocytosis to lymphadenopathy, hepatosplenomegaly, marrow failure though patients may skip stages in this progression.

Treatment is usually with single alkylating agents (chlorambucil), and combination chemotherapy in the young (COP, CHOP (see overleaf)). Local radiotherapy is appropriate for big nodes. Supportive treatment is important, including early antibiotics, blood transfusion and gamma globulin if the patient is developing frequent infections. There is an association with warm autoimmune haemolytic anaemia, idiopathic thrombocytopenic purpura and glomerulonephritis.

Hodgkin's

5.6 Non-Hodgkin's lymphomas (NHL)

Despite the general acceptance of the REAL (Revised European American Lymphoma) histological classification, the categorization of non-Hodgkin's lymphoma (NHL) remains in a state of flux. For clinical purposes the NHLs are divided into three groups:

Low grade NHL

- The cells are relatively mature and the disease pursues an indolent course without treatment. In many cases it is acceptable to watch and wait for symptoms or critical organ failure.
- Local radiotherapy to involved nodal regions effective and should always be given in Stage I disease (infrequent) as some patients can be cured by this treatment.
- Single agent chemotherapy (e.g. chlorambucil) is usually used for diffuse disease.
- Interferon may prolong remission duration.

High grade NHL

- The cells are immature and the disease is rapidly progressive without treatment.
- Combination chemotherapy is usual from the outset (e.g. CHOP regime: cyclophosphamide, adriamycin (**h**ydroxydaunorubicin), vincristine, (**o**ncovin) **p**rednisolone).
- Usual to give six (monthly) courses.
- No benefit of maintenance therapy.
- Multi-agent, alternating and hybrid regimes may be advantageous.

Lymphoblastic NHL

- The cells of the disease are very immature and have a propensity to involve the CNS.
- Treat as for ALL with CNS prophylaxis.

High-dose therapy with haemopoietic stem cell rescue may salvage some younger patients with aggressive chemotherapy-responsive lymphomas.

Prognosis

Low grade (indolent) lymphomas are readily controllable initially but relapse usually occurs even after many years of remission. Approximately 40% of high-grade lymphomas are cured.

5.7 Myeloma

A common clinical problem is the differentiation between myeloma and monoclonal gammopathy of undetermined significance (MGUS — benign monoclonal gammopathy) in patients found to have a paraprotein.

Differentiation of myeloma from MGUS

- **MGUS**
  Low level of paraprotein
    (< 20 g/l for an IgG paraprotein)
  Paraprotein level remains stable over
    a period of observation
    (months or years)
  Other immunoglobulin levels
    are normal
  No clinical evidence of myeloma
    (bone disease, renal disease)

- **Myeloma**
  High level of paraprotein
  Level rises
  Other immunoglobulin levels
    are depressed
  Clinical evidence of myeloma

5.8 Thrombocytosis (platelets > 500 x 10^9/l)

Primary (essential) thrombocythaemia

In practice it is often difficult to distinguish between essential thrombocythaemia and reactive causes of thrombocytosis unless other markers of either a myeloproliferative disorder (polycythaemia, splenomegaly, basophilia, increased bone marrow reticulin cytogenetic abnormality) or hyposplenism (due to multiple splenic infarcts) are present.

It is often necessary to treat any potential cause of secondary thrombocytosis that may be present and see what happens to the platelet count over months.

Causes of secondary (reactive) thrombocytosis

- Bleeding
- Infection
- Trauma

- Thrombosis
- Infarction
- Iron deficiency
  (even if not due to bleeding)

5.9 Uses of α interferon in haematological malignancy

This anti-viral cytokine has numerous anti-proliferative effects and has now been cloned. Side-effects of subcutaneous injection are as for viral infection — malaise, shivering, myalgia. To prevent these, the injection is given at night or paracetamol is used.

Indications for α interferon are given below:

- **CML**: prolongs chronic phase by 1–2 years in the latest MRC trials. A small proportion of patients may do especially well and become Philadelphia chromosome negative.
- **Myeloma**: used in plateau phase disease when chemotherapy has trimmed the disease bulk to an acceptable level. Helps prolong plateau.
- **Essential thrombocythaemia**: particularly useful in patients who are, or plan to be, pregnant, so that the platelet count can be controlled without the teratogenic effects of chemotherapy.
- **Hairy cell leukaemia**: a rare disease, in which the nucleoside analogues such as deoxyadenosine have replaced interferon as first-line treatment.
- **Acute myeloid leukaemia**: May prolong remission. This question is now being addressed in the latest MRC trial for older leukaemic patients who would not survive transplantation.

In other myeloproliferative disorders and lymphomas the use of interferon is experimental.

5.10 Myelodysplasias (myelodysplastic syndromes — MDS)

This group of haematological malignancies is being seen with increasing frequency as the mean age of the population rises and general practitioners perform screening blood counts more frequently on their patients. As a group, they hang together less well than other haematological malignancies, but they do have the following features in common.

- Increased frequency in the elderly, but no age is exempt.
- Cytopenias — anaemia most common, also leucopenia and thromobocytopenia or combinations of these.
- Dysplastic changes seen in blood and bone marrow. These include hypogranular neutrophils, abnormal neutrophil nuclear lobulation, changes in red cell precursors mimicking megaloblastic change ('megaloblastoid') with vacuolated erythroblasts and mononuclear megakaryocytes.
- A monocytosis in the blood. This may be found in all the myelodysplastic disorders but is most marked ($>1 \times 10^9$/l) in chronic myelo-monocytic leukaemia (CMML).
- Propensity to transform into acute myeloid leukaemia. This may be an acute transformation but usually takes a number of years.
- Cytogenetic abnormalities as seen in AML may be seen in MDS. A rare variant of MDS with a relatively good prognosis is 5q minus syndrome found mainly in women with a normal or even high platelet count and deletion of part of the long arm of chromosome 5.
- Mainstay of treatment is support — transfusion for anaemia, antibiotics for infection, platelet transfusion for bleeding.

Classification of myelodysplastic syndromes

MDS	Special features
Refractory anaemia (RA)	Dysplastic morphological features seen as above but difficult to diagnose in early stages
Refractory anaemia with excess of blasts (RAEB)	As above plus increased number of blast cells in marrow (5–20%)
Refractory anaemia with excess of blasts in transformation to AML (RAEB-t)	As above but 20–30% blasts in marrow
Chronic myelomonocytic leukaemia (CMML)	Monocytosis in marrow and blood leukaemia
Primary acquired sideroblastic	Ring sideroblasts in marrow anaemia

5.11 Bone marrow transplantation

Bone marrow or stem cell transplantation works by using a strong (myelo-ablative) treatment such as high-dose cyclophosphamide with total body irradiation to wipe out residual malignant disease. In addition, the donor's transplanted immune system may recognize malignant cells and destroy them — graft versus leukaemia (GVL) effect. The down side of GVL is that the donor immune system may attack the recipient's tissues, particularly liver, intestine and skin causing graft versus host disease (GVHD).

Peripheral blood stem cells

In the rebound after marrow recovery from chemotherapy, stem cells appear in the peripheral blood. They can be made to appear in larger numbers by using growth factors such as G-CSF. They can then be harvested using a cell separator and frozen. Peripheral blood stem cells are further down the differentiation pathway to mature cells than marrow stem cells, so their use is associated with quicker haematological recovery than seen when bone marrow is used.

Types of donor and stem cells used

Type	Advantages	Disadvantages
Autologous	Donor available!	Poor GVL, possibility of residual marrow disease being harvested and returned to patient
Syngeneic (identical twin)	Full house HLA match — no GVHD	Reduced GVL effect
HLA-matched sibling	Controllable GVHD but some GVL	GVHD unpredictable
Matched volunteer unrelated donor	Available if no family match	GVHD unpredictable

GVHD = Graft versus host disease, GVL = Graft versus leukaemia effect.

The following are conditions in which a bone marrow allograft is a useful treatment if a matched sibling is available and recipient is aged < 50 years.

- **Acute myeloid leukaemia**: in first or later remission
- **Acute lymphoblastic leukaemia**: in second or later remission unless adverse prognostic features (such as age beyond childhood)
- **Chronic myeloid leukaemia**: in first chronic phase
- **Others**: storage disease, thalassaemia major, sickle cell disease.

6. COAGULATION

6.1 The coagulation mechanism and detection of factor deficiencies

A representation of the coagulation cascades is shown opposite. It consists of an extrinsic pathway (in which tissue thromboplastin plays an important part), an intrinsic pathway (intrinsic to the blood itself — what happens when blood clots away from the body in a tube). These two pathways share a final common pathway resulting in the production of a fibrin clot.

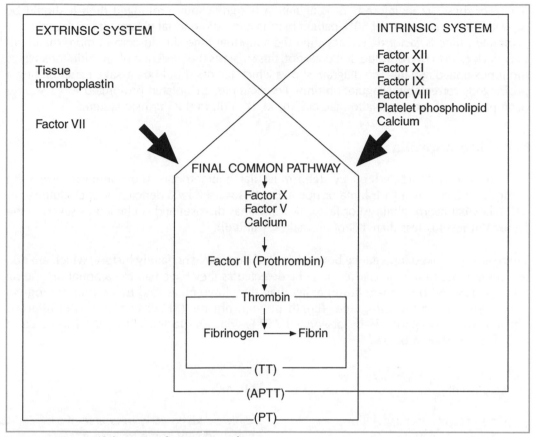

Representation of the coagulation cascades

The system can be divided into boxes, each box representing one of the following three basic screening tests of coagulation.

- **Prothrombin time** (PT) measures the extrinsic system and final common pathway.

- **Activated Partial Thromboplastin Time** (APTT) measures the intrinsic system and final common pathway. It is also known as the kaolin cephalin clotting time (KCCT) and the partial thromboplastin time (PTT) which are technical variations of the same test.

- **Thrombin time** (TT) measures the final part of the final common pathway. It is prolonged by lack of fibrinogen to convert to fibrin, and by inhibitors of this conversion, including heparin and high levels of fibrin degradation products.

If one of these screening tests of coagulation is significantly prolonged then it should be repeated using a mixture of 50% patient plasma and 50% normal plasma. If the cause of the prolonged time is factor deficiency then the abnormal time should correct more than half-way back to the control value. If it does not, this suggests the presence of an inhibitor such as the lupus anticoagulant. The diagram shows which factors should be assayed after finding a prolonged, correctable coagulation time. For example, an isolated prolonged APTT should prompt assay of the coagulation factors XII, XI, IX, VIII, in the intrinsic system.

6.2 Haemophilia

This disease is characterized by deep muscular haematomas and haemarthroses with prolonged bleeding after trauma or operation. It is caused by a deficiency of clotting factor VIII (classical haemophilia A) or factor IX (Christmas disease) and is classed as severe if the factor VIII level is less than 1% of normal (<1 unit/dl).

There is a sex-linked inheritance but one-third of cases have no family history; which are due to spontaneous mutation. Carriers may be detected as they have half the amount of clotting factor measured by a coagulation assay than they have measured by an immunological assay. Also, restriction fragment length polymorphisms (RFLP) can track the affected chromosome. Diagnosis is by prolonged APTT, with low factor VIII or IX. The range of treatments is shown below.

Treatment	Rationale
Viral inactivated coagulation factor concentrate	Should be given early in course of a bleed, ideally home treatment
DDAVP (a synthetic ADH analogue)	Releases factor VIII from storage sites in endothelial cells, so can temporarily boost blood level in mild haemophilia A
Fibrinolytic inhibitors (e.g. tranexamic acid)	Useful for bleeding wounds and tooth sockets but avoid in haemarthrosis, muscle haematomas and urinary bleeding as may lead to resolution by local fibrosis
Ancillary treatments (part of 'total haemophilia care')	Physiotherapy, hydrotherapy, immunization against hepatitis B, dental and orthopaedic advice

Complications of treatment include hepatitis, HIV, factor VIII antibodies, opiate addiction.

6.3 von Willebrand's disease

This is the commonest inherited coagulopathy in the UK. It is coded for on chromosome 12 — hence it shows an autosomal dominant inheritance pattern. It is caused by a quantitative or qualitative abnormality of von Willebrand factor (vWF) production. vWF is made in endothelial cells and forms variable size polymers in plasma.

vWF acts as a protective carrier for factor VIII in the circulation and is responsible for gluing the platelets to exposed vascular sub-endothelium. Hence, the factor VIII coagulation factor level in vWD is often reduced but (in contrast to the haemophilias) the disease manifests as a platelet-type bleeding disorder, with bruising, superficial purpura, menorrhagia, nosebleeds, and bleeding from cuts and mucous membranes.

Diagnosis

- Low factor VIIIC (C for 'clotting' activity, measured by a coagulation test)
- Low vWF Ag (von Willebrand factor antigen, measured in an immunological assay)
- Prolonged template bleeding time
- Deficient ristocetin-induced platelet aggregation.

Ristocetin is an antibiotic that clumps platelets in normal plasma but fails to clump them in vWF-deficient plasma. The disease may be divided into types according to the size of vWF multimers present.

Treatment is with DDAVP if mild, and with vWF concentrate. Many intermediate purity factor VIII concentrates contain enough vWF for treatment, otherwise cryoprecipitate is used.

6.4 Disseminated intravascular coagulation (DIC)

This disorder is caused by the release into the circulation of a pro-coagulant — something that makes the blood clot. There is massive activation of coagulation factors and platelets, with laying down of fibrin. This fibrin clot is immediately removed as the fibrinolytic system is also put into overdrive, worsening the haemorrhagic tendency.

The treatment is to remove the cause if possible, and transfuse with blood, platelets, fresh frozen plasma or cryoprecipitate.

Features and causes of disseminated intravascular coagulation (DIC)

- **Laboratory features of DIC**
  Prolongation of all coagulation times (prothrombin, APTT and thrombin)
  Activation of the fibrinolytic system leading to high fibrin degradation products
  Thrombocytopenia
  Microangiopathic blood film with fragmented red cells and helmet cells

- **Obstetric causes**   • **Other causes**
  Retroplacental haemorrhage   Crush injury
  Retained dead fetus   Septicaemia
  Amniotic fluid embolus   Haemolytic transfusion reaction
  Severe pre-eclampsia   Malignancy

6.5 Vitamin K dependent coagulation factors (II, VII, IX, X)

Vitamin K is a fat-soluble vitamin essential for the carboxylation of inactive coagulation factors into their active functional form. These coagulation factors are manufactured in the liver, consequently levels are low in liver disease, obstructive jaundice and when there is fat malabsorption (loss of vitamin K). Levels are also low in the neonate due to liver immaturity — this can lead to haemorrhagic disease of the newborn, particularly when breast-fed. These coagulation factors are also reduced by warfarin anticoagulation. Deficiency causes prolonged prothrombin time and APTT.

7. THROMBOSIS

There are many well-recognized risk factors associated with venous thombo-embolism, and in these situations it may be appropriate to take prophylactic measures.

Therapeutic ranges for warfarin anticoagulation

The necessary degree of anticoagulation will vary depending on the indication and whether the causes (e.g. bed rest, fracture) can be removed.

Indication	INR
Treatment of DVT, PE, systemic embolism, post-MI, mitral stenosis with embolism, TIAs, atrial fibrillation	2.0–3.0
Recurrent DVT and PE, arterial disease, including MI, mechanical prosthetic valves	3.0–4.5

Clinical risk factors for venous thrombosis

- Increasing age
- Immobility
- Varicose veins
- Major abdominal and hip operations
- Oestrogen/contraceptive pill therapy
- Increased blood viscosity
- Neprhotic syndrome
- Cigarette smoking
- Paroxysmal nocturnal haemoglobinuria
- Protein S or C or antithrombic III deficiency

- Obesity
- Previous family history of thrombosis
- Cancer
- Trauma to the lower limbs
- Pregnancy and puerperium
- Post-myocardial infarction or CVA
- Diabetic hyperosmolar state
- Homocystinuria
- Presence of Leiden factor V mutation

7.1 Thrombosis and the pill

Administration of oestrogen containing pills:

- Increases fibrinogen and vitamin K dependent coagulation factors
- Decreases antithrombin III levels
- Gives a four times greater risk of thrombo-embolism.

The risk of thrombo-embolism is increased by eight times if factor V Leiden is present — it is important to screen all women with a history of thrombosis if starting on the combined oral contraceptive pill.

Hormone replacement therapy is also associated with a small risk of thrombosis and patients with a previous history of thrombo-embolism should be screened for thrombophilia.

7.2 Thrombophilia

This may be defined as recurrent venous thrombo-embolism without any of the usual predisposing causes outlined above.

Groups for investigation of thrombophilia

- Venous thrombosis age < 40 years without cause
- Recurrent venous thrombosis without cause

- Arterial thrombosis age < 30 years without cause
- Family history
- Unusual anatomical site

Congenital causes of thrombophilia

The blood contains clotting factors that promote the formation of thrombus when activated. The blood also contains natural *anticoagulant* factors that inhibit the formation of clot. These factors are:

- Anti-thrombin
- Protein C
- Protein S

A congenital deficiency of these factors results in a tendency to thrombosis, so they should be tested for when screening for congenital thrombophilia.

Normally, activated clotting factor V is inhibited by the anticoagulant protein C. Approximately 3–5% of Europeans have an abnormal structure to their clotting factor V caused by a single point mutation in the factor V gene. This means that protein C cannot bind to it and inactivate it. This abnormal factor V is called **V Leiden**, after its place of discovery and it is found in 30% of patients with recurrent venous thrombosis. Screening for V Leiden may be done by PCR (looking for the abnormal gene) but this is expensive, so it is usual to screen using the **activated protein C resistance test**. In this test, protein C is added to the patient's plasma and an APTT is performed. In normal subjects the added protein C has an anticoagulant action resulting in prolongation of the APPT. In a patient with factor V Leiden the added protein C cannot bind to activated factor V so the APTT coagulation time will not be prolonged by protein C.

Other causes of inherited thrombophilia include:

- Abnormal prothrombin molecule
- Dysfibrinogenaemia
- Fibrinolytic defects.

Acquired causes of thrombophilia

- Polycythaemia and essential thrombocythaemia
- Lupus anticoagulant/anti-phospholipid antibodies.

Paradoxically, **lupus anticoagulant**, causing venous thrombosis, is detected by a prolonged coagulation test such as the APTT (or the more sensitive DRVT — dilute Russell viper venom time). The coagulation times are prolonged because anti-phospholipid antibodies neutralize phospholipids that are essential for the coagulation reaction. Although it may be found in patients with systemic lupus erythematosus (SLE), most patients with lupus anticoagulant do not have SLE. The disorder may present with recurrent venous thrombo-embolism or recurrent miscarriages. Anti-phospholipid antibodies and lupus anticoagulant have a strong association with each other and immune thrombocytopenia.

7.3 Therapeutic fibrinolysis

Therapeutic fibrinolysis

- **Action**
  Conversion of plasminogen to plasmin which dissolves fibrin to fibrin degradation products

- **Indications**
  Early stage of myocardial infarction, young patient with proximal DVT (e.g. ilio-femoral), survivors of massive pulmonary embolism, peripheral arterial thrombosis

- **Drugs**
  Streptokinase, urokinase, tissue plasminogen activator (TPA), Anisoylated Plasminogen Streptokinase Activator Complex (APSAC)

- **Unwanted effects**
  Bleeding

- **Reversal**
  Administration of tranexamic acid, cryoprecipitate

7.4 Low molecular weight heparins (LMWH)

Conventional heparin is a mixture of different sized polymers. Low molecular weight fractions can be separated by various chemical and physical methods. Low molecular weight heparin (LMWH) has a molecular weight of 5,000, compared with 15,000 for unfractionated heparin. LMWH has a strong anti-Xa and relatively weak anti-thrombin action compared with conventional heparin. It is claimed that this gives it more anti-thrombotic effect with less risk of bleeding. It certainly means that no significant prolongation of APTT is found, so this test is not used for monitoring therapy. Measurement of its anti-Xa effect is possible, though this is only necessary if prolonged treatment is required.

Advantages

- Long half-life — once or at most twice a day administration

- Laboratory assays are not required for short term administration
- Less heparin-induced thrombocytopenia and osteopenia than conventional heparin.

Disadvantages

- Expensive
- Different doses for different brands
- When given for more than a few weeks require (relatively) complicated anti-Xa assay for monitoring.

8.   THE SPLEEN

8.1 Causes of splenomegaly

- **Myeloproliferative disorders**
  Myelofibrosis
  Chronic myeloid leukaemia
  Polycythaemia rubra vera
  Essential thrombocythaemia
    (splenic atrophy also common)

- **Portal hypertension**
  Cirrhosis
  Congestive cardiac failure

- **Infection**

- **Bacterial**
  (e.g. typhoid, brucella, TB)

- **Collagen diseases**

- **Chronic haemolytic anaemias**
  Autoimmune haemolytic anaemia
  Cold haemagglutinin disease
  Hereditary spherocytosis
  Haemoglobinopathies

- **Lymphoproliferative disorders**
  Most lymphomas
  Chronic lymphocytic leukaemia
  Hairy cell leukaemia

- **Viral**
  (e.g. glandular fever, hepatitis)

- **Tropical**
  (e.g. malaria, kala-azar)

- **Storage diseases**

8.2 Splenectomy

Often performed because of traumatic injury or haematological disease, this operation results in a characteristic blood film appearance and a well-recognized predisposition to sudden overwhelming bacterial infection with capsulated organisms such as *Pneumococcus* or *Haemophilus*.

Clinical indications for splenectomy

- **Traumatic rupture**: but surgeons may preserve splenic function by surgical repair of capsular tears, omental patches, and sometimes implantation of some splenic tissue in the retroperitoneum.
- **Autoimmune destruction of blood cells**: immune thrombocytopenic purpura and warm autoimmune haemolytic anaemia after failure of steroid treatment.
- **Haematological malignancies**: low-grade lymphoproliferative disorders associated with painful splenomegaly, hypersplenism and not much disease outside the spleen. Also sometimes performed in the myeloproliferative disorders, particularly in myelofibrosis when the enlarged or painful spleen is destroying more blood cells than it is producing.
- **Congenital haemolytic anaemias**: such as hereditary spherocytosis and elliptocytosis and some cases of hypersplenic thalassaemia major.
- **Staging of Hodgkin's disease and NHL**: this is no longer performed where adequate imaging is available (CT or MRI).

Haematological and immune changes after splenectomy

- **Howell–Jolly bodies**
  (Nuclear remnants in the red cells — the spleen is responsible for removing particulate material from red cell cytoplasm — pitting function)
- **Enhanced neutrophilia** in response to infection

- **Target cells**, increased platelet count and occasionaly spherocytes with increased aniso- and and poikilocytosis
- **Decreased IgM level**

Splenectomy

8.3 Causes of hyposplenism

- Splenectomy (see above)
- Sickle cell disease
- Coeliac disease

- Myeloproliferative diseases, particularly essential thrombocythaemia
- Congenital asplenism (rare)

Infection prophylaxis necessary in hyposplenism (recent UK working party report).

Pneumococcal vaccine and one dose of haemophilia vaccine (Hib) are required at least two weeks before planned splenectomy; if the operation is unplanned then these should be given as soon as possible afterwards.

Post-operatively, prophylactic life-long penicillin V 250 mg b.d. is necessary (or erythromycin if the patient is penicillin allergic). Meticulous malaria prophylaxis is vital including insect repellant and mosquito nets. Meningococcal vaccine is necessary if the patient is going to equatorial Africa — the meningitis belt. A warning card is now available from the DHSS.

The above applies to hyposplenic patients (e.g. adult sickle cell disease) as well as previously splenectomized patients (recognized by the film comment 'Howell-Jolly bodies' on routine blood count) who have not been taking prophylaxis. If penicillin prophylaxis is refused then they should keep a supply of amoxycillin at home.

9. BLOOD TRANSFUSION

9.1 Transfusion-transmitted infection

Periodically, transfusion-transmitted infections hit the headlines, resulting in patients' reluctance to accept blood products. The infection of most concern currently is new-variant Creutzfeldt–Jakob disease, the prion protein of which is not destroyed by heat-detergent viral inactivation procedures and for which no screening test exists.

Testing donations for transfusion-transmitted infection in the UK

- HIV antibodies — small risk of viral transmission from infected donors in the period up to 8 weeks before antibody production
- Hepatitis B surface antigen
- Hepatitis C antibody
- Syphilis screen
- CMV antibody — some donations only, to ensure enough CMV-negative products for transfusion to premature neonates and immunosuppressed patients.

9.2 Blood filters

Microaggregate filters remove fibrin and aggregated dead white cell and platelet clumps. They are used when large volumes of blood are being given, usually in an operative situation. They are not efficient in removing white cells from the blood unless it has been centrifuged before administration to compact the white cell layer. Microaggregate filters may help prevent post-operative ARDS due to fibrin and cellular aggregates that would otherwise be sequestered in the lungs.

Leucocyte depletion filters

- Help prevent 'dilutional' thrombocytopenia in thrombocytopenic patients after red cell transfusion (which is really due to the patient's own platelets sticking to transfused dead white cells)
- Reduce risk of CMV transmission. After CMV infection the virus lies dormant in the genome of lymphocytes. When transfused to CMV antibody-negative (non-immune) patients it may cause CMV infection. If the recipient is immunocompromised this may be life threatening. Usually such patients are given blood products from CMV-negative blood donors, but often there are not enough of these to go round, so leucocyte depletion may help.
- Help prevent HLA sensitization. Although the white cells in transfused blood are dead, they still bear HLA antigens so can immunize the recipient. Such immunization may cause febrile non-haemolytic blood transfusion reactions and refractoriness to platelet transfusions (see below), and is unwanted in potential (especially renal) transplant recipients. These filters are available for red cells and platelets but add about £10 to the cost of each unit transfused.

9.3 Platelet support in marrow failure

This should be carried out when the platelet count is $<15 \times 10^9/l$ due to marrow underproduction. It should not be used in peripheral platelet destruction (e.g. ITP) except in cases of haemorrhagic emergency.

Give one pack of random donor platelet concentrate (5×10^{10} platelets) per 10 kg recipient weight (five platelet units for an average adult). An alternative is a single cell separator pack, prepared by placing the donor on a cell separator.

More packs will be required if there is infection, bleeding, where the patient is being given NSAIDs or in the case of poor platelet function in AML.

Platelet refractoriness is defined as an increment of platelet count less than $20 \times 10^9/l$ one hour after transfusion of an adult dose (see above). This may be due to the following.

- Non-immune consumption (e.g. bleeding, DIC, hypersplenism)
- Immune due to HLA antibodies directed against class I HLA antigens present on platelets (90%): give HLA-matched cell separator platelets, consider platelet pheresing relatives
- Immune platelet-specific antibodies (10%): use double doses of random platelets.

9.4 Indications for the transfusion of fresh frozen plasma

Indications for transfusion of FFP

- Correction of multiple coagulation factor deficits as in DIC or after massive transfusion.

- Correction of single coagulation factor deficiency where a heat-detergent virus inactivated concentrate is not available

- Emergency correction of warfarin over anticoagulation associated with bleeding, when II, VII, IX, X concentrate is not available and i.v. vitamin K would be too slow (a few hours)

The 'formula replacement' of coagulation factors by fresh frozen plasma after large volume blood transfusion is no longer recommended — it is better to perform a coagulation screen and blood count and replace as required.

Chapter 9
Immunology

CONTENTS

1. **Complement**   261
   1.1   Complement activation
   1.2   Terminal membrane attack sequence
   1.3   Regulating proteins

2. **Complement deficiency**   263
   2.1   Deficiency of complement components
   2.2   Deficiency of regulatory proteins
   2.3   Acquired deficiency

3. **Immunoglobulins**   264
   3.1   Cryoglobulins
   3.2   Cold agglutinins

4. **Cells and the immune system**   267
   4.1   Polymorphonuclear cells
   4.2   Lymphocytes

5. **Transplant immunology**   270
   5.1   The major histocompatibility complex
   5.2   The immunology of transplantation

6. **Hypersensitivity**   271

7. **Cytokines**   272
   7.1   Some patterns of cytokine production
   7.2   Therapeutic uses of cytokines

8. **Eicosanoids**   275
   8.1   Prostaglandins
   8.2   Leukotrienes

9. **Autoantibodies in diagnosis**   **277**
    9.1   Rheumatoid factor
    9.2   Antinuclear antibodies
    9.3   Extractable nuclear antigens
    9.4   Anti-neutrophil cytoplasmic antibodies (ANCA)
    9.5   Autoantibodies in gastrointestinal and liver disease
    9.6   Autoantibodies in thyroid disease
    9.7   Antiphospholipid antibodies
    9.8   Others

10. **Immunodeficiency**   **280**
    10.1   Complement deficiency
    10.2   Neutrophil disorders
    10.3   B-cell disorders
    10.4   T-cell disorders
    10.5   Combined B- and T-cell disorders
    10.6   Acquired immunodeficiency

11. **Immunization**   **282**
    11.1   Preformed antibody vaccines
    11.2   Killed organism vaccines
    11.3   Live attenuated vaccines
    11.4   Subunit vaccines

Immunology

1. COMPLEMENT

This is defined as a plasma protein sequence cascade triggered by one of two distinct pathways: classical or alternative. Both pathways produce protein complexes capable of cleaving the C3 component into its active metabolites, C3a and C3b. These activate the terminal complement components to produce a membrane attack complex (MAC) capable of cell lysis.

The complement cascade slowly 'ticks over' and is never completely inactive. This produces small quantities of active complement components that would cause tissue damage and further complement activation by positive feedback loops but for important regulatory components.

The biologically active complement products have three main effects:

- Opsonization — mediated by C3b
- Chemotaxis and inflammation — mediated by C3a, C5a
- Cell lysis (MAC) — C5, C6, C7, C8, C9.

1.1 Complement activation

The complement activation pathways are shown in the diagram overleaf.

The classical pathway   IgM / IgG   C1 – C4

- Initiated by antigen–antibody complexes containing IgM, IgG1, IgG2 or IgG3
- Components involved: C1q, C1r, C1s, C4, C2, C3
- The C4bC2b complex cleaves and activates C3

The alternative pathway   polysaccharides in cell wall / IgA

- Initiated by polysaccharides found in the cell walls of Gram-negative bacteria, pneumococci and yeasts. IgA is also a weak activator of this pathway.
- Components involved: properdin, factor D, factor B, C3
- The C3bBb complex cleaves and activates C3.

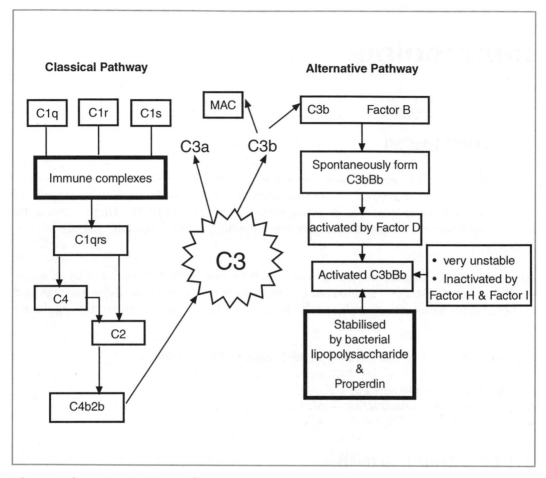

The complement activation pathways

1.2 Terminal membrane attack sequence

Components of C5, C6, C7, C8, and C9 join to form the rosette-like membrane attack complex. This structure forms on cell surfaces and will cause cell lysis unless specific inhibitors are present.

1.3 Regulating proteins

Classical pathway

- C1 inhibitor blocks C1s and C1r irreversibly
- C4 binding protein inhibits cleavage of C3.

Alternative pathway

- Factor H, decay accelerating factor (DAF) and complement receptor 1 inhibit cleavage of C3.

Others

- Factor I and membrane cofactor protein degrade C3b
- Anaphylotoxin inactivator degrades C3a and C5a
- The terminal sequence is regulated by homologous restriction factor (HRF), membrane inhibitor of reactive lysis (MIRL) and S-protein.

2. COMPLEMENT DEFICIENCY

Inherited deficiencies of complement components or regulatory proteins can produce disease states. Complement deficiency is common. Most cases, however, have only partial deficiency and are asymptomatic.

2.1 Deficiency of complement components

- Deficiencies of classical pathway components produce SLE-like disorders in some patients. This may reflect impaired clearance of immune complexes.
- C3 deficiency allows life-threatening infections by encapsulated organisms (e.g. pneumococci).
- Patients with deficiencies of the terminal complement proteins, C5, C6, C7, C8 or C9 are usually healthy but are unable to prevent Neisserial infections becoming disseminated.

2.2 Deficiency of regulatory proteins

- C1 inhibitor deficiency causes **hereditary angio-oedema**, in which there are recurrent acute episodes of non-inflammatory oedema mediated by vasoactive C2 fragments. Uncontrolled complement activation and consumption cause low levels of C2 and C4. Danazol, a synthetic anabolic steroid, can raise levels of the inhibitor sufficiently to prevent attacks. Fifteen per cent of affected patients have normal levels of C1-inhibitor — but functional assays show it to be inactive in these cases.
- **Paroxysmal nocturnal haemoglobinuria** occurs in patients who are unable to bind the regulatory proteins, DAF, HRF or MIRL on their red cell surfaces. Spontaneous complement mediated lysis of erythrocytes occurs.

2.3 Acquired deficiency

Complement consumption in inflammatory disorders such as lupus nephritis can lead to low levels of C3 and C4. This produces an increased susceptibility to severe infections with encapsulated organisms.

3. IMMUNOGLOBULINS

The functions of immunoglobulins include complement activation, stimulation of phagocytic cells and precipitation of antigen. Immunoglobulins are produced by B lymphocytes and secreted by plasma cells. They are made up of two identical light chains and two identical heavy chains joined covalently by disulphide bonds. Papain splits the Ig molecule into two antigen binding fragments (Fab) and one Fc fragment containing the complement fixation site. Isotypes (e.g. IgG, IgM) are due to differences in the heavy chains.

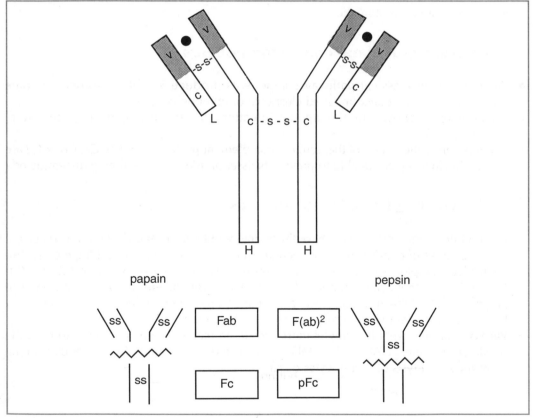

IgG molecule showing heavy (H) and light (L) chains, constant (C) and variable (V) regions and the antigen-binding site. The fragments produced by the action of papain and pepsin are shown.

IgG

This is the most abundant immunoglobulin in internal body fluids and it is important in the secondary immune response. It is also the only isotype to cross the placenta and the neonatal intestinal wall; levels fall at age 3 months as maternal IgG is catabolized.

- Fc portion activates complement by the classical pathway
- Four subclasses — differing in Fc portions of the heavy chains
- Molecular weight 150,000 daltons.

IgA

This is the major immunoglobulin of seromucous secretions, and it is produced predominantly in mucosal associated lymphoid tissue. It is present in monomeric form in plasma but as a dimer in secretions. Levels are undetectable at birth but reach adult levels by puberty. Deficiency produces autoimmune disorders, chronic diarrhoea and respiratory infections.

- Activates the Alternative complement pathway
- Two subclasses — IgA_1 and IgA_2
- Molecular weight 160,000 daltons.

IgM

This is a pentameric molecule, which is the main immunoglobulin of the primary immune response. It is very effective against bacteria which it agglutinates and then lyses by complement activation. It is undetectable at birth; adult levels are reached at 1 year of age.

- Secretion does not require help from T_H2 lymphocytes
- Includes blood group antibodies
- Molecular weight 750,000 daltons.

IgD

- Monomer present on B-cell surface and involved in B-cell activation
- Molecular weight 175,000 daltons.

IgE

- Immediate (type I) hypersensitivity reactions
- Present on mast cells and basophils, but produced by plasma cells
- Molecular weight 190,000 daltons.

3.1 Cryoglobulins

These are immunoglobulins (IgM, IgG or IgA) that precipitate when cooled to 4°C, and dissolve when reheated to body temperature. They may be monoclonal or polyclonal. Precipitation in small cool blood vessels in the peripheries and skin produces complement activation and inflammation. In high concentrations they may cause Raynaud's phenomenon or vasculitis. Treatment is of the underlying disorder. Steroids and immunosuppressives may be needed.

Causes

- Thirty-three per cent of cases are essential (i.e. unexplained)
- Lymphomas

- Hepatitis C
- Paraproteinaemia
- Connective tissue disorders, particularly SLE

Classification of cryoglobulinaemias

	Type 1	Type 2	Type 3
Frequency*	25%	25%	50%
Nature	Monoclonal proteins (usually IgM, but can be IgA or IgG) which cryo-precipitate	Mixed type Monoclone (often IgM) directed against Fc portion of IgG (e.g. rheumatoid factor activity)	Mixed polyclonal type IgM 'rheumatoid-like' factors react with IgG
Associations	Waldenstrom's macro-globulinaemia Myeloma Lymphoma Idiopathic monoclonal gammopathy	Lymphoma Chronic lymphocytic leukaemia Myeloma Waldenstrom's Sjögren's syndrome	Idiopathic Rheumatoid arthritis SLE Polyarteritis nodosa Chronic infection (e.g. hepatitis B, SBE, IM, CMV, AIDS, toxoplasmosis)
Clinical features	Vasculitis Cutaneous ulceration Raynaud's	'Immune complex disease' (e.g. vasculitis, arthritis, mesangiocapillary glomerulonephritis) (Membrano-proliferative)	Purpura Arthritis Glomerulo-nephritis

*Of all cryoglobulinaemias

3.2 Cold agglutinins

These are IgM capable of agglutinating red blood cells between 0°C and 4°C. They may be monoclonal or polyclonal. Symptoms are of Raynaud's phenomenon, acrocyanosis and mild haemolytic anaemia.

Causes

- Idiopathic (mainly in the elderly)
- Coxsackie virus
- Mycoplasma
- Lymphoma

4. CELLS AND THE IMMUNE SYSTEM

4.1 Polymorphonuclear cells

Include neutrophils, eosinophils, and basophils. Their principal actions are phagocytosis and release of inflammatory mediators.

Neutrophils

- Stored in the bone marrow and rapidly released into the bloodstream in response to infection
- Surface receptors for IgG, IgA and complement components
- Their principal action is phagocytosis and destruction of bacteria.

Basophils and mast cells

- Basophils circulate and mast cells are tissue bound
- Surface receptors for C3, C5 and IgE
- Produce histamine, prostaglandins, leukotrienes and proteases
- Involved in the immune response to parasites
- Interaction of antigen with bound IgE produces immediate hypersensitivity.

Eosinophils

- Commonly increased in patients with allergic disease
- Surface receptors for IgG, C3, and C5
- Also bind IgE but less avidly than mast cells or basophils
- Phagocytose antigen–antibody complexes.

4.2 Lymphocytes

T-lymphocytes

Characteristics of T-lymphocytes

- Form 70–80% of the total lymphocyte population
- Important in intracellular infections, tumour surveillance and graft rejection
- Arise from precursors in the bone marrow and undergo maturation in the thymus
- CD3 (part of the T-cell receptor) is present on all T-cells
- CD4 is a glycoprotein that recognizes MHC class II antigens on antigen-presenting cells. It is present on the cell surface of T-helper cells and monocytes
- CD8 is a glycoprotein on cytotoxic T-cells which recognizes class I antigens on target cells

CD4 (helper) T-cells only recognize antigen presented with class II MHC antigens. They make up 60% of the circulating T-cell population. Important in providing help for B cell differentiation and type IV hypersensitivity. The following are subsets of CD4 cells:

- T_H1 **(helper) cells** recognize antigen presented by macrophages or other specialized phagocytic cells. When activated they secrete IL-2 and interferon and produce type IV cell-mediated immunity. They are suppressed by IL-10.
- T_H2 **(helper) cells** recognize antigen presented by B lymphocytes. When activated they secrete IL-4, IL-5, IL-6 and IL-10, causing B lymphocyte proliferation and secretion of IgG, IgA or IgE, contributing to type II and type III immunity. They are suppressed by interferon.

CD8 (cytotoxic) T-cells recognize antigen presented with class I MHC antigens. They make up 35% of the circulating T-cell population. This mechanism is important in eliminating cells infected by viruses.

A schema of antigen recognition by CD4 and CD8 T-cells is shown in the figure opposite.

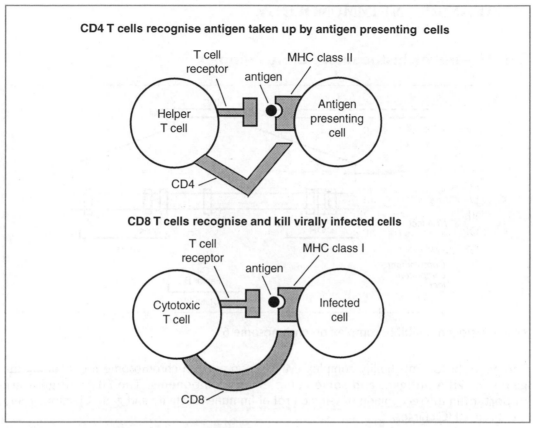

Antigen recognition by CD4 and CD8 T-cells

B lymphocytes

- Develop in the bone marrow with final maturation in the spleen and lymph nodes
- Immunoglobulin is expressed on the cell surface, but immature cells cannot secrete antibody
- Activation requires both antigen and T-helper cells but some antigens, e.g. bacterial lipopolysaccharide, can produce activation without the need for T-helper cells, but without T-helper collaboration, low affinity antibodies are produced and memory is poor.

Natural killer cells

- Large granular lymphocytes
- Recognize and lyse cells bearing viral or tumour surface markers.

5. TRANSPLANT IMMUNOLOGY

5.1 The major histocompatibility complex

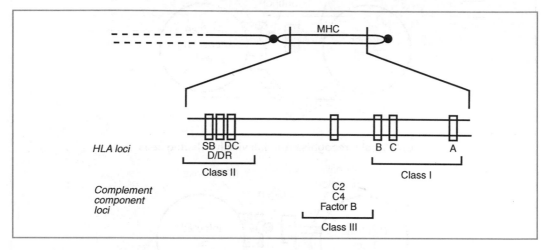

Major histocompatibility complex on chromosome 6

The major histocompatibility complex (MHC) is an area on chromosome 6 containing the genes for HLA antigens and some complement components. The HLA antigens are important in the recognition of self, control of immune reactivity and graft rejection. There are three MHC classes.

- **Class I** (HLA-A, B, C) are expressed as transmembrane peptides associated with β2-microglobulin. They are present on virtually all cells and, with antigen, signal to CD8 cytotoxic T-cells that their carrier cell is a suitable target for destruction.
- **Class II** molecules (HLA- DR, DP etc.) are heterodimers of two α and two β chains. They are present on B cells, macrophages and some endothelial cells. They signal to CD4 helper T-cells, and protect their carrier cells from destruction by cytotoxic T-cells.
- **Class III** includes the complement proteins C4 and factor B.

5.2 The immunology of transplantation

Graft rejection depends on MHC antigens and can be mediated by several mechanisms.

Rejection type	Timing	Mechanism
Hyperacute	Within minutes	Preformed antibody
Acute	Up to 10 days	CD8 lymphocytes
Acute late	After 10 days	Igs and complement
Late	Weeks, months, years	Immune complex deposition?

Privileged sites exist where rejection is rarely a problem even when there is no MHC matching:

- **Cornea**: avascular and does not sensitize the patient
- **Bone and artery**: even if the grafts die, they provide a structure for host cells to colonize.

In the kidney, HLA-DR and HLA-B matching are the most important. After these, matching for HLA-A, and to a lesser extent HLA-C, produce only small improvements in graft survival. (See Chapter 13, *Nephrology*.) Heart and liver grafts survive well with immunosuppression with only limited matching (e.g. at one HLA site).

6. HYPERSENSITIVITY

Hypersensitivity reactions are immune responses with excessive or undesirable consequences, such as tissue or organ damage. There are five types.

- **Type I: Anaphylactic or immediate**
  Antigen + IgE on mast cells and basophils leads to release of vasoactive substances, histamine, leukotrienes, interleukins and chemotactic factors. Reactions usually occur within 30 minutes of exposure to antigen.
  Clinical significance: asthma, atopy, some acute drug reactions.

- **Type II: Antibody-dependent cytotoxicity**
  Cell-bound antigen + circulating IgG or IgM antibody produce complement activation, phagocytosis, killer cell activation, and cell lysis.
  Clinical significance: transfusion reactions, rhesus incompatibility, Goodpasture's syndrome, immune thrombocytopenia.

- **Type III: Immune complex-mediated or arthus reaction**
  Free antigen + free antibody produces complement activation, platelet aggregation etc.
  Clinical significance: in *antibody excess* antigen–antibody complexes precipitate close to the site of entry into the body activate complement and cause localized disease, as in farmer's lung, pigeon fancier's lung and pulmonary aspergillosis.
  In *antigen excess* the complexes remain soluble. They are cleared by binding to red

blood cells via CR1 complement receptors. If the classical complement pathway is deficient or becomes overwhelmed, immune complexes continue to circulate and are deposited in the small blood vessels of the kidneys, skin and joints. Complement is activated producing both local tissue damage, e.g. glomerulonephritis and systemic illness. The systemic features produced are those seen in serum sickness: pyrexia, lymphadenopathy, urticarial rash, swollen joints and hypocomplementaemia about a week after injection of foreign serum.

- **Type IV: Cell-mediated or delayed type hypersensitivity**
  Antigen (with class II MHC) + sensitized (memory) T-cells — lymphokine release, T-cell activation. Reactions take 24 hours to develop.
  Clinical significance: tuberculin reaction, Kveim test, contact dermatitis, graft versus host disease, graft rejection.

- **Type V: Stimulatory**
  Antibody + cell surface receptor, e.g. Graves' disease, thyrotoxicosis.

7. CYTOKINES

Cytokines are low molecular weight peptides (10–45 kD) with non-enzymatic biological activity that are produced by lymphocytes (mainly T-cells), macrophages and fibroblasts. They include interleukins, interferons and colony-stimulating factors. The interleukin family is broadly divided into those with local (paracrine or autocrine) effects and those with systemic activity (IL-1, IL-6, TNF) which produce fever, increased CRP production, thrombocythaemia and activate osteoclasts etc. Other actions include enhancement of cytotoxic T-cells and NK cells.

7.1 Some patterns of cytokine production

Immune response	Important cytokines	Derived from
Acute phase response	IL-1, IL-6, TNF alpha	Macrophage
Cell-mediated immunity	IL-2, IFN gamma	T_H1 helper cells
Antibody-mediated	IL-4, IL-5, IL-6, IL-10	T_H2 helper cells

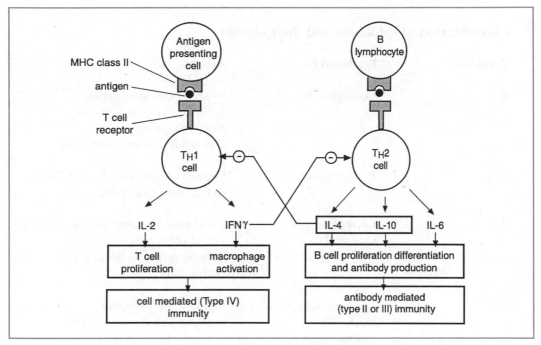

Cytokine production by T-helper cells

7.2 Therapeutic uses of cytokines

- **Interferon α**
    Hepatitis B
    Hepatitis C
    Kaposi's sarcoma in AIDS
    Hairy cell leukaemia
    Cutaneous T-cell lymphoma
    Recurrent or metastatic renal cell carcinoma
    Condylomata acuminata
- **Interferon β**
    Relapsing multiple sclerosis
- **Interferon γ**
    Serious infections in chronic granulomatous disease
- **GM-CSF**
    Correction of cytopenias, e.g. during chemotherapy.

The characteristics of individual cytokines are shown in the table overleaf.

Classification of cytokines and their actions

Cytokine	Produced by	Actions
IL-1	Macrophages	B- and T-cell stimulation Induction of IL-6, GM-CSF Acute phase response Osteoclastic bone resorption
IL-2	T$_H$1 lymphocytes	Growth of activated B- and T-cells Activation of NK cells
IL-3	T-lymphocytes Mast cells	Proliferation of activated B-, T- and mast cells Isotype switch to IgE and IgG production
IL-4	T$_H$2 lymphocytes Mast cells Macrophages	Acute phase response Immunoglobulin production
IL-5	T-lymphocytes Mast cells	Proliferation of activated B cells
IL-6	T$_H$2 lymphocytes Mast cells Macrophages	Acute phase response Immunoglobulin production
IL-7	Bone marrow cells	Proliferation of CD4 and CD8 T-cells
IL-8	Monocytes	Neutrophil chemotaxis Angiogenesis
IL-9	T-lymphocytes	Proliferation of T-cells
IL-10	T$_H$2 lymphocytes Macrophages	Inhibit production of IFN
IL-11	Bone marrow cells	Acute phase response

Continues ...

... Continued

Cytokine	Produced by	Actions
IL-12	Macrophages	Activate T_H1 lymphocytes
Interferon α/β	Leucocytes Fibroblasts Others	Anti-viral effects Expression of MHC class I
Interferon γ	T_H1 lymphocytes	Activates macrophages Inhibits T_H2 lymphocytes
TNF-α	Macrophages	Stimulates B- and T-lymphocytes Induces IL-6 Acute phase response Angiogenesis
GM-CSF	Mononuclear cells	Stimulates IL-1 production Induction of inflammation Production of granulocytes and macrophages

8. EICOSANOIDS

Eicosanoids are biologically active lipids synthesized in cells by the oxygenation of arachidonic acid. This is released from cellular lipid stores by the action of the enzyme phospholipase-A_2. Omega-3 fatty acids, from fish oils, may act as an alternative substrate. There are two main enzymatic pathways:

- 5-lipoxygenase — producing leukotrienes
- Cyclo-oxygenase — producing prostaglandins and thromboxane.

These are shown in the diagram overleaf.

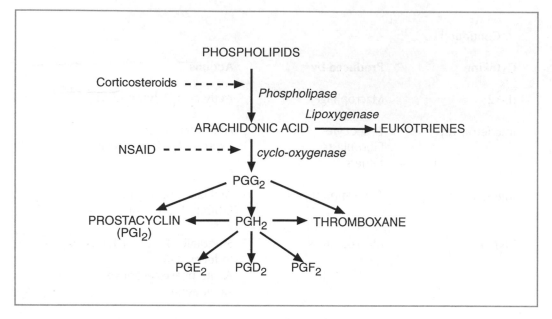

The pathway of arachidonic acid metabolism

8.1 Prostaglandins

- **PGD$_2$** is the major cyclo-oxygenase product of mast cells and produces some of the features of anaphylaxis: vasodilatation, bronchoconstriction and inhibition of platelet aggregation.

- **PGI$_2$** (prostacyclin) is a potent vasodilator and inhibitor of platelet aggregation synthesized in vascular epithelium. Used therapeutically in primary pulmonary hypertension, haemolytic uraemic syndrome and severe Raynaud's disease.

- **PGE$_2$** has predominantly immunomodulatory effects, inhibiting lymphocyte proliferation, cytokine production and neutrophil function.

NSAIDs and aspirin inhibit cyclo-oxygenase (COX) and therefore reduce prostaglandin production. There are two isoenzymes of cyclo-oxygenase: COX-1 and COX-2. COX-1 is a constitutive enzyme present in many tissues, whereas COX-2 is induced at sites of inflammation. NSAIDs which are more specific for COX-2 would be expected to have anti-inflammatory effects with less adverse gastrointestinal and renal effects.

8.2 Leukotrienes

- **LTB$_4$** causes neutrophil chemotaxis, increased mucus secretion and modulates cell growth.

- **LTC$_4$, LTD$_4$, LTE$_4$** increase vascular permeability, contract intestinal and bronchial wall smooth muscle, increase mucus production and modulate cell growth. These were previously known as slow reacting substances of anaphylaxis.

9. AUTOANTIBODIES IN DIAGNOSIS

Autoantibodies usually suggest the presence of a disease, or reflect disease activity. Some may be pathogenic through antibody–antigen interaction, such as anti-GBM in Goodpasture's syndrome. Others, such as rheumatoid factors, with cryoglobulin activity have physical properties leading to disease.

9.1 Rheumatoid factor

- Antibody against human IgG (usually the Fc portion)
- May be of any Ig class but latex and SCAT detect only IgM rheumatoid factors
- Positive in 70% of RA patients, and associated with extra-articular features and more severe articular disease
- Very high titres suggest cryoglobulinaemia.

This topic is covered in detail in Chapter 18, *Rheumatology*.

9.2 Antinuclear antibodies

Antinuclear antibodies (ANAs) are directed against a variety of nuclear antigens and may be induced by certain drugs (hydralazine). Like rheumatoid factors, ANAs can be of any Ig class (remember that IgG can cross the placenta).
A number of staining patterns are seen, though these tend to be found in particular disorders. None are specific enough to be diagnostic.

- **Homogeneous staining** suggests lupus
- **Speckled staining** suggests mixed connective tissue disease
- **Nucleolar staining** suggests scleroderma
- **Centromere staining** suggests CREST syndrome.

ANAs are found in

- Drug-induced lupus (100%)
- SLE (99%)
- Scleroderma (97%)

- Sjögren's syndrome (96%)
- Mixed connective tissue disease (93%)
- Polymyositis (78%)

ANAs in rheumatoid arthritis suggests Felty's syndrome or Sjögren's syndrome. Anti-DsDNA in high titre is virtually diagnostic of SLE.

9.3 Extractable nuclear antigens

These are specific nuclear antigens and therefore are usually associated with positive ANA tests.

- Anti-Ro — Sjögren's syndrome, congenital heart block, ANA-negative SLE
- Anti-La — primary Sjögren's syndrome
- Anti-Sm —SLE (20%, very specific: conferring a high risk of renal lupus)
- Anti-RNP — mixed connective tissue disease (100%), SLE
- Anti-Jo1 — polymyositis
- Anti-Scl70 — progressive systemic sclerosis (20%)
- Anti-centromere — CREST syndrome

9.4 Anti-neutrophil cytoplasmic antibodies (ANCA)

These antibodies are directed against constituents of the neutrophil cytoplasm, proteinase 3 (PR3) and myeloperoxidase (MPO). When neutrophils are activated PR3 and MPO move to the cell surface. Antibodies to either granule will cause activation of the respiratory burst and degranulation, particularly in the presence of TNFα, causing endothelial cell damage. ANCA may therefore play a role in the pathogenesis of its associated disorders. Titres often reflect disease activity.

- cANCA (cytoplasmic anti-PR3) is found in 90% of patients with Wegener's granulomatosis and microscopic polyangiitis (40%)
- pANCA (perinuclear anti-MPO) is found in microscopic polyangiitis (60%), connective tissue disorders, other vasculitides.

[handwritten annotations:] 10% pANCA

PAN 5% CANCA, 15% pANCA
Idiopathic crescentic glomerulonephritis 25% CANCA
65% pANCA

Churg-Strauss Syndrome 10% CANCA
60% pANCA

9.5 Autoantibodies in gastrointestinal and liver disease

- Anti-mitochondrial antibody — primary biliary cirrhosis (96%)
- Anti-smooth muscle antibody — auto-immune hepatitis, cryptogenic cirrhosis
- Gastric parietal cell antibodies — pernicious anaemia (90%), gastric atrophy (40%)
- Intrinsic factor antibodies — pernicious anaemia (70%)
- Anti-gliadin, anti-endomesial antibody — coeliac disease (continued positive anti-gliadin tests suggest inadequate dietary restriction).

9.6 Autoantibodies in thyroid disease

- Anti-thyroglobulin antibody — high titre in autoimmune thyroiditis (90%)
- Anti-microsomal antibodies — low titre in Graves' disease (35%) and in adenocarcinoma (10%).

9.7 Antiphospholipid antibodies

These are also detected as lupus anticoagulants and anticardiolipin antibodies. Other characteristics are:

- Association with arterial and venous thrombosis, transient neurological deficits, fetal loss, livedo reticularis and thrombocytopenia
- IgG and to a lesser extent IgM isotypes are pathogenic
- Interference with tests of clotting producing prolongation of the activated partial thromboplastin time. The prothrombin time and INR are not affected
- Production of false positive WR and VDRL tests
- Occurrence in connective tissue disorders, particularly SLE (up to 40% of patients), primary antiphospholipid antibody syndrome (Hugh's syndrome), infections (e.g. HIV), malignancy, but they are also found in healthy people
- Poor predictors of first thrombosis (i.e. most people with antiphospholipid antibodies do not develop thromboses etc.)
- Strongly predict recurrence of thrombosis.

9.8 Others

- Anti-glomerular basement membrane — Goodpasture's syndrome
- Acetylcholine receptor antibody — myaesthenia gravis (87%).

10. IMMUNODEFICIENCY

Primary immunodeficiency can be divided into:

- Complement deficiency
- Neutrophil disorders
- B-cell disorders
- T-cell disorders
- Combined B- and T-cell disorders.

10.1 Complement deficiency

May produce angio-oedema, SLE-like disease, or disseminated Neisseria infection.

- Hereditary angio-oedema due to C1 inhibitor deficiency
- SLE-like syndromes due to deficiencies of classical pathway components
- Paroxysmal nocturnal haemoglobinuria due to regulator protein defects.

10.2 Neutrophil disorders

Allow recurrent infections with pyogenic bacteria, especially *Staphylococcus aureus*, but also some Gram-negative bacilli and fungi, such as Aspergillus and Candida. Treatment is with antibiotics.

The following are examples:

- **Chronic granulomatous disease** where there is normal phagocytosis but an inability to kill the micro-organism intracellularly due to an X-linked defect of NADPH oxidase.
- **Chediak–Higashi disease** where there is also normal phagocytosis but inability to kill the intracellular micro-organism because lysosomes lack elastase and cathepsin G.
- **Job's syndrome** — recurrent boils.
- **Myeloperoxidase deficiency**, associated with a susceptibility to systemic candidiasis
- **Lazy leucocyte syndrome** due to defective responses to chemotactic stimuli.
- **Leucocyte adhesion deficiency** where the β-subunit of β2-integrin is absent.

10.3 B-cell disorders

These lead to failure of antibody synthesis (hypogammaglobulinaemia or agammaglobulinaemia) and recurrent infections with pyogenic bacteria and fungi such as Candida. Where necessary, regular immunoglobulin infusions are used to maintain levels of circulating immunoglobulin.

The following are examples:

- **Common variable immunodeficiency** is likely to represent more than one disorder. The marrow contains normal numbers of immature B-cells but there is a failure in maturation. Immunoglobulin levels vary from patient to patient. It is not familial.
- **IgA deficiency** is the commonest isolated Ig deficiency in the UK (one in 700), and is often asymptomatic. There is an increased susceptibility to giardiasis.
- **Bruton's X-linked agammaglobulinaemia.** No circulating B-cells are found. Usually presents between three months and two years of age.

10.4 T-cell disorders

These produce impaired cell-mediated immunity. There is an increased susceptibility to viruses, mycobacteria and fungi. Though common bacterial infections can be dealt with, infections with measles, vaccinia or even BCG immunization can prove fatal. Malignancy is increased. Treatment may require bone marrow transplants or thymus grafts.

The following are examples:

- **Di George syndrome** is a primary, non-familial, T-cell deficiency due to a defect in the development of the thymus and third and fourth branchial arches. The parathyroids are absent, causing severe hypocalcaemia and the usual presentation is with neonatal convulsions. Cardiovascular anomalies may also be present.
- **Nezelof syndrome** is due to an absent thymus though there is often some B-cell involvement.
- **Purine nucleoside phosphorylase deficiency** prevents the development of T-cells.

10.5 Combined B- and T-cell disorders

- **Severe combined immunodeficiency** (SCID) is due in some cases to lack of the enzyme adenosine deaminase. It is autosomal recessive.
- **Reticular dysgenesis** leads to lymphopenia, neutropenia and absence of monocytes.
- **Ataxia telangiectasia** is an autosomal recessive disorder presenting in childhood with cerebellar ataxia and telangiectasia. Malignancy is increased due to defective DNA repair mechanisms. There is defective cell-mediated immunity with low levels of IgE and IgA.
- **Wiskott–Aldrich syndrome**, due to lack of sialophorin, produces low IgM levels and impaired cell-mediated immunity. Malignancy is increased and there is thrombocytopenia, lymphopenia and eczema. The disorder is X-linked.

10.6 Acquired immunodeficiency

Immunoglobin deficiency

- **Drugs**
  Gold
  Phenytoin
  Penicillamine
  Unusual idiosyncratic reactions

- **Haematological malignancy**
  CLL

- **Protein loss**
  Nephrotic syndrome
  Protein-losing enteropathy

Cell-mediated immune dysfunction

- **Drugs**
  Cyclosporin
  Cyclophosphamide
  Steroids
  Common and dose-related

- **Haematological malignancy**
  Lymphoma

- **AIDS**

HIV infects T-helper cells leading to a progressive fall in the number of CD4 T-cells. The crucial immunological feature is impaired cell-mediated immunity with increased vulnerability to normally non-pathogenic organisms such as Pneumocystis but also viruses (CMV, *Herpes simplex* and EBV), fungi (Candida, Aspergillus and Cryptococcus) and protozoa (Toxoplasma). There is often an associated polyclonal activation of B-cells and hypergammaglobulinaemia.

11. IMMUNIZATION

The **benefits of immunization** depend on several factors.

- **Likelihood of contracting disease**: prevalence of disease, level of immunity in other individuals (herd immunity), presence of immunodeficiency.

- **Severity of disease**: both the disease itself and from the point of view of the host having immune deficiency.

- **Adverse effects**: more common with preformed antibodies and live attenuated vaccines.

There are several ways of enhancing the immune system to produce added protection against infection. Most are used prophylactically to prevent or reduce the severity of infection, but some can prevent the development of disease even after contact with the organism (e.g. rabies vaccine).

11.1 Preformed antibody vaccines

Preformed antibody vaccines

- Tetanus
- Hepatitis B
- Botulism
- Rabies
- Varicella
- Diphtheria

This is obtained from a previously infected individual. Used particularly in immunocompromised patients early after contact with infection and to inhibit the actions of bacterial toxins in tetanus, diphtheria and botulism. Occurs physiologically in the transfer of maternal IgG to the fetus. The antibody is catabolised, however, so protection against infection is temporary. When the source of antibody is a different species there is a risk of serum sickness with repeated doses.

11.2 Killed organism vaccines

Killed organism vaccines

- Cholera
- Pertussis
- Typhoid
- Polio (Salk)
- Influenza
- Rabies

Killed organism vaccines are widely used against both bacteria and viruses. Influenza vaccine is usually offered to those who would fare badly with infection, i.e. patients with chronic illness such as chronic obstructive airways disease (COAD), heart disease, chronic renal disease, rheumatoid arthritis and the elderly.

11.3 Live attenuated vaccines

Live attenuated vaccines

- BCG
- Vaccinia
- Measles

- Mumps
- Rubella
- Polio (Sabin)

Superior to killed vaccines. They deliver a larger sustained dose of antigen and produce a better immune response. Cytotoxic T-cell memory is acquired which needs viral replication. The immunization also occurs at the sites of natural infection. The drawback is that attenuation may fail and actual infection occur, especially in the immunocompromized.

11.4 Subunit vaccines

Subunit vaccines

- *H. influenzae*
- *N. meningitidis*

- *S. pneumoniae*
- Hepatitis B

Purified components of the infective organism. Only antigens that produce a protective response are used. The vaccinated host is not challenged with other antigens that may have deleterious effects such as hypersensitivity. Immunization against Hepatitis B is reserved for high risk groups such as health workers. Pneumoncoccal vaccination is important in asplenic patients and those with hypocomplementaemia.

Chapter 10
Infectious Diseases and Tropical Medicine

CONTENTS

1. **Basic epidemiological concepts**   287
    1.1   Herd immunity
    1.2   Modes of transmission of infection
    1.3   Pathogenesis of infection
    1.4   Predispositions to disease
    1.5   Microbial virulence factors

2. **Host defence mechanisms**   293
    2.1   Non-specific mechanisms (first line of defence)
    2.2   Humoral immunity
    2.3   Cellular immunity

3. **Specific antimicrobials**   295
    3.1   Antibacterial agents
    3.2   Antituberculous drugs
    3.3   Antiviral drugs
    3.4   Anthelmintic agents
    3.5   Other agents used to counteract infection

4. **Infections in specific situations**   300
    4.1   Pregnancy
    4.2   Alcoholism
    4.3   Splenectomy
    4.4   Sickle cell disease

5. **Major clinical syndromes**   301
    5.1   Respiratory infections
    5.2   Neurological infections
    5.3   Gastrointestinal infections
    5.4   Specific soft tissue infections

6. **Specific tropical infections**   306

    6.1   Malaria
    6.2   Enteric fevers
    6.3   Amoebiasis
    6.4   Schistosomiasis
    6.5   Leprosy

Infectious Diseases and Tropical Medicine

1. BASIC EPIDEMIOLOGICAL CONCEPTS

1.1 Herd immunity

This concept is derived from the recognition that complete protection of a given population against an infectious disease by immunization does not require 100% coverage. Partial coverage of a population, by reducing the number of susceptible people within it, will reduce the efficiency of transmission to below the levels needed to sustain a particular infectious disease.

1.2 Modes of transmission of infection

Respiratory transmission

Exhaled droplets containing organisms from infected persons will travel for up to 2 metres before falling to the ground. Inhalation of such droplets in sufficient quantity will result in infection.

Respiratory transmission: major pathogens

- *Mycobacterium tuberculosis*
- *Haemophilus influenzae*
- *Streptococcus pyogenes*
- *Neisseria meningitidis*
- *Streptococcus pneumoniae*
- Childhood respiratory viruses (e.g. measles, chickenpox)

Some pathogens are acquired via the respiratory route but hardly ever from an infected human source, for example:

- ***Legionella pneumophilia*** (aerosols from shower heads, cooling towers, air conditioning systems etc)
- ***Coxiella burneti*** (aerosols and dust from sheep/goat faeces, also products of conception from same animals).

Faecal–oral transmission

This occurs when gastrointestinal pathogens from the faeces of a human (or animal) case or carrier gain access to food, water or dairy products. The practice of anilingus can transmit many gut pathogens.

A period of amplification prior to consumption is usually required to build up sufficient inoculum to cause disease. However, the level of inoculum required to cause disease is smaller in people with reduced GA secretion, such as those on anti-ulcer medications, alcoholics, and patients with partial gastrectomy.

Some organisms are capable of causing disease with much smaller amounts of infective inoculum. **Shigella dysenteriae** can produce severe diarrhoea with as few as 12 ingested organisms, and so direct transmission from contaminated surfaces to hands to mouth is possible, particularly in children. **Giardia lamblia** also needs a relatively small inoculum of cysts (approx. 100) to cause disease. **Enteroviruses** (e.g. poliovirus and hepatitis A) are also transmitted by this route.

Animal faeces may contain human pathogens (e.g. *Salmonella* spp., *Campylobacter* spp., *Cryptosporidium parvum*, rotavirus).

Sexual transmission

Close apposition of the genito-urinary (GU) mucosa is usually required for transmission of GU tract pathogens because of their fragility. Sometimes oro-genital contact may result in sexually transmitted disease (STD), and it can occasionally occur through oral–oral contact (e.g. syphilis). A bite from an infected person may also give rise to a primary syphilitic chancre in normal skin.

- Congenital transmission of many STDs can occur either during pregnancy (e.g. syphilis) or during delivery (e.g. gonorrhoea, *Chlamydia* infection, *Herpes simplex*).

(For more information on genito-urinary and HIV infections see Chapter 7, *Genito-urinary Medicine and AIDS*.)

Congenital transmission

This may be either transplacental or perinatal. Fetal death or deformity is a variable result of transplacental infection.

Important syndromes with particular organisms are given below.

- **Rubella**: heart, eye, CNS. The fetus is nearly always affected if infection occurs in the first 7 weeks of pregnancy; after the 17th week of pregnancy specific deformities are unusual.
- **Toxoplasmosis**: affects the fetus only during maternal primary infection, except in immunocompromised mothers. There is a lower risk of transmission (but more severe disease) in the first trimester. Hydrocephalus, cerebral calcification and choroidoretinitis comprise a classic triad.
- **Chickenpox**: maternal infection in the first trimester can cause limb deformities; later infections cause infant/childhood zoster. Maternal zoster can, very rarely, cause similar problems.
- **Cytomegalovirus (CMV)**: infection may be either transplacental or by perinatal routes, as a result of primary maternal infection or reactivation. At least 75% of infected babies are undamaged. The main syndromes are neurological, including intracranial calcification, microcephaly and cerebral palsy; also cardiac syndromes (septal defects, Fallot's) and GI tract syndromes (hepatosplenomegaly, cleft palate, biliary and oesophageal atresia) can occur.
- *Herpes simplex*: infection is nearly always perinatal and gives rise to severe neonatal disease; 80% are due to type 2 virus.
- **Parvovirus B19**: either fetal death (with abortion or stillbirth) or complete recovery is the rule. Hydrops fetalis is the main intrauterine syndrome.
- **Listeriosis**: both transplacental and perinatal infection can occur. The result is abortion (early) or neonatal septicaemia (late) depending on the stage of pregnancy affected.

Blood-borne transmission

Viruses comprise the most common problem, but other organisms feature in certain situations.

- **Hepatitis B (and delta agent)**: very small amounts of blood are required for transmission of hepatitis B because of the high concentrations of virus present in most carriers or cases. Thus there is a high risk of infection from needle stick injury. In contrast, needle stick transmission is much less likely with HIV because of low virus concentrations.
- **CMV**: transmission in blood is of clinical importance in the immunosuppressed due to the risk of CMV related disease in such patients (e.g. in transplant recipients).
- **HTLV-1**: transmitted by blood (also by sexual intercourse and breast milk).
- **Other blood-borne viruses**: hepatitis C + G, Epstein–Barr virus.

Blood-borne transmission of bacterial infection

This is not a major clinical problem, but some examples are given below.

- **Syphilis**: classically from blood transfusion
- **Enterobacters**: from contaminated whole blood or platelets stored at room temperature
- **Q fever**: a few case reports
- **Protozoa**: transmitted by blood transfusion
- **Malaria**: all species are transmitted by blood and blood products such as platelets and fresh frozen plasma; infectivity may remain for up to 10 days in stored blood.
- **African and American trypanosomiasis**: both of these may be transmitted by blood transfusion. Chagas' disease is a major (late) complication of blood transfusion in South America.
- **Visceral leishmaniasis**: can be transmitted via transfused blood, particularly in the endemic parts of the Indian subcontinent where the human population acts as the main reservoir of infection and where transmission is usually insect-borne. Various animal species fulfil this role elsewhere in the world.

1.3 Pathogenesis of infection

Invasion of, or attachment to, the mucosal surfaces (i.e. respiratory, gastrointestinal, genito-urinary) is the usual first step in the establishment of an infection. Direct penetration of the epithelium may occur by trauma or by insect bite; some organisms (e.g. leptospires, cercariae (of schistosomes), larvae of hookworm and *Strongyloides*) can penetrate intact skin.

Only a minority (occasionally tiny) of infected individuals develop disease as a consequence of any given infection. The remainder remain asymptomatic and the infection clears spontaneously with an appropriate immune response. This is an almost universal principle across a large spectrum of infections (e.g. meningococcal infection, poliomyelitis, leprosy).

1.4 Predispositions to disease

Host vulnerability or (conversely) resistance to disease is multifactorial. The outcome of any infection depends upon the balance struck between the **inoculum size**, the **virulence** of the pathogen and **host factors**, listed opposite.

Host factors affecting vulnerability to disease

- **Immunological**
  Genetic deficiency
  Immunoglobulin/complement/
    T-cell deficiencies

  Prior immunity
  Naturally or articificially acquired

  Acquired deficiency
  HIV infection; malignant disease;
    transplant recipients; patients
    receiving chemotherapy

  *Miscellaneous influences on
    immune status*
    (e.g. diabetes, pregnancy, splenectomy)

- **Other factors**
  Psychological status

  Nutritional status
  (e.g. measles in under-nutrition)

  Prior antibiotic therapy
  (e.g. *Clostridium difficile*, multi-
  resistant *Staphylococcus aureus* infections)

  Foreign bodies
  (e.g. catheters; artificial heart valves)

  Behavioural factors
  (e.g. smokers, alcoholics)

1.5 Microbial virulence factors

These include the ability to invade and evade **host immune** defences, often by the production of **enzymes** and **toxins**.

As described above, penetration into host tissues usually occurs via an epithelial surface and certain microbial factors aid this process. **Invasion** through a mucosal surface first requires **attachment**. This can be relatively non-specific, mediated only by the production of a polysaccharide capsule or slime. Alternatively, specific structures on the organism's surface known as **adhesins** attach to specific glycoprotein or glycolipid **receptors** on the host cell.

Examples of receptors and attaching organisms

- **D mannose**
  Enterobacteriaceae

- **CD4 T-cell receptors**
  HIV

- **N-acetyl-d-glycosamine**
  Chlamydiae, Group B streptococci,
  Plasmodium falciparum and
  Entamoeba histolytica

- **Duffy blood group antigen**
  *Plasmodium vivax**

* Duffy blood groups are very rare in Africans, hence there is little vivax in Africa.

Following invasion, the pathogenic organism has many survival strategies.

- **Production of spreading enzymes**: (e.g. hyaluronidase, elastase, collagenase, nucleases).

- **Evasion of immune defences**: by avoidance of phagocytic killing, achieved by a variety of means such as:

  Encapsulation (*Staphylococcus aureus*, *Streptococcus pyogenes/pneumoniae*, *Neisseria* spp.);
  Inhibition of phagolysosome fusion (*Mycobacterium tuberculosis*, *Chlamydia* spp., *Legionella* spp.);
  Antigenic mimicry (*Schistosoma mansoni*);
  Antigenic shift (influenza virus, pili of *Neisseria gonorrhoeae*);
  Resistance to lysosomal enzymes (*M. leprae*, *Leishmania* spp.);
  Phagocyte destruction (streptolysin from *S. pyogenes*, alpha toxin from *Clostridium perfringens*).

Toxins

These are products of pathogenic bacteria which can be classified into endotoxins and exotoxins.

- **Endotoxin**: an **integral lipopolysaccharide** component of Gram-negative cell walls. Its active component, **lipid A** induces fever, provokes the coagulation and complement cascades, activates B lymphocytes and stimulates production of tumour necrosis factor, interleukin-1 and prostaglandins. Heavy exposure as in Gram-negative sepsis causes fever, shock and occasionally death.

- **Exotoxins**: produced by a diversity of organisms, with equally diverse effects:

    Vibrio cholerae — secretory diarrhoea (small bowel);
    Corynebacterium diphtheriae — cardiomyopathy, neuropathy;
    Clostridium tetani — tetanus;
    Clostridium perfringens — gangrene, secretory diarrhoea;
    Clostridium botulinum — paralysis.

2. HOST DEFENCE MECHANISMS

2.1 Non-specific mechanisms ('first line of defence')

Polymorphonuclear neutrophils (PMNs) circulate freely in the absence of an infectious process and do not attach to capillary endothelium. Cytokines and complement fragments which are produced at the site of an infection make local capillary endothelium and passing PMNs 'stickier'.

Glycoprotein receptors on PMNs enable them to stick to receptors on the endothelium (**margination**) prior to the process of **diapedesis** (migration through the intercellular gaps in the capillary endothelium). PMNs kill by first attaching to the pathogen (with or without the aid of opsonins) and then ingesting the pathogen, to form a **phagosome**.

Lysosomes in the PMN then discharge strong hydrolytic enzymes into the phagosome — known as a **phagolysosome**. The enzymes comprise lysozyme, elastase, a protease and myeloperoxidase. The latter reacts with H_2O_2 and chloride ion to form hypochlorous acid, and oxygen free radicals are produced. These products are highly toxic for micro-organisms. **Natural antibodies** belong mainly to the IgM class and act against pathogens which the host has not previously encountered. They are probably formed as a result of exposure to antigenically similar but harmless organisms (e.g. exposure to the commensal *Neisseria lactamica* produces protective antibody against the meningococcus).

The **acute phase response** is initiated by cytokines released by cells of the macrophage/ monocyte lineage at the site of an infection. They circulate to the liver where they trigger the release of certain proteins. These include **C-reactive protein, lipopolysaccharide binding protein** and **serum amyloid A protein**. Their concentration may increase 1000-fold or more, whereas others, such as complement factor B and alpha 1 anti-trypsin, increase by a more modest two- or three-fold. These substances have a particular role to play in the control of the immune response to infection; **transferrin** is also a major component of this response. Its major role is to mop up iron and other metals (e.g. zinc) thus denying them to invading bacteria.

The **complement system** provides protection in many ways but its main functions are:

- Direct lysis
- Opsonization
- Leucocyte chemotaxis
- Promotion of the inflammatory response.

2.2 Humoral immunity

Specific antibodies appear within 7–10 days of primary exposure to an antigen; a significant proportion of these are of the IgM class making measurement of this antibody useful in serological diagnosis.

Secondary exposure results in an accelerated response, primarily of the IgG class.

Antibody functions can be summarized thus:

- Opsonization/lysis (with complement)
- Neutralization of toxins
- Eosinophil-mediated killing
- Protective coating of host cells
- Facilitation of NK cell activity

'Secretory' IgA antibodies are produced by B cells in the lamina propria of the gut; they comprise two IgA molecules linked together and as such are resistant to digestion by small bowel enzymes.

2.3 Cellular immunity

Antibodies cannot penetrate infected cells to kill an organism that may be contained within. Sensitized T-cells perform the role of destroying infected cells. They are usually of the CD8 subtype and do so by cytolytic action following direct contact with the target cell; neither complement nor antibody is involved. Such contact can only occur when the target cell and effector cell share the same class 1 histocompatibility antigens.

Sensitized T-cells can also produce lymphokines which specifically stimulate macrophages to destroy organisms against which they are indifferent in the unstimulated state. These macrophages will then be non-specifically more active against a variety of organisms.

3. SPECIFIC ANTIMICROBIALS

3.1 Antibacterial agents

Penicillins

- **Mechanism of action**: damage to bacterial cell wall by attachment to penicillin binding proteins (PBPs) in the cell wall, inhibiting cross-linking. Resistance can be due to two different mechanisms: beta-lactamase activity which breaks the penicillin beta-lactam ring or the presence of non-penicillin-binding proteins (e.g. methicillin-resistant *S. aureus* (MRSA); also some pneumococci).
- **Serious side-effects**: anaphylaxis (rare); interstitial nephritis (rare); encephalopathy (very rare, but beware high dosage in acute meningitis).
- **Contraindications**: previous sensitivity; intrathecal injection; nearly always safe in pregnancy.
- **Excretion**: the main excretory route of most penicillins is via the kidneys; dosage adjustment is therefore required in anuria. Nafcillin is metabolized in the liver.

Cephalosporins

- **Mechanism of action**: very similar to penicillins. Most are variably resistant to different beta-lactamases from different bacterial classes. They bind to PBPs and therefore PBP mutations are resistant (as with penicillins).
- **Serious side-effects**: bronchospasm; anaphylaxis; nephrotoxicity (rare).
- **Contraindications**: previous sensitivity, nearly always safe in pregnancy.
- **Excretion**: main excretory route renal. Reduce dose in severe renal failure.

Quinolones

- **Mechanism of action**: inhibition of bacterial DNA synthesis.
- **Spectrum of activity**: broad, but better against Gram-negatives; poor anti-anaerobe activity. Can be used as second line antituberculous agents (e.g. ciprofloxacin).
- **Relevant pharmacokinetics**: well-absorbed from the gut; absorption delayed by food and also reduced by magnesium or calcium hydroxide antacids and H$_2$ blockers.
- **Serious side-effects**: hallucinations, psychotic reactions, convulsions, photosensitivity.
- **Contraindications**: pregnancy and in children (because of effects on growing cartilage in young animals).
- **Excretion**: both renal and hepatic (see Chapter 2, *Clinical Pharmacology, Toxicology and Poisoning*).

√ tendon rupture

Sulphonamides

- **Mechanism of action**: competitive inhibition of enzyme which converts para-amino benzoic acid (PABA) into folic acid.
- **Relevant pharmacokinetics**: well-absorbed from the gut.
- **Spectrum of activity**: wide, including chlamydiae, toxoplasma and plasmodia, but resistance common.
- **Serious side-effects**: agranulocytosis, thrombocytopenia, leukopenia, displacement of warfarin from plasma proteins.

Tetracyclines

- **Mechanism of action**: inhibition of bacterial protein synthesis by blocking binding of tRNA to the 30s subunit.
- **Spectrum of activity**: broad, inclusive of rickettsiae, chlamydiae, mycoplasmas.
- **Relevant pharmacokinetics**: well-absorbed but food, milk, magnesium, calcium, aluminium and iron compounds tend to reduce this.
- **Serious side-effects**: photosensitivity, exacerbation of renal failure, effects on teeth and bones: discoloration and hypoplasia of enamel (children <8 years), depression of skeletal growth — fetus and premature infant.
- **Excretion**: via kidneys.

Macrolides

- **Mechanism of action**: inhibition of bacterial protein synthesis by binding to the 50s ribosome.
- **Spectrum of activity**: broad, inclusive of mycoplasmas, chlamydiae and rickettsiae. Useful activity against pneumococci, also legionella. **Clindamycin** is particularly effective against anaerobes. **Clarithromycin** is also useful as second line antituberculous drug.
- **Relevant pharmacokinetics**: moderately absorbed from gut.
- **Serious side-effects**: thrombophlebitis (i.v. preparation), transient hearing loss, cholestatic hepatitis (erythromycin estolate), pseudomembranous colitis (particularly clindamycin).
- **Excretion**: mainly hepatic; some renal excretion. Reduced dose in severe renal failure.

Aminoglycosides

- **Mechanism of action**: inhibition of bacterial protein synthesis.
- **Spectrum of activity**: predominantly active against Gram-negative aerobic bacilli. Not active against anaerobes. Amikacin has broadest spectrum of activity.
- **Serious side-effects**: ototoxicity, renal tubular damage.
- **Excretion**: via the kidneys. Careful monitoring of plasma levels required to avoid toxicity.

3.2 Antituberculous drugs

Rifampicin

- **Mechanism of action:** inhibition of DNA-dependent RNA polymerase.
- **Spectrum of activity:** broad, inclusive of antituberculous activity. Useful prophylactic against meningococcus, also against legionella infection. Rifabutin is better against *Mycobacterium avium-intracellulare*.
- **Relevant pharmacokinetics:** well-absorbed from gut; potent inducer of hepatic enzymes causing accelerated metabolism of many drugs (e.g. warfarin and contraceptive pill).
- **Serious side-effects:** hepatic toxicity (especially in alcoholics).
- **Excretion:** hepatic.

Isoniazid

- **Mechanism of action:** inhibition of cell wall synthesis.
- **Spectrum of activity:** exclusively antituberculous.
- **Relevant pharmacokinetics:** well-absorbed; must be given with pyridoxine, particularly in slow acetylators, to prevent peripheral neuropathy. Variable activity against other mycobacteria.
- **Serious side-effects:** peripheral neuropathy, psychosis, convulsions, hepatitis-like syndrome, lupus-like syndrome.
- **Excretion:** hepatic.

Pyrazinamide

- **Mechanism of action:** poorly understood, but works best in more acid environment, i.e. inside phagosomes.
- **Spectrum of activity:** exclusively antituberculous, not effective against *Mycobacterium bovis*.
- **Relevant pharmacokinetics:** well-absorbed.
- **Serious side-effects:** hepatotoxicity (dose-related).
- **Excretion:** hepatic.

Ethambutol

- **Mechanism of action:** inhibits bacterial RNA synthesis.
- **Spectrum of activity:** good range of activity against other mycobacteria.
- **Relevant pharmacokinetics:** well-absorbed.
- **Serious side-effects:** retrobulbar neuritis, impairment of colour vision or visual acuity. (Careful monitoring of visual acuity necessary during training.)
- **Excretion:** renal.

Streptomycin

- **Mechanism of action**: inhibits bacterial protein synthesis by binding to the 50s ribosome. Now rarely used (mainly for drug-resistance or in cases of toxicity with other agents); parenteral use only, and can be given intrathecally.
- **Serious side-effects**: ototoxicity, renal tubular damage.
- **Excretion**: via the kidneys.

3.3 Antiviral drugs

Acyclovir

- **Mechanism of action**: selective activity against **herpes viruses** that encode a **thymidine kinase**. The latter phosphorylates the drug (to monophosphate), the process being continued by host cell enzymes to triphosphate. Acyclovir triphosphate competes with guanosine triphosphate causing termination of the growing viral DNA chain. Thus only virus infected cells convert acyclovir to an active form; it remains virtually inert in uninfected healthy cells.
- **Spectrum of activity**: very useful for *herpes simplex* and *herpes varicella-zoster* infections, the important principle being early commencement of therapy.
- **Serious side-effects**: renal failure (usually reversible); neurotoxicity (rare) with hallucinations, psychosis, convulsions and/or coma. May occur with drug accumulation in severe renal failure.
- **Contraindications**: very safe in most situations, including pregnancy.
- **Excretion**: excreted unchanged by the kidneys.

Ganciclovir

Similar mechanism of action, metabolism and side-effects as for acyclovir. However, gancyclovir has a greater effect against CMV; it is used to treat AIDS patients with retinitis, and also for the CMV infections which are common in transplanted patients.

Ribavirin

- **Mechanism of action**: analogue of the nucleoside guanosine; inhibits nucleoside biosynthesis, mRNA capping and other processes essential to viral replication.
- **Spectrum of activity**: useful as an aerosol in severe respiratory syncytial virus (RSV) infection, also for Lassa fever (early treatment important).
- **Serious side-effects**: bone marrow depression.

3.4 Anthelmintic agents

Benzimidazoles

(e.g. albendazole, thiabendazole, mebendazole)
- **Mechanism of action**: the net effect of various biochemical activities is a reduction or paralysis of parasite motility.
- **Spectrum of activity**: broad against intestinal nematodes (e.g. Trichuris, Necator, Ascaris, Ancylostoma, Enterobius; also cestodes such as Hymenolepis, Taenia and Echinococcus).

Piperazines

- **Mechanism of action**: induction of paralysis in target worms.
- **Spectrum of activity**: piperazine is useful against *Ascaris* and *Enterobius*. Diethylcarbamazine (DEC) is also active against the microfilariae of *Onchocerca volvulus* (cause of river blindness), *Wuchereria bancrofti* and *Brugia malayi* (both causes of lymphatic filariasis).

Praziquantel

- **Mechanism of action**: acts as calcium agonist; causes elevated intracellular calcium, tetanic muscular contraction and destruction of the tegument. This allows hitherto unexposed antigens to be attacked by host antibody.
- **Spectrum of activity**: has particularly useful activity against *Schistosoma* and *Taenia*.

3.5 Other agents used to counteract infection

Immunoglobulins

Normal human immunoglobulin has many applications, particularly in passively immunizing patients with humoral immunodeficiency. Kawasaki disease (possibly due to an infectious agent) is one clear-cut application. There are also a number of specific immunoglobulins for specific situations (e.g. tetanus, rabies, diphtheria, hepatitis B and zoster immune globulin).

Vaccines

- **Inactivated/killed vaccines**: the predominant vaccine type for bacterial disease, e.g. toxoids (diphtheria, tetanus); killed cell (pertussis, typhoid); capsular polysaccharide (*Haemophilus influenza* b, meningococcal, pneumococcal).
- **Attenuated/live vaccines**: the predominant vaccine type for viral disease (with exceptions) e.g. attenuated (measles, mumps, rubella, yellow fever, polio); subunit (hepatitis B); inactivated (rabies, Japanese encephalitis, influenza, hepatitis A).
- **Attenuated bacterial vaccines**: BCG, oral typhoid vaccine.

(See also Chapter 9, *Immunology*.)

4. INFECTIONS IN SPECIFIC SITUATIONS

4.1 Pregnancy

Because **the fetus is antigenically different from the mother**, modulation of selected aspects of the maternal immune response is necessary for the fetus to be tolerated. The placenta is responsible for this modulation.

Infections exacerbated by pregnancy

- Urinary tract infection
- Listeria
- Varicella
  (pneumonitis life-threatening,
    especially in 3rd trimester)
- Candidiasis

- Pulmonary tuberculosis
- Salmonella
- Hepatitis E
  (25% mortality)
- HIV disease
- Falciparum malaria
  (especially primigravidae in
    second trimester)

For more information on congenital infection, see modes of transmission in section 1.2.

4.2 Alcoholism

Alcoholics are more vulnerable to a number of infections because of the **immunosuppressive effects of excessive alcohol intake**. The neutropenia of alcoholism is probably due to toxic effects on the bone marrow; studies show the neutrophils themselves are less effective and less able to phagocytose foreign particles.

Important infections to which alcoholics are particularly vulnerable

- Pulmonary tuberculosis
- Legionella
- Inhalational pneumonias
- Amoebic abscess
- Salmonella

- Pneumococcal pneumonia
- Klebsiella pneumonia
- Septic shock
- Typhoid fever
- Listeria

4.3 Splenectomy

The spleen accounts for approximately 25% of the body's lymphatic tissue; absence of its function causes particular vulnerability to capsulate organisms such as:

- Pneumococcus
- *Haemophilus influenzae*
- Meningococcus
- DF-2 'Dysgonic fermenter 2' (now known as *Capnocytophaga canimorsus*) characteristically acquired from dog bites.

Splenectomized patients are also vulnerable to malaria and to **babesiosis**, a protozoal infection transmitted by ixodid ticks from an animal reservoir comprising small rodents such as field mice. The merozoite stage of the parasite invades blood cells directly after being injected under the skin by the tick. It causes a mild malaria-like disease in the immunocompetent, but is potentially life-threatening in splenectomized individuals. Diagnosis is by blood film.

4.4 Sickle cell disease

Sicklers (i.e. SS homozygotes) often have functional hyposplenism and also a reduction in complement-mediated serum opsonizing activity. This gives rise to vulnerability to:

- Pneumococcal infection (in particular)
- Other forms of bacterial sepsis
- Osteomyelitis (due to *Salmonella spp.*)
- Falciparum malaria (in contrast to AS heterozygotes who are resistant to malaria).

5. MAJOR CLINICAL SYNDROMES

In the following section short notes and lists of infective organisms are included for the more important clinical syndromes associated with infectious diseases.

5.1 Respiratory infections

Upper respiratory tract

Clinical symptoms of upper respiratory tract infections

- The common cold (coryza)
- Mastoiditis
- Pharyngitis ($\pm$ tonsillitis)
- Otitis media
- Sinusitis
- Laryngitis

Both viruses and bacteria may cause infection in these sites but virus infection usually 'prepares the ground' for a bacterial infection to follow.

Viruses responsible for upper respiratory tract infections

- Rhinoviruses
- Coronaviruses
- Adenoviruses
  (conjunctivitis is an occasional extra feature)
- Parainfluenza viruses
- Coxsackie groups A + B
- Respiratory syncytial virus (RSV)

Bacteria responsible for upper respiratory tract infections

- β haemolytic Group A streptococcus
- *H. influenzae*
- *Neisseria meningitidis*
  (usually asymptomatic)
- *Neisseria gonorrhoae*
  (as above)
- *Branhamella catarrhalis*
- *Mycoplasma pneumoniae*

Lower respiratory tract

Clinical syndromes include: tracheitis, bronchiolitis, pneumonia, bronchitis and alveolitis.

Organisms responsible for lower respiratory tract infections

- **Common**
  Streptococcus pneumoniae
  Haemophilus influenzae
  Streptococcus pyogenes
  Legionella pneumophilia
  Staphylococcus aureus
  Mycoplasma pneumoniae
  Klebsiella pneumoniae

- **Immunocompromised**
  Pseudomonas spp.
  Pneumocystis
  Aspergillus
  CMV

- **Uncommon**
  Chlamydia spp.
  Coxiella burneti
  Leptospira icterohaemorrhagiae
  Fusobacterium necrophorum
  Salmonella typhi
  Francisella tularensis
  Yersinia pestis

- **Viral**
  RSV
  Influenza
  Parainfluenza

For a description of specific pneumonias see Chapter 17, *Respiratory Medicine*.

5.2 Neurological infections

The brain and spinal cord, despite being well protected from the external environment, are prone to a large range of infections from viruses to helminths. The two main clinical syndromes are meningitis and encephalitis. Routes of access are:

- Haematogenous
- Via skull fractures/direct penetration
- Via the cribriform plate
- Via infected sinuses, mastoids or middle ear
- Via peripheral nerves

The **peripheral nerves** tend to be less susceptible to direct bacterial infection (with the exception of leprosy). Most bacterial infections that affect peripheral nerves do so by the action of specific toxins (e.g. botulinum, tetanus). Guillain–Barré syndrome may follow several different viral and bacterial infections. A number of viruses (particularly enteroviruses (e.g. poliovirus)) may seriously damage peripheral nerves.

Meningitis

- **Acute bacterial causes**
  Common in adults
    meningococcus
    pneumococcus
    Haemophilus influenzae
  Common in neonates
    Group B streptococcus
    Escherichia coli
  Rarities (characteristically with
  lymphocytic CSF)
  Listeria monocytogenes
    leptospirosis
    syphilis
    Lyme disease (due to:
    Borrelia burgdorferi)
  Rarities (characteristically with
  polymorphs in CSF)
  Mycobacterium tuberculosis (acute
    onset with CSF polymorphs)
  Staphylococcus aureus

- **Chronic bacterial causes**
  Mycobacterium tuberculosis

- **Chronic fungal causes**
  Cryptococcosis (particularly
    in the immunosuppressed)

- **Acute viral causes**
  Mumps, enteroviruses (e.g. polio),
    herpes simplex (mainly type 2)

- **Miscellaneous causes**
  Cysticercal meningitis (chronic,
    eosinophilic CSF)
  Amoebic meningitis (can be acute
    or chronic); acquired from
    contaminated water gaining access
    through cribriform plate

Encephalitis

- **Viral causes**
  Herpes simplex
    (high mortality/morbidity,
    mainly type 1)
  Enteroviruses, flaviviruses
    (e.g. Japanese encephalitis)
  Varicella
  HIV
  Rabies

- **Other causes**
  Toxoplasmosis
  Cysticercosis
  African trypanosomiasis

See also Chapter 14, *Neurology*.

5.3 Gastrointestinal infections

Bowel

The majority of gut infections cause diarrhoea; as a general rule, small bowel infection usually manifests toxin-mediated watery diarrhoea with no blood whilst large bowel infections (with exceptions) are invasive of colonic mucosa and cause bloody diarrhoea with mucus and sometimes pus — 'dysentery'. (See also Chapter 5, *Gastroenterology*.)

Small bowel, toxin-mediated, 'secretory' infective agents

- *Salmonella* spp.
  Can occasionally be invasive.
  Acquired mainly from eggs and
    chickens

- **Enterotoxigenic *E. coli* (ETEC)**
  Main cause of traveller's
    diarrhoea

- *Vibrio cholerae*

- **Some campylobacters**
  With salmonellas account for
    most acute gastroenteritis
    in UK

- *Yersinia enterocolitica*

- *Aeromonas* spp.

Large bowel, invasive infective agents

- *Shigella* spp.

- *Yersinia enterocolitica*

- Enteroinvasive *E. coli* (EIEC)

- *Entamoeba histolytica*
  NB. Amoebic dysentery is
  occasionally mistaken for
  ulcerative colitis; steroids are
  lethal in this situation

Large bowel, toxin-mediated infective agents

- *Clostridium difficile*

- Enterohaemorrhagic *E. coli* (EHEC)
  (Typical serotype is 0157) —
  verotoxin secreting; may lead
  to epidemic form of
  haemolytic–uraemic syndrome

Liver

The viral hepatitis is described in Chapter 5, *Gastroenterology*.

5.4 Specific soft tissue infections

Staphylococcus aureus and *Staphylococcus pyogenes* are mainly responsible for community-acquired soft tissue infection in otherwise healthy patients. The latter is occasionally responsible for **necrotizing fasciitis**, which requires aggressive surgical debridement as well as antibiotics (i.v. cefotaxime, metronidazole and benzyl penicillin). Necrotizing fasciitis is alternatively due to mixed **facultative anaerobes and anaerobic streptococci**. For the latter, hyperbaric oxygen is advisable; in addition to the above.

Anaerobic soft tissue infection often arises as a complication of severe trauma with destruction of tissue. Human and animal bites may do the same. Dog and cat bites may result in *Pasteurella multocida*, also DF-2 infection (see section 4.3). Anaerobes are also the predominant organism in sepsis arising from the gastrointestinal tract, from dental and gum sepsis to peri-anal abscesses.

6. SPECIFIC TROPICAL INFECTIONS

6.1 Malaria

Four species affect mankind; *Plasmodium falciparum, vivax, ovale* and *malariae. P. falciparum* is potentially lethal, the others are usually more benign.

Complications of falciparum malaria

- **Cerebral malaria**: depression of consciousness is the main feature; other neurological syndromes include seizures, focal neurological disorders and acute psychosis
- **Blackwater fever**: may cause renal failure due to massive intravascular haemolysis; the haemolysing red cells have not been parasitized but appear to become fragile through some other (unknown) mechanism. Parasites are typically scanty or even absent on blood films
- **Pulmonary oedema**: has many features in common with the adult respiratory distress syndrome of Gram-negative sepsis; neither left ventricular failure nor fluid overload contribute primarily to the pathogenesis of the oedema. Mortality is severe (80%).
- **Severe anaemia**: partly due to haemolysis, also marrow suppression, the mechanism of the latter being poorly understood
- **Splenic rupture**
- **Glomerulonephritis**
- **Hepatitis syndrome**: easily mistaken clinically for 'viral hepatitis'
- **Hyper-reactive malarious splenomegaly**: previously known as 'tropical splenomegaly' syndrome.

Treatment of falciparum malaria comprises quinine and fansidar, the other species still being sensitive to chloroquine (except for a few vivax strains found in Papua New Guinea and Indonesia).

Newer drugs include: artemesinin and atovaquone.

Complications of infection with other malaria species

- Splenic rupture
- Nephrotic syndrome in children with *P. malariae* infection 'Quartan nephropathy'.

6.2 Enteric fevers

Both typhoid and paratyphoid are included in this category. Blood cultures are usually positive in the first two weeks of illness; stool cultures in the second two weeks. The Widal test is unreliable.

Quinolones are now the treatment of choice, with most *S. typhi*, particularly from the Indian subcontinent, being chloramphenicol-resistant. High-dose steroids have been shown to be beneficial in fulminant disease, unlike other forms of Gram-negative sepsis.

6.3 Amoebiasis

The majority of infections with *Entamoeba histolytica* are benign, as evidenced by the very high asymptomatic cyst excretion rate found in many parts of the world. Factors which convert this benign state into disease are not known. The latter can vary from mild diarrhoea to fulminant colitis.

- Diagnosis is by microscopy of fresh warm stool or by serology for invasive disease (colitis or liver abscesses). The latter are usually single and unloculated, unlike pyogenic abscesses which tend to be multiple and loculated.

- **Amoebic liver abscesses hardly ever require a drainage procedure whilst pyogenic ones usually do.**

- Both types of abscess can present 'chronically', resembling malignant disease of the liver with the potential for misdiagnosis.

- Treatment comprises metronidazole or tinidazole with diloxanide furoate to eradicate intestinal cyst carriage.

6.4 Schistosomiasis

This causes much morbidity worldwide. The three principal species affecting man are:

- *Schistosoma mansoni* (bowel and liver)
- *S. haematobium* (urinary tract)
- *S. japonicum* (bowel and liver).

They are **trematodes**. According to species, the adult worms live in the venous plexuses of the portal tract or in those of the bladder. The adult worms tend not to inflict much damage. They release huge numbers of eggs which make their way through the wall of the blood vessel into the surrounding tissue; the principal pathological feature is a **granuloma around the egg**.

This results in fibrosis on a macroscopic scale giving rise to **obstructive uropathy** or **liver fibrosis** with portal hypertension. **Bladder cancer** is also a well-recognized complication of urinary schistosomiasis. Sometimes the eggs gain access to the pulmonary and systemic circulations with extra consequences such as **pulmonary hypertension** (e.g. *haematobium*), **paraparesis** (e.g. *mansoni*), or **seizures** (e.g. *japonicum*).

Diagnosis is by identification of ova in the urine or faeces or in tissue biopsy. Serological diagnosis is a useful alternative. The treatment of choice is praziquantel (see Section 3.4).

6.5 Leprosy

This is a very indolent inflammatory disease of skin and nerves with a natural history measurable in years. Most infection is subclinical without progression to disease; this can be demonstrated by positive serology in asymptomatic contacts.

Only 5% of healthy spouses of lepromatous leprosy patients (the most infective kind) eventually get the disease. Clinical expression in a given patient depends on the degree of T-cell-mediated immune response to *Mycobacterium leprae*.

- The immunological spectrum in the patient population varies from lepromatous (LL), with no measurable T-cell responses, to tuberculoid (TT), with brisk T-cell responses. There are intermediate stages termed borderline (BB), borderline lepromatous (BL), and borderline tuberculoid (BT). These immunological variants can be closely correlated with the clinical expression of the disease.

- Diagnosis requires appropriate diagnostic suspicion of any longstanding rash or neuropathy in a patient from an indigenous area (most tropical countries, including SE Asia, India, Africa, West Indies, South America). Treatment comprises remedial and protective advice (because of anaesthetic, feet, hands etc.) as well as drugs.

- Rifampicin, dapsone and clofazimine currently comprise the WHO recommended multi-drug regime. Reactions are due to a shift in the individual's immune status either up or down the spectrum.

Type 1 (reversal reactions): are towards TT and give rise to acute inflammatory, often painful episodes involving affected nerves and skin. These sometimes resemble acute cellulitis but need to be recognized and treated quickly (with steroids) because of the rapidity of the nerve damage which ensues.

Type 2 reactions: are towards LL and comprise fever, erythema nodosum leprosum and occasionally life-threatening glomerulonephritis and renal failure.

Chapter 11
Metabolic Diseases

CONTENTS

1. **Disorders of amino acid metabolism**   311
    1.1   Alkaptonuria (ochronosis)
    1.2   Cystinosis
    1.3   Cystinuria
    1.4   Homocystinuria
    1.5   Oxalosis
    1.6   Phenylketonuria (PKU)

2. **Disorders of purine metabolism**   315
    2.1   Gout
    2.2   Lesch–Nyhan syndrome

3. **Disorders of metals and metaloproteins**   316
    3.1   Wilson's disease
    3.2   Haemochromatosis
    3.3   Secondary iron overload
    3.4   The porphyrias

4. **Disorders of lipid metabolism**   321
    4.1   Lipid metabolism
    4.2   The hyperlipidaemias
    4.3   Lipid-lowering drugs
    4.4   Rare lipid disorders

5. **Disorders of bone, mineral metabolism and inorganic ions** 329
    5.1   Calcium homeostasis
    5.2   Hypercalcaemia
    5.3   Hyperparathyroid bone disease
    5.4   Hypocalcaemia
    5.5   Osteomalacia
    5.6   Paget's disease
    5.7   Osteoporosis
    5.8   Disorders of magnesium
    5.9   Disorders of phosphate

6. **Nutritional and vitamin disorders**   **341**
    6.1   Protein-energy malnutrition (PEM)
    6.2   Vitamin deficiencies

7. **Metabolic acid base disturbances (non-renal) and hypothermia**   **345**
    7.1   Metabolic acidosis
    7.2   Metabolic alkalosis
    7.3   Hypothermia

Metabolic Diseases

1. DISORDERS OF AMINO ACID METABOLISM

Inborn errors of metabolism are almost all autosomal recessive conditions resulting from enzyme defects. Although heterozygotes may synthesize equal amounts of normal and defective enzymes they are usually asymptomatic.

- Even the major inborn errors of amino acid metabolism are rare — phenylketonuria, one of the most common, has an incidence of 1/20,000.
- Complete penetrance is common and the onset is frequently early in life.
- The consequences of these enzyme deficiences are varied and frequently multisystem but expression tends to be uniform.

The more common of these conditions are listed in the box below and the major inborn errors of amino acid metabolism are then discussed.

Inborn errors of amino acid metabolism

- Albinism
- Cystinosis
- Homocystinuria
- Maple syrup urine disease
- Phenylketonuria
- Alkaptonuria
- Cystinuria
- Histidinaemia
- Oxalosis

1.1 Alkaptonuria (ochronosis)

This is a rare autosomal recessive disease with an incidence of 1/100,000. Homogentisic acid accumulates as a result of a deficiency in the enzyme homogentisic acid oxidase.

- The homogentisic acid polymerizes to produce the black–brown product, alkapton, which becomes deposited in cartilage and other tissues (ochronosis).
- Clinical features include pigmentation of the ears, arthritis, inter-vertebral disc calcification and dark sweat-stained clothing.

- The urine darkens on standing because homogentisic acid conversion to alkapton is accelerated in alkaline conditions.
- There is no specific treatment but arthritis may require symptomatic therapy.

1.2 Cystinosis

In cystinosis, cystine accumulates in the reticuloendothelial system, kidneys and other tissues. There is a defect of cystine transport across the lysosomal membrane resulting in widespread intra-lysosomal accumulation of cystine. The cystinosis gene has recently been linked to markers on the short arm of chromosome 17. Unlike cystinuria, stones do not occur in this condition.

Clinical features of cystinosis

- Severe growth retardation
- Lymphadenopathy
- Bone marrow failure
- Corneal opacities and photophobia
- Hypothyroidism
- Central nervous system involvement
- Fanconi syndrome
(often with severe hypophosphataemia and consequent vitamin D-resistant rickets)
- Insulin deficiency
- Abnormalities of cardiac conduction

Onset is usually in the first year of life and the renal disease is progressive often resulting in end stage renal failure by the age of 10 years. Corneal or conjunctival crystals usually suggest the diagnosis which can be confirmed by measuring the cystine content of neutrophils. Specific therapy with cysteamine bitartrate is effective at reducing cystine accumulation and delaying renal failure. However, this treatment is unpleasant and rarely tolerated. Supportive care, including dialysis and transplantation, is usually needed. Cystinosis does not recur in the transplant but extra-renal disease is progressive.

1.3 Cystinuria

Cystinuria is an autosomal recessive disorder with a prevalence of about 1/7000. The transport of cystine and the other dibasic amino acids lysine, ornithine and arginine is abnormal in the proximal renal tubule and the jejunum.

- No malnutrition occurs as sufficient dietary amino acids are absorbed as oligopeptides.
- Presentation is usually in the second or third decade of life with renal stones.
- Cystine is highly insoluble at acid pH resulting in the formation of radio-opaque calculi.

A urinary cystine concentration >1 mmol/l (at pH 7.0) is supersaturated and leads to calculi formation.

Diagnosis requires measurement of urinary cystine and/or chromatographic analysis of the stone.

Management

Large fluid intake, alkalinization of urine and D-penicillamine (which chelates cystine and increases its solubility). Captopril also binds to thiol groups of cystine and increases its solubility.

1.4 Homocystinuria

This autosomal recessive abnormality results from reduced activity of cystathionine β-synthase. The resulting homocysteine and methionine accumulation interferes with collagen cross-linking.

Clinical features of homocystinuria

- Downward lens dislocation
- Osteoporosis
- Arterial thromboses
- Mental retardation

Diagnosis is established by the cyanide-nitroprusside test that detects elevated urinary homocysteine.

Management

Early detection (of younger siblings). Methionine restriction and cystine supplemented diets. Pyridoxine supplements (effective in 50%). Some variants are responsive to folate or vitamin B12 supplements.

1.5 Oxalosis

There are two inborn errors of metabolism that cause overproduction of oxalate. Both are autosomal recessive and can lead to hyperoxaluria with stones and tissue deposition of oxalate.

- Type I is due to a deficiency of hepatic peroxisomal alanine:glycoxylate aminotransferase.
- Type II is due to a deficiency of D-glyceric acid dehydrogenase.

Clinical features of oxalosis

- Oxalate renal stones
- Bone disease
- Cardiac disease

- Nephrocalcinosis
- Severe arterial disease
  (due to deposition of oxalate crystals
  in the vessel wall)

Diagnosis

Oxalosis should be suspected if there is increased urinary oxalate excretion, but the latter can also occur with pyridoxine deficiency (as this is a necessary co-enzyme in oxalate metabolism), ileal disease, ethyl glycol poisoning and excess oxalate ingestion.

Confirmation of diagnosis requires:

- Liver biopsy to demonstrate enzyme deficiency in Type I
- Demonstration of enzyme deficiency in peripheral blood leucocytes in Type II.

Treatment of oxalosis

- High fluid intake
- Liver transplantation — in Type I

- Pyridoxine
- Renal replacement therapy*

*Renal transplants are often lost due to rapid crystal deposition

---

1.6 Phenylketonuria (PKU)

There are several variants of PKU due to different allelic mutations. Only severe deficiency of the enzyme results in classic PKU with neurological damage.

The biochemical abnormality is an inability to convert phenylalanine into tyrosine due to lack of phenylalanine hydroxylase. This results in hyperphenylalaninaemia and increased excretion of its metabolite, phenylpyruvic acid ('phenylketone'), in the urine.

Clinical features of PKU

- Affects children usually manifesting by 6 months of life
- Eczema

- Mental retardation
- Irritability
- Decreased pigmentation* (pale skin, fair haired and blue-eyed phenotype)

*This is due to reduced melanin formation

Diagnosis

The Guthrie screening test which detects elevated plasma phenylalanine in homozygotes in the perinatal period.

Management

Diet low in phenylalanine, with tyrosine supplementation, in infancy and childhood. PKU females should be advised to reinstitute strict dietary control prior to conception.

2. DISORDERS OF PURINE METABOLISM

Uric acid is the end product of purine metabolism. Purines can be synthesized *de novo* or salvaged from the breakdown of nucleic acids of endogenous or exogenous origin. Increased *de novo* synthesis of purines is thought to be responsible, at least partly, for primary gout. Deficiency of hypoxanthine guanine phosphoribosyl transferase (HGPRT), which is involved in the salvage pathway, results in the Lesch–Nyhan syndrome.

Disorders of purine metabolism

- Primary gout
- Secondary hyperuricaemia

- Lesch–Nyhan syndrome

(See also Chapter 18, *Rheumatology*.)

2.1 Gout

More than 10% of the population of the Western world has hyperuricaemia. Gout develops in fewer than 0.5% of the population. (See also Chapter 18, *Rheumatology*.)

- Primary hyperuricaemia is more common in males and post-menopausal females than in pre-menopausal females.
- It is rare in childhood.
- It is probably polygenic, involving both increased purine synthesis and reduced renal tubular secretion of urate.
- Gout can be precipitated by thiazide diuretics, alcohol and high purine intake.

2.2 Lesch–Nyhan syndrome

Lesch–Nyhan syndrome is an uncommon X-linked recessive disease (therefore seen only in males) due to complete lack of hypoxanthine guanine phosphoribosyl transferase (HGPRT). This results in accumulation of both hypoxanthine and guanine both of which are metabolized to xanthine and subsequently uric acid.

Clinical features of Lesch–Nyhan syndrome

- Mental retardation
- Athetosis
- Gout

- Self-mutilation
- Renal failure

3. DISORDERS OF METALS AND METALOPROTEINS

Iron and copper play central roles in the function of a number of metaloproteins, including cytochrome oxidase, which is essential in cellular aerobic respiration; haem, based on iron, is the key molecule in oxygen transport. Excessive accumulation can, however, promote free radical injury (e.g. Wilson's disease and haemochromatosis) and disorders of haem synthesis result in porphyria.

Disorders of metals and metaloproteins

- Wilson's disease
- Secondary iron overload

- Haemochromatosis
- The porphyrias

3.1 Wilson's disease

This autosomal recessive disorder has a gene frequency of 1/400 and a disease prevalence of approximately 1/200,000. The responsible gene is on chromosome 13.

In normal subjects 50% of ingested copper is absorbed and transported to the liver loosely bound to albumin. Here copper is incorporated into an alpha-2-globulin to form caeruloplasmin which is the principal transport protein for copper, and necessary for biliary excretion.
In Wilson's disease copper absorption is normal but intrahepatic formation of caeruloplasmin is defective. Total body and tissue copper levels rise due to failure of biliary excretion and urinary excretion of copper is increased.

Clinical features of Wilson's disease

- **Onset in childhood or adolescence**

- **Hepatic dysfunction**
  Acute hepatitis
  Chronic hepatitis
  Cirrhosis
  Massive hepatic necrosis

- **Kayser–Fleischer corneal rings**
  Due to copper deposition in
  Descemet's membrane

- **Hypoparathyroidism**

- **Haemolysis**

- **CNS involvement**
  Behavioural problems/psychosis
  Tremor/chorea
  Mental retardation
  Seizures

- **Fanconi syndrome**

- **Arthropathy**

Diagnosis

This is based on a decrease in serum caeruloplasmin and increases in hepatic copper content and urinary excretion of copper. Serum copper levels are of no diagnostic value.

Management

Early detection permits long term use of copper chelators (e.g. penicillamine) to prevent the accumulation of copper. Fulmant hepatic failure and end stage liver disease necessitate liver transplantation which is curative (but CNS sequelae may persist). (See also Chapter 5, *Gastroenterology*.)

3.2 Haemochromatosis

In the normal adult the iron content of the body is closely regulated. Haemochromatosis is the excessive accumulation of iron. Primary (or idiopathic) haemochromatosis is a common autosomal recessive disorder in which iron accumulates in parenchymal cells, leading to damage and fibrosis. Haemosiderin is an insoluble iron protein complex found in macrophages (it is relatively harmless to them) in the bone marrow, liver and spleen. Secondary iron overload, which has many causes, is often referred to as haemosiderosis.

- The gene for haemochromatosis is located on chromosome 6 close to the HLA locus.
- The gene frequency is 6% and disease frequency 1/220 people, but the severity of the disease seems to vary.
- Males are affected earlier and more severely than females (as menstrual loss/pregnancy protects females).
- Heterozygotes are at greater risk of secondary haemosiderosis than non-carriers if they have a predisposing condition.
- Thirty per cent of patients with cirrhosis develop hepatocellular carcinoma. (See also Chapter 5, *Gastroenterology*.)

Clinical features of haemochromatosis

- Presentation above the age of 40 years
- Hepatomegaly preceding micronodular cirrhosis
- Chondrocalcinosis and pseudogout

- Bronze skin pigmentation
- Diabetes mellitus and (rarely) exocrine pancreas failure
- Hypopituitarism, hypogonadism and testicular atrophy
- Cardiomyopathy and arrhythmias

Diagnosis

Serum iron is elevated with greater than 60% transferrin saturation. Serum ferritin > 500 µg/l. Liver iron concentration > 180 µmol/g is also indicative of haemochromatosis.

Management

- Venesection
- Chelation therapy with desferrioxamine
- Screening of first-degree relatives (serum ferritin).

3.3 Secondary iron overload

Secondary haemochromatosis is due to iron overload which can occur in a variety of conditions. The pattern of tissue injury is similar to primary haemochromatosis. In the inherited haemolytic anaemias iron overload can present in adolescence; the features are often modified by the underlying disease. Treatment is with desferrioxamine.

Secondary causes of iron overload

- **Anaemia due to ineffective erythropoiesis**
  Beta thalassaemia
  Sideroblastic anaemia
  Aplastic anaemia
  Pyruvate kinase deficiency

- **Parenteral iron overload**
  Transfusions
  Iron–dextran

- **Liver disease**
  Alcoholic cirrhosis
  Chronic viral hepatitis
  Porphyria cutanea tarda

- **Increased oral iron intake**
  (Bantu siderosis)

- **Congenital transferrinaemia**

3.4 The porphyrias

The porphyrias are a rare heterogeneous group of abnormalities of enzymes involved in the biosynthesis of haem, resulting in overproduction of the intermediate compounds called porphyrins. Excess production of porphyrins can occur in the liver or bone marrow and is classified as acute or non-acute. The haem metabolic pathway, and the type of porphyria resulting from different enzyme deficiencies, are shown in the figure overleaf. The two most important porphyrias are porphyria cutanea tarda and acute intermittent porphyria — these are described in more detail.

Porphyria cutanea tarda

This is the most common hepatic porphyria. There is a genetic predisposition but the pattern of inheritance is not established. Many sporadic cases are due to chronic liver disease, usually alcohol-related.

- There is reduced uroporphyrinogen decarboxylase activity
- Uroporphyrinogen accumulates in blood and urine
- Manifests as photosensitivity rash with bullae.

Diagnosis

Based on elevated urinary uroporphyrinogen (urine is normal in colour).

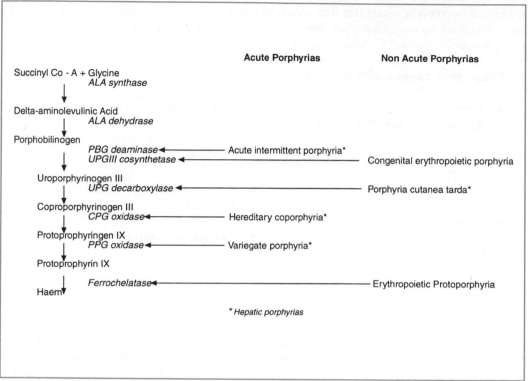

Haem synthesis and the porphyrias

Treatment

- The underlying liver disease
- Chloroquine
- Venesection.

Acute intermittent porphyria

This causes attacks of classical acute porphyria often presenting with abdominal pain and/or neuropsychiatric disorders. It is an autosomal dominant disorder.

- There is reduced hepatic porphobilinogen deaminase activity.
- The gene (and disease) frequency is between 1/10,000 and 1/50,000.
- Episodes of porphyria are more common in females (?due to the effects of oestrogens).

- There is no photosensitivity or skin rash.
- There is increased urinary porphobilinogen and aminolaevulinic acid especially during attacks.
- Urine turns deep red on standing.

Clinical features of acute intermittent porphyria

- Onset in adolescence
- Females more affected
- Polyneuropathy (motor)
- Hypertension and tachycardia

- Episodic attacks
- Abdominal pain, vomiting, constipation
- Neuropsychiatric disorders

Precipitating drugs:

- Alcohol
- Benzodiazepines
- Rifampicin
- Oral contraceptives
- Phenytoin
- Sulphonamides.

Management

- Supportive: maintain high carbohydrate intake; avoid precipitating factors.

4. DISORDERS OF LIPID METABOLISM

Hyperlipidaemia, especially hypercholesterolaemia, is associated with cardiovascular disease.

Total cholesterol (mmol/l)	Relative risk of myocardial infarct
5.2	1
6.5	2
7.8	4

Although lipid metabolism is complex, and many inherited or acquired disorders can disrupt it, the end result is usually elevated cholesterol and/or triglyceride concentrations. These can be managed by dietary and pharmacological means.

4.1 Lipid metabolism

Cholesterol and triglycerides are insoluble in plasma and circulate bound to lipoproteins. The lipoproteins consist of lipids, phospholipids and proteins. The protein components of lipoproteins are called apolipoproteins (or apoproteins) and they act as cofactors for enzymes and ligands for receptors. A schemata of lipoprotein structure is shown below.

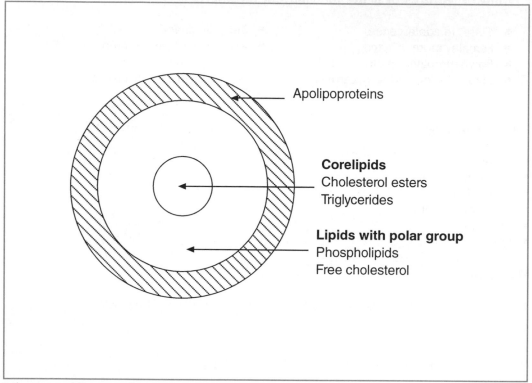

Schemata of lipoprotein structure

There are four major lipoproteins:

- **Chylomicrons**: large particles that carry dietary lipid (mainly triglycerides) from the gastro-intestinal tract to the liver. In the portal circulation lipoprotein lipase acts on chylomicrons to release free fatty acids for energy metabolism.
- **Very low density lipoprotein (VLDL)**: carries endogenous triglyceride (60%), and to a lesser extent cholesterol (20%), from the liver to the tissues. The triglyceride core of the VLDL is also hydrolysed by lipoprotein lipase to release free fatty acids. The VLDL remnants are called intermediate density lipoprotein.
- **Low density lipoprotein (LDL)**: is formed from the intermediate density lipoproteins by hepatic lipase. LDL contains a cholesterol core (50%) and lesser amounts of triglyceride (10%). LDL metabolism is regulated by cellular cholesterol requirements via negative feedback control of the LDL receptor.

- **High density lipoprotein (HDL):** carries cholesterol from the tissues back to the liver. HDL is formed in the liver and gut and acquires free cholesterol from the intracellular pools. Within the HDL, cholesterol is esterified by lecithin cholesterol acyl-transferase (LCAT). HDL is inversely associated with ischaemic heart disease.

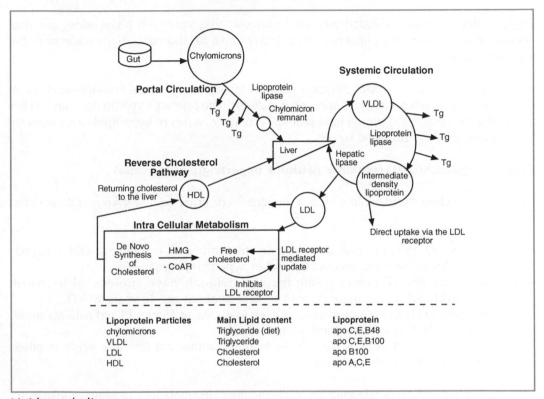

Lipid metabolism

The LDL receptor

Circulating LDL is taken up by the LDL receptor. Cells replete in cholesterol reduce LDL receptor expression. In contrast, inhibition of 3-hydroxy-3-methylglutaryl coenzyme A (HMG CoA) reductase, the enzyme that controls the rate of *de novo* cholesterol synthesis, leads to a fall in cellular cholesterol and an increase in LDL receptor expression.

Lipoprotein (a)

Lp(a) is a specialized form of LDL. Lp(a) inhibits fibrinolysis and promotes atherosclerotic plaque formation. It is an independent risk factor for ischaemic heart disease.

323

4.2 The hyperlipidaemias

Population studies have consistently demonstrated a strong relationship between both total and LDL cholesterol and coronary heart disease. HDL is protective. A total cholesterol:HDL ratio of >4.5 is associated with an increased risk. Intervention trials have now established that reduction in LDL cholesterol is associated with improvement in outcome.

Triglycerides are also associated with cardiovascular risk; very high triglycerides are also associated with pancreatitis, lipaemic serum and eruptive xanthomata. Triglycerides must be measured fasting.

A genetic classification of lipid disorders has now largely replaced the Fredrickson (WHO) classification which was based on lipoprotein patterns. The primary hyperlipidaemias can be grouped according to the simple lipid profile. Secondary causes of hyperlipidaemia need to be excluded and are discussed below.

Primary hypercholesterolaemia (without hypertriglyceridaemia)

Familial hypercholesterolaemia (FH) is a monogenic disorder resulting from LDL receptor dysfunction.

- There are many different mutations in different families all resulting in LDL receptor deficiency/dysfunction and producing isolated hypercholesterolaemia.
- Heterozygote prevalence is 1/500; these individuals have cholesterol levels of 9–15 mmol/l and sustain myocardial infarctions at about age 40 years (M=F).
- Homozygous FH is rare. Cholesterol levels are in excess of 15mmol/l and patients suffer myocardial infarction in the second or third decades.
- Other typical clinical features are Achilles tendon, xanthomata (can also occur in other extensor tendons) and xanthelasma.

In **polygenic hypercholesterolaemia** the precise nature of the metabolic defect(s) is unknown. These individuals represent the right hand tail of the normal cholesterol distribution. They are at risk of premature atherosclerosis.

Primary hypertriglyceridaemia (without hypercholesterolaemia)

- **Polygenic hypertriglyceridaemia** is analogous to polygenic hypercholesterolaemia. Some cases are familial but the precise defect is not known. There is elevated VLDL.
- **Lipoprotein lipase deficiency** and **apoprotein CII deficiency** are both rare. They result in elevated triglycerides due to failure to metabolize chylomicrons.
- These patients present in childhood with eruptive xanthomata, lipaemia retinalis, retinal vein thrombosis, pancreatitis and hepatosplenomegaly.
- Chylomicrons can be detected in fasting plasma.

Primary mixed (or combined) hyperlipidaemia

- **Familial polygenic combined hyperlipidaemia** results in elevated cholesterol and triglycerides.
- The prevalence is 1/200.
- There is premature atherosclerosis.
- **Remnant hyperlipidaemia** is a rare cause of mixed hyperlipidaemia (palmar xanthomas and tuberous xanthomas over the knees and elbows are characteristic). It is associated with apoprotein E_2. There is a high cardiovascular risk.

Secondary hyperlipidaemias are usually mixed but either elevated cholesterol or triglycerides may predominate.

Causes of secondary hyperlipidaemias

- **Predominantly increased triglycerides**
  Alcoholism
  Obesity
  Chronic renal failure
  Diabetes mellitus
  Liver disease
  High-dose oestrogens

- **Predominantly increased cholesterol**
  Hypothyroidism
  Renal transplant
  Cigarette smoking*
  Nephrotic syndrome
  Cholestasis

*Cigarette smoking reduces HDL

4.3 Lipid-lowering drugs

Cholesterol and triglyceride levels should be considered in combination with other risk factors. Potential secondary causes of hyperlipidaemia should be corrected.

Dietary intervention can be expected to reduce serum cholesterol by a maximum of 30%. Dietary measures should be continued with pharmacological therapy. The table overleaf shows the impact that can be expected with the various agents.

Impact of lipid lowering drugs

Drug class	↓LDL (%)	↑HDL (%)	↓TGs (%)
Bile acid sequestrants	15–30	No change	No change
Nicotinic acid	10–25	15–35	25–30
HMG CoA reductase inhibitors	20–40	5–10	10–20
Fibric acid derivatives	10–15	15–25	35–50
Probucol	10–15	↓20–25	No change
Neomycin	20–25	No change	No change
Fish oil	↑5–10%	No change	30–50

The side-effect profile of the older agents (see opposite) made them unpopular and reduced compliance. In the majority of cases, hypercholesterolaemia will respond to dietary intervention and statin therapy, and mixed or isolated hypertriglyceridaemia, to diet and a fibrate.

Side effects and drug interactions of lipid lowering drugs

- **Drug class**   • **Side-effects/interactions**

  Bile acid sequestrants   GIT side effects — nausea, cramping,
   cholestyramine   abnormal LFTs
   cholestipol   Impaired absorption of digoxin, warfarin,
                                        thyroxine and fat soluble vitamins

  Nicotinic acid   Flushing, headaches, upper GIT symptoms,
                                       acanthosis nigricans and myositis

  HMG CoA reductase inhibitors   Headache, nausea, insomnia, abnormal
                                       LFTs. Myositis and rhabdomyolysis
                                       (when in combination with gemfibrozil
                                       or cyclosporin A)
                                      Simvastalin (but not pravastatin)
                                       potentiate warfarin and digoxin

  Fibric acid derivates   Potentiates warfarin. Gemfibrozil absorption
   gemfibrozil   is impaired by bile acid sequestrants
   bezafibrate

  Probucol   Diarrhoea, eosinophilia, long QT syndrome,
                                       angioneurotic oedema

  Neomycin   Ototoxicity, nephrotoxicity

  Fish oil   Halitosis, bloating, nausea
                                      Impaired glycaemic control in NIDDM

4.4 Rare lipid disorders

A multitude of rare inborn errors of lipid metabolism can lead to multisystem diseases. The most common (all very rare) are shown in the table overleaf.

Disorder	Serum lipid abnormality	Clinical features	Pathogenesis	Treatment
Abetalipo-proteinaemia	Low cholesterol Low triglycerides	Onset in childhood Fat malabsoption Acanthocytosis (of RBCs) Retinitis pigmentosa Ataxia and peripheral neuropathy	Defective Apo B synthesis	Vitamin E
Tangier disease	Low cholesterol	Onset in childhood Large orange tonsils Polyneuropathy No increased IHD risk	Increased Apo A catabolism	None
LCAT deficiency	↑triglycerides Variable cholesterol	Affects young adults Renal failure	Reduced LCAT activity	Low fat diet
Cerebro-tendinous xanthomatosis	None	Affects young adults Cerebellar ataxia Dementia Tendon xanthomas Cataracts	Not known	None
β-sitosterolaemia absorption	None	Affects adults Tendon xanthomas	Increased β-sitosterol absorption	Low plant fat diet
Fabry's disease	None	Affects young male adults (mild disease in females) Angiokeratomas Periodic crises Thrombotic events Chronic renal failure	Deficiency of X-galactosidose A	Renal replacement therapy

5. DISORDERS OF BONE, MINERAL METABOLISM AND INORGANIC IONS

Bone is a unique type of connective tissue that mineralizes. Biochemically it is composed of matrix (35%) and inorganic calcium hydroxyapatite (65%). Bone and mineral homeostasis are tightly regulated by numerous factors, so as to maintain skeletal integrity and control plasma levels.

5.1 Calcium homeostasis

Calcium homeostasis is linked to phosphate homeostasis to maintain a balanced calcium phosphate product:

- Hypocalcaemia activates PTH release to restore serum ionized calcium; other stimuli to PTH release include hyper-phosphataemia and decreased vitamin D levels.
- Hypercalcaemia switches off PTH release.
- Vitamin D promotes calcium and phosphate absorption from the GI tract
- Bone stores of calcium buffer the serum changes.

The metabolism and effects of vitamin D, and the actions of parathyroid hormone (PTH) are shown schematically in the figures below.

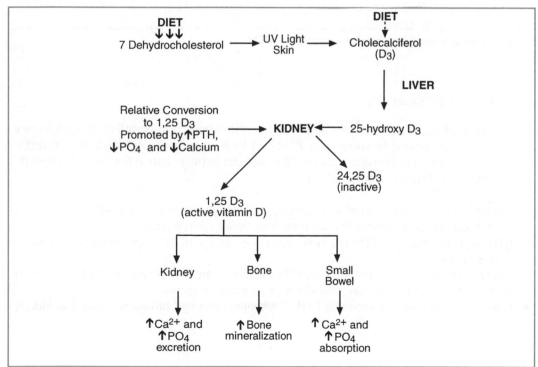

Metabolism and actions of vitamin D

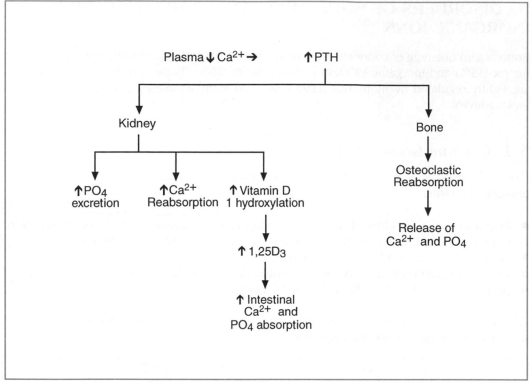

Control and actions of parathyroid hormone (PTH)

5.2 Hypercalcaemia

In over 90% of cases hypercalcaemia is due to either hyperparathyroidism or malignancy. Hypercalcaemia normally suppresses PTH and so PTH is therefore the best first test to identify the cause of hypercalcaemia — if it is detectable (in or above the normal range) the patient must have hyperparathyroidism.

- Primary hyperparathyroidism is common, especially in women aged 40–60 years. It is usually due to an adenoma of one of the four parathyroid glands.
- PTH-related protein (PTH-rP) is responsible for up to 80% of hypercalcaemia in malignancy.
- PTH-rP acts on the same receptors as PTH and shares the first (N-terminal) 13 amino acids with PTH, however, they are coded from two separate genes.
- Common malignancies secreting PTH-rP are squamous cell tumours, breast and kidney.

Causes of hypercalcaemia

- **Increased calcium absorption**
  Increased calcium intake
  Increased vitamin D

- **Increased bone reabsorption**
  Primary and tertiary hyperparathyroidism
  Malignancy
  Hyperthyroidism

- **Miscellaneous unusual causes**
  Lithium
  Thiazide diuretics
  Addison's disease
  Sarcoidosis*
  Phaeochromocytoma
  Familial hypocalciuric hypercalcaemia
  Theophylline toxicity
  Milk–Alkali syndrome

*Sarcoidosis causes hypercalcaemia due to excess production of $1,25D_3$ by macrophages in the sarcoid lesions

The symptoms of hypercalcaemia are often mild but a range of manifestations can occur as shown below.

Clinical manifestations of hypercalcaemia

- Malaise/depression
- Lethargy
- Muscle weakness
- Confusion
- Peptic ulceration**
- Pancreatitis
- Constipation

- Nephrolithiasis
- Nephrogenic DI
- Distal RTA
- Renal failure*
- Short Q-T syndrome
- Band keratopathy
- Diabetes insipidus

*Renal failure is due to chronic tubulo-interstitial calcification and fibrosis
**Peptic ulceration is due to excess gastrin secretion

The **management** of acute hypercalcaemia (serum calcium > 3mmol/l) involves:

- Adequate rehydration — 3–4 litres saline/day
- Intravenous diphosphonates (e.g. pamidronate disodium)
- Identification of the cause, and its subsequent specific treatment (e.g. corticosteroids for sarcoid) if indicated.

5.3 Hyperparathyroid bone disease

Hyperparathyroidism has a prevalence of about 1/1000. It results in bone reabsorption due to excess PTH action.

Primary hyperparathyroidism is caused by a single (80% +) or multiple (5%) parathyroid adenomas or by hyperplasia (10%). Parathyroid carcinoma is rare (<2%). It results from abnormal regulation of PTH by calcium because of an increase in the calcium set point.

Biochemically there is increased PTH, serum and urinary calcium, reduced serum phosphate and increased alkaline phosphatase. Histologically there is an increase of both osteoblasts and osteoclasts resulting in 'woven' osteoid, increased resorption cavities ('osteastitis fibrosa cystica') and marrow fibrosis.

Secondary hyperparathyroidism is physiological compensatory hypertrophy of all four glands due to hypocalcaemia (e.g. renal failure, malabsorption). PTH levels are raised, calcium is low or normal.

Tertiary hyperparathyroidism is the development of autonomous parathyroid hyperplasia in the setting of longstanding secondary hyperparathyroidism — usually in renal failure. Calcium levels are raised and parathyroidectomy is the only appropriate treatment.

5.4 Hypocalcaemia

Hypocalcaemia is usually secondary to renal failure (increased serum phosphate), hypoparathyroidism or vitamin D deficiency.

Causes of hypocalcaemia

- **Decreased calcium absorption**
  Hypoparathyroidism
  Hypovitaminosis D
  Sepsis
  Fluoride poisoning
  Hypomagnesaemia*

- **Acute respiratory alkalosis**

- **Hyperphosphataemia (by reduction in ionized calcium)**
  Renal failure
  Phosphate administration
  Rhabdomyolysis
  Tumour lysis syndrome

- **Deposition of calcium**
  Pancreatitis
  Hungry bone syndrome
  EDTA infusion

*Causes of functional hypoparathyroidism

Hypoparathyroidism can be spontaneous (autoimmune), post-surgical or due to a receptor defect (pseudo-hypoparathyroidism). Autoimmune hypoparathyroidism may be part of **autoimmune polyglandular failure type I**: mucocutaneous candidiasis, with adrenal, gonadal and thyroid failure.

In **pseudo-hypoparathyroidism** there is a characteristic phenotype with short stature, short metacarpals and intellectual impairment. The disorder is due to a G-protein abnormality (see Chapter 12, *Molecular Medicine*).

Vitamin D deficiency can occur in several settings, including:

- Dietary deficiency/lack of sunlight
- Malabsorption
- Renal failure (failure of 1-α-hydroxylation)
- I-OHase deficiency (vitamin D-dependent rickets type I)
- Vitamin D receptor defect (vitamin D-dependent rickets type II).

Rickets without vitamin D deficiency and with normal calcium may be due to hypophosphataemia, as in X-linked dominant hypophosphataemic vitamin D-resistant rickets. The symptoms of hypocalcaemia are mainly those of neuromuscular irritability and neuropsychiatric manifestations. Signs include Chvostek's (tapping the facial nerve causes twitching) and Trousseau's (precipitation of tetanic spasm in the hand by sphygmomanometer induced ischaemia).

Clinical manifestations of hypocalcaemia

- **Neuromuscular**
  Tetany
  Seizures
  Confusion
  Extrapyramidal signs
  Papilloedema
  Psychiatric
  Myopathy
  Prolonged Q-T syndrome

- **Ectodermal**
  Alopecia
  Brittle nails
  Dry skin

- **Cataracts**

- **Dental hypoplasia**

The **management** of hypocalcaemia involves:

- Intravenous calcium gluconate if severe (tetany/seizures)
- Oral calcium supplements
- Vitamin D (for hypoparathyroidism, vitamin D deficiency and renal failure).

5.5 Osteomalacia

Osteomalacia results from inadequate mineralization of osteoid. The biochemical features are elevated alkaline phosphatase (95%), hypocalcaemia (50%) and hypophosphataemia (25%). The childhood equivalent is rickets. It is usually caused by a defect of vitamin D availability or metabolism.

Causes of osteomalacia

- **Vitamin D deficiency**
  Dietary
  Sun exposure*
  Malabsorption
  Gastrectomy
  Small bowel disease
  Pancreativ insufficiency
  Pancreatic insufficiency

- **Defective 25 hydroxylation**
  Liver disease
  Anticonvulsant treatment**

- **Loss of vitamin D binding protein**
  Nephrotic syndrome

- **Defective 1 alpha hydroxylation**
  Hypoparathyroidism
  Chronic renal failure

- **Defective target organ response**
  Vitamin D-dependent rickets (Type I)

- **Mineralization defects**
  Abnormal matrix
  Osteogenesis imperfecta
  Chronic renal failure
  Enzyme deficiencies
  Hypophosphatasia

- **Inhibitors of mineralization**
  Fluoride
  Aluminium
  Biphosphonates

- **Phosphate deficiency**
  Decreased intake
  Antacids

- **Impaired renal reabsoprtion**
  Fanconi syndrome
  X-linked hypophosphataemic rickets
  (vitamin D-resistant rickets)

*Asian immigrants in Western countries are at increased risk because melanin in skin decreases D_3 formation; as vegans they may not benefit from dietary vitamin D and certain foods (e.g. chapatis) bind calcium unmasking vitamin D deficiency
**Especially phenytoin

The **management** of osteomalacia involves:

- Diagnosis and treatment of the underlying disorder
- Vitamin D therapy to correct hypocalcaemia and hypophosphataemia
- Beware iatrogenic hypercalcaemia when alkaline phosphatase begins to fall at the time of bone healing.

5.6 Paget's disease

Paget's disease is a focal (or multifocal) bone disorder characterized by accelerated and disorganized bone turnover resulting from increased numbers and activity of both osteoblasts and osteoclasts. A viral aetiology has not been confirmed.

- Rare in patients aged under 40 years
- Prevalence of 4% over the age of 40 years
- Familial clustering and HLA-linkages
- Biochemically characterized by raised alkaline phosphatase, osteocalcin and urinary hydroxyproline excretion.

Paget's disease is usually diagnosed because of asymptomatic sclerotic changes (which can mimic sclerotic bone metastasies) but a number of complications can arise.

Clinical manifestations of Paget's disease

- Bone pain
- Secondary arthritis
- Bone sarcoma (rare)
- High output congestive cardiac failure

- Skeletal deformity
- Fractures (and pseudofractures)
- Neurological compression syndromes*
- Hypercalcaemia (only with immbolization)

*Including deafness, other cranial nerve palsies and spinal stenosis

---

Treatment is indicated for bone pain, nerve compression, disease impinging on joints and immobilization hypercalcaemia. Options include:

- Biphosphonates
- Calcitonin
- Mithramycin
- Surgery.

Causes of a raised bone alkaline phosphatase

- **With high calcium**
  Hyperparathyroidism

- **With high or normal calcium**
  Malignancy
  Paget's disease

- **With normal calcium**
  Puberty
  Fracture
  Osteogenic sarcoma

- **With low calcium**
  Osteomalacia

5.7 Osteoporosis

A very common disorder characterized by reduced bone density and increased risk of fracture. The most common form is post-menopausal osteoporosis, which affects 50% of women aged 70. Common sites of fracture are the vertebrae, neck of femur (trabecular bone) and the distal radius and humerus (cortical bone); these fractures may occur with minimal trauma.

Diagnosis is by bone mineral densitometry, measured by DEXA, SPA or QCT. The measured bone density is compared to the mean population peak bone density (i.e. that of young adults of the same sex) and expressed as the number of standard deviations from that mean, the T score. The bone mineralization and serum biochemistry are normal.

- T-scores down to −1 are regarded as normal
- T-scores between −1 and −2.5 represent osteopenia
- T-scoes below −2.5 are osteoporotic.

Fracture risk

The risk of future fractures is dependent on both bone quality (strength and resilience) and the risk of falling. Fractures increase two-fold with each standard deviation of the T score and independently with age by 1.5-fold per decade.

Aetiology

From the age of 30, bone loss occurs at about 1% per year. This is accelerated to about 5% per year in the five years after the menopause. Persistent elevations of parathormone will accelerate bone loss further. This occurs both in primary hyperparathyroidism but also in secondary hyperparathyroidism arising in vitamin D deficiency, or in negative calcium balance (e.g. hypocalcaemia, hypercalcuria).

Aetiology of osteoporosis

- **Primary**
  Type 1: post-menopausal
  Type 2: age-related or involutional
  Osteoporosis of pregnancy

- **Secondary**
  Endocrine: premature menopause, Cushing's syndrome, hypopituitarism,
    hyperparathyroidism, prolactinomas, hypogonadism, hyperthyroidism
  Drugs: steroids, heparin, cyclosporin A, anticonvulsants
  Malignancy: multiple myeloma, leukaemia
  Inflammatory: rheumatoid arthritis, ulcerative colitis
  GI: gastrectomy, malabsorption, primary biliary cirrhosis
  Immbolization: space flight
  Other: osteogenesis imperfecta, homocystinuria, Turner's syndrome
    (oestrogen deficiency, rheumatoid arthritis*, scurvy)

- **Additional risk factors**
  Race: white/Asian
  Short stature and low body mass index
  Positive family history
  Nulliparity
  Amenorrhoea <6 months (other than pregnancy)
  Poor calcium and vitamin D intake
  Excess alcohol and smoking

*In rheumatoid arthritis osteoporosis is multifactoral but corticosteroids and immobility are major contributors

In the absence of a recent fracture, or secondary cause of osteoporosis, bone biochemistry should be normal.

Treatment

- **General measures**
  Correct any secondary cause
  Weightbearing exercise
  Adequate dietary calcium and
    vitamin D intake

- **Other**
  Fluoride (increases bone density, but
    can increase peripheral fractures)
  Calcitonin

- **Specific drug treatments**
  (These may reduce fractures by
    approximately 50%)
  Oestrogens (HRT)
  Vitamin D
  Testosterone (in males)
  Biphosphonates
  Calcitonin

5.8 Disorders of magnesium

Magnesium is principally found in bone (50–60%) and as an intracellular cation plasma levels are maintained within the range 0.7–1.1 mmol/l. Disorders of magnesium balance usually occur in association with other fluid and electrolyte disturbances.

Hypomagnesaemia

Hypomagnesaemia is frequently accompanied by hypocalcaemia and hypokalaemia. Patients are often asymptomatic but may complain of weakness or anorexia, and features of neuromuscular irritability have been described. Hypomagnesaemia is an important risk factor for ventricular arrhythmias.

Causes of hypomagnesaemia

- **Gastrointestinal losses**
  Diarrhoea
  Malabsorption
  Small bowel disease
  Acute pancreatitis**

- **Loop of Henle dysfunction**
  Acute tubular necrosis†
  Renal transplantation
  Post-obstructive diuresis
  Bartter's syndrome

- **Primary renal magnesium wasting††**

- **Renal losses**
  Loop and thiazide diuretics
  Volume expansion
  Alcohol*
  Diabetic ketoacidosis
  Hypercalcaemia***

- **Nephrotoxins**
  Aminoglycosides
  Amphoteracin B
  Cisplatin
  Pentamidine
  Cyclosporin A

*Alcohol acutely increases urinary magnesium excretion, in chronic alcoholism this is compounded by ketoacidosis and phosphate depletion
**Due to the formation of magnesium soaps in the areas of fat necrosis
***Hypercalciuria increases magnesium excretion. If saline and diuretics are given to treat hypercalcaemia then the three stimuli together predispose to hypomagnesaemia.
†Diuretic phase
††Primary magnesium wasting is a rare familial disorder

Hypermagnesaemia

Hypermagnesaemia is rare. It is usually due to magnesium ingestion or infusion in the setting of renal failure (i.e. when the kidney cannot excrete a magnesium load).

- At concentrations above 4 mmol/l symptoms develop including lethargy, drowsiness, areflexia, paralysis, hypotension, heart block and finally cardiac arrest.
- Toxic effects can be temporarily reversed by intravenous calcium.

Causes of hypermagnesaemia

- Renal failure
- Magnesium infusion
- Oral ingestion
- Magnesium enemas
- Familial hypocalciuric hypercalcaemia

- Adrenal insufficiency
- Milk–alkali syndrome
- Lithium
- Theophylline intoxication

5.9 Disorders of phosphate

Serum phosphate is maintained between 0.8 and 1.4 mmol/l largely by renal regulation of excretion. Bone accommodates 85% of body stores, the rest is found extracellularly as inorganic phosphate and intracellularly as phosphate esters e.g. phospholipids, nucleic acids and high energy compounds such as adenosine triphosphate (ATP).

Hypophosphataemia

Hypophosphataemia can occur in a variety of settings, either due to redistribution, renal losses or decreased intake.

- Symptoms rarely develop unless phosphate is below 0.6 mmol/l; below 0.3 mmol/l rhabdomyolysis is likely.
- Hypophosphataemia leads to reduced oxygen delivery (via reduced 2,3 DPG levels) and also impairs intracellular metabolism (by depleting ATP).
- Symptoms include weakness (especially respiratory muscles — a particular problem when weaning certain ICU patients from respiratory support), confusion, coma, heart failure and rhabdomyolysis.

Causes of hypophosphataemia

- **Internal redistribution**
  Hyperinsulinaemia
  Acute respiratory alkalosis

- **Decreased intestinal absorption**
  Inadequate intake
    (especially alcoholism)
  Antacids containing aluminium
    or magnesium
  Steatorrhoea and chronic diarrhoea

- **Increased urinary excretion**
  Primary and non-renal secondary
    hyperparathyroidism
  Vitamin D deficiency/resistance
  Fanconi syndrome
  X-linked hypophosphataemic rickets
  Miscellaneous — osmotic diuretics,
    thiazide diuretics
  Acute volume expansion

Hyperphosphataemia

Hyperphosphataemia is common in renal failure. It can also occur in massive tissue breakdown (e.g. rhabdomyolysis) and if there is increased tubular reabsorption of phosphate.

- It is usually asymptomatic. If symptoms do occur, they are secondary to a reduction in ionized calcium.

- In acute hyperphosphataemia, saline infusion and acetazolamide (a carbonic anhydrase inhibitor) can be used to increase phosphate excretion.
- In chronic renal failure a low phosphate diet, phosphate binders (e.g. calcium carbonate) and dialysis are required.

Causes of hyperphosphataemia

- **Massive acute phosphate load**
  Tumour lysis syndrome*
  Rhabdomyolysis
  Lactic and ketoacidosis
  Exogenous phosphate

- **Renal failure**

- **Increased tubular reabsorption of phosphate**
  Hypoparathyroidism
  Acromegaly
  Thyrotoxicosis
  Biphosphonates

*The tumour lysis syndrome results in release of phosphate, potassium, purines (metabolized to uric acid) and proteins (metabolized to urea). It can result in acute renal failure due to uric acid crystal deposition.

---

6. NUTRITIONAL AND VITAMIN DISORDERS

In the developed countries the most common nutritional problem is obesity. In contrast, in the developing countries, protein-energy malnutrition is common.

- Body Mass Index = weight (kg) / (height in metres)^2
- Obesity is defined as a Body Mass Index (BMI) of >30 in males and >28.6 in females.
- Obesity is associated with increased risks of cardiovascular disease, diabetes mellitus, osteoarthritis and gall stones.
- In developed countries the long term sequelae of fetal and childhood undernutrition are increased cardiovascular disease in adult life.

6.1 Protein-energy malnutrition (PEM)

Starvation is common in the developing world. In the developed countries protein-energy malnutrition frequently complicates severe sepsis, cachexia, renal failure and malabsorption. In these circumstances undernutrition is a risk factor for death.

Protein-energy malnutrition in both adults and children can be divided into undernutrition, kwashiorkor and marasmus.

Wellcome Trust classification of protein-energy malnutrition

Weight (% of standard for age)	Oedema present	Oedema absent
60–80	Kwashiorkor*	Undernutrition
<60	Marasmic kwashiorkor	Marasmus

*Kwashiorkor literally means 'disease of the displaced child'

- Marasmus results from severe deficiency of both protein and calories.
- Kwashiorkor results primarily from protein deficiency (i.e. diet entirely of carbohydrate).
- Oedema is the cardinal sign separating marasmus from kwashiorkor; fatty liver also develops in kwashiorkor.
- Growth failure is more severe in marasmus.

6.2 Vitamin deficiencies

Multiple vitamin deficiencies frequently accompany protein-energy malnutrition (PEM). Isolated or grouped vitamin deficiencies (for example, of fat-soluble vitamins) can also occur in specific circumstances.

Deficiencies of fat-soluble vitamins

Vitamin	Causes of deficiency	Roles of vitamin	Deficiency syndromes
Vitamin A	Severe PEM*	Component of visual pigment Maintenance of specialized epithelia	Night blindness Xerophthalmia** Follicular hyperkeratosis Keratomalacia***
Vitamin D	Vegans† Elderly with poor diet Renal failure	Absorption of calcium and phosphate Bone mineralization	Rickets Osteomalacia
Vitamin E	Severe (near total) fat malabsorption†† Abetalipo-proteinaemia	Antioxidant Scavenger of free radicals	Spino-cerebellar degeneration
Vitamin K	Oral antibiotics‡ Biliary obstruction	Cofactor in carboxylation of coagulation cascade factors	Bleeding tendency

*Although vitamin A is fat-soluble and deficiency can occur in any chronic malabsorptive state, this is rare unless there is severe protein-energy malnutrition
**Xerophthalmia — dryness of the cornea
***Keratomalacia — corneal ulceration and dissolution
†Vitamin D_3 is produced in the skin by photoactivation of 7-dehydrocholesterol. If sun exposure is sufficient, dietary vitamin D is not essential
††Vitamin E deficiency is rare. It can complicate biliary atresia. In abetalipoproteinaemia (see earlier section) chylomicrons cannot be formed
‡Antibacterial drugs interfere with the bacterial synthesis of vitamin K

Deficiencies of water-soluble vitamins

Vitamin	Causes of deficiency	Roles of vitamin	Deficiency syndromes
Vitamin B1* (thiamine)	Alcoholism Dietary	Nerve conduction Coenzyme in decarboxylation	Dry beri-beri — symmetrical Polyneuropathy Wernicke–Korsakoff syndrome Wet beri-beri** — peripheral vasodilatation, heart failure
Vitamin B2 (riboflavin)	Severe PEM***	Enzyme cofactor	Angular stomatitis Glossitis Corneal vascularization
Niacin (nicotinic acid)	Carcinoid syndrome† Alcoholism Low protein diets Isoniazid††	Incorporated into NAD and NADP	**Pellagra** — dementia dermatitis and diarrhoea (the three Ds)
Vitamin B6‡ (pyridoxine)	Isoniazid Hydralazine	Enzyme cofactor	Peripheral neuropathy Dermatitis Glossitis
Vitamin B12 (cyano- cobalamin)	Pernicious anaemia Post-gastrectomy Vegans Terminal ileal disease Blind loops	Coenzyme for DNA synthesis; coenzyme in myelin metabolism	Pernicious anaemia Subacute combined degeneration of the spinal cord
Vitamin C‡‡	Dietary	Redox reactions	Scurvy — bleeding, joint swelling, hyperkeratotic hair follicles, gingivitis

*Thiamine deficiency is confirmed by reduced red cell transketolase activity
**In alcoholics, wet beri-beri must be distinguished from alcoholic cardiomyopathy
***Riboflavin deficiency usually occurs with multiple deficiencies
†In the carcinoid syndrome (and to a lesser extent in phaeochromocytoma) tryptophan metabolism is diverted from nicotinamide to form amines
††Isoniazid can lead to deficiency of pyridoxine which is needed for the synthesis of nicotinamide from trypophan
‡Dietary deficiency of pyridoxine is extremely rare
‡‡Deficiency of vitamin C is confirmed by low white cell (buffy coat) ascorbic acid levels

7. METABOLIC ACID BASE DISTURBANCES (NON-RENAL) AND HYPOTHERMIA

The kidneys and the lungs are intimately involved in the regulation of hydrogen ion concentration. Metabolic acid-base disturbances arise from abnormalities in the regulation of bicarbonate and other buffers in the blood. Acidosis results from an increase in hydrogen ion concentration and alkalosis from a fall in H^+. pH is the negative logarithm of H^+ — a small change in pH represents a large change in H^+ concentration — this is often poorly appreciated in clinical practice.

7.1 Metabolic acidosis

The metabolic acidoses are conveniently divided on the basis of the anion gap.

Anion gap $= Na^+ + K^+ - (Cl^- + HCO_3^-)$

The normal anion gap is 10–18 mmol/l and represents the excess of negative charge (unmeasured anions) present on albumin, phosphate, sulphate and other organic acids.

Relationship of metabolic acidosis to anion gap

- **Normal anion gap**
  Diarrhoea (or other GI loss)
  Renal tubular acidosis
  Hypoaldosteronism
  Treatment of ketoacidosis
  Toluene ingestion

- **Increased anion gap**
  Lactic acidosis
  Ketoacidosis
  Renal failure
  Hepatic failure
  Ingestion of methanol, aspirin
    (e.g. ethylene glycol)

Specific metabolic acidoses

Metabolic acidosis with diarrhoea
The gastrointestinal secretions (below the stomach) are relatively alkaline and have a high potassium concentration. There is usually hypokalaemia, low urinary potassium loss (<25 mmol/l) and low urine pH (<5.5). Causes include:

- Villous adenoma
- Enteric fistula
- Obstruction
- Laxative abuse.

Metabolic acidosis with ureteric diversion

This results in hyperchloraemic acidosis in 80% of ureterosigmoid diversions. The mechanism is due to urinary chloride exchange for plasma bicarbonate which is then lost in the urine. Urinary ammonia is also absorbed across the sigmoid epithelium.

Metabolic acidosis accompanying poisoning

· Metabolic acidosis often accompanies poisoning (e.g. tolulene, ethylene glycol, salicylates, paracetamol). These are covered in detail in Chapter 2, *Clinical Pharmacology, Toxicology and Poisoning.*

7.2 Metabolic alkalosis

Metabolic alkalosis is less common than metabolic acidosis because metabolic processes produce acids as by-products, and also because renal excretion of excess bicarbonate is very efficient.

Metabolic alkaloses

- **Gastrointestinal hydrogen ion loss**
  Vomiting/pyloric stenosis
  Nasogastric suction
  Antacids (in renal failure)

- **Intracellular shift of hydrogen ion**
  Hypokalaemia

- **Alkali administration**

- **Renal hydrogen ion loss**
  Mineralocorticoid excess
  Loop or thiazide diuretics
  Post-hypercapnic alkalosis
  Hypercalcaemia and the milk–
    alkali syndrome

- **Contractional alkalosis**
  Volume depletion

Specific metabolic alkaloses

Gastric loss of hydrogen ions

In protracted vomiting (e.g. pyloric stenosis) or nasogastric suction there can be complete loss of up to three litres of gastric secretions per day. The gastric secretions contain:

- Hydrogen ion: 100 mmol/l
- Potassium: 15 mmol/l
- Chloride: 140 mmol/l.

Alkalosis will result, but paradoxically, acid urine is produced due to renal tubular sodium bicarbonate reabsorption to maintain plasma volume. Patients respond to volume expansion with normal saline and correction of hypokalaemia.

Milk–alkali syndrome

alkalosis

This is defined as the triad of hypercalcaemia, metabolic ~~acidosis~~ and ingestion of large amounts of calcium with absorbable alkali (traditionally for peptic ulcer pain). The hypercalcaemia increases renal bicarbonate reabsorption exacerbating the alkalosis. Clinical presentation is with symptoms of hypercalcaemia or metastatic calcification.

Post-hypercapnic alkalosis

Chronic respiratory acidosis leads to a compensatory increase in urinary hydrogen ion secretion resulting in a rise in plasma bicarbonate concentration. Rapid lowering of a raised pCO_2 (usually by mechanical ventilation) is not immediately accompanied by a fall in plasma bicarbonate. There is often an accompanying chloride loss that must be replaced before bicarbonate can fall to normal.

7.3 Hypothermia

Hypothermia is defined as a fall in core temperature to below 35°C. It is frequently fatal if the core temperature falls below 32°C.

Causes of hypothermia

- Elderly with inadequate heating
- Hypothyroidism
- Immersion in cold water
- Alcoholism
- Hypoglycaemia
- Exposure to low external temperatures (e.g. unconscious patients, mountaineers etc.)

Mild hypothermia (32–35°C) causes shivering and intense feeling of cold.

Severe hypothermia (<32°C) causes impairment in judgement and reduced awareness of the cold.

- **Clinical features of hypothermia**: include bradycardia, hypoventilation, muscle stiffness, hypotension and loss of reflexes. The pupils can be fixed and dilated in recoverable hypothermia.
- **Metabolic acidosis**: due to lactate accumulation is common, pancreatitis can complicate hypothermia.
- **Electrocardiograph changes**: include J waves, prolonged PR interval, prolonged QT and QRS complexes. Death results from ventricular arrhythmias or asystole.

Chapter 12
Molecular Medicine

CONTENTS

1. **Molecular diagnostics**   351
   - 1.1 The polymerase chain reaction (PCR)
   - 1.2 Reverse transcription PCR (rt PCR)
   - 1.3 Monoclonal antibodies

2. **Cell signalling**   354
   - 2.1 Types of receptor
   - 2.2 Protein kinases and phosphatases
   - 2.3 Nuclear hormones
   - 2.4 Transcription factors and the regulation of gene expression

3. **The molecular pathogenesis of cancer**   361
   - 3.1 Somatic evolution of cancer
   - 3.2 Oncogenes
   - 3.3 Tumour suppressor genes

4. **Apoptosis and disease**   363

5. **Mediators of vascular tone**   365
   - 5.1 Nitric oxide (NO)
   - 5.2 Endothelin-1

6. **Mediators of inflammation and repair**   368
   - 6.1 Interleukin-1(IL-1)
   - 6.2 Tumour necrosis factor (TNF)
   - 6.3 Transforming growth factor β (TGF-β)
   - 6.4 Heat shock proteins (HSPs)
   - 6.5 Free radicals

7. **Transmissible spongiform encephalopathies**   373

8. **Adhesion molecules**   374

9. **The molecular basis of some important diseases**   375
    9.1   Amyloidosis
    9.2   Alpha-1 antitrypsin deficiency
    9.3   Alzheimer's disease
    9.4   Trinucleotide repeat disorders
    9.5   Mitochondrial disorders
    9.6   Myasthenia gravis
    9.7   Duchenne muscular dystrophy
    9.8   Sickle cell disease

10. **Glossary of terms in molecular medicine**   384

Molecular Medicine

1. MOLECULAR DIAGNOSTICS

The diagnostic process in medicine is entering a new and important historical phase. In the 18th century, disease was classified by the co-existence of a number of features in a syndrome. In the 19th, and for most of the 20th centuries, diagnosis has been based on syndromic and morphological criteria, i.e. a disease is defined by what can be observed under a microscope.

Increasingly, diagnostic entities are going to be reclassified according to the molecules that are central to the disease process and also according to changes in the expression of genes that code for these molecules. This kind of diagnosis is based, therefore, on the detection of protein using antibodies and on the detection of nucleic acid (DNA and RNA), principally by using the polymerase chain reaction (PCR). It is now entering routine clinical practice.

1.1 The polymerase chain reaction (PCR)

The PCR is an amplification reaction in which a small amount of target DNA (the template) is amplified to produce enough to perform analysis. This might be the detection of a particular DNA sequence, such as that belonging to a pathogenic microorganism or an oncogene, or the detection of differences in genes, such as mutations causing inherited disease. Therefore the template DNA might consist of total human genomic DNA derived from peripheral blood lymphocytes, amniocentesis or chorionic villous sampling; alternatively, it might consist of a tumour biopsy or a biological fluid from a patient with an infection.

- Two unique oligonucleotide sequences, known as primers, are mixed with a DNA template and a thermostable DNA polymerase (Taq polymerase, derived from an organism that inhabits thermal springs). Sometimes more than two primers can be used if more than one gene is to be amplified (multiplex PCR) or the region of DNA to be amplified needs special definition ('nested' PCR), for example if it is similar to other sequences in the genome which may give spurious reaction products.
- In the initial stage of the reaction the DNA template is heated (typically for about 30 seconds) to make it single stranded and then as the reaction cools the primers will anneal to the template if the appropriate sequence is present.
- Then the reaction is heated to 72°C (for about a minute) and the DNA polymerase synthesizes new DNA between the two primer sequences. During 30 or so cycles (each typically lasting a few minutes) the target sequence will have been amplified exponentially.

The crucial feature of PCR is that to detect a given sequence of DNA it only needs to be present in one copy (i.e. one molecule of DNA): this makes it extremely powerful.

Clinical applications of PCR

- Mutation detection
- Detection of viral and bacterial sequences in tissue (*Herpes simplex* virus in CSF, hepatitis C, HIV in peripheral blood, meningococcal strains)

- Single-cell PCR of *in vitro* fertilized embryo to diagnose genetic disease before implantation

In the example below, some CSF from a patient suspected of having *Herpes simplex* encephalitis is used in a PCR reaction in an effort to detect the presence of the virus directly.

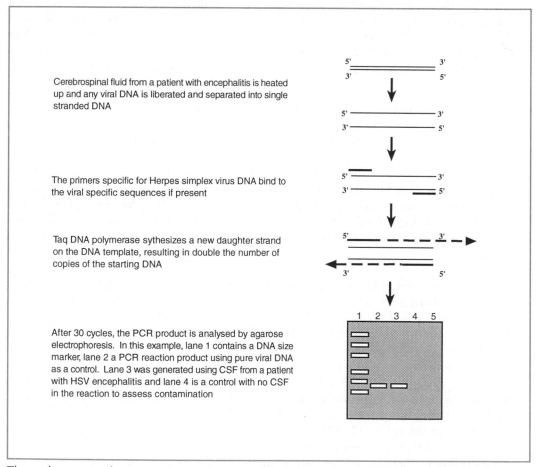

Cerebrospinal fluid from a patient with encephalitis is heated up and any viral DNA is liberated and separated into single stranded DNA

The primers specific for Herpes simplex virus DNA bind to the viral specific sequences if present

Taq DNA polymerase sythesizes a new daughter strand on the DNA template, resulting in double the number of copies of the starting DNA

After 30 cycles, the PCR product is analysed by agarose electrophoresis. In this example, lane 1 contains a DNA size marker, lane 2 a PCR reaction product using pure viral DNA as a control. Lane 3 was generated using CSF from a patient with HSV encephalitis and lane 4 is a control with no CSF in the reaction to assess contamination

The polymerase chain reaction (PCR). Small amounts of target DNA are amplified with a thermostable DNA polymerase.

1.2 Reverse transcription PCR (rt PCR)

Conventional PCR looks at genomic DNA. Every cell in our body contains our total genome in two copies. However, the phenotype of a cell (what makes a hepatocyte different from a Purkinje cell) depends on which genes are being expressed at any one time. To look at the expression of genes we must therefore analyse only those genes that are being transcribed into messenger RNA.

- RNA is too unstable to be used in PCR so it must first be converted to complementary DNA (cDNA) using reverse transcriptase, a retroviral enzyme that makes a precise copy of the mRNA.
- PCR is then performed in the normal way but, because the template reflects the mRNA of the starting material, this technique can look at gene expression in individual tissues.

Clinical applications of rt PCR

- Detection of the expression of particular genes in tumour tissue carries important prognostic information
- Basic scientific research into normal function of disease genes by understanding their spatial and temporal expression

1.3 Monoclonal antibodies

The detection of specific proteins in molecular diagnosis relies on the fact that the antibody used has a high specificity for the target protein. An immune response to an antigen consists of a polyclonal proliferation of cells giving rise to antibodies with a spectrum of specificity for the target. Therefore, useful diagnostic and therapeutic antibodies must be selected from this complex immune response, before they can be used.

Myeloma is a malignantly transformed B-cell lineage that secretes a specific antibody. This fact is used to produce unlimited amounts of specific antibodies directed toward an antigen of choice.

- A laboratory animal is injected with the antigen of choice, it mounts an immune response and its spleen, which contains B-cell precursors, with a range of specificity for the antigen, is harvested.
- The spleen cells are fused *en masse* to a specialized myeloma cell line that no longer produces its own antibody.
- The resulting fused cells, or hybridomas, grow in individual colonies, are immortal and produce antibodies specified by the lymphocytes of the immunized animal. These cells can be screened to select for the antibody of interest which can then be produced in limitless amounts.

Clinical applications of monoclonal antibodies

- Diagnosis of cancer and infections
- Imaging of tumours, radiotherapy
- As a 'magic bullet' to direct drugs to target
- Transplantation and other immune modulations (e.g. OKT3).

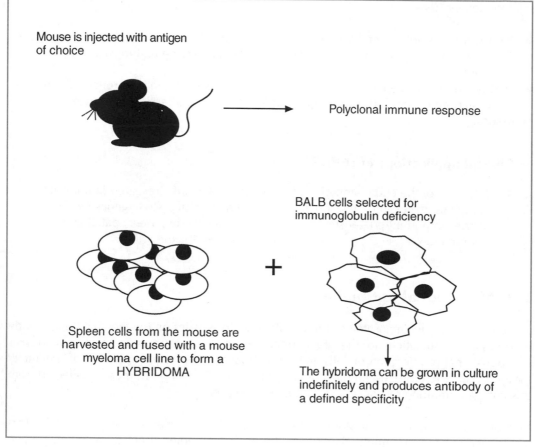

Monoclonal antibody production from mouse B-cell precursors fused with myeloma cells in culture

2. CELL SIGNALLING

Central to all cellular processes is the conversion of external signals (first messengers) via intermediates (second messengers) into changes that alter the state of that cell. This often involves adjustment in the expression of genes in the cell nucleus and new protein synthesis. In the example opposite a photon of light is the external stimulus that produces, via second messengers, a change in the resting state of the rod cell leading it to transmit a signal to the visual cortex.

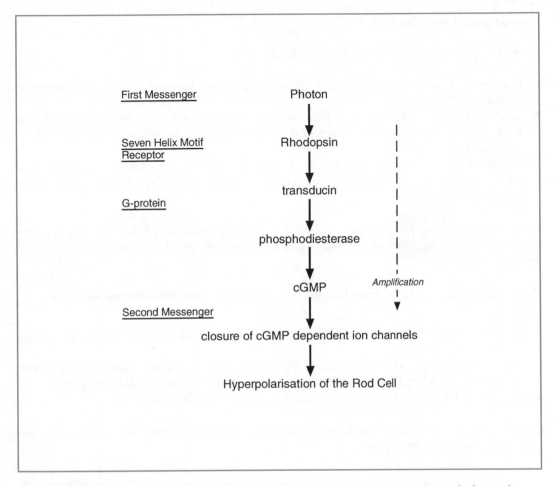

A typical signalling pathway, in the rod photoreceptor, involves G-protein-coupled membrane receptor which activates a second messenger pathway

2.1 Types of receptor

The chief function of the cell membrane is to provide a barrier to ion flux and therefore to maintain the internal milieu of the cell. There are, as described below, certain lipophilic modules which travel freely into the cell. However, most external signals can only effect changes inside the cell by interaction with membrane-bound receptor modules. This biologically ubiquitous system of signal transduction by receptors underlies the action of many hormones, growth factors and drugs.

Ligand gated ion channel

For example, acetylcholine receptor (nicotinic).

- Five non-covalently assembled subunits $\alpha_2\beta\gamma\delta$ are located at the post-synaptic neuromuscular junction.
- Each subunit is coded for by a different gene which enables mixing and matching of subunits between different tissues and in embryological development to generate a repertoire of responses.
- On binding of acetylcholine to the α subunits the whole complex undergoes a conformational change leading to the passage of sodium ions into the cell and cellular depolarization.

Other examples include some glutamate receptors (excitatory), GABA and glycine (inhibitory: the passage of chloride ions into the cell renders it more resistant to depolarization).

Receptors that contain cytoplasmic domains with protein–tyrosine–kinase activity

- **Insulin** binds to its receptor which then undergoes dimerization and autophosphorylation at a tyrosine residue.
- The tyrosine kinase activity intrinsic to the receptor is then activated and the result is the phosphorylation of cytoplasmic proteins and initiation of an intracellular cascade.
- This ultimately leads to the action of insulin on glucose uptake etc.

Other examples include platelet-derived growth factor, IGF-1, macrophage-colony stimulating factor, nerve growth factor.

G-protein-coupled receptors

Guanine nucleotide binding proteins are a ubiquitous cellular mechanism for coupling an extracellular signal to a second messenger, such as cyclic AMP.

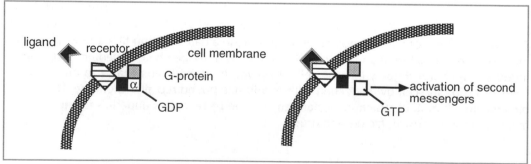

G-proteins are activated by ligand binding to a transmembrane receptor

- G-proteins have three non-covalently associated subunits: α, β, γ. In the inactive state GDP is bound to the α subunit of the G-protein.
- When the receptor is activated by ligand binding, the G-protein is activated by the exchange of GDP for GTP.
- In this active state the α subunit dissociates from the β and γ subunits. Either of these two complexes (the GTP-α or the β–γ) can then interact with second messengers.
- The α subunit is rapidly inactivated by hydrolysis of GDP to GTP (this is an intrinsic property of the α subunit, which is therefore known as a GTPase) and then re-associates with the β and γ subunits resetting the whole system to the inactive state.

G-proteins can be inhibitory (Gi) or stimulatory (Gs) and the overall activity of a second messenger like adenylate cyclase is likely to be regulated by the differential activation of these different forms. The **muscarinic acetylcholine receptor**, the α and β **adrenergic receptor** and the retinal photoreceptor **rhodopsin** are all G-protein-coupled receptors. These can be linked to a variety of second messenger systems or sometimes directly to ion channels.

Diseases associated with G-protein abnormalities

- **Cholera**: *Vibrio cholerae* secretes an exotoxin which catalyses ADP-ribosylation of an arginine residue on Gsα. This makes the subunit resistant to hydrolysis and the second messenger (in this case cAMP) remains activated and this ultimately leads to the fluid and electrolyte loss characteristic of the disease.
- **Pituitary adenomas.**
- **McCune–Albright syndrome.**
- **Albright's hereditary osteodystrophy** (or pseudohypoparathyroidism).

} See Chapter 4, *Endocrinology.*

2.2 Protein kinases and phosphatases

Protein kinases catalyse the transfer of a phosphate group from ATP to a serine, threonine or tyrosine residue on a target protein (the substrate). Phosphorylation of this amino acid residue results in an alteration in the conformation of the target protein and thus leads to its activation or inactivation. Many **growth factor receptors** are protein tyrosine kinases (see above). Many of the 'downstream' intracellular pathways which are initiated by the activation of a second messenger system involve protein kinases (usually serine kinases in the cytoplasm). In this way an external signal can, through the activation of one receptor, influence a vast array of cellular processes due to a cascade of protein interactions.

2.3 Nuclear hormones

Not all extracellular signals use second messenger systems to effect changes to the cell. Important exceptions are **steroid hormones** that bind to an intracellular receptor allowing the receptor to be freed from its cytosolic membrane-bound anchor. The receptor hormone complex then travels to the nucleus where it binds to specific regions of DNA called **hormone responsive elements,** thereby effecting alterations in the transcription of DNA.

Examples of nuclear hormones

- Corticosteroids
- Vitamin D
- Retinoic acid
- Sex steroids.

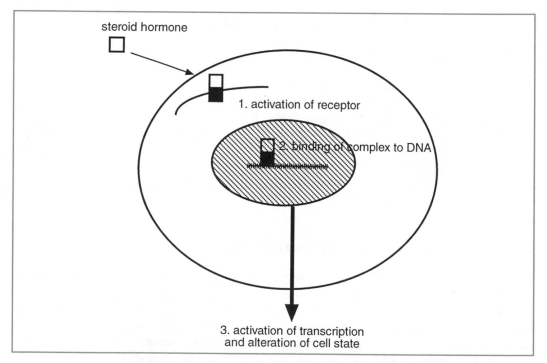

The nuclear hormone superfamily of receptors act by controlling gene transcription in the nucleus

2.4 Transcription factors and the regulation of gene expression

The human genome is present in two copies in every cell in the body, and is estimated to consist of around 80,000 genes. The spatial and temporal expression of a proportion of these genes (typically 15–20,000 genes are expressed in any one cell at any time) determines the differentiation, morphology and functional characteristics of each cell type (the cellular phenotype). Clearly, for cells to maintain a specific identity, this process must be very tightly regulated.

Eukaryotic genes consist of exons, which are transcribed into the messenger RNA template which is translated into protein. Exons are separated by introns, which do not code for protein but have a role in mRNA stability and are spliced out of the pre-mRNA prior to translation. Sometimes exons are also spliced out to produce variant forms of the protein with tissue-specific functional elements (splice variants).

Clearly some genes have a fundamental biological role and will be expressed in all cells at all times ('housekeeping genes'). However, the transcription of most genes only proceeds when a macromolecular complex (the initiation complex) binds to a region of the 5' end of genes called the promoter. The assembly of this complex is directed by the presence of transcription factors and facilitates the binding of RNA polymerase which leads to transcription. Muscle, for example, will contain specific transcription factors that lead to the expression of muscle specific genes that determine the muscle phenotype.

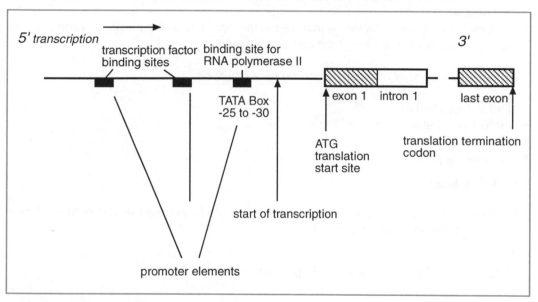

Structure of a typical gene

The promoter

- A modular arrangement of different elements that act as a binding site for RNA polymerase II and the initiation of transcription.

- The initiation of transcription involves a large complex of multimeric proteins (RNA polymerase II plus the general transcription factors (GTFs: TFII A–H).
- The GTFs can activate transcription of any gene which has a TATA box (see below).

Enhancers

- Elements that can be at the 5' or the 3' end of genes and can vary in distance from the coding sequence itself.
- Enhancers are not obligately required for the initiation of transcription but alter its efficiency in such a way as to lead to an increase in gene expression.

Transcription factors

Transcription factors are proteins that bind to sequence specific regions of DNA at the 5' end of genes called **response elements** to regulate gene expression. These elements can form part of promoters or enhancers. They can be divided into:

- Basal transcription factors — involved in the constitutive activation of so-called house-keeping genes
- Inducible transcription factors — involved in the temporal and spatial expression of genes which underlies tissue phenotype and developmental regulation.

They fall into a number of groups based on their structure:

- Helix–loop–helix
- Helix–turn–helix
- Zinc finger
- Leucine zipper.

The TATA box

A promoter element that is always located 25 to 30 base pairs from the start of transcription and serves to anchor RNA polymerase II.

Clinical applications of transcription factors

- An increasing number of diseases are being described where an inherited mutation in transcription factors leads to a developmental disorder. These are usually complex congenital malformations.

- Transcription factors can be oncogenes, e.g. c-myc, p53 (see opposite)
- Many future drugs will be developed to alter gene transcription by acting directly or indirectly on gene transcription in the manner described above for steroids

---

3. THE MOLECULAR PATHOGENESIS OF CANCER

3.1 Somatic evolution of cancer

Cancer cells are a clonal population of cells. The accumulation of mutations in multiple genes results in escape from the normally strictly regulated mechanisms that control growth and differentiation of somatic cells. It will be evident that some of these genetic 'errors' will be inherited and form the basis of a familial tendency to cancer. For cancer to develop, in most cases, an environmentally driven genetic mutation is necessary. Genotoxic damage from ionizing radiation and some of the constituents of tobacco smoke fall into this category. In addition, all somatic cell division requires the copying of DNA and this can result in spontaneous mutations of genes. It is a combination of these three types of genetic mutation (inherited, spontaneous and environmentally determined) which leads to cancer. Therefore cancer evolution is a complex, multifactorial process.

Most tumours show visible abnormalities of chromosome banding on light microscopy, suggesting that as tumours develop they become more bizarre and more prone to genetic error. Although there are some cancer genes that lead to Mendelian (i.e. monogenic) inheritance of specific tumours, most cancers result from a complex mixture of polygenetic and environmental influences.

3.2 Oncogenes

Originally identified as genes carried by cancer-causing viruses that were integrated into the host genome and, when expressed, lead to loss of growth control (viral oncogenes are denoted v-onc). They have cellular homologues, proto-oncogenes (denoted c-onc), found in the normal human genome and expressed in normal tissue, that are usually highly conserved in evolution and have central roles in the signal-transduction pathways that control cell growth and differentiation. They can be thought of as exerting a dominant effect in that they cause cancer in the presence of the normal gene product because, in mutating, they have gained a new function.

- **Ras** is a small, monomeric, G-protein and is likely to be involved in transduction of growth-promoting signals. The relative abundance of the active and inactive forms of **ras** is controlled by positive and negative regulators of GTP–GDP exchange (GAP and GNRF). Mutations affecting the GTP binding site prevent GTP hydrolysis and prolong **ras** activation. At least a third of sporadic tumours contain acquired somatic mutations in **ras**.
- Further downstream, after a number of protein kinase steps have been activated, the transduction of growth signals culminates in the activation of the transcription factors **fos** and **jun** which in turn induce the transcription of the proto-oncogene **myc** which commits the cell to a round of DNA replication and cell division. Mutant forms of these proteins can induce tumour growth.

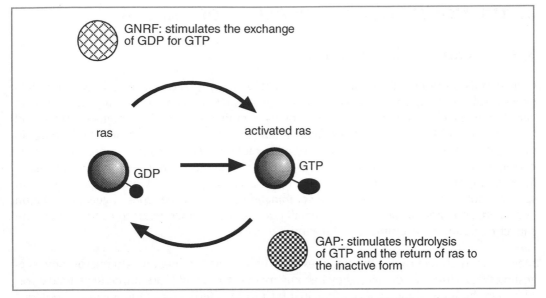

Activation of the oncoprotein *ras* is under reciprocal control by GNRF and GAP

- The 9:22 balanced translocation (Philadelphia chromosome) found in **CML** generates a composite gene comprising exons from the **bcr** locus on chromosome 22 and the **c-abl** locus on chromosome 9 generating a fusion protein with distinct biochemical properties which presumably promote tumour growth.
- In **Burkitt's lymphoma** the **c-myc** gene is transposed from its normal position into the immunoglobulin heavy chain locus on chromosome 14, resulting in a gross increase in its expression and a potent molecular signal for cells to undergo mitosis.

3.3 Tumour suppressor genes

- In contrast to oncogenes these exert a recessive effect, in that both copies must be mutated before tumorigenesis occurs.
- Mutation results in loss of function.
- These genes normally function to inhibit the cell cycle and therefore, when inactivated, lead to loss of growth control.

p53 is a protein that occupies a pivotal role in the cell cycle and is the most commonly mutated gene in tumours (breast, colon etc). It encodes a transcription factor, the normal function of which is to downregulate the cell cycle. Inactivation of **p53** is the primary defect in the Li–Fraumeni syndrome (a dominantly inherited monogenic cancer syndrome characterized by breast carcinoma, sarcomas, brain and other tumours), and is a central regulator of apoptosis (see opposite).

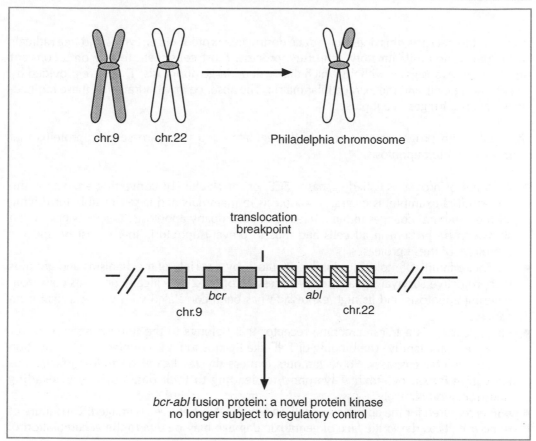

chr.9   chr.22   Philadelphia chromosome

translocation
breakpoint

bcr   *abl*

chr.9   chr.22

bcr-abl fusion protein: a novel protein kinase
no longer subject to regulatory control

In CML the Philadelphia chromosome leads to the production of an oncoprotein

4. APOPTOSIS AND DISEASE

It has only recently been fully appreciated that widespread cell death occurs in human development and in the normal regulation of cell number in the adult organism. In embryonic development cells are lost, for example, as finger webbing disappears or as neurones are 'selected' for survival by making the appropriate synaptic contact. In post-natal life, the expansion of lymphocyte numbers in response to antigen stimulation must be regulated by the subsequent death of these cells or clonal proliferation would continue unabated. It turns out that this process of naturally occurring cell death is regulated by the activation of a specific set of genes in response to external signals in a process referred to as **programmed cell death**. The morphological change that accompanies this process is called **apoptosis**.

- Cells undergo shrinkage, compaction of chromatin, nuclear and cytoplasmic budding to form membrane-bound apoptotic bodies and finally phagocytosis by surrounding macrophages.
- The activation of intracellular nucleases can be detected by the 'laddering' of DNA on electrophoresis gels, which serves as a marker for apoptosis.

In contrast to necrosis, this does not induce destructive proteolytic enzymes and free radicals and is thus a non-inflammatory, 'altruistic' process. Most cells seem to rely on a constant supply of survival signals without which they will undergo apoptosis. These are provided by neighbouring cells and the extracellular matrix. The absence or withdrawal of these molecular signals is a trigger to apoptosis.

The 'cell death programme' is genetically regulated and there are specific proteins that promote or inhibit apoptosis.

- A family of proteases called caspases (ICE, or interleukin-1β converting enzyme is the best-studied example) is central to apoptosis in mammals and is responsible for driving all the structural changes in the nucleus that accompany apoptosis. Caspases have been shown to be present in all cells and thus to prevent apoptosis there must be specific inhibitors of these proteases.
- The bcl-2 family of molecules inhibit apoptosis by a variety of mechanisms and are thus cytoprotective survival signals. Over-expression of bcl-2 specifically prevents cells from entering apoptosis and its high expression has been correlated with poor survival from cancer.
- fas, or CD95, is a transmembrane receptor that belongs to the tumour necrosis factor (TNF) receptor family. The binding of TNF-like ligands to fas is coupled to the activation of intracellular caspases. Some tumours express the fas ligand on their surface, thus activating fas on cytotoxic T-lymphocytes leading to their death (a way of evading immune surveillance).
- p53 is required for the apoptosis of cells in which DNA has been damaged. The failure of tumour cells to die in the face of genotoxic damage may be due to the accumulation of p53 mutations.

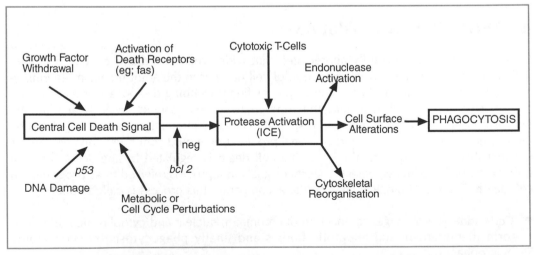

Programmed cell death can be stimulated by a variety of triggers and leads to the activation of proteases like ICE that initiate a cascade of morphological changes (collectively known as apoptosis) that result in inevitable phagocytosis.

- Certain disorders (cancer, autoimmunity and some viral illnesses) are associated with increased cell survival (and therefore a failure of programmed cell death). Metastatic tumour cells have circumvented the normal environmental cues for survival and can survive in foreign environments.

- Physiological cell death is necessary for the removal of potentially autoreactive T-cells during development and for the removal of excess cells after the completion of the immune response. Animal models of SLE (CD95/fas knockout mice) have implicated apoptosis genes in the pathogenesis of autoimmunity.

- Death by apoptosis can be seen as an evolutionary adaptation to prevent the survival of virally infected cells. Therefore viruses have developed strategies for circumventing this. Pox viruses appear to inhibit apoptosis by producing an inhibitor of ICE.

- Excessive cell death due to an excess of signals promoting apoptosis has been hypothesized to occur in many degenerative disorders where cells have been observed to die by apoptosis. Direct evidence that this actually occurs has yet to be found.

5. MEDIATORS OF VASCULAR TONE

Both the regulation of systemic arterial blood pressure and the local control of the microcirculation in organs such as the kidney and the brain are vital for the maintenance of homeostasis. Recently there has been an explosion of knowledge concerning the molecular mediators of blood flow and this is already having an impact in the therapy of some common disorders.

Two important principles should be kept in mind:

- The regulation of vascular tone is predominantly a paracrine process, where molecules are released to act in adjacent cells
- Vascular control is often a balance between competing vasodilators and vasoconstrictors.

5.1 Nitric oxide (NO)

Previously called endothelium-derived relaxant factor (EDRF), NO is an important transcellular messenger molecule which is involved in a diverse range of processes.

NO is synthesized from the oxidation of nitrogen atoms in the amino acid L-arginine by the action of NO synthase (NOS).

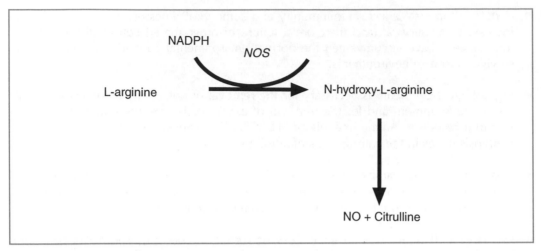

Nitric oxide is produced from L-arginine under the influence of nitric oxide synthase (NOS)

The following cell types synthesize nitric oxide:

- Vascular endothelium
- Macrophages
- Neutrophils
- Central and peripheral nerve cells
- Platelets
- Vascular smooth muscle
- Hepatocytes

NO acts on target cells close to its site of synthesis where it activates guanylate cyclase leading to a rise in intracellular cGMP which acts as a second messenger to modulate a variety of cellular processes. It has a very short half-life.

There are at least three distinct isoforms of NO synthase:

- Neuronal (constitutive)
- Endothelial (constitutive)
- Macrophage (inducible).

Constitutive NO production is involved in regulation of vascular tone and neurotransmission and is calcium/calmodulin dependent. Inducible NO production is mainly involved in cell-mediated immunity and is activated by cytokines.

Synthetic nitrates, such as GTN and sodium nitroprusside, act after their conversion into NO.

Functions of nitric oxide

- Vasodilator tone modulation in the regulation of systemic blood pressure
- CNS neurotransmission, including the formation of new memories
- Inhibition of platelet aggregation
- Cytotoxic action utilized in the generation of the host immune response in activated macrophages
- Organ-specific microregulatory control (e.g. kidney)
- PNS 'non-adrenergic, non-cholinergic neurotransmission' (NANC) mediating neurogenic vasodilatation

Diseases related to abnormalities in the generation or regulation of NO

- **Septic shock**: NO is released in massive amounts and correlates with low BP

- **Atherosclerosis**: NO synthesis may be impaired more than endothelin synthesis leading to tonic vasoconstriction and vasospasm

- **Primary and secondary pulmonary hypertension**: inhaled NO reverses pulmonary hypertension

- **Hepatorenal syndrome** and the **hypertension of chronic renal failure**: failure of breakdown and secretion of endogenous antagonists of NO leads to a microcirculatory imbalance between NO and endothelin (see below)

- **Excitotoxic cell death in the CNS**: glutamate is the principal excitatory neurotransmitter in the CNS. NO is the transduction mechanism when glutamate binds to NMDA (N-methyl-D-aspartate) receptors on neurones. The final event in the presence of excess glutamate is a rise in intracellular calcium and the cell becomes vulnerable to dying. This process, in which NO is now implicated, is thought to be important in neuronal loss in many neurodegenerative conditions such as Alzheimer's disease and also in acute brain injury such as stroke

- **Tissue damage** in acute and **chronic inflammation** (probably by interacting with oxygen-derived free radicals)

- **Adult respiratory distress syndrome** (ARDS).

5.2 Endothelin-1

This is the most potent vasoconstrictor substance yet described. It is manufactured following vascular endothelial 'stress' (shear, hypoxia, growth factors, expansion of plasma volume). It is produced from pre–pro ET by the action of endothelin converting enzyme (ETCE). Very little endothelin reaches the circulation and serum levels do not generally carry any diagnostic significance.

There are endothelin receptors:

- on the vascular endothelium and on some smooth muscle cells (gut and heart), including coronary arteries where they cause constriction
- on capillary endothelium where they cause vasodilatation.

When ET-1 is infused intravenously it causes a transient vasodilatation followed by a long period of intense vasoconstriction lasting up to two hours. The normal function of endothelin is in the regulation of vascular tone. ETCE inhibitors and receptor blockers are under development as agents for systemic arterial hypertension. More diverse functions of endothelin are indicated by the recent finding of mutations in the endothelin-B receptor in some patients with Hirschsprung's disease.

Endothelin has been implicated in the pathogenesis of the following disorders:

- Essential hypertension
- Primary pulmonary hypertension
- Renovascular hypertension
- Hepatorenal syndrome
- Acute renal failure
- Chronic heart failure
- Raynaud's phenomenon
- Vasospasm after subarachnoid haemorrhage

6. MEDIATORS OF INFLAMMATION AND REPAIR

The process of tissue injury, inflammation and subsequent repair is highly conserved in evolution and represents part of the 'primitive' repertoire of protective mechanisms against invasion by foreign organisms and other insults. This is in contrast to the more sophisticated mechanisms of defence mediated by the immune system. Some of the same molecules are involved in both processes but they are considered here to emphasize the enormous importance of inflammation as a pathological process central to many diseases. These molecular interactions are to a certain extent therefore independent of the immune system.

The principal molecules involved are termed cytokines, because they function in the immune system as products secreted by one cell to act on another cell to direct its movement ('kinesis'). In the context of inflammation it is the proinflammatory cytokines that are relevant. (See also Chapter 9, *Immunology*.)

6.1 Interleukin-1 (IL-1)

This molecule has a broad spectrum of both beneficial and harmful biological actions and, as a central regulator of the inflammatory response, has been implicated in many diseases.

There are three structurally related polypeptides in the interleukin-1 family:

- IL-1α
- IL-1β
- IL-1 receptor antagonist.

IL-1α and IL-1β are synthesized by mononuclear phagocytes that have been activated by microbial products or inflammation:

- IL-1α stays in the cell to act in an autocrine or paracrine fashion.
- IL-1β is secreted into the circulation and cleaved by interleukin-1β-converting enzyme (ICE).

IL-1β levels in the circulation are undetectable except:

- After strenuous exercise
- With sepsis
- With acute exacerbation of rheumatoid arthritis
- In ovulating women
- With acute organ rejection

IL-1 is present in the synovial lining and fluid of patients with rheumatoid arthritis and it is thought to activate gene expression for collagenases, phospholipases and cyclo-oxygenases. It is thus acting as a molecular facilitator of inflammatory damage in the joint but is not an initiator.

- The uptake of oxidized LDL by vascular endothelial cells results in IL-1 expression which stimulates the production of platelet-derived growth factor. IL-1 is thus likely to play a role in the formation of the atherosclerotic plaque.
- IL-1 has some host defence properties, inducing T and B lymphocytes and reduces mortality from bacterial and fungal infection in animal models.
- In septic shock, IL-1 acts by increasing the concentration of small mediator molecules such as platelet activating factor (PAF), prostaglandins and nitric oxide, which are potent vasodilators.

6.2 Tumour necrosis factor (TNF)

This is a pro-inflammatory cytokine that has a wide spectrum of actions. Either through neutralizing antibodies (anti-TNF-α) or inhibitor drugs it is the target of therapy in disorders such as rheumatoid arthritis and multiple sclerosis.

Two non-allelic forms of TNF, α and β, are expressed in different cells:

- TNF-α is produced by macrophages, eosinophils and NK cells
- TNF-β is made by activated T- lymphocytes.

Its name is derived from the early observation that it can have a cytotoxic effect on tumour cells *in vitro*. Trials with TNF-α as a therapeutic agent were soon stopped due to the severe toxicity of the substance. In fact in certain situations it can promote tumour growth.

Its action in diseases like rheumatoid arthritis depends on a synergistic effect with IL-1. Both are found in the synovial membrane of patients with the disease. TNF-α strongly induces monocytes to produce IL-1 at a level comparable to that stimulated by bacterial lipopolysaccaride (LPS).

- TNF-α is a potent stimulator of prostaglandin production
- TNF is a key cytokine in the pathogenesis of multi-organ failure
- It induces granulocyte-macrophage colony stimulating factor (GM–CSF) and thus is an activator of monocytes and macrophages in diseased tissue

6.3 Transforming growth factor β (TGF-β)

A key cytokine that initiates and terminates tissue repair and whose sustained production underlies the development of tissue fibrosis.

TGF-β is released by platelets at the site of tissue injury and is strongly chemotactic for monocytes, neutrophils, T-cells and fibroblasts. It induces monocytes to begin secreting fibroblast growth factor (FGF), TNF and IL-1, but inhibits the functioning of T- and B-cells and their production of TNF and IL-1. It also induces its own secretion. This autoinduction may be important in the pathogenesis of fibrosis. Other important features of TGF-β are:

- TGF-β deficient (knockout) mice die of an autoimmune disease in which levels of TNF and IL-1 are very high.
- It has a potent effect on cells to induce the production of extracellular matrix (a dynamic superstructure of self-aggregating macromolecules including fibronectin, collagen and

proteoglycans to which cells attach by means of surface receptors called integrins). Extracellular matrix is continually being degraded by proteases which are inhibited by TGF-β.

- In mesangioproliferative glomerulonephritis, glomerular immunostaining for TGF-β correlates well with the amount of mesangial deposition. In diabetic nephropathy, increased TGF-β is found in the glomeruli, and TGF-β may be central to the pathogenesis of progression of many chronic renal diseases.
- Elevated plasma levels of TGF-β are highly predictive of hepatic fibrosis in bone marrow transplant recipients. mRNA for TGF-β is found in areas of active disease in the liver biopsies of patients with chronic liver disease.
- In patients with idiopathic pulmonary fibrosis, TGF-β is increased in the alveolar walls. It is also implicated in bleomycin lung.

6.4 Heat shock proteins (HSPs)

The heat shock response is a highly conserved and phylogenetically ancient response to tissue stress that is mediated by activation of specific genes leading to the production of specific heat shock proteins that alter the phenotype of the cell, and enhance its resistance to stresses.

Some HSPs are extremely similar to constitutively activated proteins that have essential roles in unstressed cells. Their diverse functions include:

- export of proteins in and out of specific cell organelles (acting as molecular chaperones)
- catalysis of protein folding and unfolding
- degradation of proteins (often by the pathway of ubiquitination).

As well as heat, HSP expression can be triggered by cytotoxic chemicals, free radicals and other stimuli. The unifying feature that leads to the activation of HSPs in these situations is thought to be the accumulation of damaged intracellular protein.

Clinical relevance

- Tumours have an abnormal thermotolerance which is the basis for the observation of the enhanced cytotoxic effect of chemotherapeutic agents in hyperthermic subjects.
- Stress proteins are prominent amongst the bacterial antigens recognized by the immune response of humans to bacterial and parasitic infections and are thought to be involved in some autoimmune diseases.

6.5 Free radicals

Free radicals have been implicated in a large number of human diseases and are currently the subject of much interest. Therapeutic trials have been undertaken with putative free radical scavengers such as vitamin E. A free radical is literally any atom or molecule that contains one or more unpaired electrons, making it more reactive than the native species.

Free radical species produced in the human body:

- $-O\overset{\circ}{O}H$ (peroxide radical)
- $-\overset{\circ}{O}H$ (hydroxyl radical)
- $-\overset{\circ}{O}_2$ (superoxide radical)
- $-N\overset{\circ}{O}$ (nitric oxide)

The hydroxyl radical is by far the most reactive species but the others can generate more reactive species as breakdown products.

When a free radical reacts with a non-radical a chain reaction ensues which results in the formation of further free radicals and direct tissue damage by lipid peroxidation of membranes (particularly implicated in atherosclerosis and ischaemia reperfusion injury within tissues). Hydroxyl radicals can cause mutations by attacking purines and pyrimidines. Also:

- Activated phagocytes generate large amounts of superoxide within lysosomes as part of the mechanism whereby foreign organisms are killed. During chronic inflammation this protective mechanism may become harmful.
- Superoxide dismutases (SOD) convert superoxide to hydrogen peroxide and are thus part of an inherent protective antioxidant strategy. Catalases remove hydrogen peroxide. Glutathione peroxidases are major enzymes that remove hydrogen peroxide generated by SOD in cytosol and mitochondria.
- Free radical scavengers bind reactive oxygen species. Alpha-tocopherol, urate, ascorbate and glutathione remove free radicals by reacting directly and non-catalytically. Severe deficiency of alpha-tocopherol (vitamin E deficiency) causes neurodegeneration.

Clinical relevance

There is growing evidence that cardiovascular disease and cancer can be prevented by a diet rich in substances that diminish oxidative damage.

Principal dietary antioxidants

- Vitamin E
- Vitamin C
- Beta carotene
- Flavonoids

Epidemiological studies have demonstrated an association between increased intake of vitamins C and E and morbidity and mortality from coronary artery disease. This supports models where atherogenesis is initiated by lipid peroxidation of LDL.

Patients with dominant familial forms of amyotrophic lateral sclerosis (motor neurone disease) have mutations in the gene for Cu-Zn SOD-1, suggesting a link between failure of free radical scavenging and neurodegeneration.

7. TRANSMISSIBLE SPONGIFORM ENCEPHALOPATHIES

The transmissible spongiform encephalopathies (TSEs) are a group of diseases that are characterized by progressive spongiform degeneration in the brain and neuronal loss. While these conditions are rare, they are the subject of intense interest because of the fear of an epidemic of human infection in the UK from cattle with bovine spongiform encephalopathy (BSE). The biologically unique features of these diseases are, firstly, that they can be simultaneously inherited and also infectious, and secondly, that the agent of transmission is thought to be a protein only rather than an 'organism' containing DNA or RNA. This protein has been called a prion; it is encoded by the host genome and cannot replicate.

Diseases

- **Sporadic Creutzfeldt–Jakob disease (CJD):** rare (I/106), causes rapid dementia with myoclonus and characteristic EEG
- **New variant CJD (nvCJD):** less than 25 cases in total only in UK by the end of 1997. Occurs in young people with a slower course than sporadic CJD and characteristic pathological features
- **Autosomal dominant CJD:** familial form of classical CJD
- **Gerstmann–Straussler–Scheinker Syndrome (GSS):** familial spongiform encephalopathy with prominent ataxia
- **Fatal familial insomnia**
- **Kuru:** endemic in New Guinea Highlanders who performed ritual cannibalism. Now very rare.

The accidental or deliberate inoculation of affected brain tissue from a case of inherited or sporadic TSE results in the passage of the disease to the recipient. Procedures that destroy nucleic acid do not prevent this passage which has led to the proposition that the prion protein itself causes the disease by interacting with the host encoded protein, leading to its conversion to the mutant form of the protein. Other important considerations for the TSEs are:

- **Prion protein:** this is encoded by a gene on chromosome 20, exact function unknown. Curiously, mice lacking this gene only have subtle neurological defects. Prion proteins are not destroyed by boiling, UV irradiation or formaldehyde, nor do they elicit an immune response of any recognizable kind.

- **Species barrier**: this means that the diseases are, to some extent, species specific. For example, scrapie in sheep has never been passed on to humans as far as is known. Similarly, the transmission of a spongiform encephalopathy from one species to another is very difficult. If CJD brain is injected into the brain of a monkey then there is very little cell death, but if brain tissue from that same monkey is injected into another monkey (second passage) then there is severe neuronal loss. This suggests that the pathological process leading to spongiform change depends on the host protein.
- **Susceptibility polymorphism**: at codon 129 of the prion protein the amino acid can either be a valine or a glycine residue. Given that there is one copy of the gene on each chromosome we can either be heterozygous (valine/glycine) or homozygous (valine/ valine or glycine/glycine). It turns out that homozygosity at this residue is vastly over-represented in affected individuals in sporadic CJD and in new variant CJD. It would appear that the one amino acid can confer susceptibility to the disease.
- **Strain type**: when the protein from affected brains is electrophoretically separated and blotted onto a membrane (Western blotting) and then incubated with anti-prion protein antibody, different patterns can be seen. This is what is referred to as the 'strain' of the infective agent but is really a surrogate marker. It is the fact that the observed pattern with new variant CJD is identical to that observed with BSE and different to sporadic CJD that provides the strongest evidence of a link between the two.

8. ADHESION MOLECULES

The way in which cells communicate with each other is fundamental to the maintenance of homeostasis in the developing and adult organism. In particular, the molecular basis of neural connectivity, the immune response and the prevention of cancer are all dependent on adhesion molecules. Adhesion involves the interaction of one molecule, for example, a cell surface molecule, with a specific ligand which may be on another cell or a part of the extracellular matrix. These can be divided into four groups on the basis of structure and function.

- The immunoglobulin superfamily
- The cadherin superfamily
- Integrins
- Selectins.

The **immunoglobulin superfamily** is so-called because at the genetic level it has a sequence similarity that suggests that it arose from the same set of ancestral genes by duplication. These molecules are involved as cofactors in antigen presentation and are present as cell surface receptors on leukocytes (e.g. CD2, CD3, T-cell receptor) and some function as integrin ligands (e.g. ICAM, NCA: intercellular and neural cell adhesion molecule, respectively).

Cadherins are involved in the interaction between muscle and nerve in the developing embryo.

Integrins are heterodimeric (two subunits, different from each other) transmembrane glycoproteins which are widely distributed in different tissues and serve to interact with molecules of the extracellular matrix (laminin, fibronectin, collagen).

Selectins are expressed on leukocytes and are thought to be involved in leukocyte adherence to endothelium during acute inflammation and coagulation.

Expression of adhesion molecules is dynamic and can be upregulated by proinflammatory cytokines (IL-1, TNF), viral infection, T-cell activation and many other stimuli.

Clinical relevance of adhesion molecules

Adhesion molecule expression is upregulated in many forms of solid organ inflammation (e.g. autoimmune and viral hepatitis, and also in organ rejection after transplantation). The adhesion molecule, intercellular adhesion molecule-1 (ICAM-1), is a receptor for the integrin lymphocyte function associated molecule-1 (LFA-1) and may be involved in the recruitment of and maintenance of activated lymphocytes in tissue inflammation. It is theoretically possible to block these molecules to treat inflammation (e.g. in acute renal failure and in transplant rejection).

The integrin $\alpha_{IIb}\beta$ is the platelet receptor for fibrinogen.

- Mutations in its gene lead to the congenital bleeding disorder Glanzmann's thrombasthenia.
- In leukocyte adhesion deficiency (LAD), another genetic disease, lack of $\beta2$ integrins leads to failure of leukocyte migration to sites of infection and to recurrent bacterial sepsis.

Conversely, antibodies against $\alpha_{IIb}\beta$ are currently under trial as anti-thrombotic agents in coronary artery disease.

9. THE MOLECULAR BASIS OF SOME IMPORTANT DISEASES

The following conditions have been highlighted either because their molecular basis is well understood (e.g. myasthenia gravis, alpha-1 antitrypsin deficiency) or because they are caused by novel mechanisms (e.g. trinucleotide repeat disorders). Others are included because the identification of their molecular basis is historically important as for dystrophin in Duchenne muscular dystrophy, which was the first disease to be worked out by identifying the gene through positional cloning. Overall, the following diseases serve to illustrate the importance of the molecular mechanisms of disease outlined in the above sections.

9.1 Amyloidosis

A pathological process characterized by the accumulation of extracellular fibrils of insoluble protein. The aggregated protein is specific to the different amyloid diseases listed below, but in all cases the fibrillar component is associated with a non-fibrillar constituent called amyloid-P component which is derived from the acute phase protein serum amyloid P (SAP). For classification see Chapter 13, *Nephrology*.

Pathogenesis

Whilst the inherited forms of amyloid are rare, the accumulation of amyloid fibrils is a central part of the pathological process of a number of common diseases such as Alzheimer's and Type II diabetes where amyloid is found in the islets of Langerhans. Many individuals on long term haemodialysis eventually develop amyloid arthropathy. The key event in amyloid fibril formation is a change in conformation of the respective precursor protein which leads to its aggregation into an insoluble fibrillar form. The exact mechanism of this conformational change is unclear but it is thought to involve partial proteolytic cleavage of the precursor, and/or its overproduction. Using I^{131}-labelled SAP amyloid deposits can be localised using scintigraphy. Amyloid may cause organ dysfunction by progressive replacement of functional parenchyma or it may possibly be inherently cytotoxic.

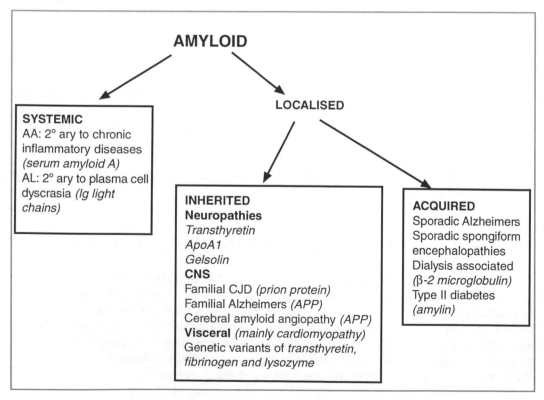

Classification of amyloidosis. The individual protein that associates with serum amyloid-P is shown in italics.

9.2 Alpha-1 antitrypsin deficiency

Deficiency of alpha-1 antitrypsin is one of the most common hereditary diseases affecting Caucasians. The prime function of the enzyme is to inhibit neutrophil elastase and it is one of the serpin superfamily of protease inhibitors. Patients with deficiency present with emphysema (see Chapter 17, *Respiratory Medicine*) because low protein levels fail to prevent the lung from proteolytic attack. A proportion of individuals also develop liver cirrhosis, but this does not appear to be directly due to enzyme deficiency.

- The most common mutation that changes a glutamate residue to a lysine at position 342 of the protein (the Z mutation) results in the accumulation of protein in the endoplasmic reticulum of the liver.
- The formation of these hepatic inclusions results from a protein–protein interaction between the reactive centre loop of one molecule and the beta-pleated sheet of a second.
- This leads to polymerization and aggregation. Similar mechanisms have been found to be responsible for deficiency of C-1 esterase inhibitor (hereditary angioneurotic angio-oedema) and anti-thrombin III.
- Since not all patients who are homozygously deficient develop liver damage, other factors, such as the way the mutant protein is broken down in the liver, must be relevant to the manifestation of the liver component.

9.3 Alzheimer's disease

A neurodegenerative disease of inexorable cognitive decline characterized histologically by intraneuronal neurofibrillary tangles and extracellular amyloid plaques. Most cases are sporadic.

- About five per cent of cases are inherited as an autosomal dominant with at least three genes responsible.
- Mutations in the amyloid precursor protein (APP) gene on chromosome 21 are a rare cause of familial Alzheimer's disease (AD). The βA4 protein is a proteolytic product of APP and the principal constituent of senile plaques.
- Mutations in two closely related genes, the presenilins PS-1 and PS-2, are responsible for other cases of AD.
- Inheritance of the ε-4 allele of apolipoprotein E is an important determinant of age of onset in familial AD and a risk factor for sporadic AD. (See also Chapter 14, *Neurology*.)

Molecular markers

Neurofibrillary tangles consist of highly ordered intraneuronal structures called paired helical filaments (PHF) which are assembled from the microtubule associated protein **tau**.

This suggests that neurones die because tau is handled in some abnormal way which leads to dysfunction of the microtubular network. Tau protein from PHFs is abnormally phosphorylated but it is not yet known whether this is part of the primary pathological process leading to AD. APP is cleaved into a β and a γ fragment. It is thought that plaque formation occurs when the Aβ fragment becomes insoluble and aggregates. Aggregated Aβ has been shown to induce free radical-mediated damage to neurones.

9.4 Trinucleotide repeat disorders

A new class of genetic disease has been recognized in recent years, in which the responsible genetic mutation is a repetitive sequence of three nucleotides which can undergo expansion (and occasionally contraction). It has therefore become known as a dynamic mutation.

Examples of trinucleotide repeat disorders

- Huntington's disease
- Fragile X syndrome*
- X-linked bulbospinal neuronopathy (Kennedy's syndrome)

- Myotonic dystrophy
- Friedriech's ataxia
- Spinocerebellar ataxias (there are a number of variants)

*See Chapter 6, *Genetics*.

As a consequence of dynamic mutation, mutant alleles arise from a population of pre-mutant alleles that have a repeat number at the upper limit of the normal range (usually < 35) which then become unstable and undergo sudden expansion into the mutant range (> 50). Two key genetic characteristics are illustrated by trinucleotide repeat disorders.

Anticipation

The phenomenon whereby the severity of a disease becomes worse, and the age of onset earlier, in successive generations.

Somatic instability

The length of the expansion continues to increase as cells divide throughout life. This may partly explain why a disease such as myotonic dystrophy gets worse as the patient gets older.

For a particular disease the length of the expansion corresponds with the age of onset of the disease

There are two main types of trinucleotide repeats.

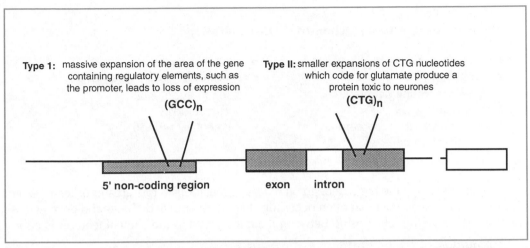

Type 1: massive expansion of the area of the gene containing regulatory elements, such as the promoter, leads to loss of expression

$(GCC)_n$

Type II: smaller expansions of CTG nucleotides which code for glutamate produce a protein toxic to neurones

$(CTG)_n$

5' non-coding region   exon   intron

Trinucleotide repeats can occur in the non-coding region or within exons, giving different effects

It will be evident from the above diagram that the consequence of a Type I expansion is loss of gene expression because the gene cannot be transcribed due to stereochemical interference from the expanded region. Type II disorders are thought to be so-called gain of function dominant mutations. That is, the trinucleotide expansion leads to the accumulation of an abnormal protein which is toxic to cells. In several of these disorders it has now been demonstrated that toxic protein accumulates in intraneuronal inclusions which stain positive for ubiquitin. (See also Chapter 6, *Genetics*.)

9.5 Mitochondrial disorders

The mitochondrial genome is circular and approximately 16.5 kb in length. It encodes genes for the mitochondrial respiratory chain and for some species of transfer RNA. Nucleic acids cannot move in and out of mitochondria, thus all of the mRNA synthesized from the mitochondrial genome must be translated in the organelle itself. However, many nuclear encoded proteins are transported into mitochondria and are absolutely necessary for mitochondrial function. (See also Chapter 6, *Genetics*.)

- Mitochondrial DNA (mtDNA) mutates 10 times more frequently than nuclear DNA; as there are no introns, a mutation will invariably strike a coding sequence.
- No mitochondria are transferred from spermatozoa at fertilization and so each individual only inherits mtDNA from the mother.
- Because there are 10^3–10^4 copies of mitochondrial DNA in each cell (each mitochondrion has 2–10 copies of mtDNA) normal and mutant mtDNA may coexist within one cell (known as heteroplasmy). This may be one explanation why mitochondrial diseases show a poor genotype–phenotype correlation.
- There is evidence that mtDNA mutations are accumulated throughout life, as mitochondrial DNA has no protective DNA repair enzymes, and that this may contribute to the changes of ageing.

Phenotypes due to mitochondrial DNA mutations

- Sensorineural deafness
- Optic atrophy
- Stroke in young people
- Myopathy
- Cardiomyopathy and cardiac conduction defects

- Diabetes mellitus
- Chronic progressive external ophthalmoplegia
- Lactic acidosis
- Pigmentary retinopathy

Virtually all tissues in the body depend on oxidative metabolism to a greater or lesser extent and thus these phenotypes can often occur together (for example, diabetes and deafness). As mentioned above the relationship between the mutations and the clinical features is poorly understood.

9.6 Myasthenia gravis

This relatively rare disease often appears in examinations because the molecular pathogenesis is well understood and it serves as a model for other autoimmune diseases.

Specific antibodies are directed against the nicotinic acetylcholine (ACh) receptor which is present on the post-synaptic membrane of the neuromuscular junction. This results in:

- complement-mediated destruction of acetylcholine receptors and a loss of the normal convolution of the muscle membrane (an important morphological hallmark of the disease); this leads to the loss of surface area for ACh to interact with its receptors
- accelerated endocytosis and degradation of receptors
- functional blockade of receptors.

These abnormalities lead to fatiguable weakness (see also Chapter 14, *Neurology*). Ptosis and diplopia are the commonest symptoms. In 10–15% of sufferers, symptoms are confined to the eyes (ocular myasthenia). Fatiguability occurs because of a combination of the normal rundown of ACh release which occurs physiologically, and a decreased number of ACh receptors.

Over 80–90% of patients have detectable antibodies to the ACh receptor and the others are presumed to have antibodies not detectable by current assays. Antibody negativity is more common in the ocular form.

- Passive transfer of antibodies from patients to mice reproduces the disease features
- Reduction of antibody levels by plasmapheresis or treatment with immune globulin ameliorates the disease

- The antibody titre in patients does not correlate with disease severity, suggesting that anti-ACh receptor antibodies have different functional consequences depending on the exact epitope to which they are directed.

The origin of the autoimmune process is controversial but 75% of patients have thymic abnormalities (hyperplasia in 85% and thymoma in 15%).

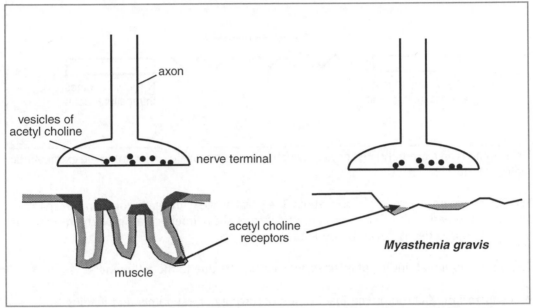

The neuromuscular junction in myasthenia gravis. There is loss of acetylcholine receptors and a decrease in post-synaptic folds.

9.7 Duchenne muscular dystrophy

This is a genetic disease which is X-linked, it has the highest new mutation rate of any X-linked gene. It is caused by mutations in a protein called dystrophin which is part of a large complex of membrane-associated proteins, defects in most of which can cause forms of muscular dystrophy.

Dystrophin is a very large protein indeed (>400 kDa) which is attached at its C-terminus to laminin on the inner aspect of the muscle membrane and at its N-terminus to actin, thus providing a connection between the extracellular matrix and the muscle cytoskeleton. Therefore its role is probably structural.

The most common mutations are large deletions which can be either of the following:

- **Inframe** in which the C-terminus and N-terminus of the molecule are preserved and a truncated form of dystrophin missing some of the rod domain is produced leading to Becker dystrophy, a milder form of the disease compatible with a normal lifespan and prolonged ambulation
- **Out of frame** which results in total abolition of dystrophin production because one or both of the binding sites for actin or laminin is disrupted.

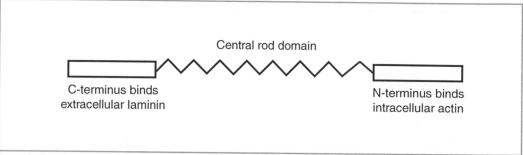

Dystrophin is an extremely large protein which links the cytoskeleton (actin) to the extracellular matrix of muscle

Weakness occurs progressively from about 3–4 years of age with death from cardiorespiratory failure in the early 20s. Thirty per cent of sufferers show intellectual impairment with the overall IQ curve being shifted to the left.

The very occasional finding of affected females can be due to the following:

- **Lyonization**: X-chromosome inactivation occurring non-randomly and leading to preferential inactivation of the normal chromosome
- Very rarely, **X-autosome translocation**. The presence of a fragment of an autosome in the region where dystrophin is normally found leads to the preferential activation of this chromosome and inactivation of the normal chromosome.

9.8 Sickle cell disease

It has been known for five decades that haemoglobin (Hb) from patients with this disease undergoes abnormal electrophoretic mobility. The basis for this is the presence, in all patients with the disease, of a single amino acid substitution of valine for glutamic acid in the HbS β-globin subunit. Hb has to be highly soluble to pack into red cells at high concentration and the sickle mutation leads to polymerization of HbS and consequent loss of solubility. The reason that polymerization takes place is that, in its deoxygenated form, the HbS β-globin subunit can bind to a partner β-subunit on another strand leading to the formation of large polymers (see diagram) which deform the red cell by damaging the membrane and interfering with ion-flux. The polymerization process is a dynamic event under the influence of the oxygenation state of the cell and the intracellular concentration of Hb which accounts in part for the variable clinical manifestations of the disease.

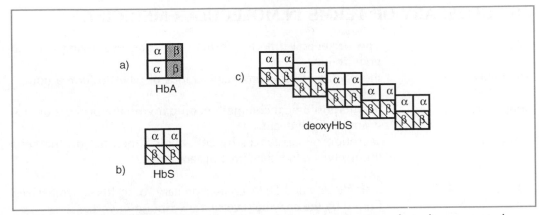

In sickle cell disease HbS undergoes abnormal depolymerization when deoxygenated

- The unpredictable nature of the vaso-occlusive events observed in patients has been explained because the SS red cells have a greater propensity for attachment to vascular endothelium. The degree of stickiness to endothelium is determined primarily by the rapidity of polymer formation which in turn is dependent on the rapidity of deoxygenation.

- The binding of sickle red cells to endothelium appears to be mediated by the interaction between integrins on the cell membrane and adhesion molecules expressed on the vascular endothelial surface.

- The presence of proinflammatory cytokines such as TNF stimulates this process, which explains why infection of any kind can provoke a sickle crisis.

- One factor that has been shown to modify the rate of polymer formation is the presence of fetal haemoglobin (HbF), which slows the rate of polymer formation.

- Certain ethnic subpopulations have higher amounts of fetal Hb persisting in the circulation and milder SS disease.

- This suggests that pharmacological upregulation of HbF could ameliorate the disease. Hydroxyurea has been shown to increase the amount of HbF and is now widely used in the prevention of sickle crises. The risk of tumours from this cytotoxic drug appears to be small and any myelosuppression is reversible.

The clinical features of sickle cell disease are discussed in Chapter 8, *Haematology*.

10. GLOSSARY OF TERMS IN MOLECULAR MEDICINE

Allele: one of several different forms of a gene occupying a given genetic locus.

Annealing: the pairing of complementary strands of DNA to form a double helix.

Apoptosis: the morphological changes accompanying the process of programmed cell death.

Autocrine: secretion of substances by cells which then act on the cells themselves rather than on a distant target.

cDNA: a single-stranded DNA complementary to an RNA, synthesized from it by the enzyme reverse transcriptase *in vitro*.

Cell cycle: the period from one cell division to the next.

Cytokines: act locally and their effect can be positive or negative depending on the environment, other cytokines, the physiological state of the cell and the extracellular matrix. This variable response of cytokines underlies the ability of the organism to maintain a wide repertoire of responses to tissue injury.

DNA polymerase: an enzyme that synthesizes a daughter strand of DNA on a DNA template.

Exon: any segment of an interrupted gene which is represented in the mature RNA product.

Gene family: consists of a set of genes the exons of which are related; the members were derived from a common ancestral gene by duplication and subsequent variation.

Gene targeting: the creation of animals (usually mice) which are null mutants for a particular gene. That is, the gene has been 'knocked out' and the 'knockout' mouse contains no copy of the gene at all.

G-protein: heterotrimeric membrane protein that is activated by the exchange of GDP for GTP and dissociates on activation into an α and $\beta\gamma$ subunits. It has intrinsic GTPase activity which mediates its inactivation.

Growth factor: a hormone that induces cell division and differentiation.

Heterozygote: an individual with different alleles on each chromosome at a given locus.

Housekeeping genes: constitutively expressed genes in all cells because they provide basic functions needed for survival of all cell types.

Hybridoma: a cell line produced by fusing a myeloma with a lymphocyte; it can indefinitely express the immunoglobulin of both cells, unless the myeloma has been selected to be deficient in Ig expression.

384

Introns: sequences of DNA that are transcribed but removed from nascent mRNA by splicing.

Isoform: one of a number of different forms of a protein that may be derived from one gene by splicing or from separate closely related members of a gene family.

Oligonucleotide: a short sequence of (synthetic) DNA, typically 18–22 base pairs in length, which acts as a primer for PCR reactions or a molecular probe when detecting gene sequences.

Oncogene: a gene whose protein product (the oncoprotein) has the ability to transform eukaryotic cells so that they grow in a manner analogous to tumour cells.

Paracrine: secretion by one cell of substances that act on adjacent cells.

Programmed cell death: the process whereby unwanted cells die under the control of a genetic programme.

Promoter: a region of DNA involved in the binding of RNA polymerase to initiate transcription.

Protein kinase: an enzyme that phosphorylates (adds a phosphate group) to a substrate (an amino acid in another protein).

Protein phosphatase: an enzyme that removes phosphate groups from substrates.

Proto-oncogene: the normal counterpart in eukaryotic genomes of retroviral genes which can transform cells.

Response elements: specific nucleotide recognition sequences in the 5' regulatory regions of genes which recognize transcription factors that have been activated by upstream signals such as steroid hormones.

Somatic cells: all the cells of an organism except the germ cells.

Transcription factor: a protein that binds to the promoter region of a gene to influence its transcription.

Tumour suppressor gene: a gene that, when activated will produce a protein that inhibits cell division. Mutations of these genes therefore lead to loss of control of cell division and contribute to tumorigenesis.

Chapter 13
Nephrology

CONTENTS

1. **Renal physiology**   389
   - 1.1   Glomerular filtration rate (GFR)
   - 1.2   Tubular physiology
   - 1.3   Renin-angiotensin-aldosterone (RAA) system

2. **Renal investigation**   392
   - 2.1   Urinalysis
   - 2.2   Renal radiology

3. **Acid-base, water and electrolyte disorders**   394
   - 3.1   Acidosis and alkalosis
   - 3.2   Renal tubular acidosis (RTA)
   - 3.3   Polyuria
   - 3.4   Hypokalaemia

4. **Acute renal failure**   398
   - 4.1   Pathogenesis and management of acute renal failure
   - 4.2   Rhabdomyolysis

5. **Chronic renal failure and renal replacement therapy**   401
   - 5.1   Chronic renal failure
   - 5.2   Anaemia of CRF
   - 5.3   Renal osteodystrophy
   - 5.4   Maintenance dialysis
   - 5.5   Renal transplantation

6. **Glomerulonephritis and associated syndromes**   408
   - 6.1   Clinical presentation of glomerulonephritis
   - 6.2   Notes on particular glomerulonephritides

7. **Inherited renal disease**   **416**
    7.1   Polycystic kidney disease (PKD)
    7.2   Other renal cystic disorders
    7.3   Alport's syndrome
    7.4   Other inherited disorders associated with renal disease

8. **Renal interstitial disorders**   **419**
    8.1   Interstitial nephritis
    8.2   Analgesic nephropathy and papillary necrosis

9. **Reflux nephropathy and urinary tract infection**   **421**
    9.1   Reflux nephropathy
    9.2   Urinary tract infection

10. **Renal calculi and nephrocalcinosis**   **424**
    10.1 Renal calculi (nephrolithiasis)
    10.2 Nephrocalcinosis

11. **Urinary tract obstruction and tumours**   **426**
    11.1 Urinary tract obstruction
    11.2 Retroperitoneal fibrosis (RPF)
    11.3 Urinary tract tumours

12. **Systemic disorders and the kidney**   **428**
    12.1 Amyloidosis
    12.2 Atherosclerotic renovascular disease (ARVD)
    12.3 Connective tissue disorders and the kidney
    12.4 Diabetic nephropathy
    12.5 Haemolytic–uraemic syndrome (HUS)
    12.6 Hypertension
    12.7 Myeloma
    12.8 Renal vasculitis

13. **Drugs and the kidney and toxic nephropathy**   **435**
    13.1 Renal elimination of drugs
    13.2 Drug nephrotoxicity
    13.3 Radio-contrast nephropathy
    13.4 Toxic nephropathy

Nephrology

1. RENAL PHYSIOLOGY

1.1 Glomerular filtration rate (GFR)

Glomerular filtration is a passive process which depends upon the net hydrostatic pressure acting across the glomerular capillaries, countered by the oncotic pressure, and also influenced by the intrinsic permeability of the glomerulus (K_f); the latter may vary due to mesangial cell contraction, such as in response to angiotensin II. The normal GFR in the adult is 100–140 ml/min/1.73m², but this can decline with age (1.73m² refers to the body surface area of an average person).

There are several means of calculating GFR:

- **Creatinine clearance**: usually calculated from a 24-hour urine collection with a consecutive blood sample.

$$\text{Creatinine clearance} = \frac{\text{Ucr x Uv x 1000}}{\text{Pcr x 24 x 60}} \quad \text{ml/min}$$

  where U = urine, P = plasma, v = volume and cr = creatinine concentration (μmol/l). This tends to overestimate GFR as some creatinine is secreted into the tubule from the post-glomerular circulation; the error increases with declining renal function.

- **Cockcroft and Gault formula**: a useful means of estimating GFR; it only requires knowledge of patient age, weight and plasma creatinine.

$$\text{GFR (ml/min)} = \frac{(140 - \text{age in years}) \text{ x weight (kg)}}{\text{plasma creatinine (μmol/l)}} \text{ x 1.23 (men) or 1.04 (women)}$$

The most accurate laboratory techniques for assessing GFR are:

- **Inulin clearance**: inulin is a small molecule, freely filtered by the glomerulus, and with no tubular secretion.
- **Chromium-labelled EDTA**: the most frequently used isotopic technique.

1.2 Tubular physiology

The renal tubule has many reabsorptive and secretory functions (see the figure below); these are energy-consuming and hence tubular cells are those most vulnerable to ischaemic damage (the ATN of ischaemic acute renal failure).

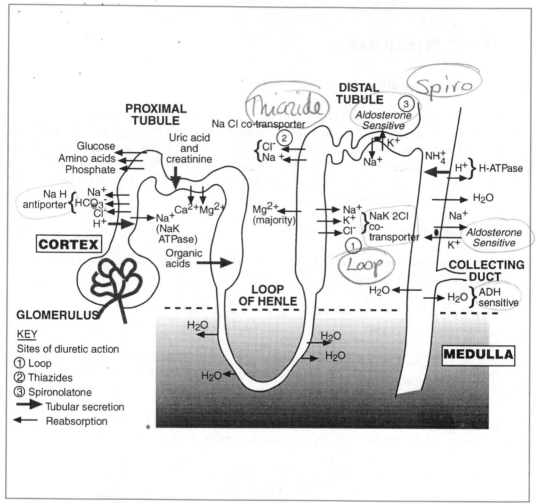

Schema of a nephron showing tubular physiology

Proximal tubule

Fifty per cent of filtered sodium is re-absorbed within the proximal tubule (via Na K ATPase); the Na H antiporter secretes H^+ into the lumen and is responsible for 90% of bicarbonate and some chloride reabsorption. All of the filtered glucose and amino acids are re-absorbed here. Other important characteristics are:

- Phosphate re-absorption occurs under the influence of parathormone (PTH)
- Some important drugs are secreted into the tubular filtrate here: trimethoprim, cimetidine, most β-lactams, and most diuretics (note that diuretics such as thiazides, amiloride and loop diuretics are highly protein-bound and are not filtered at the glomerulus)
- Creatinine and urate are secreted into the lumen.

Loop of Henle

The medullary concentration gradient is generated here; the medullary thick ascending limb (mTAL) is impermeable to water. Forty per cent of sodium is re-absorbed (via the Na K 2Cl co-transporter). Loop diuretics compete for chloride binding sites on this transporter.

Distal tubule

In this segment of the nephron 5% of sodium is reabsorbed (Na Cl co-transporter); thiazide diuretics compete for these chloride-binding sites. As loop diuretics increase sodium delivery to the distal tubule, their combination with a thiazide (e.g. metolazone) can provoke a massive diuresis in resistant oedema. There are aldosterone receptors in both the distal and collecting tubules (see below).

Collecting duct

Aldosterone-sensitive sodium channels are responsible for 2% of all sodium re-absorption; spironolactone binds to the cytoplasmic aldosterone receptor. Atrial natriuretic peptide (ANP) is also anti-aldosterone in action. Other important collecting duct functions include:

- H^+ secreted into lumen by H-ATPase, so forming ammonia/NH_4^+ (urinary acidification)
- Anti-diuretic hormone (ADH) increases water re-absorption by opening water channels; lithium enters the collecting duct cells via the sodium channels and inhibits the response to ADH (hence, nephrogenic diabetes insipidus (NDI) results).

1.3 Renin-angiotensin-aldosterone (RAA) system

This is covered in Chapter 4, *Endocrinology*. The RAA system has a central role in the pathogenesis of many cases of secondary renal hypertension (see below). Remember that intra-renal perfusion will become critically dependent upon the RAA when hypovolaemia and hypotension supervene; this explains why patients can be vulnerable to ACE-inhibitor-induced acute renal failure even in the absence of renovascular disease.

2. RENAL INVESTIGATION

2.1 Urinalysis

Urinary dipsticks

The sticks register positive for 'blood' in the presence of erythrocytes, as well as free myoglobin (e.g. in rhabdomyolysis) and haemoglobin; haemoglobinuria would be suspected by the absence of red cells at microscopy. Also:

- Standard dipsticks do not detect Bence–Jones proteins, and so if free urinary light chains are to be identified immunoelectrophoresis of urine is necessary.
- Microalbuminuria (see below) may also not be detected.

Proteinuria

Accepted ranges of proteinuria are given below:

	mg/24 hours	μg/minute
Normal range	<25	<15
Microalbuminuria	25–250	15–175
Dipstick positive	>250	>175
Nephrotic range	>3000 (i.e. 3 grams)	>2000

Non-renal causes of proteinuria:

- Normal (Tamm–Horsfall or tubular glycoprotein)
- Fever
- Severe exercise
- Skin disease (e.g. severe exfoliation, psoriasis)
- Lower urinary tract infection (e.g. cystitis).

Orthostatic proteinuria

This describes proteinuria detectable after the patient has spent several hours in the upright posture; it disappears after recumbency, and so the first morning urine should test negative. Renal biopsies are usually normal and nephrological consensus suggests this is a benign condition.

Urine microscopy

Microscopic examination of a fresh specimen of urine may yield many helpful pointers to intrinsic renal pathology.

- **Red cells**: > 2–3/high power field is pathological; cells may be dysmorphic in glomerular bleeding.
- **Leucocytes**: infection, and some cases of glomerular and interstitial nephritis.
- **Crystals**: (e.g. oxalate, struvite (see section 10.1 on renal calculi)), cystine and, with polarized light, uric acid.
- **Casts**: there are several types of cast:

  Tubular cells — acute tubular necrosis (ATN) or interstitial nephritis
  Hyaline — Tamm–Horsfall glycoprotein (i.e. in normals)
  Granular — non-specific
  Red cell — glomerulonephritis or tubular bleeding
  Leucocytes — pyelonephritis or ATN.

Causes of urinary discolouration

- Haematuria
- Myoglobinuria
- Beetroot consumption
- Alkaptonuria
- Obstructive jaundice

- Haemoglobinuria
- Drugs (e.g. rifampicin, para-aminosalicylic acid)
- Porphyria

2.2 Renal radiology

The essential first line radiological investigation for acute (ARF) or chronic renal failure (CRF), and most other nephrological conditions, is renal ultrasound. This will demonstrate:

- **Bipolar renal length**: small (<8 cm) in many cases of CRF; normal size (9–13 cm) in ARF; asymmetry (> 1.5 cm disparity) in renovascular disease
- **Obstruction**
- **Cortical scarring**: for example in reflux nephropathy or following segmental ischaemic damage
- **Calculi**: within the substance of the kidney and collecting systems
- **Mass lesions and cysts**: (e.g. renal tumour, polycystic disease or simple renal cysts).

Intravenous urography (IVU) is reserved for investigation of urinary tract bleeding (e.g. to detect urothelial tumours of the renal pelvis, ureters and bladder), UTI and for some cases of obstructive uropathy. IVU can exacerbate ARF (see section on radio-contrast nephropathy), and has very limited value in advanced CRF (poor concentration of dye).

Isotope renography

Two major types of renograms are commonly utilized:

- **Static scans (e.g. DMSA):** the isotope is concentrated and retained within the renal parenchyma, and elimination is slow. DMSA will therefore demonstrate aspects of structure (e.g. scars in reflux nephropathy) and split function of the two kidneys.
- **Dynamic scans (e.g. MAG$_3$, DTPA, Hippuran):** these isotopes are rapidly taken up and eliminated by the kidneys; such scans are used to assess renal blood flow, split function and also to investigate obstruction (e.g. to show whether urinary tract dilatation is due to obstruction).

Captopril renography

This involves a dynamic scan (e.g. MAG$_3$) which is then repeated 1 hour after an oral dose of captopril. Changes in the renographic curves (e.g. delay in time-to-peak, cortical retention of isotope) can be indicative of significant renovascular disease.

3. ACID-BASE, WATER AND ELECTROLYTE DISORDERS

3.1 Acidosis and alkalosis

Respiratory acidosis (e.g. carbon dioxide retention due to chronic or acute-on-chronic lung disease) and **alkalosis** (e.g. due to hyperventilation) are common, and well understood by all.

Metabolic alkalosis and **metabolic acidosis** are covered in detail in Chapter 11, *Metabolic Diseases*. The width of the anion gap can help differentiate the likely causes of a metabolic acidosis; the HCO$_3$ will be low, and the anion gap can be either wide (normal chloride and exogenous acid) or normal (increased chloride, and hence, hyperchloraemic acidosis). Renal failure is associated with a wide gap acidosis (due to excess ammonia and organic acids), whereas **renal tubular acidosis** is worth consideration as a cause of a normal gap acidosis.

3.2 Renal tubular acidosis (RTA)

Distal or **type 1** RTA is fairly common, and can complicate many renal parenchymal disorders, particularly those which predominantly affect the medullary regions. Note that the latter may also be associated with nephrogenic diabetes insipidus, and sometimes with salt-wasting states. **Proximal** or **type 2** RTA is uncommon. GFR is usually normal in both conditions. Calcium salts are more soluble in acid urine and hence calculi develop frequently in distal but not in proximal RTA (which is usually associated with a lower urinary pH). The two types of RTA can be differentiated by several other parameters, as shown in the following table.

	Type 1 (Distal)	**Type 2 (Proximal)**
Defect	Impaired urinary (H^+) acidification	Failure of HCO_3 reabsorption
Urine pH	>5.3 (i.e. urine never 'acidifies')	Variable
Plasma HCO$_3$	<10 mmol/l	14–20 mmol/l
Plasma K	Usually $\downarrow$	Normal or $\downarrow$
Complications	Nephrocalcinosis Calculi	Osteomalacia (phosphate wasting) Rickets
Other features	Growth failure Urine infection	Fanconi syndrome (i.e. phosphaturia, glycosuria, aminoaciduria)
Diagnostic test	Ammonium chloride load fails to acidify urine	Fractional HCO_3 rises after i.v. bicarbonate load

Causes of distal RTA	Causes of proximal RTA
• **Primary** Genetic (dominant) or idiopathic	• **Occurring alone** Idiopathic
• **Secondary to autoimmune diseases** SLE, Sjögren's syndrome, chronic active hepatitis	• **With Fanconi syndrome** Wilson's disease, cystinosis, fructose intolerance, Sjögren's syndrome
• **Tubulointerstitial disease** Chronic pyelonephritis, transplant rejection, obstructive uropathy, chronic interstitial nephritis	• **Tubulointerstitial disease** Interstitial nephritis, myeloma, amyloidosis
• **Nephrocalcinosis** Medullary sponge kidney, hypercalcaemia	• **Drugs and toxins** Outdated tetracyclines, streptozotocin, lead and mercury (and other heavy metals), acetazolamide, sulphonamides
• **Drugs and toxins** Lithium, amphotericin, toluene	

Type 4 RTA (hyporeninaemic hypoaldosteronism) describes a metabolic acidosis that is associated with hyperkalaemia and mild renal impairment (GFR usually > 30 ml/min). It is commonly associated with diabetic nephropathy, but can also complicate hypo-adrenalism, gouty nephropathy, urinary tract obstruction and treatment with NSAIDs or potassium-sparing diuretics.

3.3 Polyuria

Polyuria (urine output > 3 litres/day) may result from:

• Diuretic usage
• Large fluid intake (e.g. alcohol): inhibits ADH release
• Cranial diabetes insipidus: osmolality high
• Nephrogenic diabetes insipidus: osmolality high
• Psychogenic polydypsia: osmolality usually low
• Atrial natriuretic peptide release: post-arrhythmia, cardiac failure.

The causes of **cranial** and **nephrogenic diabetes insipidus** are listed in Chapter 4, *Endocrinology*; hyponatraemia as well as other disorders of water balance, including **SIADH**, are also discussed in that chapter.

3.4 Hypokalaemia

Acute hypokalaemia can lead to muscle weakness and direct renal tubular cell injury (vacuolation). Chronic hypokalaemia is a cause of interstitial nephritis. The causes can be classified according to the **urinary potassium excretion**, and in those with inappropriately high excretion, the **plasma renin activity**.

Causes of hypokalaemia

- **Potassium excretion
  < 30 mmol/day**

  Prior diuretic use
  Gastrointestinal tract losses

- **Potassium excretion
  >30 mmol/day**

  High plasma renin activity   *Low plasma renin activity*
    Diuretic usage   Primary hyperaldosteronism
    Renovascular disease   (Conn's syndrome)
    Accelerated-phase hypertension   Carbenoxalone
    Salt-wasting CRF   Liquorice
    Cushing's syndrome
    Renin-secreting tumour
    Bartter's syndrome (see below)

Bartter's syndrome

Severe hypokalaemia is consequent upon a salt-wasting state (increased sodium delivery to the distal tubule) that is due to defective chloride reabsorption (at the Na K 2Cl co-transporter) in the loop of Henle. Patients have normal or low blood pressure and severe hyperreninaemia (with hypertrophy of the juxtaglomerular apparatus) with consequent hyperaldosteronism; GFR is usually normal. Treatment is with large dose potassium replacement; NSAIDs may also be beneficial.

4. ACUTE RENAL FAILURE

4.1 Pathogenesis and management of acute renal failure

Acute deterioration of renal function is seen in up to 5% of all hospital admissions. The incidence of severe ARF (e.g. creatinine > 500 μmol/l) increases with age; the overall annual incidence is approximately 150/million in the UK, but this figure is six times greater in the > 80-year-old group. Dialysis-requiring ARF occurs in 70/million of the population annually. Oliguria is usual, and is defined as a daily urine output of < 400–500 ml; this is the minimum volume to enable excretion of the daily waste products.

Non-oliguric ARF occurs in 10%; this may be associated with drug-toxicity (e.g. gentamicin or amphotericin) and radio-contrast nephropathy.

The majority (55%) of cases of ARF result from renal hypoperfusion and ischaemic damage; the resulting renal histopathological lesion is **acute tubular necrosis (ATN)**. Many other patients may have similar ischaemic insults to the kidneys, with an initial period of oliguria, but renal perfusion can then be restored by vigorous haemodynamic management before severe tubular injury ensues; this is termed **pre-renal uraemia** and most cases can be managed without dialysis. In the latter, physiological mechanisms (i.e. stimulation of the RAA system), are preserved within the kidney, and so the urinary manifestations of sodium and water reabsorption allow differentiation from established ATN.

Urinary findings	ATN	Pre-renal uraemia
Urine sodium	> 40 mmol/l	< 20 mmol/l
Urine: plasma osmolality	< 1.1:1	> 1.5:1
Fractional sodium excretion (FeNa)*	> 1%	< < 1%
Urine: plasma urea	< 7:1	> 10:1
Urine volume	Oligo-anuric or polyuria (recovery phase)	< 1.5 litres

*FeNa is the percentage of sodium that is filtered at the glomerulus (normally 1000 mmol/hr) which actually appears in the urine (normal 6 mmol/hr, i.e. 0.6%)

The causes of ARF, with approximate relative frequency, are summarized below.

Classification of ARF

- **Pre-renal factors leading to renal hypoperfusion and ATN (55%)**
  Reduced circulating volume: blood loss; excess GI losses; burns
  Low cardiac output states: toxic or ischaemic myocardial depression
  Systemic sepsis
  Drugs inducing renal perfusion shutdown: (e.g. ACE inhibitors; NSAIDs).

- **Toxic ATN (5%)**
  Rhabdomyolysis with urinary myoglobin
  Drugs: (e.g. gentamicin; amphotericin)
  Radio-contrast nephropathy.

- **Structural abnormalities of renal vasculature (8%)**
  Large vessel occlusion (renovascular disease)
  Small vessel occlusion: accelerated-phase hypertension; DIC; haemolytic–uraemic syndrome; thrombotic thrombocytopenic purpura; pre-eclampsia; systemic sclerosis
  Acute cortical necrosis.

- **Acute glomerulonephritis and vasculitis (12%)**
  Idiopathic crescentic glomerulonephritis
  ANCA-positive vasculitis
  Goodpasture's syndrome
  Other proliferative glomerulonephritis (e.g. SLE; endocarditis).

- **Interstitial nephritis (4%)**
  Idiopathic, immunologically mediated
  Drug-induced hypersensitivity
  Infection (e.g. pyelonephritis; leptospirosis; Hanta virus)

- **Myeloma/tubular cast nephropathy (4%)**

- **Urinary tract obstruction (12%)**

Pathophysiology of ATN

After an ischaemic insult there is intense afferent arteriolar vasoconstriction, mediated by the release of vasoconstrictors, particularly endothelin, and by loss of intrinsic vasodilators (nitric oxide and PGI_2); this contributes to the loss of GFR and the redistribution of blood flow within the kidney. Hypoxic injury to the energy-consuming cells of the proximal tubule and thick ascending limb of Henle occurs; calcium and oxygen free-radical mediated cell necrosis results in cell shedding from the tubular basement membrane, with the formation of casts that block urine flow.

Investigation and management of ARF

The history may point to the cause of ARF (e.g. drugs, skin rash); assessment of the haemodynamic status is imperative, and appropriate fluid resuscitation should be given. A renal ultrasound scan will usually show normal sized (or swollen) kidneys, and will identify obstruction. Percutaneous renal biopsy is essential if an intrinsic lesion (e.g. vasculitis, glomerulonephritis, interstitial nephritis) is suspected, or if no ischaemic cause is apparent.

Specific immunosuppressive therapy, and sometimes plasma exchange, may be appropriate for some conditions (e.g. Goodpasture's syndrome). 'Renal dose' dopamine and loop diuretics are often given in ATN, although there is no evidence that they alter the outcome of ARF in man. The most important advances in management have involved attention to intensive nutritional support of the sicker patients, and the use of continuous renal replacement therapies (e.g. CVVH: continuous veno-venous haemofiltration) which are less likely to provoke haemodynamic instability.

Indications for urgent dialysis in ARF

- **Severe uraemia**
  (e.g. vomiting, encephalopathy)
- **Severe acidosis**
  pH <7.1
- **Pulmonary oedema**

- **Hyperkalaemia**
  K >6.5 mmol/l (or less, if ECG changes apparent)
- **Uraemic pericarditis**

The prognosis for patients with ARF remains only moderate; 55–60% of patients who require dialytic therapy survive, but this figure partly reflects the very poor outcome of patients who have ATN as a component of multi-organ failure (MOF) who are managed on the ITU. For example, only 10–20% of those with three or four organ failure will survive, yet 90% of patients with ARF in isolation survive.

4.2 Rhabdomyolysis

Muscle damage with release of myoglobin can cause severe, hypercatabolic ARF. Serum potassium and phosphate (released from muscle) rapidly rise, calcium is typically low, and the creatine kinase massively elevated; serum creatinine may be disproportionately higher than urea. Conservative treatment involves alkalinization of the urine (with i.v. bicarbonate and also acetazolamide) which solubilizes the myoglobin pigment within the renal tubules. Sometimes the source of the rhabdomyolytic process requires specific therapy (e.g. fasciotomy for compartment syndrome; amputation of severely crushed limb).

Causes of rhabdomyolysis

- **Crush injury**
  Trauma; unconsciousness with compression
- **Metabolic myopathies**
  (e.g. McArdle's syndrome)
- **Infections**
  Viral necrotizing myositis, infectious mononucleosis (e.g. Coxsackie influenza)

- **Uncontrolled fitting**
- **Drugs**
  (e.g. statins)
- **Overdose**
  Barbiturates, alcohol, heroin
- **Severe exercise, heat stroke, burns**
- **Inflammatory myopathies**
  Polymyositis
- **Malignant hyperpyrexia**

5. CHRONIC RENAL FAILURE AND RENAL REPLACEMENT THERAPY

5.1 Chronic renal failure

Chronic renal failure (CRF) is common, with an annual incidence of >150/million in the UK; approximately 75 patients/million join renal replacement therapy (RRT) programmes each year. There are several **recognized stages of CRF**:

- **Diminished renal reserve**: plasma biochemistry is normal, but GFR is reduced (to as low as 50% of normal).
- **Moderate CRF**: GFR 25–50 ml/min; also referred to as 'azotaemia' (particularly in the USA), as plasma urea and creatinine exceed normal. Renal anaemia begins to complicate this level of renal dysfunction.
- **Severe CRF**: GFR <25 ml/min; patients may have uraemic symptoms.
- **End-stage renal failure (ESRF)**: GFR 5 ml/min or less; life-threatening uraemic syndrome likely to supervene unless RRT commenced.

Although many cases of CRF progress insidiously, so that very abnormal biochemistry is relatively well-tolerated by the patient, about one-third of dialysis patients initially present as uraemic emergencies. The key parameters that **differentiate CRF from ARF** are:

- Small kidneys at imaging
- Anaemia
- Renal bone disease
- Clinical tolerance of very severe uraemia.

Causes of CRF (approximate relative frequencies)

- **Most common causes of ESRF in UK***
  Chronic glomerulonephritis (20%)
  Diabetic nephropathy (20%)
  Renovascular disease (15%)
  Chronic reflux nephropathy (15%)
  Polycystic kidney disease (10%)
  Post-obstructive (10%)
  Myeloma (3%)
  Amyloidosis (3%)

- **Other causes of CRF**
  Chronic interstitial nephritis
  Analgesic nephropathy
  Renal calculi (nephrolithiasis)
  Post-ARF
  Other hereditary disorders

*In at least 10% of cases of ESRF, the aetiology remains unknown

Although the majority of cases of CRF are slowly progressive towards ESRF, patients with particular pathologies (e.g. post-obstructive atrophy) may manifest stable CRF for many years. The general management of patients with CRF directs attention to:

- **Control of blood pressure**: this can slow progression toward ESRF (see section on diabetic nephropathy).
- **Reduction of proteinuria**: heavy urinary protein losses (e.g. >2 g/day) are associated with an increased rate of progression in some cases of CRF. Amelioration of proteinuria by use of ACE-I (and perhaps angiotensin-blockers) may slow progression.
- **Dietary modification**: it is now widely accepted that patients with advanced CRF should maintain a normal protein and high calorie intake to avoid malnutrition (and a consequent increased likelihood of morbidity) in the phase leading up to RRT. Very severely restricted protein intakes (e.g. the 18–21 g/day Giovannetti diet) are only used as a conservative means of limiting uraemia in a minority of patients.
- **Endocrine complications**: apart from uraemia, the other important complications of CRF which require consideration are anaemia and renal osteodystrophy.

5.2 Anaemia of CRF

The anaemia of CRF usually first appears when GFR is <35 ml/min; if untreated, it is a major contributor to morbidity in patients with advanced CRF. The major cause is the lack of endogenous erythropoietin (EPO) secretion by the damaged kidneys, but other factors which predispose to the anaemia are listed opposite:

- Reduced dietary iron intake due to anorexia
- Uraemia has toxic effect upon precursor cells in bone marrow
- Blood loss due to capillary fragility and platelet dysfunction (probably of minor importance)

- Impaired intestinal absorption of iron
- Reduced RBC survival (particularly in haemodialysis patients)

Patients with polycystic kidney disease are less likely to be anaemic as they tend to have greater intrinsic EPO levels than other patients with similar degrees of CRF. In general, haemodialysis patients have more severe anaemia, and a poorer response to EPO therapy, than their counterparts receiving CAPD.

Recombinant erythropoietin

Endogenous EPO is normally synthesized by renal peritubular cells; it stimulates proliferation and maturation of erythroid lines within the marrow. Recombinant EPO preparations are now widely available and are used to correct anaemia in patients receiving dialysis (and in those with low GFR (e.g. pre-dialysis; failing renal transplants)). It is imperative that these patient groups avoid repeated blood transfusion, so that future renal transplantation will not be precluded by allo-sensitization.

EPO is normally given s.c. with an initiation dose of approximately 100 iu/kg/week. The serum ferritin (and sometimes the transferrin saturation) need monitoring as many patients require supplemental i.v. iron. The target haemoglobin to be achieved with maintenance therapy is 11–13 g/dl; one of the key aims of therapy is to limit or reverse the left ventricular hypertrophy (LVH) which is prevalent in RRT patients.

Main side-effects: accelerated hypertension with encephalopathy (aim for a monthly Hb increase of <1.5 g/dl); bone aches; flu-like syndrome; fistula thrombosis (rare).

Causes of resistance to EPO therapy

- Iron deficiency
- Sepsis or chronic inflammation
- Occult GI tract blood loss

- Hyperparathyroidism
- Aluminium toxicity (rare)

5.3 Renal osteodystrophy

The regulation of vitamin D and PTH metabolism are discussed in Chapter 11, *Metabolic Diseases*. Renal bone disease (osteodystrophy) is common in patients with CRF and those receiving dialysis. The pathogenesis is fairly intricate but the most important components are:

- **Low plasma ionized calcium**: due to several factors. There is lack of 1,25 di-hydroxy vitamin D (the 1α hydroxylation, which markedly increases activity of vitamin D, normally occurs in the kidney). Malnutrition may contribute, but hyperphosphataemia (imbalancing the ionic product of Ca x P) is also very important.
- **Stimulation of parathyroid hormone (PTH) release**: secondary hyper-parathyroidism (or tertiary, if there is hypercalcaemia due to autonomous secretion from generally hyperplastic glands (90%) or an adenoma) is the direct response of the glands to hypocalcaemia, hyperphosphataemia and low 1,25 $(OH)_2$ vitamin D levels. PTH has end-organ effects upon bones (leading to osteoclastic resorption cavities) and also the heart, contributing to LVH.
- **Low vitamin D levels**: this not only results in reduced absorption of calcium by the gut, but also to osteomalacia.
- **Acidosis**: increases the severity of bone disease.

Histological findings at bone biopsy

Several different histological lesions often co-exist in the same patient:

- **Osteomalacia**
- **Hyperparathyroid bone disease**: osteoporosis and cystic resorption; also termed 'osteitis fibrosa cystica' (von Recklinghausen's disease of bone). Sub-periosteal erosions on the radial border of phalanges are characteristic
- **Osteoporosis**: due to relative malnourishment; steroid use
- **Osteosclerosis**: a component of the 'rugger jersey' spine appearance at X-ray
- **Adynamic bone disease**: bone with low turnover; PTH levels are usually sub-normal. Although the exact clinical significance is uncertain there is perhaps a greater likelihood of fracturing
- **Aluminium bone disease**: now much less common with the use of specially treated water supplies for dialysis (reverse osmosis) and non-aluminium containing phosphate binders.

Treatment of renal osteodystrophy

The basic principles are to improve the diet, reduce hyperphosphataemia and acidosis, and to reduce the PTH level toward the normal range. This is brought about by use of phosphate binders, oral bicarbonate, dialysis where necessary, and by giving the maximum dose of vitamin D that does not provoke hypercalcaemia. Parathyroidectomy may be necessary in resistant cases (usually those with large parathyroid gland mass (e.g. > 1 cm^3), who have had chronic and poorly treated secondary hyperparathyroidism) and in patients with tertiary disease.

5.4 Maintenance dialysis

In the UK, the dialysis population is 250–300/million; overall, approximately 50% receive continuous ambulatory peritoneal dialysis (**CAPD**) and a similar proportion, **haemodialysis**. Ideally, a patient should be given the opportunity to choose dialysis modality, but in practice lack of haemodialysis resource often precludes this. The dose of dialysis that is delivered to a patient can now be quantified — dialysis adequacy (Kt/V).

Factors which would favour haemodialysis in preference to CAPD

- Recent abdominal surgery, or irremediable hernias

- Recurrent or persistent (e.g. pseudomonas or fungal) peritonitis

- Peritoneal membrane failure: inability to ultra-filtrate the necessary fluid volume to maintain fluid balance in the patient

- Age and general frailty (i.e. physically or mentally incapable of CAPD)

- Severe malnutrition: protein losses in the dialysis effluent may be 3–10 g/day on CAPD (> 15 g/day during peritonitis)

- Intercurrent severe illness with hypercatabolism

- Chronic severe chest disease: respiratory function may be compromised by CAPD

- Loss of residual renal function: it is now recognized that many patients only obtain adequate dialysis with CAPD during the early stages after development of ESRF. As residual function is lost, underdialysis becomes a reality, especially in larger body weight patients

CAPD

A standard CAPD regime would involve four 2-litre exchanges/day. The concentration of dextrose within the dialysate can be altered so that differing ultrafiltration requirements, or patient characteristics, can be addressed. Automated peritoneal dialysis (APD), usually performed overnight, may be more convenient for some patients. Although a few patients manage CAPD for many years, in most there is a finite length of time (e.g. 3–6 years) for its efficacy as a form of RRT — this is determined by gradual loss of residual renal function and deterioration of peritoneal membrane function.

Haemodialysis

This therapy has been available for several decades; it is an intrinsically more efficient means of RRT than CAPD and so many patients have lived for > 20 years whilst being supported by haemodialysis.

Long-term complications in dialysis patients

Although dialytic therapies will keep patients alive and, with the additional use of EPO, relatively well, many of the metabolic abnormalities of the uraemic condition persist and these patients are at increased risk of:

- **Vascular disease**: dialysis patients have at least a 20x increased incidence of cardiovascular events and death than the general population. Contributory factors are hypertension, mixed hyperlipidaemia, anaemia, hyperparathyroidism, chronic fluid overload, LVH and homocysteinaemia. The risk is increased further in diabetic dialysis patients.
- **Dialysis-related amyloid**: (β_2 microglobulin is a small molecular weight (about 11,000 Daltons) protein normally metabolized and excreted by the kidney. Plasma levels increase greatly in patients on long-term (e.g. > 10 years) haemodialysis, and the protein is deposited as amyloid within carpal tunnels, joints and bones. Dialysis with more biocompatible membranes (e.g. polyacrylonitrile or polysulphone) can alleviate the β_2 microglobulin burden.

5.5 Renal transplantation

About 2000 UK patients benefit from renal transplantation each year. Overall graft survival is 90% at one year, and about 70% at five years. Live-related transplants account for 10–15% of all grafts. The majority of cadaveric organs are transplanted to the best available tissue match, although occasionally preference is given to less well-matched patients who are highly sensitized to the majority of HLA-allotypes, or to those with dialysis (e.g. no remaining vascular access) or co-morbid problems.

HLA typing

(See also Chapter 9, *Immunology*.)

- HLA antigens are coded from chromosome 6
- Class 1 antigens are A, B and C; class 2 are the D group antigens
- Relative importance of HLA matching: DR > B > A > C; most centres accept 1 DR or 1 B mismatch
- Beneficial match: defined as a 0 DR with 0 or 1 B mismatch.

Before transplantation can take place patients are screened for possible underlying coronary artery disease, and for peripheral vascular disease (PVD). Severe PVD may herald technical difficulty at surgery (e.g. iliac artery calcification or severe atheroma). The vast majority of recipients are aged < 70 years.

Nephrectomy prior to transplantation

- Pyonephrosis or any suppuration within the urinary tract. If this is due to bladder dysfunction (e.g. spina bifida) a resting ileal conduit may need to be created prior to transplantation

- Massive polycystic kidneys (very unusual)

- Uncontrollable hypertension (rare with modern drug therapies)

- Renal/urothelial malignancy: patients must remain free of recurrence for > 2 years before transplantation

Post-transplantation: extra-renal complications

Although the quality of life of most patients is improved after transplantation, patients are still at risk of:

- **Malignancy**: non-Hodgkin's lymphoma (EB virus-associated) and skin cancer are both increased many fold (effects of immunosuppression, especially azathioprine with skin, and cyclosporin with lymphoma); all other malignancies are slightly more prevalent.
- **Cardiovascular**: ischaemic heart disease is 10–20 times more prevalent (due to effects of immunosuppression and hyperlipidaemia) than in an age/sex-matched equivalent population.
- **Infections**: particularly opportunistic infections such as PCP, and especially cytomegalovirus (CMV). The latter occurs in about 30% and is anticipated in CMV

antibody-negative recipients of a CMV positive graft at 6–12 weeks after transplantation. Leucopenia and mild pyrexia are typical; more severe infections (in 10%) can be associated with myocarditis, encephalitis, retinitis and renal dysfunction. These cases require treatment with systemic ganciclovir.

Recurrent renal disease after transplantation

Patients with Alport's syndrome are at risk of developing anti-glomerular basement membrane antibody syndrome after transplantation, as they have no prior tolerance to the Goodpasture antigen. Vasculitis may recur, but this can be prevented by monitoring autoimmune antibody levels (e.g. ANCA). All types of primary glomerulonephritis may recur in the graft, but the most likely are:

- Focal segmental glomerulosclerosis (FSGS)
- IgA nephropathy
- Membranous glomerulonephritis
- Mesangiocapillary glomerulonephritis.

6. GLOMERULONEPHRITIS AND ASSOCIATED SYMPTOMS

6.1 Clinical presentation of glomerulonephritis

The broad definition of glomerulonephritis would be inflammatory disease primarily affecting the glomeruli — but note that no inflammation is seen in minimal change disease. Glomerulonephritis may be associated with immune complex deposition (e.g. SLE nephritis), with auto-antibody to glomerular structures (e.g. anti-GBM disease), or with other immunological abnormalities. The following are important points:

- Inflammation often leads to proliferation of cellular structures (mesangial, endothelial or epithelial cells) and/or scarring.
- Glomerulonephritis may be idiopathic, or secondary to systemic disease, drugs etc.
- The long-term clinical outcome often depends more upon the severity of tubulo-interstitial damage rather than the extent of glomerular injury.
- The type of glomerulonephritis is defined by light microscopic, immunofluorescent and electron microscopic (ultrastructural) characteristics (see below).

Screening for glomerulonephritis

- Dipstick for proteinuria; 24-hour quantification of proteinuria
- Dipstick for haematuria; urine microscopy for red cells and casts
- Hypertension.

Attenuation of progression of glomerulonephritis

- Control blood pressure: for all types of glomerulonephritis
- ACE-inhibitors: decrease proteinuria and blood pressure (see section on CRF)
- Progression depends upon degree of co-existant scarring in the tubulo-interstitium.

Classification of glomerulonephritis

The commoner forms of glomerulonephritis (GN) that are encountered in the UK are:

- Minimal change disease
- Membranous glomerulonephritis
- Focal segmental glomerulosclerosis (FSGS)
- Mesangioproliferative (IgA nephropathy) glomerulonephritis
- Diabetic glomerulosclerosis (although not truly 'glomerulonephritis')
- Crescentic glomerulonephritis (e.g. associated with Goodpasture's syndrome or vasculitis)
- Focal segmental proliferative glomerulonephritis (e.g. associated with vasculitis or endocarditis)
- Mesangiocapillary glomerulonephritis
- Diffuse proliferative glomerulonephritis (e.g. post-streptococcal).

Common renal syndromes and their relationship to glomerulonephritis

There is often confusion regarding the relationship of the various glomerulonephritides to the different renal syndromes. A particular type of glomerulonephritis may manifest several different clinical syndromes. For example, membranous glomerulonephritis may be responsible for CRF, persistent proteinuria, nephrotic syndrome and hypertension; any combination of these may be present during the course of the disease. However:

- Certain glomerulonephritides are characteristically associated with typical clinical presentations (e.g. minimal change disease and nephrotic syndrome).
- It should be borne in mind that a particular syndrome may be due to many conditions other than glomerulonephritis (e.g. CRF due to reflux nephropathy, polycystic kidney disease, renovascular disease etc.).

Definitions of the common renal syndromes

- **Asymptomatic proteinuria**
  < 3 g/day

- **Nephritic syndrome**
  Characterized by hypertension, oliguria, haematuria and oedema

- **Hypertension**

- **Nephrotic syndrome**
  > 3 g proteinuria/day; serum albumin < 25 g/l; oedema; hypercholesterolaemia

- **Haematuria**
  Microscopic or macroscopic

- **Acute and chronic renal failure**
  (Discussed in previous sections)

Causes of the nephrotic syndrome

- **Common**

  Primary glomerular disease
  Diabetes mellitus
  Infections (e.g. leprosy, malaria, hepatitis B)
  Pre-eclampsia
  Accelerated hypertension
  Myeloma
  Amyloidosis
  Drugs (e.g. gold, penicillamine, captopril, NSAIDs, mercury)
  Connective tissue disease (e.g. SLE, relapsing polychondritis)

- **Rare**

  Vesico-ureteric reflux
  Constrictive pericarditis
  Sickle cell disease
  Allergies (e.g. bee sting, penicillin)
  Hereditary renal disease (e.g. 'Finnish type' nephrotic syndrome)

Causes of macroscopic haematuria

It is usually imperative to exclude urinary tract malignancy (urine cytology, cytoscopy and IVU) in patients presenting with macroscopic haematuria, particularly those aged > 35 years.

- Urinary infections
- Acute glomerulonephritis
- IgA nephropathy
- Renal calculi

- Urinary tract malignancy
- Renal papillary necrosis
- Loin-pain haematuria syndrome
- Prostatic hypertrophy
  (dilated prostatic veins)

The frequency of association between the more common glomerulonephritides and clinical syndromes is illustrated in the table below.

Clinical presentation of glomerulonephritis

	Proteinuria	Nephrotic	Nephritic	Haematuria	ARF	CRF
Minimal change disease	+	+ + +	–	–	–	–
Membranous GN	+ +	+ + +	–	±	–	+ +
Focal segmental glomerulosclerosis	+ + +	+ +	±	–	±	+ +
Mesangial IgA	+	+	+	+ + +	±	+ +
Mesangiocapillary GN	+ +	+ +	+	+	+	+
Diffuse proliferative GN	+	±	+ + +	+ +	±	+ +
Diabetic glomerulo-sclerosis	+ + +	+ +	–	–	–	+ + +
Crescentic nephritis	+	±	+ + +	+	+ + +	+ +
Focal segmental proliferative GN	+	+ +	+ +	+ +	+ +	+

+ + + = Very common presentation; – = Never seen/extremely rare

6.2 Notes on particular glomerulonephritides

Minimal change disease

The clinical presentation is almost always nephrotic. Although most common in children (causing 80% of nephrotic syndrome due to glomerulonephritis in < 15 years), it also accounts for 28% of nephrotic syndrome in adults. Highly selective proteinuria (IgG/transferrin < 0.1) is typical, and the majority of cases are steroid-responsive. Other features include:

- Normal renal function and renal histology (by light microscopy — but epithelial cell foot-process fusion on EM)
- May be due to NSAIDs or gold; rare associations are with Hodgkin's lymphoma and thymoma
- May frequently relapse, but renal prognosis is excellent.

Urinary protein selectivity

The index of urinary protein selectivity is used mainly in paediatric nephrological practice; highly selective proteinuria is likely to result from minimal change disease, and so its detection may obviate the need to perform renal biopsy of the child. In adults the range of possible renal diagnoses usually makes biopsy essential. The index is calculated from the respective concentrations of different molecular weight proteins within the urine:

$$\frac{\text{IgG (mol. wt. 150 KD)}}{\text{Transferrin (mol.wt 40 KD)}}$$

Highly selective (i.e. minimal change) proteinuria is defined as an index of < 0.1; unselective proteinuria > 0.3.

Membranous glomerulonephritis

This is one of the commonest types of glomerulonephritis in the adult; there are two peaks of disease (patients in their mid-20s and those aged 60–70 years). The clinical presentation may be nephrotic syndrome, asymptomatic proteinuria or CRF.

- Renal histology is characterized by granular IgG and complement deposition on the glomerular basement membrane; immune complexes are sub-epithelial (outer aspect of basement membrane) and appear as 'spikes' with silver stain.
- A third of patients progress through CRF to ESRF, a third respond to immunosuppressive therapy (e.g. Ponticelli regime: chlorambucil alternating with corticosteroids), and the disease remits spontaneously in a similar proportion of patients.
- Renal vein thrombosis may occur in up to 5% of patients. Membranous glomerulonephritis recurs frequently in renal transplants.
- Membranous glomerulonephritis may be idiopathic, or secondary to other conditions.

Secondary causes of membranous glomerulonephritis

- **Malignancy**
  Bronchus, stomach, colon,
  non-Hodgkin's lymphoma, CLL
  (high suspicion of these in elderly
  patients)

- **Connective tissue disease**
  SLE, rheumatoid arthritis,
  Sjögren's syndrome,
  mixed connective tissue disease

- **Chronic infections**
  (e.g. hepatitis B, malaria, syphilis)

- **Drugs**
  Gold, penicillamine, captopril

Focal segmental glomerulosclerosis (FSGS)

FSGS usually affects the middle-aged, and presents with nephrotic syndrome, proteinuria or CRF. It is associated with obesity, and it is seen in patients with AIDS. Focal glomerular deposits of IgM are seen at biopsy. A few cases of FSGS respond to steroids. A rapidly deteriorating clinical course is seen in 2%, whereas 25% of all patients will eventually progress to ESRF. There is an extremely high rate of recurrence in transplants.

Mesangioproliferative glomerulonephritis (IgA nephropathy or Berger's disease)

This is a disease of young adults which presents with microscopic or recurrent macroscopic haematuria. The haematuric episodes are usually 'synpharyngitic' (i.e. occurring 0–3 days after URTI). It is the commonest primary glomerulonephritis in adults. There is an increased incidence in the Far East (associated with HLA DQW7). The serum IgA is increased in 50% of patients. The condition is considered to be autoimmune, perhaps due to disregulation of IgA metabolism. Other features of IgA nephropathy are:

- There is no response to immunosuppression
- Twenty-five per cent of patients will progress to ESRF by 20 years after disease onset; the disease recurs in transplants
- IgA nephropathy can be associated with cirrhosis, dermatitis herpetiformis, coeliac disease and mycosis fungoides. It occurs in the Wiskott–Aldrich syndrome
- Renal biopsy features are similar to those seen in Henoch-Schönlein nephritis. Crescents may be present during haematuric episodes.

Mesangiocapillary glomerulonephritis (MCGN)

Patients usually present with nephrotic syndrome or proteinuria. The overall prognosis is fairly poor with 50% progressing to ESRF; steroids are only occasionally effective. There is a high rate of recurrence of MCGN in transplants.

- The condition may be familial, MCGN type II (associated with partial lipodystrophy); such patients have reduced serum complement and the presence of circulating C_3 nephritic factor.
- **Secondary causes**: include shunt nephritis, sickle cell disease, α-1-antitrypsin deficiency, Kartagener syndrome and rheumatoid arthritis; the histological picture is of MCGN type I (immune-complex related).
- There is characteristic double-contouring of the basement membrane on biopsy (due to immune 'dense-deposits', seen at EM).

Diffuse proliferative glomerulonephritis

This is the histological pattern of the classic post-streptococcal glomerulonephritis which usually presents with the nephritic syndrome or ARF; children and young adults are most often affected. The disorder is typically preceded (by 10–21 days) by a sore throat, or (most often in third world countries) skin disease (impetigo).

- Serum C_3 is low and there is diffuse proliferation within glomeruli at biopsy.
- Post-infective cases usually recover spontaneously with restoration of full renal function.
- The same histological picture may be seen in SLE nephritis.

Rapidly progressive (or crescentic) glomerulonephritis (RPGN)

The terms 'rapidly progressive' and 'crescentic' glomerulonephritis are often used interchangeably. They refer to the renal lesions which excite great interest from the nephrologist, not least because patients are often very sick with hypercatabolic ARF and possibly associated systemic disease (e.g. pulmonary haemorrhage), but also because these disorders are potentially treatable provided that investigation and therapy is expedient. All age groups may be affected and the presentation is usually ARF or nephritic syndrome.

- May be idiopathic but can be associated with vasculitis (ANCA +ve or –ve), SLE, and **Goodpasture's syndrome** (anti-GBM antibodies); the latter may be triggered by inhaled hydrocarbons. The GBM antigen is a component of type 4 collagen.
- Pulmonary haemorrhage occurs in 50% of patients with Goodpasture's (especially smokers), but also in Wegener's and some patients with microscopic polyangiitis (MPA).
- Specific biopsy changes are seen in Goodpasture's (immunofluorescence: linear IgG on BM); focal segmental proliferative lesions with areas of necrosis are typical of other vasculitides. In the more severe cases there may be extensive crescent formation (epithelial cell proliferation arising from Bowman's capsule).
- The nephritis may respond to immunosuppression (steroids/cyclophosphamide), and to plasma exchange in particular cases (e.g. anti-GBM disease, pulmonary haemorrhage); treatment is essential for extra-renal manifestations. (See also section 12.8 on renal vasculitis).
- Overall mortality is > 20% (from, e.g. pulmonary haemorrhage).
- Transplantation is possible once the patient is rendered autoantibody negative.

Hypocomplementaemia and glomerulonephritis

The following disorders are often associated with glomerulonephritis coupled with **low serum complement** (C_3).

- **SLE**
  Membranous, proliferative or crescentic glomerulonephritis

- **Shunt nephritis**
  Focal segmental proliferative glomerulonephritis (or MCGN); classically associated with coagulase-negative staphylococcal infection of ventriculo-atrial shunts

- **Primary complement deficiency**
  Associated with an increased incidence of glomerulonephritis (usually the pattern of lupus nephritis) and other immune complex manifestations

- **Endocarditis**
  Focal segmental proliferative glomerulonephritis

- **Post-streptococcoal glomerulonephritis**

- **Mesangiocapillary glomerulonephritis**
  (See above)

- Cryoglobulinaemia
  Especially type II (see Chapter 9, *Immunology*, for classification)

Causes of renal vein thrombosis

- **Acute thrombosis**

  Infantile gastroenteritis
  Acute pyelonephritis (high mortality)
  Renal cell carcinoma (with renal vein invasion)

- **Chronic thrombosis**

  Amyloidosis
  Nephrotic syndrome due to glomerulonephritis (particularly membranous GM)

7. INHERITED RENAL DISEASE

The commonest inherited renal diseases are polycystic kidney disease and Alport's syndrome. Rarer disorders include other renal cystic disease, disorders of amino acids and familial glomerulonephritis; these conditions are encountered much more often in paediatric nephrology.

7.1 Polycystic kidney disease (PKD)

Adult polycystic kidney disease (APKD) is a dominantly inherited condition, and the genes have now been identified:

- **PKD1**: chromosome 16 in 86% of PKD patients (mean age of ESRF: 57 years)
- **PKD2**: chromosome 4 in 10% (ESRF mean age: 69 years).

Sporadic cases are also commonly seen. The diagnosis is usually made by ultrasound; cysts usually develop during the teenage years so that first degree relatives aged > 20 years, with a normal scan, can be > 90% confident of being disease-free; the confidence level rises to 98% at 30 years of age. The prevalence of APKD is 1 in 1000; the condition accounts for 10% of RRT patients in the UK.

- Patients may present with abdominal pain or mass, hypertension, UTI, renal calculi (10%), macroscopic haematuria or CRF.
- Cysts develop from all segments of the nephron.

Associations of APKD

- Liver cysts: 70%
- Berry aneurysms: 25%
  (with subarachnoid haemorrhage
  in 7–10% overall)
- Malignant change within cysts
  (rare; i.e. <1%)

- Pancreatic cysts: 10%
- Mitral valve prolapse or aortic
  incompetence
- Hepatic fibrosis (rare)
- Diverticular disease

7.2 Other renal cystic disorders

- **Autosomal recessive PKD**: rare (1/10,000 births). The gene is localized to chromosome 6. ESRF develops early in childhood; 100% have hepatic fibrosis. The prognosis is poor.
- **von Hippel–Lindau syndrome**: autosomal dominant, the gene is localized on chromosome 3. Renal cysts are pre-malignant (>50%) and bilateral nephrectomy is

often necessary. Patients are also at risk of spinocerebellar haemangioblastoma, retinal angiomas, pancreatic cysts, islet cell tumours and phaeochromocytoma.

- **Tuberous sclerosis**: dominantly inherited (either chromosome 9 or 16); patients develop epilepsy, mental retardation, hamartomas, renal cysts, and angiomyolipomas. Skin lesions include shagreen patches, ash-leaf spots and adenoma sebaceum.
- **Juvenile nephronophthisis ('medullary cystic disease')**: variable inheritance pattern (predominantly autosomal recessive in children); cysts occur in the renal medulla. Patients have chronic tubulo-interstitial nephritis, salt-wasting and usually develop ESRF early in life. Ten to fiften per cent of children have retinal abnormalities (a form of retinitis pigmentosa). This is a common cause of ESRF in childhood; the adult form is rare, restricted to renal disease and is dominantly inherited.
- **Medullary sponge kidney (MSK)**: sporadic; the cysts develop from ectatic collecting ducts. Patients have a benign course except that renal calculi and infections are commonly associated.
- **Acquired cystic disease**: cystic change is common in the rudimentary kidneys of dialysis patients, and especially in scarred kidneys; the cysts may undergo malignant change.
- **Simple cysts**: fluid-filled, solitary or multiple, these are usually harmless, incidental findings at ultrasound or IVU. They occasionally require percutaneous drainage because of persistent loin pain.

7.3 Alport's syndrome

The prevalence of Alport's syndrome is 1/5000 individuals; 85% have X-linked dominant inheritance, but other families may show dominant or recessive inheritance. The primary defect is an abnormal GBM (seen at electron microscopy) with variable thickness and splitting ('basket weave' appearance); the Goodpasture antigen is absent in the GBM (hence the predisposition of patients to anti-GBM glomerulonephritis after transplantation).

- Clinical presentation is with deafness, persistent microscopic haematuria, proteinuria and CRF; 30% develop nephrotic syndrome.
- Renal failure develops in all affected males; the rate of progression is heterogeneous between families (i.e. ESRF before 30 years in some, yet only by 60 years in others).
- Carrier females have slight urinary abnormalities (haematuria, proteinuria), and usually do not develop renal failure.
- Bilateral sensorineural deafness is characteristic, but the hearing loss may only be mild; familial progressive nephritis may occasionally occur without deafness.
- Other extra-renal manifestations are: ocular (lenticonus, retinal flecks or cataracts in 40%); macrothrombocytopenia; leiomyomata (rare).
- The molecular defect involves the gene encoding for the $\alpha5$-chain of type IV collagen; alteration of this chain is thought to prevent integration of the $\alpha3$-chain into the GBM.

7.4 Other inherited disorders associated with renal disease

The list is far from comprehensive as many rare disorders have been described.

- **Conditions associated with renal structural disorders**
  Cystic renal diseases (see above)
  Brachio-oto-renal syndrome (AD)
  Dandy–Walker syndrome
  (polycystic kidneys: (AR))

- **Inherited conditions with glomerular disease**
  Alport's syndrome and variants
  (see above)
  Congenital nephrotic syndrome
  (e.g. Finnish-type (AR)
  Nail–Patella syndrome (AD)
  Familial glomerulonephritis
  (e.g. some forms of FSGS or
  IgA nephropathy; Wiskott–Aldrich
  syndrome (XL))
  Inherited complement deficiency
  Charcot–Marie–Tooth disease (?AD)

- **Metabolic disorders with renal involvement**
  Fabry's disease (XL)
  Primary amyloidosis (AD)
  Familial Mediterranean Fever (AR)
  Cystinosis (AR)
  Primary oxalosis (AR)

- **Inherited tubular disorders**
  Cystinuria (AR)
  Swachman's syndrome (AR)
  Marble brain disease (AR)
  Hypophosphatasia (AR)

- **Renal diseases which have genetic influence**
  Thin membrane nephrology
  Reflux nephropathy

AD = autosomal dominant; AR = autosomal recessive; XL = X-linked.

Thin membrane nephropathy

An increasingly recognized cause of microscopic haematuria (because of awareness and measurement of GBM thickness at EM). The condition is often familial, although the gene has not been identified. Patients usually have normal blood pressure and renal function.

8. RENAL INTERSTITIAL DISORDERS

8.1 Interstitial nephritis

Inflammation of the renal tubulo-interstitium may be acute or chronic; a recognized precipitating cause can be found in the majority of patients.

Acute (allergic) interstitial nephritis

The presentation is usually with mild renal impairment and hypertension or, in more severe cases, ARF which is often non-oliguric. Urinalysis may be unremarkable (e.g. minor proteinuria), although urinary eosinophils are present in idiopathic forms. Systemic manifestations may occur and include fever, arthralgia, rash, eosinophilia, ↑IgE.

- **Renal biopsy**: oedema of interstitium with infiltration of plasma cells, lymphocytes and eosinophils; there is often ATN with variable tubular dilatation.
- **Treatment**: cessation of precipitating cause (e.g. drugs); moderate dose oral steroids in selected cases. Most patients make a near complete renal functional recovery.

Causes of acute interstitial nephritis

- **Idiopathic**

- **Infections**
  Viral (e.g. Hanta virus), bacterial
  (e.g. leptospirosis), mycobacterial

- **Drugs**
  (e.g. rifampicin, allopurinol,
  penicillin, cephalosporins,
  sulphonamides, frusemide,
  thiazide diuretics, cimetidine,
  amphotericin, **NSAIDs** (most
  common cause)

Chronic tubulo-interstitial nephritis

Many diverse systemic and local renal conditions can result in chronic inflammation within the tubulo-interstitium. Patients present with CRF or ESRF; some patients may also manifest RTA (usually type 1), nephrogenic DI or salt-wasting states. Renal biopsy findings involve a chronic inflammatory infiltrate within the interstitium, often with extensive scarring and tubular loss; the latter indicates that renal function can never be fully recovered. Other histological features may be specific to the underlying disorder (e.g. tubular casts with myeloma and light-chain nephropathy, granulomata in TB or sarcoidosis).

- **Treatment**: of the underlying condition (or drug/toxin withdrawal); steroids may be beneficial in some auto-immune or inflammatory disorders.

Causes of chronic interstitial nephritis

- **Immunological diseases**
  (e.g. SLE, Sjögren's syndrome, rheumatoid arthritis, systemic sclerosis)

- **Haematological disorders**
  Myeloma, light-chain nephropathy, sickle-cell disease

- **Heavy metals**
  (e.g. lead, cadmium)

- **Metabolic disorders**
  (e.g. hypercalcaemia, hypokalaemia, hyperuricaemia)

- **Other**
  Irradiation, chronic transplant rejection

- **Granulomatous disease**
  Wegener's, TB, sarcoidosis

- **Drugs**
  Cyclosporin A, cisplatin, lithium, iron, analgesics (see 'Analgesic nephropathy' below)

- **Chronic infections**
  Chronic pyelonephritis, (TB)

- **Hereditary disorders**
  (e.g. nephronophthisis, Alport's)

- **Endemic disease**
  Balkan nephropathy (see below)

Balkan nephropathy

A chronic interstitial renal disease endemic in villages along the tributaries of the river Danube (e.g. Romania, Bulgaria, Bosnia, Croatia). There is extensive scarring, and patients progress to ESRF.

- Urothelial malignancy is increased 200-fold
- Patients have coppery yellow pigmentation of palms and soles
- Aetiology: initially thought to be a chronic toxic nephropathy (e.g. trace metals in water) or viral infection; recent evidence suggests chronic exposure to fungal toxin (e.g. ochratoxins in stored maize).

8.2 Analgesic nephropathy and papillary necrosis

Analgesic nephropathy

In the 1950s to 1970s analgesic nephropathy was the most common cause of both ARF and CRF in parts of Europe and Australia. The condition is now in decline, especially since withdrawal of phenacetin from the pharmaceutical market. The hallmarks of the condition are the history (of chronic analgesic usage, e.g. for backache, pelvic inflammatory disease, headache), renal pain (due to papillary necrosis) and CRF; there is a classical radiological appearance on IVU — 'cup & spill' calyces due to papillary necrosis, with renal scarring.

- Renal biopsy is of no diagnostic value
- Women are affected more often than men (4:1)
- Associated with nephrogenic DI, salt-wasting and distal RTA
- Increased risk of urothelial malignancy (there may be multiple synchronous lesions).

Causes of renal papillary necrosis

- **Toxic**
  Classical analgesic nephropathy
  TB

- **Ischaemic**

Sickle cell disease	Diabetes
Acute pyelonephritis	Urinary tract obstruction
Accelerated hypertension	Hyperviscosity syndromes
Profound shock	NSAID-induced

---

9. REFLUX NEPHROPATHY AND URINARY TRACT INFECTIONS

9.1 Reflux nephropathy

Vesico-ureteric reflux (VUR) is the underlying abnormality in most cases of chronic pyelonephritis and renal scarring. VUR is common during the first five years of life (when almost all scarring occurs), but the abnormality diminishes with increasing age. In young children VUR usually presents with a complicating urinary tract infection (UTI). The end-result of severe reflux is nephropathy with hypertension, proteinuria, CRF and eventually, ESRF (when the kidneys are small and irregularly scarred: **chronic pyelonephritis**); the latter still accounts for at least 15% of patients entering RRT programmes.

- Reflux can be graded: from grade I (involving reflux into ureter only) to grade V (gross dilatation and tortuosity of ureter, renal pelvis and calyces) — see the figure overleaf.
- Diagnosis is by micturating cystography (radionuclides can be used in children); scarring can be demonstrated by ultrasound and DMSA.
- **Genetic predisposition**: first-degree relatives of patients with reflux have a greatly increased chance of VUR; it is recommended that offspring or siblings (if a child) of

affected patients undergo screening. The gene is thought to be dominant but its effect is modified by environmental factors.

- Fifteen to sixty per cent of children with UTI will have some degree of VUR; about 10% will have evidence of reflux nephropathy. All children with UTI should be investigated for VUR.
- Five per cent of women with symptomatic UTI will have reflux nephropathy; however, documented UTI occurs in <50% of adults with the nephropathy.
- Patients have an increased incidence of renal calculi.
- **Management**: anti-reflux surgery may prevent renal parenchymal damage, and so if indicated it must be performed within the first 2–3 years of life. Techniques include endoscopic injection of collagen behind the intra-vesical ureter, lengthening the sub-mucosal ureteric tunnel, and ureteric re-implantation. UTI should be promptly treated. As with all forms of chronic, potentially progressive, renal disorders hypertension must be properly controlled.

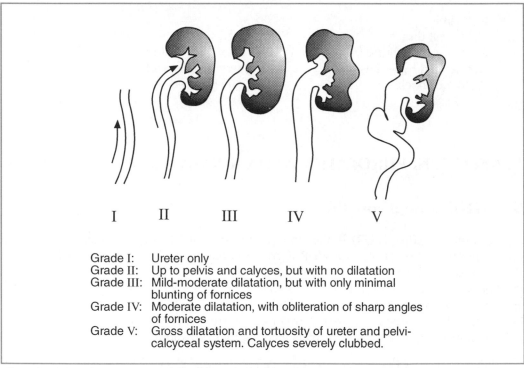

Grade I: Ureter only
Grade II: Up to pelvis and calyces, but with no dilatation
Grade III: Mild-moderate dilatation, but with only minimal blunting of fornices
Grade IV: Moderate dilatation, with obliteration of sharp angles of fornices
Grade V: Gross dilatation and tortuosity of ureter and pelvi-calyceal system. Calyces severely clubbed.

Classification of vesico-ureteric reflux

9.2 Urinary tract infection

Apart from the outer one-third of the female urethra, the urinary tract is normally sterile. UTIs are the commonest bacterial infections managed in general practice; they predominantly affect women (except in infants, patients aged >60 years, and those with co-morbid diseases). Coliforms are by far the most common pathogens.

- **Clinical presentation**: cystitis, PUO, acute pyelonephritis, urethral syndrome, asymptomatic UTI, acute prostatitis. Renal impairment is very unusual.
- **Urinary catheter-associated infection**: all patients with long-term in-dwelling catheters will have bacteriuria (organisms within the bio-film lining the catheter). Most cases do not require treatment; if lower urinary tract symptoms occur, a single antibiotic dose may be as effective as a full course of therapy (which predisposes to bacterial resistance).
- **Rotating monthly antibiotic courses**: these may be appropriate for patients prone to recurrent UTI, and especially in those with an underlying predisposition (see below).

Predispositions to urinary tract infection

- **Abnormal urinary tract**
  (e.g. calculi, VUR, reflux nephropathy, analgesic nephropathy, obstruction, atonic bladder, ileal conduit, in-dwelling catheter)

- **Impaired host defences**
  Immunosuppressive therapy (including transplanted patients), diabetes mellitus

- **Virulent organisms**
  (e.g. urease-producing *Proteus*)

Urethral syndrome

Patients have 'abacterial' cystitis. Causes include true recurrent UTI (but with low bacterial counts), and genital (e.g. *Chlamydia*), vaginal (e.g. *Trichomonas* or *Candida*) or fastidious organisms (e.g. *Ureaplasma, Lactobacillus*) infections. Post-menopausal women may develop the syndrome because of atrophic vaginitis due to oestrogen deficiency.

Asymptomatic (covert) UTI

This describes UTI detected on routine screening (e.g. at school or in pregnancy). The prevalence may be 3–5% in adult women (and 0.5% in men); it increases greatly in elderly, institutionalized patients. It should always be treated if detected in pregnant women, as 15–20% of patients will otherwise develop acute pyelonephritis.

10. RENAL CALCULI AND NEPHROCALCINOSIS

10.1 Renal calculi (nephrolithiasis)

Renal stones are common, with an annual incidence of approximately two per 1000 and a prevalence of 3% in the UK. Calcium-containing stones are commonest.

Stone composition

- Calcium oxalate: 50%
- Mixed calcium oxalate/phosphate: 15%
- Urate: 10% (radiolucent)
- Cystine: 2%
- Xanthine: 1% (radiolucent)

- Calcium phosphate: 15%
- Staghorns ('struvite' containing magnesium ammonium phosphate and sometimes calcium): 3–5%; associated with infection (e.g. *Proteus* spp.)

- **Basic investigation**: this should include stone analysis, MSU, assessment of renal function, calcium and phosphate, and a qualitative test for urinary cystine. The 24-hour urinary excretion of oxalate, calcium (should be <7.5 mmol/day), creatinine and uric acid may also be helpful, and RTA should be excluded (urine pH).

Conditions predisposing to urolithiasis

- **Metabolic abnormalities**
  Idiopathic hypercalciuria (most common)
  Primary hyperparathyroidism
    (and other causes of
    hypercalcaemia)
  Renal tubular acidosis
  Cystinuria
  Hyperoxaluria (primary or secondary)
  High dietary oxalate intake
    (e.g. glutinous rice or leafy vegetables
    in Thailand)
  Uric aciduria
  Hypocitraturia (e.g. chronic diarrhoea,
    excess laxative and diuretic use)

- **Renal structural abnormalities**
  Polycystic kidney disease
  Medullary sponge kidney
  Reflux nephropathy
  Nephrocalcinosis (see below)

- **Other causes**
  Chronic dehydration (common,
    e.g. chronic diarrhoea, warm)
    climates)
  Triamterene
  Industrial exposure to cadmium or
    beryllium

Treatment

General measures: large fluid intake and low protein diet. Associated urinary infection should be eradicated where possible (very difficult with staghorn calculi). Treat other underlying causes (e.g. allopurinol for urate stones, surgery for hyperparathyroidism).

Bendrafluazide (increases tubular absorption of calcium in patients with hypercalciuria) and **citrate** may be beneficial for calcium oxalate stones.

Stone removal: ureteric calculi <0.5 cm may be passed spontaneously. Lithotripsy alone may be used for larger ureteric stones and for pelvi-calyceal stones <4 cm (obstruction being prevented by double J-stent insertion); larger calculi can be 'debulked' by this technique before surgical extraction.

10.2 Nephrocalcinosis

This is defined as the deposition of calcium salts within the renal parenchyma; it may be associated with urinary calculi.

Causes

- **Cortical nephrocalcinosis**
  Cortical necrosis (see 'tram-line' calcification)
  Chronic glomerulonephritis

- **Medullary nephrocalcinosis**

Hypercalcaemia (e.g. primary hyperparathyroidism, sarcoidosis, hypervitaminosis D, milk-alkali syndrome)	Primary hyperoxaluria
	Berylliosis
	Thyrotoxicosis
	Sulphonamides
Idiopathic hypercalciuria	Medullary sponge kidney
Renal tubular acidosis	Tuberculosis

11. URINARY TRACT OBSTRUCTION AND TUMOURS

11.1 Urinary tract obstruction

Chronic urinary tract obstruction (most often due to prostatic disease, calculi and bladder lesions) is a common cause of CRF; obstruction must also be excluded in every case of ARF. The term **obstructive nephropathy** refers to pathological renal damage resulting from obstruction.

Acute obstruction

- May lead to anuria even when obstruction is unilateral; this is due to intense afferent arteriolar vasoconstriction (similar to that seen in ischaemic ARF).
- Ultrasound may show only minimal pelvi-calyceal dilatation in the early stages of acute obstruction.
- Temporary drainage can often be achieved by percutaneous nephrostomy or by endoscopic ureteric stenting, pending definitive surgical correction.
- Relief of obstruction may be followed by massive diuresis (temporary nephrogenic DI), but full renal functional recovery is likely, unless there is complicating pyonephrosis.
- The radiological diagnosis of obstruction is discussed in an earlier section.

Chronic obstructive nephropathy

- This is usually associated with CRF or ESRF; it is often complicated by chronic UTI. If the obstruction is relieved, however, renal functional decline may stabilize and dialysis can be prevented.
- There is permanent renal histopathological damage that results from a combination of parenchymal compression, renal ischaemia and perhaps infection. In severe cases severe tubular loss, interstitial fibrosis and cortical atrophy are observed.
- Salt-wasting nephropathy and chronic metabolic acidosis are common, the latter contributing to the advanced renal bone disease recognized in some patients.

Causes of urinary tract obstruction are given in the table opposite.

11.2 Retroperitoneal fibrosis (RPF)

A progressive condition in which the ureters become embedded in dense fibrous tissue, often at the junction of the middle and lower thirds of the ureter, leading to obstruction. The majority of cases are thought to result from an immunologically-mediated peri-aortitis, and steroids are of benefit in these 'idiopathic' forms of RPF.

- **Other associations**: retroperitoneal malignancy (e.g. colonic, bladder or prostatic cancer, lymphoma), abdominal aortic aneurysm, other fibrosing conditions (e.g. mediastinal fibrosis, sclerosing cholangitis) and drugs (e.g. methysergide and some β-blockers).

- **Investigation**: ESR is often very high, IVU shows medial deviation of the ureters and a peri-aortic mass is seen at CT scan.
- **Treatment**: ureterolysis (with tissue biopsy) with long-term steroid therapy (as relapse is common). Malignant RPF can be palliated with ureteric stenting.

Causes of urinary tract obstruction

- **Within the lumen**
  Tumour (e.g. urothelial lesions of
    bladder, ureter or renal pelvis)
  Renal calculi
  Papillary necrosis (sloughed papilla)
  Blood clot

- **External compression**
  Malignancy: retro-peritoneal neoplasia
    including para-aortic
    lymphadenopathy and pelvic cancer
    (e.g. cervical or prostatic carcinoma)
  Other 'tumours': aortic aneurysm;
    pregnancy (hydronephrosis of
    pregnancy is very common, is usually
    asymptomatic, and resolves fully
    after delivery)
  Retro-peritoneal fibrosis (e.g. malignant,
    idiopathic, peri-aortitis, drugs (see below)
  Prostatic disease: benign hypertrophy
    or malignancy
  Inflammatory disorders (e.g. diverticulitis,
    Crohn's disease, pancreatitis)
  Iatrogenic: surgical ligation of ureter

- **Within the wall of urinary tract structures**
  Neuromuscular dysfunction (e.g.
    pelvi-ureteric junction (PUJ)
    obstruction, neurogenic bladder
    (spina bifida, spinal trauma))
  Ureteric or vesico-ureteric stricture:
    TB, schistosomiasis, previous calculi,
    after surgery, congenital, irradiation
    (e.g. for seminoma of testis),
    malignancy, ureterocele
  Urethral stricture (e.g. gonococcal)
    following instrumentation
  Posterior urethral valves
  Congenital bladder neck obstruction

11.3 Urinary tract tumours

Benign renal tumours: include adenomata, which are very common (however, just as with thyroid adenoma and carcinoma, their histological differentiation from malignant lesions can be difficult), hamartomas and renin-secreting (juxta-glomerular cell) tumours.

Renal cell carcinoma (hypernephroma): arise from the tubular epithelium; they are more likely in smokers, and at least 50% of patients with von Hippel–Lindau syndrome will develop them (usually multiple and bilateral).

- The hallmark of renal cell carcinoma is its propensity to invade the renal veins, with passage of tumour emboli to lung.
- Other unusual clinical features include PUO, left varicocele (renal vein invasion leads to left testicular vein occlusion), and endocrine effects (secretion of erythropoietic factor resulting in polycythaemia (3%), PTH-like substance, renin and ACTH). Five-year survival is about 50%.

Wilm's tumour (nephroblastoma): these are tumours of early childhood, and are derived from embryonic renal tissue (so containing combinations of poorly differentiated epithelium and connective tissues). They become enormous and metastasize early. Treatment is with nephrectomy and actinomycin D, providing a three-year survival rate of 65%.

Urothelial tumours: very common and usually derived from transitional epithelium, although squamous carcinoma (far worse prognosis) is recognized. The usual presentation is with bleeding or urinary tract obstruction. Tumours are often multiple, and so investigation of the complete urinary tract is indicated.

- Several carcinogens (e.g. smoking, rubber and aniline dye exposure, analgesic nephropathy) have been aetiologically linked to this type of malignancy.
- Other risk factors include renal calculi, cystic kidney disease, chronic cystitis and *Schistosoma haematobium* infection.
- Nephro-ureterectomy is indicated for lesions of ureter or renal pelvis, and cystectomy with resection of urethral mucosa for advanced bladder cancer; surgery combined with radiotherapy provides a five-year survival of 50%.

Metastatic disease (involving the kidney): most commonly from breast, lung, stomach, lymphoma or melanoma.

12. SYSTEMIC DISORDERS AND THE KIDNEY

12.1 Amyloidosis

Renal amyloid presents with proteinuria, nephrotic syndrome or CRF; biopsy demonstrates characteristic Congo red-staining extracellular fibrillar material within the mesangium, interstitium and vessel walls. SAP scan (labelled amyloid fibrils which localize to amyloid deposits after injection) may be useful to demonstrate the full extent of disease in all organs. Amyloid is classified according to the amyloid proteins involved, as well as the underlying disease process.

Classification of amyloidosis

- **Primary amyloid**
  AL type, which is serum amyloid
  protein A coupled with
  immunoglobulin light chains

- **Secondary amyloid**
  This is usually AA type
  (fibrils composed of
  acute phase protein)

- **Secondary to chronic suppurative disorders**
  Tuberculosis, osteomyelitis, empyema, bronchiectasis, syphilis, leprosy

- **Secondary to chronic inflammatory disorders**
  Rheumatological conditions
    Rheumatoid arthritis, psoriatic arthritis, ankylosing spondylitis,
    Still's disease, Reiter's syndrome, Sjögren's syndrome, Behçet's disease
  Gastrointestinal conditions
    Whipple's disease, inflammatory bowel disease
  Para-protein-related conditions
    Myeloma (AL type), benign monoclonal gammopathy (AL type)

- **Other secondary amyloid**
  Heroin abuse, paraplegia, renal cell carcinoma

- **Hereditary amyloid (e.g. Familial Mediterranean Fever)**
  Febrils are formed from other proteins (lysozymes, apolipoproteins, fibrinogen)

- **Dialysis-related amyloid**
  Due to β_2-microglobulin (see section 5.4)

Treatment and prognosis

- Primary amyloid, myeloma and monoclonal gammopathy-related amyloid may respond to cytotoxic therapy (e.g. melphalan); bone marrow transplantation may sometimes be indicated. Progression of other forms of secondary amyloid can only be slowed by control of the underlying inflammatory or infective process. Liver transplantation can cure Familial Mediterranean Fever.
- Patients with ESRF due to amyloid have a poor prognosis, the five-year survival being <50% on RRT; this is usually due to progressive amyloid in other key organs (e.g. restrictive cardiomyopathy, lung, GI tract with bleeding and malabsorption, autonomic neuropathy, hepatosplenomegaly with bleeding tendency).

12.2 Atherosclerotic renovascular disease (ARVD)

ARVD is common with ageing and is associated with the presence of generalized vascular disease — it can be demonstrated in 30% of patients undergoing coronary angiography, 59% with peripheral vascular disease and it affects 34% of patients with CCF aged > 70 years. As older patients are now readily admitted to RRT programmes, ARVD is found to be an increasing cause of ESRF (15–20%). Prognosis is poor (5-year survival < 20%) due to co-morbid vascular events.

- **Clinical presentation**: with hypertension (it accounts for **80% of all secondary hypertension**, i.e. 4% of all cases of hypertension), CRF or ESRF, 'flash' pulmonary oedema (10%), and ARF due to acute arterial occlusion or related to ACE-I.
- The correlation between severity of proximal lesions (i.e. degree of stenosis or renal artery occlusion) and renal function is poor; this explains why vascular intervention procedures are only variably successful. Parenchymal disease, manifest by intra-renal atheroma, ischaemic change and cholesterol embolization ('atherosclerotic nephropathy'), is now being recognized as a major determinant of renal functional outcome.
- **Flash pulmonary oedema**: mechanism probably involves reduced natriuretic capability, coupled with left ventricular hypertrophy and severe hypertension, in patients who usually have severe bilateral disease.
- **Radiological diagnosis**: screening can be with captopril renography (low sensitivity in patients with CRF) or MR scanning in patients with vascular bruits or asymmetrical kidneys on ultrasound. Doppler ultrasound is time-consuming and highly observer-dependent. Conventional renal angiography remains the gold standard.
- **Intervention procedures**: renal angioplasty with or without stenting; the latter is particularly beneficial for ostial lesions (which account for 75%). A successsful result is now considered to be stabilization of CRF. Complicated lesions (e.g. related to aortic aneurysm) can be surgically treated. Patients should also receive aspirin and cholesterol-lowering therapy for their general atherosclerotic risk.
- **Fibromuscular dysplasia**: is a rare cause of renal artery stenosis and hypertension in young patients.

12.3 Connective tissue disorders and the kidney

Most of the connective tissue disorders have the propensity to cause renal disease, and characteristic features are described below (see also Chapter 18, *Rheumatology*); systemic sclerosis and lupus nephritis merit more detailed coverage.

- **Mixed connective tissue disease**: membranous or diffuse proliferative glomerulonephritis (uncommon).
- **Sjögren's syndrome**: renal involvement is most often manifest by renal tubular dysfunction with interstitial nephritis; cryoglobulinaemia and membranous or focal proliferative glomerulonephritis are less common.

- **Rheumatoid arthritis**: renal disease is common, and usually due to amyloid, or less often, the effects of drug therapy. Rheumatoid-related membranous or mesangioproliferative glomerulonephritis are rare.

Systemic sclerosis

Renal disease is always accompanied by hypertension; the hallmark presentation is 'scleroderma renal crisis' with accelerated hypertension, microangiopathic haemolytic anaemia and ARF. Prominent pathological changes are seen in the interlobular arteries (severe intimal proliferation with deposition of mucopolysaccharides — so-called 'onion skin' appearance); fibrinoid necrosis of afferent arterioles and secondary glomerular ischaemia are common. The essential treatment is ACE-I for hypertension control; many patients progress to ESRF, but renal function has been known to recover after many months of dialysis. The overall prognosis is poor because of other organ involvement (especially restrictive cardiomyopathy and pulmonary fibrosis).

SLE nephritis

Forty per cent of patients with SLE have renal involvement at presentation; lupus nephritis is commoner in black patients and in women (10-fold > than in men). Renal disease can be manifest by any syndromal picture (e.g. asymptomatic proteinuria, nephrotic syndrome, RPGN), and similarly, many different patterns of glomerular disease are recognized (the histological picture may even change, over time, within the same individual).

- **Renal histology**: the pattern is of prognostic value, with focal proliferative and membranous lesions providing a favourable renal outcome; diffuse proliferative or crescentic glomerulonephritis predicts the worst renal prognosis. 'Wire loop' lesions (thickened capillary walls — EM shows electron-dense deposits) are characteristic; immunofluorescence is positive for most immunoglobulins (IgG, IgM, IgA) and complement components (C_3, C_4, C_{1q}).
- **Treatment**: acute SLE with ARF (usually diffuse or crescentic glomerulonephritis) should be treated as for severe renal vasculitis (see below). Other forms of lupus nephritis can usually be controlled by oral steroid with azathioprine; clinical trials addressing the need for continuance of these agents in patients with quiescent disease are overdue.

12.4 Diabetic nephropathy

Diabetic nephropathy is one of the commonest causes of ESRF, occuring in 40% of IDDM patients after 20–40 years from diabetes diagnosis; at least 25% of patients with NIDDM will develop nephropathy. Approximately 600 young diabetics develop ESRF annually in the UK. The mortality of these patients is very high — patients with IDDM have a 20-fold greater mortality than the general population, and this relative risk may be magnified a further

25-fold in those with proteinuria (e.g. two-year mortality of 30% in patients with ESRF), largely due to co-morbid cardiovascular disease.

- **Clinical nephropathy (overt diabetic nephropathy)**: defined as proteinuria >0.5 g/day. Patients develop hypertension, nephrotic syndrome (30%), and CRF; there is an inexorable decline to ESRF in all patients.
- **Microalbuminuria**: albumin excretion of 10–175 µg/min (30–250 mg/day); this is a powerful predictor for the later development of clinical nephropathy in diabetics, and also of cardiovascular mortality in populations both with and without diabetes. Increased GFR implies that glomerular hyperfiltration may be important in the pathogenesis; intervention studies show that treatment with ACE-I at the microalbuminuria stage can prevent some patients progressing to clinical nephropathy. Microalbuminuria is not detected by standard Albustix.
- Nephropathy is usually associated with retinopathy (common basement membrane pathology); renovascular disease and other arterial pathology are common.
- **Renal biopsy**: Kimmelstiel–Wilson nodules (focal glomerular sclerosis) are characteristic, but mesangial matrix expansion and diffuse glomerular sclerosis, with vascular changes are more common.
- No treatment alters the eventual outcome (ESRF) of established nephropathy but blood pressure and tight glycaemic control may slow progression.
- Diabetics in certain racial groups have a far greater risk of developing nephropathy (e.g. Asians, Pima Indians).
- Combined renal and pancreatic transplantation is now feasible in selected patients; there is a high rate of recurrent nephropathy in transplanted patients

12.5 Haemolytic-uraemic syndrome (HUS)

This is the commonest cause of ARF in children, but it is also seen in adults. Children aged <4 years account for 90% of cases. The haematological abnormalities are characteristic — microangiopathic haemolytic anaemia (MAHA), with anaemia, RBC fragments and schistocytes. Two forms of HUS are recognized:

- **Sporadic**: atypical — no diarrhoea; tends to affect older children and adults. Renal failure may be insidious and progressive to ESRF; neurological disease and severe hypertension are common. Rare familial or cyclosporin A-related cases are recognized.
- **Epidemic**: 'typical' or diarrhoea-associated HUS. The onset is explosive, with ARF. A third of UK cases are due to verotoxin producing *E. coli* (VTEC); the toxin damages vascular endothelium, predisposing to the microangiopathy.
- **Renal histology**: intra-glomerular thrombi with ischaemia; arteriolar lesions.
- **Specific therapeutic options**: fresh frozen plasma, prostacyclin and plasma exchange.
- **Prognosis**: overall mortality is 10%; prognosis is worse in adults and particularly 'atypical' cases.

Thrombotic thrombocytopenic purpura (TTP): part of the same spectrum of microangiopathic disease, but ARF and haemolysis are less prominent. Adults are usually affected and relapsing chronic disease is more likely; neurological involvement and thrombocytopenia predominate, and prognosis is worse than for HUS.

12.6 Hypertension

A detailed description of hypertensive renal disease is beyond the scope of this chapter. The kidney is often damaged by essential hypertension, or it can be central to the pathogenesis of many cases of secondary hypertension.

- **Primary (essential) hypertension**: end-organ renal damage is common. Typical histological lesions include arterial fibrinoid necrosis coupled with severe tubular and glomerular ischaemia (leading to ARF in accelerated-phase or 'malignant' hypertension), or vascular wall thickening and luminal obliteration, with widespread interstitial fibrosis and glomerulosclerosis in patients with CRF due to long-standing hypertension (**hypertensive nephrosclerosis**).
- **Secondary hypertension**: renal disease accounts for the majority of cases of secondary hypertension (see Chapter 4, *Endocrinology*). The pathogenesis involves stimulation of renin release with activation of the RAA, reduced natriuretic capacity, and disorganization of intra-renal vascular structures. Most forms of renal disease can be complicated by hypertension, but ARVD is a particularly likely cause. Hypertension is evident in at least 80% of the dialysis population, and is the chief contributor to the LVH and associated high cardiovascular mortality of these patients.

12.7 Myeloma

Renal involvement in myeloma may present with ARF (about 5% of myeloma patients), CRF or nephrotic syndrome. Bence–Jones proteinuria is not detected by standard urinary dipsticks.

- **ARF**: usually associated with light chain nephropathy; hypercalcaemia, hyperuricaemia and radiocontrast agents may contribute. ARF may be reversed by vigorous rehydration (especially with regimes including bicarbonate) and chemotherapy.
- **CRF**: due to amyloidosis (see above), chronic interstitial nephritis and 'cast nephropathy'. This usually progresses to ESRF despite chemotherapy; the prevalence of myeloma patients on dialysis programmes is about 2%. Renal transplantation is not appropriate.
- **Light chain nephropathy**: free kappa (the most nephrotoxic) and lambda light chains excreted in the urine damage the tubules by direct nephrotoxicity and by cast formation. The intra-tubular casts composed of hard, needle-shaped crystals excite an interstitial infiltrate, often with multi-nucleate giant cells. ATN and tubular atrophy occur. The same pattern may also be seen in patients with benign monoclonal gammopathy.

Benign monoclonal gammopathy

See also Chapter 8, *Haematology*. This may be associated with light chain nephropathy, interstitial nephritis, amyloid and also mesangio-capillary glomerulonephritis.

Cryoglobulinaemia

Immunoglobulins which precipitate on cooling may be monoclonal or polyclonal (see Chapter 9, *Immunology*). They can induce a small vessel vasculitis, particularly affecting skin and kidneys. Type II (mixed monoclonal) and type III (polyclonal) cryoglobulinaemias are associated with glomerulonephritis (mesangiocapillary or membranoproliferative).

12.8 Renal vasculitis

The kidney is often involved in systemic vasculitic illness. Several disorders are recognized, and these are classified and described more fully in Chapter 18, *Rheumatology*.

- **Polyarteritis nodosa (PAN):** a rare, medium-sized arterial vasculitis which results in microaneurysm formation; hypertension is usually severe, and renal infarcts rather than glomerulonephritis are characteristic. Patients are usually ANCA –ve (unless there is also small vessel involvement, i.e. PAN–MPA overlap); pulmonary (infiltrates and haemorrhage), GI tract (infarcts), neurological (mononeuritis multiplex) and systemic features (myalgia, PUO) are recognized, but the condition is notoriously difficult to confirm.
- **Microscopic polyangiitis (MPA):** like Wegener's granulomatosis, this condition involves small arterioles and veins. Patients usually present with ARF and renal histology shows necrotizing glomerulitis typically associated with focal proliferative and/or crescentic glomerulonephritis. Pulmonary involvement is common (similar to PAN), but blood pressure may be normal. A purpuric vasculitic skin rash is often seen. ANCA autoantibodies are detailed in Chapter 9, *Immunology*.
- **Wegener's granulomatosis:** this is closely related to MPA, with an identical pattern of renal involvement and systemic features. In addition, characteristic necrotizing granulomata are seen in the upper respiratory tract (leading to sinusitis and nasal discharge) and lungs (with haemoptysis).

Treatment

All of the above three conditions normally merit aggressive immunosuppressive therapy; typical regimes include initiation therapy (with pulsed methyl-prednisolone and cyclophosphamide, followed by high-dose oral steroids), and then maintenance with tapering steroid doses coupled with azathioprine. Maintenance therapy is usually continued for at least 2 years. Plasma exchange may be necessary for severe disease, especially if pulmonary haemorrhage is prominent.

Henoch–Schönlein nephritis

In addition to the typical sytemic features of this condition, some patients develop renal disease as a result of small vessel (typically post-capillary venulitis with IgA deposition) vasculitis. Glomerular lesions range from mild mesangial hypercellularity (similar to idiopathic IgA nephropathy) through to crescentic nephritis.

Plasma exchange in renal disease

- **Agreed benefit**
  Goodpasture's syndrome
  ANCA +ve diseases: especially
    with pulmonary-renal presentation
    (mandatory with severe pulmonary
    haemorrhage); also for dialysis-
    requiring ARF
  Idiopathic crescentic glomerulonephritis
  Cryoglobulinaemias
  Myeloma: cases with hyperviscosity

- **Uncertain benefit**
  SLE nephritis: severe lupus ARF
  Henoch–Schönlein nephritis: with
    crescentic forms and ARF

---

13. DRUGS AND THE KIDNEY AND TOXIC NEPHROPATHY

(See also Chapter 2, *Clinical Pharmacology, Toxicology and Poisoning*.)

13.1 Renal elimination of drugs

Drugs may be eliminated via the kidneys by two main mechanisms:

- **Glomerular filtration**: a passive process; such drugs will be water-soluble.
- **Active tubular secretion**: drugs act as substrates for secretory processes that are designed to eliminate endogenous molecules; the tubular pathways are different for organic anions (basolateral tubular membrane) and cations (located on the luminal brush border).

Examples of drugs which are secreted by the tubule

- **Anionic drugs**
  Acetazolamide
  Cephalosporins
  Penicillin
  Loop diuretics
  Thiazide diuretics
  Probenecid
  Salicylates

- **Cationic drugs**
  Amiloride
  Cimetidine
  Ranitidine
  Metformin
  Morphine
  Quinine

13.2 Drug nephrotoxicity

Drugs can lead to renal damage in a number of different ways, and examples are given below.

Alterations in renal blood flow

- **NSAIDs**: alteration in prostaglandin metabolism can lead to a critical reduction in glomerular perfusion (particularly when there is reduced renal reserve or CRF). Interstitial nephritis may also result from NSAIDs.
- **ACE inhibitors (and angiotensin II receptor blockers)**: ARF or renal impairment occurring in patients who are critically dependent upon the RAA system (those with reduced renal perfusion (e.g. CCF, loop-diuretics, hypovolaemia and severe renovascular disease)) is well-recognized with these agents.
- **Cyclosporin A**: toxicity can be acute (due to renal vasoconstriction) or chronic. The latter is a common cause of transplant dysfunction, and is associated with arterial damage (intimal proliferation and hyaline degeneration of the vascular media), tubular vacuolation and atrophy and interstitial fibrosis.

Direct tubular toxicity

- **Aminoglycosides**: disturbance of renal function is seen in up to a third of patients receiving aminoglycosides. Five per cent of filtered gentamicin is actively reabsorbed by proximal tubular cells, within which the drug is concentrated; binding to phospholipid results in disturbed intracellular regulation with inhibition of microsomal protein synthesis, and eventually, ATN.
- **Cisplatin**: selectively toxic to proximal tubules, by inhibiting nuclear DNA synthesis; ATN results. The platinum component may not be the major damaging influence as carboplatin is less nephrotoxic.

- **Amphotericin**: this is toxic to distal tubular cells in a dose-dependent manner; ATN results, and is accompanied by non-oliguric ARF. Liposomal formulations minimize the nephrotoxic risk.

Glomerulonephritis

- **Gold**: proteinuria occurs (usually within 6 months of the start of therapy) in about 5% of patients receiving gold, and this is not dose-related. Therapy should be stopped if it exceeds 1 g/24 hours; resolution is then usual by 6 months. Gold is found in the mesangial cells at renal biopsy; it is believed to induce an immune-complex glomerulonephritis (usually membranous, but occasionally, minimal change nephropathy).
- **Penicillamine**: the risk of membranous glomerulonephritis is greater than with gold; it is dose-related, and the onset of proteinuria may be delayed to 18 months after the start of treatment.

Other nephrotoxic effects of drugs

Interstitial nephritis and retro-peritoneal fibrosis are covered in earlier sections, and drug-induced SLE syndromes in Chapter 18, *Rheumatology*. Nephrogenic DI is the commonest renal complication of **lithium** therapy; interstitial fibrosis and CRF are rare.

13.3 Radio-contrast nephropathy

Mild renal dysfunction may complicate up to 10% of angiographic procedures and IVUs. Radio-contrast nephropathy is manifest by non-oliguric ARF, typically occurring 1–5 days after the procedure. Intra-renal vasoconstriction, mediated largely by endothelin, and tubular cell toxicity (with ATN), are important in the pathogenesis. The ARF is fully reversible.

Risk factors for radio-contrast nephropathy

- High contrast load
- Hypovolaemia
- Myeloma
- Age
- Hyperuricaemia
- High iodine content of contrast
- Diabetes
- Hypercalcaemia
- Pre-existing CRF

13.4 Toxic nephropathy

This refers to renal damage resulting from drugs or radio-contrast media (as above) or environmental toxins (e.g. heavy metals) and poisons (e.g. paraquat).

Causes of environmental and occupational toxic nephropathy

- **Heavy metals**

  Mercury
  ARF, proteinuria and nephrotic syndrome (minimal change or membranous nephropathy)

  Lead
  Acute poisoning leads to ARF with ATN; chronic interstitial nephritis and Fanconi syndrome is seen with chronic exposure

  Cadmium
  Similar renal pathology and clinical presentation as for lead

  Arsenic
  Acute poisoning causes ARF with ATN and cortical necrosis; interstitial fibrosis leads to CRF with chronic exposure

  Bismuth
  Proteinuria, Fanconi syndrome and ARF have been described

- **Hydrocarbons and organic solvents**

  Carbon tetrachloride
  ARF

  Ethylene glycol
  This is rapidly metabolized to oxalic acid which crystallizes within the renal tubules; ATN results

  Petroleum-based hydrocarbons
  These can predispose to glomerulonephritis (e.g. Goodpasture's syndrome or membranous glomerulonephritis)

  Paraquat
  ARF, usually lethal due to irremediable pulmonary disease

- **Plant and animal toxins**

  Snake, spider and hornet venoms
  Directly nephrotoxic, or induce ATN, cortical necrosis (often associated with DIC), or muscle necrosis and rhabdomyolysis

  Bee sting
  Rare cause of nephrotic syndrome

  Mushroom poisoning
  ARF

  Poison ivy or oak
  Rare causes of nephrotic syndrome

CONTENTS

1. **Cerebral cortex**   441
    1.1   Cortical localization
    1.2   Dementia
    1.3   Multiple sclerosis
    1.4   Epilepsy

2. **Movement disorders**   449
    2.1   Tremors, myoclonus, dystonia and chorea
    2.2   Parkinsonism
    2.3   Huntington's chorea
    2.4   Wilson's disease

3. **Neuro-ophthalmology**   453
    3.1   Optic nerve and visual fields
    3.2   Pupils
    3.3   The oculomotor system and its disorders
    3.4   Nystagmus
    3.5   Cavernous sinus syndrome

4. **Other brainstem and cranial nerve disorders**   464
    4.1   Facial nerve
    4.2   Trigeminal neuralgia
    4.3   Vestibulocochlear nerve
    4.4   Lateral medullary syndrome
    4.5   Other causes of cranial nerve palsies

5. **Spinal cord disorders**   468
    5.1   Neuroanatomy
    5.2   Brown–Séquard syndrome
    5.3   Motor neurone disease
    5.4   Absent knee jerks and extensor plantars

6.   Vascular disorders, cerebral tumours and other CNS pathologies   470
    6.1   Transient ischaemic attacks
    6.2   Stroke
    6.3   Subarachnoid haemorrhage
    6.4   Headache
    6.5   Benign intracranial hypertension
    6.6   Wernicke's encephalopathy
    6.7   Cerebral tumours

7.   CNS infections   476
    7.1   Encephalitis
    7.2   Lyme disease

8.   Peripheral nerve lesions   477
    8.1   Mononeuropathies
    8.2   Polyneuropathies

9.   Disorders of muscle and neuromuscular junction   481
    9.1   Myopathies
    9.2   Neuromuscular junction

10. Investigations used in neurological disease   484
    10.1   Cerebrospinal fluid
    10.2   Neuroradiology
    10.3   Electrophysiological investigations

Neurology

1. CEREBRAL CORTEX

1.1 Cortical localization

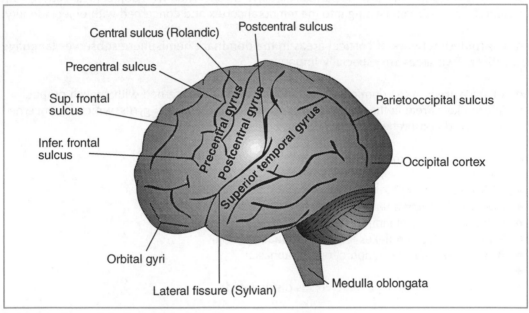

Lateral surface of the human brain

The cortical surface is divided into frontal, parietal, temporal and occipital lobes. Primary motor and sensory cortices are located as follows.

- **Motor**
  Precentral gyrus (frontal lobe)
- **Auditory**
  Superior temporal lobe (Heschl's gyrus)
- **Olfactory**
  Frontal lobe (orbitofrontal cortex)

- **Somatosensory**
  Postcentral gyrus
- **Visual**
  Occipital cortex (calcarine sulcus)

In general, primary sensory cortices receive input from subcortical structures. Signals reach the somatosensory cortex via the posterior limb of the internal capsule (the anterior limb carries descending motor output in the form of the corticospinal tracts). Auditory signals reach the temporal cortex via the medial geniculate nucleus of the thalamus. Visual signals reach the calcarine sulcus (V1) from the lateral geniculate nucleus.

After processing in primary sensory areas, corticocortical connections carry signals into secondary association cortices. The pattern of connections of the visual cortex is best understood in the following way. From primary visual cortex (V1), parallel pathways carry signals outward, with different types of processing being carried out in different functionally specialized areas. One way of thinking about visual processing is to contrast a dorsal 'where' stream, passing dorsally into the parietal cortex and concerned with object localization, with a ventral 'what' stream passing into the temporal cortex and concerned with object identity.

A distributed network of cortical areas in the dominant hemisphere subserves **language function**. Two areas are especially important.

- **Broca's area**: in the dominant frontal lobe, which is concerned with speech output.
- **Wernicke's area**: in the dominant posterior superior temporal gyrus, which is concerned with word comprehension.

Frontal lobe lesions may cause:

- Anosmia
- Abnormal affective reactions
- Difficulties with planning tasks or those requiring motivation
- Primitive release reflexes (e.g. grasp, pout, rooting)
- Broca's aphasia ('telegraphic' output aphasia)
- Perseveration
- Personality change (apathetic versus disinhibited).

Parietal lobe lesions tend to cause disorders of spatial representation or apraxias (disorders of learned movement unrelated to muscular weakness) such as those shown below. Parietal lobe lesions may also cause visual field defects, usually a homonymous inferior quadrantanopia, as the upper loop of the optic radiation (see Section 3 on neuro-ophthalmology) runs through the parietal lobe.

Parietal lobe lesions may cause:

- Visuospatial neglect (usually right parietal) or extinction
- Astereognosis (failure to recognize common objects by feeling them)
- Gerstmann's syndrome (dominant parietal) consisting of alexia (inability to read), agraphia (inability to write), right/left confusion and finger agnosia (inability to identify fingers by name)

- Apraxia (dominant)
- Acalculia (inability to perform mental arithmetic; dominant)
- Agraphia (dominant)
- Dressing apraxia (dominant)
- Constructional apraxia (non-dominant)
- Anosognosia (denial of illness; non-dominant).

Occipital lesions may cause:

- Cortical blindness
- Homonymous hemianopia
- Visual agnosia (inability to comprehend the meaning of objects despite intact primary visual perception
- Specific visual processing defects, e.g. akinetopsia (impaired perception of visual motion), achromatopsia (impaired perception of colour).

Temporal lobe lesions may cause:

- Wernicke's aphasia
- Impaired musical perception
- Auditory agnosia
- Memory impairment (e.g. bilateral hippocampal pathology)
- Cortical deafness (bilateral lesions of auditory cortex)
- Emotional disturbance with damage to limbic cortex.

Temporal lobe lesions may also cause visual field defects, usually a homonymous superior quadrantanopia, as the lower loop of the optic radiation (see Section 3 on neuro-ophthalmology) runs through the temporal lobe.

1.2 Dementia

Dementia is an acquired, progressive loss of cognitive function associated with an abnormal brain condition. It is not a feature of normal ageing.

Other disorders may masquerade as dementia, including depression, postictal states, acute confusional states (including drug-induced) and psychotic illnesses of old age.

Common causes of dementia

- Alzheimer's disease
- Chronic alcoholism
- Normal pressure hydrocephalus
- Multi-infarct dementia
- Secondary to intracranial tumours
- Huntington's chorea

> **Rarer causes of dementia**
>
> - Pick's disease
> - Progressive supranuclear palsy
> - Sequelae of acute or chronic head injury
> - Metabolic causes (e.g. hypothyroidism)
>
> - Cortical Lewy body dementia
> - AIDS-associated dementia
> - Chronic drug intoxication
> - Creutzfeldt–Jakob disease
> - After subarachnoid or subdural haemorrhage

Alzheimer's disease

The earliest symptom of Alzheimer's disease (AD) is typically forgetfulness for newly acquired information. The disease progresses to disorientation, progressive cognitive decline with multiple cognitive impairments and disintegration of personality.

The neuropathology consists of senile plaques (which contain β-amyloid) and neurofibrillary **tangles** (which contain tau protein).

Tangles and plaques occur throughout the cortex, although the hippocampus is usually disproportionally affected. There is a loss of cholinergic neurons and loss of choline acetyl transferase activity throughout the cortex, although other neurotransmitter systems are also affected.

The scores achieved by patients on neuropsychological tests have been found to correlate significantly with the number of neurofibrillary **tangles** in the cortex, but *not* with the frequency of **plaques**.

Genetic abnormalities associated with Alzheimer's disease

- A small number of cases are **familial** (autosomal dominant, with an abnormality of chromosome 21. See below and Chapter 12, *Molecular Medicine*).
- **Down's** syndrome (trisomy 21) is associated with mental retardation and the formation of senile plaques and neurofibrillary tangles in the same brain regions commonly affected by AD. Clinically, Down's syndrome patients develop progressive cognitive impairment from their fifth or sixth decade. The gene coding for amyloid precursor protein is located on chromosome 21 and it is thought that there is overproduction of β-amyloid in these individuals.
- **Apolipoprotein E** (ApoE) is a protein synthesized in the liver that serves as a cholesterol transporter. There are three major forms of ApoE that are specified by different alleles of the ApoE gene on chromosome 19 (ε2, ε3, ε4). The ε4 allele has a greatly increased frequency (around 50%) in patients with AD. The effect of this allele is to decrease the age of onset of AD.

Pick's disease

Pick's disease is also known as focal lobar atrophy, and is an example of a focal dementia predominantly affecting frontotemporal function. Atrophy is circumscribed affecting most often the frontal and/or temporal lobes. Pick bodies are seen within the cellular cytoplasm on light microscopy. Clinically, patients present with progressive language disturbance, often affecting output rather than comprehension, and behavioural changes. Frontal lobe features are prominent.

Creutzfeldt–Jakob disease

Creutzfeldt–Jacob disease (CJD) is clinically characterized by:

- Rapidly progressive dementia
- Myoclonus
- Young age of onset.

CSF examination is usually normal, though CSF protein may be mildly elevated. There is a **characteristic EEG** with biphasic high-amplitude sharp waves.

The most common cause is sporadic, but there are familial forms. A **new variant CJD** (nvCJD) has recently been reported with a neurobehavioural presentation (often depression) in people aged under 40; this form is thought to be associated with interspecies transmission of the bovine spongiform encephalopathy (BSE) agent.

Invasive brain biopsy is currently the only definitive way of diagnosing CJD ante-mortem, though serological tests show some promise. The disease is rapidly progressive and most patients die within a year of diagnosis.

CJD is a **prion** disease.

- Prion protein is a normal product of a gene found in many organisms
- It is membrane bound
- Infectious agent is resistant to heat, irradiation and autoclaving
- An abnormal isoform acculumates in the spongiform encephalopathies, and this abornal isoform is thought to be the infectious agent.

Chapter 12, *Molecular Medicine*, contains further discussion of prion diseases.

Normal pressure hydrocephalus

This should be considered in the differential diagnosis of dementia and consists of the triad of dementia, gait abnormality and urinary incontinence. Urinary symptoms are initially of urgency and frequency, and progress to frontal lobe incontinence (patients indifferent to their incontinence). Gait and posture may mimic Parkinson's disease.

The syndrome appears to be due to a defect in absorption of CSF due to thickening of the basal meninges, or in the cortical channels over the convexity and near to the arachnoid villi. The aetiology may be secondary to meningitis, head injury or subarachnoid haemorrhage. The ventricles are dilated and radiologically hydrocephalus is found, but the pressure is only intermittently high.

Headaches are not usually a complaint and papilloedema is **not** found. Treatment with a ventriculoperitoneal shunt may improve symptomatology.

1.3 Multiple sclerosis

Multiple sclerosis (MS) is a demyelinating disease that affects the central nervous system. MS can follow different courses.

- **Relapsing/remitting**: where short lasting relapses (about 4–8 weeks) are followed by complete remission. Relapsing/remitting patients average 0.8 relapses/year.
- **Primary progressive disease**: where gradual incremental progression of neurological deficit is not accompanied by remission.
- **Secondary progressive disease**: where an initial period with a relapsing/remitting course has been superseded by progression without remission.

There is a genetic component, with an increased relative risk (20–40%) in siblings compared with the general population. However the concordance rate in monozygotic twins is only 25%, suggesting a substantial environmental component.

Diagnosis typically requires:

- Two remitting episodes of two focal lesions
- Delayed visual evoked response
- Demyelinating plaques on T2 MRI that enhance with gadolinium (best single test)
- Oligoclonal bands in the CSF and not in the serum.

MS is not the only cause of oligoclonal bands in the CSF. Other causes include neurosarcoidosis, CNS lymphoma, SLE, neurosyphilis, subarachnoid haemorrhage (rare), subacute sclerosing panencephalitis (a rare late complication of measles) and Guillain–Barré syndrome.

Optic neuritis is a common presentation of MS:

- Isolated optic neuritis: 40–60% chance of subsequent MS
- A cause of painful visual loss
- Treat with steroids
- Colour vision is affected early and residual abnormality may persist after recovery.

Treatments for MS

- **Steroids**: (intravenous or oral) reduce the duration and severity of acute relapses but have no effect on their incidence.
- **β-interferon 1b**: reduces incidence in relapsing/remitting MS by one-third but this effect seems to be attenuated after two or three years of therapy.

Good prognostic factors are female sex, sensory symptoms, early age at onset and a relapsing/remitting course.

1.4 Epilepsy

An epileptic seizure is a paroxysmal discharge of neurons sufficient to cause clinically detectable events apparent either to the subject or an observer. Epilepsy is a disorder where more than one such seizure (not including febrile seizures) has occurred. The prevalence of epilepsy is relatively constant at different ages and is around 0.7%, whereas the incidence follows a U-shaped curve with the highest incidence in the young and elderly.

A simplified classification of epilepsy

- **Partial seizures**
  Simple partial seizures
  Complex partial seizures

- **Others**
  (e.g. myoclonic or atonic)

- **Generalized seizures**
  Tonic–clonic
  Absences (3 Hz spike-and-wave
    activity in ictal EEG)
  Partial seizures secondarily
    generalized

Simple partial seizures may affect any area of the brain, but consciousness is not impaired and the ictal EEG shows a local discharge starting over the corresponding cortical area. Any simple seizure may progress (for example, motor seizures may show a Jacksonian march) and become secondarily generalized with a supervening tonic–clonic seizure.

Consciousness is impaired by **complex partial seizures** that typically have a medial temporal (often hippocampal) focus. An aura (sense of *déjà vu*, strong smell or rising sensation in the abdomen) may precede the seizure, followed by loss of consciousness. There may be automatisms (repetitive stereotyped semi-purposive movements).

A typical **tonic–clonic** seizure begins without warning. After loss of consciousness and a short tonic phase, the patient falls to the ground with generalized clonic movements. There may be incontinence and there is post-ictal confusion.

Imaging is usually carried out in most if not all patients with seizures; focal seizures usually imply a focal pathology and imaging is mandatory in such circumstances.

Anticonvulsant agents are discussed in Chapter 2, *Clinical Pharmacology, Toxicology and Poisoning*.

Epilepsy and driving

Current regulations are such that following a first seizure (whether diagnosed as epilepsy or not), driving is not permitted for one year with a medical review before restarting driving. Loss of consciousness in which investigations have not revealed a cause is treated in the same way as for a solitary fit.

Patients with epilepsy may be allowed to drive if they have been free from any epileptic attack for one year, or if they have had an epileptic attack whilst asleep more than three years ago and attacks subsequently only when asleep.

To obtain a vocational (HGV etc.) driving licence patients should have been free of epileptic attacks AND off all anti-epileptic medication AND free from a continuing liability to epileptic seizures (e.g. structural intracranial lesion) for 10 years.

Epilepsy and pregnancy

Seizure rate in pregnancy is predicted by seizure rate prior to pregnancy. All epileptic drugs have teratogenic effects including:

- Cleft-lip/palate
- Congenital heart defects
- Urogenital defects
- Neural tube defects (especially valproate).

Teratogenic effects are more likely if more than one drug is used. Nevertheless, antiepileptic drugs are not contraindicated in pregnancy, as the effects of uncontrolled epilepsy may be more risky.

There is no increase in infant mortality for epileptic mothers. Folic acid supplementation decreases the incidence of malformations.

2. MOVEMENT DISORDERS

2.1 Tremors, myoclonus, dystonia and chorea

Essential tremor is a postural tremor of the hands in the absence of any identifiable cause such as drugs.

● Autosomal dominant with incomplete penetrance (35% will have no family history)
● Propranolol is the most effective medication
● Stress will worsen the tremor
● Alcohol will improve the tremor.

Resting tremor is seen when the limbs are completely supported and relaxed, and is typical of Parkinsonism ('pill-rolling').

An **action tremor** is typically caused by an ipsilateral cerebellar hemisphere lesion. **Myoclonus** is characterized by the occurrence of sudden involuntary jerks ('fragmentary epilepsy').

Causes of myoclonus

● Physiological (normal)
  hypnic jerks whilst falling asleep
● Drug-induced (e.g. amytriptilline)
● Alzheimer's disease
● Juvenile myoclonic epilepsy
● Inherited as part of other myoclonic
  epilepsies
  (e.g. Lennox–Gastaut syndrome)

● Metabolic
  (liver or renal failure)
● Creutzfeldt–Jakob disease
● Following anoxic cerebral injury
  (e.g. cardiac arrest)
● As part of a progressive myoclonic
  encephalopathy (e.g. Gaucher's
  disease)

Dystonia is characterized by prolonged spasms of muscle contraction; focal dystonias include spasmodic torticollis, writer's cramp and blepharospasm. Myotonic dystrophy is discussed in section 9.1.

Chorea is a continuous flow of small, jerky movements from limb to limb.

Causes of chorea

- Huntington's disease
- Rheumatic (Sydenham's) chorea
- SLE
- Polycythaemia rubra vera

- Neuroacanthocytosis
- Chorea gravidarum (during pregnancy)
- Thyrotoxicosis
- Drug-induced
  (e.g. oral contraceptives,
  phenytoin, neuroleptics)

Athetosis is a slow sinuous movement of the limbs, and is often seen after severe perinatal brain injury. In the past, athetosis was also used to describe movements that would now be called dystonic.

2.2 Parkinsonism

Parkinsonism refers to a triad of symptoms:

- Resting tremor
- Bradykinesia
- Rigidity.

This pattern of symptoms comprises an akinetic–rigid syndrome.

Causes of an akinetic–rigid syndrome

- Idiopathic Parkinson's disease
- Drug-induced Parkinsonism
- Normal pressure hydrocephalus
- Progressive supranuclear palsy (PSP)
- Diffuse Lewy body disease
- Dementia pugilistica
  (secondary to boxing or chronic
  minor head injury)

- Post-encephalitic Parkinsonism
- Depression with psychomotor retardation
- Parkinson's Plus syndromes
- Multiple system atrophy
  (e.g. Shy–Drager syndrome,
  olivopontocerebellar atrophy)
- Intoxications
  (e.g. carbon monoxide, MPTP,
  illegal narcotic, manganese).

The diagnosis of idiopathic Parkinson's disease is often inaccurate and there is no single diagnostic test.

Pointers include:

- An asymmetric onset
- Persistent asymmetry
- Good therapeutic response to L-dopa initially (over 90% will improve symptomatically).

In the differential diagnosis of Parkinsonism, two groups of Parkinsons Plus syndromes are of particular importance: progressive supranuclear palsy and the multiple system atrophies.

Progressive supranuclear palsy (PSP)

Also known as Steele–Richardson syndrome, this presents in the seventh decade with Parkinsonism, characteristic ophthalmoplegia and dementia.

The ophthalmoplegia is described in section 3.3.

Other features of PSP may include pseudobulbar palsy, and dementia late in the course of the illness.

Multiple system atrophies

A number of disorders fall into this category, including Shy–Drager syndrome and olivopontocerebellar atrophy. They are clinically characterized by:

- Parkinsonism
- Autonomic failure
- Cerebellar and pyramidal features (olivopontocerebellar atrophy).

2.3 Huntington's chorea

Huntington's chorea is an autosomal dominantly inherited disorder that normally begins in the third or fourth decade and is clinically characterized by the triad of:

- Chorea (which patients can temporarily suppress)
- Cognitive decline
- Positive family history.

Other motor symptoms include dysarthria, dysphagia, ataxia, myoclonus and dystonia. Childhood onset is atypical and may be associated with rigidity.

Genetics of Huntington's chorea

- Autosomal dominant with complete penetrance
- There is expansion of the CAG trinucleotide repeat within this gene (see Chapter 12, *Molecular Medicine*)
- Gene is on chromosome 4 and codes for a protein, huntingtin
- Genetic testing in asymptomatic individuals is now available

Neuropathologically the disease causes neuronal loss in cortex and striatum, especially the caudate. Treatment is unsatisfactory and relies on neuroleptics, which partially relieve chorea through interfering with dopaminergic transmission.

Other causes of chorea

- Levodopa-induced chorea in Parkinsonism
- SLE
- Antiphospholipid syndrome
- Wilson's disease
- Sydenham's chorea (autoimmune, preceded by group A Streptococcus infection)
- Neuroacanthocytosis

2.4 Wilson's disease

This is an autosomal recessive condition, the gene being on chromosome 13. Copper is deposited in the basal ganglia and elsewhere in the brain (as well as in the liver). This disorder should be considered in any young person presenting with an extrapyramidal syndrome. Psychiatric symptoms are particularly common in adults. (See also Chapter 11, *Metabolic Diseases*).

3. NEURO-OPHTHALMOLOGY

This section should be read in conjunction with Chapter 15, *Ophthalmology*.

3.1 Optic nerve and visual fields

The optic pathways, and the visual defects resulting from various lesions at different sites are illustrated overleaf.

The visual field and the retina have an inverted and reversed relationship. Optic nerve fibres from the nasal retina, and therefore the temporal field for each eye, decussate at the optic chiasm, join uncrossed temporal fibres and proceed in the optic tract to the lateral geniculate body where they synapse. The optic radiations then pass to the occipital cortex. Thus the right hemifield is represented on the left occipital cortex and *vice versa*. The macular region of the visual cortex is on the tip of the occipital lobe. This area is a vascular watershed, supplied by the posterior and middle cerebral arteries and may therefore be spared when a posterior cerebral artery CVA occurs.

Lesions of the retina and optic nerve produce field defects in the ipsilateral eye alone. Lesions at the optic chiasm typically produce **bitemporal hemianopia**. Causes include:

- Pituitary tumour (compression from below)
- Craniopharyngioma
- Intracranial aneurysm
- Meningioma
- Dilated third ventricle.

From the optic chiasm fibres run in the optic tract to the lateral geniculate nucleus (thalamus). **Retrochiasmal** lesions produce congruous (**homonymous**) field defects, the degree of congruity inceases with more posterior lesions.

From the lateral geniculate fibres pass in the optic radiation to the primary visual cortex which is located in the occipital cortex. The fibres from the lower and upper quadrants of the retina diverge, the upper fibres (lower half of the visual field) passing though the parietal lobes, the lower fibres (upper half of the visual field) through the temporal lobes. Hence:

- Temporal lobe lesions may cause superior quadrant homonymous hemianopia
- Parietal lobe lesions may cause inferior quadrant homonymous hemianopia.

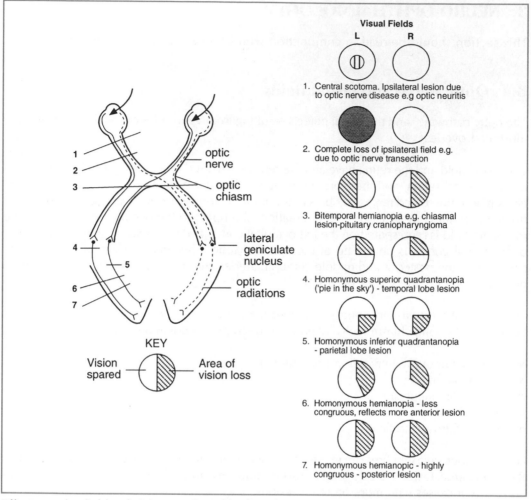

Visual Fields

1. Central scotoma. Ipsilateral lesion due to optic nerve disease e.g optic neuritis

2. Complete loss of ipsilateral field e.g. due to optic nerve transection

3. Bitemporal hemianopia e.g. chiasmal lesion-pituitary craniopharyngioma

4. Homonymous superior quadrantanopia ('pie in the sky') - temporal lobe lesion

5. Homonymous inferior quadrantanopia - parietal lobe lesion

6. Homonymous hemianopia - less congruous, reflects more anterior lesion

7. Homonymous hemianopic - highly congruous - posterior lesion

optic nerve

optic chiasm

lateral geniculate nucleus

optic radiations

KEY

Vision spared — Area of vision loss

Effects on the fields of vision produced by lesions at various points along the optic pathway

3.2 Pupils

Pupil size depends on both pupillodilator (sympathetic) and pupilloconstrictor (parasympathetic) fibres. Pupilloconstrictor fibres travel from the Edinger–Westphal nucleus in the midbrain to the orbit on the third nerve. The path of sympathetic fibres is described below.

The pupillary light reflex pathway has two parts:

- **Afferent**: retina, optic nerve, lateral geniculate body, midbrain
- **Efferent**: Edinger–Westphal nucleus (midbrain) to third nerve.

Afferent pupillary defect

This is detected by the 'swinging flashlight' test. If the amount of light information carried by one eye is less than that from the contralateral side, when the light is swung from the normal to the abnormal side, pupil dilatation is observed. This is also known as a Marcus Gunn pupil.

An afferent pupillary defect is a sign of asymmetrical disease anterior to the chiasm.

Causes:

- Retinal disease (e.g. vascular occlusion, detachment)
- Optic nerve disease (e.g. optic neuritis, glaucoma) with asymmetric nerve damage.

Causes of a small pupil (miosis)

Miosis can be caused by:

- **Senile miosis**
- **Pontine haemorrhage**
- **Horner's syndrome**: see below
- **Argyll Robertson pupil**: bilateral (may be asymmetrical) small irregular pupils which do not react to light but accommodate normally. They dilate poorly in the dark and in response to mydriatics. Lesion is in the rostral midbrain near the Sylvian aqueduct, such that the light reaction fibres are interfered with, but the more ventral near fibres are spared.
- **Drugs**: systemic (opiates); topical (pilocarpine)
- **Myotonic dystrophy**.

Horner's syndrome

Horner's syndrome is caused by interruption of sympathetic pupillomotor fibres (see the table overleaf), and is one of the causes of a small pupil (miosis).

Causes of Horner's syndrome

- **Anatomical structures**

  Brainstem or spinal cord
  1st order neurone

  Pre-ganglionic lesion
  2nd order neurone: anterior roots
  (C8T3), sympathetic chain

  Post-ganglionic lesion
  3rd order neurone: stellate ganglion
  carotid sympathetic plexus, fibres to
  eyelid in branch of III, fibres to pupil
  in ciliary nerve

- **Causes**

  Vascular, trauma, neoplastic
  demyelation, syringomyelia,
  ependymoma

  Chest lesion: apical carcinoma,
  cervical rib, mediastinal mass
  Cervical lesion: lymphadenopathy,
  trauma, thyroid neoplasm
  Surgical: thyroidectomy, carotid
  angiography, endarterectomy

  Internal carotid artery dissection,
  cavernous sinus lesions, orbital
  apex disease

Clinical characteristics of Horner's syndrome

- **Miosis**: hydroxyamphetamine differentiates between pre- and post-ganglionic. (Miosis more evident in dim light 'dilation lag'.)
- **Enophthalmos**: apparent, due to narrowing of the palpebral aperture by ptosis and elevation of the lower lid
- **Ptosis**: partial — levator palpebrae is 30% supplied by sympathetic
- **Anhidrosis**: whole face means lesion proximal to common carotid artery
- **Vasodilatation**.

Congenital Horner's syndrome is distinguished also by a difference in iris colour (heterochromia).

Causes of a large pupil (mydriasis)

Mydriasis can be due to:

- **Adie's (tonic) pupil**: idiopathic dilated pupil with poor reaction to light and slow constriction to prolonged near effort. Seventy per cent female, 80% initially unilateral, 4% per year becoming bilateral. Associated with decreased deep tendon reflexes (Holmes Adie syndrome)

- **Third nerve palsy**: see later
- **Drugs**: systemic (e.g. antidepressants, amphetamines); mydriatics (e.g. tropicamide, atropine)
- **Trauma**: sphincter pupillae rupture.

3.3 The oculomotor system and its disorders

A mnemonic to remember oculomotor innervation is:

$LR_6(SO_4)_3$

The sixth nerve supplies lateral rectus, the fourth supplies superior oblique and the third nerve innervates the others. Oculomotor palsies may affect single nerves, or the co-ordinated activity of multiple cranial nerves that produces horizontal and vertical conjugate eye movements.

Causes of oculomotor palsies

- Tumours at the base of the brain
  (e.g. glioma, metastasis,
  carcinomatous meningitis)
- Orbital cellulitis
- Myasthenia gravis
- Neurosarcoidosis
- Orbital lymphoma

- Head trauma
- Ischaemic infarction of a nerve
- Intracerebral aneurysm
- Ophthalmoplegic migraine
- Arteritides
- Meningitides
  (e.g. syphilitic or tuberculous)

Causes of bilateral ophthalmoplegia

- Dysthyroid disease
- Wernicke's encephalopathy
- Myasthenia gravis
- Ocular myopathy (chronic)

- Guillain–Barré syndrome
- Midbrain tumour or infarction
- Basal meningitides (e.g. tuberculous)
- Myositis

The effects of paresis on diplopia are predicted by three rules.

1. Paresis of horizontally acting muscles tends to cause horizontal diplopia, and vertical paresis leads to vertical diplopia.
2. The direction of gaze in which the separation of the images is maximum, is the direction of action of the paretic muscles.

3. The image seen furthest from the centre of gaze (the **false** image) belongs to the paretic eye, so when covering the paretic eye, this image will disappear.

Third nerve

The third nerve nucleus is a large nucleus located in the midbrain at the level of the superior colliculus. Fibres pass through the red nucleus and the pyramidal tract in the cerebral peduncle. The nerve then passes between the posterior cerebral and superior cerebellar arteries, through the cavernous sinus and into the orbit via the superior orbital fissure. Because of its nuclear size, it is rarely entirely affected by lesions and complete third nerve palsies tend to be caused by peripheral lesions.

A complete third nerve palsy causes:

* Ptosis
* Inability to move the eye superiorly, inferiorly or medially
* Eye deviated down (preserved superior oblique) and out (preserved lateral rectus)
* Pupil fixed and dilated.

Lateral gaze is intact and attempted downward gaze causes intorsion (inwards rotation of the eye); normal down gaze requires not only superior oblique but also inferior rectus.

The pupil may be normal (pupil-sparing or 'medical' third) or dilated and fixed to light (so-called 'surgical' third). This is because parasympathetic pupilloconstrictor fibres run on the surface of the nerve; these are fed by the pial vessels and are therefore spared in palsies of vascular aetiology. However, they are affected early by a compressive lesion (when the pupil is involved in 95% of cases).

Causes of a third nerve palsy

* Posterior communicating artery aneurysm (usually painful)
* Vasculitis
* Arteriosclerotic
* Cavernous sinus pathology (e.g. thrombosis, aneurysm, fistula, pituitary mass). Frequently associated with lesions of IV, V and VI (see Section 3.5)
* Orbital apex disease, such as tumours, thyroid disease, orbital cellulitis, granulomatous disease; often associated with palsies of IV–VI and optic nerve dysfunction

* Diabetes, usually pupil-sparing (75%)
* Trauma
* Uncal herniation; the third nerve travels anteriorly on the edge of the cerebellar tentorium and may be compressed by the uncal portion of the temporal lobe with increased intracranial pressure due to a supratentorial cause

---

Fourth nerve

The fourth nerve nucleus lies in the midbrain at the level of the inferior colliculus. The fourth nerve has the longest intracranial course; passing between the posterior cerebral and superior cerebellar arteries, lateral to the 3rd nerve and into the orbit through the cavernous sinus and superior orbital fissure. It is the only nerve to exit the dorsal aspect of the brainstem. A fourth nerve lesion is the commonest cause of vertical diplopia. Looking down and out is most difficult and classically the patient notices diplopia descending stairs or reading.

Causes of a fourth nerve palsy

- Vascular (20%)
- Diabetes
- Vasculitis
- Cavernous sinus syndrome
- Congenital (decompensation causes symptoms) (30%)

- Trauma (susceptible to contrecoup injury, for example, whiplash because of dorsal brainstem exit) (30%)
- Orbital apex syndrome

Sixth nerve

The sixth nerve nucleus lies in the mid-pons inferior to the IVth ventricle, and is motor to the lateral rectus. A sixth nerve palsy causes convergence of the eyes in primary position and diplopia maximal on lateral gaze towards the side of the lesion. The affected eye **deviates medially** due to the unopposed action of medial rectus.

Causes of a sixth nerve palsy

- Vascular
- Trauma
- Cavernous sinus syndrome
- Orbital apex syndrome

- Increased intracranial pressure (false localizing sign due to stretching of the nerve)

Disorders of conjugate gaze

Symmetrical and synchronous movements of the two eyes together are known as **conjugate eye movements**. The most important cause of horizontal conjugate gaze palsies is **internuclear ophthalmoplegia**. Internuclear ophthalmoplegia is a disorder of horizontal eye movement due to a lesion in the medial longitudinal fasciculus which connects the IIIrd and IVth nuclei in the pons (see overleaf).

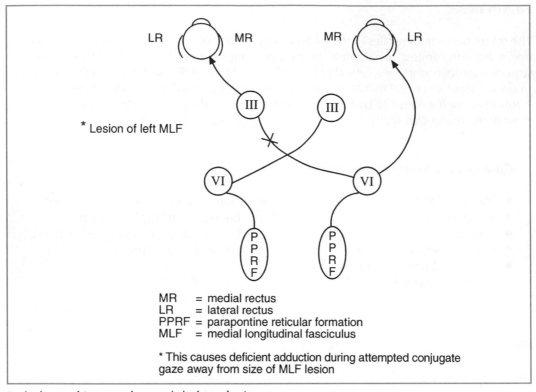

MR = medial rectus
LR = lateral rectus
PPRF = parapontine reticular formation
MLF = medial longitudinal fasciculus

* This causes deficient adduction during attempted conjugate gaze away from size of MLF lesion

Pathology of internuclear ophthalmoplegia

Features of internuclear ophthalmoplegia

- Impaired adduction of the eye ipsilateral to the lesion (complete paralysis — minor slowing)
- Horizontal nystagmus in the abducting eye contralateral to the lesion
- Convergence normal (this differentiates from a medial rectus lesion)
- Vertical gaze nystagmus occasionally present.

Bilateral internuclear ophthalmoplegia results in defective adduction (bilaterally), with nystagmus in the abducting eye.

Causes of internuclear ophthalmoplegia

- Multiple sclerosis
  (most common: may be bilateral
  in younger adults)
- Wernicke's encephalopathy
- Miller–Fisher syndrome
- Occlusion of the basilar artery
- SLE
- Drug overdose
  (barbiturates, phenytoin or
  amitriptyline)

Causes of **impaired vertical conjugate gaze** include progressive supranuclear palsy, and Parinaud's syndrome, causes of impaired vertical conjugate gaze include Graves' ophthalmopathy and thalamic or midbrain pathology.

Progressive supranuclear palsy (Steele–Richardson syndrome): the ophthalmoplegia is a paresis of vertical conjugate gaze which is supranuclear; downgaze cannot be elicited voluntarily but if the patient is allowed to fixate whilst the head is moved passively, the eyes have a full range of movements. This pattern implies that while the oculomotor nuclei are intact, in that the eyes can be driven into eccentric positions within the orbit, the supranuclear descending control of voluntary eye movements is impaired.

Parinaud's syndrome is also known as the dorsal midbrain syndrome, with damage to the midbrain and superior colliculus. It leads to:

- Impaired upgaze and accommodation
- Retraction of the eyelids
- Loss of light reflex with preserved convergence reflex
- Convergence retraction nystagmus
- Relative mydriasis.

Possible causes include pineal tumour, stroke or haemorrhage, hydrocephalus or demyelinating disease.

Other causes of upgaze palsy

- Progressive supranuclear palsy
- Thyroid ophthalmopathy
- Parinaud's syndrome
- Myasthenia gravis
- Miller–Fisher syndrome

3.4 Nystagmus

Nystagmus is a defect of control of ocular position that leads to a rhythmic involuntary to-and-fro oscillation of the eyes. There are three types.

- **Pendular**: no distinct fast and slow phases, both being of equal velocity
- **Jerk**: distinct fast and slow phases. The amplitude usually increases with gaze towards the direction of the fast phase
- **Rotatory**: combination of vertical and horizontal nystagmus.

Causes of congenital nystagmus

- X-linked or autosomal dominant; usually horizontal
- Secondary to poor vision (e.g. Albinism, congenital cataract, congenital optic atrophy).

Causes of acquired nystagmus

- **Vestibular lesions**: the lesion may be in the VIIIth nerve, inner ear, brainstem or vestibular pathway. Jerky nystagmus with fast phase away from the side of the lesion and made worse by gaze in that direction; typically improves with visual fixation
- **Cerebellar lesions**: fast phase towards the side of the lesion
- **Drug-induced** (e.g. alcohol, barbiturates, phenytoin).

Downbeat nystagmus (where the fast phase is down) is associated with foramen magnum lesions (e.g. Arnold–Chiari malformation, spinocerebellar degeneration, syringobulbia, platybasia), whereas upbeat nystagmus is typically due to intrinsic brainstem disease, or rarely cerebellar vermis lesions or organophosphates.

3.5 Cavernous sinus syndrome

The major structures passing through the cavernous sinus are the IIIrd, IVth and VIth cranial nerves, the ophthalmic division of the Vth nerve, the sympathetic carotid plexus and the intracavernous carotid artery (see figure below). Lesions in this region may therefore produce a total internal and external ophthalmoplegia.

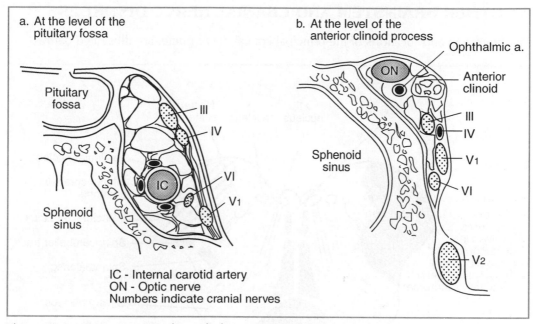

a. At the level of the pituitary fossa

b. At the level of the anterior clinoid process

IC - Internal carotid artery
ON - Optic nerve
Numbers indicate cranial nerves

The main structures passing through the cavernous sinus

The causes are:

- **Trauma**
- **Vascular**: aneurysm of intracavernous carotid artery or the posterior communicating artery; cavernous sinus thrombosis; carotico-cavernous fistula
- **Neoplastic**: primary intracranial tumours, direct spread from nasopharyngeal tumours or metastatic
- **Inflammatory**: due to infection (e.g. sinusitis, tuberculosis, or inflammatory disease such as Wegener's granulomatosis).

Carotico-cavernous fistula

This may be either a high or low pressure shunt.

- **High pressure, high flow**: shunt due to a fistula between the cavernous sinus and the intracavernous carotid artery. Usually traumatic in origin, producing marked proptosis which may be pulsatile, palsies of the IIIN, IVN and VIN, an orbital bruit with an injected chemotic eye and elevated intra-ocular pressure secondary to raised episcleral venous pressure.
- **Low pressure, low flow**: shunt occurs because of communication between the dural branches of the internal or external carotid arteries and the cavernous sinus. This type is more common in elderly patients, often occurring spontaneously in arterio-sclerotic individuals, and results in a milder clinical picture.

4. OTHER BRAINSTEM AND CRANIAL NERVE DISORDERS

The brainstem and locations of the principal cranial nerve nuclei are illustrated below.

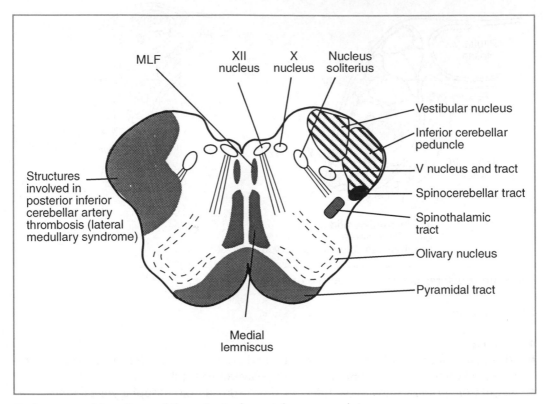

Brainstem and locations of the principal cranial nerve nuclei

4.1 Facial nerve

The facial nerve has the following functions:

- Motor to the muscles of facial expression
- Taste fibres from the anterior two-thirds of the tongue (in the chorda tympani)
- Taste from the palate (nerve of the pterygoid canal)
- Secretomotor parasympathetic fibres to parotid, submandibular and sublingual glands
- Nerve to stapedius.

Taste fibres, nerve to stapedius and to the facial muscles leave the nerve **below** the geniculate ganglion.

Causes of a facial nerve palsy

- Brainstem tumour
- Neurosarcoidosis
- Cerebello-pontine angle lesions
  (e.g. acoustic neuroma)
- Cholesteatoma
- Lyme disease

- Stroke
- Multiple sclerosis
- Otitis media
- Ramsay–Hunt syndrome
- Diabetes
- Guillain–Barré syndrome

If the palsy is bilateral, exclude myasthenia gravis, facial myopathy (look for ptosis) and neurosarcoidosis. Weakness of frontalis (forehead) indicates a nuclear or infranuclear (LMN) lesion.

Bell's palsy

An isolated facial nerve palsy of acute onset, thought secondary to viral infection.

- Unilateral facial weakness
- Pain behind ear

- Absent taste sensation on
  anterior two-thirds of tongue

Usually recovery begins by two weeks but the palsy may be prolonged and 10% have residual weakness. Electrophysiological tests can help predict the outcome and tapering dose of steroids (given from onset) improves the outcome. Tarsorraphy may be needed to prevent corneal damage

Ramsay–Hunt syndrome

Features include *Herpes zoster*, affecting the geniculate ganglion, and facial palsy with herpetic vesicles in the auditory meatus. Deafness is a complication.

4.2 Trigeminal neuralgia

This is characterized by brief lancinating pain in the distribution of one of the divisions of the trigeminal nerve. It is more common in patients over the age of 50 and in women. Maxillary and mandibular divisions are most often affected, it is almost always unilateral and trigger points are common. It may be a presenting symptom of MS in younger patients.

465

Treatment includes:

- Carbamazepine/phenytoin
- Clonazepam
- Baclofen
- Thermocoagulation of trigeminal ganglion
- Surgical section of nerve root.

4.3 Vestibulocochlear nerve

Damage to the eighth cranial nerve may result in deafness or vertigo (see below). At the bedside, sensorineural and conductive deafness are distinguished by Rinne's and Weber's tests.

Rinne's test

- Air > bone conduction normally
- Hearing decrease and bone > air conduction in conduction deafness
- Hearing decreased and air > bone conduction in sensorineural deafness.

Weber's test

- Central normally
- Lateralizes to normal side in sensorineural deafness
- Lateralizes to deaf side in conduction deafness.

Causes of deafness

Conduction

- Ear wax
- Otosclerosis
- Middle ear infection

Sensorineural

- Acoustic neuroma
- Paget's disease
- Central lesions (MS/CVA/glioma)
- Congenital (maternal infections, congenital syndromes)
- Ménière's disease
- Head trauma
- Drugs and toxins (aminoglycoside antibiotics, frusemide, lead)

Several drugs may cause tinnitus, including aspirin, frusemide and aminoglycosides.

Vertigo

Neurological disorders causing vertigo are typically due to pathology of either the labyrinthine structures of the middle ear, the brainstem vestibular nuclei, or the vestibulocochlear nerve that connects the two.

Common causes of vertigo

- **Labyrinthine (peripheral)**
  Trauma (including barotrauma)
  Ménière's disease
  Acute viral infections
  Chronic bacterial otitis media
  Occlusion of the internal auditory
    artery

- **Brainstem (central)**
  Acute vestibular neuronitis
  Vascular disease
  MS
  Space occupying lesions
    (e.g. brainstem glioma)
  Toxic causes
    (e.g. alcohol, drugs)
  Hypoglycaemia

Acoustic neuroma

Acoustic neuroma is a benign tumour arising on the eighth cranial nerve as it emerges from the brainstem in the cerebellopontine angle. It is a common cause of a cerebellopontine angle syndrome. Cranial nerve VIII affected early but the patient may not report hearing loss, tinnitus and vertigo.

- Absent corneal reflex (V)
- VII affected late
- Abnormal facial sensation (V)

Investigation is by use of MRI or high-resolution CT scanning, and treatment is surgical removal.

4.4 Lateral medullary syndrome

The lateral medullary (Wallenberg's) syndrome is usually due to vertebral artery or posterior inferior cerebellar artery occlusion, that damages the dorsolateral medulla and inferior cerebellar peduncle (see the diagram at the start of section 4).

Features of the lateral medullary syndrome

- Ipsilateral loss of pain and temperature sensation on the face (V)
- Ipsilateral paralysis of palate, pharynx and vocal cords (IX, X)
- Ipsilateral ataxia (inferior cerebellar peduncle)

- Contralateral loss of pain and temperature sensation on the body (spinothalamic tract)
- Ipsilateral Horner's syndrome (descending sympathetic outflow)
- Vertigo, nausea and vomiting, nystagmus (vestibular nuclei)

4.5 Other causes of cranial nerve palsies

The cranial nerves may commonly be involved in the following neuropathies:

- **Diabetes mellitus**: CNIII or other oculomotor
- **Guillain–Barré/Miller–Fisher**: CN VII, oculomotor
- **Diphtheria**: classically CN IX
- **Neurosarcoidosis**: CN VII and bilateral VII.

5. SPINAL CORD DISORDERS

5.1 Neuroanatomy

There is one principal descending pathway, the corticospinal tract, which crosses in the midbrain.

The two principal ascending sensory pathways are:

- **Dorsal (posterior) columns**
  Joint position sense and vibration
  Carry sensation from the same side of the body (ipsilateral — uncrossed)
  Synapse in the brainstem at the cuneate and gracilis nuclei, then decussate

- **Spinothalamic tracts**
  Pain and temperature
  Incoming fibres cross immediately or within a few segments
  Crossed tract results in *lamination* with fibres from legs outside fibres from the arms

Spinal cord ends at the lower border of L2.

5.2 Brown–Séquard syndrome

This is caused by a lateral hemisection of the spinal cord which results in:

- Ipsilateral upper motor neuron (UMN) weakness below the lesion (severed corticospinal tract)
- Ipsilateral loss of joint position sense and vibration (severed dorsal columns)
- Contralateral loss of pain and temperature sensation (crossed spinothalamic tract).

Light touch sensation is often normal below the lesion.

5.3 Motor neurone disease

Motor neurone disease is a degenerative disorder affecting both lower motor neurons (LMN) and upper motor neurons (UMN) supplying limb and bulbar muscles. There is no involvement of sensory nerves, and the aetiology is unknown. There are three principal types.

- **Progressive muscular atrophy**: typically presents with LMN signs affecting a single limb that then progresses. Best prognosis (still poor).
- **Amyotrophic lateral sclerosis**: both LMN and UMN are involved; typical clinical picture would be LMN signs in the arms and bilateral UMN signs in the legs. Intermediate prognosis.
- **Progressive bulbar palsy**: bulbar musculature affected with poor prognosis.

Examination may initially show only fasciculation but progresses to widespread wasting and weakness, spastic dysarthria and exaggerated reflexes. Diagnosis is largely clinical but confirmatory investigations include nerve conduction studies and EMG which show evidence of chronic partial denervation and widespread fasciculation with normal sensory nerves and preserved motor nerve conduction velocity (these latter features distinguish the disorder from peripheral neuropathies). CSF protein concentration may be slightly increased. Prognosis is poor with death within five years typical.

5.4 Absent knee jerks and extensor plantars

The causative lesion typically produces both LMN (diminished reflexes) and UMN (extensor plantars) signs.

Causes include:

- Friedreich's ataxia
- Subacute combined degeneration of the cord

- Motor neurone disease
- Taboparesis
- Conus medullaris compression (the conus represents the transition between spinal cord proper and the filum terminale at the lower end of the cord. Compression can cause UMN signs from cord compression and LMN signs from filum terminale — nerve root — compression).

6. VASCULAR DISORDERS, CEREBRAL TUMOURS AND OTHER CNS PATHOLOGIES

This section considers vascular disorders of the CNS, the important causes of headache, cerebral tumours and a number of metabolic disorders affecting the CNS.

6.1 Transient ischaemic attacks

A transient ischaemic attack (TIA) is a focal CNS disturbance developing and fading over minutes or hours to give full recovery within 24 hours. Most TIAs are caused by embolism.

Differential diagnosis of TIA

- Migraine
- Malignant hypertension
- MS (unusual)

- Epilepsy
- Hypoglycaemia

Modifiable risk factors for TIA include hypertension, diabetes mellitus, cigarette smoking, drug use (drugs of abuse, oral contraceptive pill, alcohol), elevated haematocrit and carotid stenosis. Medical management with oral aspirin significantly decreases the chance of subsequent TIA or stroke. If a severe (70–99%) carotid stenosis is present then the existing evidence suggests that carotid endarterectomy (by an experienced surgeon) should be undertaken. Carotid endarterectomy carries a relatively high (about 8%) risk of perioperative stroke, so the patient trades a short term increased risk of stroke for a significant long term reduction in subsequent risk.

6.2 Stroke

A completed stroke is a focal CNS disturbance due to a vascular cause where the deficit persists. The aetiology may be embolic, thrombotic or haemorrhagic. The presenting symptoms depend on the vascular territory involved.

Lacunar infarctions occur where small intracerebral arteries are occluded by atheroma or thrombosis. Typically small low density subcortical lesions are seen in the area of the internal capsule. Lacunar syndromes cause a pure motor, sensorimotor or pure sensory stroke, with no involvement of higher cortical functions. Lacunar infarcts have a low mortality and relatively good prognosis for recovery; they are primarily associated with hypertension.

Other types of stroke involve either the anterior or posterior cerebral circulation. Intracerebral haemorrhage is primarily associated with the rupture of micro-aneurysms situated in the basal ganglion or brainstem.

Risk factors for stroke

- Diabetes
- Hypertension
- Smoking
- Cocaine abuse
- Previous TIA or stroke
- Male sex
- Increased Hb, haemoglobinopathy
- Family history

Diagnosis of stroke is on clinical grounds supported by CT. Management of stroke is initially conservative, though patients with expanding cerebellar or cerebral haematoma may need surgical treatment. Aspirin is effective in secondary prevention.

Mortality from stroke is between 20 and 30%, with poorer prognosis in old patients with depressed level of consciousness.

Factors associated with a poor prognosis in stroke

- Complete paralysis of a limb (MRC grade 0 or 1)
- Loss of consciousness at onset of stroke
- Higher cerebral dysfunction
- Coma or drowsiness at 24 hours
- Old age

6.3 Subarachnoid haemorrhage

Around 5–10% of all strokes are due to subarachnoid haemorrhage (SAH). Causes include:

- Ruptured arterial aneurysm
- Trauma

- Ruptured arteriovenous malformation
- Cocaine or amphetamine abuse
- Hypertension.

Eighty per cent of intracranial aneurysms are located in the anterior circulation, most on the anterior communicating artery, and 15% are bilateral.

Subarachnoid haemorrhage is investigated with CT and lumbar puncture (LP). CT may be negative in up to 20% of suspected subarachnoid haemorrhage. LP shows xanthochromia (>4 hours from haemorrhage).

Treatment is with **nimodipine**, which reduces intracranial vasospasm, and definitive neurosurgical treatment with aneurysm clipping. Neurosurgery is contraindicated during the period of cerebral vasospasm (4–14 days). Rebleeding occurs in 30% of patients, most within the first few days.

Complications of subarachnoid haemorrhage

Neurological

- Rebleeding
- Hydrocephalus
- Focal ischaemic injury from cerebral vasospasm

Systemic

- Fever
- Tachyarrhythmias secondary to catecholamine release
- Neurogenic pulmonary oedema (rarely)
- Hyponatremia secondary to syndrome of inappropriate antidiuretic hormone

---

Other recognized findings include transient glycosuria, low CSF glucose or lengthening of the QT interval (leading to tachyarrhythmias or torsades des pointes)

Intracranial aneurysms are associated with:

- Polycystic kidney disease
- Ehlers–Danlos syndrome
- Fibromuscular dysplasia causing renal artery stenosis
- Medium vessel arteritides (e.g. polyarteritis nodosa)
- Coarctation of the aorta.

6.4 Headache

Headache is an extremely common symptom that has a multiplicity of causes. Leaving aside acute unexpected headaches caused by, for example, subarachnoid haemorrhage, important causes of chronic recurrent headache include:

- Tension headache
- Classical (accompanied by focal neurological symptoms) or common migraine
- Cluster headache
- Headaches in association with raised intracranial pressure.

Migraine

Migraine is classically preceded by a visual aura followed by a unilateral throbbing headache with photophobia and nausea.

Features of migraine

- EEG and neurovascular abnormalities associated with the headache
- Rarely may result in stroke

- May have unilateral lacrimation
- Can be associated with (reversible) neurological signs (e.g. hemiplegic migraine)

The neurological symptoms suggest a vascular origin, and a popular hypothesis is that of 'spreading depression' of cortical blood flow. However, whilst changes in cerebral perfusion undoubtedly occur, it is presently not clear whether these are primary or whether brainstem neuroregulatory abnormalities of serotonergic or noradrenergic neurotransmitters are more important. Therapy is aimed at stopping an attack (abortive) or if the frequency of attacks is high enough, regular medication is given as a prophylactic agent.

Migraine therapy

- **Abortive**
  Paracetamol
  Codeine ± antiemetic
  Ergotamine*
  Sumatriptan (5HT1 agonist)

- **Prophylactic**
  Propranolol
  Pizotifen
  Amitriptyline
  Methysergide

*Ergotamine is contraindicated with cardiovascular/peripheral vascular disease as it is a vasoconstrictor; also in pregnancy, Raynaud's or with renal impairment.

Cluster headache

Cluster headache has a distinct pattern, with attacks occurring in clusters lasting days or weeks and remissions lasting months. Males are more often affected than females, and onset of attacks is typically between 25–50 years.

Typical features of cluster headache

- Unilateral severe headache lasting up to an hour
- Lacrimation
- Partial Horner's may occur

- Pain may be retro-orbital
- Redness of ipsilateral eye
- Nasal stuffiness

The aetiology is not known and treatment is difficult. Management of the acute attack includes inhaled oxygen (face mask), ergotamine and sumatriptan. Steroids may be helpful. Lithium treatment is used for prophylaxis.

6.5 Benign intracranial hypertension

This term refers to a group of patients who present with headaches and profound papilloedema, yet have no focal neurological signs or intracranial lesion on imaging. The most common presentation is in overweight young women and comprises:

- Headache
- Blurred vision
- Dizziness
- Transient visual obscurations
- Horizontal diplopia.

Papilloedema is found on examination, with peripheral constriction of the visual fields and enlarged blind spot. The CSF pressure is elevated. Treatment is with:

- Weight loss
- Repeated lumbar puncture
- Acetazolamide
- Ventriculo-peritoneal shunt
- Optic nerve sheath fenestration.

Iatrogenic (drug-induced) causes include:

- Oral contraceptive pill
- Steroids

- Tetracycline
- Vitamin A
- Nitrofurantoin
- Nalidixic acid.

6.6 Wernicke's encephalopathy

This is a neurological syndrome of acute onset characterized by:

- Ataxia
- Ophthalmoplegia
- Nystagmus
- Global confusional state
- Polyneuropathy (in some cases).

It may evolve into Korsakoff's syndrome, with a dense amnesia and confabulation. The syndrome is commonly associated with alcoholism and may be precipitated by a sudden glucose load, but may also be caused by prolonged vomiting (e.g. hyperemesis gravidarum), dialysis or gastrointestinal cancer.

Red cell transketolase activity is reduced. Neuropathogically it is characterized by periaqueductal punctate haemorrhage. Treatment with thiamine should lead to rapid reversal of the neurological symptoms, though the memory disorder may endure. (See Chapter 16, *Psychiatry*, for further discussion.)

6.7 Cerebral tumours

Primary and secondary intracranial neoplasms have an approximately equal incidence. Both produce presenting symptoms through local neural damage giving rise to focal neurological symptoms, epilepsy or symptoms of raised intracranial pressure, such as headache. The most common presenting symptoms of a glioma are epilepsy (38%) and headache (38%).

Gliomas are the most common primary intracranial neoplasm. Most commonly gliomas are derived from the astrocyte cell line, though less commonly oligodendrogliomas, ependymomas and gangliogliomas may occur. Treatment (after confirmation of diagnosis by biopsy) is surgical removal if possible followed by radiotherapy. Adjuvant chemotherapy for high-grade gliomas is under evaluation. Prognosis is relatively poor; even grades I and II astrocytomas have survival rates of 10–30% at five years, whereas glioblastoma multiforme (grade IV astrocytoma) is usually rapidly fatal within a year.

7. CNS INFECTIONS

CSF abnormalities in bacterial and viral meningitis are discussed in section 10 of this chapter and causative organisms are listed in Chapter 10, *Infectious Diseases and Tropical Medicine*. For HIV-related neurological disease see Chapter 7, *Genito-urinary Medicine and AIDS*.

7.1 Encephalitis

Acute viral encephalitis involves not simply the meninges (a viral meningitis) but also the cerebral substance. Confusion and altered consciousness are thus prominent, and seizures and focal neurological signs may occur. Viral encephalitis is often secondary to *Herpes simplex*, but may also be secondary to infection with mumps, zoster, EBV or Coxsackie and echoviruses. See also Chapter 10, *Infectious Diseases and Tropical Medicine*.

***Herpes simplex* encephalitis** presents with:

- Fever
- Focal symptoms (e.g. musical hallucinations)
- Confusion
- Focal signs (e.g. right-sided weakness and aphasia)

Focal signs are related to anterior temporal lobe pathology, which may be visible on CT or MRI. Normal CSF findings are occasionally seen, but typically there is a lymphocytosis with red cells also present. In a minority (20%) of cases the CSF sugar may be low. Investigation with imaging or with EEG may confirm focal temporal lobe involvement, and definitive diagnosis can be made with PCR to detect viral DNA in the CSF. Treatment with aciclovir should be started on suspicion of the diagnosis.

7.2 Lyme disease

Lyme disease is caused by the tick-borne spirochaele *Borrelia burgdorferi.* It may cause (acutely) the following:

- Cranial neuropathies
- Bell's palsy
- Low-grade encephalitis
- Meningitis
- Cerebellar ataxia
- Mononeuritis multiplex

8. PERIPHERAL NERVE LESIONS

8.1 Mononeuropathies

A peripheral lesion of a single nerve is known as a mononeuropathy. Commonly mononeuropathies are associated with compressive lesions or have a vascular aetiology. Two of the most important mononeuropathies (other than oculomotor palsies) are carpal tunnel syndrome and common peroneal nerve palsy.

Carpal tunnel syndrome

The most common peripheral nerve entrapment syndrome. Symptoms are of numbness and dysaesthesia affecting median nerve (lateral three-and-a-half fingers), and weakness of median nerve innervated muscles (see below).

Conditions associated with carpal tunnel syndrome:

- Pregnancy
- Obesity
- Hypothyroidism
- Acromegaly
- Amyloidosis
- Rheumatoid arthritis.

Treatment is with wrist splintage, occasionally diuretics or surgical decompression.

Common peroneal nerve palsy

This nerve is motor to tibialis anterior and the peronei. Patients usually present with footdrop and weakness of:

- Inversion (L4) of the foot
- Dorsiflexion (L5; tibialis anterior)
- Eversion (S1; peronei).

Sensory loss over the dorsum of the foot is usually present, but not prominent. The distinction from an L5 root lesion is made by demonstrating intact eversion in a root lesion.

Causes of common peroneal palsy

- Compression at the fibula neck, where the nerve winds round the bone (below-knee plasters can cause this)
- Collagen–vascular diseases
- Weight loss
- Diabetes mellitus
- Polyarteritis nodosa
- Leprosy

Other causes of (unilateral) foot drop include diabetes mellitus (other than due to common peroneal nerve palsy), stroke, multiple sclerosis and prolapsed intervertebral disc.

Other mononeuropathies affecting the hand and arm

The **median nerve** supplies some of the muscles of the thenar eminence (abductor pollicis, flexor pollicis brevis and opponens pollicis) and the lateral two lumbricals.

The **ulnar nerve** supplies the muscles of the hypothenar eminence (abductor digiti minimi), the medial two lumbricals and all the interossei (remember dorsal abduct, palmar adduct!).

The **radial nerve** does not supply muscles in the hand. It supplies primarily the extensor compartment of the forearm.

Causes of wasting of the small muscles of the hand

- Arthritis
- Motor neurone disease
- Other cervical cord pathology
- Syringomyelia
- Polyneuropathies
- Brachial plexus injury (e.g. trauma, Pancoast's tumour)

8.2 Polyneuropathies

Polyneuropathies have a heterogeneous set of causes. Typically peripheral nerves are affected in a diffuse symmetrical fashion; symptoms and signs are most prominent in the extremities. Different aetiologies may be associated with involvement of mainly motor, mainly sensory or mainly autonomic fibres.

Mainly sensory neuropathies	Mainly motor neuropathies
Diabetes mellitus	Guillain–Barré syndrome (see below)
Leprosy	Porphyria
Amyloidosis	Lead poisoning
Vitamin B12 deficiency	Diphtheria
Carcinomatous neuropathy	Hereditary sensory and motor
Uraemic neuropathy	neuropathy (HSMN) types I and II
	Chronic inflammatory
	demyelinating polyneuropathy (CIDP)

Motor neuropathies cause partial denervation of muscle. An important sign of denervation is fasciculation, which is particularly prominent in disorders of the anterior horn cell in addition to the motor neuropathies described above.

Causes of fasciculation

- Motor neurone disease
- Thyrotoxicosis
- Cervical spondylosis
- Syringomyelia
- Acute poliomyelitis
- Metabolic — severe hyponatraemia, hypomagnesaemia
- Drugs (clofibrate, lithium, anticholinesterase, salbutamol)

Autonomic neuropathies

Autonomic neuropathy may present with:

- Postural hypotension
- Abnormal sweating
- Diarrhoea or constipation
- Urinary incontinence
- Absence of cardiovascular responses (e.g. to Valsalva's manoeuvre)
- Impotence

The principal causes of autonomic neuropathy are:

- Diabetes mellitus
- Amyloidosis
- Chronic hepatic failure
- Guillain–Barré syndrome
- Renal failure
- Multiple system atrophies (i.e. Shy–Drager syndrome/OPCA)

Palpable peripheral nerves are recognized in the following polyneuropathies:

- Charcot–Marie–Tooth (HMSN II)
- Amyloidosis
- Lepromatous leprosy
- Acromegaly

Guillain–Barré syndrome

Guillain–Barré syndrome (GBS) is a rare acute infective polyneuropathy. A progressive ascending symmetric muscle weakness (ascending polyradiculopathy) leads to paralysis, maximal by one week in more than half of patients. Symptoms frequently begin after a respiratory or gastrointestinal infection; *Campylobacter jejuni* infection is associated with a worse prognosis.

Sensory symptoms are usually not associated with sensory signs. Papilloedema may occur. The condition may be associated with urinary retention or cardiac arrhythmia (autonomic involvement). Some patients will require artificial ventilation.

Investigation reveals:

- Elevated CSF protein (often very high)
- Normal CSF white cell count
- Slowing of nerve conduction velocity and denervation on EMG.

Poor prognostic features include:

- Rapid onset of symptoms
- Age
- Axonal neuropathy on nerve conduction studies
- Prior infection with *Campylobacter jejuni*.

Treatments include plasma exchange and intravenous immunoglobulin.

Miller–Fisher syndrome is a variant of Guillain–Barré syndrome and comprises ophthalmoplegia, ataxia and areflexia.

9. DISORDERS OF MUSCLE AND NEUROMUSCULAR JUNCTION

Disorders of muscle are known as myopathies. The most important feature is muscle weakness, variably accompanied by wasting, hypertrophy, pseudohypertrophy or other symptoms, such as myotonia. Signs are invariably symmetrical. Usually myopathies, with the exception of inflammatory myopathies, are not painful.

Fasciculations are signs of muscle denervation, and indicate a disorder of motor nerves or the neuromuscular junction.

9.1 Myopathies

There are a number of different types of myopathies.

- **Inflammatory**
  (e.g. polymyositis; see Chapter 18, *Rheumatology*)

- **Metabolic**
  (e.g. mitochondrial)

- **Drug-induced**

- **Inherited — dominant**
  (e.g. dystrophia myotonica; see below); **recessive** (e.g. Duchenne; see below)

- **Secondary to endocrine disease**
  (Principally thyrotoxicosis or hypothyroidism)

Duchenne muscular dystrophy

Duchenne muscular dystrophy (see also Chapter 12, *Molecular Medicine*) is an X-linked disorder affecting about one in 3500 male births, though occasionally females may be affected (due to translocation of the short arm of the X chromosome, Xp21). The gene has now been isolated in this Xp21 region, and produces a protein named dystrophin that is normally present on the muscle sarcolemmal membrane. The function of this protein is not known.

In Duchenne dystrophy the dystrophin protein is absent (in the milder Becker dystrophy, dystrophin is seen, but at a lower level than normal; the protein is also dysfunctional). Serum creatinine kinase is elevated. There is no effective treatment at present and death usually occurs in the second or third decade.

Distinguishing features in muscular dystrophy

	Duchenne	Becker
Immunofluorescent dystrophin on muscle biopsy	Undetectable	Reduced/abnormal
Wheelchair dependence	95% at <12 years	5% at <12 years
Mental handicap	20%	Rare

Note that Gower's sign is *not* pathognomonic of Duchenne muscular dystrophy but may be seen in other dystrophies.

Dystrophia myotonica

An inherited myopathy (autosomal dominant) with onset in the third decade. Symptoms include:

- Myotonic facies
- Myotonia (delayed muscular relaxation after contraction)

- Wasting and weakness of the arms and legs

Additional features include:

- Frontal baldness
- Testicular/ovarian atrophy
- Diabetes mellitus

- Cataract
- Cardiomyopathy
- Mild cognitive impairment

Diagnosis depends on the characteristic myotonic discharge on EMG in association with the clinical features listed above. Usually severe disability results within 10–20 years, and there is no treatment available though phenytoin may be used for symptomatic relief of myotonia.

9.2 Neuromuscular junction

Neuromuscular transmission is dependent on cholinergic transmission between the terminals of motor nerves and the motor end plate.

Myasthenia gravis

This is an antibody-mediated autoimmune disease affecting the neuromuscular junction; antibodies are produced to the acetylcholine receptors. It is a relatively rare disorder with a prevalence of about 1 in 20,000. The pathogenesis is described in detail in Chapter 12, *Molecular Medicine*.

Most (but not all) patients have ptosis. Many have ophthalmoplegia, dysarthria and dysphagia, but any muscle may be affected. The pupil is never affected, but weakness of eye closure and ptosis is common. Quick lid retraction on refixation from downgaze is known as Cogan's sign.

Myasthenia gravis may mimic MND, mitochondrial myopathies, polymyositis, cranial nerve palsies or brainstem dysfunction.

- **Diagnostic tests**
  Tensilon test
  ACh receptor antibodies
  (present in 85–90%)
  Electrophysiology (repetitive stimulation
  gives rise to diminution in the
  amplitude of the evoked EMG response)
  Thyroid function tests (up to 10% have
  co-existent thyrotoxicosis)
  CT mediastinum

- **Treatment**
  Cholinesterase (ChE) inhibitors
  (e.g. pyridostigmine)
  Thymectomy
  Steroids
  Immunosuppression — azathioprine,
  cyclophosphamide, cyclosporin
  Plasmapheresis
  Intravenous immune globulin

The primary treatment is with cholinesterase inhibitors, and some patients will achieve control on these agents alone. Common practice nowadays is to attempt to modify the course of the disease with treatments directed at the immune system. In those with thymoma or hyperplasia, up to 60% will improve or achieve remission after thymectomy. The benefits of this treatment are greatest in patients aged less than 40.

Lambert–Eaton myasthenic syndrome (LEMS)

The clinical features of this syndrome are:

- Fatiguability
- Hyporeflexia
- Ocular and bulbar muscles
  rarely affected

- Autonomic symptoms
  (e.g. difficulty with micturition,
  dry mouth, impotence

Unlike myasthenia gravis, ophthalmoplegia and ptosis are not features. Like myasthenia gravis, LEMS is an autoimmune disorder with antibodies produced to voltage-gated calcium channels in the muscle membrane. On examination, reflexes are absent but return **after** exercise (c.f. MG). EMG with repetitive stimulation shows an improvement in response.

LEMS is commonly a paraneoplastic syndrome, most commonly associated with small cell carcinoma of the lung (also breast and ovarian cancer). However in a variable proportion (up to 50%) of patients no cancer is found.

10. INVESTIGATIONS USED IN NEUROLOGICAL DISEASE

10.1 Cerebrospinal fluid

Normal CSF findings

- **Pressure**
  60–150 mm of CSF
  (patient recumbent)

- **Protein**
  0.2–0.4 g/l

- **Cell count**
  Red cells 0, White cells <5/mm³
  (few monocytes or lymphocytes)

- **Glucose**
  More than 2/3 blood glucose

Abnormal CSF findings

- **Elevated protein**
  Very high; >2 g/l
    Guillain–Barré syndrome
    Spinal block
    TB meningitis
    Fungal meningitis
  High
    Bacterial meningitis
    Viral encephalitis
    Cerebral abscess
    Neurosyphilis
    Subdural haematoma
    Cerebral malignancy

- **Polymorphs**
  Bacterial meningitis

- **Lymphocytes**
  Viral encephalitis/meningitis
  Partially treated bacterial meningitis
  Behçet's syndrome
  CNS vasculities
  HIV-associated
  Lymphoma
  Leukaemia
  Lyme disease
  Systemic lupus erythematosus

Continues ...

... Continued

- **Low CSF glucose**
  Bacterial meningitis
  TB meningitis
  Fungal meningitis
  Mumps meningitis (20%)
  Herpes simplex encephalitis (20%)
  Subarachnoid haemorrhage
    (occasionally)

- **Oligoclonal bands in CSF**
  Multiple sclerosis
  Neurosarcoidosis
  CNS lymphoma
  Systemic lupus erythematosus
  Subacute sclerosing panencephalitis
    rare, late complication of measles
  Subarachnoid haemorrhage (unusual)
  Neurosyphilis
  Guillain–Barré syndrome

10.2 Neuroradiology

Causes of intracranial calcification on head CT or skull X-ray:

- Oligodendroglioma
- Craniopharyngioma
- Pineal gland (may be normal finding)
- Sturge–Weber syndrome
- Aneurysm

- Meningioma
- Tuberculoma
- Tuberous sclerosis
- Toxoplasmosis
- Hypoparathyroidism (basal ganglia)

10.3 Electrophysiological investigations

EEG

Characteristic EEG findings:

- **Absence seizures**: 3 Hz spike-and-wave complexes
- **Creutzfeldt–Jakob**: periodic bursts of high-amplitude sharp waves.

Nerve conduction tests

Nerve conduction tests are used to investigate peripheral neuropathies. The technique involves stimulating a peripheral nerve (sensory or motor) and recording the action potential latency and amplitude further along the same nerve. This allows calculation of the conduction velocity of the nerve. These measures can be used to distinguish (amongst other things) between axonal and demyelinating neuropathies.

- **Axonal**: reduced amplitude (loss of axons) but **preserved** conduction velocity
- **Demyelinating**: preserved amplitude but **reduced** conduction velocity (loss of myelin).

Electromyography (EMG)

EMG is useful in disorders of the neuromuscular junction or investigation of myopathic processes. The technique involves stimulating the motor nerves while recording the compound action potential from muscles.

Characteristic abnormalities:

- **Myasthenia gravis**: diminished response to repetitive stimulation
- **Lambert–Eaton syndrome**: enhanced response to repetitive stimulation
- **Polymyositis**: fibrillation due to denervation hypersensitivity, reduced amplitude and duration of motor units
- **Myotonic syndromes**: 'dive bomber' discharge (high-frequency action potentials).

Chapter 15
Ophthalmology

CONTENTS

1. **Basic anatomy of the eye** 489
   1.1 Orbit
   1.2 Extraocular muscles
   1.3 The globe

2. **Retinal disorders** 490
   2.1 Retinal venous occlusion
   2.2 Retinal arterial occlusion
   2.3 Hypertensive retinopathy
   2.4 Diabetic retinopathy
   2.5 Retinitis pigmentosa

3. **Lens abnormalities** 496
   3.1 Cataract
   3.2 Lens dislocation

4. **Optic nerve disorders** 497
   4.1 Optic neuritis
   4.2 Causes of optic atrophy
   4.3 The swollen optic nerve head

5. **Uveitis and scleritis** 500
   5.1 Uveitis
   5.2 Scleritis
   5.3 Causes of a painful red eye

6. **Miscellaneous disorders** 502
   6.1 Thyroid eye disease
   6.2 Myotonic dystrophy
   6.3 Ocular features of the phacomatoses
   6.4 Sarcoidosis
   6.5 Keratoconus
   6.6 Glaucoma

Pupillary and eye movement disorders, nystagmus and visual field defects are all covered in the neuro-ophthalmology section of Chapter 14, *Neurology*.

Ophthalmology

Pupillary and eye movement disorders, nystagmus and visual field defects are all covered in the neuro-ophthalmology section of Chapter 14, *Neurology*.

1. BASIC ANATOMY OF THE EYE

1.1 Orbit

The orbit houses the globe, extraocular muscles, lacrimal gland, orbital fat and attendant arteries, veins and nerves.

1.2 Extraocular muscles

The four rectus muscles and the superior oblique arise at the orbital apex and pass forward to insert into the globe. The inferior oblique arises from the anteromedial orbital floor and runs along the lower surface of the globe to insert into its posterolateral aspect.

The innervation and primary action of each muscle is shown below — note all other movements are composite, i.e. due to the action of two muscles acting together.

Muscle	Nerve supply	Primary action
Superior rectus	3rd	Elevation in abduction
Inferior rectus	3rd	Depression in abduction
Medial rectus	3rd	Adduction
Lateral rectus	6th	Abduction
Inferior oblique	3rd	Elevation in adduction
Superior oblique	4th	Depression in adduction

1.3 The globe

Key features of the constituent parts are:

- **Cornea**: clarity maintained by avascularity, the regular structural array of component fibrils and its relative dehydrated state (maintained by endothelium).

- **Conjunctiva**: thin mucous membrane covering anterior sclera and lining eyelids.

- **Sclera**: tough fibroelastic coat.

- **Uveal tract**: anterior uvea comprises iris and ciliary body. Posterior uvea is the choroid, a vascular layer lining the sclera which nourishes outer retinal layers.

- **Retinal pigment epithelium**: cellular monolayer composing outermost layer of retina.

- **Retina**: light-sensitive innermost layer of the globe. Converts light energy into electrical energy. It comprises (i) Rods — more plentiful in peripheral retina, sensitive to low light and movement detection; (ii) Cones — concentrated within the macular region, particularly at the fovea, important for acuity and colour vision. Vascular supply is from the central retinal artery. Capillaries have non-fenestrated endothelium and tight junctions forming a blood-retinal barrier (analogous to the blood-brain barrier), preventing the passage of large molecules.

- **Lens**: positioned posterior to the iris and anterior to the vitreous, anchored by the zonules. It is enclosed by a capsule, the basement membrane of the lens epithelium. New lens fibres are continuously produced throughout life and the older fibres are compressed to form the lens nucleus. Reduced accommodation is found in later life due to the lens being less deformable.

2. RETINAL DISORDERS

2.1 Retinal venous occlusion

Retinal vein occlusion probably occurs due to a dynamic change in blood flow at arteriovenous crossings and may affect the central retinal vein (CRVO) or one of its branches (BRVO).

Aetiology

- Systemic hypertension (most common)
- Increased intraocular pressure (central occlusion only)
- Diabetes
- Hyperviscosity states
- Vasculitides.

Clinical signs of retinal venous occlusion

- **Loss of vision**
  Variable extent depending on macular involvement and degree of retinal ischaemia produced

- **Multiple retinal haemorrhages**
  Mainly superficial, in nerve fibre layer ('blood and thunder' appearance)

- **Retinal venous dilatation**

- **Cotton wool spots**

- **Vascular sheathing**

- **Relative afferent pupillary defect**
  With retinal ischaemia

- **Neovascularization**
  May occur in 20% CRVO and 1% BRVO due to ischaemia, i.e. similar pathogenesis to diabetic retinopathy. This may affect anterior segment producing neovascular glaucoma or the retina causing vitreous haemorrhage or retinal traction. Treatment is by retinal laser to abolish the ischaemic stimulus

2.2 Retinal arterial occlusion

As the central retinal artery is an end artery, occlusion of the central artery or one of its branches produces retinal infarction and visual loss in the area supplied.

Aetiology

- **Embolic**

- **Sudden rapid increase in intraocular pressure**
  To above central retinal arterial pressure

- **Arteritic**
  Most commonly giant cell arteritis (GCA). However, visual loss in GCA is only due to central retinal artery occlusion in 10% of cases; it usually affects vision by producing anterior ischaemic optic neuropathy which damages the optic nerve head

Clinical signs of retinal arterial occlusion

- **Sudden, profound, painless loss of vision**
  (Corresponding sector field loss if branch occlusion)

- **Neovascular complications (occur later)**
  Much rarer than with venous occlusions, probably because the retina is too severely damaged to produce angiogenic factor

- **Relative afferent pupillary defect**

- **Pale oedematous retina with cherry red spot at fovea (only lasts c. 48 hours)**
  This is due to the choroidal reflex showing through at the fovea as the retina is thinner here

Treatment is sometimes possible to dislodge the embolus if presentation occurs within a few hours of onset.

2.3 Hypertensive retinopathy

Retinal abnormalities represent the severity of hypertension and are characterized by:

- Vascular constriction causing focal retinal ischaemia
- Leakage leading to retinal oedema, haemorrhage and lipid deposition.

Arteriosclerotic changes reflect the duration of the hypertension. These include vessel wall thickening secondary to intimal hyalinization, medial hypertrophy and endothelial hyperplasia.

Classification of hypertensive retinopathy

- **Grade 1**
  Arteriolar attenuation

- **Grade 2**
  Focal arteriolar attenuation
  (with 'ateriovenous nipping')

- **Grade 3**
  Haemorrhages, cotton wool spots (due to infarction of nerve fibre layer of retina)

- **Grade 4**
  Disc swelling — 'malignant' or 'accelerated' phase

Grades 3 and 4 are associated with severe target organ damage and high mortality (accelerated phase hypertension). Treatment is purely aimed towards the hypertension and any underlying cause.

2.4 Diabetic retinopathy

Diabetic retinopathy is related to the duration and control of the disease. It is the most common cause of blindness in patients aged 30–60 years. It is unusual in Type I diabetes until 10 years after diagnosis, but eventually occurs in nearly all patients. It is present in 10% of Type II patients at diagnosis, 50% after 10 years' disease and 80% after 20 years' disease.

Diabetic retinopathy is a **microvascular** disease. The following pathological changes are known to occur.

- **Loss of vascular pericytes**: thought to be responsible for the structural integrity of the vessel wall. A decrease therefore results in disruption of the blood-retinal barrier and leakage of plasma constituents into the retina.
- **Capillary endothelial cell** damage.
- **Basement membrane thickening** with carbohydrate and glycogen deposition.

Changes in red cell oxygen carrying capabilities and increased platelet aggregation are also thought to contribute. The production of an angiogenic factor by ischaemic retina is the likely cause of neovascularization. At all stages good control of diabetes, of any coexisting hypertension and stopping smoking have been shown to reduce serious sequelae.

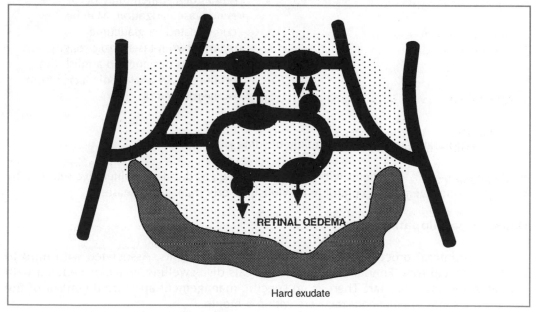

RETINAL OEDEMA

Hard exudate

Consequences of retinal vascular leakage

Classification of diabetic retinopathy

- **Background retinopathy**
  Does not affect visual acuity
  Microaneurysms — first clinical change, saccular pouch, either leaks or resolves due to thrombosis
  Haemorrhages — dot, blot and flame-shaped
  Exudates — leakage of lipid and lipoprotein
  No local treatment required; adequate control of diabetes only

- **Diabetic maculopathy**
  Most common cause of visual loss
  More common in Type II diabetes
  Retinopathy within the macular region
  Oedematous retina may require laser treatment

- **Preproliferative retinopathy**
  Cotton wool spots — represent areas of axonal disruption secondary to ischaemia
  Venous changes — dilatation and beading
  Large deep haemorrhages
  Treatment controversial. Some advocate prophylactic laser treatment, others recommend improving disease control and more frequent monitoring

- **Proliferative retinopathy**
  More common in Type I diabetes
  Retinal neovascularization. New vessels occur in thin-walled friable clumps on the venous side of the retinal circulation. New vessels on the disc are more ominous than those on the vascular arcades. Vitreous haemorrhage, fibrosis and tractional retinal detachment may occur
  Iris neovascularization. May be complicated by glaucoma
  Treatment with laser photocoagulation to retina is designed to abolish the production of angiogenic factor from ischaemic retina

Diabetic retinopathy may progress rapidly in some situations:

- Pregnancy — 5% of patients with background changes develop proliferative retinopathy
- Sudden improvement in control in previously poorly managed disease.

Diabetic papillopathy

Typically bilateral process in young Type I diabetic patients. Associated with mild to moderate visual loss. Fundai examination reveals disc swelling, macular oedema with exudates and macular star. There is no specific management apart from control of the diabetes. Usually spontaneous recovery within 6 months.

Non-retinal eye disease in diabetics

The eye may be affected by diabetes in several other ways:

- **Visual changes**
  Secondary to osmotic lens changes
  with fluctuating glucose levels

- **Mononeuropathies**
  Leading to ophthalmoplegia

- **Snowflake cataract**
  Poorly controlled juvenile diabetes

- **Early onset senile cataract**

- **Increased external eye infections**
  (e.g. conjunctivitis, styes)

2.5 Retinitis pigmentosa

Retinitis pigmentosa (RP) is a term describing a group of progressive inherited diseases affecting the photoreceptors and the retinal pigment epithelium. It is characterized by the triad of:

- **Night blindness**: due to loss of rod function.
- **Tunnel vision**: loss of peripheral field also due to rod dysfunction. Central visual acuity loss due to cone disease may also occur but tends to be a later feature.
- **Pigmented bony spicule**: fundal appearance with associated disc pallor and blood vessel attenuation.

There are three inheritance patterns: autosomal recessive, autosomal dominant and X-linked recessive.

Disease onset and progression varies between different groups and also between affected members within families. Autosomal recessive and X-linked recessive tend to be more severe.

Important systemic associations include the following:

- **Abetalipoproteinaemia (Bassen Kornzweig syndrome)**: autosomal recessive disease typically affecting Ashkenazy Jews. Treatment with high-dose vitamin E may help neurological and retinal disease. (See Chapter 11, *Metabolic Diseases*.)
- **Refsum's disease**: autosomal recessive disorder of phytanic acid metabolism leading to its accumulation in tissues, causing peripheral neuropathy, cerebellar ataxia, ichthyosis and deafness. Serum phytanic acid levels are elevated and examination of the CSF reveals elevated protein in the presence of a normal cell count. Refsum's disease is responsive to a phytanic acid-free diet which excludes animal fats, dairy products and green leafy vegetables.

- **Usher's syndrome**: autosomal recessive condition with non-progressive sensorineural deafness.
- **Barder–Biedl (Laurence–Moon–Biedl syndrome)**: autosomal recessive disease with mental retardation, obesity, hypogonadism, polydactyly, deafness and renal cystic disease.
- **Kearns Sayre syndrome**: disorder of mitochondrial inheritance with progressive external ophthalmoplegia, ptosis and heart block.

3. LENS ABNORMALITIES

3.1 Cataract

Cataract is an opacity of the lens. It is the most common cause of blindness world-wide. Many classifications exist according to type, aetiology and associations. Surgical intervention is indicated:

- When patient function is impaired because of decreased vision
- If the view of the fundus is impaired when monitoring or treating another condition (e.g. diabetes).

Causes of cataracts

- **Congenital**
  Autosomal dominant (25%)
  Maternal infection — rubella,
    toxoplasmosis, CMV,
    herpes simplex, varicella zoster
  Maternal drug ingestion —
    corticosteroids, thalidomide
  Metabolic — galactosaemia,
    hypocalcaemia, Lowe's syndrome,
    hypoglycaemia
  Chromosomal abnormalities
    (e.g. Down's syndrome,
    Turner's syndrome)

- **Toxic/drug-induced**
  (e.g. steroids, chlorpromazine,
    busulphan, gold, amiodarone)

- **Senile**

- **Secondary to ocular disease**
  (e.g. uveitis, high myopia)

- **Metabolic**
  Diabetes, hypoglycaemia,
    mannosidosis, Fabry's disease,
    Lowe's syndrome, Wilson's disease
    hypocalcaemia, galactokinase
    deficiency

- **Traumatic**
  Penetrating or blunt injury,
    infra-red radiation, radiotherapy,
    electric shock

- **Miscellaneous**
  Myotonic dystrophy, progeria,
    atopic dermatitis

3.2 Lens dislocation

Lens dislocation results from disruption of the zonules which anchor it in position. Depending on the lens shift this may produce myopia or hypermetropia, or elevated intraocular pressure.

Causes of lens dislocation

- Marfan's syndrome: up and out
- Homocystinuria: down and in
- Ehlers–Danlos syndrome
- Autosomal recessive ectopia lentis
- Trauma
- Uveal tumours.

4. OPTIC NERVE DISORDERS

4.1 Optic neuritis

Inflammation of the optic nerve may affect the:

- **Nerve head**: producing **papillitis** with optic disc swelling, hyperaemia and haemorrhages
- **Retrobulbar portion of the nerve**: in which the nerve appears normal ('the patient sees nothing, the doctor sees nothing').

It is the presenting feature of 25% of patients with multiple sclerosis (MS), up to 70% of patients who have an attack of optic neuritis will develop MS (20% in the first 2 years).

Clinical signs of optic neuritis

- **Reduced visual acuity**
  Usually monocular (90%), progresses rapidly over a few days; improves over 4–6 weeks, achieving virtually normal vision in 90%

- **Paracentral or central scotoma**

- **Visual evoked potential prolonged**
  Reflecting delayed conduction in optic pathway

- **Pain**
  Precedes visual loss by a few days; worsened by eye movements

- **Red colour desaturation**

- **Relative afferent pupillary defect**

- **Variable degree of optic atrophy**
  Occurs after recovery

Causes of optic neuritis/papillitis

- **Infections**: viral encephalitis (measles, mumps, chicken-pox), infectious mononucleosis, herpes zoster.
- **Inflammatory**: contiguous with orbital inflammation sinusitis or meningitis secondary to granulomatous optic nerve inflammation (e.g. TB, sarcoid, syphilis).
- **Demyelination**: (also post-viral syndromes).
- **Other systemic disease**: (e.g. diabetes).

4.2 Causes of optic atrophy

Causes of optic atrophy

- **Congenital**
  Dominant or recessive

- **Secondary to optic nerve compression**
  (e.g. pituitary mass, meningioma,
    orbital cellulitis)

- **Drugs**
  Ethambutol, isoniazid,
    chloramphenicol, digitalis,
    chlorpropamide

- **Radiation neuropathy**

- **Carcinomatous**
  Due to microscopic infiltrates of the
    nerve and its sheath

- **Post papilloedema**

- **Post-optic neuritis**
  See above

- **Post-trauma**

- **Toxic neuropathy**
  (e.g. tobacco (cyanide), arsenic,
    lead, methanol)

- **Nutritional**
  Vitamins B1, B2, B6, B12, folic acid
    and niacin deficiencies.
    Tobacco amblyopia may
    be toxic or nutritional with a good
    prognosis for recovery

- **Infiltrative neuropathy**
  (e.g. sarcoid, lymphoma, leukaemia)

4.3 The swollen optic nerve head

Papilloedema

Papilloedema means optic nerve head swelling **secondary to increased intracranial pressure**. This may be due to:
- Space occupying lesion
- Hydrocephalus
- CO_2 retention
- Benign intracranial hypertension.

Papilloedema is usually bilateral. Features include:

- Hyperaemia of the disc: due to capillary dilatation
- Splinter haemorrhages of retina
- Blurring of the disc margins: due to nerve fibre layer swelling
- Exudates and cotton wool spots
- Loss of spontaneous venous pulsation: absent in 20% of normal people
- Loss of the cup is a late feature.

On clinical examination papilloedema produces an enlarged blind spot. **Transient visual obscurations**, with blacking out of vision lasting a few seconds, often due to positional change, also occur. Visual loss occurs late.

Foster–Kennedy syndrome is unilateral papilloedema with contralateral optic atrophy. It is due to a mass lesion compressing the optic nerve on one side causing ipsilateral atrophic changes and resulting in increased intracranial pressure and contralateral papilloedema.

Papillitis

This refers to inflammation of the optic nerve head (as distinct from retrobulbar neuritis) and is most frequently due to a demyelinative episode (see section 4.1 above).

Ischaemic optic neuropathy

Infarction of the anterior portion of the optic nerve results in acute severe visual loss which generally does not improve. This is the usual method by which giant cell arteritis affects vision (90%), retinal artery occlusion occurring in the other 10% cases. It is essential to exclude this condition as it rapidly becomes bilateral. Giant cells and loss of the internal elastic lamina are evident histologically on temporal artery biopsy.

Ischaemic optic neuropathy is not always due to inflammatory arteritis; it may be due to arteriosclerosis or to hypotensive events.

Other causes of swelling of the optic nerve head

- Central retinal vein occlusion
- Orbital mass
  (e.g. optic nerve glioma,
  nerve sheath meningioma, thyroid
  eye disease and metastases)

- Accelerated phase hypertension
  (see above)
- Infiltrative neuropathy
  (e.g. lymphoma)
- Toxic neuropathy

---

5. UVEITIS AND SCLERITIS

5.1 Uveitis

Uveitis is inflammation of the uveal tract, which may affect the anterior and/or posterior uvea.

Anterior uveitis typically presents with pain, photophobia, a red eye, lacrimation and decreased vision.

Posterior uveitis presents with floaters (due to inflammatory debris in the vitreous) or impaired vision, (secondary to choroiditis if the inflammatory lesion is within the macula).

Uveitis of any cause may be complicated by cataract or glaucoma. Anterior uveitis is most commonly idiopathic but there are also many associations with systemic diseases.

Systemic diseases associated with uveitis

- **Ankylosing spondylitis**

- **Reiter's syndrome**

- **Malignancy**
  Non-Hodgkin's lymphoma
  Retinoblastoma
  Ocular melanoma

- **Psoriatic disease**

- **Sarcoidosis**

- **Inflammatory bowel disease**
  (10% of colitics, 3% Crohn's patients)

- **Behçet's disease**

- **Juvenile chronic arthritis**

- **Infections**
  TB, syphilis, herpes simplex,
  herpes zoster, toxoplasmosis,
  toxocariasis, AIDS, leprosy

500

Characteristics of uveitis associated with particular systemic diseases are:

- **Ankylosing spondylitis**: recurrent anterior uveitis occurs in approximately 30% of patients with ankylosing spondylitis, and about 30% of males with unilateral uveitis will have ankylosing spondylitis. The uveitis may precede or follow the joint involvement and does not correlate with disease severity.

- **Sarcoidosis**: acute or granulomatous. Anterior or posterior. Frequently bilateral and complicated. (See following section.)

- **Reiter's syndrome**: anterior uveitis occurs in 30% of patients. Other ocular features include conjunctivitis and keratitis.

- **Behçet's disease**: ocular disease occurs in 70% of patients. Anterior uveitis is often severe and bilateral. Conjunctivitis and episcleritis are seen and the retina may also be affected by retinal vasculitis with infarction, secondary venous occlusion, retinal oedema, exudates and neovascularization.

- **Juvenile chronic arthritis**: ocular involvement typically occurs in pauciarticular disease, particularly those patients who are ANA positive. Uveitic activity bears no relation to that of the arthropathy. The disease is usually bilateral and asymptomatic and therefore regular screening is required because of the high incidence of complications. These are cataract in 35% of patients, secondary glaucoma in 20% and band keratopathy in 40%.

Common causes of **posterior uveitis** (chlorido-retinitis) are:

- **Inflammatory**: sarcoid
- **Infections**: TB, syphilis (congenital and tertiary), leprosy, toxoplasmosis, toxocariasis and AIDS.

5.2 Scleritis

Inflammation of the sclera may be caused by:

- Herpes zoster
- Ankylosing spondylitis
- Sarcoidosis
- Inflammatory bowel disease
- Gout
- Vasculitis: PAN, SLE, Wegener's, relapsing polychondritis, dermatomyositis, Behçet's

501

5.3 Causes of a painful red eye

- **Conjunctivitis**
  bacterial is irritable, viral is painful

- **Uveitis**

- **Scleritis**
  causes listed above

- **Corneal damage**
  abrasion, keratitis (e.g. herpes simplex and herpes zoster)

- **Acute glaucoma**
  due to angle closure or rubeosis

6. MISCELLANEOUS DISORDERS

Ophthalmic features of HIV/AIDS are covered in Chapter 7, *Genito-urinary Medicine and AIDS*.

6.1 Thyroid eye disease

The ocular manifestations of Graves' disease may pre-date, coincide or follow the systemic disease. The classic triad is the association of ocular changes with thyroid acropachy and pretibial myxoedema. Eye disease may be divided according to Werner's classification ('NO SPECS'), although it is important to appreciate that there is not necessarily a step-like progression from one stage to the next, and not all steps occur in all patients.

No signs or symptoms
Only signs (e.g. lid retraction/lag)

Soft tissue swelling
Proptosis — orbital fat proliferation and muscle changes. Auto-decompresses orbital contents
Extraocular muscle changes — usually affect inferior and/or medial recti. Lymphocytic infiltrate.
Corneal exposure
Sight loss — secondary to corneal disease or optic nerve compression.

Management of ocular manifestations may be divided into:

- **Surface abnormalities**: ocular lubricants, tarsorrhaphy
- **Muscle changes**: prisms to control diplopia, surgery after defect stable for minimum of 6 months

- **Optic nerve compression**: systemic steroids, radiotherapy, surgical decompression
- **Cosmetic**: improve lid position, remove redundant tissue.

6.2 Myotonic dystrophy

Autosomal dominant condition characterized by failure of relaxation of voluntary muscle fibres.

Ophthalmic features of myotonic dystrophy

- Ptosis, poor lid closure and orbicularis weakness
- Retinal pigmentary changes
- Presenile cataract
- Miotic pupils

6.3 Ocular features of the phacomatoses

This group of disorders affect the nervous system, skin, eye and other organs and are characterized by the presence of hamartomatous lesions.

Sturge–Weber syndrome

Glaucoma occurs on ipsilateral side to cutaneous angioma in 50%. Cavernous haemangioma may be seen in the choroid.

Neurofibromatosis

- The eyelid may be affected by cutaneous neuroma.
- In the anterior segment, iris nodules are seen and glaucoma is more common.
- Choroidal naevi may be seen on fundoscopy.
- The optic nerve may be affected by glioma, and a pulsatile globe suggests a defect of the greater wing of the sphenoid.

von Hippel–Lindau syndrome

Autosomal dominant condition with incomplete penetrance and variable expressivity, the abnormality being on the short arm of chromosome 3.

- Retinal haemangiomas develop bilaterally in 25% of patients and may leak (producing exudates or a serous retinal detachment), or rupture (leading to vitreous haemorrhage). These are histologically identical to the cerebellar haemangioblastomas which also occur.

- Indirectly, increased inracranial pressure due to posterior fossa haemangioblastoma may lead to papilloedema, hypertensive changes may be seen when phaeochromocytoma is present.

Tuberous sclerosis

- Autosomal dominant condition linked to several chromosomal abnormalities; 50% are new mutations. Ocular features include retinal hamartomas and rarely papilloedema or VIth nerve palsy due to increased intracranial pressure secondary to CNS lesions.

6.4 Sarcoidosis

This multisystem granulomatous disease affects the eye and ocular adenexae in about 30% of cases, and of these 25% will have posterior segment disease.

Ocular effects of sarcoidosis

- **Lids**
  Lupus pernio, cutaneous granuloma

- **Lacrimal glands**
  Granulomatous infiltrate, may cause sicca syndrome (Mikulicz's syndrome when combined with parotid involvement)

- **Uveitis**
  Acute or granulomatous, frequently bilateral, and complicated by glaucoma and cataract

- **Retinal involvement**
  With periphlebtic 'candle wax exudates', haemorrhages, oedema and neovascularization

- **Choroiditis and choroidal granulomas**

- **Optic nerve granuloma**

- **Disc oedema**

- **Nerve palsies: III, IV, VI**

6.5 Keratoconus

Keratoconus is an ectatic condition of the inferior paracentral cornea. Onset is usually in the teens with progressive myopic astigmatism.

Systemic associations are:

- Atopy
- Down's syndrome
- Turner's syndrome
- Marfan's syndrome
- Ehler–Danlos syndrome.

6.6 Glaucoma

Glaucoma describes the group of conditions in which intra-ocular pressure is sufficient to cause visual damage with a characteristic optic neuropathy. The normal intraocular pressure is < 22 mmHg. Aqueous humour is formed by the ciliary body, passes through the pupil and drains, via the trabecular meshwork, into the venous circulation through the episcleral venous system.

Acute glaucoma

- Rapid decrease in visual acuity associated with severe pain and vomiting.
- More common in hypermetropes (long-sightedness).
- Due to closure of the drainage angle resulting in massive sudden elevation in intra-ocular pressure.
- Cornea appears cloudy with a mid-dilated non-reacting pupil.
- Failure to treat pressure rapidly results in permanent visual loss.

Chronic glaucoma

- Insidious asymptomatic disease.
- Intra-ocular pressure elevated (usually not as markedly as in acute glaucoma), resulting in cupping of the optic nerve head and loss of visual field.
- Classically an arcuate scotoma develops which progress to generalized field constriction.
- Familial tendency but no strict inheritance.
- More common in women and myopes (short-sighted).

Secondary glaucoma

Glaucoma is a possible complication of almost any ocular disorder. Secondary glaucomas may be generally classified as follows.

- **Pre-trabecular**
  (e.g. fibrovascular membrane in rubeosis)

- **Trabecular**
  clogging of meshwork by (e.g. inflammatory cells in uveitis) meshwork
  alteration due to inflammation in uveitis or scleritis

- **Post-trabecular**
  raised episcleral venous pressure preventing outflow
  (e.g. carotico-cavernous fistula, or cavernous sinus thrombosis)

Chapter 16
Psychiatry

CONTENTS

1. **Schizophrenia** 509
   1.1   First rank symptoms
   1.2   Principles of treatment

2. **Mood disorders** 511
   2.1   Hypomania/mania (bipolar affective disorder)
   2.2   Depression
   2.3   Depression in the elderly
   2.4   Differentiation of depression from dementia
   2.5   Principles of treatment

3. **Anxiety disorders** 515
   3.1   Generalized anxiety disorder
   3.2   Panic disorder
   3.3   Phobic disorders

4. **Obsessive compulsive disorder** 516

5. **Unexplained physical symptoms** 518
   5.1   Somatoform disorders
   5.2   Conversion disorder
   5.3   Factitious disorder

6. **Eating disorders** 519
   6.1   Anorexia nervosa and bulimia nervosa: diagnostic criteria
   6.2   Medical complications of anorexia nervosa
   6.3   Principles of treatment

7. **Deliberate self-harm** 523

8. **Organic psychiatry**   525
    8.1   Acute organic brain syndrome
    8.2   Dementia
    8.3   Physical illnesses particularly associated with mental disorders
    8.4   Drug-induced mental disorders

9. **Alcohol abuse**   529
    9.1   Social consequences of alcohol abuse
    9.2   Acute withdrawal consequences
    9.3   Psychological consequences of alcohol abuse
    9.4   Neuropsychiatric consequences of alcohol abuse

10. **Sleep disorders**   532
    10.1   Normal sleep
    10.2   Insomnia
    10.3   Narcolepsy

11. **Treatments in psychiatry**   534
    11.1   Antipsychotics
    11.2   Antidepressants
    11.3   Benzodiazepines
    11.4   Electroconvulsive therapy (ECT)
    11.5   The psychotherapies

Psychiatry

1. SCHIZOPHRENIA

Schizophrenia is characterized by disturbances of thought, perception, mood and personality. These lead to 'positive' symptoms, such as delusions, hallucinations and disorganization of thoughts and speech, and 'negative' symptoms, including decreased motivation, poor self-care and social withdrawal. Patients do not have a 'spilt personality'. The lifetime risk is about 1% for men and women, although men consistently have an earlier age of onset. There is strong evidence of genetic predisposition, but not through a simple Mendelian model of inheritance (see table).

Lifetime risk of schizophrenia in relatives of patients with schizophrenia

Relationship	Per cent schizophrenic
Monozygotic twin	50
Children (both parents schizophrenic)	46
Children	13
Dizygotic twin	10
Sibling	10
Uncles/aunts	3
Unrelated	0.9

Schizophrenia is a heterogeneous condition; signs and symptoms present to a highly variable degree between individuals. Despite this, generalizations can be made about certain 'core features'. Schneider's first rank symptoms were an attempt to tighten diagnostic practice.

1.1 First rank symptoms

Originally described by Schneider, these represent an attempt to identify symptoms that occur exclusively in schizophrenia. In clinical practice they occur in approximately 70% of schizophrenic patients and in approximately 10% of manic patients. However, for the purpose of medical examinations, including the MRCP, they *should* be considered to be 'diagnostic of' or 'characteristic of' schizophrenia in the absence of obvious organic brain disease. A mnemonic for first rank symptoms follows.

First rank symptoms mnemonic:

ATPD — Aim To Pass Definitely

Auditory hallucinations of a specific type:

- Third person (i.e. two or more voices heard discussing the patient)
- Running commentary
- Thought echo

Thought disorder of a specific type (passivity of thought):

- Thought withdrawal
- Thought insertion
- Thought broadcasting

Passivity experiences (delusions of control):

- Actions/feelings/impulses under external control
- Bodily sensations being due to external influence

Delusional perception (two-stage process):

- Perception of commonplace object/sight, leads to ...
- Sudden, intense, self-referential attribution of new meaning
  (e.g. finding coin on the ground leads to belief of messianic role)

There are many other important clinical features of schizophrenia, including impaired insight, suspiciousness, flat/blunted or incongruous effect, decreased spontaneous speech and other motor activity and general lack of motivation and poor self-care.

Auditory hallucinations which are not of the type covered by the first rank symptoms may occur, as can other types of delusions, often bizarre and non-mood-congruent. These symptoms can be divided into two categories:

- Positive: delusions, hallucinations, formal thought disorder
- Negative: flat/blunted effect, decreased motor activity and speech, poor motivation and self-care.

1.2 Principles of treatment

Treatment of schizophrenia involves a biopsychosocial model, but compliance with medication is the best predictor of relapse. Atypical antipsychotics are now widely prescribed and three independent trials have recently shown that cognitive behaviour therapy is a valuable adjunctive treatment for patients with persistent hallucinations and delusions.

- **Antipsychotics** may be given orally, i.m. or depot i.m.; depot preparations aid compliance. Use of traditional antipsychotics (chlorpromazine, haloperidol, trifluoperazine, pimozide etc.) is limited by extrapyramidal side effects. Tardive dyskinesia occurs in >30% of patients on long term traditional antipsychotics. Atypical antipsychotics (clozapine, olanzapine, risperidone, sertindole) have a preferential side effect profile, particularly with regard to extrapyramidal side effects.

- 'Positive' symptoms respond better than 'negative' symptoms to antipsychotics; the atypical antipsychotics are probably better for negative symptoms. Only clozapine has increased efficacy.

- Electroconvulsive therapy (ECT) may be needed for catatonic stupor.

- Psychosocial treatments are also important. Cognitive behaviour therapy may help psychotic symptoms and aid compliance, whereas social interventions should target accommodation, finances and daytime activities. Both patients and relatives may benefit from supportive psychotherapy, counselling and education.

2. MOOD DISORDERS

Mood disorders are conditions in which a pathologically depressed or elated mood is the core feature. Depression is much more common than mania; those who suffer with mania almost invariably have one or more periods of depression at some stage in the course of their illness. The genetic contribution to mood disorders is strongest for bipolar disorder.

2.1 Hypomania/mania (bipolar affective disorder)

Hypomania and mania are mood disorders characterized by pathologically elated or irritable mood. Lifetime prevalence is about 1% with a slight female predominance. Hypomania is a slightly less severe form of mania and psychotic symptoms should be absent. The majority of symptoms in both are 'mood congruent', i.e. understandable in the context of the pathological mood change. There is usually a previous episode of depression or episodes of depression in the future, hence hypomania/mania is part of a bipolar affective disorder. The main differential diagnoses are usually organic psychoses or schizophrenia. The clinical features of hypomania/mania are listed overleaf.

Clinical features of hypomania/mania

- **Mood**
  Predominantly elevated/
    elated ± irritable
  Expansive (but note transient
    depression common)

- **Behaviour**
  Insomnia
  Over-activity
  Loss of normal social inhibitions:
    overfamiliar, sexual promiscuity, risk-taking,
    overspending
  Increased libido
  Increased appetite, decreased weight.

- **Speech and thoughts**
  Pressured (fast)
  Flight of ideas
  Inflated self-esteem/grandiosity
  Over-optimistic ideas
  Poor attention, concentration

- **Psychotic symptoms (mania)**
  Mood-congruent (e.g. delusions of special
    ability or status, grandiose delusions)

Perhaps the most crucial decision to make in the management of bipolar disorder is the timing of the introduction of long term prophylactic mood stabilizing medication (typically lithium or anticonvulsants). There are no hard and fast rules; this is a matter of clinical judgement.

Lithium is the most commonly prescribed mood stabilizer and it is particularly important to remember its therapeutic window. (See Chapter 2, *Clinical Pharmacology, Toxicology and Poisoning.*)

Biological/physical treatments of hypomania/mania

- **Short term, acute episode**
  Antipsychotics
  Benzodiazepines
  Lithium (plasma level 1.0 mmol/l)
  ECT

- **Long term, prophylaxis**
  Lithium (plasma level 0.5 mmol/l)
  Carbamazepine
  Depot antipsychotics

2.2 Depression

Depression occurs with a wide range of severity and has a multifactorial aetiology. Lifetime incidence of depression varies from 1% to 20% according to severity. Evidence for a genetic contribution is most compelling in the most severe illness, whereas mild and moderate depression is usually best explained by psychosocial models. These latter disorders are rarely treated by psychiatrists unless they are complicated by co-morbidity with substance misuse or personality disorder. The variation in severity and symptomatology of depression has led to a number of classification systems:

- Endogenous versus reactive
- Melancholic versus neurotic
- Unipolar versus bipolar.

Clinical features of depression

'Biological' symptoms (shown in italics) are especially important because their presence predicts response to physical treatments. They are also known as 'somatic', 'endogenous' or 'melancholic' symptoms.

- **Mood**
  Pervasively lowered
  Loss of reactivity
  Diurnal variation (worse a.m.)
  Variable anxiety/irritability

- **Speech and thoughts**
  Slowed speech, low volume
  Reduced attention/concentration
  Reduced self-esteem
  Reduced confidence
  Ideas of guilt, worthlessness,
    hopelessness
  Bleak, pessimistic outlook
  Ideas and acts of self-harm

- **Behaviour**
  Insomnia (early morning wakening)
  Psychomotor agitation or retardation
  Decreased social interactions
  Reduced libido
  Loss of enjoyment (anhedonia)
  Reduced energy
  Increased fatigue
  Decreased activity
  Decreased appetite
  Weight loss

- **Psychotic symptoms**
  Mood-congruent
  Delusions of guilt, physical illness
  Auditory hallucinations with
  derogatory content

2.3 Depression in the elderly

Depression in the elderly is often missed. This is in part due to the prejudice that depression is an inevitable consequence of increasing age, but also because older patients tend to present less with depressed mood and more with physical complaints. It is likely to be associated with social isolation, bereavement, financial problems or physical ill health. The most common presentations are physical symptoms (or hypochondriasis), insomnia and psychomotor disturbances. Cognitive impairment may mimic dementia (see overleaf).

Treatment

- Physical: beware of sensitivity to side effects of tricyclics. ECT may be preferable in severe illness
- Psychological: cognitive therapy
- Social: decrease isolation.

2.4 Differentiation of depression from dementia

The cognitive impairment seen in severe depression, sometimes called depressive pseudodementia, can lead to a misdiagnosis of primary depression, particularly in elderly patients. The table below details differentiating clinical features.

Clinical features	Depression	Dementia
Family history	Affective disorder	Alzheimer's disease (in some)
Illness duration	Short	Long
Progression	Rapid	Slow
Patient features previous depression	Yes	No
c/o poor memory	Yes	No
History given	Detailed	Vague
Effort at testing	Poor	Good
Response at test results	Picks on faults	Pleased
Other behaviour	Contrary	Compatible
Examination of concentration/attention	Poor	Lapses
Orientation tests	'Don't know'	Poor
Memory loss	Global	Recent
Primitive reflexes	Absent	Present
Apraxias	Absent	Present
Word intrusions	Corrects	Present
Neuropsychological tests		
test performance	Variable	Always poor
Pattern	Nil specific	Verbal IQ > performance IQ

2.5 Principles of treatment

Treatments in depression target the biological, psychological and social aetiologies. If biological symptoms are present then physical treatments are indicated, whatever the apparent psychosocial precipitants. See also section 11.

Biological/physical treatments

- Antidepressants
- Lithium (for augmentation of antidepressant effect or long term prophylaxis)
- Thyroid hormone (T_3; augmentation therapy in resistant depression)
- ECT (for severe or resistant depression)
- Antipsychotics (if psychotic symptoms present)

Psychological treatments

- Supportive psychotherapy/counselling
- Cognitive therapy

Social interventions

- Accommodation, finances, day-time activities

3. ANXIETY DISORDERS

3.1 Generalized anxiety disorder

The clinical features of generalized anxiety disorder are persistent and generalized. Patients never completely return to a baseline level of zero anxiety.

Cognitive symptoms

- Apprehension
- Fear of death, losing control or going mad
- Hypervigilance.

Somatic symptoms

- Palpitations
- Shortness of breath and hyperventilation
- Butterflies in the stomach, nausea, loose bowel motions
- Urinary frequency
- Muscle tension
- Headaches, dizziness, lightheadedness, tingling in fingers and around mouth.

Treatment may include physical interventions and psychological approaches. Short term use of benzodiazepines (with care), tricyclic antidepressants and beta-blockers are appropriate physical treatments. Psychological treatments might include cognitive behaviour therapy and anxiety management.

3.2 Panic disorder

These patients suffer paroxysms of intense anxiety (panic) interspersed with periods of complete remission. Typical attacks last several minutes and occur without situational cues. Somatic symptoms are prominent. Patients may develop an anticipatory fear of the next attack.

Physical treatment includes short term use of benzodiazepines with care, and selective serotonin re-uptake inhibitors. Cognitive behaviour therapy is an appropriate psychological treatment.

3.3 Phobic disorders

These patients suffer from intense anxiety which is reliably precipitated by a situational cue. The fear they experience is out of proportion to the situation and cannot be reasoned or explained away. This results in the avoidance of the feared situation and related situations.

Specific/simple phobias include fear of flying, heights, animals etc. Agoraphobia is anxiety about being in places or situations from which escape may be difficult, for example in crowds, on public transport, on a bridge etc. Social phobia is a persistent fear of humiliation or embarrassment in social situations.

Appropriate physical treatments include short term use of benzodiazepines 'with care', tricyclic antidepressants and beta-blockers. Patients may also benefit from psychological treatments including:

- Behavioural psychotherapy: systematic desensitization, flooding, modelling
- Supportive psychotherapy
- Psychodynamic psychotherapy (see section on 'the psychotherapies').

4. OBSESSIVE COMPULSIVE DISORDER

Obsessive compulsive disorder may also be called obsessional illness, or obsessional neurosis. Mild obsessional symptoms are very common and may actually be helpful for certain occupations (e.g. accountancy). Pathologically severe symptoms may be secondary to other psychiatric or neuropsychiatric disorders (see below). The lifetime prevalence of primary obsessive compulsive disorder is between 1.9% and 3.1%, with a slight excess of females affected.

Obsessions are ideas, thoughts (ruminations) or images, that are:

- Recurrent
- Persistent
- Occur against the patient's will
- Regarded as absurd, but insight maintained
- Recognized as product of patient's own mind
- Resisted → anxiety.

Compulsions are:

- Impulses to carry out a particular activity
- Usually triggered by an obsessional thought.

OBSESSION	→	**COMPULSION**	→	**RITUAL**
hands dirty		must wash hands		washing

Compulsions and ritualized behaviours are sometimes referred to together as 'compulsions'.

- 30% of patients with obsessive compulsive disorder have associated depression
- 25% of patients with depression develop obsessions.

Other associations include:

- Schizophrenia (3–5%)
- Anorexia nervosa
- Organic brain disease (Sydenham's chorea, Tourette's syndrome (obsessional symptoms in 11–80%)).

Appropriate biological/physical treatments include antidepressants which increase 5HT neurotransmission (clomipramine, SSRIs), and antipsychotics if the patient is resistant to antidepressant alone. Psychosurgery may be effective for the most severely disabled patients.

Cognitive behaviour therapy (CBT) includes habituation training and thought stopping (obsessions), and exposure with response prevention (compulsions).

5. UNEXPLAINED PHYSICAL SYMPTOMS

Within a general hospital or general practice setting psychiatric referral may occur because no organic cause is found for physical symptoms. Somatic symptoms may be a manifestation of depression, anxiety or schizophrenia (rare) and these diagnoses should be excluded before a diagnosis of somatoform, conversion or fictitious disorder is made.

5.1 Somatoform disorders

In this group of disorders there is repeated presentation of physical symptoms accompanied by persistent requests for medical investigations. If physical disorders are present, they do not explain the nature or extent of symptoms. Repeated negative findings and reassurance have little effect and patients usually refute the possibility of psychological causation.

Somatization disorder

- More than two years of multiple physical *symptoms* without adequate explanation
- Persistent refusal to accept advice or reassurance re: no physical explanation
- Functional impairment due to nature of symptoms and resulting behaviour
- Affects women much more often than men
- Tend to excessive drug use.

Particularly common symptoms include gastrointestinal sensations (pain, belching, vomiting, nausea), abnormal skin sensations (itching, burning, tingling) and sexual and menstrual complaints.

Hypochondriacal disorder

- Persistent belief in presence of at least one serious physical *illness* despite repeated negative investigations
- Typical illnesses include cancer, AIDS
- Persistent refusal to accept advice or reassurance
- Fear of drugs and side effects.

The principles of treatment for somatoform disorders are to exclude an organic basis for the complaint, acknowledge that the symptoms exist and then educate the patient about basic physiology and elicit and challenge the assumptions leading from the symptoms. Self-monitoring (by keeping a diary) can assist with the re-attribution of physical experiences.

5.2 Conversion disorder

This is a **rare** cause of unexplained physical symptoms. The theory is that intolerable psychic anxiety is 'converted' to physical symptoms. The extent of 'motivation' or voluntary control is usually hard to assess, but there is a clear alteration or loss in physical function which is usually acute, but may be chronic.

Such 'psychogenic' symptoms usually follow an unresolved stressful event and their existence may lead to a reduction in psychological distress ('primary gain') and to a resolution of the stressful event. Although some patients experience the 'secondary gain' of attention from others, others may be indifferent to their loss of function ('la belle indifference'). Isolated conversion symptoms may occur in schizophrenia or depression.

Convincing evidence of psychological causation may be difficult to find. It is vital to exercise caution in making a diagnosis of conversion disorder, especially in the presence of a known CNS or peripheral nervous system disorder.

Treatment involves detection of the underlying conflict and may require hypnosis/abreaction.

5.3 Factitious disorder

Also known as Munchausen's syndrome, this is the intentional production of physical or psychological symptoms. It is usually associated with severe personality disorder and treatment is extremely difficult.

6. EATING DISORDERS

Anorexia nervosa and bulimia nervosa share many clinical features and patients may satisfy criteria for anorexia or bulimia at different stages of their illness. Eating disorders are much more common in women, but 5–10% of cases of anorexia are male.

Anorexia nervosa is largely restricted to social groups in which thinness is coveted. Presentation is usually in adolescence. The long term outcome is poor, with only 20% making a full recovery and long term mortality is around 15–20%.

Bulimia nervosa has a prevalence in young women of 1–2% and usually presents in the 20s. About one-third of patients have a previous history of anorexia. Outcome is highly variable but is worse if there is preceding anorexia or if the bulimia is part of a multi-impulsive personality disorder.

Differentiation of eating disorders

	Anorexia nervosa (restricting subtype)	Anorexia nervosa (bulimic subtype)	Bulimia nervosa
'Nervosa' psychopathology	Yes	Yes	Yes
Behaviour to control weight	Yes	Yes	Yes
Bulimic episodes	No	Yes	Yes
Low weight (<15% average body weight)	Yes	Yes	No
Amenorrhoea	Yes	Yes	Possible

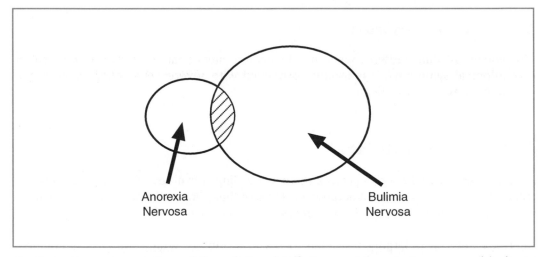

Anorexia Nervosa

Bulimia Nervosa

A schematic representation of the relationship between anorexia nervosa and bulimia nervosa. In clinical practice a diagnosis of bulimia is restricted to those with greater than average body weight. Those in the overlap are considered to have anorexia, bulimic subtype.

6.1 Anorexia nervosa and bulimia nervosa: diagnostic criteria

Anorexia nervosa: diagnostic criteria

Loss of (>15%) normal body weight which is self-induced.

- Extreme avoidance of foods considered 'fattening'
- Aggravated by self-induced vomiting, purging or exercise.

A specific psychopathology ('nervosa'):

- Overvalued idea that fatness is a dreadful state
- Extremely harsh definition of fatness
- Will not let weight rise above very low threshold.

Specific endocrine associations:

- Female
  amenorrhoea
  delayed puberty if very young (primary amenorrhoea)
- Male
  loss of sexual interest and potency
  delayed puberty if very young; arrest of secondary sexual characteristics.

Bulimia nervosa: diagnostic criteria

Key features:

- Episodes of binge eating
- Persistent preoccupation with eating
- Irresistible craving for food.

- **Attempts to counteract the 'fattening' effects of food**

  Self-induced vomiting
  Periods of starvation
  Purgative and diuretic abuse
  Abuse of appetite suppressants
  Abuse of thyroid hormones
  Neglect to use insulin (diabetics)

- **Specific psychopathology ('nervosa')**

  Morbid fear of fatness
  Sharply defined weight threshold
  ± earlier episode of anorexia nervosa

6.2 Medical complications of anorexia nervosa

These are mostly physiological adaptations to starvation and usually revert with refeeding.

Medical complications of anorexia nervosa

- **Cardiovascular**
  Bradycardia (87%)
  Hypotension (85%)
  Ventricular arrhythmias
  ECG abnormalities
  Congestive cardiac failure

- **Gastroenterological**
  Eroded dental enamel/caries
    (secondary to vomiting)
  Enlarged salivary glands (secondary
    to vomiting)
  Oesophagitis
  Erosions
  Ulcers
  Oesophageal rupture
  Acute gastric dilatation with refeeding
  Decreased gastric emptying
  Constipation
  Duodenal dilatation
  Irritable bowel syndrome
  Melanosis coli (secondary to laxatives)

- **Renal**
  Decreased GFR
  Decreased concentration ability
  Hypokalaemic nephropathy
  Pre-renal uraemia

- **Haematological**
  Pancytopenia
  Hypoplastic marrow
  Low plasma proteins

- **Musculoskeletal**
  Early onset leads to shorter stature
  Osteoporosis
  Pathological fractures
  Proximal myopatht
  Cramps
  Tetany
  Muscle weakness

- **Metabolic**
  Hypothermia and dehydration
  Electrolyte disturbance
    (especially hypokalaemia)
  Hypercholesterolaemia and
    carotinaemia
  Hypoglycaemia and raised
    liver enzymes

- **Neurological**
  Reversible brain atrophy
    (on CT scan)
  Abnormal EEG and seizures

- **Endocrine**
  Low FSH, LH, oestrogens,
    testosterone
  Low T_3
  Raised cortisol and positive
    dexamethasone suppression test
  Raised GH

6.3 Principles of treatment

Anorexia nervosa   **Bulimia nervosa**

Biological/physical treatments

- Restoration of weight as an inpatient, ideally in a specialist eating disorder unit
- Drugs have a limited place in management
- Enteral/parenteral nutrition is rarely indicated

- Selective serotonin re-uptake inhibitor (SSRI) may be useful
- Reduce bingeing and self-induced vomiting
- Effect not related to presence of depressive symptoms

Psychological treatments

- Supportive psychotherapy
- Family therapy
- Cognitive behaviour therapy

- Cognitive behaviour therapy
- Cognitive analytic therapy
- Self-help manuals

7. DELIBERATE SELF-HARM

A good deal is known about the epidemiology of and risk factors for deliberate self-harm, both fatal and non-fatal. These are presented in the table overleaf. A decrease in the rate of suicide, particularly in patients with mental illness, is a target of the *'Health of the Nation'* policy.

523

Features of suicide and non-fatal self-harm

	Suicide	Non-fatal self-harm
Annual incidence in UK	1/10,000 (5000 total)	20–30/10,000
Sex	M:F = 3:1	F > M
Age	Young males, late middle age	Young < 35 years
Socioeconomic class	I,V	IV,V
Childhood	Parental death	Broken home
Physical health	Chronic or terminal illness, handicapped, pain	Nil specific
Mental illness	Depression ~ 60% Alcoholism ~ 20%	Depression ~ 10%
Pre-morbid personality	Usually good	Antisocial, borderline personality disorder
Precipitants	Guilt, hopelessness	Situational
Setting	Premeditated, alone, warnings	Impulsive, other present

The incidence of completed suicide is reduced during wartime and in certain religious groups (e.g. Roman Catholics). The incidence is increased in springtime, amongst those working in certain high-risk occupations, such as farmers and doctors, and amongst those who are unemployed, have a family history of suicide and have the means available to carry it out (i.e. weapons/drugs).

- Approximately 20% of non-fatal deliberate self-harm cases repeat within one year.
- 1–2% per year of non-fatal deliberate self-harm cases will lead to suicide within one year.
- 10–20% eventually commit suicide.

Prevention of the above involves the identification and treatment of mental illness, increased awareness among GPs and in hospital staff, and the removal of the means to commit suicide (firearms restrictions, limit sales of paracetamol, catalytic converters).

8. ORGANIC PSYCHIATRY

Organic brain disorders can mimic any other functional mental disorder. Features that raise the possibility of an organic disorder include visual perceptual abnormalities (illusions or hallucinations), cognitive deficit clearly preceding other symptoms, neurological signs, fluctuating symptoms.

8.1 Acute organic brain syndrome

This is also known as acute confusional state, or delirium. The young and the elderly are especially vulnerable. A breakdown of the blood–brain barrier is implicated. There are multiple possible aetiologies, both intra- and extra-cranial.

Causes of acute organic brain syndrome

- **Extra-cranial**
  Hypoxia (cardiac, respiratory)
  Infection (respiratory, urinary, septicaemia)
  Metabolic (electrolyte imbalance, uraemia, hepatic encephalopathy porphyria, hypoglycaemia)
  Hypovitaminosis (thiamine B12)
  Endocrine (hypo/hyperthyroid, hypo/hyperparathyroid, diabetes, Addison's/Cushing's, hypopituitarism)
  Toxic (alcohol intoxication, alcohol withdrawal, all other illicit drugs, prescribed drugs (many), heavy metals)

- **Intra-cranial**
  Trauma (head injury)
  Infection (meningitis, encephalitis)
  Vascular disease (TIA/stroke, hypersensitive encephalopathy, subarachnoid haemorrhage)
  Space occupying lesion (tumour, abscess, subdural haemorrhage)
  Epilepsy

Characteristic clinical features of acute organic brain syndrome

- Clouding of consciousness
- Disorientation

- Poor attention (digit span)
- Memory deficits
- Disturbed behaviour (especially at night)
- Mood abnormalities
- Disordered speech and thinking
- Abnormal perceptions (especially visual)
- Abnormal beliefs.

EEG tests for this condition are sensitive but not specific; results may be abnormal (slowing of rhythm, low voltage trace) in the absence of clear cognitive abnormalities.

Principles of treatment are:

- Specific — to treat cause of confusional state
- General — to optimize immediate environment and reduce disorientation
- Symptomatic — careful use of sedatives if necessary.

8.2 Dementia

Dementia is the global deterioration of higher mental functioning. Characteristic clinical features of dementia include coarsened personality with aggression or disinhibition, but clear consciousness (c.f. acute confusional state). Delusions and hallucinations may occur with mild to moderate disease severity.

Aetiology:

- Alzheimer's disease ~ 50%
- Lewy body dementia ~ 20%
- Vascular dementia (multi-infarct dementia) ~ 20%.

For differentiation of dementia from depression, see section 2.4

Features of Alzheimer's disease and multi-infarct dementia

Clinical feature	Alzheimer's	Multi-infarct dementia
Age of onset	70–90 years	60–80 years
Sex	F > M	M > F
Family history	FAD* less than 1%	–
Aetiology	Genetic + environmental	Embolic
Onset	Insidious	Acute
Presenting symptoms	Cognitive	Emotional
Cognitive impairment	Diffuse	Patchy
Insight	Early loss	Preserved
Personality	Early loss	Preserved
Course of progression	Relentless	Stepwise
Focal neurological signs	Unusual	Common
Previous CVA or TIA	–	+ + +
Hypertension	–	+ + +
Associated ischaemic heart disease	–	+ + +
Seizures	+	+ + +
Most common cause of death	Infection	Ischaemic heart disease
Time to death from diagnosis	2–5 years	4–5 years

*FAD = familial Alzheimer's disease

8.3 Physical illnesses particularly associated with mental disorders

Physical illnesses particularly associated with mental disorders

Intracranial
- Parkinson's disease (depression, dementia)
- Huntingdon's disease (depression, suicide, dementia)
- Neurosyphilis (dementia, depression, grandiosity)
- Epilepsy (depression, psychosis)
- Multiple sclerosis (depression, elation, dementia)
- Wilson's disease (affective disorder, aggression, cognitive impairment)
- Prion diseases (dementia)
- Brain tumour (location determines early symptoms)

Systemic
- Systemic lupus erythematosus (SLE) (acute confusional state, affective or schizophreniform psychosis) may be further complicated by effect of steroids
- Vitamin deficiency (b1: Wernick–Korsakoff syndrome; B1: acute confusional state, depression)
- Porphyria (especially AIP): (acute confusional state, depression, paranoid psychosis)
- Endocrine
  Cushing's syndrome — psychiatric disturbance in about 50% of hospital cases, depression, euphoria, confusion, paranoid psychoses, cognitive dysfunction in 66%
  Addison's disease — psychiatric features in virtually 100%, depression, withdrawal, apathy, memory difficulties in up to 75%
  Hyperthyroidism — psychological disturbance in 100%, restlessness, agitation, confusional state (rare), psychosis (very rare)
  Hypothyroidism — mental symptoms universal at presentation, lethargy, cognitive slowing, apathy > depression, irritability, confusional state, dementia, affective or schizophreniform psychosis (very rare)

8.4 Drug-induced mental disorders

Many drugs can lead to psychiatric conditions.

Anxiety	**Depression**	**Paranoid psychosis**
Amphetamines	Reserpine	Amphetamines
Cocaine	Beta-blockers	LSD
Alcohol	Calcium antagonists	Cocaine
Phenylcyclidine	Oral contraceptive pill	Marijuana
	Corticosteroids	
	Alcohol	

9. ALCOHOL ABUSE

The complications of alcohol are wide-ranging and cross social, psychological and neuropsychiatric domains. General medical problems are not covered here.

9.1 Social consequences of alcohol abuse

- Family/marital problems
- Incest
- Absenteeism from work
- Accidents (major factor in ≥10% of road traffic accidents)
- Crime (associated with acute abuse)
- Vagrancy.

9.2 Acute withdrawal consequences

Acute withdrawal causes a wide spectrum of symptoms. The fully developed syndrome is known as delirium tremens.

Delirium tremens

- **Definition of full syndrome**
  Vivid hallucinations (often visual)
  Delusions
  Profound confusional state
  Tremor
  Agitation
  Sleeplessness
  Autonomic overactivity
    (inc. pyrexia)

- **Other clinical features**
  Associated trauma or infection in 50%
  Prodromal features may occur
  Onset usually after 72 hours of abstinence
  Visual illusions/hallucinations prominent
  Duration ≤3 days in majority
  Hypokalaemia common
    ± hypomagnesaemia
  Mortality up to 5%

Treatment

- In-patient
- Rehydration, antibiotics, vitamins, sedation
- Sedative drugs which facilitate GABAergic neurotransmission (chlormethiazole oral/i.v. , chlordiazepoxide — avoid phenothiazines: risk of seizure (haloperidol if antipsychotic required)).

9.3 Psychological consequences of alcohol abuse

These include dysphoric mood, pathological jealousy (Othello syndrome) and sexual problems (impotence, decreased libido). Other symptoms are alcoholic hallucinosis and alcohol dependence syndrome.

Alcohol dependence syndrome — seven key features

Sense of compulsion to drink
Stereotyped pattern of drinking
Prominent drink seeking behaviour
Increased tolerance to alcohol
Repeated withdrawal symptoms
Relief drinking to avoid withdrawal symptoms
Reinstatement after abstinence

Suicide is more common amongst this group (16% with full dependence syndrome) as is parasuicide (used acutely by 35%).

9.4 Neuropsychiatric consequences of alcohol abuse

The most likely neuropsychiatric consequences of alcohol abuse are Wernicke's encephalopathy and Korsakoff's syndrome/psychosis. This group is also more likely to suffer seizures, head injury and dementia.

Rarer conditions associated with alcohol abuse include cerebellar degeneration, central pontine myelinosis and Marchiafava–Bignami disease (demyelination of the corpus callosum, optic tracts and cerebral peduncles).

Wernicke's encephalopathy (WE)

A disorder of acute onset featuring:

- Nystagmus
- Abducens and conjugate gaze palsies (96%)
- Ataxia of gait (87%)
- Global confusional state (90%).

It is caused by thiamine deficiency, most commonly secondary to alcoholism, but more rarely due to:

- Carcinoma of the stomach
- Toxaemia
- Pregnancy
- Persistent vomiting
- Dietary deficiency.

Pathology:

- Macroscopic: petechial haemorrhages
- Microscopic: dilatation and proliferation of capillaries, small haemorrhages, pale staining parenchyma, reactive change in astrocytes and microglia, neurons relatively spared.

Structures affected:

- Mamillary bodies
- Walls of IIIrd ventricle
- Floor of IVth ventricle
- Periaqueductal grey matter
- Certain thalamic nuclei — med dorsal, anteromedial, pulvinar
- Brain stem
- Cerebellum anterior lobe/vermis
- Cortical lesions rarely seen.

Treatment: Parenteral thiamine. Up to 80% of sufferers go on to develop Korsakoff's syndrome.

Korsakoff's syndrome

A marked memory disorder with good preservation of other cognitive functions.

Clinical features:

- Chronic disorder usually following Wernicke's encephalopathy
- Inability to consolidate new information
- Retrograde amnesia of days/years
- Patchy preservation of long term memory
- Confabulation not complaints of poor memory
- Apathy
- Lack of insight.

Pathology: as for Wernicke's encephalopathy.

Treatment: thiamine. There may be a response in only 20% of sufferers.

10. SLEEP DISORDERS

10.1 Normal sleep

In normal sleep, drowsiness first gives way to increasingly deep non-REM (Rapid Eye Movement) sleep. The first REM period occurs after 50–90 minutes and lasts for 5–10 minutes. The cycle repeats at approximately 90-minute intervals so that there are 4–6 REM periods each night. In total, REM occupies 20–25% of a night's sleep.

REM sleep	Non-REM sleep
Asynchronous, mixed frequency EEG	EEG synchronous, with sleep spindles,
Bursts of rapid conjugate eye movements	K-complexes, generalized slowing with
Prominent autonomic changes —	delta waves
increased heart rate, blood pressure —	Four stages recognized; stages 3 and 4
penile tumescence	characterized as 'slow wave' sleep
Decreased muscle tone	
Extensor plantar responses may occur	

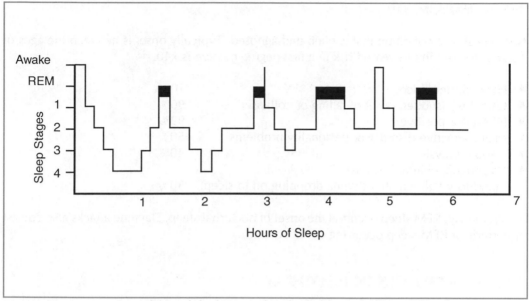

Pictorial representation of the adult sleep cycle. Shaded areas indicate REM sleep.

10.2 Insomnia

Insomnia is seen in a wide range of psychiatric disorders. Psychiatric disorders may account for up to 36% of patients with insomnia. Paradoxically sleep deprivation may be used to treat depression and may precipitate mania.

The following table describes the pattern of insomnia in various disorders.

Disorder	Pattern of insomnia
Major depression	Initial and late insomnia (early morning waking)
Mania	in up to 80%
Generalized anxiety disorder	Globally reduced sleep
Post-traumatic stress disorder	Initial and middle insomnia
Acute confusional state	Intrusive nightmares about trauma
	Disturbed sleep cycle

10.3 Narcolepsy

Narcolepsy is a condition that is often undiagnosed. Typically onset is between the ages of 10 and 20, and the increased risk in a first-degree relative is x40.

- Hypersomnolence   100%
- Cataplexy (sudden onset of falling or collapse)   90%
- HLA-DR2 positive   99%
- Major affective disorder or personality problems   50%
- Sleep paralysis   40%
- Hypnogogic hallucinations
    (auditory hallucinations while dropping off to sleep)   30%

In narcolepsy, REM sleep occurs at the **onset** of nocturnal sleep. Daytime attacks also consist of periods of REM sleep occurring out of context.

11. TREATMENTS IN PSYCHIATRY

11.1 Antipsychotics

Antipsychotics are indicated in schizophrenia, mania, other paranoid psychoses and psychotic depression.

Antipsychotics are most effective against the 'positive' symptoms of schizophrenia. They have an immediate sedative action but the antipsychotic action may be delayed for three weeks. They play an important role in preventing relapse. 'Atypical' antipsychotics have preferable side effect profiles, and clozapine is effective in treatment-resistant schizophrenia.

Class	Example	Side effects*
Phenothiazines	chlorpromazine, thioridazine	**Extrapyramidal** — acute dystonia, Parkinsonism, akathisia, tardive dyskinesia
Butyrophenones	haloperidol droperidol	**Anticholinergic** — dry mouth, constipation etc. **Antiadrenergic** — postural hypotension
Thioxanthenes	flupenthixol clopixol	**Antihistaminergic** — sedation **Endocrine** — hyperprolactinaemia, photosensitivity (especially phenothiazines) **Lowered seizure threshold** **Neuroleptic** malignant syndrome
Atypical	clozapine olanzapine sertindole risperidone	Blood dyscrasia (clozapine) Other side effects vary from drug to drug

*Seen with all three classes of drug.

11.2 Antidepressants

Antidepressants are indicated in depressive illness, anxiety disorders (especially panic disorder and phobic disorders) and obsessional illness.

In depressive illness, antidepressants have a response rate of around 65%, with a delay in action of between 10 days and 6 weeks. The presence of 'biological' symptoms can help in the prediction of response. Antidepressants also play a prophylactic role in recurrent depressive disorders.

Drugs which inhibit 5HT reuptake are particularly useful in obsessional illness.

Class	Example	Side-effects
Tricyclic	Amitriptyline Imipramine Clomipramine	Anticholinergic — dry mouth, constipation etc. Antiadrenergic — postural hypotension Antihistaminergic — sedation Weight gain Lower seizure threshold Cardiac arrhythmias
SSRI*	Citalopram Fluoxetine Fluvoxamine Paroxetine Sertraline	Nausea Sexual dysfunction Headache Sleep disturbance (early) Increased anxiety (early)
SNRI**	Venlafaxine	Nausea Hypertension
MAOI	Phenelzine	Anticholinergic Antiadrenergic Hypertensive reaction with tyramine-containing foods Important drug interactions
RIMA***	Moclobemide	Potential tyramine interaction

*SSRI = Selective serotonin re-uptake inhibitor.
**SNRI = Selective noradrenaline re-uptake inhibitor.
***RIMA = Reversible inhibitor of monoamine oxidase A.

The side-effects and toxicity of lithium are described in detail in Chapter 2, *Clinical Pharmacology, Toxicology and Poisoning.*

11.3 Benzodiazepines

Benzodiazepines are only indicated for the short term relief of severe, disabling anxiety. The BNF recommends only 2–4 weeks of use. They are not indicated for 'mild' anxiety but can be used as adjunctive treatment for anxiety, agitation and behavioural disturbance in acute psychosis. They are only indicated for insomnia if the condition is severe, disabling or subjecting the subject to extreme distress.

Longer half-life	Diazepam equivalent*	Half-life (hours)	Shorter half-life	Diazepam equivalent	Half-life (hours)
Diazepam	5 mg	20–90	Lorazepam	0.5 mg	8–24
Chlordiaze- poxide	15 mg	20–90**	Oxazepam	15 mg	6–28
			Temazepam	10 mg	6–10
Nitrazepam	5 mg	16–40	Alprazolam	–	6–16
Chlorazepate	–	50–100			
Flurazepam	–	50–100			

*Approximate equivalent doses to diazepam 5 mg.
**Includes active metabolites.

Benzodiazepine withdrawal syndrome may not develop for up to three weeks, but can occur within a few hours for short-acting drugs. Symptoms include insomnia, perspiration, anxiety, tinnitus, decreased appetite, decreased weight, perceptual disturbances and tremor.

The recommended withdrawal regime involves transferring the patient to an equivalent dose of diazepam, preferably taken at night. Ideally the dose should be decreased by approximately 1/8 of the daily dose every two weeks. If withdrawal symptoms occur, the dose is maintained until symptoms improve.

11.4 Electroconvulsive therapy (ECT)

ECT is indicated in depression to treat psychotic symptoms, stupor and elderly (especially agitated) patients. 'Biological' features help predict the likely response. It is also indicated to treat catatonia associated with schizophrenia and in treatment-resistant cases of mania.

Side effects of ECT

- **Early**
  Headache
  Temporary confusion
  Impaired short term memory
    (bilateral ECT worse than unilateral)
  (Rare) fractures, dislocation,
    fat embolism

- **Late (6–9 months)**
  No memory impairment detected
  Subjective impairment

- **Contraindications to ECT**: raised intra-cranial pressure, cardiac < 2 years, other cardiac disease, pulmonary disease, history of CVA.

ECT has a mortality rate of 3–5 deaths per 100,000 (c.f. minor surgery + general anaesthesia). The mortality rate of untreated major depression is 10%.

11.5 The psychotherapies

Type	Frequency	No. of sessions	Indications
Counselling	Weekly–monthly	6–12	Mild depression Anxiety Bereavement
Cognitive behavioural	Weekly	8–12	Depression Anxiety Somatoform disorder Eating disorders
Behavioural	Weekly	6–12	Phobias Anxiety Obsessional illness Sexual dysfunction
Psychoanalytic	1–5/week	50–indefinite	Neurosis Personality disorders Psychosexual
Group	Weekly	6–12	Anxiety Substance misuse Eating disorders

Chapter 17
Respiratory Medicine

CONTENTS

1. **Lung anatomy and physiology** 541
   1.1 Ventilation
   1.2 Perfusion
   1.3 Control of respiration
   1.4 Pulmonary function tests (PFTs)
   1.5 Gas transfer
   1.6 Adaptation to high altitude

2. **Diseases of large airways** 547
   2.1 Asthma
   2.2 Chronic obstructive pulmonary disease (COPD)
   2.3 Long-term oxygen therapy (LTOT)
   2.4 Respiratory failure
   2.5 Ventilatory support

3. **Lung infections** 555
   3.1 Pneumonia
   3.2 Empyema
   3.3 Tuberculosis
   3.4 Bronchiectasis
   3.5 Cystic fibrosis
   3.6 Aspergillus and the lung

4. **Occupational lung disease** 567
   4.1 Asbestos-related disease
   4.2 Coal-workers' penumoconiosis
   4.3 Silicosis
   4.4 Berylliosis
   4.5 Byssinosis
   4.6 Occupational asthma
   4.7 Extrinsic allergic alveolitis

5. **Tumours**   **570**
    5.1   Lung cancer
    5.2   Mesothelioma

6. **Granulomatous lung disease and pulmonary fibrosis**   **574**
    6.1   Sarcoidosis
    6.2   Histiocytosis
    6.3   Pulmonary fibrosis

7. **Pulmonary vasculitis and eosinophilia**   **579**
    7.1   Wegener's granulomatosis
    7.2   Churg–Strauss syndrome
    7.3   Polyarteritis and Henoch–Schönlein vasculitis
    7.4   Connective tissue disorders
    7.5   Pulmonary eosinophilia

8. **Miscellaneous respiratory disorders**   **581**
    8.1   Pleural effusion
    8.2   Obstructive sleep apnoea (OSA)
    8.3   Adult respiratory distress syndrome (ARDS)
    8.4   Rare lung disorders

Respiratory Medicine

1. LUNG ANATOMY AND PHYSIOLOGY

The human lung is composed of approximately 300 million alveoli each around 1/3 mm in diameter. Gas exchange takes place in the alveoli, and air is transported to these via a series of conducting airways. It is warmed and humidified in the upper airways and transported through the trachea, main bronchi, lobar and segmental bronchi to the terminal bronchioles, the smallest of the conducting tubes. These airways take no part in gas exchange and constitute the anatomical dead space (approximately 150 ml). The terminal bronchioles lead to the respiratory bronchioles which have alveoli budding from their walls. Lung tissue distal to the terminal bronchiole forms the primary lobule.

1.1 Ventilation

The most important muscle of inspiration is the diaphragm, a muscular dome which moves downwards on inspiration. The external intercostal muscles assist inspiration by moving the ribs upwards and forwards in a 'bucket-handle' movement.

- The accessory muscles of respiration include the scalene muscles, which elevate the first two ribs, and the sternocleidomastoids, which elevate the sternum; these are not used during quiet breathing.
- Expiration is passive during quiet breathing.
- During exercise, expiration becomes active and the internal intercostal muscles and the muscles of the anterior abdominal wall are utilized.
- The greatest ventilation is achieved at the lung bases and this is matched by increased perfusion in these areas.

Normal lung is very compliant. **Compliance** is reduced by pulmonary venous engorgement and alveolar oedema and in areas of atelectasis. Surfactant, secreted by type 2 alveolar epithelial cells, substantially lowers the surface tension of the alveolar lining fluid, increasing lung compliance and promoting alveolar stability. Lack of surfactant leads to respiratory distress syndrome.

Resistance to airflow is related to the radius of the airway, but the greatest overall resistance to flow occurs in medium-sized bronchi. Airway calibre is influenced by lung volume; at low lung volumes small airways may close completely leading to areas of atelectasis, particularly at the lung bases.

1.2 Perfusion

The pulmonary vessels form a low pressure system conducting deoxygenated blood from the pulmonary arteries to the alveoli where they form a dense capillary network. The pulmonary arteries have thin walls with very little smooth muscle; the mean pulmonary artery pressure is 15 mmHg.

- Pulmonary vascular resistance is 1/10 systemic vascular resistance.
- Hypoxic vasoconstriction refers to contraction of smooth muscle in the walls of the small arterioles in a hypoxic region of lung; this helps to divert blood away from areas with poor ventilation so maintaining ventilation and perfusion matching.

1.3 Control of respiration

The respiratory centre comprises a poorly defined collection of neurones in the pons and medulla; to a certain extent, the cortex can override the function of the respiratory centre. Chemoreceptors are crucial to the control of respiration, and these may be **central** or **peripheral**:

- **Central chemoreceptors** are located on the ventral surface of the medulla. They respond to increased hydrogen ion concentration in the CSF, generated by increased pCO_2 in the blood.
- **Peripheral chemoreceptors** are located in the carotid bodies (at the bifurcation of the common carotid arteries) and the aortic bodies (near the aortic arch); they respond to hypoxaemia, hypercapnia and pH changes.

In people with normal respiratory function the most important factor for control of ventilation is the pCO_2 which is maintained to within 3 mmHg of baseline (normal range 35–45 mmHg). However, in patients with severe lung disease, chronic CO_2 retention develops and the hypoxic drive to ventilation becomes very important.

- Ventilation may increase by 15 times the resting level during severe exercise.
- Cheyne–Stokes respiration is characterized by periods of apnoea separated by periods of hyperventilation; it occurs in severe heart failure or brain damage, and at altitude.

1.4 Pulmonary function tests (PFTs)

Spirometry

- FEV_1 refers to the volume of gas expired in the first second of a forced expiration
- FVC refers to the total volume of gas expired on forced expiration
- The normal ratio of FEV_1/FVC is 70–80%

- Reduction in FEV_1 with a preserved FVC occurs in airways obstruction (e.g. asthma or COPD)
- Restriction refers to a reduction in FVC with a preserved FEV_1/FVC ratio and occurs in conditions such as pulmonary fibrosis.

Flow volume loops

A flow volume loop is produced by plotting flow on the y axis against volume on the x axis.

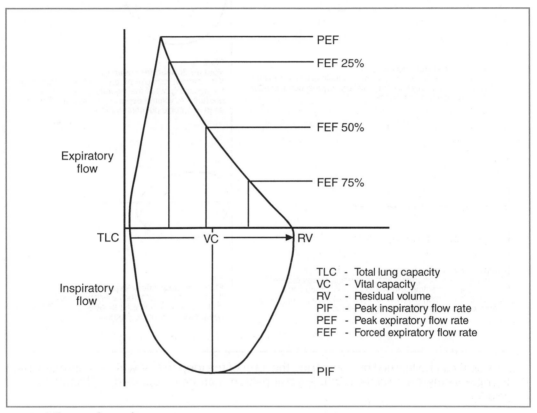

Typical flow volume loop

If a subject inspires rapidly from residual volume (RV) to total lung capacity (TLC) and then exhales as hard as possible back to residual volume, then a record can be made of the maximum flow volume loop. This loop shows that expiratory flow rises very rapidly to a maximum value, but then declines over the rest of expiration. During the early part of a forced expiration the maximum effort-dependent flow rate is achieved within 0.1 s, but the rise in transmural pressure leads to the airways being compressed and therefore to the flow rate being reduced. The flow rate is then said to be effort-independent.

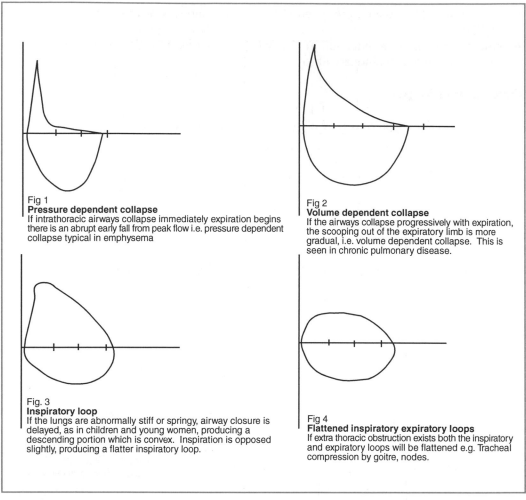

Fig 1
Pressure dependent collapse
If intrathoracic airways collapse immediately expiration begins there is an abrupt early fall from peak flow i.e. pressure dependent collapse typical in emphysema

Fig 2
Volume dependent collapse
If the airways collapse progressively with expiration, the scooping out of the expiratory limb is more gradual, i.e. volume dependent collapse. This is seen in chronic pulmonary disease.

Fig. 3
Inspiratory loop
If the lungs are abnormally stiff or springy, airway closure is delayed, as in children and young women, producing a descending portion which is convex. Inspiration is opposed slightly, producing a flatter inspiratory loop.

Fig 4
Flattened inspiratory expiratory loops
If extra thoracic obstruction exists both the inspiratory and expiratory loops will be flattened e.g. Tracheal compression by goitre, nodes.

A great deal can be learned by comparing the form of the loop to that which is normally seen ('a triangle sitting on a semi-circle'). Several patterns can be recognized, reflecting various disorders.

Lung volumes

- Tidal volume, inspiratory and expiratory reserve volumes and vital capacity can all be measured by use of a spirometer.
- Total lung capacity, residual volume and functional residual capacity can be measured using a helium dilution method, nitrogen washout or body box.

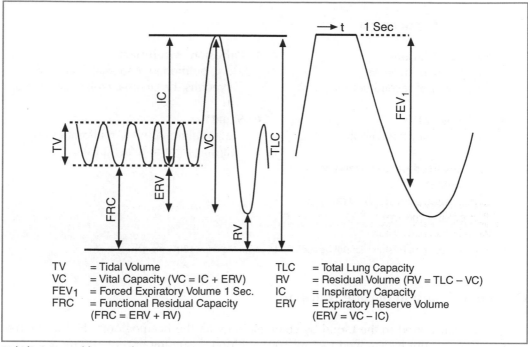

TV   = Tidal Volume
VC   = Vital Capacity (VC = IC + ERV)
FEV_1 = Forced Expiratory Volume 1 Sec.
FRC = Functional Residual Capacity
       (FRC = ERV + RV)

TLC = Total Lung Capacity
RV   = Residual Volume (RV = TLC – VC)
IC   = Inspiratory Capacity
ERV = Expiratory Reserve Volume
      (ERV = VC – IC)

Subdivision of lung volume

1.5 Gas transfer

Transfer of carbon monoxide is solely limited by diffusion and is used to measure gas transfer. Either a single breath hold or a steady state method can be used. Results are expressed both as total gas transfer (DLCO) or gas transfer corrected for lung volume (KCO, i.e. KCO = DLCO/VA where VA is alveolar volume).

Causes of hypoxaemia

- **Hypoventilation**
  (e.g. opiate overdose,
  paralysis of respiratory muscles)

- **V/Q mismatch**
  (e.g. pulmonary embolus)

- **Low inspired partial pressure
  of oxygen**
  (e.g. high altitude, breathing a
  hypoxic mixture)

- **Diffusion impairment**
  (e.g. pulmonary oedema, fibrosing
  alveolitis, bronchioalveolar carcinoma)

- **Shunt***
  (e.g. pulmonary A-V malformations,
  cardiac right to left shunts)

*Hypoxaemia caused by shunt cannot be abolished by administering 100% oxygen.

Oxygen and carbon dioxide transport

Oxygen is transported in the blood by combination with the haemoglobin (Hb) in the red cells. A tiny amount is dissolved (0.3 ml/100 ml blood, assuming pO_2 of 100 mmHg). The oxyhaemoglobin dissociation curve is sigmoidal in shape and the amount of oxygen carried by the Hb increases rapidly up to a pO_2 of around 50 mmHg; above this level the curve becomes much flatter.

- The curve is **shifted to the right** by high temperature, acidosis, increased pCO_2 and increased levels of 2,3-diphosphoglycerate (2, 3-DPG); this encourages offloading of oxygen to the tissues
- The curve is **shifted to the left** by changes opposite to those above, and by carboxyhaemoglobin and fetal haemoglobin.

Carbon dioxide is transported in the blood as bicarbonate, in combination with proteins as carbamino compounds, and it is also dissolved in plasma. Carbon dioxide is 20 times more soluble than oxygen and about 10% of all CO_2 is dissolved. CO_2 diffuses into red blood cells where carbonic anhydrase facilitates the formation of carbonic acid which dissociates into bicarbonate and hydrogen ions. Bicarbonate diffuses out of the cell and chloride moves in to maintain electrical neutrality.

Acid-base control

The normal pH of arterial blood is 7.35–7.45. Blood pH is closely regulated and variation outside this pH range results in compensation either by the lung or the kidney to return pH to normal. Failure to excrete CO_2 normally results in a respiratory acidosis; this is usually due to hypoventilation. Hyperventilation causes lowering of the pCO_2 and alkalosis.

pH can also be altered by metabolic disturbance. Metabolic acidosis and alkalosis are considered in Chapter 12, *Metabolic Diseases*. Mixed respiratory and metabolic acid-base disturbances are common.

1.6 Adaptation to high altitude

The barometric pressure decreases with altitude; at 18,000 feet it is half the normal 760 mmHg. Hyperventilation, due to hypoxic stimulation of peripheral chemoreceptors, is an early response to altitude. The respiratory alkalosis produced is corrected by renal excretion of bicarbonate.

- Hypoxaemia stimulates the release of erythropoietin from the kidney, and the resultant polycythaemia allows increased carriage of oxygen by arterial blood.
- There is an increased production of 2,3-DPG, which shifts the oxygen dissociation curve to the right, allowing better offloading of oxygen to the tissues.
- Hypoxic vasoconstriction increases pulmonary artery pressure causing right ventricular hypertrophy. Pulmonary hypertension is sometimes associated with pulmonary oedema — altitude sickness.

2. DISEASES OF LARGE AIRWAYS

2.1 Asthma

Asthma is a chronic inflammatory disorder of the airways. In susceptible individuals this inflammation causes symptoms which are usually associated with widespread but variable airflow obstruction that is often reversible either spontaneously or with treatment. There is an increase in airway sensitivity to a variety of stimuli.

The prevalence of asthma has been increasing in recent years, principally among children. Approximately 3.4 million people suffer from asthma in the UK — 1.5 million of these are children. Around 1500 asthma deaths occur annually in the UK.

The development of asthma is almost certainly due to a combination of genetic predisposition and environmental factors. Atopy is strongly associated with asthma. The most important allergens are the house dust mite (*Dermatophagoides pteronyssinus*), dog allergen (found in pelt, dander and saliva), cat allergen (predominantly in sebaceous glands), pollen and moulds.

Asthma attacks may be provoked by the following.

- Exposure to sensitizing agents
- Infection
- Drugs, including aspirin, non-steroidal anti-inflammatory agents, beta-blockers
- Exercise
- Gastro-oesophageal reflux
- Cigarette smoke, fumes, sprays, perfumes etc.
- Failure to comply with medication

In patients with asthma the airways are narrowed by a combination of contraction of bronchiolar smooth muscle, mucosal oedema and mucus plugging. In the early stages changes are reversible; however, in chronic asthma structural changes (including thickening of the basement membrane, goblet cell hyperplasia and hypertrophy of smooth muscle) develop and ultimately lead to irreversible fibrosis of the airways. Asthma is regarded as a complex inflammatory condition and mast cells, eosinophils, macrophages, T-lymphocytes and neutrophils are all involved in the pathogenesis. A variety of inflammatory mediators are released including histamine, leukotrienes, prostaglandins, bradykinin and platelet activating factor (PAF).

Chronic asthma

The hallmark of chronic asthma is variable airflow obstruction. This causes:

- Shortness of breath
- Wheeze
- Cough.

At times the cough may be productive of sputum which may be clear, or yellow/green, due to the presence of eosinophils. The normal diurnal variation in airway calibre is accentuated in asthmatics and symptoms may be worse at night.

Physical signs of asthma

- Hyperinflation of the chest
- Nasal polyps (particularly in aspirin-sensitive asthmatics)
- Wheezing, most marked in expiration
- Atopic eczema

Lung function tests may show:

- Significant (>25%) peak expiratory flow rate (PEFR) variability
- Increased lung volumes
- Significant improvement in PEFR and FEV_1 post-bronchodilator
- Reduced FEV_1
- FEV_1/FVC ratio <70%
- Gas trapping

Diagnosis of asthma

The diagnosis of asthma is often confirmed by diary recordings of PEFR. Challenge tests with histamine or methacholine can be used to assess airways' responsiveness where the diagnosis is unclear. Responsiveness is expressed as the concentration of provoking agent required to decrease the FEV_1 by 20%.

Skin prick tests

Skin prick tests can be use to assess atopy. Many asthmatic subjects make IgE in response to common allergens. A tiny quantity of allergen is introduced into the superficial layers of the dermis and tests are read at 20 minutes. The diameter of the weal is measured in mm, the size of the weal correlating well with bronchial challenge testing. Serum total IgE is commonly raised in asthmatics. Specific IgE may be measured by radio-allergo-sorbent testing (RAST).

Treatment

The mainstay of treatment is inhaled corticosteroid with short acting β-agonists to relieve symptoms. The dose of inhaled steroid should be stepped up until symptoms are controlled, and reduced once adequate control has been achieved. Long-acting β-agonists (e.g. salmeterol or eformoterol) can be added in patients inadequately controlled with a moderate dose of inhaled steroid (≤800 µg/day of beclomethasone dipropionate). Oral theophylline preparations or inhaled cromoglycate are of benefit in some patients. Recently available leucotriene receptor antagonists may be particularly useful for exercise-induced asthma, and in patients with aspirin sensitivity.

By the year 2003 all inhalers will be required to be CFC-free.

Acute severe asthma

Asthma symptoms may worsen acutely necessitating prompt treatment to relieve the attack. An immediate assessment is essential, looking for signs of severity which include the following.

- Speech impairment
- Tachycardia (pulse >115/min)
- Respiratory rate >30/min
- Hypoxaemia
- PEFR <33% predicted

- Fatigue
- Bradycardia (pulse <60/min)
- Silent chest
- Normal or raised pCO_2

Arterial blood gases should be performed if the patient is hypoxic on air (saturations <92%) and a chest X-ray is necessary to exclude pneumothorax.

Management consists of controlled oxygen therapy, nebulized bronchodilators (β-agonists ± ipratropium), steroids and, if infection is considered likely, antibiotics. PEFR should be measured regularly to assess the response to treatment. If there is no improvement with nebulizers, then intravenous infusions of either salbutamol or aminophylline should be used.

If the patient is severely ill, or not improving with treatment, they should be promptly transferred to an Intensive Care Unit.

Allergic bronchopulmonary aspergillosis

Most patients with allergic bronchopulmonary aspergillosis are asthmatics but the condition may occur in non-asthmatics.

The disease is due to sensitivity to *Aspergillus fumigatus* spores mediated by specific IgE and IgG antibodies. The allergic response results in airways becoming obstructed by rubbery mucus plugs containing aspergillus hyphae, mucus and eosinophils; plugs may be expectorated.

- Lobar or segmental collapse of airways occurs
- Fleeting chest X-ray shadows due to intermittent obstruction of airways
- Positive skin-prick tests and RAST to Aspergillus
- May result in proximal bronchiectasis
- Treatment is with oral corticosteroids which may be required long-term.

2.2 Chronic obstructive pulmonary disease (COPD)

COPD is defined as a chronic, slowly progressive disease characterized by airflow obstruction that does not markedly change over several months. Most of the lung function impairment is fixed although some reversibility can be produced by bronchodilator therapy. Long-term prognosis is determined by post-bronchodilator FEV_1.

The diagnosis is made by:

- History of cough, wheeze and shortness of breath
- Reduced FEV_1/FVC ratio.

Causes of COPD

- Smoking (usually a history of at least 20 pack-years)
- Dust exposure
- Alpha-1 antitrypsin deficiency
- Air pollution

COPD is due to a combination of chronic bronchitis and emphysema.

Chronic bronchitis is defined as chronic cough and sputum production for at least 3 months of 2 consecutive years in the absence of other diseases recognized to cause sputum production.

Emphysema is characterized by abnormal, permanent enlargement of the air spaces distal to the terminal bronchioles, accompanied by destruction of their walls without obvious fibrosis. Emphysema may be centriacinar (predominantly affecting the upper lobes and associated with smoking), panacinar, paraseptal or predominantly localized around scars (scar emphysema).

COPD caused > 26,000 deaths in 1992 in England and Wales, accounting for 6.4% of male deaths and 3.9% of female deaths.

Signs of COPD

- Hyperinflation
- Weight loss
- Flapping tremor
- Pursed-lip breathing
- Wheeze
- Central cyanosis
- Cor pulmonale: raised JVP, right ventricular heave, loud P_2, tricuspid regurgitation, peripheral oedema

Investigations

- **PFTs**: FEV_1 <80% predicted, FEV_1/FVC < 70%; patients have large lung volumes and reduced gas transfer factor (KCO) in emphysema.

- **Chest X-ray**: may be normal or show evidence of hyperinflation, bullae or prominent vasculature due to pulmonary hypertension.
- **Arterial blood gases**: may indicate type 1 or type 2 respiratory failure.
- **FBC**: possible polycythaemia.
- **ECG**: may show p pulmonale, right axis deviation, right bundle branch block.
- **Sputum culture**: *Haemophilus influenzae, Streptococcus pneumoniae* or less commonly *Staphylococcus, Moxharella catarrhalis* or Gram-negative organisms.

Treatments available for COPD

- Smoking cessation
- Inhaled anticholinergic drugs
- Inhaled or systemic steroids
- Long-term oxygen therapy (LTOT)
- Lung volume reduction surgery (for patients with severe emphysema)

- Inhaled short-acting β_2-agonists
- Theophyllines
- Diuretics
- Pulmonary rehabilitation
- Transplantation

Treatment of acute exacerbations

Antibiotics are indicated for acute exacerbations if two of the following are present:

- Increased breathlessness
- Increased sputum volume
- Increased sputum purulence.

In addition, short courses of oral steroids and controlled oxygen therapy may be used. Doxapram is only useful if significant acidosis is present (pH < 7.26) and/or hypercapnia and hypoventilation. Non-invasive positive pressure ventilation (NIPPV) via face mask may also be useful for those with hypoventilation, hypercapnia and acidosis.

2.3 Long-term oxygen therapy (LTOT)

Two trials have established the benefit of LTOT. In the MRC trial, oxygen via nasal cannulae was given to raise the pO_2 to 8 kPa (60 mmHg) for at least 15 hours per day compared to patients with COPD receiving conventional therapy. After 3 years of treatment, survival was 50% better in the group receiving oxygen.

The NOTT trial compared 12 and 24 hours of continuous oxygen therapy and was terminated prematurely due to better survival in the group receiving 24-hour therapy.

Patients are eligible for LTOT if they **exhibit all of the following**:

- pO_2 on air <7.3 kPa (55 mmHg)
- Normal or elevated pCO_2
- FEV_1 <1.5 litres
- pO_2 7.3–8 kPa (55–60 mmHg) with evidence of pulmonary hypertension, peripheral oedema or nocturnal hypoxaemia.

Arterial blood gases must be measured when the patient is clinically stable, and on two occasions which are at least 3 weeks apart. pO_2 on oxygen should be >8 kPa without an unacceptable rise in pCO_2. Oxygen should be given via a concentrator for at least 15 hours per day.

Alpha-1 antitrypsin deficiency

Many different phenotypes of alpha-1 antitrypsin are known, the common ones being designated M, S and ZZ. MM confers 100% protease inhibitor activity while the most severe deficiency is produced by ZZ. Panlobular emphysema develops, which is most marked in the basal areas of the lungs. The decline in lung function is accelerated in smokers.

- PFTs show airflow obstruction, large lung volumes and reduced KCO.
- Cirrhosis of the liver is more common, particularly in those of ZZ phenotype.
- Smoking cessation is imperative.
- Trials involving the administration of alpha-1 antitrypsin are being undertaken.
- Lung transplantation may be an option for some patients.
- Genetic counselling should be offered and siblings of index cases should be genetically tested.

2.4 Respiratory failure

Respiratory failure is an inability to maintain adequate oxygenation and carbon dioxide excretion. There are two recognized types of respiratory failure.

- **Type 1** respiratory failure is present when there is hypoxaemia with normal or low levels of carbon dioxide.
- **Type 2** respiratory failure is hypoxaemia with high pCO_2.

Causes of respiratory failure

- **Reduced ventilatory drive**
  Opiate overdosage, brainstem
  injury

- **Mechanical problems**
  Chest trauma causing flail chest,
  severe kyphoscoliosis

- **Alveolar problems**
  Barriers to diffusion
  Pulmonary oedema
  Pulmonary fibrosis
  V/Q mismatch
  Pulmonary embolus
  Shunt (cardiac or pulmonary)
  *Reduced inspired partial pressure
  of oxygen*
  High altitude

- **Neurological conditions
  (affecting chest wall muscles)**
  Guillain–Barré syndrome
  Polio

- **Upper airway obstruction**
  Laryngeal tumour
  Obstructive sleep apnoea

- **Lower airway obstruction**
  Bronchospasm
  Sputum retention

- **Type 1 respiratory failure** may be corrected by increasing the inspired oxygen concentration.
- **Type 2 respiratory failure** may require mechanical ventilatory support. Respiratory stimulants such as doxapram may be useful for those with reduced respiratory drive.

2.5 Ventilatory support

This may be invasive or non-invasive.

Non-invasive positive pressure ventilation

This involves the use of a tightly fitting nasal or full face mask. The technique has been used to provide long-term respiratory support in the community for patients with respiratory failure due to conditions such as severe chest wall deformity or old polio. It is used increasingly to manage episodes of acute respiratory failure due, for example, to exacerbations of COPD as an alternative to (and often more appropriate than) ventilation on the Intensive Care Unit.

Positive pressure ventilation

Conventional ventilation requires access to the airway, either by means of an endotracheal tube or tracheostomy. Indications for positive pressure ventilation include the following.

- Type 2 respiratory failure from any cause
- Paralysis of respiratory muscles (e.g. Guillain–Barré syndrome)
- Multiple organ failure
- Trauma cases, including injury to the chest or cervical spine
- Inability to maintain a clear airway
- Reduced conscious level — Glasgow coma scale < 5
- During and after certain surgical procedures

Ventilation should be considered when there is failure to maintain oxygenation (pO_2 < 8 kPa (60 mmHg)) despite high inspired oxygen concentrations (usually associated with hypercapnia and acidosis). It is often necessary in patients with multiple organ dysfunction associated with sepsis or trauma.

Continuous positive airways pressure (CPAP)

CPAP is delivered through a tightly fitting face mask or it may be used in conjunction with conventional ventilation. It provides a pneumatic splint to the airway and is the treatment of choice for obstructive sleep apnoea. CPAP improves oxygenation in patients requiring high concentrations of oxygen through a conventional mask. It may, however, cause hypotension, the rise in mean intrathoracic pressure inhibiting venous return and reducing cardiac output.

3. LUNG INFECTIONS

HIV/AIDS-associated respiratory disease is covered in Chapter 7, *Genito-urinary Medicine and AIDS*.

3.1 Pneumonia

Pneumonia is an acute inflammatory condition of the lung usually caused by bacteria, viruses or, rarely, fungi.

Community acquired pneumonia

The incidence is 1–3/1000 adult population per year. Causal organisms are shown overleaf.

- *Strep. pneumoniae* (60–70%)
- Atypical organisms, including
  Mycoplasma pneumoniae (5–19%),
  Legionella pneumophilia,
  Chlamydia psittaci,
  Chlamydia pneumoniae and
  Coxiella burnetii (Q fever)

- *H. influenzae*
- *S. aureus*
- Gram-negative organisms
- Viruses, including influenza,
  varicella-zoster, CMV

Signs of severity

- Respiratory rate >30/minute
- Diastolic BP <60 mmHg

- Urea >7 mmol/l

Two or more of the above findings are associated with a 21-fold increase in mortality. Marked leucopenia (<4 x 10^9/l) and marked leucocytosis (>30 x 10^9/l) are also bad prognostic signs.

Specific pneumonias

Streptococcus pneumoniae
There is an abrupt onset of illness, with high fever and rigors. Examination reveals crackles or bronchial breathing, and herpetic cold sores may be present in >1/3 cases.

- Elderly patients may present with general deterioration or confusion.
- Capsular polysaccharide antigen may be detected in serum, sputum, pleural fluid or urine.
- Increasing incidence of penicillin resistance, particularly in countries such as Spain
- Vaccine available.

Mycoplasma pneumoniae
Mycoplasma tends to affect young adults; it occurs in epidemics every 3–4 years. There is typically a longer prodrome, usually of 2 or more weeks, and the white cell count may be normal. Cold agglutinins occur in 50%; the mortality is low.

- Extrapulmonary complications include: peri/myocarditis, erythema multiforme, erythema nodosum, Stevens–Johnson syndrome, haemolytic anaemia, DIC, thrombocytopenia, meningo-encephalitis, cranial and peripheral neuropathies, bullous myringitis, hepatitis and pancreatitis.

Legionella pneumophila

Outbreaks are usually related to contaminated water cooling systems, showers, or air conditioning systems, but sporadic cases do occur. Legionnaires' disease usually affects the middle-aged and elderly, patients often having underlying lung disease. Males are affected more than females (3:1). Diagnosis is by direct fluorescent antibody staining or serological tests; antigen may be detected in the urine.

Clinical and laboratory features

- Gastrointestinal upset common; jaundice, ileus and pancreatitis may occur
- WCC often not elevated with lymphopenia; thrombocytopenia/ pancytopenia may occur
- Hyponatraemia due to SIADH

- Headache, confusion and delirium are prominent and focal neurological signs may develop
- Abnormal liver and renal function in approximately 50%
- Acute renal failure, interstitial nephritis and glomerulonephritis may develop

---

Staphylococcus aureus

Staphylococcus aureus pneumonia may follow a viral illness; it has a high mortality (30–70%). The disease is more common in intravenous drug addicts.

Specific features include:

- Toxin production with extensive tissue necrosis
- Staphylococcal skin lesions may develop
- Chest X-ray shows patchy infiltrates with abscess formation in 25% and empyema in 10%
- >25% of patients have positive blood cultures.

Treatment of pneumonia

Treatment is with oral amoxycillin or erythromycin for non-severe cases and with a third-generation cephalosporin and clarithromycin intravenously in severe cases. This can be stepped down to oral treatment after 48 hours provided the patient is improving. If a specific organism is isolated the appropriate antibiotic is given.

Nosocomial (hospital-acquired) pneumonia

This is defined as pneumonia that develops 2 or more days after admission to hospital (0.5–5% of hospitalized patients). The organisms usually involved include:

- *Staphylococcus aureus*
- Gram-negative bacteria: Klebsiella, Pseudomonas, *E. coli, Proteus* spp., *Serratia* spp., *Acinetobacter* spp.
- Anaerobes
- Fungi
- *Streptococcus pneumoniae* (and other streptococci) are less common.

Treatment is with broad spectrum agents (e.g. third-generation cephalosporins).

Aspiration pneumonia
Aspiration pneumonia may complicate impaired consciousness and dysphagia. Particulate matter may obstruct the airway, but also chemical pneumonitis may develop from aspiration of acid gastric contents, leading to pulmonary oedema.

- Anaerobes are the principal pathogens, arising from the oropharynx.
- There are typically 2–3 separate isolates in each case.
- Multiple pulmonary abscesses or empyema may result.
- Treat with metronidazole in combination with broad spectrum agent (e.g. third-generation cephalosporin).

Cavitation may develop with the following infections:

- *Staphylococcus aureus*
- *Klebsiella pneumoniae*
- *Legionella pneumophila* (rare)
- Anaerobic infections
- *Pseudomonas aeruginosa*
- *Mycobacterium tuberculosis* and atypical mycobacterial infections

3.2 Empyema

A collection of pus in the pleural space may complicate up to 15% of community acquired pneumonias and is more common when there is a history of excess alcohol consumption, poor dentition, aspiration or general anaesthesia.

- A diagnosis of empyema is suspected if a patient is slow to improve, has a persistent fever or elevation of the white cell count and has radiological evidence of a pleural fluid collection.
- Untreated, extensive fibrosis occurs in the pleural cavity, weight loss and clubbing develop and the mortality rate is high.
- The mainstay of treatment is drainage of the pleural space combined with continuous high-dose antibiotic treatment. Daily intra-pleural administration of streptokinase has been shown to liquefy the pus and facilitate percutaneous drainage with improved resolution rates.

- For those who fail to resolve with medical therapy, thoracotomy and decortication of the lung may be necessary.

3.3 Tuberculosis

The number of new cases of tuberculosis (TB) has been declining in the UK throughout the 20th century mainly due to the improvement in living standards. In recent years, however, the incidence of TB has begun to increase again (there was a 27% increase in notifications between 1987–1990).

Those at risk include:

- Those on low incomes
- Homeless persons
- Alcoholics
- HIV-positive individuals
- Immigrants from countries with a high incidence of TB.

The most commonly involved site is the lung — with lymph node, bone, renal tract and GI tract being less common. Tuberculous meningitis is the most serious complication.

Primary TB

Primary infection occurs in those without immunity. A small lung lesion known as the Ghon focus develops in the mid or lower zones of the lung and is composed of tubercle-laden macrophages. Bacilli are transported through the lymphatics to the draining lymph nodes which enlarge considerably and caseate. Infection is often arrested at this stage and the bacteria may remain dormant for many years. The peripheral lung lesion and the nodes heal and may calcify. The entire process is often asymptomatic, however, specific immunity begins to develop and tuberculin skin tests become positive.

Post-primary TB

Organisms disseminated by the blood at the time of primary infection may reactivate many years later. The most common site for post-primary TB is the lungs, with bone and lymph node sites being less common. Reactivation may be precipitated by a waning of host immunity, for example due to malignancy or immunosuppressive drugs including steroids.

Clinical picture

Primary infection is often asymptomatic, but may cause mild cough and wheeze or erythema nodosum.

Reactivation or reinfection may cause:

- Persistent cough
- Night sweats
- Pleural effusion
- Meningitis
- Weight loss
- Haemoptysis
- Pneumonia

Miliary TB

This is caused by widespread dissemination of infection via the blood stream. It may present with non-specific symptoms of malaise, pyrexia and weight loss. Eventually hepatosplenomegaly develops and choroidal tubercles may be visible on fundoscopy. The chest X-ray shows multiple rounded shadows a few millimetres in diameter. It is universally fatal if left untreated.

Diagnosis of TB

- **Chest X-ray**
  May show patchy shadowing in the upper zones with volume loss and cavitation, and ultimately fibrosis

- **Pleural fluid aspiration and biopsy**

- **Lymph node biopsy**

- **Bone marrow aspirate**

- **Morning sputum collections**
  For acid–alcohol fast bacilli smear

- **Bronchoscopy and lavage**
  Used for those unable to expectorate; transbronchial biopsy if miliary disease is a possibility

- **Early morning urine specimens**
  For renal tract disease

- **CSF culture**

Specimens are examined for AAFB using Ziehl–Neelsen or auramine stains and then cultured on Löwenstein–Jensen medium. Cultures are continued for at least 6 weeks as the organism is slow growing. PCR for tuberculous DNA can be used to provide a rapid diagnosis.

Treatment

This is with a combination of four drugs:

- Rifampicin
- Isoniazid
- Pyrazinamide
- Ethambutol.

Ethambutol can be omitted if the patient is Caucasian, has not had previous treatment for TB, is HIV-negative and has no known contact with drug-resistant disease.

All drugs are given for 2 months and isoniazid and rifampicin are continued for a further 4 months. Sensitivity testing will identify drug resistance and second line agents (e.g. ethionamide, propionamide, streptomycin, cycloserine) may be needed. Compliance can pose major problems and directly observed therapy (DOT) is used when poor compliance is anticipated.

- Side-effects are common, rifampicin, isoniazid and pyrazinamide all causing hepatitis, whereas ethambutol may cause optic neuritis — visual acuity should be checked before treatment is initiated. Isoniazid may cause peripheral neuropathy, 10 mg of pyridoxine daily being given in those at particular risk of this complication (e.g. alcoholics).

- Multi-drug resistant TB (MDR-TB) signifies resistance to rifampicin and isoniazid and currently accounts for 2% of tuberculous infections.

Prevention

BCG vaccination is given to most children aged 13 years provided that a Heaf test shows grade 0–1 reactivity. BCG provides approximately 70% protection against TB and prevents disseminated disease developing. In infants at particular risk, vaccination is given at birth.

Chemoprophylaxis (isoniazid for 6 months or rifampicin and isoniazid for 3 months) is given to those with evidence of recent infection (Heaf conversion) but no disease. TB is a notifiable disease and contacts of all notified cases are screened for infection.

Atypical tuberculous infections

These account for 10% of all mycobacterial infections. Organisms causing atypical TB include the following.

- *Mycobacterium kansasii*
- *Mycobacterium xenopi*
- *Mycobacterium malmoense*
- *Mycobacterium avium intracellulare*

These organisms cause disease which is clinically and radiologically identical to TB. They are ubiquitous in the environment and are low grade pathogens. Opportunistic mycobacterial infections constitute a relatively higher proportion of tuberculous infections in AIDS patients. The onset of symptoms is usually gradual. Treatment programmes are generally longer than for TB, and are often continued for 18 months to 2 years. Rifampicin and ethambutol are the main agents used, but for those not responding streptomycin, clarithromycin or ciprofloxacin may be added. Atypical infections do not need to be notified. Contact tracing is unnecessary as person to person infection is very rare.

3.4 Bronchiectasis

This is the permanent dilatation of sub-segmental airways which are inflamed, tortuous, flabby and partially/totally obstructed by secretions. Bronchiectasis may be follicular, saccular or atelectatic.

Causes

- Congenital
- Post-infective (e.g. following episodes of childhood measles, pneumonia or pertussis)
- Immune deficiency
- Post-tuberculosis
- Allergic bronchopulmonary aspergillosis (ABPA) — proximal
- Complicating sarcoidosis or pulmonary fibrosis
- Idiopathic — 60%

- Distal to an obstructed bronchus
- Secondary to bronchial damage resulting from a chemical pneumonitis (e.g. inhalation of caustic chemicals)
- Mucociliary clearance defects: primary ciliary dyskinesis or associated with situs inversus (Kartagener's syndrome) or associated with azoospermia and sinusitis in males (Young's syndrome)

Clinical features

There is a history of chronic sputum production which is often mucopurulent and accompanied by episodes of haemoptysis. Exertional dyspnoea and wheeze may be associated. Patients complain of malaise and fatigue; one-third have symptoms of chronic sinusitis. There may be few abnormal clinical findings other than occasional basal crackles on chest examination; clubbing may be present.

Investigations

- **Sputum microbiology**: most commonly shows *Haemophilus influenzae, Streptococcus pneumoniae* or *Pseudomonas aeruginosa*
- **Chest X-ray**: may be normal or may show thickening of bronchial walls and in saccular bronchiectasis, ring shadows ± fluid levels. The upper lobes are most frequently affected in ABPA, cystic fibrosis, sarcoidosis and tuberculosis
- **Pulmonary function tests**: may be normal or show an obstructed/restricted pattern (or both)
- **High-resolution CT scanning**: is diagnostic in >90% of cases
- **Immunoglobulin levels**: may demonstrate deficiency of humoral immunity.

Associated conditions

- Rheumatoid arthritis
- Yellow nail syndrome
  and primary lymphoedema
- Malignancy (childhood acute
  lymphoblastic leukaemia,
  adult chronic lymphocytic leukaemia)

- Inflammatory bowel disease
  (usually ulcerative colitis)
- Infertility

Treatment

As far as possible the aetiology of the bronchiectasis should be established in every case. If there is an underlying immune deficiency state, treatment with intravenous immunoglobulin therapy is beneficial. Regular physiotherapy with postural drainage or forced expiratory 'huffing' helps to clear the airways. Antibiotics are usually given in response to an exacerbation, however, some patients require continuous oral treatment, usually three antibiotics in rotation. Inhaled corticosteroids may be of benefit in those patients with marked airways obstruction; mucolytics are generally not helpful. Surgery is reserved for those with localized severe disease; lung transplantation has been successful.

Complications

Infective exacerbations are the principal problem. Haemoptysis usually settles with treatment of the infection but occasionally embolization of the bleeding vessel is required. Chest pain over an area of bronchiectatic lung is not uncommon. In the long term, systemic amyloid may result.

3.5 Cystic fibrosis

Cystic fibrosis affects 1:2500 children and is the most common fatal inherited disease. One in 25 adults are carriers. The gene for cystic fibrosis has been localized to the long arm of chromosome 7 and codes for the cystic fibrosis transmembrane regulator protein (CFTR), which functions as a chloride channel. Over 300 mutations have been identified, the most common being $\Delta508$. The basic defect involves abnormal transport of chloride across the cell membrane; in the sweat gland there is a failure to reabsorb chloride and in the airway there is failure of chloride secretion. Diagnosis is made by detection of an abnormally high sweat chloride (>60 mEq/l).

Pulmonary disease

The lungs are normal at birth. The airways become obstructed by thick mucus due to decreased chloride secretion and increased sodium reabsorption, and so bacterial infection becomes established in early life.

Infection occurs in an age-related fashion: infants and young children become colonized with *Staphylococcus aureus* and subsequently *Haemophilus influenzae*. In the teenage years: infection with *Pseudomonas aeruginosa* occurs.

The other major pathogens involved are:

- *Streptococcus pneumoniae*
- *Burkholderia cepacia*
- *Mycobacterium tuberculosis*
- Atypical mycobacteria
- *Aspergillus fumigatus*
- Viruses.

Chronic infection and inflammation causes lung damage with bronchiectasis affecting predominantly the upper lobes. Patients have breathlessness and reduced exercise tolerance, cough with chronic purulent sputum production, and occasional haemoptysis. Physical signs include clubbing, cyanosis, wheeze and scattered coarse crackles. Slight haemoptysis is often associated with infection but major haemoptysis may occasionally necessitate embolization.

- Pulmonary function tests show airflow obstruction; chest X-ray may show hyperinflation, atelectasis, visible thickened bronchial walls, fibrosis and apical bullae; pneumothorax occurs in up to 10% of patients.

- In the terminal stages of disease, respiratory failure develops.

Gastrointestinal tract

Pancreatic insufficiency is present in approximately 80% of patients and malabsorption causes bulky offensive stools, with weight loss and deficiency of fat-soluble vitamins. Babies may present with meconium ileus and adults may develop an equivalent syndrome with obstruction of the small bowel due to poorly digested intestinal contents causing abdominal pain, distension, vomiting and severe constipation.

- Obstruction of the biliary ductules in the liver may eventually lead to cirrhosis with portal hypertension, splenomegaly and oesophageal varices.
- Gallstones (in 15% of patients), peptic ulcer and reflux oesophagitis are all more prevalent.
- Pancreatitis may develop in older patients.

Involvement of other systems

- **Diabetes**: occurs in 8–15% of patients; there is a gradual loss of pancreatic islet cells with fibrosis developing. Ketoacidosis is very uncommon.
- **Upper airway disease**: nasal polyps occur frequently (up to 1/3 of patients): chronic purulent sinusitis may develop.
- **Fertility**: virtually all males are infertile due to abnormal development of the vas deferens and seminiferous tubules, but fertility in women is only slightly reduced. Although many women with cystic fibrosis have had successful pregnancies, pregnancy may lead to life-threatening respiratory complications.

Treatment

Antibiotics and respiratory treatments

In the UK most centres give antibiotics when sputum becomes increasingly purulent, pulmonary function tests are deteriorating or the patient is generally unwell with weight loss. Most patients become chronically colonized with *Pseudomonas aeruginosa* and so two different antibiotics (e.g. ceftazidime and tobramycin) are used in combination to prevent resistance developing.

- Up to 25% of patients become colonized with *Burkholderia cepacia*, an organism which is highly transmissible from one individual to another and associated with a worse prognosis. These patients are therefore segregated from patients colonized with *Pseudomonas*, both in hospital, at outpatient clinics and socially.
- Most patients need continuous anti-staphylococcal treatment.

Nebulized antibiotics reduce the microbial load and are useful in those who need frequent courses of intravenous antibiotics; colomycin or tobramycin are used continuously in a twice daily regimen.

- DNase helps to liquefy viscous sputum and is helpful in some patients. Bronchodilators and inhaled steroid are given to treat airflow obstruction. Physiotherapy, using the active cycle of breathing technique, should be tailored to individual needs.

Pancreatic enzyme supplements

Given with main meals and snacks to those with pancreatic insufficiency. Meconium ileus equivalent is treated with vigorous rehydration and regular oral gastrografin. Good nutritional status is associated with improved prognosis; supplementary overnight feeding with nasogastric tube or via gastroenterostomy can help to maintain body weight.

Transplantation

Either double-lung or heart–lung transplantation may be appropriate for some patients with terminal respiratory failure. Non-invasive positive pressure ventilation may be utilized to support a patient before transplantation. The timing of lung transplantation is difficult and must be assessed in each individual case.

3.6 Aspergillus and the lung

Aspergillus causes three distinct forms of pulmonary disease:

Allergic bronchopulmonary aspergillosis

(See section 2.1)

Colonizing aspergillosis

Fungal colonization of cavities in the lung parenchyma, of dilated bronchi or the pleural space.

A mass or ball of fungus develops known as an aspergilloma. *A. fumigatus* is usually responsible, but occasionally *A. niger, A. flavus* or *A. nidulans* may be implicated. The most common predisposing condition is TB, but cavities of other aetiology may be colonized. Cough and sputum production often occur and are features of the underlying disease. Haemoptysis is a common complication, and this may be massive.

- An aspergilloma is usually suspected by chest X-ray which demonstrates a cystic space containing a rounded opacity. An air space is visible between the fungal mass and the cavity wall — the 'halo' sign.
- Precipitating antibodies are nearly always present but response to skin testing is variable.
- Sputum examination may reveal fungal hyphae.

Many aspergillomas require no specific treatment. Treatment is indicated for recurrent haemoptysis, systemic symptoms and where there is evidence of fungal invasion of surrounding tissue. Resection of the affected area of lung may be curative. Intra-cavity instillation of amphotericin paste is useful, but systemic antifungal treatment is generally unhelpful.

Invasive aspergillosis

Fungal infection spreads rapidly through the lung causing granulomas, necrosis of tissue and suppuration. It occurs most commonly in the immunosuppressed host and may be rapidly fatal. Progressive chest X-ray shadowing (which may cavitate), associated with fever and malaise which does not settle promptly with antibacterial agents, suggests invasive aspergillosis.

- Cough with copious sputum production, often with haemoptysis, is usual.
- Examination of sputum or bronchio-alveolar lavage fluid may demonstrate fungal hyphae. High resolution CT scanning shows pulmonary infiltrates with the 'halo' sign. Treatment is with systemic antifungal agents, usually amphotericin.

4. OCCUPATIONAL LUNG DISEASE

4.1 Asbestos-related disease

Exposure to asbestos was previously commonplace in many occupations including ship building, laggers, building, dockers and factories engaged in the manufacture of asbestos products.

Effects of asbestos on the lung

Pleural plaques
These appear 20 or more years after low-density exposure. They develop on the parietal pleura of the chest wall, diaphragm, pericardium and mediastinum, and commonly calcify. Pleural plaques are usually asymptomatic but they may cause mild restriction.

Diffuse pleural thickening
This can extend continuously over a variable proportion of the thoracic cavity, but is most marked at the lung bases. It causes exertional dyspnoea; PFTs show restriction, decreased compliance, reduced total lung capacity, but the KCO is normal.

Pleural effusions may occur in asbestos-related disease.

Asbestosis
The onset of asbestosis is usually > 20 years after exposure (but with higher levels of exposure fibrosis occurs earlier). Fibrotic changes are more pronounced in the lower lobes; patients present with exertional dyspnoea and dry cough and clinical examination reveals fine inspiratory crackles in the lower zones. Clubbing may occur.

- Chest X-ray shows small irregular opacities, horizontal lines, and, in more advanced disease, honeycomb and ring shadows.
- PFTs show a restrictive defect with reduced KCO.
- There is an increased risk of lung cancer (see below).
- Sufferers are entitled to industrial compensation.

Lung cancer
Asbestosis is associated with a substantially increased risk of lung cancer (see later section), and the predisposition is synergistic with smoking. The risk of mesothelioma is also markedly increased.

4.2 Coal workers' pneumoconiosis (CWP)

The incidence of this pneumoconiosis is related to total dust exposure. Dust particles 2–5μm in diameter are retained in the respiratory bronchioles and alveoli. Simple CWP is characterized by small rounded opacities (<1.5 mm in diameter) on chest X-ray, and is associated with focal emphysema. The lesions are asymptomatic.

- **Progressive massive fibrosis** (PMF) involves the development of larger opacities (>1 cm in diameter) on a background of simple CWP.
- PMF lesions are usually in the upper zones and may cavitate.
- Cough, sputum production and dyspnoea occur with reduced life expectancy, deaths occurring from progressive respiratory failure.
- PFTs show a mixed obstructive/restrictive pattern with reduced KCO.

Coal mining is now recognized as a cause of COPD.

Caplan's syndrome is the development of multiple round pulmonary nodules in patients with rheumatoid arthritis and a background of coal workers' pneumoconiosis. Nodules may develop before the joint disease, and occur in crops in the periphery of the lung. They may be associated with pleural effusion and may ultimately calcify.

4.3 Silicosis

This is caused by inhaling silicon dioxide, a highly fibrogenic dust, and it affects quarry workers, hard rock miners, civil engineers, etc. Silicosis was commonly associated with TB in the first half of the 20th century.

- An acute illness characterized by dry cough and breathlessness occurs within a few months of exposure to very high levels of dust.
- With more chronic exposure silicotic nodules form, which are 3–5 mm in diameter and predominantly affect the upper lobes.
- Eggshell calcification occurs around enlarged hilar glands.
- Gradually worsening breathlessness is associated with restrictive lung physiology and a fall in gas transfer.
- There is no effective treatment (other than lung transplantation in patients with respiratory failure), but the disease is compensatible.

4.4 Berylliosis

The inhalation of fumes from molten beryllium causes an acute alveolitis. However, most cases of berylliosis are due to chronic low level exposure, causing a tissue reaction similar to sarcoidosis. Non-caseating granulomata form in the lungs and lymph nodes surrounded by fibrous tissue; the chest X-ray shows fine nodulation evenly distributed throughout the lung fields with bilateral hilar lymphadenopathy.

- A positive blood and BAL beryllium lymphocyte proliferation assay is strongly associated with the presence of chronic beryllium disease.

- Interstitial fibrosis develops with shrinking of the lungs.
- Patients develop progressive breathlessness with death ultimately occurring due to respiratory and right heart failure.

4.5 Byssinosis

This is caused by exposure to cotton dust, flax and hemp. Acute exposure causes airways narrowing in 1/3 of affected individuals. However, chronic byssinosis develops after years of heavy exposure to cotton dust; symptoms are worse on the first day back after a break from work, and include chest tightness, cough, dyspnoea and wheeze.

- There is a progressive decline in FEV_1 during the working shift, most marked on the first day of the week.
- Prevention is by reducing the levels of cotton dust to which employees are exposed.
- Bronchodilators may provide some relief of symptoms.

4.6 Occupational asthma

A large number of agents encountered at work cause asthma and are officially recognized for industrial compensation. These include the following.

Causes of occupational asthma

- Isocyanates
- Platinum salts
- Stainless steel welding
- Epoxy resins
- Azodicarbonamide (PVC, plastics)
- Glutaraldehyde
- Wood dust
- Laboratory animals and insects
- Dyes
- Acid anhydride and amine hardening agents
- Resin used in soldering flux
- Proteolytic enzymes
- Pharmaceuticals
- Many other chemicals
- Any known sensitizing agent in the workplace
- Flour/grains

Occupational asthma develops after a period of asymptomatic exposure to the allergen, but usually within two years of first exposure. Detection depends on a careful history, and PEFR monitoring both at work and at home. Once occupational asthma has developed, bronchospasm may be precipitated by other non-specific triggers such as cold air, exercise etc. Occupational asthma may develop in workers with previously diagnosed asthma. In order to identify the substance involved specific IgE levels may be measured or occasionally bronchial provocation testing may be performed. Early diagnosis and removal of the individual from exposure to the allergen is essential if they are to make a full recovery. Asthma symptoms may persist despite termination of exposure.

4.7 Extrinsic allergic alveolitis

This is a hypersensitivity pneumonitis caused by a specific immunological response (usually IgG-mediated) to inhaled organic dusts.

- **Farmers' lung** is due to the inhalation of thermophilic actinomycetes, (usually *Micropolyspora faeni* and *Thermoactinomyces vulgaris*), when workers are exposed to mouldy hay.
- **Bird fanciers' lung** is caused by inhaled avian serum proteins, present in excreta, and in the bloom from feathers; it primarily affects those who keep racing pigeons and those keeping budgerigars as pets.
- **Ventilation pneumonitis** occurs in inhabitants of air-conditioned buildings where thermophilic actinomycetes grow in the humidification system.
- **Bagassosis** is due to exposure to *Thermoactinomyces sacchari* in sugar cane processors.
- **Malt workers' lung** is due to the inhalation of *Aspergillus clavatus*.
- **Mushroom workers' lung** is due to the inhalation of *Thermophilic actinomyces*.

The clinical features depend on the pattern of exposure. An acute allergic alveolitis develops several hours after exposure to high concentrations of dust. Breathlessness and 'flu-like' symptoms occur, sometimes associated with fever, headaches and muscle pains. The symptoms are short-lived and usually resolve completely within 48 hours. Inspiratory crackles may be heard on chest auscultation.

- **Chest X-ray** may show a generalized haze sometimes associated with nodular shadows.
- **Spirometry** becomes restrictive and gas transfer is reduced. With chronic exposure irreversible pulmonary fibrosis develops.
- The diagnosis is made by establishing a history of exposure to antigen and the demonstration of precipitating antibodies in the patient's serum. Histology of lung biopsy shows a mononuclear cell infiltrate with the formation of granulomas.
- Once the diagnosis is established the patient should be isolated from the antigen; if this is impossible respiratory protection should be worn. Corticosteroids accelerate the rate of recovery from an acute attack but are generally not helpful once established fibrosis develops.

5. TUMOURS

5.1 Lung cancer

Lung cancer is the most prevalent cancer in the Western world and accounts for 1:3 cancer deaths in men and 1:6.5 cancer deaths in women. In Scotland, the female mortality rate from lung cancer now exceeds that from breast cancer. Twenty per cent of smokers will develop lung cancer. The prognosis is poor, with 90% of those diagnosed being dead within 12 months. The five-year survival rate has changed little over the past 20 years.

Causes of lung cancer

- **Smoking**
  Over 95% of lung cancers occur
  in current or ex-smokers

- **Atmospheric pollution**
  Persistently higher lung cancer rates
  in urban populations;
  passive smoking

- **Industrial exposures**
  Asbestos fibre, aluminium industry
  arsenic compounds, benzoyl chloride,
  beryllium

- Increased incidence in patients
  with cryptogenic fibrosing alveolitis
  and systemic sclerosis

Smoking is the leading cause of lung cancer. Although smoking rates have declined amongst adult men and to a lesser extent among women, there are an increasing number of teenage smokers, particularly girls.

Cell types:

- **Squamous cell**: usually arise from a central airway.
- **Small cell ('oat cell')**: arise in central airways and grow rapidly producing both intra-thoracic and metastatic symptoms.
- **Adenocarcinoma**: may be peripheral and slow-growing.
- **Undifferentiated** large cell.
- **Bronchiolar-alveolar** cell carcinoma.

Intra-thoracic complications of lung cancer

- Recurrent laryngeal nerve palsy
  causing hoarseness
- Dysphagia due to compression of
  the oesophagus by enlarged
  metastatic lymph nodes or tumour
  invasion
- Pericarditis with effusion
- Phrenic nerve palsy with raised
- hemidiaphragm
- Pleural effusion

- Superior venacaval obstruction
  causing headache, distension of the
  veins in the upper body, fixed
  elevation of the JVP, facial suffusion
  with conjunctival oedema,
  Pemberton's sign (breathlessness
  due to narrowing of airway on
  raising arms above the head)
- Rib metastases
- Spontaneous pneumothorax

Metastases can occur throughout the body but the most commonly involved sites are:

- Supraclavicular and anterior cervical lymph nodes, adrenal, bones, liver and brain.

Paraneoplastic syndromes

- **SIADH**: chiefly associated with small cell lung cancer. May resolve with chemotherapy but recurs with tumour progression. Treatment involves fluid restriction initially and demeclocycline for resistant cases.
- **Ectopic ACTH**: mainly associated with small cell lung cancer.
- **Hypercalcaemia**: usually associated with multiple bony metastases, but ectopic PTH secretion occurs in a few squamous cancers.
- **Gynaecomastia**: associated with squamous cell lung cancer; may be painful.
- **Hyperthyroidism**: rare (due to ectopic TSH) — squamous cell lung cancer.
- **Eaton–Lambert syndrome**: most commonly associated with small cell lung cancer; produces a proximal myopathy, reduced tendon reflexes and autonomic features.
- **Clubbing**: occurs in 10–30% of lung cancers; may resolve after resection.
- **Hypertrophic pulmonary osteoarthropathy (HPOA)**: produces periostitis, arthritis and gross finger clubbing. Most commonly associated with squamous cell lung cancer and involves the long bones (tibia/fibula, radius/ulna, femur/humerus). It is associated with subperiosteal new bone formation visible on plain X-ray and is often painful.

Pancoast's syndrome

This is due to a tumour at the thoracic inlet. The most common presenting complaint is pain (due to involvement of the eighth cervical and first thoracic nerve roots) extending down the medial side of the upper arm to the elbow. Horner's syndrome may develop. Chest X-ray demonstrates a shadow at the extreme apex, and there may be destruction of the first and second ribs.

Diagnosis of lung cancer

- Sputum cytology
- CT thorax
- Peripheral lung nodules are usually resected as biopsy is technically difficult and often unsuccessful

- Bronchoscopy
- Biopsy of metastatic deposit (including lymph nodes)

Treatment

Surgery offers the only chance of cure. At the time of presentation only 20% of patients with non-small cell lung cancer will be operable. Despite apparently curative surgery the five-year survival rate is only 25% due to the high incidence of undetected disseminated disease. Patients whose tumour is technically operable, but who are unfit for surgery due to coexisting medical conditions or poor lung function, may be treated with **radical radiotherapy.**

- **Palliative radiotherapy** is very effective in relieving pain from bony metastases, controlling haemoptysis and cough. Dyspnoea and dysphagia due to oesophageal compression by lymph nodes respond well to radiotherapy.
- **Superior vena caval obstruction** can also be treated with radiotherapy, however, stenting provides more immediate relief of symptoms.
- **Chemotherapy** for non-small cell lung cancer offers only a very small survival benefit but has been shown to provide effective palliation.

Small cell lung cancer is associated with an extremely poor prognosis if left untreated, with a median survival of only 8 weeks. The tumour is, however, much more sensitive to chemotherapeutic agents than other types of lung cancer, and cycles of chemotherapy can result in remission in up to 50% of cases. Median survival is now 14–16 months for limited disease and 8–10 months for extensive disease.

5.2 Mesothelioma

This is most common in men between the ages of 50–70 years. The lesion arises from mesothelial cells of pleura, or less commonly, the peritoneum. **Asbestos exposure** is responsible for at least 85% of malignant mesotheliomas, and the risk of mesothelioma increases with the dose of asbestos received. Crocidolite (blue) is more potent than amosite (brown) and both are more potent than crysotile (white asbestos) in causing mesothelioma.

There is usually a latent period of >30 years between asbestos exposure and development of mesothelioma. The tumour arises from the visceral or parietal pleura, and expands to encase the lung. Pleural mesothelioma presents with chest pain and dyspnoea and may cause pleural effusion.

- Annual incidence of mesothelioma in the UK exceeds 1000 cases and is rising; it is expected to peak in the year 2020.
- Chest X-ray and CT thorax usually show an effusion progressing to lobulated pleural thickening and contraction of the hemithorax.
- Diagnosis is made by pleural biopsy often done as a VATS procedure (see section 6.3); the main differential diagnosis is adenocarcinoma of the pleura.
- Treatment is unsatisfactory; there is no known cure even with radical surgical procedures. Radiotherapy is helpful for pain relief and for prevention of seeding of

biopsy track. There are no randomized trials demonstrating a survival advantage from chemotherapy.

- Median survival from presentation is 12–18 months for pleural mesothelioma and 7 months for peritoneal mesothelioma.
- Patients with mesothelioma may be eligible for industrial compensation.

Pulmonary causes of clubbing

- Carcinoma of the bronchus
- Asbestosis
- Lung abscess
- Cystic fibrosis

- Cryptogenic fibrosing alveolitis
- Bronchiectasis
- Empyema
- Mesothelioma

Causes of haemoptysis

- **Common causes**
  Carcinoma of the bronchus
  Pneumonia
  Bronchiectasis
  Pulmonary tuberculosis
  Pulmonary embolus
  Mitral valve disease
  Infective exacerbation of COPD

- **Rarer causes**
  Vascular malformations
  Mycetoma
  Connective tissue disorders
  Vasculitis
  Goodpasture's syndrome
  Cystic fibrosis
  Bleeding diathesis
  Idiopathic pulmonary haemosiderosis

---

6. GRANULOMATOUS LUNG DISEASE AND PULMONARY FIBROSIS

6.1 Sarcoidosis

Sarcoidosis is a multisystem granulomatous disorder primarily affecting young adults. The aetiology is unknown. The prevalence varies among different populations but in the UK it is 20–30 /100,000, being highest among West Indian and Asian immigrants. The characteristic histological lesion is the granuloma composed of macrophages, lymphocytes and epithelioid histiocytes which fuse to form multinucleate giant cells. The disease may present acutely with erythema nodosum and bilateral hilar lymphadenopathy on the chest X-ray (good prognosis with most patients showing radiological resolution within a year) or insidiously with multi-organ involvement. Ninety per cent of patients have intra-thoracic involvement.

Chest X-ray changes are graded as:

- **Stage 0**: clear chest X-ray
- **Stage 1**: bilateral hilar lymphadenopathy (BHL)
- **Stage 2**: bilateral hilar lymphadenopathy and pulmonary infiltration
- **Stage 3**: diffuse pulmonary infiltration.

Patients may have no respiratory symptoms or complain of dyspnoea, dry cough, fever, malaise and weight loss. Chest examination is frequently normal; finger clubbing is rare.

Diffuse parenchymal lung involvement may progress to irreversible fibrosis; the mid and upper zones of the lungs are most frequently affected. Calcification of the hilar nodes or the lung parenchyma may occur with chronic disease. Pleural effusion is rare.

Upper airway involvement (infrequent): the nasal mucosa may become hypertrophied and cause obstruction, crusting and discharge; perforation of the nasal septum and bony erosion are rare.

Extra-pulmonary disease

- **Lymphadenopathy**: painless, rubbery lymph node enlargement is more common in Black patients; the cervical and scalene lymph nodes are most frequently affected.
- **Splenomegaly** (25%).
- **Liver involvement**: common, but usually subclinical; liver biopsy is of diagnostic value in 90% (typical sarcoid granulomata).
- **Skin**: erythema nodosum (usually in Caucasian females) in disease with BHL; skin plaques, subcutaneous nodules and lupus pernio (violaceous lesions on the nose, cheeks and ears) seen in chronic disease.
- **Acute anterior uveitis (25%)**; chronic iridocyclitis affects older patients and responds poorly to treatment.
- **Heerfordt–Waldenström syndrome**: consists of parotid gland enlargement, uveitis, fever and cranial nerve palsies.
- **Neurological manifestations** (uncommon): cranial nerve palsies (facial nerve most often affected), meningitis, hydrocephalus, space occupying lesions and spinal cord involvement; granulomata infiltrating the posterior pituitary may produce diabetes insipidus, hypothalamic hypothyroidism or hypopituitarism.
- **Cardiac sarcoid** may result in cardiac muscle dysfunction or involve the conducting system, producing arrhythmias, bundle-branch block or complete heart block.
- **Bone cysts**: with overlying soft tissue swelling occur most often in the phalanges, metacarpals, metatarsals and nasal bones; arthritis is common.

Diagnosis

The combination of BHL with erythema nodosum in a young adult is virtually diagnostic of acute sarcoidosis. In other cases, tissue biopsy (transbronchial or endobronchial) is useful. Elevated serum angiotensin-converting enzyme and calcium are consistent with the diagnosis but are non-specific. The Kveim–Siltzbach test (intradermal injection of extract of spleen from patient with active sarcoidosis with skin biopsy at 4–6 weeks demonstrating a granulomatous response) is now rarely used.

Treatment

The best prognosis is associated with acute sarcoidosis which frequently undergoes complete remission without specific therapy. Steroids are the mainstay of therapy for chronic disease but response is unpredictable. Hypercalcaemia and hypercalciuria despite dietary calcium restriction is a definite indication for steroid therapy. Other immunosuppressive agents (e.g. azathioprine and methotrexate) may be used as steroid-sparing agents.

6.2 Histiocytosis

Three clinical entities are recognized:

- **Eosinophilic granuloma**: solitary bone lesions occurring in children and young adults. Lung disease is known as Langerhans cell histiocytosis.
- **Letterer–Siwe disease**: a diffuse multisystem disorder of infancy which is rapidly lethal.
- **Hand–Schüller–Christian disease**: characterized by exophthalmos, bony defects and diabetes insipidus (in children and teenagers). Diffuse nodular shadows occur in the lung with hilar lymphadenopathy.

In adults histiocytosis is often confined to the lung. It is rare and most likely in young and middle-aged males.

- Strongly associated with smoking.
- Chest X-ray shows multiple ring shadows on a background of diffuse reticulo-nodular opacities mainly in the upper and mid-zones; the lung bases are spared.
- With disease progression larger cysts and bullae form and interstitial fibrosis develops.
- Diagnosis is by high-resolution CT scanning and lung biopsy.
- Treatment includes smoking cessation and steroids; spontaneous remission occurs in 25% of patients, however, in a further 25% the disease may be rapidly fatal.

6.3 Pulmonary fibrosis

Interstitial lung disease is associated with many conditions including the connective tissue diseases (particularly SLE and systemic sclerosis), rheumatoid arthritis and sarcoidosis. When pulmonary fibrosis develops without obvious cause it is known as cryptogenic fibrosing alveolitis. Extrinsic allergic alveolitis also causes diffuse interstitial fibrosis.

Cryptogenic fibrosing alveolitis (CFA)

The prevalence of CFA is increasing (currently 20–30 per 100,000 in some areas). It is a disease of the elderly, more common in men, and is possibly the result of an inhaled environmental antigen; metal and wood dusts have been implicated but no causal relationship has been identified. There may be an association with Epstein–Barr virus (EBV). Patients present with a dry cough and breathlessness, and signs include cyanosis, finger clubbing and fine late inspiratory crackles.

- **Lung function tests**: small lung volumes, with reduction in gas transfer and restrictive spirometry.
- **Blood gas analysis**: typically shows type 1 respiratory failure with hypoxaemia and a normal or low pCO_2.
- **Chest X-ray**: reveals interstitial shadowing most marked at the bases and peripheries, and CT scanning is useful to determine the degree of inflammatory change and the likelihood of response to steroids.
- **VATS** (video-assisted thorascopic surgery) or open lung biopsy confirms the diagnosis and histology shows variable degrees of established fibrosis and acute inflammation.
- **Treatment**: is with steroids and other immunosuppressive agents such as azathioprine or cyclophosphamide; only 20% of cases respond.

Extrinsic allergic alveolitis (EAA)

(See section 4 on occupational lung disease.)

Multiple episodes of acute exposure to agents causing EAA, or long-term low-grade exposure, as occurs in budgerigar owners, can lead to irreversible lung fibrosis. Patients present with breathlessness, weight loss and inspiratory crackles over the lung fields.

- **Chest X-ray**: shows honeycombing and lung shrinkage mainly involving the upper lobes; calcification or cavitation does not develop.
- **Spirometry**: as for CFA.

See section 4.7 for diagnostic strategy.

Drugs causing pulmonary fibrosis

- **Amiodarone**
  Causes an alveolitis (which may be reversible on drug cessation), progressing to diffuse fibrosis; commoner when higher doses are used
- **Sulphasalazine**

- **Methotrexate**
- **Busulphan**
- **Bleomycin**
- **Cyclophosphamide**
- **Nitrofurantoin**
- **Gold**
- **Melphelan**

Causes of reticular-nodular shadowing on chest X-ray

- **Upper zone**
  Extrinsic allergic alveolitis
  Sarcoidosis
  Coal-workers' pneumoconiosis
  Silicosis

- **Basal zone**
  Idiopathic pulmonary fibrosis
  Lymphangiitis carcinomatosis
  Drugs
  Connective tissue disorders

Causes of calcification on chest X-ray

- **Lymph node calcification**
  Sarcoidosis
  Silicosis
  Tuberculosis

- **Parenchymal calcification**
  Healed tuberculous lesions
  Calcified pleural plaques following asbestos exposure, and pleural calcification due to previous haemothorax (pleural)
  Healed fungal infections
  Previous varicella pneumonia
  Mitral stenosis*
  Chronic left ventricular failure*

  Hyperparathyroidism
  Chronic renal failure
  Vitamin D intoxication
  Benign tumours
  Busulphan lung
  Caplan's syndrome
  Alveolar microlithiasis

*Results in secondary pulmonary haemosideroisis

7. PULMONARY VASCULITIS AND EOSINOPHILIA

7.1 Wegener's granulomatosis

Small/medium sized arteries, veins and capillaries are involved with a granulomatous inflammation. Upper airway involvement includes crusting and granulation tissue on the nasal turbinates producing nasal obstruction and a bloody discharge; collapse of the nasal bridge produces a saddle-shaped nose; c-ANCA is present is 90% of cases (see also Chapter 9, *Immunology*).

- Large rounded shadows may be visible on the chest X-ray and these often cavitate.
- Untreated the median survival is 5 months; cyclophosphamide and steroids can now induce lasting remission in 90%.

7.2 Churg–Strauss syndrome

A syndrome of necrotizing vasculitis, eosinophilic infiltrates and granuloma formation there is often a prior history of asthma, and sometimes allergic rhinitis. Peripheral blood eosinophilia occurs with eosinophilic infiltrates of the lungs and often the gastrointestinal tract. Vasculitic lesions appear on the skin (purpura, erythema or nodules).

- p-ANCA is positive in 50%.
- Chest X-ray shows nodular or confluent shadows without cavitation.
- Treatment is with steroids and/or azathioprine.

7.3 Polyarteritis and Henoch–Schönlein vasculitis

- Microscopic polyangiitis (MPA) produces pulmonary haemorrhage, haemoptysis and occasionally pleurisy; granulomas are not a feature.

- Lung involvement is uncommon in polyarteritis nodosa; it consists of pulmonary infiltrates (composed mainly of neutrophils) without granuloma formation.

- Pulmonary involvement is a rare feature in Henoch–Schönlein purpura (HSP). The disorder can be associated with streptococcal or hepatitis B (less often with viral or fungal) infections.

7.4 Connective tissue disorders

- **Rheumatoid disease:** has many pulmonary associations which include bronchiectasis, obliterative bronchiolitis, pulmonary fibrosis, nodules, Caplan's syndrome and pleurisy with effusion.

- **SLE**: pulmonary fibrosis, bronchiolitis obliterans organizing pneumonia, pleural effusion and shrinking lung syndrome can all occur.
- **Systemic sclerosis**: associated with bronchiectasis, pulmonary fibrosis and aspiration pneumonia (due to dysphagia).

All may cause pulmonary hypertension.

Pulmonary vasculitis occurs in association with

- Ulcerative colitis
- Takayasu's disease
- Multiple pulmonary emboli

- Giant cell arteritis
- Behçet's disease
- Infection

7.5 Pulmonary eosinophilia

Eosinophilic pneumonia

This describes chest X-ray shadowing accompanied by peripheral blood eosinophilia. Lung biopsy shows airspace consolidation with an inflammatory infiltrate having a preponderance of eosinophils. The condition responds to steroids.

Causes:

- Allergic aspergillosis
- Other infections
- Drugs (nitrofurantoin, imipramine, sulphasalazine)
- Parasites
- Other agents (e.g. smoke inhalation)
- It is also associated with asthma.

Chronic pulmonary eosinophilia

Persistent peripheral blood eosinophilia occurs with pulmonary infiltrates. There is usually a polymorphonuclear leucocytosis and raised ESR.

- Clinical features: cough, dyspnoea, weight loss, fever, anaemia, night sweats, hepatomegaly and diffuse lymph node enlargement.
- Chest X-ray shadowing most marked in the peripheral and apical areas.
- Symptoms and chest X-ray shadows improve with steroids.

Hypereosinophilic syndrome

Characterized by very high eosinophil counts (mean 20 x10^9/l), the syndrome has clinical manifestations (weight loss, fever, night sweats, hepatomegaly and lymphadenopathy) similar to chronic pulmonary eosinophilia. Cardiac involvement occurs in 60% (producing arrhythmias and cardiac failure). See also Chapter 8, *Haematology*.

- Thrombo-embolism occurs in two-thirds of patients.
- Other organ involvement: central nervous system (intellectual deterioration and peripheral neuropathies), GI tract, and the kidney (proteinuria and hypertension).
- Steroids are effective.

8. MISCELLANEOUS RESPIRATORY DISORDERS

8.1 Pleural effusion

Transudates are usually clear or straw-coloured, whereas exudates are often turbid, bloody and may clot on standing. Fluid protein content should be examined; protein levels >30 g/l (or fluid to serum ratio >0.5) and lactic dehydrogenase (LDH) levels >200 IU (fluid to serum ratio of >0.6) are consistent with an exudate. pH <7.1, also suggests an exudate.

- Low concentrations of glucose in the pleural fluid compared to serum glucose are found in infection and with rheumatoid arthritis.
- In pancreatitis the amylase level may be higher in pleural fluid than in blood.
- **Cell content should be examined**. Transudates contain <1000 white cells made up of a mixture of polymorphs, lymphocytes and mesothelial cells. Exudates usually have a much higher white cell count. In bacterial infection this is usually polymorphs but in established TB, lymphocytes predominate.
- Malignant cells from a primary bronchial carcinoma or from metastatic disease may be found in approximately 60% of malignant pleural effusions.

Causes of pleural effusion

Transudates

- **Common**
  LVF
  Cirrhosis of the liver
  Nephrotic syndrome
  Acute glomerulonephritis
  Other causes of hypoproteinaemia

- **Uncommon**
  Myxoedema
  Pulmonary emboli
  Sarcoidosis
  Peritoneal dialysis

Exudates

- **Common**
  Pulmonary embolism

- **Uncommon**

Infections

Bacterial pneumonia
TB

Fungal
Viral
Parasitic

Malignancy

Primary carcinoma of bronchus
Metastatic carcinoma

Lymphoma
Pleural tumours

Connective tissue disorders

Rheumatoid arthritis
Systemic lupus erythematosus

Wegener's granulomatosis
Sjögren's syndrome
Immunoblastic lymphadenopathy

Subdiaphragmatic

Pancreatitis
Subphrenic abscess

Hepatic abscesses

Trauma

Haemothorax
Chylothorax

Ruptured oesophagus

- **Other rare causes**
  Meigs syndrome
  Asbestos exposure
  Familial Mediterranean fever
  Yellow nail syndrome
  Post-thoracotomy syndrome
  Dressler's syndrome

8.2 Obstructive sleep apnoea (OSA)

It is estimated that approximately 4% of adult men and 2% of women suffer from obstructive sleep apnoea, but the true incidence may be rather lower. The cardinal symptom is daytime somnolence due to the disruption of the normal sleep pattern. This leads to poor concentration, irritability and personality changes and a tendency to fall asleep during the day. Road traffic accidents are more frequent in this group of patients. The problem is exacerbated by night-time alcohol intake and sedative medication.

Pathogenesis

During sleep, muscle tone is reduced and the airway narrows so that airway obstruction develops between the level of the soft palate and the base of the tongue. Respiratory effort continues but airflow ceases due to the obstructed airway; eventually the patient arouses briefly and ventilation is resumed. The cycle is repeated several hundreds of times throughout the night.

- Over 80% of men with OSA are obese (BMI > 30). Hypothyroidism and acromegaly are also recognized causes. Retrognathia can cause OSA, and large tonsils may obstruct the airway.
- Patients (or their partners) give a history of loud snoring interrupted by episodes of apnoea. There may be a sensation of waking up due to choking. Sleep is generally unsatisfying.
- Patients suspected of suffering from OSA should have some measure of daytime somnolence made (e.g. using the Epworth scoring system).
- Diagnosis is made by demonstration of desaturation (SaO_2 below 90%) associated with a rise in heart rate and arousal from sleep. This can be made in most patients by home pulse oximetry recordings, but where the diagnosis is in doubt, full polysomnography may be needed.

Treatment involves:

- Nocturnal continuous positive airways pressure (CPAP) administered via a nasal mask
- Tonsillectomy if enlarged tonsils are thought to be the cause
- Correction of underlying medical disorders (e.g. hypothyroidism)
- Weight loss for individuals who are obese
- Anterior mandibular positioning devices are useful in some patients
- Tracheostomy (only as a last resort)

Uvulopalatopharyngoplasty is not generally of benefit.

Once a patient has been diagnosed as suffering from OSA he/she should refrain from driving and inform the Licensing Authorities. Patients may resume driving once their OSA has been satisfactorily treated. Holders of HGV licences may have their licence reinstated once adequately treated.

8.3 Adult respiratory distress syndrome (ARDS)

This is a syndrome comprising:

- Arterial hypoxaemia
- Bilateral fluffy pulmonary infiltrates on chest X-ray
- Non-cardiogenic pulmonary oedema (pulmonary capillary wedge pressure < 18 cm H_2O)
- Reduced lung compliance.

Causes include:

- Sepsis
- Burns
- DIC
- Pneumonia
- Aspiration of gastric contents
- Near drowning
- Drug overdoses (e.g. diamorphine, methadone, barbiturates, paraquat)

- Trauma
- Pancreatitis, uraemia
- Cardiopulmonary bypass
- Pulmonary contusion
- Smoke inhalation
- Oxygen toxicity

Management

No specific treatment is available and management is essentially supportive. Supplemental oxygen is given and patients frequently require mechanical ventilation. Pressure-controlled inverse ratio ventilation is used as this lowers peak airway pressure, reduces barotrauma and creates better distribution of gas in the lungs. With the addition of positive end-expiratory pressure (PEEP) there is greater alveolar recruitment, increased functional residual capacity, better lung compliance and reduced shunt. Turning the patient into the prone position inter- mittently allows those dependent parts of the lung which are susceptible to atelectasis to reexpand and improves blood flow to the ventilated parts of the lung.

- Inhaled nitric oxide (NO) is a potent vasodilator which causes selective vasodilatation of the ventilated areas of the lung when inhaled at low concentrations.
- Use of exogenous surfactant in adult patients has no proven value.
- Corticosteroids have been shown to be beneficial in the latter stages of ARDS that is characterized by progressive pulmonary interstitial fibro-proliferation.

8.4 Rare lung disorders

Lymphangioleiomyomatosis

This is a disease of women in their reproductive years. Patients present with dyspnoea complicated by recurrent pneumothoraces, chylous effusions and pulmonary haemorrhage.

- **Pathogenesis**: immature muscle cells infiltrate the bronchiolar and alveolar walls; the alveolar walls weaken forming multiple areas of emphysema which in advanced disease leads to gross honeycomb change throughout the lung.
- **Treatment**: unsatisfactory; hormonal manipulation is often tried but ultimately lung transplantation may be necessary.

Alveolar proteinosis

A disorder characterized by the accumulation of phospholipid and proteinaceous material in the alveoli and distal airways. The male:female ratio is 3:1, with age of onset 30–50 years. Patients present with dyspnoea of effort and cough; occasionally constitutional symptoms (fever, weight loss and malaise) develop. Haemoptysis and chest pain may occur.

- Chest X-ray shows bilateral infiltrates with air bronchograms in a butterfly pattern.
- Bronchoalveolar lavage establishes the diagnosis, yielding milky fluid.
- Treatment consists of interval whole lung lavage under general anaesthesia.

Pulmonary amyloidosis

The lungs are frequently involved in systemic amyloidosis (most often in primary amyloidosis); either the lung parenchyma or the tracheobronchial tree may be predominantly affected. The diagnosis is usually confirmed by biopsy.

- **Bronchial tree**: plaques visible on bronchoscopy; leads to breathlessness, wheezing, stridor and haemoptysis.
- **Nodules**: may develop throughout the lung parenchyma or a solitary nodule may occur.
- **Diffuse parenchymal amyloidosis**: may develop with amyloid deposited along the alveolar septa and around blood vessels; this form is extremely rare.

Chapter 18
Rheumatology

CONTENTS

1. **Rheumatoid factor**   589

2. **Rheumatoid arthritis**   590
    2.1   Clinical features
    2.2   Musculoskeletal features
    2.3   Extra-articular manifestations
    2.4   Investigations
    2.5   Disease-modifying drugs

3. **Spondyloarthropathies (HLA-B27-associated disorders)**   596
    3.1   Ankylosing spondylitis
    3.2   Reiter's syndrome
    3.3   Psoriatic arthritis

4. **Inflammatory connective tissue disorders**   600
    4.1   Autoantibodies in diagnosis
    4.2   Systemic lupus erythematosus (SLE)
    4.3   Dermatomyositis and polymyositis
    4.4   Systemic sclerosis
    4.5   Sjögren's syndrome
    4.6   Mixed connective tissue disease/overlap syndromes

5. **Vasculitis**   608
    5.1   Overview of vasculitis
    5.2   Classification of vasculitis
    5.3   Polymyalgia rheumatica, giant cell and other large vessel arteritis
    5.4   Wegener's granulomatosis
    5.5   Churg–Strauss syndrome (allergic angiitis and granulomatosis)
    5.6   Polyarteritis nodosa
    5.7   Microscopic polyangiitis (microscopic polyarteritis)
    5.8   Kawasaki disease
    5.9   Behçet's syndrome

6. Crystal arthropathies and osteoarthritis   **613**

    6.1   Gout

    6.2   Calcium pyrophosphate deposition disease (CPDD)

    6.3   Osteoarthritis

7. Arthritis in children   **617**

Rheumatology

1. RHEUMATOID FACTOR

Rheumatoid factors (RF) are antibodies to human IgG, usually reacting with the Fc portion. Routine hospital tests detect IgM rheumatoid factors, but RF may be of any immunoglobulin isotype (IgM/IgG/IgA).

- **Agglutination tests (Latex/SCAT)**: detect only IgM RF
- **RIA/ELISA tests**: can detect any class of RF (IgA, IgG, IgM).

IgM RF is found in:

- **Normal population**
  (4% overall; 25% of the elderly)

- **Chronic infections**
  (usually low titre)
  Syphilis 10%
  Leprosy 50%
  Bacterial endocarditis 25%
  Pulmonary tuberculosis 5–20%

- **Other 'immunological' diseases**
  Autoimmune liver disease
  Sarcoidosis
  Paraproteinaemias
  Cryoglobulinaemias
  Transplant recipients

- **Connective tissue disorders**
  (often high titre, i.e. >1/160)
  Rheumatoid arthritis 70%
  Rheumatoid arthritis with
    extra-articular features 100%
  Sjögren's syndrome >75%
  Systemic lupus erythematosus
    (SLE) 20–40%
  Scleroderma 30%
  Polyarteritis nodosa 0–5%
  Dermatomyositis 0–5%

- **Miscellaneous**
  Relatives of rheumatoid arthritis patients
  Increasing age
  Transiently during acute infections

In rheumatoid arthritis, the RF is an assessment of prognosis rather than a diagnostic test.

2. RHEUMATOID ARTHRITIS

Rheumatoid arthritis (RA) is a chronic symmetrical inflammatory polyarthritis. It characteristically involves small joints, and can be both erosive and deforming. Soft tissues and extra-articular structures may also be involved in the disease process. RA is the most common form of inflammatory arthritis. It affects 1–3% of the population in all racial groups, with a female:male ratio of 3:1. It may start at any age but onset is most commonly in the 40s.

The cause is not known but both genetic and environmental factors are thought to play a part, with genetic factors accounting for 10–30% of the risk of developing RA. There is an association with HLA-DR4 and patients with DR4 tend to have more severe disease.

Prognosis is variable and difficult to predict in individual cases:

- 50% are too disabled to work 10 years after diagnosis
- 25% have relatively mild disease
- There is excess mortality.

The following are associated with a worse prognosis:

- Positive rheumatoid factor
- Extra-articular features
- HLA-DR4
- Female sex
- Early erosions
- Insidious onset
- Severe disability at presentation.

2.1 Clinical features

The onset of disease may take several forms:

- Insidious (weeks/months)   55–70%
- Intermediate   15–20%
- Acute (days)   8–15%.

Other rare patterns of onset:

- **Palindromic**: episodic with complete resolution between attacks
- **Systemic**: presentation with systemic/extra-articular features
- **Polymyalgic**: symptoms initially similar to polymyalgia rheumatica.

2.2 Musculoskeletal features

Joints

Symmetrical MCP joint and wrist arthritis is characteristic but any synovial joint can be involved. RA tends to start in the hands and feet but, in time, most joints of the upper and lower limbs become affected. The cervical spine is involved in more than 30%. Hip or DIP joint involvement is unusual in early disease.

Characteristic deformities

- Ulnar deviation of MCP joints
- Swan-neck deformities of fingers
- Boutonnière deformities of fingers
- Z deformity of thumbs

Soft tissue involvement in RA

- **Tenosynovitis**
  Tendon rupture (extensor more frequently than flexor)
  Carpal tunnel syndrome (common)
- **Ligament laxity**
  Atlanto-axial subluxation (most are asymptomatic)
  Sub-axial subluxation
- **Lymphoedema**
  Rare

2.3 Extra-articular manifestations

Extra-articular features may arise in several ways:

- True extra-articular manifestations of the rheumatoid process
- Extra-articular manifestations of joint/tendon disease (not specific to RA)
- Systemic effects of inflammation (not specific to RA) (e.g. amyloidosis)
- Adverse drug effects.

True extra-articular manifestations of rheumatoid disease:

- Present in approximately 30% of patients with RA
- Rheumatoid factor is always positive
- Arthritis tends to be more severe.

Rheumatoid nodules are the most characteristic extra-articular feature.

Rheumatoid nodules

- 20–30% of cases
- Rheumatoid factor always positive
- Any site — most commonly subcutaneous at extensor surfaces and pressure points
- Mimic malignancy in the lung and may cavitate
- Associated with more severe arthritis

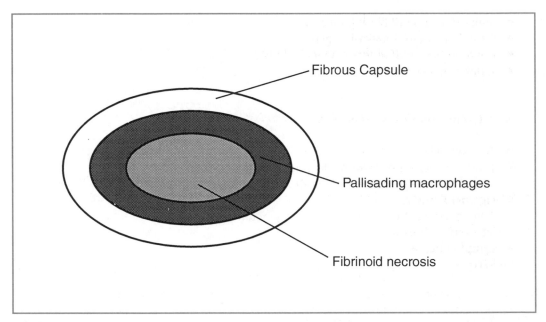

Pathology of a rheumatoid nodule

Eye involvement is common; 20–30% of patients have keratoconjunctivitis sicca (Sjögren's syndrome). Episcleritis (painless reddening of the eye lasting about a week) is likely to be as common but usually goes unnoticed. Scleritis (reddening and pain) is a manifestation of vasculitis and is uncommon. Repeated attacks of scleritis produce scleromalacia (blue sclera) and the eye may perforate (scleromalacia perforans). This is very rare. In contrast to the spondyloarthropathies, iritis is not a feature.

Vasculitis is usually benign, manifesting as nail fold infarcts and mild sensory neuropathy in association with active joint disease. The much rarer systemic rheumatoid vasculitis carries a significant mortality. Its features include cutaneous ulceration, mononeuritis multiplex, and involvement of the mesenteric, cerebral and coronary arteries. Renal vasculitis is unusual.

Cardio-respiratory manifestations. Pleural and pericardial disease is common (30%) but asymptomatic in all but a few cases. Less common features include interstitial lung disease and the very rare, and often rapidly fatal, obliterative bronchiolitis. Caplan's syndrome (massive lung fibrosis in RA patients with pneumoconiosis) is very rare.

Felty's syndrome (splenomegaly, neutropenia and RA) is rare. Patients with Felty's syndrome usually have a positive ANA and may have associated leg ulcers, lymphadenopathy and anaemia.

Systemic effects of inflammation

- Malaise, fever, weight loss, myalgia
- Anaemia of chronic disease
- Osteoporosis (immobility also contributes)
- Lymphadenopathy

Non-articular manifestations of joint/tendon disease

- Entrapment neuropathy, most commonly carpel tunnel syndrome, may occur in up to 30% of patients, but is usually mild. It may be the first symptom of RA.
- Cervical myelopathy due to atlanto-axial subluxation (rare, but high mortality)
- Hoarseness and stridor due to cricoarytenoid arthritis (rare, but dangerous).

Adverse drug effects

- **Skin rashes**: may be due to NSAIDs or disease modifying drugs. Rashes occur in about 10% of patients treated with gold or penicillamine.
- **Renal impairment**: due to prostaglandin inhibition, or the much rarer acute interstitial nephritis, may be due to NSAIDs. Proteinuria occurs in about 10% of patients receiving gold or penicillamine but only a few develop nephrotic syndrome. The proteinuria usually resolves after cessation of treatment.
- **Gastrointestinal**: NSAIDs commonly cause peptic and intestinal ulceration. Gold may cause stomatitis (common) and enterocolitis (rare).

Other extra-articular features/associations of RA

- Palmar erythema (common)
- Recurrent respiratory infections
- Pyoderma gangrenosum
- Depression (30%)

2.4 Investigations

The diagnosis of RA is based primarily on the history and examination. Laboratory tests and X-rays may be helpful but are rarely diagnostic in early disease. In clinical studies, RA can be diagnosed when four or more of the following are present:

- Morning stiffness > 1 hour for more than 6 weeks
- Arthritis of hand joints (wrist, MCP or PIP) for more than 6 weeks
- Subcutaneous nodules
- Characteristic X-ray findings
- Arthritis of three or more joint areas for more than 6 weeks
- Symmetric arthritis for more than 6 weeks
- Positive rheumatoid factor

Radiology

- **Early changes**
  Soft tissue swelling
  Juxta-articular osteoporosis

- **Intermediate changes**
  Joint space narrowing (due to cartilage loss)

- **Late changes**
  Bone and joint destruction
  Subluxation
  Ankylosis (rare nowadays)

Laboratory studies

- Rheumatoid factor is positive in 70%
- Most laboratory abnormalities are secondary to active inflammation or drug effects and are not specific to RA. They are used to monitor disease activity and screen for adverse drug effects
- ESR, CRP and plasma viscosity reflect disease activity
- Alkaline phosphatase is often mildly raised in active disease
- Raised AST and ALT are more likely to be drug-induced
- Anaemia is common and may be:
  Iron deficient: gastric blood loss from NSAIDs
  Normochromic: with active disease (often with thrombocytosis)
  Aplastic: rare drug effect (e.g. aurothiomalate, NSAIDs)
  Haemolytic: rare as a manifestation of RA, but mild forms common with sulphasalazine
- Immunoglobulin levels may be raised

- Complement levels are usually normal, or elevated as an acute phase response
- Ferritin may be elevated in an acute phase response and can not be used to assess iron status
- Synovial fluid examination is rarely helpful in diagnosis but is often done to exclude other diagnoses (e.g. sepsis, gout). Rheumatoid effusions, like those of most other inflammatory arthropathies, contain large numbers of polymorphs.

2.5 Disease-modifying drugs

Drugs used in the treatment of RA fall into two categories: **symptom-modifying** and **disease-modifying**. The disease-modifying drugs are also referred to as slow acting anti-rheumatic drugs or second-line drugs.

- **Symptom-modifying** drugs (e.g. NSAIDs) will reduce pain, stiffness and swelling
- **Disease-modifying** drugs have additional actions and will:
  Reduce pain, swelling and stiffness
  Reduce ESR and CRP
  Correct the anaemia of chronic disease
  Possibly slow disease progression
- Other extra-articular features do not respond to disease-modifying drugs, though nodules may regress. Methotrexate is unusual in that it can increase the formation of rheumatoid nodules
- Corticosteroids, although effective at reducing the acute phase response and synovitis, are not thought to be truly 'disease-modifying'
- Disease-modifying drugs in common use are listed below, together with the necessary parameters for monitoring.

Disease-modifying drugs in common use

Drug	Monitoring
Antimalarials (chloroquine/hydroxychloroquine)	Ophthalmological
Sulphasalazine	FBC, LFT
Methotrexate	FBC, LFT
Azathioprine	FBC, LFT
Gold (sodium aurothiomalate)	FBC, urinalysis
D-penicillamine	FBC, urinalysis
Cyclosporin A	FBC, U&Es, BP

3. SPONDYLOARTHROPATHIES (HLA-B27-ASSOCIATED DISORDERS)

This group of disorders is characterized by seronegative (i.e. rheumatoid factor negative) inflammatory arthritis and/or spondylitis. The peripheral arthritis is typically asymmetrical, involving larger joints, especially the knees and ankles. Characteristic articular features include enthesitis (inflammation at sites of tendon insertion), sacroiliitis and dactylitis. These arthropathies should not be confused with seronegative RA, which is a symmetrical small joint arthritis.

The spondyloathropathies include:

- Ankylosing spondylitis
- Reiter's syndrome/reactive arthritis
- Undifferentiated spondyloarthropathy
- Psoriatic arthritis
- Enteropathic arthritis
  (with ulcerative colitis or Crohn's disease)

Associated conditions:

- Psoriasis
- Anterior uveitis (independently associated with HLA-B27)
- Inflammatory bowel disease
- Erythema nodosum

There is an association with HLA-B27 and a tendency for relatives to have other conditions within the group.

Prevalence of HLA-B27 in spondyloarthropathies (%)

Normal Caucasian population	8
Ankylosing spondylitis	90
Reiter's syndrome	70
Enteropathic spondylitis	50
Psoriatic arthritis	20
Psoriatic arthritis with sacroiliitis	50

3.1 Ankylosing spondylitis

Typically begins with the insidious onset of low back pain and stiffness in a young man. The age of onset is usually between 15 and 40 years and the male:female ratio is about 5:1. It is less common than RA, with a prevalence of about 0.1%. The prognosis is good.

Clinical features of ankylosing spondylitis

- **Articular**
  Sacroiliitis is the characteristic feature,
    but radiological changes may not
    be evident for several years
  Spondylitis (100%)
  Peripheral joints (35%)
  Inter-vertebral discitis (rare)

- **Extra-articular**
  Anterior uveitis (25%)
  Aortic incompetence (4%)
  Apical lung fibrosis (rare)
  Aortitis (rare)
  Heart block (rare)
  Amyloidosis (rare)

Investigations:

- ESR/CRP may be elevated
- Normochromic anaemia
- Alkaline phosphatase often mildly elevated.

HLA-B27 in diagnosis

This should not be a routine test in back pain. Although a negative result makes ankylosing spondylitis unlikely, a positive result is of little help.

Radiology

- **Sacro-iliac joints**
  Irregular/blurred joint margins
  Subchondral erosion
  Sclerosis
  Fusion

.

- **Spine**
  Loss of lumbar lordosis
  Squaring of vertebrae
  Romanus lesion (erosion at the
    corner of vertebral bodies)
  Bamboo spine (calcification in anterior
    and posterior spinal ligaments)
  Enthesitis (calcification at tendon/
    ligament insertions into bone)

Treatment

- Physiotherapy and regular home exercises
- NSAIDs
- Disease-modifying drugs (e.g. sulphasalazine, methotrexate) help peripheral arthritis but have no effect on spinal disease.

3.2 Reiter's syndrome

Reiter's syndrome is a form of reactive arthritis characterized by a triad of arthritis, conjunctivitis and urethritis. A reactive arthritis usually begins 1–3 weeks after an initiating infection at a distant site. Antigenic material from the infecting organism may be identified in affected joints but complete organisms cannot be identified or grown, and the arthritis does not respond to treatment with antibiotics.

Reiter's syndrome is said to be 20 times more frequent in men than in women. This is likely to be an over-estimate because cervicitis may go unrecognized. The true male:female ratio is more likely to be 5:1. Post-dysenteric reactive arthritis has an equal sex distribution. The age of onset is 15–40 years.

Recognized precipitating infections:

- **Post-urethritis**: (*Chlamydia trachomatis* — 50%)
- **Post-dysenteric**: (*Yersinia, Salmonella, Shigella, Campylobacter*).

Clinical features of Reiter's syndrome

- **Classical triad**
  Arthritis
  Conjunctivitis
  Urethritis

- **Rare features**
  Heart: pericarditis, aortitis,
    conduction defects
  Lung: pleurisy, pulmonary infiltrates
  CNS: meningoencephalitis,
    peripheral neuropathy

- **Other features**
  Circinate balanitis (25%)
  Buccal/lingual ulcers (10%)
  Keratoderma blenorrhagica (10%)
  Iritis (chronic cases only — 30%)
  Plantar fasciitis/Achilles tendinitis
  Fever/weight loss

Prognosis

- Complete resolution, no recurrence in 70–75%
- Complete resolution, recurrent episodes in 20–25% (usually B27 +ve)
- Chronic disease in <5% (usually B27 +ve).

Treatment

- Mild disease: NSAIDs
- Chronic disease may need disease-modifying drugs
- Prominent systemic symptoms may need corticosteroids.

3.3 Psoriatic arthritis

Chronic synovitis occurs in about 8% of patients with psoriasis. The arthritis may precede the diagnosis of psoriasis in 1 in 6 of these patients. Males and females are equally affected.

Patterns of psoriatic arthritis:

- Polyarthritis similar to RA (most common type)
- Distal interphalangeal joints (5–10%)
- Sacroiliitis and spondylitis (20–40%)
- Asymmetric oligoarthritis (20–40%)
- Arthritis mutilans (<5%).

Characteristic features of psoriatic arthritis

- Nail pitting and onycholysis
- DIP joint arthritis
- Telescoping fingers in arthritis mutilans
- Paravertebral calcification
- Dactylitis

4. INFLAMMATORY CONNECTIVE TISSUE DISORDERS

4.1 Autoantibodies in diagnosis

This topic is covered in detail in Chapter 9, *Immunology*.

Anti-nuclear antibodies (ANA)

Indirect immunofluorescence is the routine method for detecting ANA. It is highly sensitive and the fluorescence pattern can give some indication of the type of ANA/disease present. (See also Chapter 9, *Immunology*.)

Anti-double stranded DNA antibodies

- Specific for systemic lupus erythematosus (SLE) (except low titres on ELISA assay)
- Present in approximately 80% of patients with SLE.

Methods:

- Radioimmunoassay (Farr assay)
- Crithidia lucillae immunofluorescence
- Enzyme linked immunosorbent assay (ELISA).

(See also Chapter 9, *Immunology*.)

Antibodies to extractable nuclear antigens (ENA)

Methods:

- Counter immunoelectrophoresis/ELISA.

Many ENA antibodies have been described in the literature; they are covered in Chapter 9, *Immunology*.

Anti-phospholipid and anti-neutrophil antibodies

These are covered in Chapter 9, *Immunology*.

4.2 Systemic lupus erythematosus (SLE)

A multi-system inflammatory connective tissue disorder with small vessel vasculitis and non-organ specific auto-antibodies. It is characterized by skin rashes, arthralgia and antibodies against double-stranded DNA. Young women are predominantly affected with a female:male ratio of 10:1. It is more common in West Indian populations. Ten-year survival exceeds 90%.

Clinical features of SLE

- **Common** (>80% of cases)
  Arthralgia or non-erosive arthritis
  Rash (malar, discoid or photosensitive)
  Fever

- **Others**
  Serositis (30–60%): pericarditis, pleurisy, effusions
  Renal* (30–60%): glomerulonephritis, nephrotic syndrome
  Neuropsychiatric (10–60%): psychosis, seizures
  Haematological (up to 50%): leucopenia, thrombocytopenia, haemolysis
  Alopecia (up to 50%)
  Raynaud's phenomenon (10–40%)
  Oral or nasal ulcers(10–40%)
  Respiratory (10%)**: pneumonitis, shrinking lung syndrome
  Cardiac (10%)**: myocarditis, endocarditis

*Proteinuria is present in 30–60% of patients with SLE.
**Up to 60% of lupus patients will have respiratory and cardiac involvement but in the majority this is pleural and pericardial disease (i.e. serositis). Pneumonitis, myocarditis etc. are less common.

Investigations for SLE

FBC may show:

- Anaemia of chronic disease (normal MCV)
- Neutropenia
- Thrombocytopenia
- Haemolytic anaemia (high MCV, reticulocytosis)
- Lymphopenia
- Aplastic anaemia (rare)

ESR reflects disease activity, whereas CRP may not. This discrepancy can be used to differentiate between a flare of SLE and intercurrent infection.

Low C3 and C4 suggest lupus nephritis.

Antibodies

- ANA-positive in 95% of cases, usually with a homogeneous staining pattern
- Anti-double stranded DNA antibodies in high titre are very specific for SLE
- Anti-Sm antibodies are found in only 20% but are very specific for lupus
- Anti-Ro or anti-La are found in ANA-negative subacute cutaneous lupus
- Antiphospholipid antibodies in 40%, but only a minority have thrombotic events
  False positive VDRL

Lupus variants

Drug-induced lupus is more common in men than in women. It is usually mild and always resolves on stopping the drug. CNS and renal disease are rare. ANA is positive but antibodies to double-stranded DNA are not usually present. The pathogenesis is not known, and antibodies to the drug do not occur. The drugs commonly implicated (procainamide, isoniazid, and hydralazine) all have active amido groups. See also Chapter 2, *Clinical Pharmacology, Toxicology and Poisoning*.

Antiphospholipid antibody syndrome (Hughes' syndrome): recurrent venous or arterial thromboses, fetal loss and thrombocytopenia. Libman–Sacks endocarditis and focal neurological lesions (such as CVA or TIA) in lupus are usually due to antiphospholipid antibodies.

Treatment of lupus depends on severity and organ involvement.

Treatment of SLE

- **Sunscreens**
  Sunburn can provoke a generalized
  flare in disease

- **Plasma exchange**
  In difficult cases with most
  aggressive disease

- **NSAIDS and anti-malarials**
  (e.g. chloroquine) used for arthritis

- **Corticosteroids and**
  immunosuppressive drugs
  For vital organ involvement

- **Anticoagulation**
  For thrombotic features

4.3 Dermatomyositis and polymyositis

Polymyositis is an idiopathic inflammatory disorder of skeletal muscle. When associated
with cutaneous lesions it is called dermatomyositis. These conditions are rare (5/1,000,000).
Five-year survival is 80% with treatment. Myositis may also occur with other connective
tissue disorders.

Clinical features of dermatomyositis and polymyositis

- **Muscle disease**
  Proximal weakness
  Swelling and tenderness of muscles

- **Others**
  Pulmonary muscle weakness
  Interstitial lung disease
  Oesophageal dysfunction
  Arthralgia
  Weight loss
  Fever

- **Skin rash**
  Heliotrope discoloration
   of the eyelids
  Gottron's papules (scaly papules
   over MCP/PIP joints)
  Periungual telangiectasia
  Erythematous macules

Juvenile dermatomyositis differs from the adult form. Vasculitis, ectopic calcification and
lipodystrophy are commonly present.

Malignancy

The elderly with dermatomyositis and polymyositis have a higher prevalence of malignancy than would be expected by chance and this is most pronounced in dermatomyositis. There is no association between dermatomyositis/polymyositis and malignancy in children or adults of young and middle age.

Laboratory tests include:

- **Muscle**
  Elevated muscle enzymes:
    CK, AST, LDH
  Abnormal EMG
  Biopsy showing inflammation,
    muscle fibre necrosis and regeneration

- **Autoantibodies**
  Antinuclear antibodies may be
    present
  Anti-Jo-1 is associated with a specific
    syndrome of: acute onset myositis;
    interstitial lung disease; fever;
    arthritis; Raynaud's phenomenon;
    mechanics' hands (fissuring of the
    digital pads without ulceration and
    periungual infarcts)

Treatment

- **Corticosteroids:** CK falls rapidly but muscle power takes many weeks to improve.
- **Immunosuppressives**: in resistant cases.

4.4 Systemic sclerosis

Systemic sclerosis is a connective tissue disorder characterized by thickening and fibrosis of the skin (scleroderma) with distinctive involvement of internal organs. It is a rare condition, occurring in all racial groups, with an incidence of 4–12/million/year. It is more common in women (female:male ratio 4:1) and may start at any age.

Some cases may be due to exposure to substances such as vinyl chloride.

Clinical features of systemic sclerosis

- **Raynaud's phenomenon**
  Initial complaint in 70%
  Associated digital ulcers and calcinosis
  (very unusual in primary Raynaud's
  phenomenon)

- **Musculoskeletal**
  Arthralgia
  Erosive arthritis in about 30%
  Myositis (usually mild, often
  asymptomatic with raised CK)
  Flexion deformities of fingers due
  to skin fibrosis

- **Pulmonary**
  Fibrotic interstitial lung disease
  Pulmonary hypertension

- **Renal**
  Scleroderma renal crisis
  (malignant hypertension,
  rapid renal impairment with
  'onion skin' intra-renal vasculature)

- **Scleroderma**
  Early oedematous phase
  Later indurated and hidebound
  Affected areas may become
  pigmented and lose hair

- **Gastrointestinal**
  Motility can be impaired at any
  level (smooth muscle atrophy
  and fibrosis)
  Oesophagus (reflux, dysphagia,
  peptic strictures)
  Gastric dilatation

- **Gastrointestinal**
  Intestine (bacterial overgrowth,
  malabsorption, steatorrhoea,
  pseudo-obstruction
  Colon (constipation)

Laboratory tests include:

- **Elevated ESR or CRP**

- **Autoantibodies**
  Rheumatoid factor positive in 30%
  Antinuclear factor positive in 90% (homogeneous, speckled or nucleolar staining)
  Anticentromere and Anti-Scl-70 are quite specific
  Anticentromere positive in 50–90% of limited and 10% of diffuse scleroderma
  Anti-Scl-70 (anti-topoisomerase-I) positive in 20–40%.

Disease patterns

Limited scleroderma with systemic involvement — CREST
- Scleroderma limited to the face, neck and limbs distal to the elbow and knee
- Usually begins with Raynaud's phenomenon
- CREST (Calcinosis, Raynaud's, oEsophageal dysmotility, Sclerodactyly, Telangiectasia)
- Anti-centromere antibody positive in most
- Renal crisis rare, pulmonary hypertension more common
- Better prognosis.

Diffuse scleroderma with limited involvement
- Scleroderma involving trunk and proximal limbs as well as face and distal limbs
- Usually begins with swelling of fingers and arthritis
- Anti-Scl-70 antibodies 20–40%
- Pulmonary hypertension rare, renal crisis more common
- Worse prognosis.

Scleroderma without internal organ disease
- Plaques: morphea
- Linear: coup de sabre.

Treatment

- **Supportive**
  NSAIDs for arthralgia/arthritis
  Proton pump inhibitors for reflux
  Intermittent antibiotics for bacterial
    overgrowth in the small bowel
  Vasodilators for Raynaud's phenomenon
  Prostacyclin or Iloprost infusions for
    severe Raynaud's phenomenon and
    digital ischaemia

- **Specific**
  D-penicillamine can slow the
    progression of skin disease
  Steroids and immunosuppressives
    for interstitial lung disease
  Steroids do not help the skin

4.5 Sjögren's syndrome

A connective tissue disorder characterized by lymphocytic infiltration of exocrine glands, especially the lacrimal and salivary glands. The reduced secretions produce the dry eyes and dry mouth of the sicca syndrome. Secondary Sjögren's syndrome describes the presence of sicca syndrome and either RA or a connective tissue disorder. About 30% of rheumatoid patients have secondary Sjögren's syndrome.

Clinical features of Sjögren's syndrome

- **Dryness from atrophy of exocrine glands**
  Eyes (xerophthalmia) which may allow
    corneal ulceration
  Mouth (xerostomia) with increased
    dental caries
  Respiratory with hoarseness,
    dysphagia, respiratory infections
  Vaginal producing dyspareunia

- **Arthralgia or arthritis**
  Which may be erosive

- **Raynaud's phenomenon**

- **Lymphadenopathy**

- **Gland swelling**
  In the early stages (e.g. parotid)

- **Vasculitic purpura**

- **Neuropathies**

- **Renal tubular acidosis (30%)**

- **Pancreatitis**

Laboratory tests:

- Anaemia and leucopenia
  are common
- ANA frequently present
- Anti-Ro or anti-La present in
  primary Sjögren's syndrome

- ESR and CRP reflect disease activity
- Rheumatoid factor positive in
  most cases
- Polyclonal hypergammaglobulinaemia

Treatment

- **Artificial tears**: plugging of lacrimal punctae in severe cases.
- **Moistening sprays**: for the mouth.
- **NSAIDs**: and sometimes hydroxychloroquine for arthritis.

4.6 Mixed connective tissue disease/overlap syndromes

Some patients have features of more than one connective tissue disorder and are said to have overlap syndromes. One specific overlap syndrome, mixed connective tissue disease, is associated with anti-RNP antibodies. The clinical features are Raynaud's phenomenon, swollen hands and other features from at least two connective tissue disorders (SLE, scleroderma or polymyositis).

5. VASCULITIS

5.1 Overview of vasculitis

Systemic vasculitis usually presents with constitutional symptoms such as general malaise, fever and weight loss, combined with more specific signs and symptoms related to specific organ involvement. The diagnosis is based on a combination of clinical and laboratory findings, and is usually confirmed by biopsy and/or angiography.

Aetiology

Infections, malignancy and drugs may all produce vasculitic illness but, in many cases, the trigger for endothelial injury is unknown. The following mechanisms of endothelial cell injury have been proposed in the pathogenesis of vasculitis:

- **Immune complex deposition**: hepatitis B-associated polyarteritis nodosa
- **Direct endothelial cell infection**: HIV
- **Anti-endothelial cell antibodies**: Kawasaki's disease, Behçet's disease
- **ANCA-mediated neutrophil activation**: Wegener's granulomatosis
- **T-cell dependent injury**: giant cell arteritis.

Clinical features of vasculitis

- **General**
  Constitutional (fever, weight loss, fatigue, anorexia)
  Musculoskeletal (arthralgia, arthritis, myalgia)
  Skin (livedo reticularis, urticaria)

- **Related to specific organ involvement**
  Kidney (proteinuria, hypertension, glomerulonephritis)
  Respiratory (alveolitis, infiltrates, haemorrhage, sinusitis)
  Neuropathy (mononeuritis multiplex, sensory neuropathy)
  Gastrointestinal (diarrhoea, abdominal pain, perforation, haemorrhage)
  Cardiovascular (jaw or extremity claudication, angina, myocardial infarction)
  Central nervous system (headache, visual loss, stroke, seizures)

5.2 Classification of vasculitis

The vasculitides are classified according to the size of vessel involved and the pattern of organ involvement.

- **Large vessels**
  Takayasu's arteritis
  Giant cell/temporal arteritis
  Aortitis associated with ankylosing
  spondylitis

- **Small/medium-sized vessels**
  Granulomatous:
  Wegener's granulomatosis
  Churg–Strauss syndrome
  Granulomatous angiitis of the CNS
  Non-granulomatous:
  Polyarteritis nodosa
  Kawasaki disease
  Arteritis/vasculitis of RA, SLE,
  Sjögren's syndrome
  Microscopic polyangiitis

- **Small vessel vasculitis**
  Leucocytoclastic vasculities
   allergic or hypersensitivity vasculitis
  Henoch–Schönlein syndrome
  Cryoglobulinaemia
  Drug-induced vasculities
  Vasculitis of RA, SLE, Sjögren's
   syndrome
  Microscopic polyangiitis

- **Others**
  Behçets syndrome (vasculitis and
   venulitis)

Laboratory tests:

- ESR/CRP are invariably elevated in active disease
- Normochromic anaemia and leucocytosis (usually a neutrophilia) are common
- Eosinophilia is characteristic of Churg–Strauss syndrome but may occur in any vasculitis
- Serum creatinine and urinary protein assessments are essential if vasculitis is suspected since renal involvement is one of the most important factors affecting prognosis
- Autoantibodies:
  cANCA is useful in identifying Wegener's disease and microscopic polyangiitis
  pANCA may be positive in any vasculitis
  ANCA titres may reflect the activity of vasculitis and titres may begin to rise before a flare in disease activity.

Treatment

- **Large vessel group**: corticosteroids only for most cases
- **Medium/small vessels**: corticosteroids and immunosuppressives (cyclophosphamide and/ or azathioprine)

- **Small vessel group**: some conditions benign, corticosteroids and immunosuppressives in some cases.

Prognosis

The size of vessel involved and presence of renal involvement are the most important factors determining prognosis. Despite treatment with immunosuppressive agents and steroids, up to 20% of patients with systemic vasculitis of the small/medium vessel group die within 1 year of diagnosis. Patients with large or small vessel vasculitis have a much more favourable outlook.

5.3 Polymyalgia rheumatica, giant cell and other large vessel arteritis

Giant cell arteritis is a vasculitis of large vessels, usually the cranial branches of arteries arising from the aorta. Polymyalgia rheumatica is not a vasculitis, but is found in 40–60% of patients with giant cell arteritis. Both are disorders of the over 50s and both are relatively common. Polymyalgia has an incidence of 52/100,000 persons aged over 50, and giant cell arteritis of 18/100,000 persons over 50. Treatment is with corticosteroids.

Features of polymyalgia rheumatica and giant cell arteritis

- **Polymyalgia rheumatica**
  Female:male ratio 3:1
  Age > 50 years
  Proximal muscle pain
    (shoulder or pelvic)
    without weakness
  Early morning stiffness
  Raised acute phase response
    (ESR/CRP)
  Abnormal liver function tests
    (alkaline phosphatase/GGT)
  CK normal
  Synovitis of knees, etc. may occur
  Response to corticosteroids is dramatic
    and prompt (within 24–48 hours)

- **Giant cell arteritis**
  General malaise, weight loss, fever
  Temporal headache with tender,
    enlarged non-pulsatile temporal
    arteries
  Scalp tenderness
  Jaw claudication
  Visual disturbance/loss
  Polymyalgia rheumatica
  Positive temporal artery biopsy
    (patchy granulomatous necrosis
    with giant cells)

Takayasu's arteritis (pulseless disease)

This rare condition presents with systemic illness such as malaise, weight loss and fever. The main vasculitic involvement is of the aorta and its main branches, producing arm claudication, absent pulses and bruits. Thirty per cent of patients have visual disturbance. Diagnosis is by angiography and treatment involves corticosteroids.

5.4 Wegener's granulomatosis

A rare disorder (incidence 0.4/100,000) characterized by a granulomatous necrotizing vasculitis. Any organ may be involved but the classical Wegener's triad includes:

- **Upper airways (sinuses, ears, eyes)**: saddle nose, proptosis
- **Respiratory**: multiple pulmonary nodules
- **Renal**: focal proliferative glomerulonephritis often with segmental necrosis.

Treatment is with corticosteroids and immunosuppressives. c-ANCA is present in 90% of cases (see also Chapter 13, *Nephrology*).

5.5 Churg–Strauss syndrome (allergic angiitis and granulomatosis)

A rare systemic vasculitis with a similar pattern of organ involvement to polyarteritis nodosa but with associated eosinophilia and asthma. Though corticosteroids are required, the condition of most patients can be controlled without immunosuppressives. In some cases, the disease is triphasic. See also Chapter 17, *Respiratory Medicine*.

- **Prodromal**: allergic features of asthma, rhinitis
- **Eosinophilia**: with eosinophilic pneumonia or eosinophilic gastroenteritis
- **Systemic vasculitis**.

5.6 Polyarteritis nodosa

Primary necrotizing vasculitis of small/medium-sized vessels with formation of microaneurysms. It is uncommon with an incidence of 5–9 per million, but it may be as much as ten times more frequent in areas where hepatitis B is endemic. Presentation is usually with constitutional symptoms. Any organ may be involved but commonly skin, peripheral nerves, kidney, gut and joints are affected. Treatment is with corticosteroids and immunosuppressives.

- Hepatitis B surface antigen is present in 30% of cases world-wide, but <10% in the UK
- Mild eosinophilia may be present
- LFTs often abnormal
- ANCA is positive in <10%.

5.7 Microscopic polyangiitis (microscopic polyarteritis)

Usually presents between the ages of 40 and 60 with constitutional illness and renal disease. Though classified with the medium/small vessel disorders, microscopic angiitis tends to affect small arteries and arterioles of the kidney. Organs involved include:

- **Kidney**: glomerulonephritis as for Wegener's disease
- **Skin**: palpable purpura
- **Lung**: infiltrates, haemoptysis, haemorrhage
- **Gut, eye or peripheral nerves** can also be involved.

ANCA is positive in most cases: pANCA in 60% and cANCA in 40% (see Chapter 13, *Nephrology*).

5.8 Kawasaki disease

An acute febrile illness with systemic vasculitis which mainly affects children less than five years old. The peak onset is at 1.5 years and it has an incidence of about 6/100,000 in the under fives. It is more common and more severe in males. The cause is not known but its occasional occurrence in mini-epidemics suggests an infectious agent. (Rickettsia has been implicated.)

Clinical features of Kawasaki disease

- **Fever**
  (Followed by thrombocytosis)

- **Mucocutaneous**
  Rashes, red cracked lips,
    strawberry tongue, conjunctivitis

- **Vasculitis**
  With coronary aneurysm formation
  Myocardial infarctions in 2.5%

- **Lymphadenopathy**
  (Especially cervical)

Treatment differs from most other vasculitides. Corticosteroids are contraindicated since they increase coronary aneurysms. Anti-inflammatory doses of aspirin are used during the acute febrile phase and anti-platelet doses once the fever resolves and thrombocytosis occurs. Intravenous immunoglobulin is also effective.

5.9 Behçet's syndrome

Behçet's syndrome is a rare condition most commonly found in Turkey and the eastern Mediterranean where there is a strong association with HLA B5. There is an equal sex ratio but the disease is more severe in males. The pathological findings are of immune-mediated occlusive vasculitis and venulitis. The diagnosis is based on clinical features.

- **Main clinical features**
  Recurrent oral ulceration (100%)
  Recurrent painful genital ulceration (80%)
  Recurrent iritis (60–70%)
  Skin lesions (60–80%)

- **Other features**
  Cutaneous vasculitis
  Thrombophlebitis
  Pathergy reaction (red papules >2 mm at sites of needle pricks after 48 hours)
  Erythema nodosum
  Arthritis (usually non-erosive, asymmetrical, lower limb)
  Neurological involvement (aseptic meningitis, ataxia, pseudobulbar palsy)
  Gastrointestinal involvement

6. CRYSTAL ARTHROPATHIES AND OSTEOARTHRITIS

6.1 Gout

Hyperuricaemia is common and usually asymptomatic, but in some individuals uric acid crystals form within joints or soft tissues to produce a variety of diseases.

Clinical features of gout

- **Acute crystal arthritis**
  Particularly affecting the small joints
  of the feet (e.g. 1st MTP usually
  recurrent)

- **Gouty nephropathy**
  Tubulo interstitial disease due to
  parenchymal crystal deposition
  Acute intratubular precipitation
  resulting in acute renal failure
  Urate stone formation (radio-luscent)

- **Chronic tophaceous arthritis**
  These are aggregations of urate
  crystals affecting articular,
  periarticular and non-articular
  cartilage (e.g. ears)

Aetiology

Uric acid is a breakdown product of purine nucleotides. Purines can be synthesized from precursors, but significant amounts are ingested in normal diets and released at cell death. Hyperuricaemia arises because of an imbalance in uric acid production/ingestion and excretion.

Causes of gout

- **Primary (innate)**
  Idiopathic (90% of these are due to undersecretion)
  Rare enzyme deficiencies: e.g. HGPRT deficiency (Lesch–Nyhan syndrome)

- **Secondary hyperuricaemia**
  Increased uric acid production/intake
    Myeloproliferative and lymphoproliferative disorders
    High purine diet: e.g. purines in beer (even non-alcoholic)
    Cytolytic therapy
    Acidosis: e.g. the ketosis of starvation or diabetes
    Extreme exercise status epilepticus
    Psoriasis
  Decreased uric acid excretion
    Renal failure
    Drugs (diuretics, low-dose aspirin, cyclosporin, pyrazinamide)
    Alcohol
    Lead intoxication (saturnine gout)
    Down's syndrome

Diagnosis

- Negatively birefringent needle-shaped crystals must be identified in joint fluid or other tissues for a definitive diagnosis.
- In chronic tophaceous gout the X-ray appearances (large punched-out erosions distant from the joint margin) are characteristic and may allow diagnosis.
- In clinical practice, a characteristic history with hyperuricaemia is often thought sufficient, but there are pitfalls: uric acid may fall by up to 30% during an acute attack; hyperuricaemia is common and may be coincidental.

Treatment

- **Acute attack**
  NSAIDs or colchicine

- **Prophylaxis**
  Allopurinol, a xanthine oxidase inhibitor, is the drug of first choice. It may precipitate acute attacks at the outset of treatment unless an NSAID or colchicine is given
  Probenecid and sulphinpyrazone are less effective

Indications for prophylaxis

- Recurrent attacks of arthritis
- Tophi
- Uric acid nephropathy
- Nephrolithiasis
- Cytolytic therapy
- HGPRT deficiency.

6.2 Calcium pyrophosphate deposition disease (CPDD)

This is a spectrum of disorders ranging from asymptomatic radiological abnormalities to disabling polyarthritis. The underlying problem is the deposition of calcium pyrophosphate crystals in and around joints. This is most commonly idiopathic and age-related, but may occur in metabolic disorders especially those with hypercalcaemia or hypomagnesaemia. Calcium pyrophosphate forms positively birefringent brick shaped crystals — 'Pseudogout'.

Variants:

- **Asymptomatic**: radiological chondrocalcinosis (30% of over 80s)
- **Acute monoarthritis**: pseudogout (usually knee, elbow or shoulder)

- **Inflammatory polyarthritis**: mimicking RA (10% of CPDD)
- **Osteoarthritis**: often of hips and knees but with involvement of the index and middle MCP joints (rarely seen in primary osteoarthritis).

Causes of CPDD

Hyperparathyroidism
Wilson's disease
Bartter's syndrome
Hypomagnesaemia

Haemochromatosis
Hypophosphatasia
Ochronosis

Treatment of CPDD

Chondrocalcinosis alone needs no treatment
NSAIDs for arthritis
Correction of metabolic disturbances (if possible)

6.3 Osteoarthritis

Osteoarthritis (OA) is the most common joint disease. It is characterized by softening and disintegration of articular cartilage, with secondary changes within adjacent bone. The prevalence of OA on X-ray rises with age and affects 70% of 70-year-olds. Many individuals with radiological OA, however, are asymptomatic.

Common joints involved are:

- Distal interphalangeal joints (Heberden's nodes)
- Proximal interphalangeal joints (Bouchard's nodes)
- Base of thumb (1st carpometacarpal joint)
- Hips
- Knees
- Spine.

Metacarpophalangeal joint OA suggests a secondary cause (e.g. CPDD disease).

OA subsets

- **Primary**
  Localized (one principal site, e.g. hip)
  Generalized (e.g. hands, knees, spine)

- **Secondary**
  Dysplastic disorders
  Mechanical damage
    (e.g. osteonecrosis,
    post-meniscectomy)
  Metabolic (e.g. ochronosis,
    acromegaly)
  Previous inflammation
    (e.g. sepsis, gout, RA)

7. ARTHRITIS IN CHILDREN

Classifications:

- Juvenile chronic arthritis (JCA)
- Systemic connective tissue disease
- Reactive arthritis (e.g. rheumatic fever)
- Other (psoriatic, viral, leukaemic).

Juvenile chronic arthritis

Juvenile chronic arthritis is persistent arthritis of more than 3 months' duration in children under the age of 16. It is one of the more common chronic disorders of children and is a major cause of musculoskeletal disability and eye disease. The cause is not known. A number of distinct clinical patterns of onset are recognized.

Clinical patterns of onset of JCA

	Systemic	*Polyarticular*	*Pauciarticular*
Frequency (%)	10	30	60
Number of joints	Variable	5 or more	4 or less
Female:male ratio	1:1	3:1	5:1
Extra-articular	Prominent	Moderate	Rarer
Uveitis (%)	Rare	5	20
Rheumatoid factor (%)	Rare	15	Rare
Antinuclear factor (%)	10	40	85
Prognosis	Moderate	Moderate	Good

Systemic (classical Still's disease)

The hallmark is a high spiking fever which, with the salmon pink evanescent rash, is virtually diagnostic. There is usually visceral involvement with hepatosplenomegaly and serositis. Initially the arthritis may be flitting as in rheumatic fever, but in 50% of cases, this develops into a chronic destructive arthropathy. This is usually a disease of the under fives, but adult cases do occur.

Polyarticular

Arthritis of more than four joints. This is probably two distinct disorders. Younger children with negative rheumatoid factor have a symmetrical arthritis of large joints (especially the knees), though the small joints can be affected. Older children, usually teenagers, with a positive rheumatoid factor have, in fact, early onset rheumatoid arthritis.

Pauciarticular

Arthritis of between one and four joints. Again there are two distinct groups. Older boys with sacroiliitis and HLA-B27 who probably have juvenile onset ankylosing spondylitis and younger girls, usually ANA positive who may have uveitis. Regular ophthalmological screening is required in this group.

Treatment of arthritis in children

- Physiotherapy
- Splintage
- NSAIDs

- Disease-modifying agents (e.g. methotrexate) in persistent polyarticular disease
- Corticosteroids may be needed for systemic disease

Chapter 19
Statistics

CONTENTS

1. **Study design**   621
   1.1   Research questions
   1.2   Experimental studies
   1.3   Crossover studies
   1.4   Observational studies
   1.5   Confounding

2. **Distributions**   624
   2.1   Types of data
   2.2   Skewed distributions
   2.3   Normal distribution
   2.4   Standard deviation

3. **Confidence intervals**   626
   3.1   Standard error (SE or SEM)

4. **Significance tests**   628
   4.1   Null hypotheses and p values
   4.2   Significance, power and sample size
   4.3   Parametric and nonparametric tests

5. **Correlation and regression**   630
   5.1   Correlation coefficients
   5.2   Linear regression

6. **Screening tests**   634

Statistics

1. STUDY DESIGN

1.1 Research questions

A research study should always be designed to answer a particular research question. The question usually relates to a specific population. For example:

- Does taking folic acid early in pregnancy prevent neural tube defects?
- Is a new inhaled steroid better than current treatment for improving lung function amongst cystic fibrosis patients?
- Are those who smoke more likely to develop cancer?

Random samples of the relevant groups are taken. For example: pregnant women, cystic fibrosis patients, those who do and do not smoke.

Based on the outcome in the samples, inferences are made about the populations from which they were randomly sampled. Statistical analysis enables us to determine what inferences can be made.

Studies are either experimental or observational.

1.2 Experimental studies

In experimental studies, individuals are assigned to groups by the investigator. For example, pregnant women will be assigned to take either folic acid or a placebo; cystic fibrosis patients will be assigned to either the new or current treatment. In both of these examples the second group is known as a control group.

Note that a control group does not necessarily consist of normal healthy individuals. In the second example the control group comprises cystic fibrosis patients on standard therapy.

Individuals should be randomized to groups to remove any potential bias. Randomization means that each patient has the same chance of being assigned to either of the groups, regardless of their personal characteristics. Note that random does not mean haphazard or systematic.

Experimental studies may be:

- **Double-blind**: neither the patient, nor the researcher assessing the patients, nor the treating clinician knows which treatment the patient has been randomized to receive
- **Single-blind**: either the patient or the researcher/clinician does not know (usually the patient)
- **Unblinded** (or open): both the patient and the researcher/clinician know.

Clinical trials are experimental studies.

1.3 Crossover studies

In a crossover study, each patient receives treatment and placebo in a random order. Fewer patients are needed because many between-patient confounders may be removed. For example, even though pairs of cystic fibrosis patients may be chosen and randomized to groups on the basis of their disease severity this does not ensure that the groups will be of similar age or sex.

Crossover studies are only suitable for chronic disorders that are not cured but for which treatment may give temporary relief. There should be no carryover effect of the treatment from one treatment period to the next.

1.4 Observational studies

In observational studies the groups being compared are already defined (e.g. smokers and non-smokers) and the study merely observes what happens.

Case-control, cross-sectional and **cohort** are particular types of observational studies that, respectively, consider features of the past, the present and the future to try and identify differences between the groups.

- If we take groups of individuals with and without cancer with the aim of identifying different features in their past that might explain a causal route for the cancer this is a **case-control** study.
- If we take groups of smokers and non-smokers and follow them forward in time to see whether one group is more prone to cancer then this is a **cohort** study.

1.5 Confounding

Confounding may be an important source of error. A confounding factor is a background variable (i.e. something not of direct interest) that:

- is different between the groups being compared

and

- affects the outcome being studied.

For example, in a study to compare the effect of folic acid supplementation in early pregnancy on neural tube defects, age will be a confounding factor if:

- either the folic acid or placebo group tends to consist of older women

and

- older women are more, or less, likely to have a child with a neural tube defect.

When studying the effects of a new inhaled steroid against standard therapy for cystic fibrosis patients, disease severity will be a confounder if:

- one of the groups (new steroid/standard therapy) consists of more severely affected patients

and

- disease severity affects the outcome measure (lung function).

In the comparison of cancer rates between smokers and non-smokers, diet will be a confounder if:

- smokers eat less fruit and vegetables

and

- eating more fruit and vegetables reduces the risk of contracting cancer.

If a difference is found between the groups (folic acid/placebo, new steroid/standard therapy and smokers/non-smokers) we will not know whether the differences are, respectively, due to folic acid or age, to the potency of the new steroid or the severity of disease in the patient, or to smoking or diet.

Confounding may be avoided by matching individuals in the groups according to potential confounders. For example, we could age-match folic acid and placebo pairs or deliberately recruit smokers and non-smokers with similar fruit and vegetable consumption. We could find pairs of cystic fibrosis patients of similar disease severity and randomly allocate one of each pair to receive the new steroid while the other receives standard therapy.

2. DISTRIBUTIONS

2.1 Types of data

Data may be either categoric (qualitative) or numeric (quantitative).

- With **categoric** variables each individual lies in one category
- **Numeric** data is measured on a number scale.

Ranks give the order of increasing magnitude of numeric variables. For example:

Sample of seven readings:

| 2.3 | 5.0 | 3.9 | 1.3 | −2.1 | 1.3 | 4.2 |

In order of magnitude:

| −2.1 | 1.3 | 1.3 | 2.3 | 3.9 | 4.2 | 5.0 |

Ranks:

| 1 | 2.5 | 2.5 | 4 | 5 | 6 | 7 |

Note that there are seven values in the sample and the largest value has rank 7. Where there are ties (for example, the two values 1.3), the ranks are averaged between the tied values.

The **mode** is the value that occurs most often. In the example above:

Mode = 1.3

The **median** is the middle value when the values are ranked. In the example above:

Median = 2.3

The **mean** is the arithmetic average. In the example above:

$$\text{Mean} = \frac{2.3 + 5.0 + 3.9 + 1.3 - 2.1 + 1.3 + 4.2}{7} = \frac{15.9}{7} = 2.27$$

2.2 Skewed distributions

The distribution of a set of values may be asymmetric or skewed.

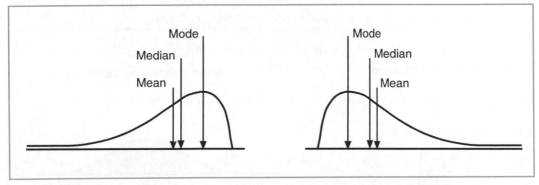

(a) Negative or downward or left skew   (b) Positive or upward or right skew

In a sample of this type the mean is 'pulled towards' the values in the outlying tail of the distribution and is unrepresentative of the bulk of the data.

Note that the skew is named according to the direction in which the tail points. In the left-hand diagram (a), the tail points to the left, to negative values and downwards.

If the distribution is skewed then the median is preferable as a summary of the data.

2.3 Normal distribution

The Normal distribution is symmetric and bell-shaped. The Normal distribution is sometimes called the Gaussian distribution.

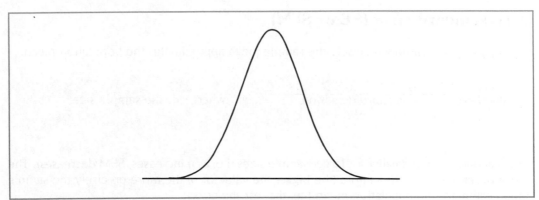

Normal distribution

2.4 Standard deviation

The standard deviation ($= \sqrt{variance}$) gives a measure of the spread of the distribution values. The smaller the standard deviation (or variance) the more tightly grouped the values.

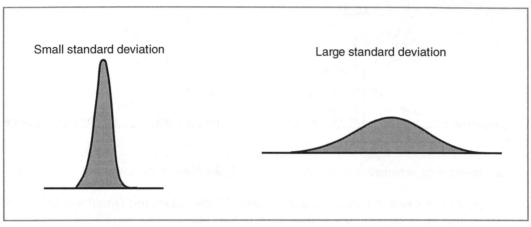

| Small standard deviation | Large standard deviation |

(a) Small standard deviation (b) Large standard deviation

If the values are normally distributed, then:

- approximately 68% of the values lie within ± 1 standard deviation of the mean
- approximately 95% of the values lie within ± 2 standard deviations of the mean
- exactly 95% of the values lie within ± 1.96 standard deviations of the mean (hence 2.5% lie in each tail).

3. CONFIDENCE INTERVALS

3.1 Standard error (SE or SEM)

This is a measure of how precisely the sample mean approximates the population mean.

Standard error $= \dfrac{\text{standard deviation}}{\sqrt{n}}$ where n is the sample size.

The standard error is smaller for larger sample sizes (i.e. as n increases, SEM decreases). The more observations in the sample (the bigger the value of n) the more precisely the sample mean estimates the population mean (i.e. the less the error).

The SEM can be used to construct **confidence intervals**.

- The interval (mean $\pm$ 1.96 SEM) is a 95% confidence interval for the population mean.
- The interval (mean $\pm$ 2 SEM) is an approximate 95% confidence interval for the population mean.
- The interval (mean $\pm$ 1.64 SEM) is a 90% confidence interval for the population mean.

There is a 5%, or 0.05, or a 1 in 20, chance that the true mean lies outside the 95% confidence interval.

- 'We are 95% confident that the true mean lies inside the interval.'

There is a 10%, or 0.1, or 1 in 10, chance that the true mean lies outside the 90% confidence interval.

- 'We are 90% confident that the true mean lies inside the interval.'

Note the difference between the standard deviation and the standard error.

- Standard deviation (SD) gives a measure of the spread of the data values.
- Standard error (SE) is a measure of how precisely the sample mean approximates the population mean.

For example, FEV_1 is measured in 100 students. The mean value for this group is 4.5 litres with a standard deviation of 0.5 litres. If the values are normally distributed then:

approximately 95% of the values lie in the range $(4.5 \pm 2(0.5))$
= (4.5 ± 1)
= $(3.5, 5.5$ litres$)$
Standard error = $\dfrac{0.5}{\sqrt{100}} = \dfrac{0.5}{10} = 0.05$

An approximate 95% confidence interval for the population mean FEV_1 is given by:

$(4.5 \pm 2(0.05)) = (4.5 \pm 0.1) = (4.4 - 4.6$ litres$)$

i.e. we are 95% confident that the population mean FEV_1 of students lies in the range 4.4–4.6 litres.

Confidence intervals can similarly be constructed around other summary statistics, for example, the difference between two means, a single proportion or percentage, the difference between two proportions. The standard error always gives a measure of the precision of the sample estimate and is smaller for larger sample sizes.

4. SIGNIFICANCE TESTS

Statistical significance tests, or hypothesis tests, use the sample data to assess how likely some specified null hypothesis is to be correct. The measure of 'how likely' is given by a probability (p) value. Usually, the null hypothesis is that there is 'no difference' between the groups.

4.1 Null hypotheses and p values

To answer the research questions in Section 1 we test the following null hypotheses:

- There is no difference in the incidence of fetuses with neural tube defects between the groups of pregnant women who do and do not take folic acid supplements
- Lung function is similar in cystic fibrosis patients who receive the new inhaled steroid when compared with the patients on current treatment
- Smokers and non-smokers have equal chances of contracting cancer.

Even if these null hypotheses were true we would not expect the averages or proportions in our sample groups to be identical. Because of random variation there will be some difference. The **p value** is the probability of observing a difference of that magnitude if the null hypothesis is true.

Since the p value is a probability, it takes values between 0 and 1. Values near to zero suggest that the null hypothesis is unlikely to be true. The smaller the p value the more significant the result:

- $p = 0.05$, the result is significant at 5%.
  The sample difference had a 1 in 20 chance of occurring if the null hypothesis were true.
- $p = 0.01$, the result is significant at 1%.
  The sample difference had a 1 in 100 chance of occurring if the null hypothesis were true.

Statistical significance is not the same as clinical significance. Although a study may show that the results from drug A are statistically significantly better than for drug B we have to consider the magnitude of the improvement, the costs, ease of administration and potential side effects of the two drugs etc. before deciding that the result is clinically significant and that drug A should be introduced in preference to drug B.

4.2 Significance, power and sample size

The study sample may or may not be compatible with the null hypothesis. On the basis of the study results, we may decide to disbelieve (or reject) the null hypothesis. In reality, the null hypothesis either is or is not true.

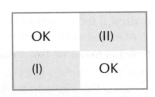

Null hypothesis:

	True	False
Decision based on study results: 'Accept' null hypothesis	OK	(II)
'Reject' null hypothesis	(I)	OK

The study may lead to the wrong conclusions:

- A low (significant) *p* value may lead us to disbelieve (or reject) the null hypothesis when it is actually true — Box (I) above. This is known as a **type I error**.
- The *p* value may be high (non-significant) when the null hypothesis is false — Box (II) above. This is known as a **type II error**.

The **power** of a study is the probability (usually expressed as a percentage) of correctly rejecting the null hypothesis when it is false.

Larger differences between the groups can be detected with greater power. The power to identify correctly a difference of a certain size can be increased by increasing the sample size. Small samples often lead to type II errors (i.e. there is not sufficient power to detect differences of clinical importance).

In practice there is a grey area between accepting and rejecting the null hypothesis. The decision will be made in the light of the *p* value obtained. We should not draw different conclusions based on a *p* value of 0.051 compared with a value of 0.049. The *p* value is a probability. As it gets smaller the less likely it is that the null hypothesis is true. There is no sudden changeover from 'accept' to 'reject'.

4.3 Parametric and nonparametric tests

Statistical hypothesis tests are either parametric or nonparametric. Choosing the appropriate statistical test depends on:

- the type of data and its distribution
- whether the data is paired or not.

Parametric tests usually assume the data is normally distributed. Examples are:

- *t*-test (sometimes called 'Student's *t*-test' or 'Student's paired *t*-test')
- Pearson's coefficient of linear correlation.

An unpaired (or 2-sample) *t*-test is used to compare the average values of two independent groups (e.g. patients with and without disease, treated versus placebo etc.).

A paired (or 1-sample) *t*-test is used if the members of the groups are paired. For example, each individual with disease is matched with a healthy individual of the same age and sex; in a crossover trial the measurements made on two treatments are paired within individuals.

Nonparametric tests are usually based on ranks. Examples are:

- Wilcoxon
- Sign
- Mann–Whitney U
- Kendall's S
- Spearman's Rank Correlation
- Chi-squared (χ^2)

Chi-squared is used to compare proportions (or percentages) between two groups.

5. CORRELATION AND REGRESSION

Sometimes measurements are made on two continuous variables for each study subject, e.g. CD4 count and age, blood pressure and weight, FRC and height. The data can be displayed in a scatterplot.

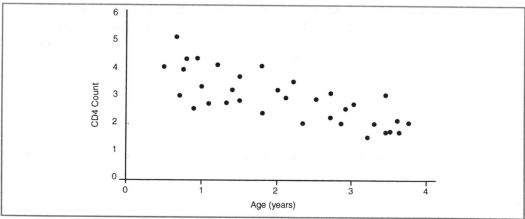

Scatterplot of CD4 count versus age

5.1 Correlation coefficients

The correlation coefficient (sometimes called Pearson's coefficient of linear correlation) is denoted by *r* and indicates how closely the points lie to a line.

r takes values between −1 and 1, the closer it is to zero the less the linear association between the two variables. (Note that the variables may be strongly associated but not linearly.)

Negative values of *r* indicate that one variable decreases as the other increases (e.g. CD4 count falls with age).

Values of −1 or +1 show that the variables are perfectly linearly related, i.e. the scatterplot points lie on a straight line.

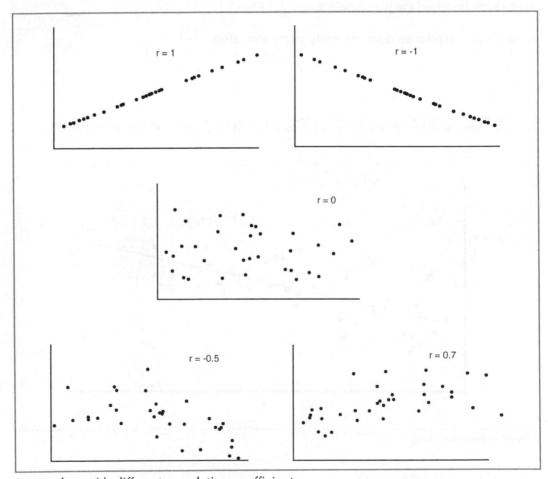

Scatterplots with different correlation coefficients

Correlation coefficients:

- show how one variable increases or decreases as the other variable increases
- do not give information about the size of the increase or decrease
- do not give a measure of agreement.

Pearson's *r* is a parametric correlation coefficient. Spearman's Rank Correlation and Kendall's S are nonparametric correlation coefficients.

- Parametric correlation coefficients quantify the extent of any linear increase or decrease.
- Nonparametric correlation coefficients quantify the extent of any tendency for one variable to increase or decrease as the other increases (for example, exponential increase or decline, increasing in steps etc.).

A *p* value attached to a correlation coefficient shows how likely it is that there is no linear association between the two variables.

A significant correlation does not imply cause and effect.

5.2 Linear regression

A regression equation ($y = a + bx$) may be used to PREDICT one variable from the other.

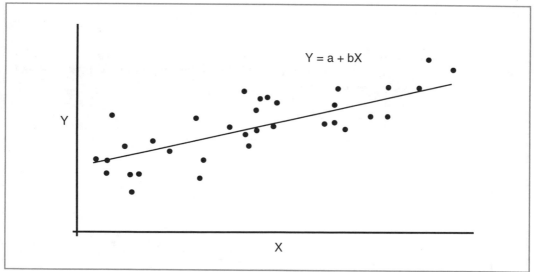

Linear regression line

- 'a' is the intercept — the value y takes when x is zero.
- 'b' is the slope of the line — sometimes called the **regression coefficient**. It gives the average change in y for a unit increase in x.
- If 'b' is negative then y decreases as x increases.

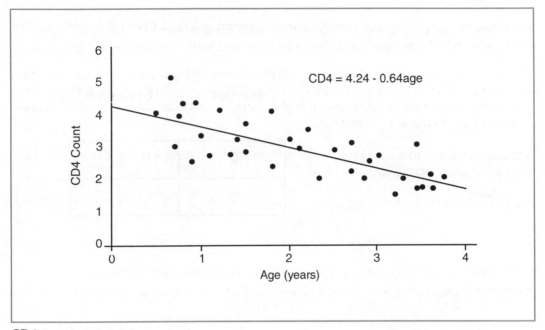

CD4 count versus age

If the units of measurement change then so will the regression equation. For example, if age is measured in months rather than years then the value of the slope (the average change in CD4 for a unit increase in age) will alter accordingly.

6. SCREENING TESTS

Screening tests are often used to identify individuals at risk of disease. Individuals who are positive on screening may be investigated further to determine whether they actually have the disease.

- Some of those who screen positive will not have the disease.
- Some of those who have the disease may be missed by the screen (i.e. test negative).

	Diseased	Disease-free
Screening test result:		
Positive — indicating possible disease	a	b
Negative	c	d

- **Sensitivity** is the proportion of true positives correctly identified by the test
$$= \frac{a}{a+c}$$

- **Specificity** is the proportion of true negatives correctly identified by the test
$$= \frac{d}{b+d}$$

- **Positive predictive value** is the proportion of those who test positive who actually have the disease
$$= \frac{a}{a+b}$$

- **Negative predictive value** is the proportion of those who test negative who do not have the disease
$$= \frac{d}{c+d}$$

Note that the positive and negative predictive values depend on the **prevalence** of the disease and may vary from population to population.

Bibliography

Cardiology
Heart Disease, A Textbook of Cardiovascular Medicine: Braunwald E, 5th edition. WB Saunders 1996.
Pocket Consultant in Cardiology: Swanton RH, 4th edition. Blackwell Science 1997.

Clinical Pharmacology
Clinical Pharmacology: Laurence DR, Bennett PN and Brown MJ, 8th edition. Churchill Livingstone 1994.
Oxford Textbook of Medicine: Wetherall DJ, Ledingham JGG and Warrell DA (eds), 3rd edition. Oxford University Press 1995.

Dermatology
Clinical Dermatology: Hunter JAA, Savin JA and Dahl MV, 2nd edition. Blackwell Science 1994.
Textbook of Dermatology: Champion RH, Burton JL and Ebling FJG, 6th edition. Blackwell Science 1998.

Endocrinology
Endocrine Secrets: McDermott MT, 1st edition. Hanley & Belfus 1995.
Textbook of Diabetes: Pickup JC and Williams G, 2nd edition. Blackwell Science 1996.

Gastroenterology
Bockus Gastroenterology: Haubrich WS, Schaffner F (eds), 5th edition. WB Saunders 1994.
Gastrointestinal Disease: Pathophysiology, Diagnosis, Management: Sleisenger MH, Fordtran JS and Feldman M (eds), 6th edition. WB Saunders 1997.

Genetics
Human Molecular Genetics: Strachan T and Read AP, 1st edition. Bios Scientific 1996.
Practical Genetic Counselling: Harper PS, 4th edition. Butterworth Heinemann 1993.

Genito-urinary Medicine and AIDS
Atlas of Differential Diagnosis in HIV Disease: Lipman, Gluck and Johnson, 1st edition. Parthenon 1995.

Haematology
Essential Haematology: Hoffbrand A and Petit J, 3rd edition. Blackwell Publishing 1992.
Handbook of Transfusion Medicine: McClelland DBL (Ed.), 2nd edition. HMSO 1996.

Immunology
Essential Immunology: Roitt I, 9th edition. Blackwell Science 1997.
Oxford Textbook of Medicine: Wetherall DJ, Ledingham JGG and Warrell DA (eds), 3rd edition. Oxford University Press 1995.

Infectious Diseases
Pathogenesis of Infectious Diseases: Mims C, 4th edition. Harcourt Brace 1995.
Principles and Practice of Infectious Diseases: Mandell, Douglas and Bennett, 4th edition. Harcourt Brace 1994.

Metabolic Diseases
Clinical Medicine: Kumar PJ and Clark ML (eds), 3rd edition. WB Saunders 1994.
Oxford Textbook of Medicine: Wetherall DJ, Ledingham JGG and Warrell DA (eds), 3rd edition. Oxford University Press 1995.

Molecular Medicine
Molecular Medicine: Trent RJA, 1st edition. Churchill Livingstone 1997.
The Molecular Biology in Medicine: Cox T and Sinclair J (eds), 1st edition. Blackwell Science 1997.

Nephrology
Oxford Textbook of Clinical Nephrology: Cameron S et al. (eds), 2nd edition. Oxford University Press 1997.
Oxford Textbook of Medicine: Wetherall DJ, Ledingham JGG and Warrell DA (eds), 3rd edition. Oxford University Press 1995.

Ophthalmology
Medical Cases in Ophthalmology: Kanski JJ, 1st edition. Butterworth Heinemann 1998.
The Eye in Systemic Disease: Kanski JJ, 1st edition. Butterworth Heinemann 1990.

Psychiatry
Problem-based Psychiatry: Green B. Churchill Livingstone 1996.
Psychiatry at a Glance: Katona CLE and Robertson MM, Blackwell Science 1995.

Respiratory Medicine
Oxford Textbook of Medicine: Wetherall DJ, Ledingham JGG and Warrell DA (eds), 3rd edition. Oxford University Press 1995.
Respiratory Medicine: Brewis RAL, Corrin B, Geddes DM, Gibson GJ, 2nd edition. WB Saunders 1996.

Rheumatology
Oxford Textbook of Rheumatology: Maddison PJ, 2nd edition. Oxford University Press 1998.
Textbook of Rheumatology: Kelley, Harris, Ruddy and Sledge (eds), 5th edition. WB Saunders 1996

Statistics
Essential Statistics for Medical Examinations: Faragher B and Marguerie, 1st edition. PasTest 1998.
Practical Statistics for Medical Research: Altman DG, 1st edition. Chapman & Hall 1991.

PASTEST INTENSIVE REVISON COURSES

PASTEST: the key to exam success, the key to your future.

PasTest is dedicated to helping doctors pass their professional examinations. We have over 25 years of specialist experience in medical education and over 4000 doctors attend our revision courses each year.

Experienced lecturers:
Many of our lecturers are also examiners who teach in a lively and interesting way to ensure you

✔ are familiar with current trends in exams
✔ receive essential advice on exam techniques
✔ are taught how to avoid the common pitfalls
✔ have plenty of mock exam practice.

Outstanding accelerated learning:
Our up-to-date comprehensive course material includes hundreds of sample questions similar to those you will experience in the exam. You will also receive detailed explanations, including charts and diagrams.

Choice of courses:
PasTest has developed a wide range of high-quality courses in various cities around the UK to suit your individual needs.

What other candidates have said about our courses:

'The information needed and techniques gained on the course gave me the extra marks needed to pass.'
Dr Copeland, Aberdeen.

'Vital for passing MRCP and also highly informative and updating.'
Dr Flynn, Kent.

'Good fun, well taught and organized and extremely helpful.'
Dr Morgan, Londonderry.

For further details contact:

PasTest, Egerton Court, Parkgate Estate, Knutsford, Cheshire WA16 8DX, UK

Telephone: 01565 752000 Fax: 01565 650264
E-mail: courses@pastest.co.uk Web site: http:\\www.pastest.co.uk

Index

α Interferon 273
  in viral hepatitis 181
  in haematological malignancy 243
Acalculia 443
Acanthosis nigricans 97
  causes 97
Achalasia 148
Acid-base control 345, 394
Acidosis 394
  metabolic 345
  renal tubular 395
Acromegaly 105, 115
ACTH 121
Activated partial thromboplastin time 247
Acute organic brain syndrome 525
Acyclovir 298
Adhesion molecules 374
Adie's (tonic) pupil 456
Adrenal disease 120
Adrenal hyperplasia, congenital 123
Adrenal steroids 109
Adrenalism, hypo 124
Adult respiratory distress syndrome 584
  causes and management 584
Afferent pupillary defect 455
Agglutinins, cold 267
Agraphia 443
AIDS 206–219
  Centre for Disease Control 208
  dermatological associations 95, 216, 217
  epidemiology 206
  gastrointestinal tumours 212
  malignant disease 216
  neurological features 213
  other respiratory diseases 210
  ophthalmic disorders 215
  Pneumocystis carinii pneumonia 209
  pulmonary tuberculosis 209
  related skin disease 216
  respiratory diseases and AIDS 209, 210
  seroconversion and HIV antibody test 208

  virus 207
  See also HIV
Albright's hereditary osteodystrophy 105, 357
Alcohol abuse 529–532
  acute withdrawal 529
  delirium tremens 529
  neuropsychiatric consequences 530
  psychological consequences 530
  social consequences 529
Alcohol and the heart 45
  mechanisms 46
Alcohol dependence syndrome 530
Alcoholism and infections 300
Aldosterone 110
Alkalosis 394
Alkaptonuria 311
Allopurinol 74
Alopecia 97
Alpha-1 antitrypsin deficiency 377
Alport's syndrome 417
Alveolar proteinosis 585
Alveolitis
  cryptogenic fibrosing 577
  extrinsic allergic, types 570, 577
Alzheimer's disease 377, 444, 526
Amantadine 70
Ambiguous genitalia 198
Amino acid metabolism disorders 311–315
  alkaptonuria 311
  cystinosis 312
  cystinuria 312
  homocystinuria 313
  oxalosis 313
  phenylketonuria (PKU) 314
Aminoglycosides 296
Amoebiasis 307
Amyloidosis 376, 428
Anaemia 223–227
  aplastic 227
  microangiopathic haemolytic 231
  sideroblastic 229

with rheumatoid arthritis 594
Analgesic nephropathy 420
Angelman syndrome 197
Angina 34
causes of non-anginal chest pains 35
Angiodysplasia 159
Angiotensin 110, 111
Anion gap 345
Ankylosing spondylitis 597
Anorexia nervosa 519, 521
complications 522
treatment 523
Anosognosia 443
Anthelmintic agents 299
Antibodies
antinuclear 277
antiphospholipid 279
Antibody vaccines, preformed 283
Antidepressants 535
Antidiuretic hormone 138
Antipsychotics 511, 534
Anti-thyroid drugs 118
Antitrypsin deficiency, Alpha-1 553
Antituberculous drugs 297
Antiviral drugs 298
Anxiety disorders 515
Aortic dissection 53
associations 54
investigations 54
Aortic regurgitation 17
causes 17
eponymous signs associated 17
features 18
Aortic stenosis 18
indicators of severe 19
Aplastic anaemia 227
Aplastic crisis 226
Apoptosis 363
Apraxia 443
Argyll Robertson pupil 455
Arrhythmias
atrial 28
re-entrant tachycardia 27
ventricular 29, 250
associations of ventricular tachycardia 29
prolonged QT intervals 31
Arterial pulse associations 10
causes of an absent radial pulse 11
Arteritis
giant cell 610
microscopic polyangiitis (polyarteritis) 612

polyarteritis nodosa 611
Takayasu's 611
Arthritis
in children 617
juvenile chronic 500, 617
psoriatic 599
rheumatoid 93
systemic 618
Asbestos
asbestosis 567
diffuse pleural thickening 567
lung cancer 567, 573
pleural plaques 567
Ascites 174
Aspergillosis 550
allergic bronchopulmonary 550
aspergilloma 566
colonizing 566
invasive 566
Astereognosis 442
Asthma 547–550
acute severe 549
bronchopulmonary aspergillosis 550
chronic 548
diagnosis 549
lung function tests 549
occupational 569
signs of severity 550
treatment 549
Ataxia telangiectasia 97, 281
Atherosclerotic renovascular disease 430
Atrial fibrillation 28
Atrial natriuretic peptide 112
Atrial septal defect 22
primum 22
secundum 22
sinus venosus 22
Autoantibodies 277–279
anti-neutrophil cytoplasmic 278
antinuclear 277
extractable nuclear antigens 278
gastrointestinal & liver disease 279
rheumatoid factor 277
thyroid disease 279
Autonomic neuropathy 136, 479
Autosomal recessive conditions 194

Babesiosis 301
Balkan nephropathy 420
Barrett's oesophagus 149
Bartter's syndrome 397

Basophils 267
Bassen Kornzweig syndrome 495
B-cell disorders 280
Becker muscular dystrophy 481
Behçet's disease 501, 613
Bell's palsy 465
Benign monoclonal gammopathy 242
Benzimidazoles 299
Benzodiazepines 536
Berger's disease 413
Berylliosis 568
Bipolar affective disorder 511
Blackwater fever 306
Blood filters 256
Blood pressure monitoring 9
Blood stem cells, peripheral 245
Blood transfusion 256–258
   fresh frozen plasma 258
   transmitted infection 256
Bone marrow, transplantation 245
Bone, mineral metabolism 329
Bowel disorders
   large bowel 163–168
   small bowel 157–160
Brainstem and cranial nerve disorders 464
Breast feeding, drugs 63
Broca's area 442
Bronchiectasis 562
   associated conditions 563
   causes 562
   investigation 562
Bronchitis, chronic 551
Brown–Séquard syndrome 469
Bruton's X-linked agammaglobulinaemia 281
Bulimia nervosa 519–523
Bullous eruptions 92
Burkitt's lymphoma 362
Byssinosis 569

Cadherins 375
Calcium homeostasis 329
Calcium pyrophosphate deposition disease 615
Campylobacter 169
Cancer, molecular pathogenesis 361
   oncogenes 361
   somatic evolution 361
   tumour suppressor genes 362
Capnocytophaga canimorsus 301
Carbamazepine 71
Carbon dioxide, transport 546
Carcinoid tumours 158

Carcinoma
   cholangio 185
   colorectal 166
   gallbladder 185
   gastric 154
   hepatocellular 184
   lung 570–574
   pancreatic 156
   oesophageal 150
   small bowel 158
Cardiac apex 11
Cardiac catheterization pressures 55
Cardiac failure 41
Cardiac functions, indices 55
Cardiac investigations 9–13
Cardiac physiological values, normal 55
Cardiac tamponade 48
   common signs 49
Cardiac transplantation 46
Cardiac tumours 45
Cardiomyopathy
   dilated 43
   hypertrophic 42
   restrictive 44
Carotico-cavernous fistula
   high pressure, high flow 463
   low pressure, low flow 463
Carpal tunnel syndrome 477
Cataracts 496
   causes 496
   types 496
Cavernous sinus syndrome 462
Cell signalling 354–360
   nuclear hormones 358
   protein kinases and phosphatases 357
   receptor, types 355
   transcription factors 358–360
Cells and the immune system 267–269
   lymphocytes 268
   polymorphonuclear 267
Central nervous system
   AIDS and HIV 213
   infections 476
   pathologies 470–475
Cephalosporins 295
Cerebral cortex 441–448
Cerebral toxoplasmosis 214
Cerebral tumours 475
Cerebrospinal fluid 484
   abnormal and normal findings 484
Chédiak–Higashi syndrome 97

Chemoreceptors, central and peripheral 542
Chest X-ray
    causes of calcification 578
    reticular-nodular shadowing 578
Chickenpox 287
Chlamydia 206
Chlorpromazine 72
Cholangiocarcinoma 185
Cholangiopathy 212
Cholecystokinin-pancreozymin 146
Cholera 169, 357
Cholestasis 78
Christmas disease (factor IX deficiency) 248
Chromosomes 189–193
    acrocentric 189
Chronic bronchitis 551
Chronic obstructive nephropathy 426
Chronic obstructive pulmonary disease 550–552
Churg–Strauss syndrome 579
Cicatricial pemphigoid 92
Ciprofloxacin 74
Cirrhosis 175
    causes 176
    clinical signs 176
    primary biliary 183
    treatment 176
Clostridium difficile 165
Clubbing, pulmonary causes 574
Coagulation 246–250
Coal workers' pneumoconiosis 567
    progressive massive fibrosis 568
Caplan's syndrome 568
Coarctation of the aorta 24
Cockcroft and Gault formula 389
Coeliac disease 157
Cognitive behaviour therapy 517
Colchicine 74
Cold agglutinins 267
Colitis, pseudomembranous 165
Colon 145
Colorectal cancer 166
Common peroneal nerve palsy 477
Complement 261
    activation 261
    alternative pathway 261
    classical pathway 261
    deficiency 263
    regulating proteins 262
    terminal membrane attack sequence 262
Complete heart block 27
Compulsion 517

Confidence intervals 626
Confounding, in statistical studies 623
Congenital adrenal hyperplasia 123
Congenital heart disease
    acyanotic 22
    cyanotic 22
Connective tissue disorders 579
    and the kidney 430
    mixed 607
    pulmonary vasculitis 580
    rheumatoid disease 579
    SLE 580
    systemic sclerosis 580
Conversion disorder 519
Coombs' test 231
Coronary artery interventional procedures 40
Correlation 630
    coefficients 631
Cortical localization 441
    frontal lobe lesions 442
    occipital lesions 443
    parietal lobe lesions 442
    temporal lobe lesions 443
Cowden's disease 96
Cranial nerve palsies 464
Craniopharyngiomas 114
Creatinine clearance 389
Creutzfeldt–Jakob disease 373, 445
Crohn's disease 163
Cryoglobulins 266
Cryptococcal meningitis 214
Cushing's syndrome 120, 121, 528
    tests 122
Cyclic AMP proteins 104
Cyclosporin A 75
Cystic fibrosis 200, 563–565
Cystinosis 312
Cystinuria 312
Cytokines 272–275
    production patterns 272
    therapeutic uses 273
Cytomegalovirus 289
Cytotoxics, specific side-effects 7

Data, types 624
Delayed puberty, causes 129
Delirium tremens 529
Dementia 514, 526
Depression 512
    clinical features 513
    in the elderly 513

treatment 514
Dermatitis
  atopic 90
  herpetiformis 92
  seborrhoeic 90
Dermatomyositis 93, 603
  juvenile 603
Dermis 85
Di George syndrome 281
Diabetes insipidus 114
  cranial 114
  nephrogenic 114
Diabetes mellitus 131–137
  clinical features 131
  complications 135
  diagnostic criteria 133
Diabetic nephropathy 431
Dialysis 405
Diarrhoea 161
Diazepam 71
Dimorphic blood picture 225
Disseminated intravascular coagulation 249
Distributions, statistical 624
  normal/Gaussian 625
  skewed 625
DNA (deoxyribonucleic acid) 196
Down's syndrome 192
Drug metabolism 61–63
  genetic polymorphisms 61
Drug therapies in HIV/AIDS 218
  anti-retroviral therapy 218
Drugs, specific adverse effects
  bronchospasm 76
  dyskinesia and dystonia 77
  gynaecomastia 77
  hypothyroidism 77
  liver disease 77
  myasthenia 78
  nephrotoxicity 436
  photosensitivity 78
  secondary amenorrhoea 76
Duchenne muscular dystrophy 381, 481
Dystrophia myotonica 482

Eating disorders 519–523
Echocardiography 6
  diagnostic uses 6
  potential uses 6
Eczema 90
Edward's syndrome 193
Eicosanoids 275–277

leukotrienes 277
prostaglandins 276
Eisenmenger's syndrome 25
Electrocardiographs (ECG) 3
  common abnormalities 3
  causes of tall R waves in V1 4
Potassium and ECG changes 6
Electroconvulsive therapy 537
Electrophysiological investigations 485
EEG 485
  electromyography 486
Emphysema 551
Empyema 558
Enteric fevers 306
Entero-hepatic circulation of bile salts 145
Eosinophilia 233
Eosinophils 267
Epidermolysis bullosa 92
Epilepsy 447, 448
Erythema
  multiforme 90
  nodosum 91
Erythroderma 89
Erythropoiesis 223
  normoblastic 223
  megaloblastic 223
Erythropoietin, recombinant 403
Ethambutol 297
Exercise stress testing 7
Experimental studies
  double-blind 622
  single-blind 622
  unblinded 622
Eye 489

Facial nerve 464
  Bell's palsy 465
  Ramsay–Hunt syndrome 465
Factitious disorder 519
Felty's syndrome 593
Fibrinolysis, therapeutic 253
Flow volume loops 543
Focal neurological disease 214
Folate metabolism 147
Forced alkaline diuresis 79
Foster–Kennedy syndrome 499
Fragile X syndrome 197
Free radicals, oxygen 371–373

G Proteins 104, 356, 384
Gallstone disease 174

Ganciclovir 298
Gardner's syndrome 96
Gastric carcinoma 154
Gastric inhibitory peptide 146
Gastrin 146
Gastroenteritis 168
Gastrointestinal diseases with HIV/AIDS 211
  ano-rectal conditions 212
  biliary and pancreatic disease 212
  diarrhoea/abdominal pain 211
  oral/oesophageal conditions 211
Gastrointestinal infections 168–170
  amoebiasis 168
  bowel 304
  Campylobacter 169
  cholera 169
  gastro-enteritis 168
  giardiasis 169
  liver 305
  salmonella 169
  shigella 169
Gastrointestinal tract
  anatomy & physiology 143–148
  upper, haemorrhage 152
Gastrointestinal tuberculosis 170
Gene family 384
Gene transcription factors 358
Genetics, molecular 196
Genitalia, ambiguous 198
Genomic imprinting 197
Gerstmann's syndrome 442
Gerstmann–Straussler–Scheinker syndrome 373
Giardiasis 169
Glaucomas 505
Glomerular filtration rate 389
  creatinine clearance 389
  inulin clearance 389
Glomerulonephritis 408–415
  classification 409
  clinical features 408
  diffuse proliferative 414
  focal segmental 413
  hypocomplementaemia 415
  membranous 412
  mesangiocapillary 413
  mesangioproliferative 413
  particular glomerulonephritides 412
  rapidly progressive 414
Glorin's syndrome 96
Glycated haemoglobin 105
Gonorrhoea 205

Gout 316
  prophylaxis 615
Graft versus host disease 245
Graft versus leukaemia 245
Granulomatous lung disease 574–578
Growth factor receptors 356
Growth hormone deficiency, adults 116
Guillain–Barré syndrome 480
Gut, hormones 146
Gynaecomastia 77, 109

Haematinics, metabolism of 147
Haematuria, macroscopic 410
Haemochromatosis 183, 318
Haemodialysis for overdosing or poisoning 82
Haemolysis, causes and general features 230
Haemolytic–uraemic syndrome 432
Haemophilia 248
Haemoptysis 574
Haemorrhage, subarachnoid 471
Haemosiderosis 318
Hair, disorders 86
Headache 473
  cluster 474
Heart sounds 12
  causes of valvular clicks 13
Heat shock proteins 371
Helicobacter pylori 152
Henoch–Schönlein purpura 579
Heparins, low molecular weight 253
Hepatic
  adenoma, benign 185
  encephalopathy 179
  haemangioma 185
Hepatic tumours
  cholangiocarcinoma 185
  gallbladder 185
  hepatocellular 184
Hepatitis 180
  B, serology 181
  chronic 182
  delta agent 289
  drug-induced 77
  viral 180
Hepatorenal syndrome 367
Herd immunity 287
Hereditary angio-oedema 263
Herpes simplex encephalitis 476
High altitude, adaptation to 547
Hirsutism 86, 125
Histiocytosis 576

eosinophilic granuloma 576
Hand–Schüller–Christian Disease 576
HIV
    anti-retroviral therapy 218
    CDC classification 208
    drug therapies 218
    enteropathogens 211
    See also AIDS
HLA-B27 596
Homocystinuria 313
Hormones 103–111
    action 103–106
    growth hormone 108
        deficiency in adults 116
    gut 146
    investigations in endocrinology 107
    physiology 106–112
        in illness 106
        in obesity 107
        in pregnancy 107
    resistance syndromes 106
Horner's syndrome 455
Host defence mechanisms 293
    cellular immunity 294
    humoral immunity 294
    non-specific mechanisms 293
Howel–Evans syndrome 96
Howell–Jolly bodies 255
HTLV-1 289
Huntington's chorea 451, 452
Hybridoma 384
Hydrocephalus, normal pressure 443
Hyperbilirubinaemia, congenital 172
Hypercalcaemia 330
Hypercholesterolaemia 324
    familial 324
    polygenic 324
Hypereosinophilic syndrome 234, 581
Hyperlipidaemias 324
    familial polygenic combined 325
    remnant 325
    secondary 325
Hypermagnesaemia 338
Hyperparathyroid bone disease 332
Hyperparathyroidism 332
    primary 332
    secondary 332
    tertiary 332
Hyperphosphataemia 340
Hypersensitivity Type I–V 271
Hypertension 53

    intracranial, benign 474
    kidney 433
Hyperthyroidism 116–117
Hypertrichosis 86
Hypertriglyceridaemia, polygenic 324
Hypoadrenalism 333
Hypocalcaemia 333
Hypochondriacal disorder 518
Hypoglycaemia 137
Hypokalaemia 397
Hypomagnesaemia 338
Hypomania 511
Hyponatraemia 138
    pseudohyponatraemia 139
    dilutional 139
Hypoparathyroidism 332
    pseudo-hypoparathyroidism 333
Hypophosphataemia 340
Hypopigmentation 98
Hyposplenism 255
Hypothermia 347
Hypothesis tests 628
    See statistical significance tests
Hypothyroidism 116–117

IgA deficiency 281
Immunization 282–284
Immunodeficiency 280–282
Immunoglobulin deficiency 282
Immunoglobulins 264
Infarctions 470
    lacunar 471
    myocardial 35
Infection
    modes of transmission 287
    pathogenesis 290
    predispositions 290
    prophylaxis in hyposplenism 255
Infections in specific situations 300
Infective endocarditis 20
    indications for surgery 21
    poor prognostic factors 21
Inflammation and repair, mediators 368–373
    free radicals 371
    heat shock proteins 371
    interleukin-1 369
    transforming growth factor β 370
    tumour necrosis factor 370
Inflammatory connective tissue disorders 600–608
Insomnia 533
Integrins 375

Interferon 273
Interleukin-1 (IL-1) 369
Intersex 131
Interstitial nephritis 419
    acute (allergic) 419
    Balkan nephropathy 420
    chronic tubulo- 419
Intestine, small 145
Iron 229
    metabolism 147, 228
    overload, secondary 319
    status 229
Irritable bowel syndrome 166
Ischaemic attacks, transient 470
Ischaemic heart disease 33
    risk factors for coronary heart disease 33
    summary of important trials 56
Isoniazid 297

Jaundice 170–173
    liver function tests 173
Job's syndrome 280
Jugular venous pulse 9
    normal waves 9
    pathological waves 10

Kallman's syndrome 130
Kaposi's sarcoma 216
Kawasaki disease 612
Kearns Sayre syndrome 496
Keratoconus 504
Kidney and drugs 435–438
    nephrotoxicity 436
Kidney disease, polycystic 416
Kidney
    hypertension 433
    myeloma 433
    tubular physiology 390
Killed organism vaccines 283
Klinefelter's syndrome 130, 191
Knee jerks, absent 469
Köbner phenomenon 89
Korsakoff's syndrome 475, 531
Kuru 373
Kussmaul's sign 9
Kveim–Siltzbach 576
Kwashiorkor 341

Lambert–Eaton myasthenic syndromes 483
Lamotrigine 71
Large bowel, disorders 163–168

Lateral medullary syndrome 467
Laurence–Moon–Biedl syndrome 496
Leber's hereditary optic neuropathy 197
Legionella pneumophila 557
Lens abnormalities 496
    cataract 496
    dislocation 497
Leprosy 308
Lesch–Nyhan syndrome 316
Leucocyte
    depletion filters 257
    disorders 232
Leucocytosis 232
Leucoerythroblastic change 235
Leukaemias 236–241
    acute (ALL and AML) 236
    chromosome abnormalities 238
    chronic lymphocytic 241
    chronic myeloid 240
    FAB classification 239
    promyelocytic (AML M3) 240
Leukotrienes 277
Levodopa 70
LH/FSH 107
Lichen planus 90
Ligand gated ion channel 356
Lipid metabolism 322
    chylomicrons 322
    LDL receptor 323
    lipoproteins 322
    rare disorders 327, 328
    schemata of lipoprotein structure 322
Lipid-lowering drugs 325
Listeriosis 289
Lithium carbonate 72
Lithium 72, 512
    side-effects 73
    toxicity 73
Liver enzyme
    induction 62
    inhibition 62
Liver 145
    disease and drug therapies 64
    tumours 78
Loop of Henle 391
Lung
    anatomy and physiology 541
    aspergillus 550, 566
    connective tissue disorders 579
    cancer 570–574
    infections 555–566

Lung compliance 541
Lupus anticoagulant 253
Lupus, drug-induced 602
Lyme disease 476
Lymphangioleiomyomatosis 585
Lymphocytes 268
Lymphocytosis 232
Lymphogranuloma venereum 206
Lymphomas
    lymphoblastic 242
    non-Hodgkin's 241

Macrocytosis 223
Macrolides 296
Magnesium concentration disorders 338
Malabsorption 162
Malaria 306
Mania 511
Marasmus 341
Marfan's syndrome 201
Materno-fetal transmission 206
McCune–Albright syndrome 105, 129, 357
Mendelian inheritance 193
Mental disorders
    associated with physical illness 528
    drug-induced 528
Mesothelioma 573
    asbestos exposure 567, 573
Metabolic acidosis 345
Metabolic alkalosis 346
    milk-alkali syndrome 347
    post-hypercapnic alkalosis 347
Metals and metalloproteins, disorders 346
Microaggregate filters 256
Microangiopathic haemolytic anaemia 231
Microbial virulence factors 291
Microcytosis 224
Microdeletion syndromes 193
Migraine 473
Miller–Fisher syndrome 480
Miosis 455
Mitochondrial disorders 197, 379
    phenotypes due to mutations 380
Mitosis 189
Mitral regurgitation 15
    mitral valve prolapse 16
Mitral stenosis 14
    features of severe 15
Molecular diagnostics 351–354
Monoclonal antibodies 353
    clinical applications 354

Monocytosis 234
Mononeuropathies 477
Mood disorders 511–515
Motilin 146
Motor neurone disease 469
    amyotrophic muscular atrophy 469
    progressive bulbar palsy 469
    progressive muscular atrophy 469
Movement disorders 449–452
    akinetic-rigid syndrome 450
    athetosis 450
    chorea 450
    dystonia 449
    myoclonus 449
    Parkinsonism 450
    tremors 449
Multiple sclerosis 446
Multiple endocrine neoplasia 126
    medullary thyroid cancer 128
Munchausen's syndrome 519
Murmurs 13
Myasthenia gravis 380, 483
Mycobacterium tuberculosis 559
Mydriasis 456
Myelodysplastic syndromes 244
Myeloma, renal involvement 433
Myocardial infarctions 35–37
Myocardial perfusion imaging 7
Myocarditis 44
    rheumatic fever 44
Myoclonic epilepsy 197
Myopathies 481
Myotonic dystrophy 503
    ophthalmic features

N-acetyl cysteine 81
Nails, changes/skin disorders 87
Narcolepsy 534
Negative predicative value 634
Nelson's syndrome 114
Nephritis
    chronic tubulo-interstitial 419
    interstitial 419
Nephrocalcinosis 425
Nephropathy
    analgesic 420
    chronic obstructive 426
    diabetic 431
    radio-contrast 437
    reflux 421
    thin membrane 418

toxic 438
Nephrotic syndrome 409
Nerve conduction tests 485
Nerve lesions, peripheral 477–480
Nerve palsy
    common peroneal 477
    facial 465
Nerves in the hand
    causes of wasting in small muscles 478
    median, radial and ulnar 478
Neuralgia, trigeminal 465
    treatment 466
Neuritis, optic 497
    causes 498
    clinical signs 497
    in multiple sclerosis 446
Neuroanatomy 468
Neurofibromatosis 96, 200, 503
Neurological infections 303
Neuroma, acoustic 467
Neuromuscular junction 482
    disorders 482–484
Neuro-ophthalmology 453–463
Neuroradiology 485
    intracranial calcification 485
Neurosyphilis 215
Neutropenia 235
Neutrophilia 232
Neutrophils 267, 280
Nezelof syndrome 281
Nitric oxide 365
    functions 367
Non-gonococcal urethritis 206
Non-Hodgkin's lymphoma 241
Nonparametric tests 629
Nuclear antigens 278
Nuclear hormones 358
Null hypotheses 628
Nutrition 160–163
    enteral 160
    malabsorption 162
    oral 160
    parenteral 160
Nutritional disorders 341
Nystagmus 462

Obesity 341
    endocrine causes 123
Obsessions 517
Obsessive compulsive disorder 516
Oculomotor system 457–461

bilateral ophthalmoplegia 457
conjugate gaze, disorders 457
fourth nerve 459
impaired vertical conjugated gaze 461
internuclear ophthalmoplegia 460
sixth nerve 459
third nerve 458
Oesophagitis 149
Oesophagus 143
    Barrett's 149
    carcinoma 150
    disorders 148–151
Oligonucleotide 385
Oncogenes 361
Onycholysis 88
Ophthalmic disorders in AIDS 215
Optic nerve 453
    disorders 497
    optic atrophy 498
    optic nerve head, swollen 499
    optic neuritis 497
    visual field defects 453
Oral contraceptive pill, failure of 62
Organic brain syndrome, acute 525
Osteoarthritis 616
Osteodystrophy, renal 404
Osteomalacia 334
Osteoporosis 336–338
Oxalosis 314
Oxygen therapy, long term 552
Oxygen, transport 546
Oxyhaemoglobin dissociation curve 546

p value (probability) 628
Paget's disease 335
Pancoast's syndrome 572
Pancreas 144
    carcinoma 156
    disorders 154–156
    secretions 144
Pancreatic polypeptide 146
Pancreatitis
    acute 154
    and HIV 212
    chronic 155
Panic disorder 516
Papillary necrosis 420
Parametric tests 629
Paraneoplastic syndromes 572
Parathyroid hormone 111
Parietal lobe 442

Parinaud's syndrome 461
Parkinsonism 450
Paroxysmal nocturnal haemoglobinuria 263
Parvovirus B19 289
Patau syndrome 193
Patent ductus arteriosus 24
Pemphigoid
    bullous 92
    cicatricial 92
Pemphigus 92
Penicillins 295
Peptic ulcer disease 151
Pericardial effusion 48
Pericarditis, constrictive 47
Peripheral nerve lesions 477–480
Peripheral nerves, palpable 480
Peutz–Jeghers syndrome 96, 166
Phacomatoses, ocular features 503
Phaeochromocytoma 24, 126
Phenylketonuria
Philadelphia chromosome 241
Phobic disorders 516
Phosphate concentration disorders 340
Pick's disease 445
Pigmentation 98
Piperazines 299
Pituitary gland 112–116
    adenomas 113
    anatomy 112
    apoplexy 114
    tumours 113
Platelet refractoriness 257
Platelet support in marrow failure 257
Pleural effusion 581
Pneumoconiosis 567
Pneumocystis carinii pneumonia 209
Pneumonia 555–558
    aspiration 558
    causal organisms 556
    cavitation 558
    Legionella pneumophila 557
    Mycobacterium tuberculosis 559
    Mycoplasma pneumoniae 556
    nosocomial 557
    Pneumocystis carinii 209
    Staphylococcus aureus 557
    Streptococcus pneumoniae 555
Poikilocytosis 224
Poisoning 79–82
    aspirin overdose 79
    carbon monoxide 80

    ethylene glycol 80
    paracetamol overdose 81
    quinidine and quinine 81
    theophylline overdose 82
    tricyclic antidepressant overdose 82
Polyangiitis 579, 612
    microscopic 579
Polyarteritis nodosa 579, 611
Polychromasia 225
Polycystic kidney disease 416
Polycystic ovarian syndrome 125
Polymerase chain reaction 196, 351
    clinical applications 352
Polymorphism, susceptibility 374
Polymorphonuclear cells 267
Polymyalgia rheumatica 610
Polymyositis 603
Polyneuropathies 478–480
    autonomic neuropathies 479
    motor neuropathies 479
    sensory neuropathies 479
Polyposis coli, familial 166
Polyuria 396
Porphyrias 319
    and mental disorders 528
    effects on skin 94
    haem synthesis 320
    precipitating drugs 321
Portal hypertension & varices 177
Positive predictive value 634
Prader–Willi syndrome 197
Praziquantel 299
Pregnancy
    drug therapies 63
    infections 300
Priapism 226
Primary biliary cirrhosis 183
Prion protein 373
Prolactin 107, 108
Prostaglandins 276
Prosthetic valves 19
Protein kinases 357
Proteinuria 392
Prothrombin time 247
Pruritus 95
Pseudohypoparathyroidism 105
Pseudomembranous colitis 165
Psoriasis 87, 88
Psoriatic arthritis 599
Psychosocial, treatment 511
Psychotherapies 538

Puberty
 delayed 129
 normal 128
 precocious 129
 short stature 129
Pulmonary amyloidosis 585
Pulmonary embolism 51
Pulmonary eosinophilia 580
Pulmonary fibrosis 577
 drugs causing 578
Pulmonary function tests 542
Pulmonary hypertension 49
 primary 49
Pulmonary tuberculosis 209
Pulmonary vasculitis 579–581
Pupils 454
Purine metabolism disorders 315
 gout 316
 Lesch–Nyhan syndrome 316
 purine nucleoside phosphorylase deficiency
  281
Pyoderma gangrenosum 94
Pyrazinamide 297

Quinolones 295

Ramsay Hunt syndrome 465
Receptor tyrosine kinases 104
Red cell morphology 224
Red eye, causes 224
Refsum's disease 495
Regression coefficient 633
Regression, linear 632
Reiter's syndrome 598
Renal calculi and nephrolithiasis 424
Renal cystic disorders 416
Renal disease, inherited 416–418
Renal failure
 acute 398–401
 chronic 401–406
Renal
 osteodystrophy 404
 papillary necrosis 421
 physiology 389–391
 radiology 393
Renal transplantation 406
 complications 407
Renal tubular
 acidosis 395
 necrosis 398
Renal vein thrombosis 415

Renin–angiotensin–aldosterone system 391
Respiratory disease and HIV 209
Respiratory distress syndrome, adult 584
Respiratory failure 553
Reticular dysgenesis 281
Retinal disorders 490–496
Retinitis pigmentosa 495
Retinoids 76
Retroperitoneal fibrosis 426
Rhabdomyolysis 400
Rheumatoid arthritis 590–595
 disease-modifying drugs 595
 extra-articular manifestations 593
 investigations 594
 musculoskeletal features 591
 palindromic 590
 polymyalgic 590
Rheumatoid factor 277, 589
Rheumatoid nodules 592
 eye involvement 592
Ribavirin 298
Ribonucleic acid 196
Rifampicin 297
Rinne's test 466
Rubella 289

Salmonella 169
Sarcoidosis 94, 504, 574–576
 effect on skin 94
 ocular effects 504, 575
 treatment 576
Schilling test 148
Schistosomiasis 307
Schizophrenia 509–511
 symptoms 509
 treatment 511
Scleritis 501
Scleroderma 604
Sclerosis, systemic 93
Secretin 146
Selectins 375
Selegiline 70
Self-harm, deliberate 523
Seroconversion illnesses 208
Severe combined immunodeficiency 281
Sexually transmitted disease 205
 chlamydia infections 206
 gonorrhoea 205
 syphilis 205
Shigella 169
Shy–Drager syndrome 451

SIADH 138
Sickle cell disease 225, 301, 382
Sickle dactylitis 226
Sideroblastic anaemia 229
Significance tests 628–630
Silicosis 568
Sjögren's syndrome 606
Skin
    drug eruptions 96
    hypopigmentation 85
    internal malignancy 98
    pigmentation disorders 98
    structure 85
    paraneoplastic features 97
Sleep
    apnoea, obstructive 583
    disorders 532–534
    insomnia 533
    normal 532
Small intestine 145
    carcinoid tumours 158
    disorders 157–160
Sodium valproate 71
Somatoform disorders 518
Somatostatin 146
Specificity 534
Spherocytes 225
Spinal cord disorders 468, 469
Splenectomy 254, 301
    clinical indications 255
Splenic sequestration crisis 226
Splenomegaly 254, 301
Spondyloarthropathies 596–599
    ankylosing spondylitis 597
    psoriatic arthritis 599
    Reiter's syndrome 598
Spongiform encephalopathies 373
Standard deviation 626
Standard error 626
Staphylococcus aureus 557
Statistical studies
    design 621–623
    observational 622
    significance tests 628–630
    types 622
Steele–Richardson syndrome 451
Still's disease 618
Stomach 143
    disorders 151–154
Streptococcus pneumoniae 556
Streptomycin 298

Stroke 470
    risk factors 471
    poor prognosis factors 471
Sturge–Weber syndrome 96, 503
Subarachnoid haemorrhage 471, 472
    complications of 472
    intracranial aneurysms 472
Subunit vaccines 284
Suicide 524
Sulphonamides 296
Sumatriptan 71
Supranuclear palsy 451
Syphilis 205
Systemic lupus erythematosus 528, 601
Systemic sclerosis 604

Target cells 225
T-cell disorders 281
Temporal lobe 443
Temporary pacing 32
Teratogenic drug effects 63
Tetracyclines 296
Tetralogy of Fallot 25
T_H1 (helper) and T_H2 (helper) cells 296
Thrombin time 247
Thrombocytosis 243
Thrombolysis 38
    contraindications 38
Thrombophilia 251
Thromboplastin time, activated partial 247
Thrombosis 250–254
    and the pill 251
    risk factors 251
Thyroid axis 107
Thyroid binding globulin 120
Thyroid disease
    autoimmunity 119
    eye disease 502
Thyroid gland 116–120
    cancer 118
    drugs 119
    function tests 120
    nodules 118
Thyroid hormone, metabolism 110
Thyrotoxicosis 118
Tissue disorders 600–608
Torre–Muir syndrome 96
Toxoplasmosis 289
Trachoma 206
Transcription factors 358–360
    clinical applications 360

Transferrin saturation 229
Transforming growth factor β 370
Transient ischaemic attacks 470
   differential diagnosis 470
Transplant immunology 270
   histocompatibility complex 270
   transplantation 270
Tricuspid regurgitation 19
Trigeminal neuralgia 465
Trinucleotide repeat disorders 196, 378
Triple X syndrome 191
Tropical infections 306–308
T-test 630
Tuberculosis 559–561
   atypical 561
   BCG vaccination 561
   gastrointestinal 170
   infections, atypical 561
   miliary 560
   post-primary 559
   prevention 561
   primary 559
   pulmonary in AIDS 209
   treatment 560
Tuberose sclerosis 96, 201, 504
Tumour necrosis factor 370
Turner's syndrome 130, 190

Ulcerative colitis 163
Urethral syndrome 423
Urinalysis 392
Urinary tract
   infection 423
   obstruction 426
   tumours 427
Urolithiasis 424
Urticaria 99
Usher's syndrome 496
Uveitis 500
   anterior 500
   posterior 500

Vaccines 299
   killed organism 283
   live attenuated 284
   subunit 284
Variceal haemorrhage 178
Vascular tone, mediators 365
   endothelin-1 368
   nitric oxide 365–367
Vasculitis 592, 608

drug-induced 79
polymyalgia rheumatica 610
pulmonary 579–581
renal 434
treatment 609
See also arteritis
Vasoactive intestinal peptide 146
Ventilation 541
   compliance 541
   positive pressure ventilation 555
   ventilatory support 554
Ventricular septal defects 23
Vertigo 467
Vestibulocochlear nerve 466
Vigabatrin 71
Villous atrophy 158
Viral hepatitis 180–182
Virulence factors, microbial 291
Visual agnosia 443
Vitamin B12 147
Vitamin D 111
Vitamin deficiencies 342–344
   fat-soluble vitamins 343
   vitamin D 334
   water-soluble vitamins 344
von Willebrand's disease 249
von-Hippel Lindau syndrome 503

Wallenberg's syndrome 467
Warfarin, therapeutic ranges 250
Weber's test 466
Wegener's granulomatosis 579, 611
Wernicke's area 442
Wernicke's encephalopathy 475, 531
Whipple's disease 159
William's syndrome 193
Wilms' tumour 428
Wilson's disease 184, 317, 452
Wiskott–Aldrich syndrome 96, 281

X-linked recessive conditions 195
   dominant conditions 195

Yellow nail syndrome 88

Zollinger-Ellison syndrome 153

PASTEST REVISION BOOKS FOR MRCP PART 1 & 2

PasTest are the specialists in study guides and revision courses for professional medical qualifications. For 25 years we have been helping doctors to achieve their potential.

MRCP PART 1 REVISION BOOKS

- **MCQs in Basic Medical Sciences for MRCP Part 1**
  300 exam-based MCQs with answers and detailed explanatory notes.

- **MRCP Part 1 Practice Exams, 2nd edition**
  Five complete MCQ papers (300 MCQs) covering favourite Royal College topics.

- **MRCP 1 MCQ Revision Book, 3rd edition**
  300 MCQs arranged by subject with correct answers and teaching notes, plus one complete mock exam.

- **MRCP 1 Past Topics: A Revision Syllabus, 2nd edition**
  Contains authoritative lists of past topics which have occurred in the Royal College examination over the past 7 years.

- **Explanations to the RCP Past Papers**
  Correct answers and teaching notes related to the Royal College Green and Blue books of actual past exam questions.

- **MRCP Part 1 MCQs with Key Topic Summaries, 2nd edition**
  200 MCQs related to current examination syllabus with 200 comprehensive topic summaries.

- **Oxford Textbook of Medicine MCQs, 3rd edition**
  375 new MCQs related to the 1995 *Oxford Textbook of Medicine*, ideal for subject-based revision.

- **MRCP Part 1 MCQ Pocket Books**
  Each pocket-sized book contains 100 MCQs on favourite Membership topics. Answers and detailed teaching notes included for every question:

  Book 1: Cardiology and Respiratory Medicine
  Book 2: Neurology and Psychiatry
  Book 3: Gastroenterology, Endocrinology and Renal Medicine
  Book 4: Rheumatology, Immunology, Haematology and Infectious Diseases
  Book 5: Basic Sciences, Applied Sciences and Therapeutics
  Book 6: Clinical Pharmacology

MRCP PART 2 REVISION BOOKS

- **Radiology for MRCP: 101 Cases with Discussion**
  Incorporates a collection of radiological plates and discussion points. Contains X-rays, MRI scans and CT scans with a section on understanding the principles of interpretation.

- **MRCP Part 2 Preparation for the Clinical Examination**
  Systematic approach to preparation for the long case, short cases and viva. Over 120 popular Short Case topics.

- **Data Interpretation for the MRCP, Revised edition**
  10 Data Interpretation practice papers with strong clinical orientation.

- **MRCP Part 2 Pocket Books**
  Each pocket-sized book contains Case Histories and Data Interpretations for selected subject areas:

Book 1: Cardiology and Respiratory Medicine
Book 2: Gastroenterology and Endocrinology
Book 3: Haematology, Rheumatology and Neurology

For full details contact:

**PasTest
FREEPOST
Knutsford
Cheshire
WA16 7BR**

**Telephone: 01565 752000 Fax: 01565 650264
E-mail: books@pastest.co.uk**